MW00388884

Classic Data Structures in Java

Classic Data Structures in Java

Timothy Budd
Oregon State University

Boston San Francisco New York
London Toronto Sydney Tokyo Singapore Madrid
Mexico City Munich Paris Cape Town Hong Kong Montreal

Senior Acquisitions Editor: *Susan Hartman*
Assistant Editor: *Lisa Kalner*
Executive Marketing Manager: *Michael Hirsch*
Production Supervision: *Diane Freed*
Cover Illustration: *© 2000, Susan Cyr*
Cover Design: *Leslie Haimes / Regina Hagen*
Interior Design: *Mark Ong, Side by Side Studios; Windfall Software*
Composition: *Windfall Software, using ZzTEX*
Technical Art: *LM Graphics*
Copyeditor: *Evelyn Pyle*
Proofreader: *Diane Wood*
Design Manager: *Regina Hagen*
Manufacturing Coordinator: *Caroline Fell*

Access the latest information about Addison-Wesley titles from our World Wide Web site: *http://www.awl.com/cs*

Library of Congress Cataloging-in-Publication Data

Budd, Timothy.
Classic data structures in Java / Timothy A. Budd.
p. cm.
ISBN 0-201-70002-6
1. Java (Computer program language) 2. Data structures (Computer science) I. Title.
QA76.73.J38 B83 2001
005.7'3—dc21 00-022798

ISBN 0-201-70002-6

1 2 3 4 5 6 7 8 9 10—MA—03 02 01 00

CONTENTS

PREFACE

The study of data structures is historically one of the first steps a student takes in the process of learning computer science as a discipline. Data structures play a fundamental role in almost every aspect of computer science and are found in almost every nontrivial computer program. Furthermore, the analysis of data structures may represent the first time the student encounters a number of key concepts:

- The relationship between an *algorithm* (an abstract approach used to solve a specific problem) and a *method* (the code written in a specific language, such as Java, that embodies the ideas of an algorithm)
- The division of a large program into smaller independent units and, more important, the idea that these units can be characterized by an interface independently of their implementation
- The extension of this separation of interface and implementation to the concept of an *abstract data type,* or ADT
- The reuse of standard software components in the development of new applications
- The fact that several different reusable software abstractions may satisfy the same interface and how one goes about selecting the proper component for a particular application
- The use of formal techniques to reason about both algorithms and programs—for example, how to argue that an algorithm will always terminate, regardless of its input values
- The techniques used to frame a proof of correctness for an algorithm or a method and the observation that such a proof is an essential part of software development
- The idea that an algorithm can be characterized by its execution-time performance in a fashion that is independent of any particular machine or programming language

- The relationship between mathematical concepts, such as induction, and software concepts, such as recursive procedures

And last, but not least, the student becomes familiar with a variety of specific tools that have proved themselves, over a period of many years, to be useful techniques for maintaining large collections of elements. The ideas embodied in these tools and techniques are so ingrained in computer science that they can truly be said to represent the essential foundation on which all the rest of computer science is built and the essential vocabulary in which all of computer science is discussed.

FEATURES OF THIS BOOK

Features of this book that make it different from many other data structures textbooks in common use include the following:

- The object-oriented mindset is applied throughout. Object-oriented organization is discussed from the very beginning, and object-oriented techniques are used in the development of all examples.
- The clear separation between ADT (interface) and implementation is emphasized throughout. The various categories of containers are first described as data types, independent of any implementation. These ADT descriptions are given as narrow (that is, small) interfaces. Data structures are then introduced as realizations of the interfaces. Most data structures implement several different interfaces, showing that the same container can be used in many different ways.
- A rigorous approach to development is encouraged. Techniques for developing formal proofs of programs are presented, and proofs of programs appear throughout the text.
- Sprinkled throughout the book are suggested experiments that will lead the student in exploring further aspects of data structures in more detail. A typical experiment will investigate, for example, the impact that data ordering will have on the execution time of a sorting procedure.
- As an aid to performing these experiments, the book provides tools that make it easy to create a visual record of execution time. The combination of a hands-on experiment coupled with a visual display is an effective tool for reinforcing the lessons gained from an analytical dissection of the algorithms embedded in a data structure.
- Important software patterns are highlighted, and the use of patterns is emphasized from the beginning.

- Graphical elements of Java are used to the reader's advantage. Many students are attracted to the graphical elements of Java. Yet graphical applications can quickly become complex, and the important lessons about data structures must not be lost in the process of creating a nice visual output. The graphical examples have been carefully chosen to minimize the unnecessary detail and to emphasize the important lessons.
- Sidebars are used for additional information. Throughout the text, a key linear narrative is almost always being presented. Often, additional or incidental information would help the reader but might detract from the narrative flow. In these situations, the information has been placed into boxes. Readers can then peruse the additional information as they choose.
- Each chapter ends with a chapter summary, a collection of key terms, and a series of study questions that the student can use to evaluate his or her understanding of the material. Study questions are designed so that a student who understands the material should be able to give an immediate and simple answer. In constrast, exercises require more thought and time, even if a student has understood the chapter. Finally, each chapter ends with a series of programming projects. These can be used as jumping-off points for instructors in the creation of projects for their own courses.

Assumed Background

It is assumed that the student using this book will have had at least one course that introduced programming using Java. The book also assumes that the student has some mathematical background, generally no more than is typically found in high school mathematics. For example, we assume that the student has seen the definition of a logarithm and is familiar with the terms polynomial and exponential. Students who have some background in programming but not in Java should read Appendix A to learn more about the language.

How This Book Is Organized

- **Tools and techniques:** Chapters 1 through 5 provide the foundation on which everything else will be built. These chapters define the essential concept of the abstract data type (ADT) and describe the tools used in the evaluation and analysis of data structures.

- **Basic data abstractions:** Chapters 6 and 8 provide detailed descriptions of the two most important fundamental data abstractions: the vector and the linked list. Chapters 7 and 9 each provide an explanation of some of the more common variations on these fundamental ideas. Many of the sections in these latter chapters are marked as optional material and can be omitted at the discretion of the instructor.
- **Insertion order—preserving containers:** Chapters 10, 11, and 12 consider data structures applicable to problems in which the order that values are added to a collection is important. These data structures can be divided into three broad categories, each considered in a separate chapter.
- **Trees and their uses:** Chapters 13, 14, and 15 consider the various ways in which binary trees are used in the creation of data structures. Binary trees are important in providing a natural way to repeatedly reduce the size of a problem by half and thus permit efficient solution to many problems.
- **Advanced data structures:** Chapters 16 through 19 consider a sequence of more advanced data structures. Most are constructed as *adapters* built on top of earlier abstractions. Hash tables are introduced first as a technique for implementing simple collections and only later (in Chapter 17) as a tool for developing efficient maps. Many data structure texts explore hash tables only as a key/value data structure, leaving the mistaken impression that this is their only use.
- **Algorithms:** Chapter 20 considers the graph data type. Here, several alternative data structure representations are in common use, and the emphasis in this chapter is more on the development and analysis of useful algorithms than on any particular data structuring technique.

Appendix A provides a quick overview of Java syntax. This material is useful for students who come to this course with a background in a different programming language.

TOPICS BY PREREQUISITES

No one order of presentation can hope to suit all situations. Students in different institutions will have different backgrounds. Some instructors will want to take a more mathematical approach to this material; others, a more software engineering approach. Some instructors will think that `SkipLists` (to take just one example) are eye opening and therefore fundamental to the purpose of this course; others may think that the same abstraction is far too complex and should be omitted altogether.

I have endeavored to satisfy these diverse requirements in a number of ways. Many of the interesting but nevertheless tangential ideas encountered during the development of the classic data structures have been placed in sidebars, which can be emphasized or ignored at the instructor's discretion. Similarly, many sections are marked as optional. The instructor is free to pick and choose those optional sections as interest and schedules dictate.

Even the order of entire chapters can be rearranged. The order given here seemed most natural to me, but I nevertheless realize that natural in some cases may reflect more than a little personal bias. I will therefore explicitly describe the prerequisite chain, leaving open the possibility of approaching the material in a slightly different order.

The first five chapters are fundamental and should be covered in the order presented. However, the amount of time one elects to spend on these chapters can be adjusted, depending on the background the students will have acquired in their earlier courses. (The same can be said of the first appendix. Appendix A can be omitted if students have had previous courses in Java programming, but may need to be covered in detail if students' previous programming has been in a different language.)

Once past the introductory material, the order of dependencies between chapters can be described as follows:

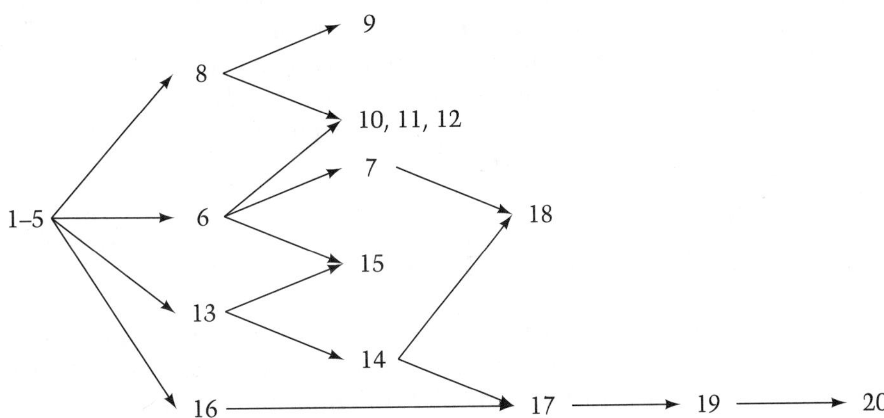

Chapters 6 (vectors) and 8 (linked lists) need no more than an understanding of abstract data types, which is developed in Chapter 2. Chapter 7 (sorted vectors) presents variations on the topics of Chapter 6. In a similar fashion, Chapter 9 (list variations) discusses variations on the theme of linked lists introduced in Chapter 8. Much of the material in Chapters 7 and 9 is marked as optional; although interesting, it can be omitted with little impact on understanding the rest of the material in the text.

Chapters 10, 11, and 12 (stacks, deques, and queues, respectively) represent one large unit divided over three chapters. They require only the basic ideas developed in Chapters 6 and 8. The order of Chapters 11 and 12 is largely arbitrary. Doing 12 before 11 makes more sense from a formal or mathematical perspective, whereas doing 11 before 12 makes more sense from a software engineering perspective. However, either order is possible.

Chapter 13, on trees, is fundamental to both Chapters 14 (binary search trees) and 15 (priority queues, heaps). However, the order of the latter two chapters is arbitrary and can easily be reversed.

Chapter 16, on hash tables, does not depend on anything other than the basic ADT definitions (from Chapter 2) and a certain level of comfort in the analysis of algorithms (as will be gained throughout the book). Chapter 16 can be easily moved earlier in the course if the instructor so desires.

Chapter 17, on maps, depends loosely on Chapter 16 and more strongly on Chapters 8 and 14. Chapter 17, too, could easily be moved earlier in the course if the instructor so desires.

Chapter 18, on sets, depends on Chapter 7 and slightly more loosely on Chapters 8 and 14. If the material in Chapter 7 was slighted or omitted earlier in the course, it can easily be brought forth into this chapter.

Chapter 19, on matrices, depends only loosely on Chapter 17. Many instructors like to present the first part of this chapter much earlier, linking the matrix idea to the concept of the vector developed in Chapter 6. This can be accommodated by omitting Sections 19.7 and 19.8, which contain the only real dependencies on Chapter 17.

Finally, Chapter 20 does build on the matrix concepts discussed in Chapter 19. However, if Chapter 19 is moved earlier in the course, so too can Chapter 20.

ADVANTAGES OF USING JAVA

As a vehicle for teaching, Java is a great advance over many of the alternative langauges, such as C++ or Pascal. Unlike Pascal, Java forces the student to adopt an object-oriented mindset. The error messages from Java compilers are typically much more useful than error messages from, for example, the majority of C++ compilers. Similarly, Java performs many more run-time checks, making debugging less of a burden.

Java is a relatively simple language, having far fewer subtle dark corners than does C++. And Java is largely platform independent. This allows textbooks, such as this one, to be independent of any platform. It also allows students to move their code from one system to another. Many colleges now permit students to develop programs on any platform of their choice, so a single class will have some students working on Windows systems, others on Macintoshes, and others on UNIX or Linux variants.

Java also allows students to create graphical applications much more easily than in most other languages. Students often find these graphical programs more appealing than the traditional text-centered example programs. Of course, it is important that the instructor ensure that the message does not become lost in the medium.

PROBLEMS INHERENT IN JAVA

Both students and instructors who have used Java in an earlier course will have encountered the fact that the language imposes the need to explain many ideas far earlier than an instructor might desire. Consider this classic first program:

```
class HelloWorld {
  public static void main (String [ ] args) {
    System.out.println("hello world!");
  }
}
```

Understanding it requires an explanation of `static` methods, classes and objects, command line arguments, and system output. Similarly, a few concepts must be mentioned in the early part of this book, although they are not relevant to the point at hand and are not used until much later. The three most notable concepts in this category are serialization, synchronization, and stream I/O.

Declaring an object as `Serializable` simply means that it can be written in binary form to a stream: for example, placed into a file. Because this is a useful property for objects to have, we declare, in Chapter 2, all our containers as subclasses of `Serializable`. However, having made this statement, nothing more is made of this property until Chapter 17, and there only fleetingly.

Similarly, honesty dictates that when it is important for a method to be declared `synchronized`, we do so, even if it occurs in an early chapter—despite the fact that few students will have ever written a program that uses multiple threads, and we will not ourselves create such a program until Chapter 12. But although we don't expect the student to be able to write multithreaded applications right from the start, the idea that such a thing is *possible* is not difficult to grasp, and hence our discussion of the problems that the `synchronized` modifier is intended to solve should be accessible to all students, regardless of their background.

The Java I/O library is structured differently from similar libraries found in other languages. Seen in the right light, it is an excellent illustration of object-oriented design and reuse. However, at least initially, it is simply a confusingly large collection of seemingly unrelated classes. This has been made doubly so by the introduction, in Java 1.2, of two parallel libraries: one based on streams (for processing bytes) and one based on `Readers` (for processing characters). We have tried to minimize this confusion by introducing features slowly and one at a time.

An attraction of Java is that it permits the creation of graphical interfaces with far less effort than is required by many other languages. Nevertheless, it takes some time to master the AWT (Abstract Windowing Toolkit), the Java GUI building library. The author (not to mention the instructor) is faced with a quandary. Students like creating more graphical programs, such as games, but time devoted to teaching GUI concepts comes at the expense of time that could be spent teaching data structures. The examples presented in this book try to walk a middle ground. Some examples are graphical, but many are not. Those that are tend to use very simple graphics, so that the issues relating to data structures do not become lost.

WHY NOT USE THE STANDARD LIBRARY?

When I started contemplating writing a data structures textbook using Java, my first thought was to base the material on an examination of the data types found in the Java standard library as distributed by Sun Microsystems. Doing so would have many advantages. The library would be found as part of any Java implementation, thereby avoiding the necessity of distributing code along with the text. Students would be much more likely to use the standard library after finishing the course than to continue to use a textbook-specific set of classes, and so on.

However, after carefully examining the Java collection classes, I decided that to limit myself to these abstractions would simply not do justice to the material. My reasons for coming to this conclusion were as follows:

The Java library is incomplete. Major abstractions, even whole families of data types, are not covered by the code found in the standard library.

The Java library is misleading and in some places poorly designed. A good example is the `HashTable` data type. In the Java library, this is a dictionary-like data structure that is indeed one of the classic *applications* for this data type, but it prevents any discussion of the equally historical use of the data type as a simple *set*. Furthermore, the data type is an odd mishmash of the two classic hash table techniques.

The library has wide interfaces. This is perhaps an understandable decision on the part of the designers of the Java library, as they want to get the most mileage out of the fewest data structures. But for a student audience, wide interfaces tend to obscure the important points. In my own data structures, I have purposely made very narrow interfaces, thus permitting me to spend the majority of my time addressing the key concepts.

The library confuses interfaces and implementations. Although the Java library has both interfaces and implementations, they tend to be very close to each other. Thus, there is a great tendency to program to an implementation rather than selecting the appropriate interface. It is difficult to say what, in the Java library, corresponds to an abstract data type. In my own code, I have used a larger number of smaller interfaces and consistently in my example programs illustrate the idea of programming to an interface (an ADT) rather than to an implementation.

The library shows too much evidence of evolution. The code in the standard library underwent a major revision in the 1.2 version of the language yet retained backward compatibility with the earlier library. This introduced several inconsistencies into the library, such as in naming conventions. By writing my own library, I can use a consistent and, I hope, easy-to-remember set of conventions.

The library has unsupported operations. A key idea in the Java standard library is that an implementation may claim to support an interface and nevertheless decline to respect all the methods specified by the interface. The implementation can do this by throwing an `UnsupportedOperationException` when asked to perform a method it is unable to honor. Although occasionally useful, this is a bad idea to hold up to the student as a paradigm. In the library of abstractions I describe in this book, only when I discuss open hashing and the `remove` operation do I not provide a working implementation for a method declared in the interface.

Nevertheless, I have provided, in Appendix C, a discussion of the data structures found in the Java standard library and how they relate to the categories described in this text.

Obtaining the Code

I can be reached by e-mail at `budd@cs.orst.edu`. My personal Web pages are found at `http://www.cs.orst.edu/~budd/`. The library of abstractions described in this book can be downloaded from `ftp://ftp.cs.orst.edu/pub/budd/jds`.

Supplementary material for qualified instructors is available. Contact your Addison-Wesley representative or send e-mail to `\verb+aw.cse @awl.com+` for details.

ACKNOWLEDGMENTS

Many people have seen earlier drafts of this text, and their comments and suggestions have been most helpful. In particular, I wish to acknowledge Paul Benjamin (Pace University), Rebecca Djang (Oregon State University), Peter Gabrovsky (California State University), Dean Kelley (Minnesota State University, Mankato), Martha Klems (Western Illinois University), Robert Moll (University of Massachusetts, Amherst), Jim Morrison (Mankato State University), Thaddeus F. Pawlicki (University of Rochester), Carolyn Schauble (Colorado State University), Frank Tompa (University of Waterloo), Jane Turk (La Salle University), Jack Wileden (University of Massachusetts), and Salih Yurttas (Texas A&M University).

Of course, a great deal of rewriting occurred after I received all of these comments, so any remaining errors are solely my responsibility.

My editor from Addison-Wesley has once again been Susan Hartman, now Susan Hartman Sullivan. Despite some important changes going on in her life, she somehow still found time to discuss *Data Structures* with me and with the reviewers. I wish her and her new husband, Pat, all the best. Her able assistant has been Lisa Kalner, with whom I have also had the pleasure to work with on previous projects. As always, I have found Susan and Lisa, and all the rest of the Addison-Wesley team, to be professional and a pleasure to work with. As with several of my recent books, composition and layout has been produced by Paul Anagnostopoulos of Windfall Software. I am continually amazed at how Paul and his team make a job that I know is so complex look so easy.

Classic Data Structures in Java

CHAPTER 1

THE MANAGEMENT OF COMPLEXITY

An exploration of any field must always begin by placing the topic in context and relating the new information to the body of existing knowledge that the author assumes is already familiar to the reader. So it is with this book. We are setting out to explore the concept of a data structure. But to do so, we must first pull together ideas you will have undoubtedly seen but may not have pondered in detail.

First of all, we assume that you have at least a passing familiarity with the programming language Java, which we will use as the vehicle for our exposition. This is not to say that data structures are limited to Java. Indeed, the basic ideas found at the heart of most data structures transcend programming languages and can be rewritten in a host of other forms. But ideas are most easily understood with the help of concrete examples, and concrete examples require the use of a specific programming language. We have selected Java as our language. Appendix A provides a short summary of the essential features of Java for the benefit of readers who come to this material with a background in other programming languages.

Data structures are one of the simplest tools used to help structure and control the complexity of large applications. The beginning computer science student may never have thought about the problems inherent in large computer programs. Fortunately, most of the techniques used by computer scientists mirror techniques the student will have experience with in everyday life. In this chapter, we will explore some of the techniques used both to develop large computer applications and to understand existing large systems.

1.1 The Control of Complexity

Most students embarking on the study of data structures will have created a program of at most 100–200 lines in length. Programs of this size can be easily understood by one person and can be constructed with a bit of insight, a dash of perseverance, and maybe just a tad bit of luck. Unfortunately, luck, and sometimes even insight, do not always suffice as pro-

Programming in the Small versus Programming in the Large

The difference between the development of individual projects and more sizable software systems is often described using the terms "programming in the small" and "programming in the large." Briefly, programming in the small characterizes projects with the following attributes.

- Code is developed by a single programmer or perhaps by a very small collection of programmers. A single individual can understand all aspects of a project: from top to bottom, beginning to end.
- The major problem in the software development process is the design and development of algorithms for dealing with the problem at hand.

Programming in the large, on the other hand, characterizes software projects with features such as the following.

- The software system is developed by a large team of programmers. Individuals involved in the specification or the design of the system may differ from those involved in the coding of individual components, who may differ as well from those involved in the integration of various components into the final product. No single individual can be said to be responsible for the entire project or even necessarily understand all aspects of the project.
- The major problem in the software development process is the management of details and the communication of information among members of the programming team.

Although the beginning student will initially practice programming in the small, aspects of the Java language are best understood as responses to the problems of programming in the large. Thus, some appreciation of the difficulties involved in developing large systems is a helpful prerequisite to understanding the Java language.

Increasingly, even beginning students are experiencing some aspects of programming in the large through the use of software frameworks. A software framework, such as a graphical user interface system, may handle a significant portion of the functionality involved in using a windowing system. The user of a software framework seldom understands the details about how operations are implemented, instead merely needing to know how the new software component connects and interacts with the framework. Thus, even relatively simple programs are generated as a component connected to a larger system.

grams become ever larger.[1] Instead, the creation of significant software systems requires discipline, organization, and systematic management skills.

Nowadays, the typical computer application requires thousands, if not millions, of lines of code. Furthermore, these applications are created by groups of programmers working together as a team. In such an environment, proper organization and the management of communication are keys for success. Even when working alone, a solitary programmer will, more often than not, have to connect code to large libraries of software written by others. For example, the Java programmer very quickly encounters the vast libraries for developing user interfaces and for performing file I/O. Effective programming requires making use of these libraries without necessarily understanding the exact steps they use to perform their tasks. So once again, it is organization and communication that are of greatest concern, not coding.

Many of the features of Java, and more generally of the style of programming embodied by Java (termed *object-oriented* programming), have evolved in response to the need to manage and to control these large and complex software development efforts. Although we do not expect that readers will have had previous experience in writing large Java programs, we do expect that most readers will have had to understand and to solve complex problems, as complexity is a natural part of everyday life. Therefore, in order to motivate the need for the tools and techniques we will use in the development of software, we first consider ways that people manage and understand complex systems in real life.

1.2 Abstraction, Information Hiding, and Layering

If you open an atlas, you will often first see a map of the world. This map will show only the most significant features. For example, it may show the various mountain ranges, the ocean currents, and other extremely large structures. But small features will almost certainly be omitted.

A subsequent map will cover a smaller geographical region and will typically possess more detail. For example, a map of a single continent, such as South America, may now include political boundaries and perhaps the major cities. A map over an even smaller region, such as a country, might then include towns and cities and smaller geographical features, such as the names of individual mountains. A map of an individual large city might include the most important roads leading into and out of the city.

1. Although perseverance is almost always helpful.

Note how, at each level, certain information has been included and certain information purposely omitted. Fundamentally, people use only a few simple tools to create, understand, or manage complex systems. One of the most important techniques is termed *abstraction*.

→ **Abstraction** Abstraction is the purposeful suppression, or hiding, of some details of a process or an artifact in order to bring out more clearly other aspects or details.

Consider the average person's understanding of an automobile. My view of an automobile engine, for example, is as a device that takes fuel as input and produces a rotation of the drive shaft as output. This rotation is too fast to connect to the wheels of the car directly, so a transmission is the mechanism used to reduce a rotation of several thousand revolutions per minute to a rotation of several revolutions per minute. This slower rotation can then be used to propel my car. This description is not exactly correct, but it is sufficiently close for everyday purposes. We sometimes say that by means of abstraction, I have constructed a *model* of the actual system.

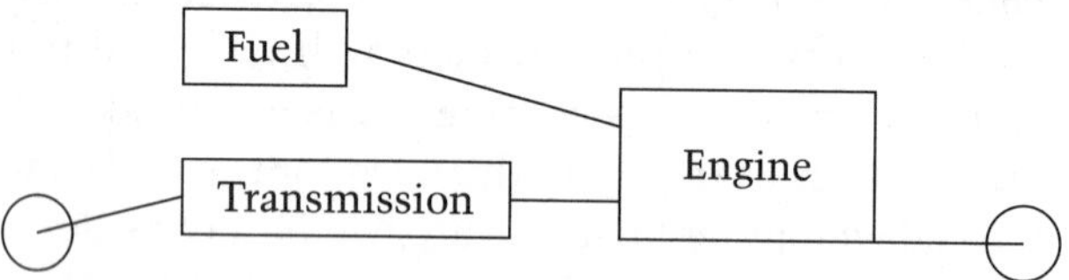

In forming an abstraction, or model, we purposely avoid the need to understand many details, concentrating instead on a few key features. We often describe this process with another term, *information hiding*.

→ **Information Hiding** Information hiding is the purposeful omission of details in the development of an abstract representation.

The appropriate level of information hiding may vary from user to user. My mechanic, for example, requires a much more detailed model of an automobile than do I. The automobile example also illustrates another important technique commonly used to manage the understanding of complex systems. This is the idea of *layering*.

→ **Layering** Layering is the imposition of structure over a model.

Layering is used to help understand a system. The structure I impose may reflect some real aspects of the system (my car really does have both an engine and a transmission), or it may simply be a mental abstraction we use to aid our understanding.

This idea of layering can be further subdivided into a variety of forms (Figure 1.1). A common technique is to divide a layer into constituent

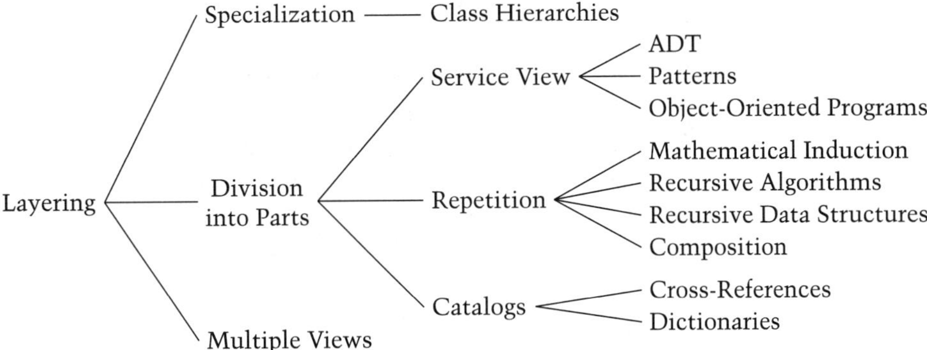

FIGURE 1.1 Some Techniques for Handling Complexity, with Examples

parts. This is the approach I used when I described my automobile as being composed of the engine, the transmission, the body, and the wheels. The next level of understanding is then achieved by examining each of these parts in turn. This is nothing more than the application of the old maxim *divide and conquer*.

Other times, we use different types of layering. Another form is the idea of layers of specialization (Figure 1.2). My understanding of an automobile is based, in part, on my knowledge that it is a *wheeled vehicle*, which is in turn a *means of transportation*. I know other information about wheeled vehicles, and that knowledge is applicable to both my automobile and my bicycle. I have other knowledge about various means of transportation, and that information is also applicable to pack horses and to bicycles. Object-oriented languages make extensive use of this form of layering.

Yet another form of layering is to provide multiple views of the same artifact. Each of the views can emphasize certain details and suppress others and thus bring out different features of the same object. My view of a car, for example, is very different from the view used by my mechanic. Let us consider each of these techniques in turn.

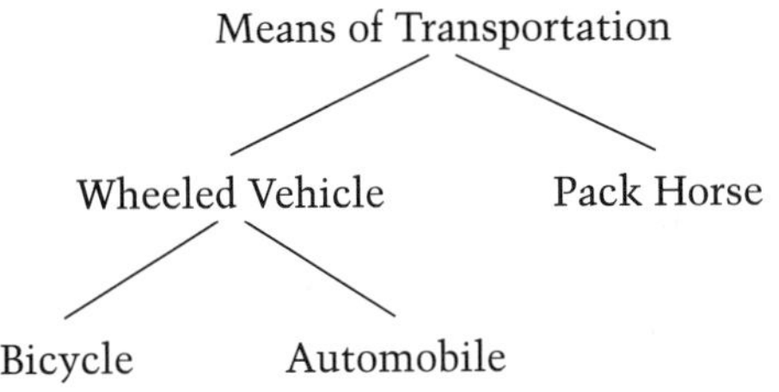

FIGURE 1.2 Layers of Specialization

1.3 Division into Parts

The most common technique people use to help understand complex systems is to combine abstraction with a division into component parts. My description of an automobile is an example of this. The next level of understanding is then achieved by taking each of the parts and performing the same sort of analysis at a finer level of detail. A slightly more precise description of an engine, for example, views it as a collection of cylinders, each of which converts an explosion of fuel into a vertical motion, and a crankshaft, which converts the up-and-down motion of the cylinder into a rotation.

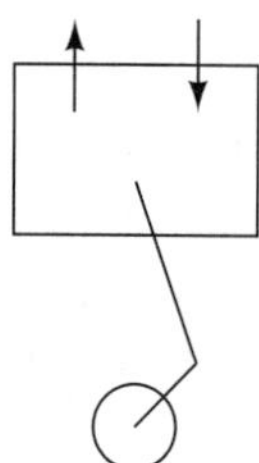

Another example might be organizing information about motion in a human body. At one level, we are simply concerned with mechanics, and we consider the body as composed of bone (for rigidity), muscles (for movement), eyes and ears (for sensing), the nervous system (for transferring information), and skin (to bind it all together). At the next level of detail, we might ask how the muscles work and consider such issues as cell structure and chemical actions. But chemical actions are governed by their molecular structure. And to understand molecules, we break them into their individual atoms.

Any explanation must be phrased at the right level of abstraction. Trying to explain how a person can walk, for example, by understanding the atomic-level details is almost certainly difficult, if not impossible.

1.3.1 Encapsulation and Interchangeability

A key step in the creation of large systems is the division into components. Suppose that instead of writing software, we are part of a team working to create a new automobile. By separating the automobile into the parts *engine* and *transmission*, it is possible to assign people to work on the two aspects more or less independently of each other. We use the term *encapsulation* to mean that the inner and the outer views are strictly divided; those members of the team working on the engine need only an abstract (outside, as it were) view of the transmission, whereas those working on the transmission need the more detailed (inside) view.

An important benefit of encapsulation is that it permits us to consider the possibility of *interchangeability*. When we divide a system into parts, a desirable goal is that the interaction between the parts is kept to a minimum. For example, by encapsulating the behavior of the engine from that of the transmission, we permit the ability to exchange one type of engine with another without incurring an undue impact on the other portions of the system.

For these ideas to be applicable to software systems, we need a way to discuss the task that a software component performs and to separate this from the way in which the component fulfills this responsibility.

1.3.2 Interface and Implementation

In software, we use the terms *interface* and *implementation* to describe the distinction between the *what* aspects of a task and the *how* features: between the outside view and the inside view. An interface describes what a system is designed to do. This is the view that *users* of the abstraction must understand. The interface says nothing about how the assigned task is being performed. So to work, an interface is matched with an *implementation* that completes the abstraction. The designers of an engine will deal with the interface to the transmission, whereas the designers of the transmission must complete an implementation of this interface.

Similarly, a key step along the path to developing complex computer systems will be the division of a task into component parts. These parts can then be developed by different members of a team. Each component will have two faces: the interface that it shows to the outside world and an implementation that it uses to fulfill the requirements of the interface.

CATALOGS

When the number of components in a system becomes large, it is often useful to organize the items by means of a catalog. We use many different forms of catalog in everyday life. Examples include a telephone directory, a dictionary, or an Internet search engine. Similarly, a variety of catalogs are used in software. One example is a simple list of classes. Another might be the list of methods defined by a class. A reference book that describes the classes found in the Java standard library is a very useful form of catalog. In each of these cases, the idea is to give the user a mechanism to quickly locate a single part (be it class, object, or method) from a larger collection of items.

The division between interface and implementation makes it easier to understand a design at a high level, as the description of an interface is much simpler than the description of any specific implementation. This division also makes possible the interchangeability of software components, as I can use any implementation that satisfies the specifications given by the interface.

1.3.3 The Service View

The idea that an interface describes the service provided by a software component without describing the techniques used to implement the service is at the heart of a much more general approach to managing the understanding of complex software systems. When we break a complex system into smaller components, one very useful way of describing the interfaces among the various parts is by the services they provide to the other elements. This, too, is very close to the way people frequently describe their interactions in real life. For example, suppose that I wish to send flowers to my friend Sally, who lives in another city. To do this, I talk with my local florist (who is named Flora), who will in turn telephone another florist in Sally's city. That florist will have obtained her flowers from a wholesaler, will perhaps make use of an arranger, and will see that the flowers are delivered to Sally by means of a delivery person. So a whole community of people is involved in the process of sending flowers.

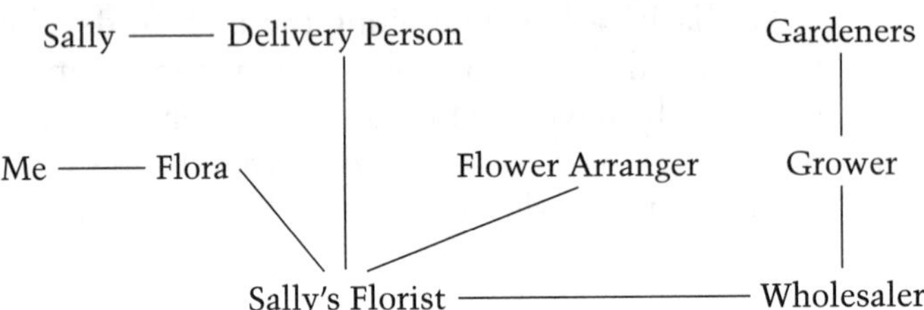

We can describe each of these individuals by the service the person provides to the other members of the community. We often use a similar technique to describe object-oriented programs. A complex application will be viewed as a "community" of interacting objects. Each object will have a role to play, and each object will provide a service to the other members of the community. The benefit of the service view is that it permits us to concentrate on describing the "what"—the task that needs to be done—without needing to understand the "how"—the way in which each of the individual behaviors will be realized. As with all forms of abstraction, we purposely hide some details in order to emphasize others.

1.3.4 Repetition and Recursion

An important special form of breaking into parts occurs when we have *repetition* of a number of identical or nearly identical components. Repetition permits us to divide the understanding between a level where we consider a single component in isolation and a level where we consider the overall structure of an entire collection. We used this approach in describing an engine as a collection of cylinders and then proceeded to describe the actions of just a single cylinder.

We will see many examples of repetition in this book. For example, in Chapter 8, we will explore the concept of a linked list. A linked list is formed out of links. Each link is simply a structure that holds a single value and a reference to the next link.

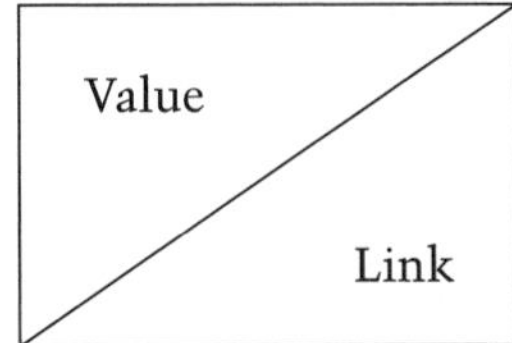

In Java, a reference is either another object or the special element `null` that indicates an uninitialized reference. A list can therefore be constructed by creating a collection of links, the last link holding a `null` reference, and each link other than the last referring to the next.

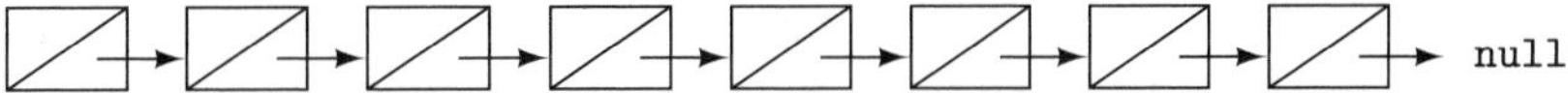

A similar arrangement is the idea of a *binary tree*, which we will explore in Chapter 13. A binary tree is composed of nodes. Each node contains a value and two references: a left child and a right child. As with the linked list, the children can be `null` or they can be another binary tree.

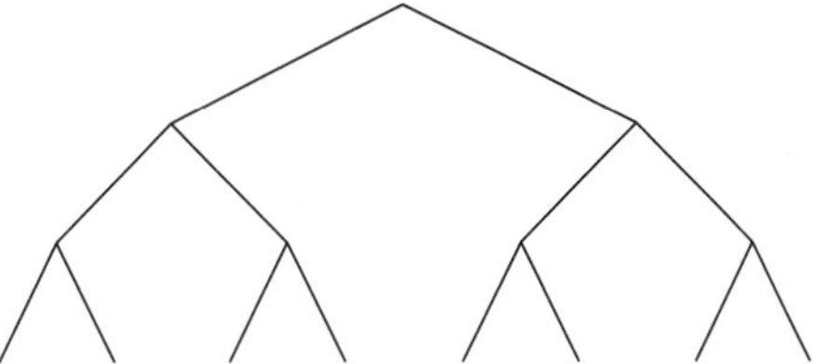

Repetition may not always involve separable artifacts. A good example is the concept of mathematical induction, a topic we will also return to in a later chapter. Here, as in the linked list, the important idea is that there are two levels of understanding. We can understand the individual parts in isolation, and then we can step back and understand how the resulting proof applies to all numbers, regardless of their magnitude.

To illustrate, consider the proof that the sum of the integers from 1 to n is $\frac{n(n+1)}{2}$. To prove this, we start with a base case, simply observing that the sum of the values from 1 to 1 is $\frac{1(1+1)}{2}$. (If we are cautious or doubt our claim, we might try a few more numbers, such as 2 and 3). We then present an induction step, whereby we *assume* that the claim is true for all values up to n, then prove it true for $n+1$.

$$\begin{aligned} 1+2+\cdots+(n+1) &= 1+2+\cdots+n+(n+1) \\ &= (1+2+\cdots+n)+(n+1) \end{aligned}$$

which, by our assumption, can be rewritten as follows:

$$\begin{aligned} &= \frac{n(n+1)}{2}+(n+1) \\ &= \frac{n^2+n}{2}+\frac{2n+2}{2} \\ &= \frac{n^2+3n+2}{2} \\ &= \frac{(n+1)(n+2)}{2}, \qquad q.e.d. \end{aligned}$$

These two parts—the base case and the induction argument—can be understood in isolation. When we step back and examine the larger picture, the amazing result is that the claim must be true for any positive value n, regardless of its size.

The same technique used to understand mathematical induction can also be applied to understanding recursive methods. In the case of a recursive method, it is the execution that is being repeated. As with mathematical induction, there is a base case and a recursive case. Imagine, for example, that we are developing a procedure to print a positive integer value. Assume that we have the ability to print a single character value for the digit characters between 0 and 9. A recursive procedure might be written as follows:

```
public void printInt(OutputStream out, int val) {
    // pre: val is greater than or equal to zero
    // post: will print textual representation of val on out
  if (n < 10)
    out.write(digitChar(val)); // base case, print one digit
```

```
  else {
    printInt(n/10); // recursive call, print all but last digit
    out.write(digitChar(n%10)  // then print last digit
  }
}
```

We can understand this procedure by verifying the base case (numbers less than 10) and then the induction case (all other numbers). To print the value 456, for example, we divide the number into the two parts 45 and 6. The former is then printed recursively, whereas the latter is a single-digit number we know how to print. As any number must eventually be reduced to a single digit, the desired output is eventually produced.

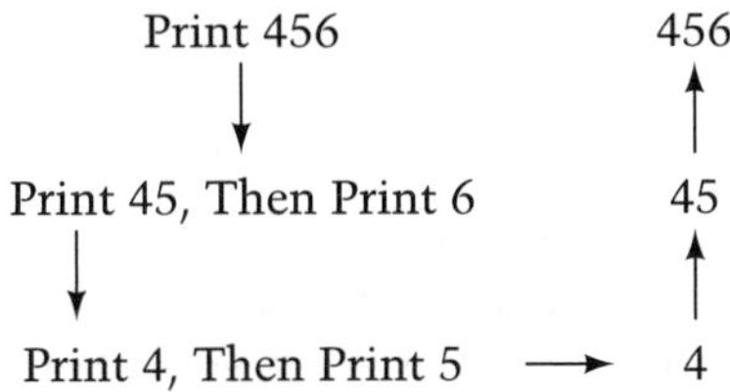

The common theme in recursive procedures, mathematical induction, and recursive data structures is to reduce complexity by dividing a problem into two levels. At a high level is a collection of similar components (or ideas). At a lower level, we then consider just a single instance. We can examine the artifact first at the lower level and then step back and consider how all the pieces fit together.

1.4 Composition

Composition is another powerful technique used to create complex structures out of simple parts. The idea is to begin with a few primitive forms and to add rules for combining forms to create new forms. The key insight in composition is to permit the combination mechanism to be used both on the new forms and on the original primitive forms.

A good illustration of this technique is the concept of regular expressions. Regular expressions are a simple technique for describing sets of values and have been extensively studied by theoretical computer scientists. The description of a regular expression begins by identifying a basic alphabet, such as the letters a, b, c, and d. Any single example of the alphabet is a regular expression. We next add a rule that says that the composition of two regular expressions is a regular expression. By applying this rule repeatedly, we see that any finite string of letters is a regular expression:

abaccaba

The next combining rule says that the alternation (represented by the vertical bar |) of two regular expressions is a regular expression. Normally, we give this rule a lower precedence than composition, so that the following pattern represents the set of three-letter values that begin with ab and end with an a, c, or d:

aba | abc | abd

Parentheses can be used for grouping, so the previous set can also be described as follows:

ab(a | c | d)

Finally, the * symbol (technically known as the Kleene star) is used to represent the concept "zero or more repetitions." By combining these rules, we can describe quite complex sets. For example, the following describes the set of values that begin with a run of a's and b's followed by a single c, or a two-character sequence dd followed by the letter a.

(((a | b) * c) | dd)a

This idea of composition is also basic to the Java type system. We begin with the primitive types, such as `int` and `boolean`. The idea of a `class` then permits the user to create new types.[2] These new types can include data fields constructed out of previous types, either primitive or user-defined. As classes can build on previously defined classes, very complex structures can be constructed piece by piece.

```
class  Box { // a box is a new data type
   .
   .
   .
  private int value; // built out of the existing type int
}
```

Yet another application of the principle of composition is the way the Java GUI (graphical user interface) library facilitates the layout of windows. A window is composed from a few simple data types, such as buttons,

2. Appendix A gives a summary of the basic concepts found in the Java programming language. In the next chapter, we will also discuss in more detail the creation of new software abstractions, using classes and interfaces.

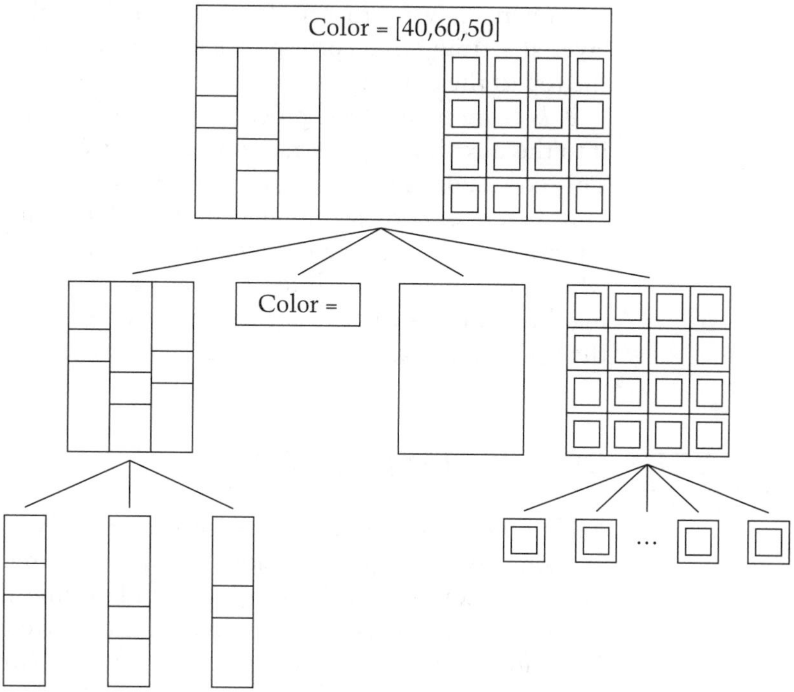

FIGURE 1.3 Composition in the Creation of User Interfaces

sliders, and drawing panels. Various types of layout managers create simple structures. For example, a grid layout defines a rectangular grid of equal-sized components; a border layout manager permits the specification of up to five components in the north, south, east, west, and center of a screen. As with regular expressions, the key is that windows can be structured as part of other windows. Imagine, for example, that we want to define a window that has three sliders on the left, a drawing panel in the middle, a bank of sixteen buttons organized four by four on the right, and a text output box running along the top. We can do this by laying simple windows inside of more complex windows (Figure 1.3).

Many computer programs can themselves be considered a product of composition, whereby the method or procedure call is the mechanism of composition. We begin with the primitive statements in the language (assignments and the like). With these we can develop a library of useful functions. Using these functions as new primitives, we can then develop more complex functions. We continue, each layer being built on top of earlier layers, until eventually we have the desired application.

To either construct or understand a system constructed using composition, we can proceed in either a top-down or a bottom-up fashion. A *top-down* analysis proceeds from the final complete system and unwraps a layer at a time. This corresponds to, for example, reading Figure 1.3 from the top to the bottom.

A *bottom-up* analysis proceeds from the primitive parts, building each into the next level of abstraction, until the complete system is developed. This corresponds to reading Figure 1.3 from the bottom to the top.

In practice, both techniques are used for both understanding and construction. Analysis or construction can advance from the bottom, seeing what is feasible to do, while a similar analysis proceeds from the top, seeking direction for what it is that needs to be done. When the two meet in the middle, a clear path from tools to task is then formed.

1.5 Layers of Specialization

Yet another approach to dealing with complexity is to structure abstraction by using layers of specialization. This is sometimes referred to as a *taxonomy*. For example, in biology, we divide living things into animals and plants. Living things are then divided into vertebrates and invertebrates. The category vertebrates eventually includes mammals, which can be divided into (among other categories) cats and dogs, and so on.

The key difference between this and the earlier layering is that the more specialized layer of abstraction (for example, a cat) is indeed a representative of the more general layer of abstraction (for example, an animal). This was not true when, in an earlier example, we descended from the characterization of a muscle to the description of different chemical interactions. These two types of relations are sometimes described using the heuristic keywords "is-a" and "has-a." The first relationship, that of parts to a whole, is a has-a relation, as in the sentence "A car has an engine." In con-

Handling Exceptions

Phyl and his friends, the furry creatures shown on the cover, remind us that generalizations almost never occur without exceptions. A platypus (such as Phyl) is a mammal that lays eggs. Thus, although we might associate the tidbit of knowledge "gives birth to live young" with the category `Mammal`, we then need to amend this with the caveat "lays eggs" when we descend to the category `Platypus`.

Object-oriented languages also need a mechanism to *override* information inherited from a more general category. We will explore this in more detail once we have developed the idea of class hierarchies.

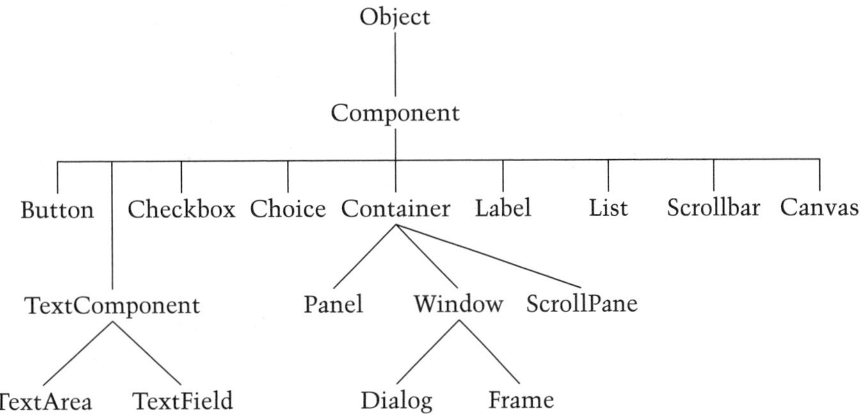

FIGURE 1.4 The AWT Class Hierarchy

trast, the specialization relation is described using is-a, as in "A cat is a mammal."

But in practice, our reason for using either type of layering is the same. The principle of abstraction permits us to suppress some details so that we can more easily characterize a smaller number of features. We can say that mammals are animals that have hair and nurse their young, for example. By associating this fact at a high level of abstraction, we can then apply the information to all more specialized categories, such as cats and dogs.

The same technique is used in object-oriented languages. New interfaces can be formed from existing interfaces. A class can be formed by using inheritance from an existing class. In doing so, all the properties (data fields and behavior) we associate with the original class become available to the new class.

Readers familiar with the Java AWT (Abstract Windowing Toolkit) library will have seen this form of inheritance.[3] When a programmer creates a new application using the AWT, the main class is declared as a subclass of `Frame`, which in turn is linked to many other classes in the AWT library (Figure 1.4). A `Frame` is a special type of application window, but it is also a more specialized type of the general class `Window`. A `Window` can hold other graphical objects and is hence a type of `Container`. Each level of the hierarchy provides methods used by those below. Even the simplest application will likely use the following:

3. Readers unfamiliar with the AWT will learn more about this library in Chapter 6.

Method	Hierarchy
setTitle(String)	Inherited from class Frame
setSize(int, int)	Inherited from class Component
show()	Inherited from class Window
repaint()	Inherited from class Component
paint()	Inherited from Component, Overridden in the programmer's new application class

1.6 MULTIPLE VIEWS

Yet another technique for dealing with complex systems is the idea of looking at the same artifact from a number of perspectives. When we think about an automobile, for example, we sometimes want to dwell on its styling, sometimes on its carrying capacity, and sometimes on its power. Yet it's the same object in all three cases. But the different views, like all abstraction mechanisms, allow us to suppress some details and to bring out others.

We often do the same with software systems. A complex object, such as the LinkedList data structure (a data structure we will develop in Chapter 8), might be viewed at one point as an embodiment of the interfaces it supports. Later, we might want to emphasize the speed with which it performs certain of the actions described by the interface. So we have two views of the same object. However, neither of these views highlights how the list operations work. Hence, yet another view might open up the implementation and discuss how the operations are realized.

1.7 PATTERNS

When faced with a new problem, most people will first look to previous problems they have solved that seem to have characteristics in common with the new task. These previous problems can be used as a model and the new problem attacked in a similar fashion, making changes as necessary to fit the different circumstances.

This insight lies behind the idea of a software *pattern*. A pattern is nothing more than an attempt to document a proven solution to a problem so that future problems can be more easily handled in a similar fashion. However, in their application to computer science, patterns have evolved their own special format. A pattern will typically be described by a narrative divided into the following sections:

name The term that will be used to describe the pattern. By means of these names, a collection of patterns creates a vocabulary with which various design alternatives can be discussed.

synopsis A short description of the problem the pattern is designed to solve.

forces A description of the requirements for a pattern, or the considerations that must be taken into account in the use of the pattern.

solution The essence of the solution.

counterforces A description of reasons that might need to be considered in deciding to *not* use a pattern.

related patterns Descriptions of related patterns the user might want to consider in the solution to the problem.

Not all sections need be found in all patterns. The idea of a pattern is perhaps best illustrated by an example. One of the easiest patterns to describe is the *Adapter*. Suppose that you have one object in your community (a client) that needs a service and requires a specific interface for the provider for that service. Imagine that you have another object that provides the functionality you need but does not happen to support the desired interface. Rather than rewriting either the client or the service provider, you can get the two to communicate with each other by creating an adapter. The adapter simply speaks the language of the requester but rather than doing the work itself, it then translates into the interface used by the service provider.

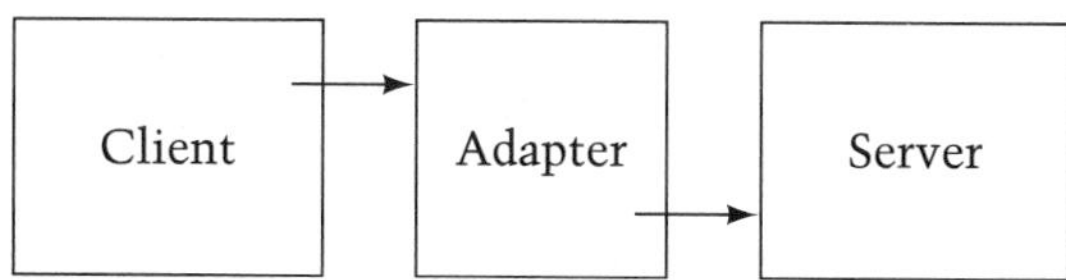

The following describes an adapter in pattern format:

name The Adapter pattern. (The term is derived from a comparison to electrical outlet adapters, such as the type one might use when traveling abroad.)

synopsis Used to connect a client that needs a service described using one interface with a provider that implements the desired functionality but uses a different interface.

solution The Adapter implements the interface as specified by the client but rather than performing the given operations, passes the work on to the service provider.

counterforces Adds one layer of indirection between the client and the provider; also introduces another class of object.

The greatest benefit comes from gathering and cataloging a large collection of common patterns. New problems can then be compared to previous situations; when common features are noted, a solution that has worked well in the past can be applied in a new way. We will see several types of patterns during the course of our investigation.

1.8 Chapter Summary

Key Concepts

- Abstraction
- Information hiding
- Division into components
- Encapsulation
- Interface and implementation
- Repetition
- Induction and recursion
- Composition
- Inheritance hierarchy
- Multiple views
- Pattern

People deal with complex artifacts and situations every day. Thus, although most readers may not yet have created complex computer programs, they nevertheless will have experience in using the tools that computer scientists use in managing complexity.

The most basic tool is *abstraction*, the purposeful suppression of detail in order to emphasize a few basic features. *Information hiding* describes the part of abstraction in which we intentionally choose to ignore some features so that we can concentrate on others.

Abstraction is often combined with a division into *components*. For example, we divided the automobile into the engine and the transmission. Components are carefully chosen so that they *encapsulate* certain key features and interact with other components through a simple and fixed *interface*.

The division into components means that we can divide a large task into smaller problems that can then be worked on more or less independently of each other. It is the responsibility of a developer of a component to provide an *implementation* that satisfies the requirements of the interface.

A point of view that turns out to be very useful in developing complex software systems is the concept of a *service provider*. A software component is providing a service to other components with which it interacts. In real life, we often characterize members of the communities in which we operate by the services they provide. (A delivery person is charged with transporting flowers from a florist to a recipient.) Thus, this metaphor allows one to think about a large software system in the same way that we think about situations in our everyday lives.

Another form of division into parts is *repetition*. With repetition, we have several artifacts of the same type working together. Repetition therefore allows us to understand a system by considering it on two levels: as a single object in isolation and as the entire collection of values. Examples of repetition include data structures, such as linked lists, mathematical induction, or recursive procedures.

Yet another powerful tool for creating complex systems out of simple parts is *composition*. Composition begins with a small set of primitive values, such as the basic types in the Java programming language, and rules for creating new values out of existing values, such as the `class` mechanism. The composition technique then allows new artifacts to be created from the existing elements. These new artifacts then become available for further use, and thus complex systems are constructed layer by layer.

Another form of layering is a taxonomy, in object-oriented languages more often termed an *inheritance hierarchy*. Here, the layers are more detailed representatives of a general category. An example of this type of system is a biological division into categories, such as Living Thing-Animal-Mammal-Cat. Each level is a more specialized version of the previous one. This division simplifies understanding, as knowledge of more general levels is applicable to many more specific categories. When applied to software, this technique also simplifies the creation of new components, because if a new component can be related to an existing category, all the functionality of the older category can be used for free. (Thus, for example, by saying that a new component represents a `Frame` in the Java library, we immediately get such features as a menu bar, as well as the ability to move and to resize the window.)

Another tool we will use in the understanding of complex systems is the concept of *multiple views*. Here, the idea is that we can consider the same artifact in different ways at different times, using abstraction to bring out certain details one time and to bring out other details the next time.

Finally, a particular tool that has become popular in recent years is the *pattern*. A pattern is simply a generalized description of a solution to a problem that has been observed to occur in many places and in many forms. The pattern describes how the problem can be addressed and the reasons both for adopting the solution and for considering other alternatives. We will see several types of patterns throughout this book.

Further Information

In the sidebar on page 7, we mention software catalogs. For the Java programmer, a very useful catalog is *The Java Developer's Almanac* by Patrick Chan [Chan 99].

The concept of *patterns* grew out of work in architecture, specifically the work of Christopher Alexander [Alexander 77]. The application of patterns to software is described by Gabriel [Gabriel 96]. The best-known catalog of software patterns is by Gamma et al. [Gamma 95].

An interesting book that deals with the relationship between how people think and the way they form abstractions of the real word is Lakoff [Lakoff 87].

Study Questions

1. What are some features that characterize programming in the small? How are they different from the features of programming in the large?
2. What is abstraction? What are some ways we use abstraction in real life?
3. What is information hiding? How does information hiding relate to abstraction?
4. What are some of the various forms of layering?
5. How does division into parts simplify the understanding of a complex system?
6. What do we mean by encapsulation? How does encapsulation relate to division into parts?
7. What is the difference between an interface and an implementation?
8. What is the service view of a collection of objects?
9. How is a division into component parts that use repetition different from a division into parts more generally?
10. When we use repetition, what are the two natural levels of explanation or understanding?
11. What is the relationship between mathematical induction and recursive procedures?
12. What is composition? Give two examples.
13. What is the difference between a top-down and a bottom-up analysis of a system formed using composition?
14. In what way is an inheritance hierarchy different from a division into parts?
15. What is a pattern? What are the basic parts of a pattern description?
16. Has this chapter presented a top-down or a bottom-up analysis of methods for controlling complexity?

Exercises

1. In an object-oriented inheritance hierarchy, each level is a more specialized form of the preceding level. Give an example found in everyday life of a hierarchy that has this property. Some types of hierarchy found in everyday life are not inheritance hierarchies. Give an example of a hierarchy that is not an inheritance hierarchy.
2. Take a real-world problem, such as the task of sending flowers described earlier, and describe its solution in terms of agents (objects) and responsibilities.
3. Consider an object in the real world, such as a pet animal. Describe some of the classes, or categories, to which the object belongs. Can you organize these categories into an inheritance hierarchy? What knowledge about the object is represented in each category?
4. Prove, by mathematical induction, that the sum of powers of 2 is one less than the next-higher power. That is, for any nonnegative integer n:

$$\sum_{i=0}^{n} 2^i = 2^{n+1} - 1$$

Programming Projects

1. The procedure `printInt` does not work correctly with negative numbers. Explain how this problem can be remedied; then write a program to execute the method and to verify that it does indeed work. (You will need to also develop an implementation of the method `digitChar` or look ahead to Chapter 3, where we will discuss this method.)

CHAPTER 2

ABSTRACT DATA TYPES

In Chapter 1, we described how a large and complex system can be broken down into component parts. Each of these parts can then be further examined in isolation. But this isolation cannot be complete; each member of the community of components must interact with at least one other member of the group. For this reason, we need a way to formalize the *interface* between two components.

Another useful metaphor introduced in Chapter 1 is the idea of thinking about the relationships between components in terms of the services they provide. Recall the flower example: The local florist provided the service of sending flowers, the driver provided the service of delivery, the grower provided the service of fresh flowers, and so on.

When we carry this idea to computer programs, we must formalize the description of these services. In the field of data structures, this formal description is given the name *abstract data type*, or ADT. Not surprisingly, the idea of an ADT builds on the programming language notion of a type. The reader may never have thought there was anything beyond the obvious in the mechanism of a programming language type. So a part of our exploration in this chapter is an examination of the properties of types. We then extend this to the exposition of the concept of an abstract data type. Having developed the idea of an ADT, we next outline and summarize the various data types that will, for the most part, constitute the body of this text.

2.1 WHAT IS A TYPE?

What does the concept of a *type* represent in a computer programming language? For an idea that, at least with experience, seems so intuitive, the answer may seem surprisingly complicated. When we say that a value, such as 17, is an integer type, what are we asserting?

One answer is that we are asserting that the value is a member of a set of values. The name int is the handle by which we describe this set. In Java, for example, the set of integers represents the whole numbers that range from −2147483648 (which is -2^{31}) to 2147483647 (which is $2^{31} - 1$). Other types denote similar sets of values. The following table shows a few of these:

Set	Range of Values
int	−2147483648 to 2147483647
short	−32768 to 32767
long	−9223372036854775807 to 9223372036854775808
byte	−128 to 127
boolean	true, false

But there is more that we know by virtue of the assertion that a value is an int. We know, for example, that we can perform a set of *operations* on the value. Integers are arithmetic quantities, and so we can perform addition, subtraction, multiplication, and division. We are not permitted to perform these operations on a value of type boolean, as the definition of the boolean data type does not include these tasks.

So in one sense, a type is simply a set of values and a set of operations. But we know yet more about integers. We expect integers to satisfy a set of *properties*. If we add the values 3 and 5, we expect to yield the value 8. This we expect always to be true. Note that some of the properties of integer values differ from our experience with whole numbers in the real world; if we add the value 2,147,483,646 and 5, for example, the computer will produce the negative number −2147483645 and not 2147483651. But we expect this, as it is defined as the behavior of the data type in this situation, and we can count on the operation's always generating the same value.

We expect this behavior because another aspect of type is that it describes the layout of values in memory. An integer is defined as a 32-bit binary number. A short is a 16-bit quantity, and so the addition of two short values 32765 and 5 will yield the result −32766, not 32770 as it would were the values known to be integer.

The notion of type has more features, but these three—values, operations, and properties—will be the most important aspects for our discussion of abstract data types.

2.1.1 Classes

The types int, short, long, byte, char, and boolean are called *primitive types*. They are, in a sense, "built in" to the language. Their operations are part of the basic language grammar and cannot be changed.

New types can be created by using the class mechanism. A class declaration performs several tasks at one time. It adds a new type name to the program vocabulary. It explicitly describes the set of operations associated with this new type. By describing the data fields used by this type, it tells the compiler how instances of the type can be represented in memory and implicitly defines the set of values the type can represent (namely, the collection of bit values that match the memory layout).

TYPED VARIABLES

All programming languages include the concept of type, but not all programming languages use types in the same way. Some languages—LISP and Smalltalk are probably the two best-known examples—associate types with values but not with variables. That is, a value, such as 17, is recognized as an integer type, but a variable, such as x, is simply declared as a name. A variable can hold any type of value. So a variable may at one instance be holding an integer and some time later be holding a floating-point value. Such languages are termed *dynamically typed.*

The alternative is termed a *statically typed* language. Java follows this approach. In a statically typed language, all variables must be associated with a type when they are declared. The statement

```
int maxValue;
```

asserts not only that the variable maxValue can be used as a legal variable in our program but also that it will always maintain an integer variable. Using statically typed languages has many advantages.[a] For example, the compiler can ensure that operations performed on maxValue are only the legal operations permitted by the integer data type. It also means that many errors can be caught at compile time. An example would be to assign a value from one type to a variable of a different type:

```
maxValue = false; // will produce a
                  // compiler error
```

The only exception to the strong typing of variables in Java is the idea of a polymorphic variable defined using an interface or through inheritance, both topics we will discuss later in this chapter.

[a] Advocates of dynamically typed languages would be quick to point out that there are many disadvantages as well, but this is not an issue we want to discuss here.

```
class Box {
  public void insert(int newValue) {
    v = newValue;
  }

  public int extract() {
    return v;
  }

  private int v = 0;
}
```

Having provided the class definition of Box, we can declare variables, create instances using the new operator, and perform any of the operations defined as part of the class:

```
Box joe; // joe is the name of the box
joe = new Box();  // the new operator creates a new instance
joe.insert(12);
System.out.println("box value is " + joe.extract());
```

The Java standard library provides a rich set of class definitions that the programmer can use in his or her code. In addition, a Java programmer will define new types by creating class definitions.

Of our trio *values*, *operations*, and *properties*, the weakest attribute supported by the simple class mechanism is the notion of properties. What exactly do we know to be true after performing one of the operations using an instance of a class? For example, the class Box is a simple holder for an integer value. We (the readers) know that if we insert a value into the box, we will, on a subsequent extract, retrieve the most recently inserted value. But nothing in the code for the extract operation (taken in isolation) tells us that this is true: The compiler knows only that the result is an integer. To help communicate this additional information, programmers often describe the most important properties by using comments:

```
/*
  class Box -
  A container for holding an integer value.
  An insert places a value into the box.
  An extract returns the most recently inserted value.
  The box initially holds the value zero.
*/
class Box {
   .
   .
   .
}
```

Comments should always be written to convey any information that is not obvious from a cursory examination of the code.[1]

2.1.2 Interfaces and Polymorphism

Oftentimes, we will need to discuss related families of similar types. For example, the types `integer` and `short` can be considered to be similar types, as they both support the arithmetic operations, and a value of type `short` can be assigned to a variable of type `int`, or vice versa.

```
int bigValue;
short littleValue;
littleValue = 17;
bigValue = littleValue;
```

Java provides two mechanisms that programmers can use to create families of types in their own code. These are the concepts of *interface* and *inheritance*.

An `interface` is similar to a `class` but defines only the operations the type will support, not their representation. As with classes, interface properties that cannot be written as code are often described by using comments:

```
/*
  interface insertAndExtract
  represents containers for getting and setting integer values
  An insert will place the value,
  and subsequent extract will return the value
*/

interface GetAndSet {
  public void insert (int v);
  public int extract ();
}
```

Note that the interface describes only the argument and return types but does not provide a body for any method. Using an interface, one can declare a variable and perform any of the provided operations; however, it is not legal to create an instance of an interface by using the `new` operator:

```
GetAndSet sam;
sam = new GetAndSet(); // error -- not legal
sam.insert(17);
```

---

1. Despite this remark, the code in this text will purposely use very few comments, in order to force the reader to examine the *code*, not the comments.

TYPE SIGNATURE

The term *type signature* means the combination of method name, argument types, and return type for a function. The term is used mainly when discussing the possibility of two or more methods having the same name:

```
interface StringBox {
  public void insert (int v);
     // can place one integer
  public void insert (int v, int w); // or two
  public void insert (double d); // or a double
  public void insert (String s); // or a string
  public String extract ();
}
```

In this example, four methods have the same name, but they are distinct because they have different type signatures.

Instead, instances of an interface must be created by defining a class that explicitly states that it supports the interface. A class definition makes this assertion, using the `implements` keyword:

```
class OneTimeBox implements GetAndSet {
  public void insert (int newValue) {
    if (notSetYet) { // set only the first time called
      v = newValue;
      notSetYet = false;
    }
  }

  public int extract() {
    return v;
  }

  protected int v = 0;
  private boolean notSetYet = true;
}
```

It is legal to assign a class *value* to any interface *variable* that it supports:[2]

```
GetAndSet alice;
alice = new OneTimeBox(); // legal, OneTimeBox supports GetAndSet
alice.insert(17);
```

Another mechanism that can be used to create families of related types is the idea of *inheritance*. A class can declare that it `extends` from another class. This means that all the operations and data fields defined as part

2. Note that a OneTimeBox and a simple Box differ in some fundamental ways. We are here playing with these examples but will shortly have a more formal way to describe these differences. Exercise 1 will explore the ways we could document these differences in more detail.

of the previous class are then automatically included in the new class. In addition, the new class can define further operations and/or data fields. It can even replace the definition of a method inherited from the parent class, by overriding it with another method having the same type signature.

```
/*
  class SuccessorBox
  a type of box that increments its value each
  time it is accessed, and can also
  return the next value larger than the current contents
*/
class SuccessorBox extends OneTimeBox {
  public int extract() {
    v = v + 1;
    return v;
  }

  public int successor() {
    return 1 + extract();
  }
}
```

Instances of the new class (often called the *child* class) can be created, and they can use operations provided by the earlier class (the *parent* class):

```
SuccessorBox helen;
helen = new SuccessorBox();
helen.insert(17);
  // perform an inherited operation
System.out.println("box value is " + helen.extract());
  // or perform a newly defined operation
System.out.println("box value is " + helen.successor());
```

Software Reuse: Composition and Inheritance

We have described two techniques for leveraging existing software components in order to create new components. Using *composition*, an old component is declared as a data field inside the new object. Using *inheritance*, the old class is declared as the parent to the new class. How does one decide which technique to use?

The answer lies in the two types of hierarchies we described in Chapter 1. Composition is appropriate when we divide a system into parts and the parts are a subunit of the whole. We described this as the "has-a" relationship. Thus, for example, a Box has an integer value, and thus composition is the appropriate technique.

Inheritance, on the other hand, represents the "is-a" relationship. It is appropriate when the new abstraction is a more specialized form of the older component. A `SuccessorBox` is a `OneTimeBox`, meaning that it has all the properties and attributes of the class `OneTimeBox`. And thus inheritance is the appropriate technique.

Because the new class supports all the operations defined as part of the parent and also includes all the parent's data fields, a *value* of the child class can be assigned to a *variable* declared using the parent class:

```
oneTimeBox sam;
sam = helen;
System.out.println("box value is " + sam.extract());
```

Any new operations defined by the child class are, however, lost to variables declared using the parent class:

```
  // error -- sam cannot perform successor operation
System.out.println("box value is " + sam.successor());
```

The `class` mechanism has more features, such as the concept of class *constructors*. However, this brief description will suffice for the moment. Further information on many features of Java can be found in Appendix A.

2.2 Abstract Data Types

The traditional data structure abstractions are mechanisms that have proved themselves useful, over a period of many years, as tools for maintaining collections of values. In this book, we will present these techniques first as a series of interfaces and properties that describe the operations the data types must support and later as a variety of implementations for the various categories of collections.

The fact that we find it necessary to define a number of families of data types can be viewed as a consequence of the idea of abstraction we described in the previous chapter. For example, the name of the simplest collection we will consider, a Bag, is intended to convey a mental image, such as a bag of marbles. Only the most basic operations are provided for the Bag data type. You can place something into the bag, you can see whether the bag contains a specific element, and you can remove an item from the bag. Characteristics, such as the order in which you placed the

Types versus Structures

There is an important distinction between an abstract data *type* and a data *structure*. We will consistently use the term ADT, or data type, to refer to an object that is characterized by its behavior: its operations and properties. An example is the Bag ADT. The characterization of an ADT is made without reference to any concrete implementation. A data *structure*, on the other hand, is the term used to describe a specific approach to provide the services described by an ADT. A `LinkedList` or an `AVLTree` are examples.

items into the bag or the order that elements are stored in the bag, have all been abstracted away.

But sometimes these other features *are* important. Generally not all of them, but the features that are of interest will vary from problem to problem. Thus, the various families of containers are distinguished by the features they elect to not abstract away or, alternatively, by the additional behavior they provide.

For example, sometimes it *is* important that the elements in a collection be maintained in a specific order. This requirement has two broad subdivisions. In the first, the order is given by the elements. We say that the collection is *sorted*. A sorted list of numbers would maintain their values in increasing order; a sorted list of words would maintain the values in the fashion of a dictionary.

But another order of importance may be given not by the elements but by the time or sequence in which they were inserted. It may be critical to know that one value was placed into the collection before another. Elements are then removed from the collection, based on the order in which they were inserted. Two variations on this idea are the *stack*, in which the most recently inserted value is the one removed, and the *queue*, in which the value held in the collection the longest is the one removed.

Another source of variation is the ability to search for a value based on a property rather than simply being able to ask whether the collection does or does not contain a given element. A `FindMin` collection allows one to easily find the smallest element in the collection, whereas a `FindNth` collection allows one to find the *n*th smallest element.

Yet another source of variation is to provide an alternative way to access the elements in a collection. In the simple `Bag`, we are permitted to examine the values only one by one. In an `Indexed` collection, each element is given a position. In addition to sequencing through the values, you can ask for the element stored in position *i*. This *random-access* feature allows the user to jump around in the collection very quickly and is essential to many programming techniques. An alternative method of access is the `Map`. Here, elements are stored as key/value pairs and can be quickly accessed by using the key. An analogy is the way that a dictionary allows you to quickly find a definition, using a word as a key.

Each of the broad categories of collection will be represented by an interface. The interfaces are part of an *abstract data type*, or ADT. As we have seen, interfaces and classes are the two mechanisms a Java programmer can use to create a new data type. An interface is abstract in that it defines only the tasks the type will perform, not their implementation. But unfortunately, an interface defines only the type signatures for a given set of operations. To complete the description of an ADT, we must not only give an interface that describes the operations the type can perform but also describe the properties that those operations must obey.

Let us illustrate this by considering what is the simplest of our data abstractions: the Bag. This ADT is represented in part by the following interface:

```
public interface Bag extends Collection {
  public void addElement (Object newElement);
  public boolean containsElement (Object testElement);
  public Object findElement (Object testElement);
  public void removeElement (Object oldElement);
}
```

The interface `Collection` from which Bag inherits is defined as follows:

```
public interface Collection extends Serializable {
  public Enumeration elements ();
  public boolean isEmpty ();
  public int size ();
}
```

What properties do we expect from a Bag? We can ask, for example, what we expect to be true following an execution of `addElement(newElement)`. One answer is that we would expect that a call on `containsElement` using the same value would yield a `true` result. That is, if a value is inserted into a Bag, the collection contains the value. Properties such as these, which assert statements that we expect to be true following the execution of a method, are described as *postconditions*. You will sometimes see them written as comments documenting a method:

```
public interface Bag extends Collection {
  /*
    addElement -- insert element into set
    postcondition: containsElement (newElement) is true
  */
  public void addElement (Object newElement);
    .
    .
    .
}
```

Of course, we could also make many other assertions. Here are just a few.

- An invocation of `isEmpty` will yield `false` (because the collection now has at least one element).
- The `size` of the collection is one larger than the size it was prior to the insertion.

- A search (using `findElement`) using an argument that is equal to the newly inserted value will be successful and will not throw a `NoSuchElementException`.
- An enumeration of the values (as yielded by *elements*) will now include the newly inserted value.

Sometimes, it is also necessary to note what conditions are required to be true *before* a method can invoked. These are described as *preconditions*. For example, before the method is even started, we expect that the argument value is comparable to the elements already held in the collection.

Just as important as understanding what properties *are* true following an operation is understanding what properties may *not* be true. A good example is the value returned by `findElement`. If a value is placed into a container and then subsequently a search is performed using `findElement` with an argument equal to the original value, we are not guaranteed that the item found will be the value that was just inserted. The reason is that nothing in the definition of Bag prevents the collection from maintaining two values that are equal. (See sidebar on identity and equality.) Furthermore, nothing specifies which of these two values will be the first encountered during the course of a search. Thus, if we insert a value that

OBJECT IDENTITY AND OBJECT EQUALITY

The discussion of the `findElement` method talks about inserting a value into a container, searching for the value, and finding a different element. How can this happen? The following joke helps illustrate what can occur. A man walks into a pizza parlor, sits down, and tells the waiter, "I'll have what that lady is eating." The waiter then picks up the pizza that is resting in front of the lady and sets it down on the man's table.

This joke is funny because it confuses two related issues: *identity* and *equality*. Identity is a property that says that two objects are exactly the same thing. For example, the planet Venus is known as both the morning star and the evening star, and thus we can say that the morning star is identical to the evening star. Equality, on the other hand, is a property that says that two objects are, for all practical purposes, the same, although they may not be the same object. One pepperoni pizza is generally pretty much equal to another. Of course, the exact meaning of equality may differ from one problem area to another.

This distinction between identity and equality is reflected in Java in two separate methods: == and `equals()`. The == method is used to test object identity and it cannot be overridden in new classes. The method `equals`, inherited from class `Object`, is used to test object equality. Although it is defined in `Object` to mean the same thing as ==, it can be overridden to have other meanings. For example, it is overridden in class `String` to mean string equality (character-by-character equality).

The search for an element performed using `findElement` uses equality, not identity. Thus, it is possible for two values to test equal to each other even if they are not exactly the same value.

is equal to another value already in the collection, a subsequent search might uncover the first or the second; we have no way of knowing which. Another feature left undefined in the Bag data type is the order of elements yielded by the enumeration constructed using the method `elements`. We insist only that all values eventually be generated and that no value be generated more than once, but the exact order is unspecified.

2.3 THE FUNDAMENTAL ADTs

Throughout this book, our exposition of data structures will jump between examining data types at the abstract level and examining specific implementation techniques that will provide the behavior specified by an ADT. It is useful, therefore, to begin by summarizing the various abstract data types we will examine. For each, we will outline some of the properties that describe the behavior expected from instances of the data type. In each of the categories, note carefully how few of the properties are conveyed by the type signatures of the operations.

2.3.1 Collection

The `Collection` interface is the root for most of the collection classes we will examine. The `Collection` interface itself is seldom useful on its own, as it merely provides a means to discover whether the collection is empty, the number of elements held by the collection, and a mechanism to access the elements in the collection as part of a loop. In fact, none of the methods defined in `Collection` can make any permanent change to the collection at all. The interface has the following definition:

```
public interface Collection extends Serializable {
  public Enumeration elements ();
  public boolean isEmpty ();
  public int size ();
}
```

The `Serializable` parent is simply the standard Java way of saying that instances of this class can be stored in a binary format in files.[3] The three methods that constitute the class can be described as follows:

3. Values must be declared as `Serializable` before they can be stored on an `ObjectOutputStream`. For an example of the use of this feature, see the sidebar on page 460.

REUSABLE CONTAINERS AND POLYMORPHISM

To be a useful tool, a collection class must be something that can be carried from one program to the next and reused in a variety of situations. Such a tool cannot be too closely tied to any particular application.

If we wish to build a reusable collection class, what type should be used for the elements being held by the container? In Java, the solution to this problem is provided through the use of *polymorphic variables.*[a] A polymorphic variable, you will recall, is a variable that can be declared as one type but can hold a value from a different type.

Polymorphic variables in Java come in two forms. The first is created using interfaces. A variable declared using an interface as a type, such as a variable declared as a `Bag`, can hold any data value that is declared as implementing the interface:

```
Bag aCollection = new LinkedList();
    // a LinkedList implements Bag
```

The second form comes about through the use of *inheritance*. A variable using a class name as a type can be assigned a data value that was derived from a *subclass* of the class. For example, because the class `ObjectInputStream` is a subclass of `InputStream`, an instance of the former can be assigned to a variable declared as the latter:

```
InputStream in = new ObjectInputStream(fin);
```

In Java, all classes ultimately inherit from the single root class `Object`. Thus, a variable declared as `Object` can hold any object value:

```
Object test;
test = aCollection;  // can hold a linked
                     // list
test = in; // or an object input stream
```

This property is the key we will use in creating new collection classes. The values stored in the collection will be held by variables that are declared as `Object`. This will allow our containers to hold a wide variety of values.

[a] The reader interested in the study of computer languages should note that the Java approach is not the only solution to this problem. In particular, the language C++, although similar to Java in many regards, uses an entirely different approach in its library of collection classes.

`elements` Returns an `Enumeration` that can be used to access the elements held in the collection.[4] The property we expect of an enumeration is that every value is yielded, no value is yielded more than once, and hence the number of values yielded by the enumeration is the same as the size of the collection. Unless noted otherwise (see the `Sorted` interface), the order in which elements are yielded by an enumeration is undefined. The effect of adding or removing elements from a collection while it is being enumerated is also undefined.

`isEmpty` Returns `true` if the collection is empty and returns `false` otherwise. This method will always return `true` when applied on a newly

---

4. The class `Enumeration` is part of the standard Java library, whereas the class `Collection` was specifically created for this book. In the preface, I explain why I believe that the collection classes in the Java standard library are not suitable for *teaching* data structures, although they may be very useful as programming tools. However, in Appendix C, I discuss the data structures that are found in the Java standard library.

created collection. Invoking this method will not change the state of the collection in any way.

`size` Returns an integer value that indicates the number of elements held by the collection. This method will always return zero when applied on a newly created collection. Invoking this method will not change the state of the collection in any way.

The `Enumeration` interface defines two methods: `hasMoreElements` and `nextElement`. They are typically used in combination to form a loop, as in the following:

```
  // print all the items in a collection
for (Enumeration e = data.elements(); e.hasMoreElements(); )
  System.out.println("Value is " + e.nextElement());
```

2.3.2 Bag

A Bag is the simplest type of collection. As noted earlier, all features, such as the order in which elements are maintained inside the collection and the order in which they were inserted, have been abstracted away. The simple Bag, which provides the ability to add and to remove elements from the collection and to search for a value, has the following interface:

```
public interface Bag extends Collection {
  public void addElement (Object newElement);
  public boolean containsElement (Object testElement);
  public Object findElement (Object testElement);
  public void removeElement (Object oldElement);
}
```

The properties associated with this ADT are the following:

`addElement` *Pre:* The argument must be comparable to the existing elements in the collection. (See sidebar on equality and identity.) *Post:* Adds an element to a collection. The size of the collection is increased by one. Because the collection is therefore larger than zero, a call on `isEmpty` will return `false`. The location of the element in relation to existing elements (as, for example, revealed by an enumeration) is undefined.

`containsElement` *Pre:* The argument must be comparable to the existing elements in the collection. *Post:* Returns `true` if the collection contains the indicated element and `false` otherwise. Invoking this method will not change the state of the collection in any way.

`findElement` *Pre:* The argument must be comparable to the existing elements in the collection. *Post:* Returns a value held in the collection that is equal to the argument, if one exists. Will throw a `NoSuchElementException` if no value in the collection matches the argument. If two or more values in the collection are equal to the argument, the selection of which value will be returned is undefined. Invoking this method will not change the state of the collection in any way.

`removeElement` *Pre:* The argument must be comparable to the existing elements in the collection. *Post:* Will remove a value from the collection that is equal to the argument. Will throw a `NoSuchElementException` if no value in the collection matches the argument. Assuming that execution is successful, the size of the collection will be reduced by one.

2.3.3 Set

The `Set` ADT defines operations with the same type signature as `Bag`, with one important change in the property of the `addElement` method. In particular, the `Set` corresponds to the mathematical notion of a set, in which every element is unique. Thus, for example, performing an `addElement` operation may not increase the size of the collection, if the element is already part of the set. In addition to redefining the meaning of `addElement`, the set incorporates methods that permit a set to be combined with other sets in a number of ways. The interface for this class is as follows:

```
public interface Set {
    // single-element operations
  public void addElement (Object newElement);
  public boolean containsElement (Object testElement);
  public Object findElement (Object testElement);
  public void removeElement (Object oldElement);
    // set-set operations
  public void unionWith (Set aSet);
  public void intersectWith (Set aSet);
  public void differenceWith (Set aSet);
  public boolean subsetOf (Set aSet);
}
```

We can describe the operations as follows. Three of the four operations that the `Set` has in common with `Bag` have the same definition.

`addElement` *Pre:* The argument must be comparable to the existing elements in the collection. (All implementations require at least the ability to compare using the `equals` operator; some implementations also require the ability to order elements.) *Post:* Ensures that the argument value is contained in the collection. If the argument value is already present in the collection prior to the invocation, the collection is unchanged; otherwise, it is added to the collection.

`unionWith` *Pre:* Assumes that all values in the argument set are comparable with elements in the collection. *Post:* Forms the union of the current set with the argument set. All values in the argument set that are not already members of the current set are added. The argument set is not modified.

`intersectWith` *Pre:* Assumes that all values in the argument set are comparable with elements in the collection. *Post:* Forms the intersection of the current set with the argument set. All elements in the current set that are not members of the argument set are deleted. The argument set is not modified.

`differenceWith` *Pre:* Assumes that all values in the argument set are comparable with elements in the collection. *Post:* Forms the difference between the current set with the argument set. In the current set, all elements that are members of the argument set are deleted. The argument set is not modified.

`subsetOf` *Pre:* Assumes that all values in the argument set are comparable with elements in the collection. *Post:* Returns `true` if all members of the current set are members of the argument set, returning `false` otherwise. The argument set may include additional elements that are not members of the current set. The argument set is not modified.

2.3.4 Sorted, Comparator, and Comparable

In some cases, it is important that we *not* abstract away the order in which elements are maintained in the collection. The `Sorted` ADT redefines properties associated with methods inherited from the parent class, without changing the interface. In particular, an instance of the `Sorted` ADT is guaranteed to enumerate its values (using the `elements` method) in order, smallest to largest.

```
public interface Sorted extends Collection {
  // no new methods
}
```

Typically, classes combine support for the `Sorted` interface with support for other interfaces, such as `Bag`. Examples of classes that support the `Sorted` interface are the `SortedVector` (Section 7.2), the `SortedList` (Section 9.1), and the various forms of binary search tree (Chapter 14).

Elements stored in a sorted collection must have the ability to be ordered by comparison. This is enforced by requiring that the user supply an object that satisfies the Comparator interface:[5]

```
public interface Comparator extends Serializable {
  int compare (Object left, Object right);
}
```

The compare method should return −1 if the left object is larger than the right, 0 if they are equal, and 1 if the right object is larger than the left. A standard comparator, the DefaultComparator, will work with objects that implement the Comparable interface:

```
public interface Comparable extends Serializable {
  public int compareTo (Object value);
}
```

Since version 1.2, the Java standard library has made standard objects, such as Integer and String, to be subclasses of Comparable.

2.3.5 Stack, Queue, and Deque

Another category of containers arises from the need to remember the *order* in which elements were inserted rather than ignoring this information, as we do with a Bag. Elements are then removed from the collection in relation to the order in which they were inserted. This type of container is sometime called a *linear* collection.

The Stack, Queue, and Deque interfaces each describe a different type of linear collection ADT in which elements are maintained in the order in which they were inserted. An enumeration of a linear collection will yield the elements in sequence, from the first element inserted to the most recent.

The Stack interface allows the user to remove the element that was most recently inserted. This data abstraction will be examined in more detail in Chapter 10.

```
public interface Stack extends Collection {
  public void addLast (Object newElement);
  public Object getLast ();
  public void removeLast ();
};
```

---

5. The Comparator and Comparable classes are from the Java standard library. They were introduced in version 1.2 of the language.

The element returned by the getLast operation is the value that has been held by the container the shortest time, that is, the element that was most recently inserted into the container.

addLast *Post:*[6] Adds an element to the top (last end) of the stack. The relative position of all other elements in the collection remains unchanged. The inserted value will become the new topmost element. Note that, unlike the Bag and Set ADTs, there is no requirement that the argument value be comparable to elements already held by the collection.

getLast Returns the element that has been in the stack the shortest period of time. Because values can be inserted only at one end of the stack, this will naturally be the element at the top. This method will throw NoSuchElementException if the stack is currently empty. Invoking this method will not change the state of the collection in any way.

removeLast Removes the current top of the stack. This method will throw NoSuchElementException if the stack is currently empty.

elements The properties of this method are changed from those inherited from Collection, in order to ensure that values are enumerated in sequence.

The Queue interface adds elements to one end and removes them from the other. This data abstraction is examined in Chapter 12.

```
public interface Queue extends Collection {
  public void addLast (Object newElement);
  public Object getFirst ();
  public void removeFirst ();
};
```

Unlike the stack, the value returned by a Queue in response to the getFirst method is the value that has been in the container the longest time, that is, the first element that was inserted.

addLast Inserts a new element by placing it at the back of the queue. The relative positions of all other elements in the queue remain unchanged.

getFirst Returns the element that has been in the queue the longest period of time. Because values can be inserted only at the end of the queue, this will naturally be the element at the front. This method will throw NoSuchElementException if the queue is currently empty. Invoking this method will not change the state of the collection in any way.

---

6. If there are no preconditions, the explicit *post* directive will be omitted.

`removeFirst` Removes the current front of the queue. This method will throw `NoSuchElementException` if the queue is currently empty.

`elements` As with `Stack`, the properties of this method are modified so as to ensure that elements are enumerated in sequence.

The `Deque` interface combines the features of the `Stack` and the `Queue` and adds the ability to insert a value to the front of a collection, thereby providing support for adding and removing elements from both sides. The `Deque` data type will be examined in Chapter 11.

```
public interface Deque extends Stack, Queue {
  public void addFirst (Object newElement);
};
```

2.3.6 FindMin and FindNth

The simple `Bag` permits the user to ask only whether a specific element is contained in the collection. But for many problems, it is important to be able to search for an element by a property and not simply by value.

The `FindMin` ADT defines the ability to add new elements to a collection and to find and remove the smallest (or minimum) value in a collection. This interface is supported by priority queues (Chapter 15) and many ordered collections (see the `Sorted` interface).

```
public interface FindMin extends Collection {
  public void addElement (Object newElement);
  public Object getFirst ();
  public void removeFirst ();
}
```

`addElement` *Pre:* Assumes that the argument is comparable with any elements currently in the collection. *Post:* Adds an element to a collection. The size of the collection is increased by one. Because the collection is therefore larger than zero, a call on `isEmpty` will return `false`. The location of the element in relation to existing elements (as, for example, revealed by an enumeration) is undefined.

`getFirst` Returns the smallest value in the collection. (See the earlier discussion of sorted collections for a description of how smallest is defined.) Will throw `NoSuchElementException` if the collection is empty. Invoking this method will not change the state of the collection in any way.

`removeFirst` Removes the smallest value from the collection. Will throw `NoSuchElementException` if the collection is empty.

The FindNth ADT provides the ability to find the *N*th smallest value in a collection. Values are counted like index positions, starting with zero up to one less than the number of elements in the collection. Because this interface does not provide any means to add or to remove elements from the collection, it is generally combined with another interface. Both the SortedVector and the Partition (Chapter 7) implement this interface.

```
public interface FindNth {
  public Object findNth (int index);
}
```

2.3.7 Indexed Collections and Sorting Algorithms

A Bag permits values to be accessed only in a sequence, from beginning to end. For many types of problems, it is useful to be able to access elements in a random order. The Indexed ADT defines a type of object that can be indexed using an integer key, in the fashion of arrays. The interface defines methods that permit the size of the collection to be set, as well as accessing and setting elements at specific locations.

```
public interface Indexed extends Collection {
  public void setSize (int size);
  public Object elementAt (int index);
  public void setElementAt (Object value, int index);
  public void addElementAt (Object value, int index);
  public void removeElementAt (int index);
}
```

`setSize` Sets the size of the collection. Any value that was previously set using an index larger than the argument becomes inaccessible. Any position smaller than the argument size that has not been previously set (using `setElementAt`) will have a `null` value.

`elementAt` If the index is smaller than the collection size and the given position has previously been set (by `setElementAt`), this method will return the most recent value stored. If the position has not yet been set, the method will return `null`. If the index is out of range, the method will throw `ArrayIndexOutOfBoundsException`.

`setElementAt` If the index is smaller than the collection size, this will set the argument value in the given position. If the index is out of range, the method will throw `ArrayIndexOutOfBoundsException`. Note that there is no requirement that the argument be comparable to elements already in the collection.

`addElementAt` Places the argument value at the given location and moves the current value at that position and all successively higher positions up by one. Note that this increases the size of the collection by one. If the index is out of range, the method will throw `ArrayIndexOutOfBoundsException`.

`removeElementAt` Removes the element stored at the given position. Moves all elements with successively higher index positions down by one. Note that this decreases the size of the collection by one. If the index is out of range, the method will throw `ArrayIndexOutOfBoundsException`.

`elements` Although this method is inherited from `Collection`, its property is changed so as to guarantee that elements are enumerated in their index order, from first to last.

The `Vector` data type is the most commonly used abstraction that supports this interface,[7] although by no means the only one. Other classes that support this interface are the `IndexedDeque` described in Chapter 11 and the `SparseVector` described in Chapter 19. The latter can be used to create a collection that is essentially infinite in extent.

An important task associated with indexed collections is the rearrangement of elements so that they form a nondecreasing sequence. This process is known as *sorting*. Hundreds of sorting algorithms have been developed, and many are described in this text. We will identify a sorting algorithm as a class that supports the `SortAlgorithm` interface, which is described as follows:

```
public interface SortAlgorithm {
  public void sort (Indexed data);
}
```

A sorting algorithm produces no result but as a side effect will rearrange the argument collection so that its elements are ordered. A subsequent enumeration of the values in the collection will then yield the values in sequence.

2.3.8 Map

Like the `Indexed` ADT, the `Map` ADT provides an alternative to a sequential examination of elements in a collection. However, the way that values are accessed is different. A `Map` ADT is a collection that permits values to be accessed by key. The key can be any object type, as can the value. (Some

7. Note that the `Vector` class described in this book is slightly different from the class of the same name found in the Java library as distributed by Sun. See Appendix C for a further discussion on this point.

implementations of the Map interface restrict the key to quantities that can be compared to each other and ordered.)

```
public interface Map extends Collection {
  public boolean containsKey (Object key);
  public Object get (Object key);
  public void removeKey (Object key);
  public void set (Object key, Object newValue);
}
```

`set` *Pre:* Assumes that the argument is comparable with the other keys currently being maintained by the collection. *Post:* Creates an association between the key and the value. A subsequent retrieval using the same key will yield the value. Overwrites any previous associations that used the same key.

`get` *Pre:* Assumes that the argument is comparable with the other keys currently being maintained by the collection. *Post:* If the container currently maintains an association with the given key, the value portion is returned. Otherwise, the method will throw `NoSuchElementException`.

`removeKey` *Pre:* Assumes that the argument is comparable with the other keys currently being maintained by the collection. *Post:* If the container currently maintains an association with the given key, the association is deleted. If the key does not denote a currently valid association, the method will throw `NoSuchElementException`.

`containsKey` *Pre:* Assumes the argument is comparable with the other keys currently being maintained by the collection. *Post:* Indicates whether the collection is currently maintaining an association with the given key. Does not change the collection.

We will examine implementations of the Map data type in Chapter 17.

2.3.9 Matrix

The `Matrix` interface describes a two-dimensional structure. Instead of a size, separate methods are provided to determine the number of rows and the number of columns.

```
public interface Matrix extends Serializable {
  public void setSize (int rows, int columns);
  public int numberRows ();
  public int numberColumns ();
  public Object elementAt (int row, int column);
  public void setElementAt (Object val, int row, int column);
}
```

`setSize` Defines the number of rows and the number of columns in the collection. The initial value of each position is undefined.

`numberRows` Returns the number of rows in the collection. Invoking this method will not change the state of the collection in any way.

`numberColumns` Returns the number of columns in the collection. Invoking this method will not change the state of the collection in any way.

`elementAt` Returns the most recent element stored at the given position. The result is undefined if no value has yet been stored at the location. Invoking this method will not change the state of the collection in any way.

`setElementAt` Places the value into the position specified. Any previous value stored at the given location is lost.

We will examine the `Matrix` data type in Chapter 19.

2.4 Chapter Summary

Key Concepts

- Aspects of type:
  - Values
  - Operations
  - Properties
- Class
- Interface
- Polymorphic variable
- Abstract data type
- Pre- and postconditions

We began our exploration of data structures with an examination of the concept of *type* in programming languages. A type denotes a set of values, a set of operations, and a set of properties we expect the values and operations to possess. This is true both for the primitive types defined by the language and for user-defined types. Types in Java are formed by using the mechanisms of either a `class` or an `interface`. The former includes an implementation of the operations defined for the type, whereas the latter does not. A polymorphic variable is a variable that is declared as one type but can hold as a value a different type—for example, a variable declared using an interface but holding a value that implements the interface.

An abstract data type is defined by the operations it supports and the properties it maintains, not by the way those operations are implemented. In Java, the operations required by an ADT can be specified using an interface. However, an interface can describe only the type signatures of the operations, not the properties that the methods must support. A useful way to describe these nonsyntactic aspects is with pre- and postconditions. A precondition specifies properties that must be true prior to the execution of a method if it is to operate properly. A postcondition specifies properties that will be true subsequent to the execution of a method.

Further Information

Many good tutorials are available for those unfamiliar with the Java programming language. Examples include *Java by Dissection* by Pohl and McDowell [Pohl 00], *The Java Tutorial* by Campione and Walrath [Campione 98], and *Core Java* by Cornell and Horstmann [Cornell 96]. Readers with slightly more background may find it useful to consult a reference manual. The most complete reference manual is the one written by the developers of the language [Gosling 96]. Another tool useful for most programmers is the annotated description of the Java class library presented by Chan [Chan 96]. A more complete exploration of the meaning of types in programming languages is given by Wegner [Wegner 86].

Study Questions

1. What are the three most important aspects of the notion of *type* in programming languages?
2. Give an example that shows how integers in programming languages differ from natural numbers in mathematics.
3. What is a primitive type? What are the primitive types in Java?
4. How does a `class` definition document the properties associated with the class?
5. How is an `interface` different from a `class`?
6. What is the difference between a data type and a data structure?
7. What is the difference between object identity and object equality?
8. How is an ADT different from an interface?
9. How is an ADT different from a data structure?
10. What operations are associated with the `Bag` ADT?
11. In what ways is the `Set` interface different from the `Bag`?
12. In what ways does an `Enumeration` of a `Sorted` collection differ from that of other collections?
13. What does it mean to say that the `Stack`, `Queue`, and `Deque` ADTs all represent *linear* collections?
14. In what way is a `Map` similar to a `Vector`?

Exercises

1. Give pre- and postcondition characterizations of the methods in the interface `GetAndSet`. Does your specification allow for the following implementation?

```
class FortyTwoBox implements GetAndSet {
  public void insert (int v) { } // throw it away
  public int extract () { return 42; }
}
```

How would you write the properties if you wanted to allow this? How would you write them differently if you wanted to rule this out?

2. Rewrite the class Box so that it implements the `GetAndSet` interface; then provide pre- and postcondition characterizations of the three classes `Box`, `OneTimeBox`, and `SuccessorBox`. Note that each of the three is different from the others. Are these differences brought out in your pre- and postcondition descriptions?
3. In Chapter 1, we discussed the concept of an adapter. The following is an adapter that takes a different type of container, a `DataBox`, and uses it to implement the Bag interface.

```
class MyCollection implements Bag {
  private DataBox data = new DataBox();

    // the collection interface
  public Enumeration elements () { return data.elements(); }
  public boolean isEmpty () { return data.count() == 0; }
  public int size () { return data.count(); }

    // the Bag interface
  public void addElement (Object newElement) {data.add(newElement); }
  public boolean containsElement (Object test)
    { return data.find(test) != null; }
  public Object findElement (Object test) { return data.find(test); }
  public void removeElement (Object old) { return data.delete(old); }
}
```

Just by examining this code, what can you infer is the interface to the class `DataBox`? What properties must be associated with the methods in this class?

Programming Projects

1. The Fibonacci numbers are defined by the relations:

$$F_0 = 0$$
$$F_1 = 1$$
$$F_{n+1} = F_{n-1} + F_n$$

Write a method that satisfies the `Enumeration` interface and that on each call will return the next larger Fibonacci number. Halt when the numbers exceed the value 100.

CHAPTER 3

ALGORITHMS

In Chapter 1, we explained how complex systems could be constructed and/or understood in layers of abstraction. A typical program written in the object-oriented style of Java has four important levels of abstraction. At the highest level, a program is viewed as a "community" of objects that must interact in order to achieve their common goal.

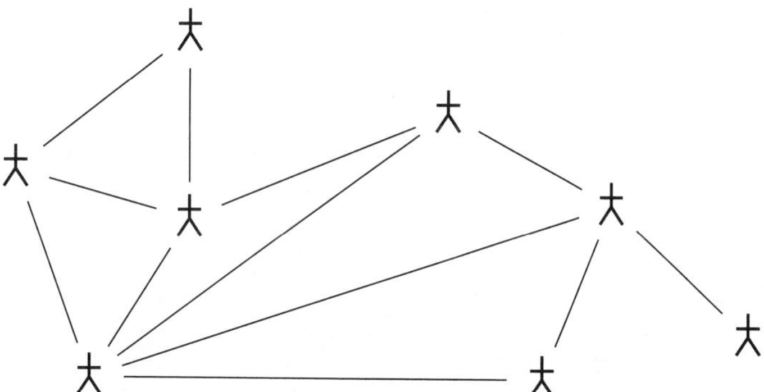

Each object in this community provides a service that is used by other members of the organization. At this highest level of abstraction, the important features to emphasize are the lines of communication and cooperation and the way in which the members must interact.

At the next level of abstraction, we consider a single element in isolation and examine the services it provides to the rest of the organization. In a good design, we can describe and discuss those services with only minimal reference to the clients who will be making use of the behavior. Our description of an ADT is an example of an analysis performed at this level. We can describe a Bag as an object that implements a given interface, without knowing either who is using the data abstraction or how the services will be provided:

```
public interface Bag extends Collection {
  public void addElement (Object newElement);
  public boolean containsElement (Object testElement);
  public Object findElement (Object testElement);
  public void removeElement (Object oldElement);
}
```

Descending further, the next level of understanding considers a concrete implementation of the abstract behavior. For example, in Chapter 8, we will investigate the idea of a `LinkedList`, a data structure that supports the Bag interface:

```
public class LinkedList implements Bag, ... {
   .
   .
   .
}
```

Finally, the last level of abstraction considers a single task in isolation and examines the precise sequence of operations used to perform just this one activity. For example, we might investigate the technique used to perform a search for an element in a linked list. It is this level of abstraction that we examine in this chapter.

3.1 Characteristics of Algorithms

An *algorithm* is a description of how a specific problem can be solved, written at a sufficient level of detail that it can be reproduced and reused. An algorithm is used to solve a single problem or, more commonly, to solve a general class of similar problems. Terms that have a similar meaning are *process*, *technique*, *procedure*, *routine*, *outline*, *pattern*, and even, as we will illustrate in a moment, *recipe*.

An algorithm should be distinguished from a *method*, which is a set of instructions written in Java and attached to a specific class. A method will often embody an algorithm, but the essence of the algorithm transcends the method, transcends even the programming language. I can describe, for example, how a search can be performed on a linked list, and the details of the algorithm will remain the same no matter what programming language is used to write the code.[1]

Once we have uncovered an algorithm, the solution to a problem is simply a matter of executing each instruction of the algorithm in turn. If this process is to be successful, an algorithm must possess, in general, several characteristics. Among these are

- *Accurate specification of the input.* The most common form of algorithm is a transformation that takes a set of input values and performs some manipulations to yield a set of output values. An algorithm must make clear the number and type of input values and the essential initial conditions those input values must possess to achieve successful operation. This is what, in Chapter 2, we termed the *preconditions.*
- *Precise specification of each instruction.* Each step of an algorithm must be precisely defined. There should be no ambiguity about the actions to be carried out at any point. As we will see shortly, algorithms presented in an informal descriptive form are sometimes ill-defined for exactly this reason, due to the ambiguities in English and other natural languages.
- *Correctness.* An algorithm is expected to solve a problem. For any putative algorithm, we must demonstrate that, in fact, the algorithm will solve the problem. Often, this will take the form of an argument, mathematical or logical in nature, to the effect that *if* the input conditions are satisfied and the steps of the algorithm executed, *then* the desired outcome will be produced.
- *Termination, time to execute.* It must be clear that for any particular input values, the algorithm is guaranteed to terminate after a finite number of steps. We will postpone a more precise definition of the informal term "steps." It is usually not necessary to know the exact number of steps an algorithm will require, but it will be convenient to provide an upper bound and to argue that the algorithm will always terminate in fewer steps than the upper bound. Usually, this upper bound will be given as a function of some values in the input. For example, if the input consists of two integer values n and m, we might be able to say that a particular algorithm will always terminate in fewer than $n + m$ steps.
- *Description of the result or effect.* Finally, it must be clear exactly what the algorithm is intended to accomplish. Most often, this can be expressed as the production of a result value having certain properties. Less

1. Despite this, most people learn best by using concrete examples. For this reason, we will throughout the text present algorithms as bits of code written in Java, leaving to the reader the task of abstracting the more general concepts out of the Java-specific realizations.

frequently, algorithms are executed for a *side effect*, such as printing a value on an output device. In either case, the expected outcome must be completely specified. This is what, in Chapter 2, we termed the *postconditions*.

In the rest of this chapter and in Chapter 4, we will examine a number of algorithms and explain how we can evaluate each in terms of the characteristics given.

3.2 RECIPES AS ALGORITHMS

Probably the most common form of algorithm the reader is likely to have encountered is a recipe. A recipe is a structured set of instructions used to transform an input (the ingredients) into a finished product (the edible). Consider the recipe for lemon soufflé shown in Figure 3.1. Let us evaluate this recipe with respect to the characteristics of an algorithm described in the previous section.

- *Input:* The recipe begins with a list of ingredients that define the basic set of initial conditions required before the steps provided by the recipe can be undertaken. Note that input conditions consist of both a set of input objects (gelatin, water, eggs, sugar) and a set of conditions (the water must be cold, the cream heavy).
- *Result:* The primary result of the recipe is usually described by the name—in this case, *Lemon Soufflé*. Incidental consequences of executing the recipe procedure, such as producing a messy kitchen, are usually of little interest and are left unstated.
- *Correctness:* It takes a talented cook to be able to simply look at a recipe and tell whether the outcome will be tasty or even edible if the recipe is correctly followed. For most people, it is a matter of experimentation. As the saying goes, the proof of the pudding (or soufflé) is in the tasting.
- *Time to execute:* It is somewhat difficult to guarantee from a mere examination of the steps involved in a recipe that the preparation can be carried out in a finite amount of time. In step 1, are we guaranteed that when beating the egg yolks and sugar, they will eventually become thick and light or that when the result is cooked over a low heat, it will always become thick and hot? What if it never becomes thick? Perhaps in realization of this potential difficulty, the author of the recipe has provided an estimated amount of time this operation should take. If the time estimate is greatly exceeded and the desired outcome has not yet been achieved, the cook knows that something is wrong.

Lemon Soufflé

Ingredients / Input

1 envelope unflavored gelatin
¼ cup cold water
6 egg yolks
1 cup sugar
⅔ cup lemon juice
1 tablespoon grated lemon rind
4 egg whites
1½ cup heavy cream

Actions

1. Soften the gelatin in water. Beat egg yokes and sugar until thick and light. Stir in lemon juice and cook over low heat, beating steadily with a whisk until thickened and hot but not boiling (10–15 minutes).
2. Pour mixture into large bowl, mix in gelatin until dissolved, and then add lemon rind. Stir occasionally until cool.
3. Beat egg whites until stiff but not dry. Fold into lemon mixture, then whip the cream and fold in. Pour into a two-quart soufflé dish (or large bowl) and refrigerate at least 12 hours.

FIGURE 3.1 A Recipe for Lemon Soufflé

- *Instruction precision:* It is in the area of definiteness, or instruction precision, that we see perhaps the greatest weakness of a recipe as an algorithm and the significant differences between preparing a set of instructions for a human being to follow versus preparing instructions for a computer. What exactly is "thick and light" in step 1? Does "light" refer to light in texture or light in color? How long should the mixture be whipped in step 3? The success of the operation will depend on answers to questions such as these, but the details are simply not found in the recipe itself. Instead, good cooks rely on experience and intuition to fill in any missing information.

3.3 Analyzing Computer Algorithms

In the next several sections, we will analyze the features we have noted and will investigate how they are manifest in relation to computer algorithms.

Two of the topics—the question of describing the amount of time it takes to execute a program and the question of correctness for programs—are sufficiently complex, so we will devote the following two chapters to each of them.

3.3.1 Specification of the Input

An algorithm will, in general, produce the desired outcome only when it is used in a proper fashion. Restrictions may be placed not only on the input values manipulated by the algorithm but also on other conditions. In the case of computer algorithms, two general techniques are used to specify these restrictions.

The first mechanism is *type checking*. Input to an algorithm is usually provided in the form of parameters, class variables, or instance data fields. In each case, a *type* is associated with the value, and the functioning of the algorithm is guaranteed only if the input values are drawn from the proper type. An algorithm for manipulating integer values—for example, the following algorithm—will not work correctly when the arguments are floating-point quantities. Such errors, however, are usually easily caught by the compiler.[2]

```
public int min (int a, int b) {
    // return smaller of two integer arguments
  int smallest;

  if (a < b)
    smallest = a;
  else
    smallest = b;
  return smallest;
}
```

As we have seen in Chapter 2, not all requirements can be captured by type signatures. Often, stronger input conditions, which we termed preconditions, are necessary. A common form is a restriction on the range of values that can be processed. For example, the following procedure converts an integer into the corresponding character value but is effective only for the integers between 0 and 9. One approach would be to simply note the restriction in a comment:

---

2. Because a method is an embodiment of an algorithm and our intent in this chapter is to discuss algorithms, we will usually omit a surrounding class definition unless it is needed in order to discuss more global features, such as instance variables.

```
public char digitChar (int val) {
    // pre: val must be between zero and nine
    // post: return the character equivalent for argument value
  switch (val) {
    case 0: return '0';
    case 1: return '1';
    case 2: return '2';
    case 3: return '3';
    case 4: return '4';
    case 5: return '5';
    case 6: return '6';
    case 7: return '7';
    case 8: return '8';
    case 9: return '9';
    }
}
```

Unfortunately, comments may not be read, and hence the restrictions may not be applied. One approach to solving this is to have the algorithm check the validity of the input and indicate to the programmer if they are not satisfied. A common mechanism to do this is an *exception*. The following program illustrates this and also shows how character values can be used as small integers:

```
public char digitChar (int val) {
    // pre: argument must be between 0 and 9
    // post: return the character equivalent for argument
  if ((val < 0) || (val > 9))
    throw new Exception("digitChar argument out of range");
  int d = '0' + val;
  return (char) d;
}
```

There are other situations in which restrictions on input values are necessary but cannot be checked by using types or even exceptions. One example is an assumption that the input values are such that numeric overflow will not occur during the course of execution. This is illustrated in the following, which raises a floating-point value to an integer exponent value. Where these conditions are important, they should be documented, as comments, along with the code:

```
public double power (double base, int n) {
    // pre: n is larger than or equal to zero
    // post: return the value yielded by raising the
    // double-precision base to the integer exponent
    // assumes floating-point overflow does not occur
```

```
  double result = 1.0; // base raised to zero

    // raise base to new powers
  for (int i = 1; i <= n; i++) {
    result *= base;
    }

  return result;
}
```

3.3.2 Description of the Result

Just as input conditions for computer programs are specified in a number of ways, the expected results of execution are also frequently documented in a variety of fashions. The most obvious result is that yielded by a function. The name of the function identifies the result, whereas the return type indicates the form the value will take. If other characteristics are important, they can be indicated in comments. An example is the `min` function, which was described in an earlier section:

```
public int min (int a, int b) {
  // return the smaller of two arguments
  .
  .
  .
}
```

Sometimes, programs are executed not for their result but for a *side effect* that occurs during the course of execution. Because it may not be obvious from the procedure heading, this side effect should be documented in a comment. An example is the recursive procedure `printInt`, used to print the representation of a nonnegative integer value:

```
public void printInt (OutputStream out, int val) {
    // print the character representation of
    // the argument value
  if (val < 10)
    out.write(digitChar(val));
  else {
    printInt(val/10);
    out.write(digitChar(val%10));
  }
}
```

Besides output, other frequent side effects are the modification of class variables or instance variables. These, too, should be documented with comments.

3.3.3 Instruction Precision

The computer is a true *idiot savant*. It is an extremely simple-minded device, notable only for its ability to perform simple instructions with almost unbelievable rapidity. For example, even relatively inexpensive computers can add several million integers in 1 second. This speed, however, is possible only when commands are precisely specified. Computer algorithms can have none of the ambiguity we find in English-language descriptions. Whereas English descriptions tend to describe more the objective being sought (the "what"), computer algorithms must specify in exacting detail the technique to be used in reaching those objectives (the "how").

For example, a reasonable request to another human being might be "Go to the store and buy something to make lunch." Here, it is the objective that has been stated, not the means. We rely on the person receiving the command to know from previous experience the steps necessary to achieve the goal (not only what elements are needed for a lunch but also how to operate a car, how to purchase the items, and so on). Not only is the process poorly specified, but even the objective is unclear. Is the request being conveyed that the second individual should purchase the items that together will constitute a lunch, or is the request that a "lunch-making" device be purchased (perhaps a personal robotic servant)? To a computer, every step of the process necessary to achieve the goal must be outlined in detail.

3.3.4 Time to Execute

We will divide our discussion of execution time into two parts, often the course followed in practice. The first question to address with any algorithm is whether it terminates at all. Once we are satisfied that an algorithm *will* terminate for all legal input values, the next question is whether we can develop a more accurate characterization about the amount of time it will take to execute. We will consider the second question in more detail in the next chapter. In this section, we address the first question.

A basic assumption is that all primitive operations in the language, with the exception of procedure calls and loops, will execute in a finite amount of time, and thus the question of termination for those procedures that consist only of such elements is trivially addressed. The majority of loops, as well, can be easily characterized as depending on some input value, and thus termination is ensured.

Only in rare cases must termination of an algorithm be explicitly addressed. Most often, this occurs through the use of `while` loops or through the use of recursion. By far the most common technique used to prove termination of an algorithm, when it is not immediately obvious, is to identify a property or a value that possesses the following three characteristics.

1. The property or value can be placed in one-to-one correspondence with integer values. (Most commonly, we simply use an integer quantity that appears in the problem; in other cases, it is necessary to construct a mapping from a quantity in the problem to the integers.)
2. The property or value is nonnegative.
3. The property or value decreases steadily as the algorithm executes. (Often, we say that such a quantity is *monotonically decreasing*.)

If we can discover such a quantity, the argument for finite termination can be expressed as follows: This quantity must begin with a value, even if we don't know precisely *what* that value might be. Over time, the quantity is always decreasing. Because the quantity can never be negative, the algorithm must necessarily terminate before the quantity is reduced below zero.

Loops that increment or decrement a value can frequently be characterized by identifying a formula involving the termination condition. The integer exponential algorithm, for example, will continually decrease the quantity $n - i$ as the variable i increases, so we can use this quantity to guarantee that the program will always terminate.

```
public double power (double base, int n) {
  double result = 1.0;

  for (int i = 1; i <= n; i++) {
    result *= base;
  }

  return result;
}
```

An example in which termination may not be immediately obvious is Euclid's Greatest Common Divisor (GCD) algorithm, first developed in third-century B.C. Greece.[3] Donald Knuth, a computer scientist who has done a great deal of research into the history of algorithms, has claimed that the sequence of operations presented by Euclid in Propositions 1 and 2 of Book 7 of the *Elements* is the earliest-known nontrivial completely specified mathematical algorithm. The algorithm is intended to compute,

---

3. Readers not immediately convinced that Euclid's algorithm will work as advertised must wait patiently until Chapter 5, when the topic of proving correctness will be addressed.

given two positive integer values n and m, the largest positive integer that evenly divides both values. The algorithm can be written as follows:

```
public int gcd (int n, int m) {
    // pre: assume arguments are greater than or equal to zero
    // post: compute the greatest common divisor of arguments
  while (m != n) {
    if (n > m)
      n = n - m;
    else
      m = m - n;
  }
  return n;
}
```

Because we have no definite limit on the number of iterations for the `while` loop, termination may not seem ensured. To prove termination, we

ZENO'S PARADOX

The most nonintuitive of the three properties required for proving termination is the first: that the quantity or property being discussed can be placed into a one-to-one correspondence with a diminishing list of integers. To illustrate the necessity of this requirement, consider the following "proof" that it is possible to share a single candy bar with all your friends, no matter how many friends you may have. Take a candy bar and cut it in half, giving one half to your best friend. Take the remaining half and cut it in half once more, giving a portion to your second-best friend. Assuming that you have a sufficiently sharp knife, you can continue in this manner, at each step producing ever smaller pieces, for as long as you like. Thus, we have no guarantee of termination for this process. Certainly, the sequence here ($\frac{1}{2}, \frac{1}{4}, \frac{1}{8}, \ldots$) consists of all nonnegative terms and is decreasing. But a one-to-one correspondence with the integers would need to increase, not decrease.

In the fifth century B.C., the Greek philosopher Zeno used similar arguments to show that no matter how fast the famous hero Achilles runs, he cannot overtake a Tortoise, if the Tortoise is given a head start. Suppose, for example, that the Tortoise and Achilles start at time A. When, at time B, Achilles reaches the point from which the Tortoise started, the Tortoise will have proceeded some distance ahead of this point. When Achilles reaches this farther point at time C, the Tortoise will have proceeded yet farther ahead. At each point, when Achilles reaches a point from which the Tortoise began, the Tortoise will have proceeded at least some distance farther. Thus, it is impossible for Achilles to ever overtake and pass the Tortoise.

Achilles A ⟶ B ⟶ C ⟶ D
Tortoise A ⟶ B ⟶ C ⟶ D

The paradox arises from an infinite sequence of ever smaller quantities and the nonintuitive possibility that an infinite sum can nevertheless be bounded by a finite value. By restricting our arguments about termination to use only a decreasing set of *integer* values, we avoid problems such as those typified by Zeno's paradox.

must first observe that not only must n and m be initially nonzero but also they can never be assigned the values zero or less. (To see this, we must argue that the loop is evaluated only while m differs from n and that the subtractions can never produce a negative result.) But even this observation does not directly give us a value we can use in our monotonically decreasing argument, because on each iteration, one of n or m changes, but the other does not. To prove termination, we can consider the sum $n+m$ and note that this sum, although it does not occur anywhere in the algorithm, must nevertheless always decrease, as well as satisfy the other properties we require.

Recursive functions—functions that in certain circumstances invoke themselves—are another programming construct in which termination may not be immediately obvious. An example is the procedure `printInt`, described in Section 3.3.2. Here, termination is ensured once we note that the value being passed as argument in the recursive call is both positive and always strictly smaller than the original argument. Because for any input values, there are only a finite number of times one can continue to find a quantity with these properties, termination must eventually occur.

3.3.5 Space Utilization

Most of the time, the amount of space required in the solution of a problem is determined by the problem itself, and the programmer will have little room for variation. Occasionally, however, differences in space utilization will be important, and we will point them out.

Many sorting algorithms, for example, operate by copying the input into an auxiliary structure, performing certain transformations, and then copying the results back into the original container. This doubles the amount of memory needed for this task. Other sorting algorithms are able to make their changes in place in the original container and thereby reduce this memory load.

In some cases, it is possible to improve execution time (improve speed) by increasing the amount of memory devoted to a process, and vice versa. This is known as a *time/space tradeoff*. We will see examples of this later in the book. When time/space tradeoffs are present, deciding which of many alternatives makes best use of limited resources (both time and space) may be subtle.

3.4 Recursive Algorithms

A procedure that under certain situations invokes itself is called *recursive*. The use of recursive procedures is a powerful programming technique, one we will use frequently throughout the book.

A recursive procedure must always involve a conditional test that divides execution into two or more cases. At least one case must be handled without resort to the recursive call, because to do otherwise would result in an infinite sequence of procedure executions. These are often known as the *base cases*. In the printing procedure examined in Section 3.3.2, the base case occurs when the input value is less than 10.

For values larger than or equal to 10, the *recursive case* operates by dividing the number by 10, thereby producing a value with one fewer digit. The function then calls *itself* in order to print this smaller number, followed by another call to print the low-order character. Thus, to print the value 456, the procedure recursively calls itself to print the value 45, which in turn recursively calls itself once more in order to print the value 4. With the argument 4, the base case is finally encountered, and execution starts to return. Once the 4 has been printed, we return to the procedure that was printing 45; this procedure then prints the low-order digit (the 5). Returning from this procedure, we get back to the procedure printing the 456, which then prints its low-order character (the 6). In this manner, all three characters are finally produced.

In trying to understand how a recursive procedure can operate, it is important to remember that every time a procedure is invoked, new space is allocated for pass-by-value parameters and local variables. Each time the `min` procedure from Section 3.3.1 is executed, for example, new space is created for the parameters named `a` and `b`. This is true for recursive procedures as well. The only difference is that now there may be several parameters with the same name, but all copies are nonetheless distinct. In the case of printing the value 456, one copy of the parameter named `val` holds the value 456, a second maintains the value 45, and a third is manipulating the value 4. This all happens automatically, with no instruction or assistance necessary on the part of the programmer.

We will illustrate the development of another recursive algorithm by considering a classic puzzle, the *Towers of Hanoi*. In this puzzle, three poles are labeled A, B, and C. A number of disks of decreasing sizes are, initially, all on pole A.

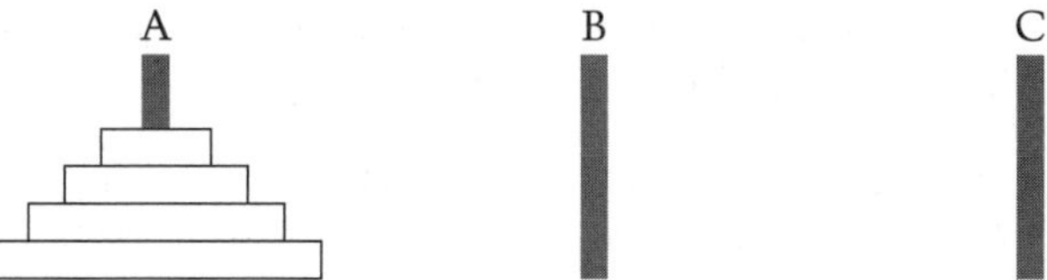

The goal of the puzzle is to move all disks from pole A to pole B without ever moving a disk onto another disk with a smaller size. The third pole can be used as a temporary during this process. At any point, only the topmost disk from any pole may be moved.

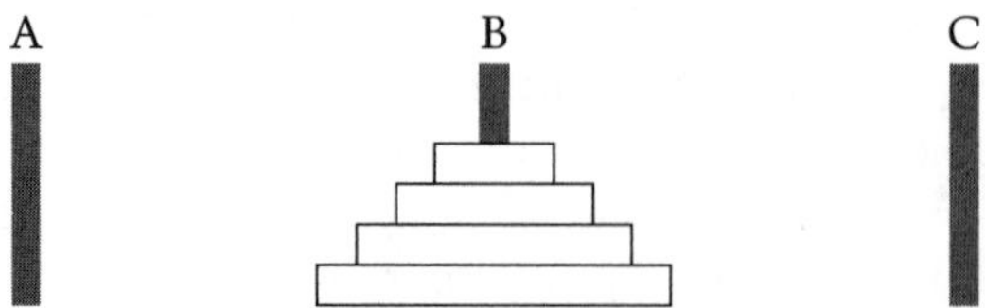

Only two first steps are legal: (1) moving the smallest piece from pole A to pole B or (2) moving the same piece from pole A to pole C. However, there does not seem to be any good way to discover which of these alternatives is the correct choice without first solving the puzzle!

As is often the case with the development of recursive algorithms, a greater insight can be found by considering a point in the *middle* of execution. For example, consider the point we must be at one step *before* we move the largest disk. For this to be a legal move, we must have already moved all the disks except for the largest from pole A to pole C:

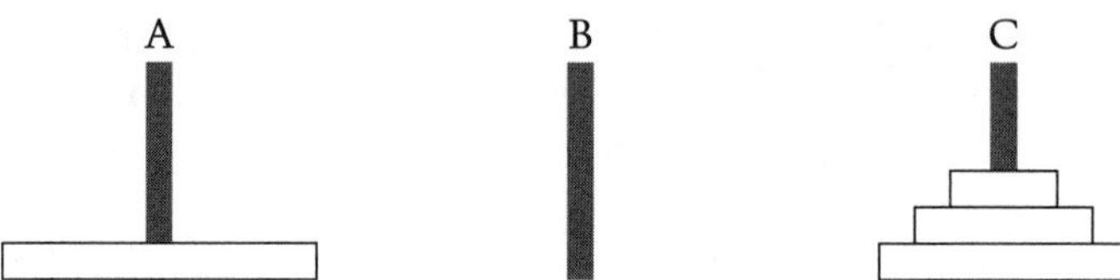

This observation gives us a hint as to how a solution can be developed. What we have discovered is that *if* we could move every disk *except* the largest disk from pole A to pole C, we could then move the largest disk from pole A to pole B. But then pole A would be empty, and so we could use it as a temporary. So, if we could *then* move all *but* the largest disks from their new location on pole C back to pole B, we would be finished.

It might not seem that we have accomplished very much, but indeed we have. The reason is that the new problem we have hypothesized is the same form as the original but slightly smaller (inasmuch as it involves a stack holding one fewer disk). If we could do this consistently, we might have a solution. So, our first stab at an algorithm for the Hanoi problem might be something like this:

```
public void solveHanoi (int n, char a, char b, char c) {
  // move n disks from tower a to tower b, using tower c
    // first move all but last disk to tower c
  solveHanoi(n-1, a, c, b);
    // then move one disk from a to b
```

```
  System.out.println("move disk from tower " + a + " to " + b);
    // then move all disks from c back to b
  solveHanoi(n-1, c, b, a);
}
```

If we try executing this program with a few simple values of *n*, we immediately see a problem. It never halts! It simply calls itself repeatedly forever. To avoid this problem, a recursive algorithm must always eventually reach a *base case,* which is handled directly. In the present problem, the obvious base case occurs when we have a pile with just one disk.[4] Moving one disk does not require first moving any disks stacked above and hence can be performed directly. Adding the condition to test for this situation gives us the following revised program:

```
public void solveHanoi (int n, char a, char b, char c) {
    // move n disks from tower a to tower b, using tower c
  if (n == 1) { // can move smallest disk directly
    System.out.println("move disk from tower " + a + " to " + b);
    }
  else {
      // first move all but last disk to tower c
    solveHanoi(n-1, a, c, b);
      // then move one disk from a to b
    System.out.println("move disk from tower " + a + " to " + b);
      // then move all disks from c back to b
    solveHanoi(n-1, c, b, a);
    }
}
```

If we simulate the execution of this algorithm for three disks, we get the following sequence of moves. You can check that the moves satisfy the game rules and result in the expected outcome:

```
move disk from tower A to tower B
move disk from tower A to tower C
move disk from tower B to tower C
move disk from tower A to tower B
move disk from tower C to tower A
move disk from tower C to tower B
move disk from tower A to tower B
```

4. A less obvious base case is the handling of a stack with *no* elements. Moving a stack of zero elements is even easier than moving a stack that has only one disk. Programming project 2 at the end of this chapter explores writing the algorithm that uses 0 instead of 1 as the base case.

We will return to this puzzle and develop a graphical display when we consider the Stack ADT in Chapter 10.

3.5 CHAPTER SUMMARY

KEY CONCEPTS

- Properties of algorithms
- Specification of input conditions
- Definiteness of each instruction
- Correctness of the algorithm
- Termination of an algorithm
- Running time of an algorithm
- Result of execution
- Recursive procedures

An algorithm is a set of instructions used to solve a specific problem. To be useful, an algorithm must possess certain characteristics.

- The algorithm must accurately describe the input values.
- Each step of the algorithm must be completely specified.
- The algorithm must make the correct transformation of the inputs to the outputs.
- The algorithm must be guaranteed to terminate on all input values.
- The result, or effect, of the algorithm must be completely characterized.

An argument that an algorithm must terminate for all input values can be provided by finding an integer quantity that is nonnegative and that decreases steadily as the algorithm executes.

A recursive algorithm is a procedure that calls itself during the course of execution. Recursive algorithms always consist of at least two parts:

- A base case that is handled in a conventional fashion. In the printing algorithm, the base case occurred in the printing of a number less than 10. In the Towers of Hanoi puzzle, the base case involved moving a stack that contains only one disk.
- A recursive case that is solved in part directly and in part by invoking the procedure on a problem of slightly smaller size. In the printing algorithm, the recursive case involved printing numbers greater than or equal to 10. The bottommost digit was removed and the algorithm invoked recursively to print the resulting digit. After this task was performed, the final digit was printed. In the Towers of Hanoi, when the procedure was invoked to move a tower of n elements, it recursively invoked itself in order to move a tower of $n - 1$ elements.

Further Information

The study of algorithms, as well as the term "analysis of algorithms," was popularized by Donald Knuth in his three-part series [Knuth 97, Knuth 98a, Knuth 98b]. The characteristics of algorithms described at the beginning of this chapter are adapted from Volume 1. A discussion of Euclid's GCD algorithm appears in both Volumes 1 and 2.

Since the 1970s, the study of algorithms has emerged as an important subdiscipline in computer science. More recent descriptions of the field can be found in the works by Sedgewick [Sedgewick 92], Cormen et al. [Cormen 90], and Harel [Harel 92].

I acquired the lemon soufflé recipe from another graduate student when I participated in an international dining club during my dissertation studies. Some would argue that no soufflé algorithm that uses gelatin can be considered correct, but the results are generally satisfactory.

Study Questions

1. What is an algorithm?
2. What is the relationship between an algorithm and a method?
3. What are two techniques used to specify the input conditions for an algorithm?
4. What are some ways used to describe the outcome, or result, of executing an algorithm?
5. What is a recursive procedure?
6. What quantity describes the number of times the procedure `printInt` will recursively call itself for any given integer value?
7. Assume that the recursive procedure `printInt` has been invoked to print the value 456. Show the runtime activation stack at the point where the procedure is finally printing the character 4, and label the name and value of each local variable in the action stack sections.
8. In what way does the precision of instructions needed to convey an algorithm to another human being differ from that needed to convey an algorithm to a computer?
9. In considering the execution time of algorithms, what are the two general types of questions one can ask?
10. What are some situations in which termination of an algorithm would not be immediately obvious?
11. What three properties must a value possess in order to be used to prove termination of an algorithm?
12. What two sections must be part of every recursive procedure?

Exercises

1. Examine a recipe from your favorite cookbook. Evaluate the recipe with respect to each of the characteristics described at the beginning of this chapter.

2. Select an activity that you perform every day. Examples might be getting ready for the day, studying for an exam, making a dinner, or driving to work. Describe this activity as an algorithm, being as precise as possible. Do you think that somebody else would be able to replicate your actions by reading your algorithm?
3. Show that each of the three properties identified in Section 3.3.4 is necessary to ensure termination of an algorithm. Do this by exhibiting three algorithms that each satisfy two of the three properties but nevertheless do not terminate. Your descriptions need not be precise; they can just be informal directions.
4. Rewrite the GCD algorithm as a recursive procedure.
5. List the sequence of moves the Towers of Hanoi problem would make in moving a tower of five disks from the source pole to the destination pole.
6. Assume that a person could move one disk in the Towers of Hanoi puzzle every second. What is the largest number of disks that could be solved as a puzzle in 1 hour?

Programming Projects

1. Write a recursive procedure to print the hexadecimal (base-16) representation of an integer value. Present an argument for termination of your algorithm. What quantity characterizes the number of times your procedure will invoke itself recursively? Can you generalize your procedure to one that will print a base-n representation, where n is any value between 2 and 36?
2. Rewrite the Towers of Hanoi problem so that the base case corresponds to moving a stack of size zero. Is the resulting program smaller or larger than the one given in the text? Is it easier to understand?
3. Binomial coefficients (the number of ways that n elements can be selected out of a collection of m values) can be defined recursively by the following formula:

$$\binom{n}{m} = \binom{n-1}{m} + \binom{n-1}{m-1}$$

$$\binom{n}{0} = \binom{n}{n} = 1$$

Write a recursive procedure named `comb(n, m)` to compute this value.

4. Write a program that will accept as argument an integer value and print the value of the integer spelled out as English words. For example, the input −3472 would produce the output "negative three thousand four hundred seventy-two." After removing any initial negative signs, this program is most easily handled in a recursive fashion. Numbers greater than millions can be printed by printing the number of millions (via a recursive call), then printing the word *million*, then printing the remainder. Similarly, numbers between a thousand and a million can be produced by printing the number of thousands (again, a recursive call), then the word *thousand*, then the remainder. The same can be done with hundreds. Take care to deal with special cases (zero, numbers between 10 and 20).

CHAPTER 4

Execution-Time Measurement

In comparing two implementations of the same ADT, an important question to address is their relative execution times. It might appear, at first, that describing the execution time of a computer algorithm should be easy: One merely runs the algorithm with a stopwatch in hand (or any number of technological variations of a similar theme) and records the results. And indeed, such a value, called a *benchmark*, is occasionally useful. We will examine benchmarks later in this chapter.

Most of the time, however, a benchmark is not a good characterization of a computer algorithm. A benchmark describes only the performance of a program on a specific machine on a given day. Different processors can have dramatically different performances. (Computer manufacturers go to great lengths to remind users of this fact in hopes of enticing them to purchase faster and more costly machines.) Even working on a single machine, there may be a selection of many alternative compilers for the same programming language. These compilers will produce slightly different machine code instructions for the same source language and thus have varying execution times. Finally, execution timings for multiprocessing computers (computers that can perform many tasks simultaneously) will be altered by the other tasks being performed at the same time.

In this chapter, we introduce the concept of *algorithmic analysis* (or *analysis of algorithms*), a technique used to characterize the execution behavior of algorithms in a manner independent of a particular platform, compiler, or language. Many of the data structures described in this book provide similar functionality but differ in their execution times for various operations. Thus, selecting the appropriate type of container for any particular problem involves an understanding of not only a container's capabilities but also how execution times are determined and contrasted.

4.1 ALGORITHMIC ANALYSIS AND BIG-OH NOTATION

Rather than measuring the execution time of computer programs, we will henceforth speak of measuring computer *algorithms*. An algorithm will generally be embodied in one or more methods. Thus, our measurements will be based on an examination of the execution time for the invocation of a single method. Of course, making individual methods faster can only help to improve the execution speed of entire programs.

We would like a technique to abstract away small variations and to describe the performance of algorithms in a more idealized, processor-independent fashion. It is clear that alternative approaches for the same problem can have dramatically different execution times. Ask yourself, for example, why dictionaries list words in alphabetical order. The reason, we know, is that doing so permits the reader to discover a word by repeatedly moving back and forth over increasingly small sections of the book (a process we will later label *binary search*). If dictionaries were not ordered, to discover whether a particular word appeared in the collection, the reader would have to examine the list in sequence from one end to the other, comparing the test word against each entry in turn; obviously, this process would be considerably slower than finding a word in a normal dictionary.

The technique we use to capture this more or less intuitive notion of complexity is an idea called *algorithmic analysis*. In algorithmic analysis (sometimes termed *asymptotic analysis*), we gain power by, ironically, losing precision. By systematically ignoring constant amounts and instead concentrating on an abstract characterization of the *size* of a problem, we can make more intelligent comparisons.

Determining whether a word appears in an unorganized list of n alternatives requires, for example, comparing each word against the target and therefore uses approximately n comparisons. We assume that each of these comparisons can be performed in a constant amount of time (the particular constant is unimportant, being greater or smaller depending on the machine being used). In total, the running time of the process is therefore $c \times n$ for an unknown constant c. On the other hand, if the list is ordered and we can easily move to any position in the collection, we will see (later in this chapter) that the search can be performed using only $\log n$ comparisons. Thus, the real running time is a function $d \times \log n$ for an unknown value d.

Because the constants involved are unknown and, largely, irrelevant, we can eliminate them from our description. We use a notation, called "big-Oh" notation, which captures this intuitive idea. We say that searching an unorganized list requires $O(n)$ steps (read "big-Oh of n steps"), whereas searching a sorted and randomly accessible dictionary can be performed in $O(\log n)$ steps (read "big-Oh of $\log n$ steps"). We call the big-Oh characterization the *asymptotic execution time* for the operation.

The formal definition of big-Oh states that if $f(n)$ is a function that represents the *actual* execution time of an algorithm, the algorithm is $O(g(n))$ if, for all values n larger than a fixed constant n_0, there exists a constant c, such that $f(n)$ is always bounded by (smaller than or equal to) the quantity $c \times g(n)$. Although this formal definition may be of critical importance to theoreticians, an intuitive feeling for algorithmic execution is of more practical importance. (For those readers who insist on a more formal approach, several of the exercises at the end of the chapter are designed to place the concept of algorithmic analysis on a firm foundation.)

4.2 Execution Time of Programming Constructs

In the following sections, we will discuss the most common programming constructs and illustrate the analysis of the running times by using several algorithms.

4.2.1 Constant Time

The Java language provides a number of primitive data types, such as integers and floating-point numbers. We begin by assuming that operations on such values (addition, subtraction, and the like) can be performed within a constant amount of time. Assignment also requires only constant time. A fixed sequence of constant-time operations, such as a sequence of assignments, still requires only constant time. The following is from a playing card abstraction, a class we will use in many of our examples:

```
public class Card {
  Card (int is, int ir) { // initialize a new Card
    suit = is; // suit
    rank = ir; // rank
  }

  public final int suit; // suit
  public final int rank; // rank

  public static final int diamond = 1;
  public static final int club = 2;
```

```
  public static final int spade = 3;
  public static final int heart = 4;
.
.
.
}
```

The maximum time it takes to perform a conditional `if` statement is the sum of the times it takes to perform a test and the maximum time required by either alternative. If all three can be performed in constant time, the time to execute the `if` statement can still be bounded by a constant value:

```
public class Card {
.
.
.
  public Color color () {
    if ((suit == diamond) || (suit == heart))
      return Color.red;
    else
      return Color.black;
  }
}
```

Even when procedures are quite lengthy, if they do not include loops or procedure calls, the total execution time must remain constant.

4.2.2 Simple Loops

A loop that performs a constant number of iterations is still considered to be executing in constant time. An example might be the following, which creates a deck of playing cards and places them into an array:

```
public class CardDeck {
  CardDeck () {
    int topCard = 0;
    for (int i = 1; i <= 13; i++) {
      cards[topCard++] = new Card(Card.diamond, i);
      cards[topCard++] = new Card(Card.club, i);
      cards[topCard++] = new Card(Card.spade, i);
      cards[topCard++] = new Card(Card.heart, i);
    }
  }

  private Card [ ] cards = new Card[52];
.
.
.
}
```

Such loops, however, are relatively rare in comparison to loops in general. More commonly, the number of iterations a loop will perform is determined in some fashion by the input values. To describe the running time of a loop, we need to characterize how many iterations the loop will perform and then multiply this value by the running time of the body of the loop. The simplest case occurs when the limits of the loop are fixed by the input value and the body of the loop uses constant time. An example in which this occurs is a procedure that takes as arguments an array of values and returns the smallest value in the collection:

```
public double minimum (double [ ] values) {
    // pre: values has at least one element
    // post: returns smallest value in collection
  int n = values.length;
  double minValue = values[0];

  for (int i = 1; i < n; i++) {
      // if current value is less then minimum so far
```

THE ARRAY IN JAVA

The *array* is the only data structure the Java language provides that is designed specifically to hold a collection of values. (Other data structures are provided by the standard Java *library*, but they are not part of the basic Java language.)

Although many computer languages have an array data type, the array in Java is slightly more general than most. For example, when declaring a variable as an array, the programmer need not specify an upper bound. This can be seen, for example, in the declaration of command line arguments that must be present in the `main` procedure in any program:

```
public class AnApplication {
  public static void main (String [ ] args) {
      ⋮
  }
}
```

The brackets signify that `args` is an array of `String` values yet do not specify how many elements the array will hold. Instead, the size of an array is established when the value of the variable is first created. Here, too, Java is different from most other computer languages. In Java, creating an array is a two-step process. First, the variable that will hold the array must be declared. Second, the space for the variable must be allocated by using the `new` operator. This can be seen in the `CardDeck` example:

```
Card [ ] cards = new Card[52];
    // create an array with 52 elements
```

Values in an array are accessed by using the subscript operator. The index values used with this operator must be greater than or equal to zero and less than the number of elements in the array. Again, Java is unlike some other languages (such as C++) in that index bounds *are* checked, and an exception will be raised if they are not valid.

```
      if (values[i] < minValue)
        minValue = values[i]; // then save it
    }
    return minValue;
}
```

Here, the loop will clearly execute $n - 1$ times. Because at each iteration we are performing at most one comparison and one assignment, the execution time for the body of the loop is constant. The total running time for the procedure is therefore $O(n)$. (Note that the n in $O(n)$ need not correspond to any variable in the program; it is just a convenient way to indicate that the execution time is proportional to the size of the input. Even if we had used a different variable in the program, we would still say that the execution time was $O(n)$.)

Loops need not always have a simple terminating condition, and therefore a careful analysis of the algorithm may be necessary in order to characterize the number of iterations a loop will perform. A good example of this is a procedure to determine whether an integer value represents a prime number. To do this, we need only test integers that are smaller than the square root of the value, because if a value has any factors, it must have at least one factor smaller than this amount. This can be accomplished by the following procedure, which returns a `true` value if the integer argument is prime and `false` otherwise:

```
public boolean isPrime (int n) {
      // pre: n is greater than or equal to 2
      // post: true if n is prime, false otherwise
    for (int i = 2; i * i <= n; i++) {
        // if i is a factor, then not prime
      if (0 == n % i) return false;
    }
      // if we end loop without finding factor
      // then n must be prime
    return true;
}
```

In this case, the loop terminates when the value of the loop variable exceeds the square root of the original value. Thus, the number of iterations is at most $\sqrt{n}$. Because each iteration of the loop is performing only a constant amount of work, the entire algorithm is said to be $O(\sqrt{n})$. Note in this case that the loop could very well terminate early (it will almost always do so, unless the number is prime). We say in this case that the algorithmic execution time represents a bound on the *worst-case* execution time. When it is difficult to characterize the execution time for every instance, a worst-case bound is often the next-best thing. Between these two lies a third possibility: a characterization of the *average* (or *expected*) execution time. We will later see examples in which the average execution time is the characterization of greatest interest.

4.2.3 Nested Loops

As noted earlier, the execution time of a loop is the number of iterations of the loop multiplied by the execution time for the body of the loop. This becomes more complex for nested loops.

The simplest case occurs when the limits of the loops are independent of one another. In this situation, the execution time is the product of the values representing the number of times each loop will iterate multiplied by the execution time of the body. An example of this is the classic algorithm for multiplying two n by n matrices, to produce a new n by n matrix product.

```
void matprod (double [ ][ ] a, double [ ] [ ]  b, double [ ] [ ] c) {
  int n = a.length;
  for (int i = 0; i < n; i++) {
    for (int j = 0; j < n; j++) {
      c[i][j] = 0.0;
      for (int k = 0; k < n; k++) {
        c[i][j] += a[i][k] * b[k][j];
      }
    }
  }
}
```

The number of iterations in each loop is n. The body of the innermost loop, which performs only a multiplication, an addition, and an assignment, is constant time. Therefore, the total running time is $O(n^3)$.

A more complex analysis is required when the limits of iteration for the inner loops are linked to an outer loop. An example of this behavior is found in the procedure `bubbleSort`, which places the values of an array into sorted order. An outer loop provides the index for the value to be placed. An inner loop then compares elements against each other, "bubbling" larger elements to the top of the array. By the end of each iteration of the inner loop, the largest remaining value will have been moved into position.

```
void bubbleSort (double [ ] v) {
  int n = v.length;
    // find the largest remaining value
    // and place into v[i]
  for (int i = n - 1; i > 0; i--) {
      // move large values to the top
```

```
            for (int j = 0; j < i; j++) {
                if (v[j] > v[j+1]) { // if out of order
                    double temp = v[j]; // then swap
                    v[j] = v[j + 1];
                    v[j + 1] = temp;
                }
            }
        }
    }
```

To determine the running time of this procedure, we can simulate execution on a few values. The pattern that quickly becomes apparent is that on the first iteration of the outermost loop, the inner loop will execute $n - 1$ times. On the second iteration of the outermost loop, the inner loop will execute $n - 2$ times, and so on, until on the final iteration, the inner loop executes one time. The number of iterations is therefore the sum of $(n - 1) + (n - 2) + \ldots + 1$.

In order to determine the size of the sum $(n - 1) + (n - 2) + \ldots + 1$, we use a powerful technique, called *mathematical induction*. We will encounter mathematical induction (or induction, for short) in many different places and guises in our investigations of data structures, and thus it is useful to be well versed in the technique.

To apply mathematical induction, one first forms a *hypothesis*, a statement of the result you think will hold. In this case, our hypothesis will be that the sum of the values from 1 to n is given by the formula $\frac{n(n+1)}{2}$. Discovering a hypothesis is sometimes the most difficult part of a mathematical induction proof. Sometimes, the hypothesis will be provided for you naturally in the problem statement; other times, it can be discovered only by, for example, looking for patterns in several different cases.

Mathematical Induction and Recursion

The technique of mathematical induction and the use of recursion as a programming technique are closely related.

- Both begin by identifying one or more *base cases* that are handled by using some other means.
- Both proceed by showing how a large problem can be *reduced* to a slightly smaller problem *of the same form.*
- The analysis then proceeds by showing first that the base cases are correct. This is followed by a conditional argument of the form that *if* the induction formula (or recursive function call) is correct, *then* the larger expression must be correct.

We will see more of both mathematical induction and recursive algorithms in later chapters.

The next step is to verify this formula for one or more *base cases*. If we select 1 for n, for example, we have 1 for the sum, and $\frac{2}{2}$ for the fraction, so the result holds. If we select 2 for n, we have 3 for the sum, and $\frac{2\times 3}{2}$ for the fraction, so the result again holds.

The final step is to verify the formula for all remaining integers. We do this by *assuming* that the hypothesis holds for all integers smaller than or equal to an indeterminate value n, then proving that it must therefore hold for the value $n+1$. Doing so generally requires understanding how the hypotheses for n and $n+1$ are linked and *reducing* the $n+1$ case to the size n situation.[1]

For example, in our present problem, we assume that the summation of values from 1 to n is $\frac{n(n+1)}{2}$. We then inquire as to the sum of the values from 1 to $n+1$. But this can be written as $(1+2+\ldots+n)+(n+1)$. Our *induction hypothesis* tells us that we can substitute $\frac{n(n+1)}{2}$ for the first term. The resulting expression is $\frac{n(n+1)}{2}+(n+1)$, or $\frac{n(n+1)}{2}+\frac{2(n+1)}{2}$, which simplifies to $\frac{(n+1)(n+2)}{2}$. Because this matches our induction hypothesis for $n+1$, we are done.

From this analysis, we can deduce that the number of iterations of the body of the loop in the bubble sort algorithm is $\frac{(n-1)n}{2}$. This is $\frac{n^2+n}{2}$. As we will see when we discuss the addition of terms in algorithmic analysis, this therefore shows that the running time of this algorithm is $O(n^2)$.

4.2.4 While Loops

The analysis of `while` loops is similar to that of `for` loops. The key is to determine the number of iterations the loop will perform. If the `while` loop is doing a linear traversal over a range, this may be straightforward. An example is the insertion sort algorithm, which can be written as follows:

```
void insertionSort (double [ ] v) {
  int n = v.length;
  for (int i = 1; i < n; i++) {
    // move element v[i] into place
    double element = v[i];
    int j = i - 1;
    while (j >= 0 && element < v[j]) {
      v[j+1] = v[j]; // slide old value up
      j = j - 1;
    }
```

1. Sometimes, it is easier to *assume* that the hypothesis holds for integers smaller than $n-1$ and then to *prove* that it must therefore hold for n.

```
    // place element into position
    v[j+1] = element;
  }
}
```

Unlike the bubble sort algorithm, the insertion sort algorithm places the lower portion of the array into sequence first. Each new value is inserted into place, sliding elements over until the proper location for each new value is established.

The outer loop clearly executes $n - 1$ times. The inner loop *may* terminate early, but in the worst case must shift elements all the way to the bottom. (This worst case occurs if the input is initially sorted backward, and thus each value in turn is swapped until it reaches the zeroth element.) We see, therefore, that in the worst case, the number of iterations of the inner loop follows the pattern $1 + 2 + 3 + 4 + \ldots + (n - 1)$. As we have seen, the sum of this series is $\frac{(n-1)n}{2}$, and thus the algorithm is $O(n^2)$. (An optimist might argue that this worst-case performance is rare, citing that in the best case, the inner loop executes only one step and that therefore in this situation, the insertion sort algorithm is $O(n)$. Unfortunately, although the mathematics is more complicated than we can present here, it is possible to show that the average-case behavior of insertion sort is still $O(n^2)$.)

More complicated uses of the `while` loop occur when the variables involved are not simply tracing out an arithmetic progression. A classic example of a nontrivial `while` loop occurs in the binary search algorithm. Here, we assume that the input array is an already ordered collection of values. The task is to determine whether a particular value occurs in the list and, if not, the position immediately above the location where the element would be placed.

```
int binarySearch (double [ ] data, double testValue) {
  // pre: elements in argument data are ordered smallest to largest
  // post: returns the index in data where testValue is found,
  // or index of next larger element if not in collection
  int low = 0;
  int high = data.length;

    // repeatedly reduce the area of search
    // until it is just one value
  while (low < high) {
    mid = (low + high) / 2;
    if (data[mid] < testValue)
      low = mid + 1;
    else
      high = mid;
```

```
    }
    return low;
}
```

The program works by repeatedly dividing in half the range of values being searched. Because there were originally n values, we know that the number of times the collection can be subdivided is no larger than roughly $\log n$ (see sidebar on logarithms). This is sufficient to tell us that the entire procedure is $O(\log n)$.

4.2.5 Function Calls

When function or procedure calls occur, the running time of the call is taken to be the running time of the associated procedure. For example, suppose that we wished to print the values of all prime numbers less than n. We could use an algorithm such as the following:

```
public void printPrimes (int n) {
  for (int i = 2; i <= n; i++) {
    if (isPrime(i))
      System.out.println("value " + i + " is prime");
    else
      System.out.println("value " + i + " is not prime");
  }
}
```

We know that the execution time of the `isPrime` routine is $O(\sqrt{n})$. (In fact, we can make the even stronger statement that it is $O(\sqrt{i})$, but doing

LOGARITHMS

To the mathematician, a *logarithm* is generally envisioned as the inverse of the exponential function, or perhaps it is associated with the integral calculus (that is, $\log_e a = \int_1^a \frac{1}{x} dx$). To a computer scientist, the intuition about the log function should be something very different.

Logarithm (base n) The log (base n) of a positive value x is *approximately* equal to the number of times that x can be divided by n.

Most often, the log function will arise when quantities are repeatedly split in half. This is why logarithms in computer science are, almost invariably, used with a base value 2.

Logarithm (base 2) The log (base 2) of a positive value x is *approximately* equal to the number of times that x can be divided in half.

The word "approximately" is used because the log function yields a fractional value, and the exact figure can be as much as one larger than the integer ceiling of the log. But, as we have already noted, integer constants can be safely ignored when discussing asymptotic bounds.

so results in a summation that is difficult to analyze, so we will bound each call by the larger limit.) Because we are making roughly n calls, the total running time of the procedure is no greater than $O(n\sqrt{n})$.

4.3 Summing Algorithmic Execution Times

Consider the following procedure for initializing an n by n matrix as an identity matrix:

```
public void makeIdentityMatrix (double [ ] [ ] m) {
  int n = m.length;
    // first make matrix of all zeros
  for (int i = 0; i < n; i++) {
    for (int j = 0; j < n; j++) {
      m[i, j] = 0.0;
    }
  }

    // then place ones along diagonal
  for (i = 0; i < n; i++) {
    m[i, i] = 1.0;
  }
}
```

Clearly, the first set of loops has an $O(n^2)$ execution time, and just as clearly, the latter loop has $O(n)$ behavior. One might be tempted to assert that the entire process therefore has $O(n^2 + n)$ performance. Instead, in this section, we will argue for a simpler rule: *When adding algorithmic complexities, the larger value dominates.* Therefore, the entire algorithm is $O(n^2)$.

To know what functions will dominate others, we must have some sort of ranking. The following table gives one such ordering, with the fastest-growing functions listed near the top and the slower-growing functions listed below. Formally, we say that a function $f(n)$ dominates a function $g(n)$ if there exists a constant value n_0 such that for all values $n > n_0$, it is the case that $g(n) < f(n)$.

This table also shows the common name used to describe the algorithmic behavior. We use such names when we say, for example, that the matrix multiplication algorithm given in Section 4.2.3 is cubic or that the bubble sort algorithm is quadratic.

Function	Common Name
$n!$	Factorial
2^n	Exponential
$n^d, d > 3$	Polynomial
n^3	Cubic
n^2	Quadratic
$n\sqrt{n}$	
$n \log n$	
n	Linear
$\sqrt{n}$	Root-n
$\log n$	Logarithmic
1	Constant

In the following discussion, we will motivate this rule in a variety of fashions. The first is intended merely as an intuitive illustration. You have probably had the experience of sitting in a car during a rainstorm and noting that small raindrops will stay fixed on the angled front window, even if the car remains at rest. If more water collects in the drop, however, it eventually falls off. There is a certain limit in size beyond which drops seemingly cannot remain fixed on the window.

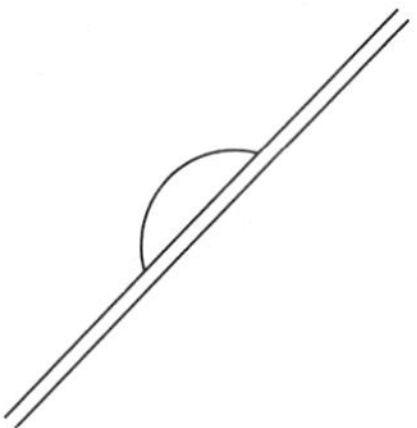

The force pulling the drop down is gravity, whereas the force permitting the drop to remain on the windshield is friction, or the surface tension between the drop and the glass. We can idealize the situation slightly and consider the drop to be a perfect hemisphere. If r represents the radius of the drop, the surface area between the drop and the window is πr^2. Gravity, on the other hand, operates on the entire volume of the drop, which is

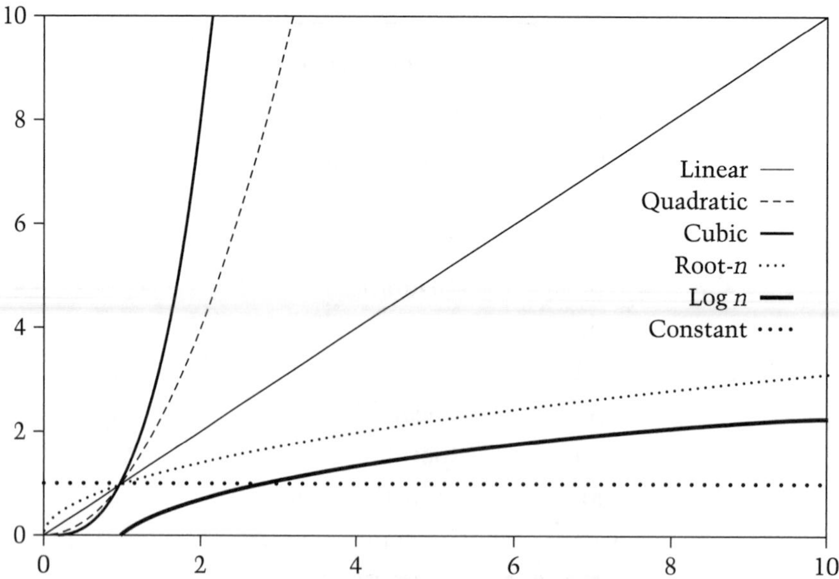

FIGURE 4.1 Characteristic Curves for Various Functions

proportional to r^3. Thus, the force of gravity can be described by $c \times r^3$, for an unknown constant c, and the force of surface tension is similarly described by $d \times r^2$, making use of an unknown constant d.

The observed phenomenon is that small drops will remain on the surface. This is the situation when the force of the surface tension is greater than that of gravity. As the drop becomes larger, its radius increases. Eventually, no matter what the constants may be, a cubic (r^3) function will always become larger than a quadratic (r^2) function. Thus, we would predict that large drops must always fall off the surface, because gravity prevails over surface tension. This, of course, matches what we observe.

We can see this behavior in a graphical fashion by noting the curves given by various functions. All functions possess a certain characteristic curve. Figure 4.1 illustrates these curves for various functions. An n^3 function will always grow faster than, and thus always eventually surpass, an n^2 function, regardless of the constant values involved either as a coefficient on the function or as an additive amount. This is shown in Figure 4.2, where the function $\frac{n^2}{4}$ is compared against the amount $200 + n \times \log n$. Although the latter is initially much larger, the n^2 function must always eventually dominate.

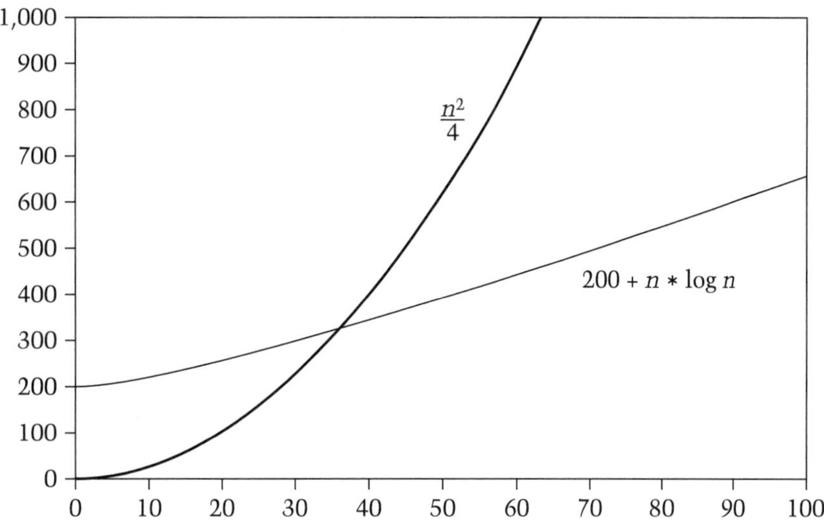

FIGURE 4.2 Comparing $n \log n$ and n^2 Growth

When two functions of different orders of magnitude are combined, the larger function will dominate the smaller one, so that the characteristic shape of the result matches the larger and not the smaller. This is shown in Figure 4.3, which compares the functions n and n^2 and the combination $n^2 + n$.

Another way to understand this is to consider a few values for the various functions. Assume, for example, that we can perform one operation every microsecond (that is, 10^6 operations per second) and that we have a task that requires an input of size 10^5. The figures in Table 4.1 illustrate how long it would take to perform this task, assuming various running times. The multiplication of the dominant function by a constant will, of course, change the running time but only by a constant factor. Consider a task that requires $n^2 + n \log n$ steps. The n^2 part means that the task will require several hours to complete, whereas the $n \log n$ component will add an insignificant few seconds to the execution time. Taking all these arguments into consideration, it seems intuitive that when we add algorithmic execution times, it is safe to ignore all terms except the dominant function. (For those who have a natural dislike of intuitive arguments, some of the exercises at the end of the chapter will place this assertion on a more formal grounding.)

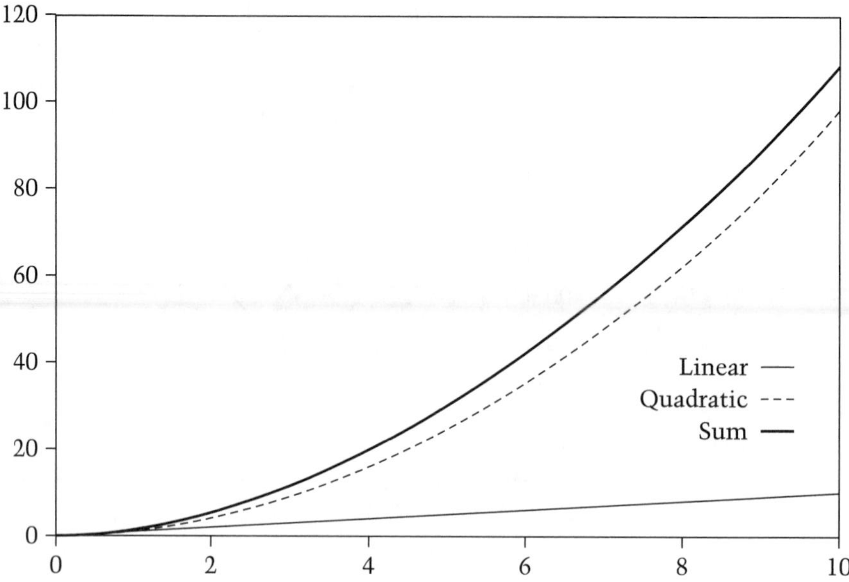

FIGURE 4.3 Addition of a Linear and a Quadratic Function

TABLE 4.1 EXECUTION TIMES ($n=10^5$ INPUT VALUES, ASSUMING 10^6 OPERATIONS PER SECOND)

Function	Running Time
2^n	More than a century
n^3	31.7 years
n^2	2.8 hours
$n\sqrt{n}$	31.6 seconds
$n \log n$	1.2 seconds
n	0.1 seconds
$\sqrt{n}$	3.2×10^{-4} seconds
$\log n$	1.2×10^{-5} seconds

4.4 THE IMPORTANCE OF FAST ALGORITHMS

The following story will help illustrate both the importance of finding fast algorithms and data structures and that the most obvious approach to solving a problem may not necessarily be the best. Several years ago, a student working in genetic research was faced with a task involved in the analysis of DNA sequences. The problem could be reduced to a relatively simple form. The DNA is represented as an array of n integer values, where n is very large (on the order of tens of thousands). The problem was to discover whether any pattern of length m, where m was a fixed and small constant (say 5 or 10) is ever repeated in the array of values.

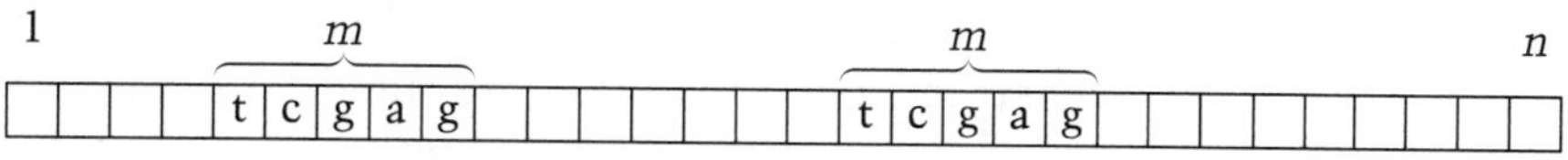

1 m m n

				t	c	g	a	g								t	c	g	a	g								

The programmer dutifully sat down and wrote a simple and straightforward program, something like the following:

```
for (int i = 0; i < (n-m); i++)
  for (int j = i+1; j < (n-m); j++) {
    boolean found = true;
    for (k = 0; k < m; k++) {
      if (x[i+k] != x[j+k])
        found = false;
    }
    if (found) {
      .
      .
      .
    }
  }
```

The student was somewhat disappointed when trial runs indicated that his program would need several days to complete. He discussed his problem with a second student, who suggested a different approach. Rather than working with an array of n elements, the second student reorganized the data into a matrix with roughly n rows and m columns:

x_1	x_2	...	x_m
x_2	x_3	...	x_{m+1}
...			...
x_{n-m}	...	...	x_{n-1}
$x_{n-(m-1)}$	...	x_{n-1}	x_n

The second student then wrote a program to sort this matrix by rows. If any pattern was repeated, two adjacent rows in the sorted matrix would have identical values. It was a trivial matter to check for this condition.

As we will see in later chapters, sorting can be made an $O(n \log n)$ time operation. Sorting a matrix can be performed by an algorithm that is $O(m \times n \log n)$, whereas the original program was $O(m \times n^2)$. This was a considerable improvement, reducing the estimated execution time from several days to slightly less than one day.

At this point, a third student entered the room and said that she had a technique that could reduce the execution time even further. Her approach was to take each section of m values and reduce it to a single integer value—for example, by adding the elements. This is a technique called *hashing*, and we will examine it in detail in Chapter 16. The student then constructed another array of roughly n elements. For each hashed entry, she placed a string representing the run of m characters at the location given by the remainder yielded after dividing the hash value by the size of the array:

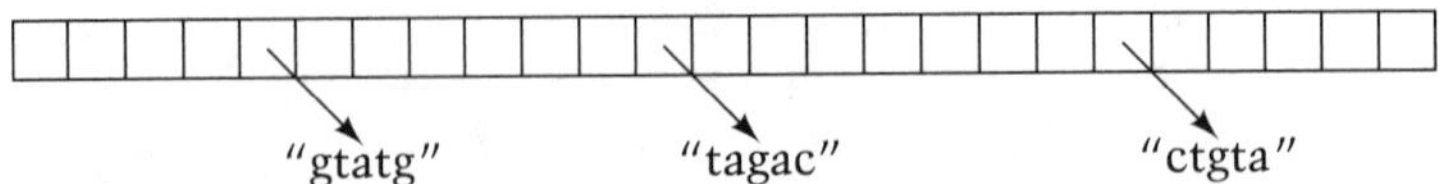

If two elements were equal, they would have the same hash value. It was therefore a simple matter to examine the array prior to placing each value to see whether the same value had already been seen. Because all this could be performed in one pass through the original data array, it was $O(m \times n)$, which was even faster than the $O(m \times n \log n)$ solution. Using this technique, the first student was able to reduce the data analysis phase of his work from several days to well under one day of execution time.

4.5 BENCHMARKING EXECUTION TIMES

Although an asymptotic characterization is normally the first and best way to describe the execution-time behavior of a complex algorithm, it is not the final word. For example, how do we compare the execution time of bubble sort and insertion sort once we have determined that they are both $O(n^2)$ algorithms? For that, we must compare the two algorithms by their running times on a machine.

The library of classes described in this book contains a simple utility, `GraphMaker`, that we will use to perform timings of algorithms. A `GraphMaker` is a `Canvas`, which means that it can be used as a standard Java graphical object. Typically, the `GraphMaker` is a central portion of an application display. The constructor for the class `GraphMaker` takes two integer arguments, which represent the maximum x and maximum y values for the graph to be displayed. Elements are added to a graph by means of a `Reporter`, a helper class that accepts x and y pairs.

Another utility class, `TaskTimer`, will simplify the creation of graphs. This class, shown in Figure 4.4, provides three methods in addition to

```
public class TaskTimer {

  public TaskTimer (Reporter ioutput) { output = ioutput; }
  private Reporter output;

  public void initialize (int i) { } // default is nothing

  public void doTask (int i) { } // override this method

  public void run (int start, int stop, int step) {
    for(int i = start; i <= stop; i += step) {
      initialize(i);
      System.gc(); // do garbage collection
      long startTime = System.currentTimeMillis();
      doTask(i);
      long stopTime = System.currentTimeMillis();
      int time = (int) (stopTime - startTime);
      output.addPoint(i, time);
    }
  }
}
```

FIGURE 4.4 The Class TaskTimer

the constructor. The constructor requires a reporter that will be used to plot the values. The methods `initialize` and `doTask` are overwritten by the user to specify the task to be performed. The method `run` repeatedly executes the given tasks, computing the execution time and recording the execution times using the reporter.

The code in Figure 4.5 shows how we can create a subclass of `TaskTimer` to compute the running time of the bubble sort algorithm described in Section 4.2.3. This figure also shows how to create the main application that combines the `GraphMaker` and the `TaskTimer`. Running the `BubbleExperiment` program produces output like that shown in Figure 4.6. Note that although the execution timings for the two algorithms show clear trends, they are not precise. This is characteristic of execution timings. Memory management, the need for the hardware to respond to other processes, and other uncertain factors can combine to make small (or, sometimes, very large) deviations in execution timings. Thus, no single timing should ever be taken to be representative of the performance of an algorithm. Instead, a number of repeated timings should be obtained, so as to smooth out any transient effects.

```
class BubbleTime extends TaskTimer {
  BubbleTime (Reporter out) { super(out); }

  public void initialize (int n) {
    data = new double[n]; // create new array
    for (int i = 0; i < n; i++) // fill with random values
      data[i] = n * Math.random();
  }

  public void doTask (int n) { bubbleSort(data); }

  private double [ ] data;

  private void bubbleSort (double [ ] v) { ... }
}

public class BubbleExperiment extends Frame {

  public static void main (String [ ] args) {
    BubbleExperiment world = new BubbleExperiment();
    world.show(); world.run();
  }

  public BubbleExperiment () {
    setTitle("Bubble Sort and Insertion Sort Comparison");
    setSize(500, 300);
    add("Center", graph);
  }

  private GraphMaker graph = new GraphMaker(5000, 3000);

  public void run() {
    BubbleTime bTimer = new BubbleTime(graph.getReporter("Bubble"));
    bTimer.run(0, 5000, 100);
    InsertionTime iTimer =
      new InsertionTime(graph.getReporter("Insertion"));
    iTimer.run(0, 5000, 100);
  }
}
```

FIGURE 4.5 The Class BubbleExperiment

THE JAVA BIG BANG

In Chapter 1, we noted that an object-oriented program can be envisioned as a universe of interacting objects. It is helpful to keep this image in mind when considering how a Java program typically starts execution. The procedure `main` must be declared both `public` and `static`. The latter characteristic is necessary because only `static` methods can be executed prior to the creation of any instances of a class.

Often, as in Figure 4.5, the most important action the `main` program must perform is to create the first object that will occupy the object-oriented universe. (Sometimes, it is the *only* action.) The constructor for this class will then proceed to create other objects until all the necessary elements in the universe are formed. In this program, we create a `GraphMaker` and instances of two subclasses of `TaskTimer`. The `GraphMaker` will, in turn, create instances of `Reporter`. Finally, the program is set in motion, and the output is displayed.

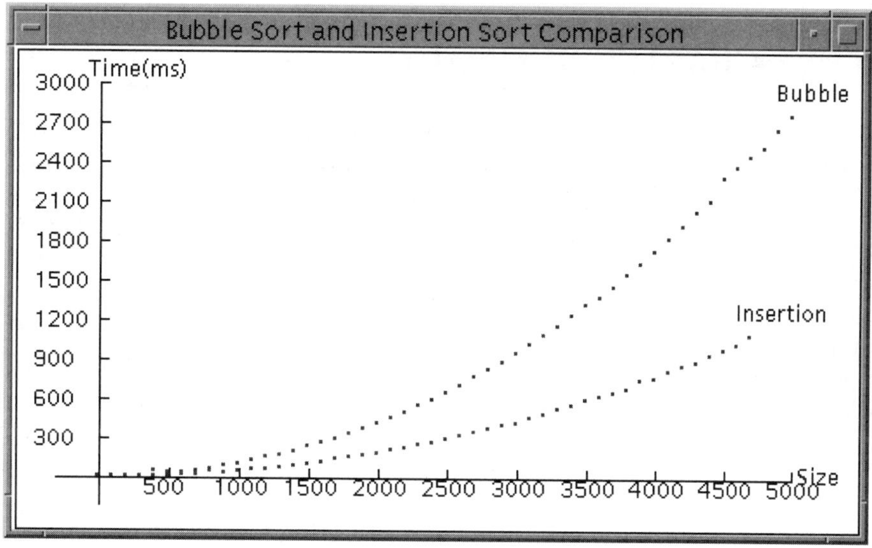

FIGURE 4.6 Execution Timings for Bubble Sort and Insertion Sort

We can see from Figure 4.6 that although bubble sort and insertion sort have the same asymptotic execution time (they are both $O(n^2)$), in practice, insertion sort tends to be slightly faster.

EXPERIMENT: CHANGING THE INPUT DISTRIBUTION

Throughout the book, we will suggest experiments that you may wish to perform in order to gain a deeper understanding of various topics. One interesting experiment relevant to the output shown in Figure 4.6 is to consider the impact of the distribution of values in the original unsorted array and whether an alternative distribution will produce radically different results. We noted, for example, that the execution time of the `InsertionSort` algorithm will vary considerably, depending on the characteristics of the input values.

We can create an "almost sorted" input array by changing the way that we initialize the `data` array in Figure 4.5. Consider the following:

```
public void initialize (int n) {
  data = new double[n]; // create new array
  for (int i = 0; i < n; i++)
    data[i] = i + 3 * Math.random();
}
```

Because `Math.random` returns a value larger than or equal to 0 and smaller than 1, if we multiply this by 3, we get a value between 0 and 3. If we add this to i, we get a value between i and $i+3$. Because the values are random, we are not guaranteed that they will be monotonically increasing, but they should generally get larger. Will this change the result we see in Figure 4.6? Can you figure out how to create a array that is "almost reverse sorted"?

4.6 CHAPTER SUMMARY

KEY CONCEPTS

- Algorithmic complexity
- Big-Oh notation
- Recursion
- Mathematical induction
- Benchmarks

On a coarse level, algorithms can be compared by their algorithmic complexity. The algorithmic characterization of an algorithm is usually given by a "big-Oh" expression. This expression characterizes the behavior of the algorithm as input values grow ever larger. However, even with relatively small inputs, an algorithm with a smaller algorithmic complexity will usually execute more quickly than one with a larger algorithmic complexity.

Mathematical induction is a powerful analysis technique used in proving properties of general formulas. In computer science, mathematical induction is used in the analysis of program fragments that are executed repeatedly, either as loops or as recursive algorithms. Mathematical induction is used in proving termination, analyzing execution time, and proving correctness.

Mathematical induction and the development of recursive algorithms are very similar. Some of the common features of both are

- The discovery of base cases that can be handled by other mechanisms and to which all larger problems will ultimately be reduced
- The discovery of how a larger problem can be reduced to a slightly smaller problem of the same form

In comparing two algorithms with the same algorithmic complexity, running times, or benchmarks, may be used. Although a benchmark can provide an accurate time estimate for a particular machine and particular input conditions, it is sometimes difficult (frequently impossible) to extrapolate such a number to new machines or to different input values.

Further Information

The basic concepts of computational complexity were originally developed by Juris Hartmanis and Richard E. Stearns [Hartmanis 65], for which they were awarded the ACM Turing award in 1993. As we noted in Chapter 3, the study of algorithms was popularized by Donald Knuth in his three-part series [Knuth 97, Knuth 98a, Knuth 98b].

Study Questions

1. Why is a benchmark not generally a good characterization of the running time of an algorithm?
2. What does it mean to say that an algorithm is $O(f(n))$ for a function $f(n)$?
3. What formula describes the algorithmic execution time of a conditional (`if`) statement? How about a `switch` statement?
4. What is the algorithmic running time of the procedure named `power`, used to raise a double-precision value to an integer exponent, that we described in Section 3.3.1?
5. What parts of an argument use mathematical induction?
6. What is the best- and worst-case algorithmic running time of the insertion sort algorithm?
7. To a computer scientist, what should be the intuitive meaning of the log function?
8. What two pieces of information are needed to characterize the algorithmic running time of a recursive procedure?
9. What rule is used in adding two algorithmic complexity formulas?
10. What are some situations in which a benchmark provides more useful information than an algorithmic complexity characterization?

Exercises

1. The three parts of this exercise are intended to place the concept of algorithmic analysis on a slightly firmer theoretical foundation. In particular, these exercises will help support the idea that (a) additive constants can be ignored, (b) constant coefficients can be ignored, and (c)

when adding two algorithmic complexities, only the dominant function need be considered.

Recall that the definition of big-Oh notation said that a function $f(n)$ is $O(g(n))$ if there exist constants n_0 and c such that for all values $n > n_0$, $f(n) < c \times g(n)$.

a. Assume that $f(n)$ is $O(g(n))$, where $f(n)$ and $g(n)$ are both functions of n, $g(n) > 1$ for all n. Demonstrate that $f(n) + c$, for any constant c, is still $O(g(n))$. *Hint:* Show that there exists a new constant, c_2, that bounds $f(n) + c$.

b. Assume that $f(n)$ is $O(g(n))$. Demonstrate that $c \times f(n)$, for any constant c, is still $O(g(n))$.

c. Assume $f_1(n) < f_2(n)$ for all values larger than some n_0 and that $f_2(n)$ is $O(g(n))$. Show that $f_1(n) + f_2(n)$ is $O(g(n))$.

2. Prove that the function ax^i is $O(x^{i+j})$ for any value $j >= 0$.
3. Using the proof from the previous question, prove that any polynomial $a + bx + cx^2 + \ldots + hx^i$ is $O(x^i)$, that is, that the largest polynomial term will dominate.
4. Prove that the function $\log_a n$ is $O(\log_2 n)$ for any constant value a (hence, we need not state the base of a log when using big-Oh notation).
5. Prove, using mathematical induction, that a common multiplier can be factored out of a summation. That is, for any constant c and nonnegative integer n:

$$\sum_{i=1}^{n} c \times f(i) = c \times \sum_{i=1}^{n} f(i)$$

6. Prove, by mathematical induction, that the sum of powers of 2 is one less than the next-higher power. That is, for any nonnegative integer n:

$$\sum_{i=0}^{n} 2^i = 2^{n+1} - 1$$

7. Suppose that by careful measurement, we have discovered a function that describes the precise running time of an algorithm. For each of the following such functions, describe the algorithmic running time in big-Oh notation.

a. $3n^2 + 3n + 7$

b. $(5 * n) * (3 + \log n)$

c. $\frac{5n+4}{6}$

d. $1 + 2 + 3 + 4 + \ldots + n$

e. $n + \log n^2$

f. $\frac{(n+1)\log n}{2}$

8. For each of the following program skeletons, describe the algorithmic execution time as a function of n. You can assume that the remaining portions of the loops require only constant execution time.

a.
```
for (int i = 0; i < n; i++) {
   .
   .
   .
}
for (int j = n; j >= 0; j--) {
   .
   .
   .
}
```

b.
```
for (int i = 0; i < n; i++) {
   for (int j = 0; j < n; j++) {
      .
      .
      .
   }
}
```

c.
```
for (int i = 0; i < n; i++) {
   for (int j = 0; j < i; j++) {
      .
      .
      .
   }
}
```

d.
```
for (int i = n; i > 0; i = i / 2) {
   .
   .
   .
}
```

e.
```
for (int i = 0; i < n; i++) {
   for (int j = 0; j * j < n; j++) {
      .
      .
      .
   }
}
```

f.
```
for (int i = n; i > 0; i = i >> 1) {
   for (int j = 0; j < n; j++) {
      .
      .
      .
   }
}
```

9. Suppose that we have an n^2 algorithm that for $n = 80$ runs slightly longer than 1 hour. One day, we discover an alternative algorithm that runs in time $n \log n$. If we assume that the constants of proportionality are about the same, about how long would we expect the new program to run?
10. Simulate the execution of bubble sort (Section 4.2.3) on the array of value 7 2 3 9 4. Show the state of the array at the end of each iteration of the outermost loop.
11. Simulate the execution of insertion sort (Section 4.2.4) on the array of value 7 2 3 9 4. Show the state of the array at the end of each iteration of the outermost loop.

Programming Projects

1. Can you rewrite the binary search algorithm as a recursive procedure? Perform execution timings on the resulting algorithm to compare the running time to that of the original.
2. The *selection sort* algorithm is similar to bubble sort, but rather than swapping elements in the inner loop, it merely locates the position of the currently largest value, then performs one swap in the outer loop. Implement this algorithm and compare the running time to that of bubble sort and insertion sort. Is it better than bubble sort? Is it faster than insertion sort?
3. Convert the insertion sort algorithm so that it will work on an array of `Object` values, using a `Comparator` (see Section 2.3.4) to determine the ordering of the elements.
4. Using the `TaskTimer` class, plot the execution time for the method `isPrime` for all integer values between 1 and 1,000. Does the resulting curve appear to be $\sqrt{n}$? (Because the total execution time is so small, you may need to repeatedly execute the function call 100 times to get a meaningful value.)
5. Using the `TaskTimer` class, plot the number of moves required to solve the Towers of Hanoi puzzle as a function of n. What type of curve do you think this represents?
6. Using the `TaskTimer` class, provide evidence that `binarySearch` is an $O(\log n)$ algorithm. To do this, in the initialization phase of `TaskTimer`, create an array of n random integers between 1 and n and sort them so that they will be in order. Then, in the timed section, search for a random value between 1 and n. Perform this task for a sequence of increasing values of n, and plot the execution times.

7. The Fibonacci numbers are described by the formula $F(0) = 0$, $F(1) = 1$, and the recursive formula $F(n) = F(n-2) + F(n-1)$. Write two routines for computing the nth Fibonacci number. The first routine should compute the value iteratively; given an argument value n, it first computes $F(0)$, then $F(1)$, and from these each value $F(i)$ until i reaches n. The second algorithm should work recursively. Given an argument n, if n is larger than 1, it will recursively call itself to compute the two earlier Fibonacci numbers, then return their sum. Calculate and compare execution timings for these two algorithms. Can you explain the difference in execution times?
8. The `GraphMaker` utility can be used to plot any type of graph, not simply those generated using the `TaskTimer`. Write an application that will take an array of integer values and determine the size of the array and the maximum and minimum values in the array; then create a graph of the appropriate size and plot the values.
9. A number of interesting mathematical problems involve random walks. Here is a simple one-dimensional example that can be solved using an array. Imagine that a drunken cockroach is placed in the middle square of an array of n elements. The bug wanders randomly back and forth. Assuming that at each step, the bug will move with *equal probability* to either the next-higher or the next-lower square, how long will it take for the bug to reach the end of the array? How many times will it cross each square?

   Although difficult to solve mathematically, this type of problem is easily solved by using a simulation. Program a simulation for the one-dimensional drunken cockroach problem for an array of size n. Then, using the plotting utility you developed in the previous programming project, display the number of times the bug stepped on each square.

CHAPTER 5

INCREASING CONFIDENCE IN CORRECTNESS

In this chapter, we investigate techniques that are used to increase confidence in the likelihood that a program will execute correctly. There are two primary approaches to this task. One is the mechanism of *testing*, whereby a function or a procedure is executed with test values. The second is the process of *proving correctness*, whereby a more or less formal proof is developed to demonstrate that an algorithm will perform the desired task. Both techniques are useful, and neither should be considered a substitite for the other.

Techniques used in developing arguments for the correctness of programs include *pre-* and *postconditions*, *assertions*, and *invariants*. After introducing the tools used in program proving, this chapter concludes with a discussion of program-testing techniques and objectives. Major topics are

- Program proofs
- Assertions
- Invariants
- Program testing

5.1 PROGRAM PROOFS

Programmers use proofs of programs to increase their own confidence in the correctness of their algorithms and to discover and to highlight those places where such confidence is misplaced (that is, find errors). To properly understand the role of program proofs, you should remember that, in the large, programming is a social activity pursued by a team of individuals working cooperatively on a given task. A program proof is not for the benefit of the computer; indeed, the greater portion of the proof is documented by comments in the program text, which are not processed by the computer at all. Similarly, a proof is intended only partially for the benefit of the original programmer. Most often, programmers examine one another's code in a structured setting, called a *code walk-through*. In such a walk-through, a programmer traces the execution of an algorithm and presents arguments to justify the contention that the particular section of code under scrutiny will perform as expected. Proofs of program correctness are an essential part of this process.

Whereas the role of the programmer is to argue for the correctness of the program, the roles of the other members participating in a code walk-through are to try to anticipate ways in which failure can occur and to highlight potential weakness. Although it is not our place here to discuss in detail principles of software engineering, we note in passing that great care must be taken during code walk-through to ensure that the atmosphere remains one of cooperation and that programmers are not permitted to have the feeling that they are defending their code against "attacks" by other programmers.

5.1.1 Invariants

The major tool used in formulating an argument that can be used to justify belief in the correctness of an algorithm is the *invariant*. Like a *precondition*, an invariant is nothing more than a comment, but it is a comment that describes the state of the computation at the point where the comment would be encountered during the course of execution. The art of using invariants lies in finding statements that are most meaningful to a human audience. To do so, an invariant should describe the processing being performed in the high-level language of the problem domain and not necessarily in the low-level language of the calculation being performed.

Here is a program that contains an error. Let us see how the use of invariants could be used to uncover the bug. The program purports to characterize three sides of a triangle, returning 1 if the triangle is equilateral (all sides equal), 2 if isosceles (two sides equal), and 3 if scalene (no sides equal).

```
int triangle (int a, int b, int c) {
    // pre: input a, b, and c are sides of a triangle
    // post: returns a characterization of the triangle
    // 1 if equalateral, 2 if isosceles, and 3 is scalene
```

```
  if (a == b) {
    if (b == c) {
      // inv: a equals b, b equals c,
      // so a equals c and all are equal
      return 1; // equilateral
      }
    else {
      // inv: a equals b, but b does not equal c
      // so only two sides are equal
      return 2; // isosceles
      }
    }
  else {
    if (b == c) {
      // inv: a not equal to b, but b equals c,
      // so two sides are equal
      return 2; // isosceles
      }
    else {
      // inv: so no sides are equal
      return 3; // scalene
      }
    }
}
```

To form an argument to justify belief in the correctness of an algorithm, we first assume that the preconditions, if any, are valid. We then trace execution from beginning to end, following all possible paths, and demonstrate that the invariants must be true when execution reaches the point where they are placed. Finally, we can argue that the invariant establishes the correct result.

If we imagine a test case that fails the first `if` statement and also the second, we can see the error in the program. At the point of the invariant immediately prior to returning the value 3, the information we have is that `a` is not equal to `b` and that `b` is not equal to `c`, as both these conditions have failed. But we do not therefore know that all sides are unequal, as it is possible for `a` to be equal to `c`. Thus, the invariant we have written (which, if it were true, would justify the subsequent statement) cannot be supported by an argument. (This illustrates that invariants should not be assumed to be true until proven by argument.)

Invariants become more useful, but also more complicated, when programs contain loops. In a program with loops, we cannot simply execute all possible paths. However, the concept of an invariant remains the same. That is, an invariant simply describes the state of execution at the point the invariant appears. In Chapter 4, we described an algorithm that could be used to find the minimum value from a vector of n floating-point quantities. This function could be augmented with invariants in the following fashion:

```
public double minimum (double [ ] values) {
    // pre: values has at least one element
    // post: returns smallest value in collection
  int n = values.length;
    // return the minimum value found
    // in the vector of double precision values
  double minValue = values [0];
    // inv 1: minValue is the minimum value found in
    // the range 0 .. 0
  for (int i = 1; i < n; i++) {
    // inv 2: minValue is the minimum value found in
    // the range 0 .. i-1
    if (values[i] < minValue)
      minValue = values[i];
    // inv 3: minValue is the minimum value found in
    // the range 0 .. i
    }
  // inv 4: minValue is the minimum value found in
  // the range 0 .. n-1
  return minValue;
}
```

In the next section, we will describe how invariants are used in formulating an argument to increase confidence in the correct functioning of an algorithm.

5.1.2 Analyzing Loops

To create an argument that can be used to increase confidence in an algorithm, the programmer traces through a program all possible execution paths that lead from one invariant to the next. In each case, the programmer creates an argument that asserts that *if* the first invariant is true, and *if* the intervening statements are executed, *then* the second invariant must be true. We will illustrate this process with the function given in the previous section.

The first step is to verify the initial invariant. We assume that the precondition has been satisfied and that therefore the assignment statement used to initialize the variable `minValue` to the first element will succeed without raising an indexing exception. The variable, therefore, holds the minimum value of the vector in the range 0 to 0 (indeed, it holds the only value in this range).

```
    .
    .
    .
double minValue = values [0];
  // inv 1: minValue is the minimum value found in
  // the range 0 .. 0
for (int i = 1; i < n; i++) {
  // inv 2: minValue is the minimum value found in
  // the range 0 .. i-1
    .
    .
    .
```

We next argue from invariant 1 to invariant 2. Just as we did with induction, we are now making the *assumption* that invariant 1 is true and arguing that if this is the case, invariant 2 must be true when execution reaches the point at which it has been placed. Between these two points, the only value that is changed is the variable i, which is assigned the value 1 and has been tested to ensure that it is less than n. But the quantity i − 1 is therefore 0, and if invariant 1 was previously true, invariant 2 must now be true, because it is asserting the same fact.

```
    .
    .
    .
  // inv 2: minValue is the minimum value found in
  // the range 0 .. i-1
  if (values[i] < minValue)
    minValue = values[i];
  // inv 3: minValue is the minimum value found in
  // the range 0 .. i
    .
    .
    .
```

Loop Invariants and Mathematical Induction

The validity of the use of loop invariants can be demonstrated by turning a proof based on invariants into a proof using mathematical induction. To do so, we simply let the *number of times execution has passed through the loop* be the induction value.

Consider how invariants are used in the analysis of the minimum-value function considered in Section 5.1.2. Cases in which the loop is executed zero times and in which the loop is executed one time are handled as base cases. For the induction case, we assume that the loop has been executed n times and will loop at least $n + 1$ times (that is, at least one more time). The argument presented in the text then demonstrates that if invariant 3 is true during the nth iteration, invariant 2 must be true on the $n + 1$ iteration.

This shows that no matter how many times the loop iterates, invariant 3 will always be true when it is encountered. A separate argument then traces the flow from invariant 3 to invariant 4, and we are finished.

Next, we consider the flow of execution between invariant 2 and invariant 3. This time, instead of assuming that we are on the first iteration (as we did between invariant 1 and invariant 2), we now assume that we are on an indefinite iteration. We therefore have no specific information about the value `i` other than that it must have a value between 1 and `n` (the limits of the loop). Invariant 2 tells us that the variable `minValue` holds the minimum value in the vector for indices in the range 0 to `i - 1`. If we examine the code between invariants 2 and 3, we see that we can divide our argument into two cases. Either the value held by the vector at index position `i` is smaller than this minimum, or it is not. In the former case, the variable `minValue` is updated to hold this new value. Therefore, in either case, by the time we reach invariant 3, we can argue that the value held by `minValue` is now the smallest element in the range of data values indexed by 0 through the position `i`.

Note that invariant 2 and invariant 3 are very similar. We often say that invariant 2 has been *strengthened* in order to reach invariant 3. In this case, strengthening means that we have extended the range of values under consideration from $(0 .. i - 1)$ to $(0 .. i)$.

From invariant 3, execution could flow in two possible directions. Both must be investigated. In both cases, the variable `i` will be incremented. The new value of `i` then either is or is not greater than or equal to the limit value `n`. If it is not, the loop will iterate once more, and invariant 2 will once again be reached. In this circumstance, we are assuming that invariant 3 is true and arguing that invariant 2 must now be true. But invariant 3 is asserting the same condition as invariant 2, under the condition that variable `i` has been incremented.

The second possibility is that the loop terminates, and execution flows from invariant 3 to the final invariant 4. But this will occur only if the updated value of `i`, which is monotonically increasing, is now `n`. Therefore, invariant 3 is transformed into invariant 4 with the substitution of `n - 1` for `i`. (We must subtract 1 to "undo" the fact that `i` was incremented prior to the test.)

```
  .
  .
  .
  // inv 1: minValue is the minimum value found in
  // the range 0 .. 0

for (int i = 1; i < n; i++) {
    .
    .
    .
    // inv 3: minValue is the minimum value found in
```

```
    // the range 0 .. i
  }

  // inv 4: minValue is the minimum value found in
  // the range 0 .. n-1
```

The last flow of control is the easiest to forget. It is possible to move directly from invariant 1 to invariant 4 without encountering any other invariants. This will occur only when the size of the vector is exactly 1, and therefore the condition controlling the loop is false when it is first encountered. But in this circumstance, the value n must be 1, and therefore invariant 4 is asserting the same condition as invariant 1.

5.1.3 Asserting That the Outcome Is Correct

The final invariant in any procedure should always assert the conditions corresponding to the desired outcome—that is, the result specified by the postconditions. These may be addressed only indirectly by the actions of the program. For example, the invariants in the `isPrime` procedure deal with finding factors of the input value. Only if no factors are found is the number known to be prime. Note that, as in the minimum-number procedure, the invariant at the end of the loop is a simple conjunction of the invariant at the start of the loop and the negation of the looping condition.

```
public boolean isPrime (int n) {
    // pre: n is greater than or equal to 2
    // post: true if n is prime, false otherwise
  for (int i = 2; i * i <= n; i++) {
      // inv 1: n has no factors between 2 and i-1

    if (0 == n % i) {
        // inv 2: i divides n
        // therefore n is not prime
      return false;
      }

      // inv 3: n has no factors between 2 and i
    }

    // inv 4: n has no factors between 2 and
    // ceiling(sqrt(n)), therefore number must be prime
  return true;
}
```

5.1.4 Progress toward an Objective

Invariants inside a loop describe an intermediate stage within a calculation. In such situations, only partial progress has been made toward an ultimate objective. To describe such invariants, it is necessary to understand not only the ultimate objective but also how the intermediate stage relates to the intended outcome. (When viewed in this light, a loop is therefore one more example of the abstraction device we termed *repetition* in Chapter 1.)

For example, in the binary search procedure, we initially know only that the target value, if it appears at all, appears in positions indexed between 0 and $n - 1$ (that is, the entire vector). By repeatedly examining the middle value in a range, we divide in half the region in which the value can potentially be found. This continues until the region is reduced to a single element.

```
int binarySearch (double [ ] data, double testValue) {
  // pre: elements in argument data are ordered smallest to largest
  // post: returns the index in data where testValue is found,
  // or index of next larger element if not in collection
  int low = 0;
  int high = data.length;

  while (low < high) {
    // inv: data[0 .. low-1] less than testValue
    // data[high .. max] greater than or equal to testValue
    mid = (low + high) / 2;
    if (data[mid] < testValue)
      low = mid + 1;
    else
      high = mid;
  }
  // inv: data[0..low-1] less than testValue
  // and testValue less than or equal to data[low+1]
  return low;
}
```

When loops are nested, each loop may be pursuing its own objective, and each may therefore have a different set of invariants. In the bubble sort procedure, for example, the outer loop is placing elements into position, starting from the top. The inner loop is designed to ensure that the largest remaining value is moved into the topmost position. This is accomplished by moving the loop variable j upward through all possibilities and maintaining the condition that the largest value seen so far is kept at position j+1. We could augment this procedure with invariants, as follows:

```
void bubbleSort (double [ ] v) {
  // exchange the values in the vector v
  // so they appear in ascending order
  int n = v.length;

  for (int i = n - 1; i > 0; i--) {
    // inv: elements indexed i+1 to n-1 are correctly ordered

    for (int j = 0; j < i; j++) {
      // inv: v[j] holds largest value from range (0..j)

      if (v[j+1] < v[j]) { // if out of order, then swap
        double temp = v[j];
        v[j] = v[j + 1];
        v[j + 1] = temp;
        }

      // inv: v[j+1] holds largest value from range (0..j+1)
      }

    // inv: v[i] holds largest value from range (0..i)
    // inv: therefore, elements i to n-1 are correctly ordered
    }

  // inv: elements indexed 0 to n-1 are correctly ordered
}
```

5.1.5 Manipulating Unnamed Quantities

When using invariants, it is often necessary to discuss quantities that are not explicitly named in the program. An example occurs in the Greatest Common Divisor program from Chapter 3. To argue that this procedure is correct, we require the observation that if d is a divisor for both n and m and if n is larger than m, d must also be a divisor for $n - m$. (To see this, note that $\frac{n}{d}$ must be integer, as must $\frac{m}{d}$, and therefore $\frac{n}{d} - \frac{m}{d}$ must be integer, but this is the same as $\frac{n-m}{d}$). The invariants for the loop must therefore assert that although we have changed n and m, the GCD of the original values, which is not a quantity that has been given a name by the program, has not been altered.[1]

1. To be precise, all we have demonstrated by this argument is that the result will be *a* divisor of the original n and m values. To assert that the result is the largest possible divisor requires a more subtle mathematical argument, which is not relevant to our discussion here.

```
public int gcd (int n, int m) {
    // pre: assume arguments are greater than or equal to zero
    // post: compute the greatest common divisor of arguments

  while (m != n) {
    if (n > m)
      n = n - m;
      // inv: gcd of n and m
      // has not been altered
    else
      m = m - n;
      // inv: gcd of n and m
      // has not been altered
    }

    // n equal to m,
    // so n is divisor of both
  return n;
}
```

5.1.6 Function Calls

When a procedure invokes another procedure, the argument about the correctness of the first procedure is always expressed conditionally, based on the assumption that the invoked procedure is performing in the correct manner. Although it is not necessary to repeat the argument for the correctness of the called procedure, it *is* necessary to address the question of whether the arguments that are being passed to the underlying procedure are valid—that is, within the range of elements the procedure is prepared to handle.

For example, the `printPrimes` procedures can be shown to be correct, based on the assumption that the `isPrime` procedure operates correctly. The precondition to `isPrime` requires the index value to be larger than 2. It is easy to verify that this condition is satisfied, and so we assume that `isPrime` is producing the correct outcome. But with this assumption, it is then easy to argue that `printPrimes` must be correct.

```
void printPrimes (int n) {
    // print numbers between 2 and n
    // indicating which are prime
  for (int i = 2; i <= n; i++) {
    if (isPrime(i))
      System.out.println("value " + i + " is prime");
```

```
    else
      System.out.println("value " + i + " is not prime");
    }
}
```

5.1.7 Recursive Algorithms

The analysis of recursive algorithms is simply an extension of the technique used for ordinary procedure calls. As we noted in Chapter 4, the execution of recursive procedures is always divided into two cases. One or more *base cases* can be handled without recursive invocation. The *recursive* (or *inductive*) cases are handled by the procedure's calling itself.

The base cases are analyzed as any other procedure, using invariants, if necessary. To handle the recursive case, we simply *assume* that the recursive invocation will perform correctly and argue the remainder of the procedure accordingly. For example, consider the procedure from the previous chapter to print a positive integer value:

```
public void printInt (OutputStream out, int val) {
    // print the character representation of the argument value
  if (val < 10)
    out.write(digitChar(val));
  else {
    printInt(val/10); // print all but final character
    out.write(digitChar(val%10)); // print last character
  }
}
```

If the parameter value is less than 10, it is easy to see that the procedure performs as expected, assuming that the two procedures `digitChar` and `write` operate properly. The recursive case is hardly any more complex; we assume that the recursive call will work, and the remainder is simply another set of calls on `write` and `digitChar`.

Once again, to place this technique on firm formal footing requires relating the analysis to mathematical induction. One argues that in situations in which no recursive calls are invoked, the correct results are produced. One then assumes that the correct result is produced in all situations in which n recursive calls are necessary. Based on this, one then formulates an argument that if $n + 1$ recursive calls are necessary, the correct result will be produced, because this reduces to a case in which n calls are necessary.

In both proving mathematical formulas using induction and in analyzing recursive algorithms, the following steps must be performed:

1. Identify the base cases and establish that the formula or algorithm works for these cases.
2. Argue that, in all situations, the reduction being performed must eventually reach one of the base cases.
3. Provide a conditional argument that asserts that *if* the recursive call produces the correct outcome, *then* the remainder of the program must produce the correct result.

The recursive version of the integer exponential algorithm illustrates that invariants are related more to the problem domain than to the mechanics of execution. In this case, the only invariant necessary is used to assert that although the recursive calculation being performed is different, the resulting value is the same as the original request.

```
public double power (double base, int n) {
    // pre: n is larger than or equal to zero
    // post: return the value yielded by raising the
    // double-precision base to the integer exponent
    // assumes floating-point overflow does not occur
  if (n == 0)  // anything raised to zero power is 1
    return 1.0;
  else if (even(n))
      // base ^ n is same as
      // (base ^ 2) ^ (n / 2) for even n
    return power(base * base, n / 2);
  else
      // base ^ n is same as
      // base * (base ^ 2) ^ (n / 2) for odd n
    return power(base * base, n / 2) * base;
}
```

The Towers of Hanoi puzzle gives us an even more dramatic example of how the analysis of recursive algorithms is performed by conditionally assuming the correct functioning of the recursive case. This algorithm could be augmented with invariants as follows:

```
void solveHanoi (int n, char a, char b, char c) {
  // move n disks from tower a to tower b, using tower c

  if (n == 1) {
    System.out.println("move disk from tower " + a + " to " + b);
      // inv: have moved stack of size 1
      // from tower a to tower b
    }
```

```
  else {
    solveHanoi(n-1, a, c, b);
      // inv: have moved stack of size n-1 from
      // stack a to stack c

    System.out.println("move disk from tower " + a + " to " + b);
      // inv: have moved largest disk from stack a
      // to stack b

    solveHanoi(n-1, c, b, a);
      // inv: have moved stack of size n-1 from
      // stack c back to stack b, on top of
      // disk previously moved,
      // therefore now have stack of size n
      // on stack b

    }
}
```

We *assume* that the recursive call will perform the task we describe. Based on that assumption, we then prove that the current task is correctly executed. The base cases are handled by a separate argument. If all these arguments are correct, the entire algorithm must be correct, regardless of the input values.

5.2 PROGRAM TESTING

Testing is the process of executing computer code on actual values and verifying the resulting output for correctness. As a side effect, programming errors are often uncovered when the expected output is not produced. Testing should always be an intrinsic part of any software development effort.

Testing can, and should, be performed at all levels.

- Individual functions or methods can be tested as they are written.
- A class can be tested in isolation from the remainder of a program.
- Finally, a complete program can be tested as an application.

In the first two cases, we are testing small portions of a program, independent of the remainder of the application. To do this, it is often necessary to write short-term, temporary code to "harness" the software being tested. This harness code can be divided into two categories.

- *Driver* code acts as the calling procedure. This code sets up the argument values, global variables, or whatever input is necessary for the code under test; then the code invokes the procedure and, finally, validates the result (or prints the result, leaving it to the programmer to perform the validation).

- *Stub* code simulates the actions of any procedures that may be called by the algorithm under test. Although stub code simulates the actions that will be found in the resulting application, they need not perform exactly the same process. For example, a stub might merely print the argument values and then prompt the programmer to supply the result that will be returned.

Functions should always be tested using a number of different input values. The following guidelines can be considered in creating good test values.

- Make sure that every statement in the function is exercised by at least one test value.
- Make sure to use test data that exercises both the true and false alternatives for every `if` and `while` expression. Test each legal label of a `switch` statement.
- If there is a minimal legal input value, such as an empty array or a smallest integer value, use it as one of your test cases.
- If the function (or program) has both legal and illegal inputs, a set of test cases should include both clearly legal values and clearly illegal values, as well as values that are "barely" legal and "barely" not legal.
- If the program involves loops that can exercise a variable number of iterations, try to develop a test case in which the loop executes zero times.

Testing Alone Can Never Show Correctness

It has been said that testing can show the presence of errors but never their absence. What this means is that a test case that produces an incorrect result clearly shows that the program is wrong, but a single test case (or even many test cases) that is correctly handled does not show that the program is right. Testing should never be used as a substitute for a proof of correctness. (A programming project described at the end of this chapter has you explore this idea by investigating exactly how many random test cases you would need to generate before you might uncover the error in the triangle program.)

Neither testing nor a proof of correctness should be taken to be definitive evidence that a program is valid. Program proofs can be misleading if preconditions are not satisfied or if the postconditions do not capture all the necessary properties required by the rest of a program. These are features that are often caught more easily by testing. So both techniques are useful mechanisms for increasing confidence in the validity of a program.

Several more specific guidelines have also been suggested. The readings cited at the end of the chapter can be examined for further details.

5.3 Chapter Summary

Key Concepts

- Program proofs
- Invariants
- Using invariants in tracing execution flow
- Relationship between recursion and mathematical induction
- Software testing

An invariant is a statement that describes the state of computation when execution reaches a particular point in a program. By tracing the flow of execution from invariant to invariant, invariants can be used to structure arguments used to increase confidence in the validity of an algorithm or a function.

Even when a proof of correctness has been presented, software testing should be used as an alternative technique to increase the confidence in the correct performance of a function or an application.

Further Information

The argument that programming (and, indeed, mathematics) is a social activity was given forceful exposition in a classic paper by Richard DeMillo, Richard Lipton, and the late Alan Perlis [DeMillo 79].

The notion of program invariants was developed by Robert Floyd. For this contribution (among others), he was presented with the 1979 Alan Turing award by the Association for Computing Machinery, a major computer science professional organization [Floyd 62].

Many researchers have tried to raise the level of program proofs to a formal mathematical process. Such proofs tend to be many times more complex than the arguments we develop in this book. A good introduction to program proving can be found in the book by David Gries [Gries 81]. Another prominent advocate of program proving is Edsger Dijkstra [Dijkstra 76].

A good description of the art of software testing is [Beizer 90].

Study Questions

1. What are the two primary mechanisms for increasing confidence in the correctness of programs?
2. For whom is a program proof created? That is, who will read a program proof?
3. What is a code walk-through?

4. What is an invariant?
5. Explain the steps used in proving a program correct using invariants.
6. Assume that an algorithm consists of a single loop, such as the `minimum` algorithm presented in Section 5.1.1. Assume that within the loop are invariants at both the beginning and the end of the loop body, as well as prior to and after the loop. How many different arguments must be given that move from invariant to invariant?
7. What is the objective toward which "progress" is being made in the binary search algorithm?
8. What is the unnamed quantity that is referred to by the invariants for the GCD algorithm?
9. What are the steps involved in proving the correctness of a recursive algorithm?
10. What is the unnamed quantity that is referred to by the invariants for the `power` procedure described in Section 5.1.7?
11. At what point in the development process should testing be performed?
12. What is a testing harness? A driver? A stub?
13. What are some basic guidelines for developing good test cases?

Exercises

1. Complete the task of arguing the correctness of the `isPrime` procedure described in Section 5.1.3. That is, give arguments to move from each invariant to each possible succeeding invariant.
2. Complete the task of arguing the correctness of the `binarySearch` procedure described in Section 5.1.4. That is, give arguments to move from each invariant to each possible succeeding invariant.
3. Provide invariants for the linear time `power` procedure from Chapter 4.

```
double power (double base, int n) {
  double result = 1.0;
    // inv 1:

  for (int i = 1; i <= n; i++) {
      // inv 2:
    result *= base;
      // inv 3:
    }

    // inv 4:
```

```
  return result;
}
```

4. Using the invariants you developed in the previous question, give arguments that support the validity of the invariants by tracing possible execution flows.

5. Complete the loop invariants for the following procedure that sums the values of an array.

```
//
//  sum the elements of a double array
//

double sumArray (double [ ] data) {
  int size = data.length;
  double sum = 0.0;
  // inv:
  for (int i = 0; i < size; i++) {
    // inv:
    sum += data[i];
    // inv:
    }
  // inv:
  return sum;
}
```

6. Using the invariants you developed in the previous question, give arguments that support the validity of the invariants by tracing possible execution flows.

7. Complete the loop invariants for the following procedure that computes the factorial function for a positive integer argument.

```
//
//  compute the factorial of an integer value
//

double factorial (int val)
{
  double result = 1.0;
  // inv:
  for (int i = 1; i <= val;  i++) {
    // inv:
    result *= i;
    // inv:
    }
  // inv:
  return result;
}
```

8. Using the invariants you developed in the previous question, give arguments that support the validity of the invariants by tracing possible execution flows.
9. Provide a set of invariants for the insertion sort algorithm described in Section 4.2.4. Using these invariants as a base, give arguments that support the validity of the invariants by tracing possible execution flows.
10. What are some test cases one might use to exercise the function `minimum` described in Section 5.1.1?
11. What are some test cases one might use to exercise the function `isPrime` described in Section 5.1.3?
12. What are some test cases one might use to exercise the function `binarySearch` described in Section 5.1.4?
13. Augment with invariants the main program in the application developed in Chapter 9, and with these provide an informal proof of correctness.

Programming Projects

1. Write a program that will generate three random integer values, and compare the output produced by the incorrect version of the `triangle` to that of the corrected program. How many random elements must you examine before you find a set of inputs that exposes the error in the algorithm?
2. Using the `TaskTimer` utility described in Chapter 4, compare the execution time of the looping version and the recursive version of the integer `power` algorithm. Do this by raising the value `1.02` to ever larger integer exponents and plotting the execution times.
3. The key idea of binary search—repeatedly dividing a search area in half—is applicable to more than simply searching an ordered list of values. For example, we can use binary search to quickly discover the approximate value of a root for a continuous function. (A root is a point where the function has value zero; a continuous function is one that has no "gaps," that can be drawn without lifting a pen from the paper.) The idea is to start with two values that we know surround the root, because the function is positive at one point and negative at the other. Repeatedly divide the area in half, and move either the lower or the upper bound. Repeat until the difference between the lower and upper bounds is very small, at which point you have the approximate location of the root. The following shows this process

applied to the function $x^2 - 14x^2 + 59x - 65$, using the initial values 0 and 8. The numbers represent the values of the midpoints. Implement a root-finding program based on these ideas.

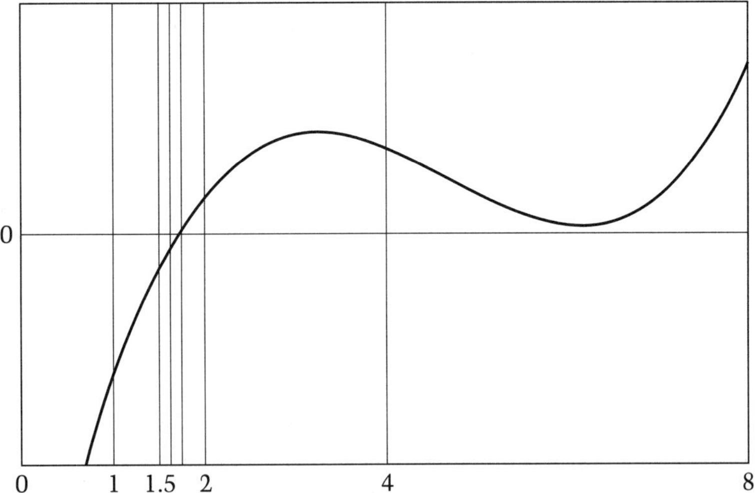

4. Another application of the binary search technique is an algorithm for finding the square root of a positive value. For a given value n, we bound the square root by two values `low` and `high`. We can initially set `low` to zero and `high` to n. We repeatedly compute the midpoint between `low` and `high` and change either the low or the high value, depending on whether the midpoint squared is greater than or less than the value n (that is, whether the midpoint is greater than or less than the real square root). The process halts when the difference between the low and the high values becomes sufficiently small (for example, less than 0.0001).

   Develop an algorithm for computing the square root using this process, and provide a proof of correctness. What type of inputs would you use to test your algorithm?

CHAPTER 6

VECTORS

As we noted in Chapter 4, the *array* is the only data structure the Java language provides that is designed specifically to hold a collection of elements. The power of the array comes from the fact that the time required to access any element in the collection is constant, regardless of the size of the array. We say that the array permits *random access*, as the order that elements are accessed can be entirely arbitrary.

But this power is purchased only at a cost. The constant-time access derives from the fact that the elements in an array are stored in a block, a single piece of memory in which the elements are placed end to end:

element [0]	element [1]	element [2]	element [3]	element [4]	element [5]	element [6]

Management of this block makes some operations difficult. For example, what if we need to make the collection larger? What if we need to insert elements into the interior of the collection? What if we need to hold an assortment of different types of values? Thus, although an array is an exceedingly powerful and useful programming tool, it is not appropriate for all problems. It is for these and similar reasons that we investigate the design of alternative data structures.

6.1 THE VECTOR DATA STRUCTURE

Before we describe the implementation, let us consider first a simple program that will illustrate the use of the `Vector` data structure. The program shown in Figure 6.1 will read a file of words, one word to a line, and compute the frequency of use for each word. The program does this in three steps. In step 1, the words are inserted into a vector in the order they are found in the file. In step 2, the vector of words is sorted, thereby placing repeated occurrences of the same word adjacent to each other. In step 3, the vector is traversed, and each adjacent word is compared to the previous one; either a count is incremented (if they are the same), or a frequence is generated (if they are different).

The program in Figure 6.1 begins with a sequence of `import` statements. Those statements beginning with `java` represent the standard Java runtime library, whereas those that begin with `jds` represent features we will develop in this text.

The code for step 1 illustrates how file input is performed in Java. The method `readLine` is found only in the class `BufferedReader`. However, to form a `BufferedReader`, we must first construct a `FileReader` that will be used to obtain the character values. Once we have a `BufferedReader`, lines are read one by one and placed into the vector, using the method `addLast`, which will insert a new value at the end of the vector. The `BufferedReader` will return a `null` value when the end of file is encountered.

Because both opening the file and reading from the file could potentially result in an `IOException`, the file actions are placed inside a `try` block. In this case, we simply print an error message if the exception occurs.

In step 2, the vector is sorted, using the `ShellSort` algorithm we will describe later in this chapter. After the list has been sorted, a special end marker—an entry that will not match any word—is appended to the end of the list.

In step 3, the frequencies are determined by using the sorted vector of words. A loop cycles over the vector. Each word is compared to the previous one. If they are the same, a count is incremented. This count will therefore keep track of the number of times the same word has been repeated. If the current word is different from the previous entry, the number of occurrences of the previous word is printed. Because the end marker is guaranteed to not match any word, this ensures that the frequency for the final word will be printed.

As with all data structures, the `Vector`[1] can be viewed from two levels. To the programmer who must use the `Vector` data structure, the class is simply a realization of two of the abstract data types we described in

---

1. Again we note that the `Vector` data structure described here is similar to, but not exactly the same as, the `Vector` data structure provided by the Java standard library.

```
import java.io.*;
import jds.SortAlgorithm;
import jds.collection.Vector;
import jds.sort.ShellSort;
import jds.util.StringCompare;

class WordFreq {
  static public void main (String [ ] args) {
    Vector v = new Vector();
    try {
      // step 1. first read the input
      FileReader fin = new FileReader(args[0]);
      BufferedReader in = new BufferedReader(fin);
      String line = in.readLine();
      while (line != null) {
        v.addLast(line);
        line = in.readLine();
      }

      // step 2. sort the words, add end marker
      SortAlgorithm alg = new ShellSort(new StringCompare());
      alg.sort(v);
      v.addLast(" "); // add end marker

      // step 3. print out the frequency
      int count = 1;
      for (int i = 2; i < v.size(); i++) {
        if (v.elementAt(i).equals(v.elementAt(i-1)))
          count++;
        else { // new word, print old count
          System.out.println("word " + v.elementAt(i-1) +
            ":" + count);
          count = 1;
        }
      }
    } catch (IOException e) {
      System.out.println("received IO Exception " + e);
    }
  }
}
```

FIGURE 6.1 Program to Compute Word Frequencies

Chapter 2. At this level of understanding, it is necessary to examine only the interface. On the other hand, to truly understand the `Vector`, we must also examine the data structure on a more detailed level—from the *inside*, as it were—in order to better understand how this functionality is implemented.

The two interfaces supported by the `Vector` data structure are the `Indexed` ADT and the `Stack` ADT. The first says simply that elements held by the collection can be accessed by using an integer key, which ranges from zero up to one less than the size of the collection. New elements can be inserted into or removed from any point. It is in this sense that the `Vector` is similar to an array.

`aVec.elementAt(1)` Yields 17

12	17	3	29	6	31	22	49

When viewed as an embodiment of the `Stack` interface, the range of operations is much more limited. With a `Stack`, elements can be inserted into and removed from only one end of the container.

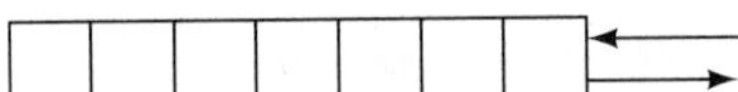

To see *how* this is done, we must examine the implementation of the data structure. The first thing we note is that the `Vector` is constructed by using an array. The array is used to hold the elements being stored by the collection. For this purpose, the array is declared as maintaining values of type `Object`. The use of an array will permit the efficient random-access behavior we desire for the `Indexed` data abstraction. But the use of an array will also require that we handle the problems mentioned at the beginning of this chapter—for example, what should happen when a new element is inserted and the array is completely full. By wrapping the array inside another data abstraction, we can hide the memory management details and leave the programmer free to view the container at a higher level of abstraction.

```
public class Vector implements Indexed, Stack {
    // two internal data fields
  private int elementCount = 0;
  private Object [ ] elementData = new Object[10];
     .
     .
     .
}
```

Fundamental to the internal operation of the Vector is the idea that two integer values can characterize the memory utilization of this internal array. The *size* of a vector represents the number of elements that are currently being maintained in active use by the collection. The size is maintained by the variable elementCount. The *capacity* of a vector represents the number of elements that can be held in the underlying array. The capacity will always be larger than or equal to the size:

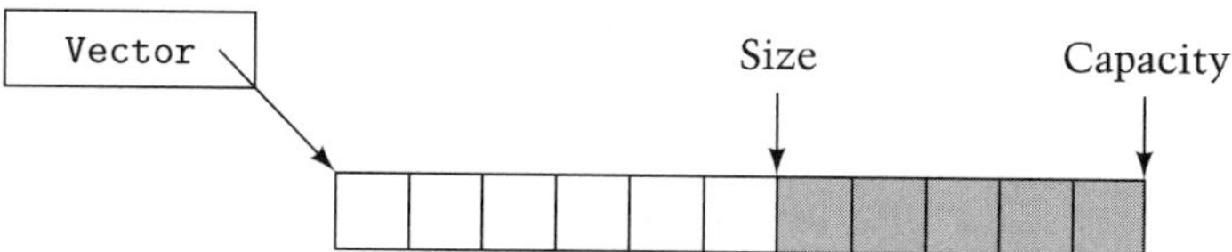

A simple use of the elementCount data field is the implementation of methods from the Collection interface:

```
  // the Collection interface
public boolean isEmpty () { return elementCount == 0; }
public int size () { return elementCount; }
```

Access to elements in the collection can be provided through the use of subscripts on the underlying array. We must first, however, compare the index against the count. It is illegal to access a position that has not yet been set, even if the field is within the legal index range for the underlying array. An attempt to access an illegal position will generate an ArrayIndexOutOfBoundsException.

Polymorphism, Containers, and Wrappers

With the exception of arrays, all the containers in the Java standard library store their elements in variables declared as Object. Because all classes must ultimately descend from Object, the polymorphic assignment rule (the rule that you can assign instances of a child class to variables of a parent class) means that containers can store any type of object.

We note two consequences to this use of Object. The first is that primitive types (integer, real, and the like) cannot be stored directly in containers, as they are not objects. In order to store these values, it is necessary to first enclose them in *wrapper* classes. The class Integer, for example, is a wrapper for the primitive int. The following shows how an integer can be stored in a vector:

```
int idx = 17;
aVec.addElement(new Integer(idx)); // wrap idx in
                                   // an Integer
```

The second implication of the use of Object is that when an element is *removed* from a container, it must be cast back to the correct type. The following illustrates removing an element from a vector, casting the result to an Integer, and then using a method to unwrap the original int:

```
Integer ele = (Integer) aVec.elementAt(0);
int x = ele.intValue(); // x now has same value
                        // as idx
```

```
public Object elementAt (int index) {
  if ((index < 0) || (index >= elementCount))
    throw new ArrayIndexOutOfBoundsException(index);
  return elementData [index];
}

public void setElementAt (Object val, int index) {
  if ((index < 0) || (index >= elementCount))
    throw new ArrayIndexOutOfBoundsException(index);
  elementData[index] = val;
}
```

The method addElementAt is more complex. The reason is that it is used to add an element into the interior of the collection. Imagine, for example, that we want to insert a new element into position 2 of the following collection:

2	7	3	1	6					

First, the existing elements must be moved upward to make a hole for the new element:

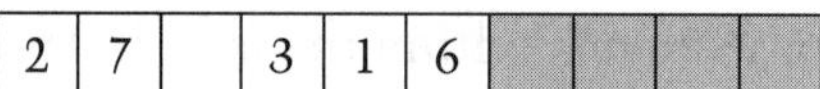

Synchronized and Nonsynchronized Methods

Note that the methods setSize, addElementAt, removeElementAt, and ensureCapacity are all declared synchronized. This modifier is important whenever data structures could potentially be accessed by two or more threads running at the same time. No two synchronized methods from the same object are ever allowed to be executing at one time.[a]

To see what troubles this declaration prevents, imagine that the synchronized modifiers have been removed. Now imagine that one thread of execution is performing an ensureCapacity operation and has completed the loop that copies elements into the new array but is then suspended before it can perform the final assignment. Meanwhile, a second thread is executing an addElementAt operation. This change will be made in the old array. When the first thread resumes, it will remove the old array, and so the effect of the addElementAt will be lost. (See exercise 10.)

Although the synchronized attributes cannot ensure that two threads will not interfere with each other (for example, one thread can undo an operation just performed by another), they should always be used to guarantee that a data structure cannot be left in an inconsistent state.

[a] Readers unfamiliar with multithreading may wish to gloss over the discussion of synchronized methods until Chapter 8, where we will explain in greater detail how a program can make and use more than one thread of execution.

It is only after we have created a hole that the new element can be placed:

2	7	5	3	1	6				

The code to perform this operation is as follows:

```
public synchronized void addElementAt (Object val, int index) {
  if ((index < 0) || (index > elementCount))
    throw new ArrayIndexOutOfBoundsException(index);
  setSize(elementCount+1);
  for (int i = elementCount-1; i > index; i--)
    elementData[i] = elementData[i-1];
  elementData[index] = val;
}
```

Note that it is legal for the index supplied to this method to be one larger than the largest legal subscript. This allows elements to be inserted at the end of a vector. In a three-element vector, for example, four positions are valid for inserting a new element:

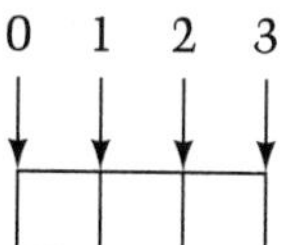

Of course, if too many elements are added to the collection, the size will eventually exceed the capacity. At this point, a *reallocation* must take place. This involves allocating a new and larger array, then copying the elements from the old array into the new one. But, unlike with the array, we can encapsulate (that is, hide) the details of this reallocation inside a method. By doing so, the user of the `Vector` data structure need not be aware that this reallocation is taking place.

The `addElementAt` method uses `setSize` to ensure that there is space for the new element. In practice, it is useful to give the programmer control over both the size and the capacity. The method `ensureCapacity` is used to set the capacity. (This method is specific to the `Vector` data structure and is not part of any interface.) Of course, we want to ensure that the capacity is never smaller than the size. For reasons we will describe when we discuss the `Stack` interface, when a size that is larger than the current size is requested, the capacity is repeatedly doubled until enough space can be found. The code to perform these two tasks is as follows:

```
public synchronized void setSize (int newSize) {
    // repeatedly double capacity until larger than size
  while (newSize > elementData.length)
```

```
    ensureCapacity(2 * elementData.length);
  elementCount = newSize;
}

public synchronized void ensureCapacity (int newCapacity) {
  if (newCapacity <= elementData.length) return;
  Object [ ] newArray = new Object[newCapacity];
    // copy elements from old array into new
  for (int i = 0; i < elementCount; i++)
    newArray[i] = elementData[i];
  elementData = newArray;
}
```

Both because a reallocation can potentially occur as a result of calling `setSize` and because elements must be moved, the `addElementAt` method is $O(n)$. The method `removeElementAt` must solve a problem that is the reverse of that faced by `addElementAt`. To remove an element, all the elements above the given position must be moved downward:

```
public synchronized void removeElementAt (int index) {
  if ((index < 0) || (index >= elementCount))
    throw new ArrayIndexOutOfBoundsException(index);
  elementCount--;
  for (int i = index; i < elementCount; i++)
    elementData[i] = elementData[i+1];
  elementData[elementCount] = null;
}
```

Like `addElementAt`, the `removeElementAt` method is, in the worst case, $O(n)$. We can summarize the algorithmic execution times for the `Indexed` operations as follows:

Operation	**Execution Time**
`elementAt`	$O(1)$ *always*
`setElementAt`	$O(1)$ *always*
`addElementAt`	$O(n)$ *worst case*
`removeElementAt`	$O(n)$ *worst case*

Now let us consider the other face presented by the `Vector` data abstraction: that of a `Stack`. The `Stack` interface is easily implemented, using the ability to set and to remove elements from arbitrary locations.

```
  // the Stack interface
public void addLast(Object val) { addElementAt(val, elementCount); }
public Object getLast() { return elementData[elementCount-1]; }
public void removeLast() { removeElementAt(elementCount-1); }
```

To place a new element into the collection, the element is simply added to the end of the vector:

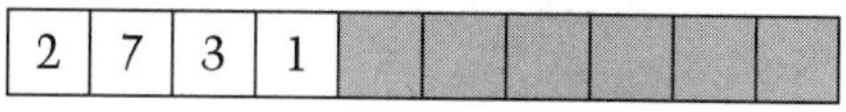

2	7	3	1						

after addLast(6)

2	7	3	1	6					

Because the Stack methods use the $O(n)$ operations we have already examined, it is tempting to imagine that the worst-case execution times for addLast and removeLast must be $O(n)$. However, a more careful examination will show that things are not that bad. Consider the removal method. Because the last element is being removed, the loop in the method removeElementAt will never iterate more than one time. All other operations are constant time, showing that removeLast will be a constant-time operation.

The analysis of addLast is more subtle. Although the loop in addElementAt will not be executed more than once, it is possible that a reallocation will occur as a result of invoking addLast on an already completely full vector. So indeed we have to admit that addLast is $O(n)$ in the worst case. But how often will this occur? A call that results in this unfortunately slow behavior will double the size of the vector. Thus, it will take at least n more calls on addLast before we again require another reallocation. Thus, although the worst-case execution time for addLast is $O(n)$, the *average* (or *expected*) execution time is constant. (This is why it is important that the size of the vector be doubled. If we simply increased the capacity to fit the new size, a series of addLast operations could force a reallocation on every call. Doubling the vector size reduces the chance of this occurring. See exercise 5.)

The following chart summarizes the execution time for Stack operations performed using the Vector:

Operation	**Execution Time**
addLast	$O(1)$ *expected*, $O(n)$ *worst case*
getLast	$O(1)$ *always*
removeLast	$O(1)$ *always*

Implementation of the Enumeration protocol is provided by a helper class named IndexedEnumeration. This class is also used by other containers that satisfy the Indexed interface:

```
public class Vector implements Indexed, Stack {
    .
    .
    .
  public Enumeration elements () { return new IndexedEnumeration(this); }
    .
    .
    .
}

public class IndexedEnumeration implements Enumeration {
  public IndexedEnumeration (Indexed d) { data = d; }
  private Indexed data;
  private int index = 0;

  public boolean hasMoreElements () { return index < data.size(); }

  public Object nextElement () { return data.elementAt(index++); }
}
```

An instance of IndexedEnumeration maintains two data fields: an Indexed container and an index. Each time an element is requested, the object at the indexed position is returned, and the index is incremented. Note that the specification of the Enumeration interface requires calls on hasMoreElements and nextElement to be intermixed. Exercise 8 investigates what can occur if this rule is not followed. It is also not a good idea to make additions or removals from a collection (of any type) in the middle of an enumeration. Exercise 9 explores what can happen if this is tried with a Vector.

WHAT IS THIS?

The method elements makes use of the variable this. In Java, the variable this always refers to the object that is responding to the current message. In this case, the vector wants to create a new value, an instance of IndexedEnumeration, and have this object point back to the vector. The variable this permits the vector to pass *itself* as argument to the constructor for IndexedEnumeration.

*6.2 ENUMERATION

To *enumerate* a collection is to examine all the elements in turn, one at a time, without repetition. Normally, an enumeration is performed using a loop. With a `Vector`, there are several ways to perform this task. The simplest enumeration uses an integer variable that cycles over the range of legal index values:

```
for (int i = 0; i < aVec.size(); i++) {
  Object v = aVec.elementAt(i);
  ... // do something with v
}
```

Although this is easy to write, it creates a loop that works only with vectors (or, more precisely, only with `Indexed` data types). A more general loop can be created by using an `Enumeration`:

```
for (Enumeration e = aVec.elements(); e.hasMoreElements(); ) {
  Object v = e.nextElement();
  ... // do something with v
}
```

The advantage of the enumeration loop is that the same loop will work for any type of data structure: a linked list, a binary tree, or anything that supports the `Enumeration` protocol.

But index loops and enumerations are not the only techniques one can use to examine all the elements of a collection. The `Vector` data structure supports a third approach, called a *visitor*. Intuitively, the idea behind the visitor technique is to hand to the list a bit of code that will then

THE VISITOR DESIGN PATTERN

name Visitor.

forces A visitor pattern can be used whenever it seems most natural to define only the action to be performed on every element in a collection.

synopsis A visitor defines only the actions to be performed on every element in a collection. The visitor is handed to the collection. The collection performs a loop and executes the visitor function repeatedly, passing each element in turn.

counterforces Requires the creation of a new class that has no other purpose than to define the actions to be performed on every element.

related patterns The visitor is usually considered as an alternative to forming an `Enumeration`. A special type of visitor specific to binary trees is the Euler tour (Section 13.5).

be executed on every element: that will *visit* every value in the vector. The programmer using the visitor mechanism does not need to write any looping code whatsoever but merely describes the actions to be performed.

A visitor is any class that implements the Visitor interface, which is defined as follows:

```
interface Visitor {
  public void apply (Object v);
}
```

To begin a visit, the Vector method named visit is invoked, passing the visitor as an argument. For example, suppose that we have a vector of integer values and wish to compute their sum. To use the visitor loop, we would first define a class that will take one element and add it to a running sum:

```
class SumMaker implements Visitor {
  public int total = 0;
  public void apply (Object v) {
    Integer i = (Integer) v;
    total += i.intValue();
  }
}
```

To compute the value, we simply create an instance of this class and pass it to the vector:

```
SumMaker sum = new SumMaker();
aVec.visit(sum);
...// total is now in sum.total
```

The implementation of the visit method hides the loop inside the vector itself:

```
class Vector ... {
  .
  .
  .
  public void visit (Visitor task) {
      // visit every element, performing task
    for (int i = 0; i < size(); i++)
      task.apply(elementAt(i));
  }
}
```

* 6.3 Application—Silly Sentences

We will illustrate the use of the Vector data structure with three example programs. The first is a simple application that will generate a string of silly sentences of the form subject-verb-object. To make the output easy to modify, we will read the sample values for these categories from three different files. Some example phrases of each category might be the following:

Subject	Verb	Object
alice and fred	love	dogs
cats	hate	cats
people	eat	donuts
teachers	hassle	people

Our example program is shown in Figure 6.2. The `main` program simply creates an instance of the class, so the major flow of control is found in the constructor. The constructor uses the method `readFromFile` to read the three categories of terms into three different vectors. The method `randomElement` is then used to select a random element from each.

The method `readFromFile` illustrates how file input streams are manipulated in Java. Recall from the word frequency example at the beginning of this chapter that the method `readLine` is found only in the class `BufferedReader`. However, to form a `BufferedReader`, we must first construct a `FileReader` that will be used to obtain the character values.

Streams and Decorators

The Java I/O library is structured in part using two basic ideas. The first is the notion of a `stream`, which is simply a sequence of characters. A stream can be generated in many ways; for example, the characters could come from a keyboard, from a file, or across a network. The class `FileReader` creates a stream for reading a file.

The second idea is the notion of a `decorator`. A decorator is a design pattern, similar to the Adapter design pattern we discussed in Chapter 1. A decorator[a] wraps around an existing object, preserving the interface of the original but adding new functionality. A `BufferedReader`, for example, adds the ability to read an entire line using the method `readLine`. Simple streams can read only one character at a time. By separating these into two classes, the functionality provided by `BufferedReader` can be used with a variety of streams, not just files.

In Chapter 17, we will encounter another powerful decorator for streams: the `ObjectOutputStream`. This stream will add the ability to copy out an entire structured object with a single command. The object can subsequently be read back, using an instance of `ObjectInputStream`.

[a] Decorators are also sometimes called `wrappers`, but this term should not be confused with the wrapper classes such as `Integer` and `Double`.

```
import java.io.*;
import jds.collection.Vector;

public class SillySentence {
  static public void main (String [ ] args)
    { SillySentence world = new SillySentence();  world.run(); }

  public SillySentence () {
    Vector subjects = readFromFile("subject");
    Vector verbs = readFromFile("verb");
    Vector objects = readFromFile("object");
  }

  public void run () {
    for (int i = 0; i < 5; i++)  // generate five sentences
      System.out.println(randomElement(subjects) + " "  +
        randomElement(verbs) + " " + randomElement(objects));
  }

  private Vector readFromFile (String fileName) {
    Vector result = new Vector();
    try {
      FileReader fin = new FileReader(fileName);
      BufferedReader din = new BufferedReader(fin);
      String line = din.readLine();
      while (line != null) {
        result.addLast(line);
        line = din.readLine();
      }
    } catch (IOException e) { } // do nothing on exception
    return result;
  }

  private String randomElement (Vector v) {
    int index = (int)(v.size() * Math.random());
    return (String) v.elementAt(index);
  }
}
```

FIGURE 6.2 Silly-Sentence Generation Program

Once we have a BufferedReader, lines are read one by one and placed into a vector, which is then yielded as the output for the method. Because both opening the file and reading from the file could potentially result in an IOException, the file actions are placed inside a try block. In this case, we do no actions in response to an exception, simply returning whatever values have been found so far.

The method randomElement contains two examples of a *cast* expression. A cast is used to convert a value from one type to another. In the first case, a cast is being used to convert a value from double-precision floating point to integer. The expression Math.random() will return a floating-point value between 0 and 1. Multiplying this by the size of the argument vector will result in a random value between 0 and the vector size. Converting this to an integer will truncate all but the integer part, yielding a random index. This index is then used as a subscript for the vector. The result of the elementAt operation, you will recall, is a value of type Object. The second cast is used to convert this value from Object to type String. Another way to think about this is that the cast is being used to verify that the expression in question is really a value of type String.

Example output from the program might be as follows:

```
alice and fred hate dogs
teachers hassle cats
alice and fred love cats
people hassle donuts
people hate dogs
```

*6.4 Application–Memory Game

Our second example program is a memory game. Figure 6.3 shows a screen shot from the application. The computer will display a number of ever increasing length. The user then clicks the OK button, the number is erased, and the user tries to repeat the number. If the user succeeds in repeating the number, the score is increased, and a longer number is tried. This continues until the user makes a mistake.

As with many graphical applications, at the highest level, the program is concerned mainly with laying out the graphical components. Throughout this text, our applications will use the simple border layout manager, with graphical objects placed either in one of the four compass points (north, west, east, or south) or in the center of the window. Here, we place a text box in the center, a Label in the north, and a panel of buttons in the south.

FIGURE 6.3 Screen Shot of Memory Game

```
import java.awt.*;
import jds.collection.Vector;
import jds.util.ButtonAdapter;

public class Memory extends Frame {
  static public void main (String [ ] args)
    { Memory world = new Memory(); world.show(); }

  public Memory () {
      // Frame initialization
    setSize(400, 120); setTitle("Memory Game");
      // application initialization
    add("North", scorebox);
    add("Center", text);
    Panel p = new Panel();
    p.setLayout(new GridLayout(1, 4));
```

THE AWT

Java's Abstract Windowing Toolkit, or AWT, is a library that greatly simplifies the creation of graphical user interfaces. The parent class `Frame`, from which Java applications will inherit, supplies the code needed to create a window, including such operations as setting the size of the window, the window title, and moving the window around on the screen. The inherited command `show` specifies that the window is ready to be displayed.

The AWT supplies many classes that can be used to create simple graphical interface devices, such as buttons and text boxes. Depending on the layout manager selected, objects are placed either at the compass points of the window (east, west, north, or south) or in a grid pattern. The memory game shows an example of both of these.

Although not used in this example, we will see in later programs that to display a window, the AWT invokes the method named `paint`, giving as argument a helper object of class `Graphics`. The `Graphics` class provides a large number of simple drawing commands.

```
    p.add(new ResetButton());
    p.add(new OkButton());
    p.add(new DoneButton());
    p.add(new QuitButton());
    add("South", p);
  }

  private Label scorebox = new Label("score = 0:");
  private TextField text = new TextField("Press Reset to begin");
  private int score = 0;
  private int size = 2;
  private Vector answers = new Vector();

  private void makePuzzle () { ... }
  private class ResetButton extends ButtonAdapter { ... }
  private class OkButton extends ButtonAdapter { ... }
  private class DoneButton extends ButtonAdapter { ... }
  private class QuitButton extends ButtonAdapter { ... }
}
```

The `Panel` allows us to create a grid consisting of four buttons. You may recall that buttons, as well as key presses and other user events, are handled in Java by creating a *listener* that does nothing more than sit and wait for an event to occur. The class `ButtonAdapter` is a useful utility that enters itself as a listener, then invokes the method `pressed` when the button is activated. This utility has the following definition:

```
public class ButtonAdapter extends Button implements ActionListener {
  public ButtonAdapter (String name) {
    super(name);
    addActionListener(this); // register ourselves as listener
  }

  public void actionPerformed (ActionEvent e) { pressed(); }

  public void pressed () { }
}
```

The class `ButtonAdapter` greatly simplifies the creation of new buttons. For example, here is the definition of the `Quit` button:

```
private class QuitButton extends ButtonAdapter {
  QuitButton () { super("Quit"); }
  public void pressed () { System.exit(0); }
}
```

THE LISTENER PATTERN

In the Java AWT library, button presses, mouse commands, and keyboard presses are all handled using a facility that matches the *Listener* design pattern. A listener is simply an object that sits and waits for something to happen, then wakes up and responds to it. For each type of listener that Java recognizes, there is a different command to register an object as a listener, a different interface for the listener object, and a different method that will be invoked to wake the listener up. These are summarized in the following table:

GUI Command	Class	Example Method
addActionListener	ActionListener	actionPerformed(ActionEvent)
addMouseListener	MouseAdapter	mousePressed(MouseEvent)
addKeyListener	KeyAdapter	keyPressed(KeyEvent)
addWindowListener	WindowAdapter	windowClosing(WindowEvent)

A listener is in fact a form of *adapter*. A listener satisfies the interface required by the Java system, then translates the action into a form specific to the given application. The class ButtonAdapter illustrates another use of the Adapter pattern. Programs in later chapters will make extensive use of listeners and other adapters.

The logic for the game is contained in the other three buttons. Note that all four buttons are formed using *inner classes* (see sidebar). The game begins when the user clicks the Reset button. This button resets the values of the size and score and then creates an initial puzzle by invoking the method makePuzzle in the outer class. The puzzle is both displayed in the text box and stored in a vector so that the user's answer can be compared.

```
private void makePuzzle () {
  answers.setSize(0);
  String line = "";
```

INNER CLASSES

A class definition that appears inside another class definition is called an *inner class*. Instances of an inner class are objects, but they are also allowed to invoke methods defined in the surrounding, or *outer*, class. This feature makes an instance of an inner class extremely useful as a listener object. The inner class can implement the appropriate listener interface but when invoked can then translate the action into a call on a method in the outer class.

```
  for (int i = 0; i < size; i++) {
    int d = (int)(10 * Math.random());
    char cd = Character.forDigit(d, 10);
    line = line.concat(String.valueOf(cd));
    answers.addLast(new Character(cd));
  }
  text.setText(line);
}

private class ResetButton extends ButtonAdapter {
  public ResetButton () { super("Reset"); }
  public void pressed () {
    size = 2;
    score = 0;
    makePuzzle();
    scorebox.setText("score = 0: Press OK to proceed");
  }
}
```

After studying the number, the user clicks the OK button. In response, the text box is cleared, and instructions are given in the score box:

```
private class OkButton extends ButtonAdapter {
  public OkButton () { super("OK"); }
  public void pressed () {
    text.setText("");
    scorebox.setText("Enter Numbers, Press Done When Finished");
  }
}
```

Once the user has entered the text and clicked the Done button, the contents of the text box are compared against the value previously stored in the answer vector. If they match, a new and more difficult puzzle is presented; otherwise, the user has failed, and the final score is displayed.

```
private class DoneButton extends ButtonAdapter {
  public DoneButton () { super("Done"); }
  public void pressed () {
    String line = text.getText();
    if (line.length() != answers.size())
      { failed(); return; }
    for (int i = 0; i < line.length(); i++) {
      if (! answers.elementAt(i).equals(
        new Character(line.charAt(i)))) {
          failed();
```

```
            return;
          }
        }
        score = score + 1;
        scorebox.setText("score = " + score +
          ": Next level. Press OK to proceed");
        size = size + 1;
        makePuzzle();
      }

      private void failed () {
        scorebox.setText("sorry, you failed: score = " + score);
        text.setText("Press Reset to try again");
      }
    }
```

In the programming exercises at the end of the chapter, we suggest various improvements to this game.

*6.5 Application—Shell Sort

As we noted in Chapter 4, sorting is one of the most common and most important tasks computers perform. In Chapter 4, we described two techniques—bubble sort and insertion sort—that can be used to sort an array of integers. To generalize the sorting task, we need to first examine what it means to compare two elements. We can assign a clear meaning to a comparison between two integers or between two floating-point numbers, but it is much less clear how to compare two strings or two instances of a user-defined data type.

The containers we will examine in this book will follow those in the Java standard library in defining sorting by means of a comparator object. A comparator is simply an object that satisfies the `Comparator` interface (see Section 2.3.4). This interface provides for a method that will take two values and return −1, 0, or 1, depending on whether the first is less than the second, they are equal, or the first is larger than the second.

An example comparator object is the class `IntegerCompare`, which will compare two objects held in `Integer` wrappers:

```
public class IntegerCompare implements Comparator {
  public int compare (Object left, Object right) {
    Integer ileft = (Integer) left;
    Integer iright = (Integer) right;
    if (ileft.intValue() == iright.intValue())
      return 0;
```

```
    if (ileft.intValue() < iright.intValue())
      return -1;
    return 1;
  }
}
```

Another example is the `StringCompare` class, used to compare two `String` values. We used this class in the example presented at the beginning of this chapter:

```
public class StringCompare implements Comparator {
  public int compare (Object left, Object right) {
    String sleft = (String) left;
    return sleft.compareTo((String) right);
  }
}
```

We will illustrate the use of a comparator object by presenting yet another sorting algorithm. In 1959, Donald Shell noticed that one problem with both bubble sort and insertion sort was that elements moved only one location at a time. Imagine an array that starts out in exactly reverse order and ends up sorted. If you think about how far each element must move before it finds the correct location, it is not surprising that these algorithms are $O(n^2)$.

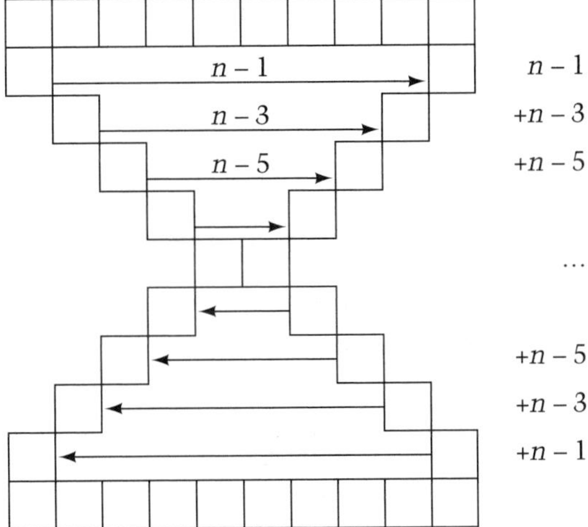

To make a significant improvement in the execution speed for sorting, elements must be able to jump several locations in the search for their final location. Shell proposed a simple modification to insertion sort to accomplish this. The outermost loop in the insertion sort procedure would be surrounded by yet another loop, called the *gap* loop. Rather than moving elements one by one, the outer loop would, in effect, perform an insertion sort every gap values. Thus, elements could jump gap steps rather than just a single step. For example, assume that we are sorting the following array of eight elements:

4	7	0	3	1	6	2	5

Imagine that we are sorting using a gap of 3. We first sort the elements with index positions 0, 3, and 6, placing them into order:

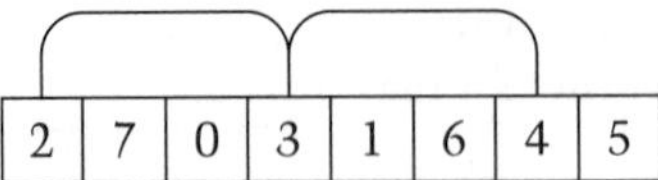

Next, we order the elements with index positions 1, 4, and 7:

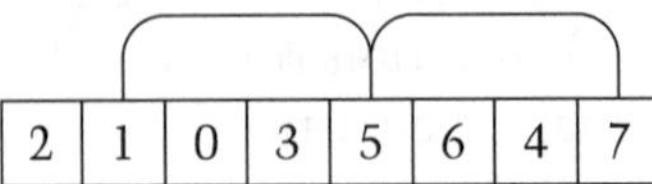

Elements in index positions 5 and 2 are then compared, but they are already ordered. Imagine that we next reduce the gap to 2. Now elements will jump two positions before finding their final location. First, we sort the elements with odd-numbered index positions:

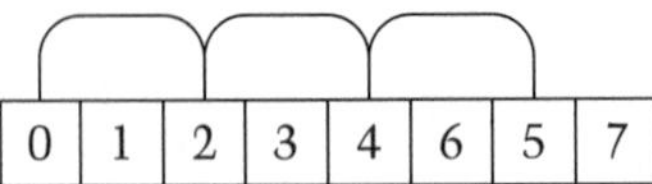

Next, we do the same with elements in even-numbered index positions (but here there is no change):

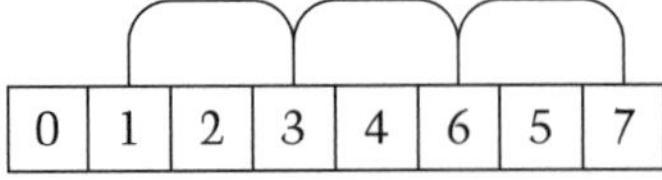

The final step is to sort with a gap of 1, which is the same as our original insertion sort. However, remember that insertion sort was very fast if elements were "roughly" in the correct place. Placing elements into their approximate location is exactly what the previous loops will have done. Note that only one element is now out of place, and it moves only one position:

```
import java.util.Enumeration;
import jds.SortAlgorithm;
import jds.Indexed;
import jds.util.Comparator; // or java.util.Comparator after Java 1.2

public class ShellSort implements SortAlgorithm {
  public ShellSort (Comparator t) { test = t; }
  private Comparator test;

  public void sort (Indexed v) {
    int n = v.size();
    for (int gap = n/2; gap >= 1; gap = gap / 2) {
      for (int i = gap; i < n; i++) {
        Object element = v.elementAt(i);
        int j = i - gap;
        while (j >= 0 &&
          (test.compare(element,v.elementAt(j)) < 0)) {
          Object val = v.elementAt(j);
          v.setElementAt(val, j+gap);
          j = j - gap;
        }
        v.setElementAt(element, j+gap);
      }
    }
  }
}
```

FIGURE 6.4 The Shell Sort Algorithm

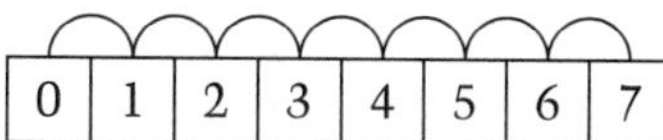

The gap size can be any decreasing sequence of values, as long as they end with 1. Shell suggested the sequence $n/2$, $n/4$, $n/8$, ...1. This results in the technique illustrated in Figure 6.4.

The analysis of the average execution time for Shell sort is subtle, as it depends on the mechanism used in selecting the gaps. However, in practice, it is considerably faster than simple insertion sort—despite the fact that Shell sort contains three nested loops rather than the two found in the insertion sort algorithm. Figure 6.5 compares the two procedures on random vectors of various sizes.

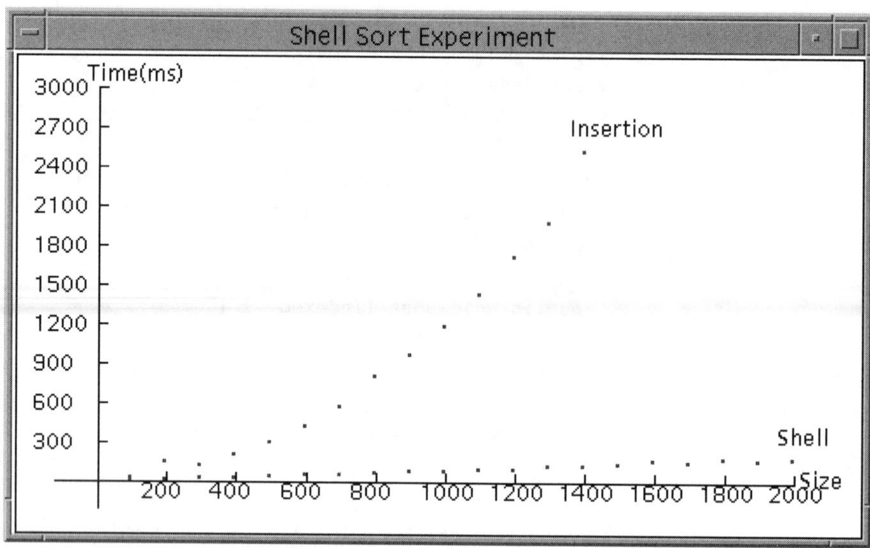

FIGURE 6.5 Comparison Timing of Shell Sort and and Insertion Sort

EXPERIMENT: IMPACT OF INPUT DISTRIBUTION ON SHELL SORT

In the previous chapter, we noted that the distribution of values in the original vector will have a major impact on the execution time for insertion sort. Vectors that are "almost" sorted will result in almost linear execution time, whereas vectors that are exactly backward will yield cubic execution time. Does the same property hold for Shell sort? Compare the execution time of Shell sort on three distributions: random elements, an almost sorted vector, and an almost reverse sorted vector.

*6.6 A VISUAL VECTOR

Many algorithms, particularly sorting techniques, are much easier to understand if you can visualize how the data is being rearranged as it occurs. The class `VisualVector` permits you to do this. A `VisualVector` takes as argument an `Indexed` data structure, which is used to hold the elements. This vector is permitted to hold only `Integer` data values. But the `VisualVector` itself recognizes the `Indexed` interface and so can be manipulated like a `Vector`. However, the class also provides a method, `getPanel`, that will return a graphical panel that can be placed into a user interface. As changes are made to the vector, the display is updated.

The following program illustrates how the `VisualVector` can be created and used to visualize a sorting procedure:

```
import java.awt.*;
import jds.SortAlgorithm;
import jds.collection.Vector;
import jds.util.VisualVector;
import jds.util.IntegerCompare;
import jds.util.CloseQuit;
import jds.sort.ShellSort;

public class VisualSort extends Frame {
  public static void main (String [ ] args)
  { VisualSort world = new VisualSort(); world.show(); world.run(); }

  public VisualSort () {
      // set up application
    setTitle("Shell Sort Test");
    setSize(500, 300);

      // create visual panel
    add("Center", vv.getPanel());
    addWindowListener(new CloseQuit());
  }

  private Vector data = new Vector();
  private VisualVector vv = new VisualVector(data);
  private final static int numberOfElements = 100;
```

STOP! I WANT TO GET OFF!

Unless the programmer has provided some special mechanism, graphical applications in Java are often difficult to halt. Sometimes, there are platform-specific solutions to this problem. On UNIX systems, for example, a program can always be halted by pressing the Control and C keys simultaneously.

A more elegant solution is to halt the program when the user closes the application window. This can be done by creating and registering a window event listener and performing an `exit` in response to the close window event. For this purpose, the `jds` library supplies a class named `CloseQuit`, which is defined as follows:

```
import java.awt.event.*;

class CloseQuit extends WindowAdapter {
  public void windowClosing (WindowEvent e)
                          {System.exit(0); }
}
```

To add the ability to halt a program, all that is necessary is to register an instance of `CloseQuit` as a window listener:

```
addWindowListener(new CloseQuit());
```

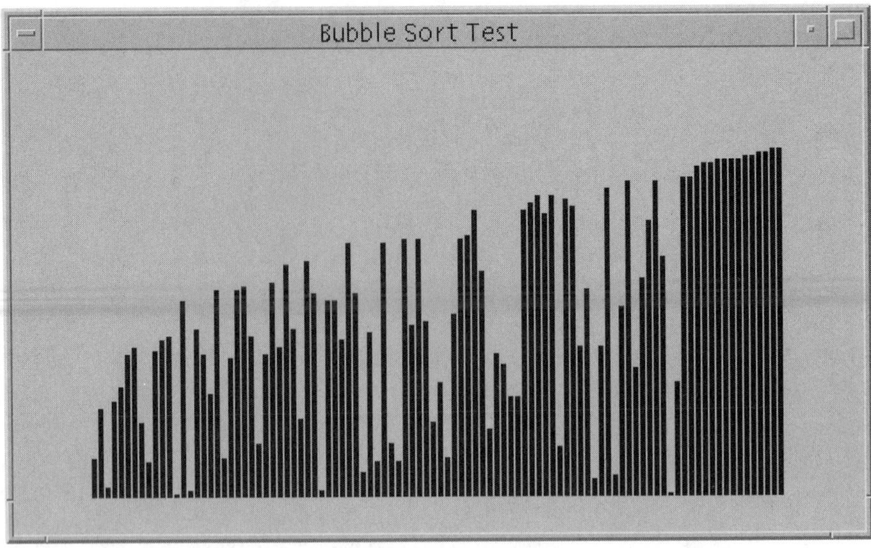

FIGURE 6.6 Snapshot Execution of Bubble Sort

```
  public void run () {
      // create initial data
    for (int i = 0; i < numberOfElements; i++) {
      int d = (int)(numberOfElements * Math.random());
      data.addLast(new Integer(d));
      }

      // now sort
    SortAlgorithm sortAlg = new ShellSort(new IntegerCompare());
    sortAlg.sort(vv);
  }
}
```

We can examine sample output from this program by using the three sorting algorithms we have seen so far. Figure 6.6 shows a snapshot of a bubble sort. Note how elements to the right have been sorted, whereas elements to the left are relatively unchanged. Figure 6.7 is a snapshot execution of insertion sort. Here, the elements to the left have been sorted, whereas elements to the right are waiting to be placed. Note that in both figures, the unexamined values remain in relatively random order.

In contrast, Figure 6.8 shows a snapshot taken from the middle of execution of Shell sort. Note that although elements are not exactly ordered, they have migrated to a point that is near their final location. It is this rapid migration that makes Shell sort so much faster than bubble or insertion sort.

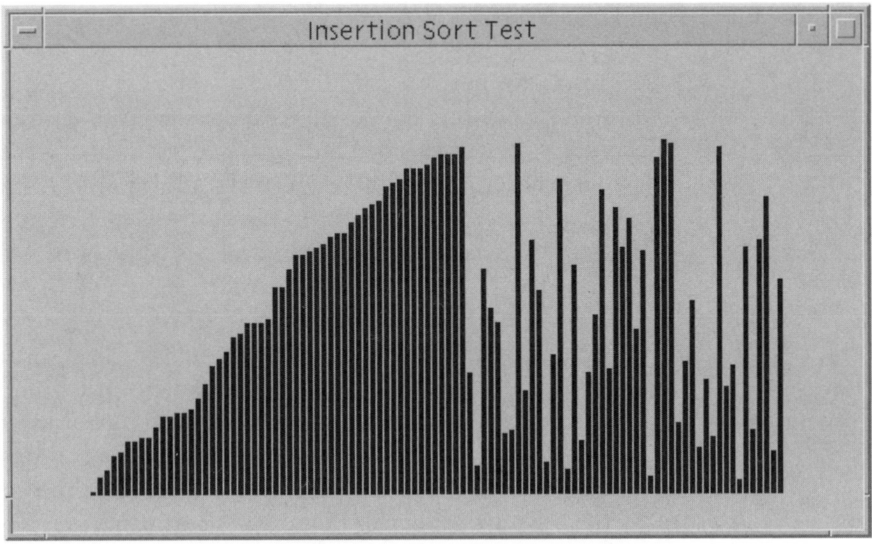

FIGURE 6.7 Snapshot Execution of Insertion Sort

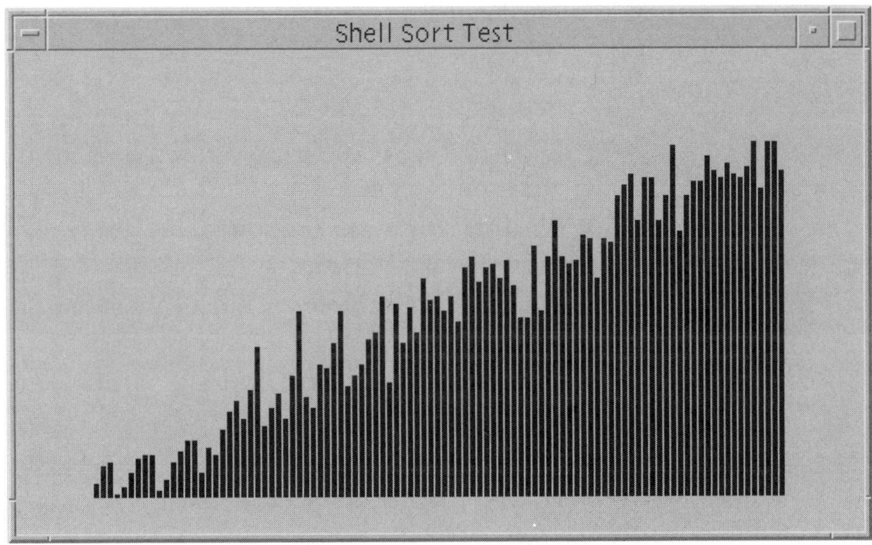

FIGURE 6.8 Snapshot Execution of Shell Sort

6.7 CHAPTER SUMMARY

KEY CONCEPTS

- Array
- Random access
- Polymorphic variable
- Wrapper class
- `Vector`
- Expected time performance
- Listener
- `Comparator`
- Shell sort

An array permits efficient (constant-time) access to each element in a collection, but it does not easily accommodate collections that grow in size over time. The `Vector` data structure solves this problem. As an abstraction, the `Vector` permits a programmer to view a container as a simple indexed collection but to hide the memory management details that are necessary if the container is to be permitted to grow. The `Vector` can also be viewed as a realization of the `Stack` ADT.

The implementation of the method `addLast` illustrates the concept of expected time performance. Although the best estimate we can give for any single invocation of `addLast` is a linear $O(n)$ time, the *average* execution time in any sequence of invocations will be constant, or $O(1)$.

We have illustrated the use of the `Vector` data structure with three applications. One of these, `ShellSort`, is the first sorting algorithm we have seen with better than $O(n^2)$ performance.

Further Information

A more detailed analysis of Shell sort is presented by Weiss [Weiss 96].

Study Questions

1. In what ways is the array in Java different from arrays in other programming languages?
2. What does it mean to say that the array data type supports random access?
3. What is a polymorphic variable? What are the two types of polymorphic variables in Java?
4. What purpose is served by the wrapper classes in the Java standard library?
5. What two interfaces does the `Vector` data structure support?
6. What is the size of a vector? What is the capacity? How are these two values different?
7. Why do we say that `elementAt` is $O(1)$ always, whereas `addElementAt` is $O(n)$ worst case? What is the best-case performance of `addElementAt`?
8. Fill in the asymptotic execution times for the following operations. For each, indicate whether the execution time will always be required, is an expected (or average) time, or is worst case.

Operation	Execution Time
`isEmpty`	$O(\_)$
`size`	$O(\_)$
`setSize`	$O(\_)$
`elementAt`	$O(\_)$
`addElementAt`	$O(\_)$
`removeElementAt`	$O(\_)$
`addLast`	$O(\_)$
`getLast`	$O(\_)$
`removeLast`	$O(\_)$
`ensureCapacity`	$O(\_)$

9. What does it mean to declare a method as `synchronized`?
10. Why does the `addElementAt` method permit the index argument to be larger than the corresponding argument in `removeElementAt`?
11. What is the meaning of the variable `this` when used in the body of a method?
12. What task is performed by a cast expression?
13. What task is performed by a *listener* object?
14. What method is used to register a listener with a `Button` object?
15. What is an inner class? What is an inner class permitted to do that other classes cannot?
16. What task is performed by a `Comparator` object? What is the name of the method used to perform this task?
17. What is the key idea used in Shell sort to achieve better than $O(n^2)$ performance?

Exercises

1. Describe the state of a `Vector` after the following sequence of operations:

```
Vector v = new Vector();
v.setSize(4);
v.setElementAt("A", 3);
v.setElementAt("B", 1);
```

```
v.removeLast();
v.addElementAt("C", 2);
v.addLast("D");
v.setSize(6);
```

2. What happens when `setSize` is used to reduce the size of a `Vector`? Can this ever result in a reallocation?
3. Using invariants, provide an informal proof of correctness for the `addElementAt` method. Make sure that you handle the following special cases:
   a. An element is placed in an empty vector.
   b. An element is placed at the first location of a nonempty vector.
   c. An element is placed in a middle position of a nonempty vector.
   d. An element is placed at the end of a nonempty vector.
4. Using invariants, provide an informal proof of correctness for the `removeElementAt` method. Make sure that you handle the removal of the last element from a one-element vector, as well as the nonempty special cases noted for the previous exercise.
5. To illustrate that the expected execution time for `addLast` is constant, imagine that we start with an empty vector and perform 25 successive `addLast` operations. To estimate the execution time for each, assign a value of 1 to those executions that can be performed in constant time and a value equal to the size of the new vector to those executions that require a reallocation. Then sum the values and divide by 25. How large is the resulting average?
6. Suppose that instead of doubling the size of the vector when an reallocation occurred, we simply increased the size of the vector by 1. Perform the same analysis as described in the previous question. How large is the resulting average execution now?
7. Programming project 4 suggests adding a version of the constructor that would take an object of type `Collection` as interface and initialize the vector using this value. Show how this could be used to make a copy, or clone, of a vector. An alternative technique for making copies is the `Clonable` interface in the standard library. What are the advantages and disadvantages of these two approaches?
8. The specification of the `Enumeration` interface requires calls on `nextElement` and `hasMoreElements` to be intermixed. Each call on `nextElement` must be preceded by a call on `hasMoreElements`, and each call on `hasMoreElements` must, if it returns `true`, be followed by a call on `nextElement`. To discover what trouble can occur if this is not

followed, imagine a three-element vector and execute the following loop, which tries to print two elements at a time. Explain what error will occur:

```
for (Enumeration e = vec.elements(); e.hasMoreElements(); ) {
  System.out.println(e.nextElement()); // print one
  System.out.println(e.nextElement()); // print two
}
```

9. In general, making changes to a collection at the same time it is being accessed using an `Enumeration` can result in unpredictable consequences. For example, imagine that an `IndexedEnumeration` is iterating over the following five-element vector:

3	7	2	4	9

Assume that the enumeration has already produced the values 3, 7, and 2 and that before the next value is accessed, a new element is added at position 1. What will be the remaining sequence of values produced by the enumeration?

10. To see why `addElementAt` must be synchronized, perform the following thought experiment. Imagine that we have a vector with a five-element array currently holding the three integer values 2, 5, and 8. Assume that the `synchronized` modifier has been removed from `addElementAt` and that two threads are both trying to insert values into index position 1. The first thread gets halted after the `for` loop in `addElementAt` but before it can complete the assignment. The second thread then runs to completion before the first thread resumes. Describe the final state of the vector. Is this what you would expect?

11. To see why both `setSize` and `ensureCapacity` must be synchronized, perform the following thought experiment. Assume that the `synchronized` modifiers have been removed. Assume that we have a vector with a capacity of ten elements and that two threads are simultaneously working with this collection. The first invokes `setSize(12)` but gets suspended in the middle of the method `ensureCapacity` after it has allocated the new array but before it can fill it. The second invokes `setSize(16)` but gets suspended right before the final assignment. The first thread then runs to completion, followed by the second. What is the state of the vector at this point? What is its size? What is its capacity? What problems can arise as a result of this condition?

12. Show the various intermediate steps in a bubble sort algorithm being applied to the following nine-element vector:

3	7	2	4	1	0	5	6	8

13. The pattern suggested for the worst-case number of swaps for bubble sort or insertion sort seems to be twice the sum of the odd integers between 0 and n. Using mathematical induction, derive a formula for this quantity.
14. A sorting algorithm is said to be *stable* if the relative positions of two equal elements are the same in the final result as in the original vector. Show that bubble sort is not stable. Do this by simulating the execution on the following five-element vector:

0	4	2_1	2_2	5

    The subscripts will help you keep track of the two otherwise equal elements. Show that in the final vector, the relative positions of these two elements have been reversed.
15. Is insertion sort stable? Either give an argument showing that it is, or give an example showing that it is not.
16. Is Shell sort stable? Either give an argument showing that it is, or give an example showing that it is not.
17. Using invariants, provide an informal proof of correctness for Shell sort.
18. In Section 4.4, we described how the problem of searching for repeated patterns in a DNA strand was speeded up by rearranging the data into a two-dimensional matrix. Unfortunately, this matrix would require much more memory than the original vector (m times as much memory, to be precise). Show how this could be reduced to only two times the original memory by sorting a `Vector` of index values using a specialized `Comparator` object. The vector to be sorted will initially contain the values 0, 1, 2, ... n in order. Write a `Comparator` object that will, when given two `Integer` values from this matrix, compare the next m positions in the original data matrix, starting at the two given positions. Explain how the sorted result can then be used to answer the original question about the DNA sequence. (This technique is often called *indirect sorting*.)

Programming Projects

1. Rewrite both the bubble sort and the insertion sort algorithms so that they will operate on a vector of `Object` values rather than on an array of integers. Compare once more the execution times for these two procedures. Do the results reported in the previous chapter still hold?
2. Modify the `Vector` data structure so that it will support the `Bag` interface. What is the asymptotic complexity of the methods you need?
3. Modify the `Vector` data structure so that it will support the `FindMin` interface. What is the asymptotic complexity of the methods you need?
4. Modify the `Vector` data structure and add the following operations:
   a. A constructor that takes a `Collection` as argument and initializes the vector using the data from the collection. (This is a simple way to make a copy of a vector or any other container.)
   b. The method `firstIndexOf`, which returns the index of the first element that will test equal to the argument value. Throw a `NoSuchElementException` if no value can be found.
   c. The method `lastIndexOf`, which returns the index of the last element that will test equal to the argument value.
   d. The method `trimToSize`, which will reduce the capacity of the vector so that it is equal to its size.
   e. The method `subVector`, which takes two integer index values and returns a vector containing the elements between the two points.
   f. The method `clear`, which removes all elements from a vector. This should be done in constant time.
5. The most recent version of the Java standard library includes the idea of an `Iterator`. Unlike an `Enumeration`, an `Iterator` includes a method that will remove the current element from a container:

```
public interface Iterator {
  boolean hasMoreElements();
  Object nextElement();
  void remove(); // remove current value
}
```

   Show how to modify the `IndexedEnumeration` so that it will satisfy the `Iterator` interface. What problems does the removal of the current element cause?
6. Modify the memory game so that it uses letters rather than digits as the puzzle values.

7. Using a collection of English words, modify the memory puzzle so that it presents a series of words and asks the user to repeat the sequence of words in order. You may wish to investigate the `StringTokenizer` in the standard Java library; this tool provides a simple way to break a line of text into individual words.
8. There are times when you need a sorting procedure to rearrange the values in a `Vector` so that they appear in decreasing order rather than in increasing order. Show how you can achieve this result by means of a `Comparator` object without modifying the sorting algorithm.
9. Various authors have reported that the execution time for Shell sort can be improved by using a different sequence of values. Select one of the following and implement the new algorithm; then compare the execution time to the algorithm given in the text.
   a. Shell's sequence, but add 1 to the gap if it is even
   b. The values $1, 3, 7, \ldots, 2^k - 1$
   c. The values $1, 4, 13, \ldots, (3^k + 1)/2$
10. Using an array as the underlying data structure, create a data structure that implements the `Matrix` interface (see Section 2.3.9). Elements should be stored in the array one row after the other. For example, a 2 by 3 matrix would be represented as follows:

0,0	0,1	0,2	1,0	1,1	1,2

    What should be the effect when an array is resized by a new `setSize` command?
11. An alternative representation of a matrix is as an array, each element of which is itself an array:

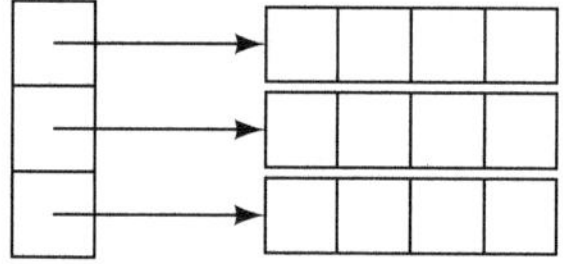

    Create a data structure that implements the `Matrix` interface using this approach.
12. In Programming project 7 in Chapter 4, a recursive program to compute the Fibonacci numbers was compared with an iterative one. In that case, the recursive version was considerably slower. Many students mistakenly believe that examples such as this show that recursion is an inherently inefficient technique. This is not true. The problem with the recursive solution was not the recursion but the fact that the

same values were being repeatedly regenerated. This can be observed by writing a third Fibonacci calculator, one that does not recalculate values if they have already been computed. (This technique is sometimes known as *dynamic programming*.)

This Fibonacci routine allocates a `Vector` of $n + 1$ values. It then calls a recursive routine to fill in the elements of this vector, finally returning the last computed value. It can be written as follows:

```
int Fibonacci (int n)
{
  Vector values = new Vector();
  values.setSize(n+1);
  fibCalculator(values, n);
  return values.elementAt(n);
}
```

The routine `fibCalculator` first checks the vector to see whether the entry indexed by the second argument is something other than `null`. If so, it merely returns the integer value. If not, it computes the value by making recursive calls, wraps the result into an `Integer`, and assigns the result to the appropriate index position. Write the routine `fibCalculator`, and then compare its execution time with the two algorithms you wrote in the earlier chapter.

13. Programming project 4 in Chapter 3 described how to take an integer value and translate it into the textual representation. Using this, describe how to make a `Comparator` object that will order two `Integer` values based on their textual representation, not their value. For example, *one* comes before *ten*, which comes before *zero*. Using this comparator, order the integer values from zero to one hundred.

CHAPTER 7

SORTING VECTORS

In Chapter 6, we explored the `Vector` as an implementation of several different abstract data types. In this chapter, we will examine some of the more important variations on the theme of the vector data type. In particular, we will examine ways of sorting vectors, as well as applications for the resulting sorted vectors.

7.1 DIVIDE AND CONQUER

As a prelude to discussing the `SortedVector` abstraction, it is useful to first consider the leverage that ordering provides. In Chapter 4, we asked, Why, for example, do dictionaries list their words in sequence? The answer to the question may seem obvious, but the general implication is significant. Let us consider a small example. Suppose that we have the following sorted list of names:

0	1	2	3	4	5	6	7	8	9	10
Abigail	Abner	Adam	Adela	Aiyana	Alex	Alice	Allen	Amina	Arthur	Audrey

Imagine that we are attempting to discover whether the name *Amanda* occurs in the list. We could just walk through the list, checking each entry in turn. If the list were unordered, this would, in fact, be our only alternative. Such a linear search would require 11 comparisons before we could say for certain that the name was not present.[1] An alternative strategy is to compare the element we are searching for to the *middle* element of the vector. In our case, this is element number 5, which holds the value *Alex*. With a single comparison—*Alex* to *Amanda*—we can tell (because *Alex* is lexicographically smaller than *Amanda*) that the value *Amanda* cannot occur in the first six elements. Thus, in one stroke, we have eliminated more than half the possibilities for a match and thus reduced the size of the problem by half.

0	1	2	3	4	5	6	7	8	9	10
Abigail	Abner	Adam	Adela	Aiyana	Alex	Alice	Allen	Amina	Arthur	Audrey

This is an example of the general problem-solving heuristic termed *divide and conquer*.[2] The basic idea of divide and conquer is to choose an initial step that divides the problem roughly in half and that allows us to eliminate one or the other possibility. The greatest benefit of the heuristic occurs when we apply the technique repeatedly. We know now that *Amanda* must occur, if it occurs at all, in the latter half of the list. Thus, our second query attempts to divide this in half, by comparing *Amanda* to position 8, which contains *Amina*. Because the name *Amanda* is ordered as a word before *Amina*, we know that the name does not occur any later than position 8.

0	1	2	3	4	5	6	7	8	9	10
Abigail	Abner	Adam	Adela	Aiyana	Alex	Alice	Allen	Amina	Arthur	Audrey

The next comparison is to position 6. When no match occurs, we know that the only possibility is position 7. This comparison is then sufficient to tell us that the name *Amanda* does not occur in the list. The most important feature is that we have been able to discover this fact with only 4 comparisons instead of the 11 required by the brute-force approach.

1. To be totally accurate, the search could be abandoned after nine comparisons if we remembered that the list was ordered.

2. We have encountered divide and conquer already in Chapter 1 as a guiding principle for abstracting the structure of complex systems. Here, we develop the same idea as a tool for creating algorithms.

```
public class SortedVector implements
    Bag, Sorted, FindMin, FindNth, SortAlgorithm
{
  protected Indexed elementData;
  protected Comparator test;
  .
  .
  .
    // pre: assumes elementData is ordered
    // post: returns index position (idx) so that
    // all elements indexed less than idx are smaller than argument,
    // and all elements indexed greater than idx are greater
    // than or equal to argument
  protected int binarySearch (Object key) {
    int low = 0;
    int high = elementData.size();
      // invariant is true here
    while (low < high) {
      int mid = (low + high)/2;
      if (test.compare(elementData.elementAt(mid), key) < 0)
        low = mid + 1;
      else
        high = mid;
        // invariant is true here
      }
    // invariant is true here
    return low;
    }
}
```

FIGURE 7.1 The Binary Search Algorithm as It Appears in SortedVector

7.1.1 Binary Search

This example illustrates the technique known as a *binary search*. An application of this technique can be found in the class SortedVector, which we will describe in Section 7.2. The class SortedVector will hold its elements in a data field named elementData. The insertion and removal algorithms, to be described shortly, will ensure that the elements are maintained in sequential order. The binary search algorithm is shown in Figure 7.1. This is a rewriting of the algorithm we first presented in Chapter 4. We have added comments to indicate code locations we will refer to in the proof of correctness.

Following the technique outlined in earlier chapters, we will analyze this algorithm in three steps. First, we establish that the algorithm will always terminate, regardless of the argument value or the distribution of elements stored in the inner collection. Next, we characterize the running time of the algorithm. Finally, we consider the validity of the result produced as output by the algorithm.

To prove termination, we must find a quantity that changes each iteration of the loop, is integer, decreasing, and strictly positive. Neither `low` nor `high` has the property we seek, as there is no guarantee that either will change in any particular iteration of the loop. However, the expression `high` − `low` will suffice. The verification of this depends on a property of integer division: that for nonnegative values, integer division rounds *down* to the next-lower integer in cases where a fractional value would result. Thus, if `low` is less than `high`, the expression `(low` + `high)/2` must be strictly smaller than `high`, although it could be the same as `low`. With this assumption, we know that either `low` is being set to `mid` + `1`, in which case it is clearly increasing in value, or `high` is being set to `mid`, in which case it is decreasing.

To characterize the running time, we note that the range of positions in which the index might be found is cut in half in each iteration of the `while` loop. As we pointed out in Chapter 4, if we begin with n elements in the collection held by `elementData`, the number of times that we can cut this value in half is no larger than $\lceil \log n \rceil$.

The most important task is to prove that the result satisfies certain conditions. In particular, the integer yielded by this procedure should satisfy the following three conditions:

1. The value should be larger than or equal to zero and less than or equal to the number of elements in `elementData`. Note carefully that we permit the output to be equal to the size of `elementData`, which is one greater than the largest legal index value.
2. All elements stored at index positions less than the result are strictly smaller than the argument value.
3. All elements stored at index positions greater than or equal to the result are greater than or equal to the argument value.

To prove this, we will establish that the following two invariants hold at three places: before the `while` loop is executed, at the end of the `while` loop, and after the `while` loop terminates.

1. The elements stored in index locations less than `low` are themselves less than the argument.
2. The elements stored in index locations greater than or equal to `high` are themselves greater than or equal to the argument.

It is easy to see that this condition must be satisfied before we begin execution of the `while` loop. Because `low` is initially zero and `high` is initially one larger than the highest legal index, both the sets mentioned in the invariant are empty.

Next, we assume that the invariants are true at the beginning of an iteration of the `while` loop and that we have executed the body of the loop. After computing a new index `mid`, the body of the loop compares the element stored at this position to the argument. If the element is strictly less than the argument, which is the condition being tested by the call on the method `compare`, all elements with index positions less than or equal to `mid` must be strictly less than the argument. In this case, `low` can safely be set to `mid + 1`, and the invariant will be preserved. On the other hand, if the condition being tested is false, it means that the element stored at location `mid` must be greater than or equal to the argument. Because the collection is ordered, all elements stored at index positions greater than `mid` must similarly be greater than or equal to the argument. In this case, we can assign the variable `high` the value `mid`, and the invariant will still be preserved.

The last step is to verify that the invariant is true at the termination of the `while` loop. If the loop was executed zero times and the invariant was true before the loop was executed, it must be true afterwards. If the loop was executed some number of times, the invariant must have been true on the last iteration of the loop and hence will be true after the loop terminates.

To finally prove that the result yielded by the procedure has the properties we want, we simply combine the invariant with the observation that the loop will terminate when the variable `high` is less than or equal to `low`. Because we know that `high` can never be less than `low`, it must be that they are equal. This is sufficient to establish the three result conditions.

EXPERIMENT: EARLY TESTING FOR EQUALITY

The binary search algorithm shown in Figure 7.1 will continue searching until the variables `low` and `high` meet at the same value, even if by chance the element being targeted is discovered sooner. For example, if we were searching the vector of names for the value *Alex*, we would discover the element on the first comparison. Modify the algorithm so that it will halt if the element is discovered. Then conduct an experiment in which you perform n search operations for increasing values of n to measure the change on the execution time of the algorithm. Does the altered program still satisfy the postcondition? Why not? How must the postcondition be modified?

*7.2 Sorted Vectors

The SortedVector data abstraction stores elements in an underlying indexed data structure and uses the binary search algorithm described in the previous section to maintain ordering as values are added to and deleted from the collection. The fact that elements are ordered makes it easy to support a number of important interfaces. We will describe the data structure in stages, by means of these various interfaces.

The constructor for the SortedVector class can take a Comparator, an initial set of data items, or both. Default values are used if either is omitted. Should a vector be supplied, it need not be initially sorted, and so the sort operation is executed to ensure that the elements are put into place.

```
public class SortedVector implements Sorted, ...
{
  protected Indexed elementData;
  protected Comparator test;

  public SortedVector (Indexed v, Comparator c)
    { test = c; sort(v); elementData = v;}

  public SortedVector (Comparator c)
    { test = c; elementData = new Vector();}

  public SortedVector ()
  { test = new DefaultComparator(); elementData = new Vector(); }
    .
    .
    .
}
```

Comparators

As we noted in Chapter 2, the Java standard library defines ordering by means of the classes Comparator and Comparable. These two classes are linked by a small utility class named DefaultComparator, a form of Comparator. A DefaultComparator assumes that its arguments are both instances of Comparable and passes the message compare to the left argument, using the right argument as value:

```
public class DefaultComparator implements
                              Comparator {
  public int compare (Object left,
                            Object right) {
    Comparable cleft = (Comparable) left;
    return cleft.compareTo(right);
  }
}
```

Using a DefaultComparator, it is necessary to ensure only that the elements held in the container satisfy the Comparable interface.

The first abstract data type we will consider is represented by the `Sorted` interface. The properties of this ADT simply assert that the data abstraction will honor all the methods associated with the `Collection` interface and that, furthermore, the elements—when enumerated by `elements`—will be ordered. Ignoring, for the moment, the requirement that elements are ordered, we will examine the implementation of these methods. The implementation is simplified by making use of operations provided by the underlying `Indexed` data type:

```
  // collection interface
public Enumeration elements () { return elementData.elements(); }

public boolean isEmpty () { return elementData.isEmpty(); }

public int size () { return elementData.size(); }
```

Note that the property of the method `elements` in the `Sorted` interface is different from that of `Collection`. In particular, the sorted list is obligated to enumerate its elements in sequence. The fact that the method will do so depends on two observations. First, the underlying vector is being maintained in sequence. Second, an enumeration for an `Indexed` data type produces elements in the order of their index positions.

The next two interfaces we consider are `FindMin` and `FindNth`, which require the ability to add new elements to the collection. To add an element, we perform a binary search and insert the value at the indicated location. This ensures that the elements will retain their ordered property. Furthermore, the minimum value will always be found in the first location. Because the collection is both ordered and indexed, the nth value will always be found at location n.

```
  // FindMin and FindNth interfaces
public void addElement (Object obj)
  { elementData.addElementAt(obj, binarySearch(obj)); }

public Object getFirst () { return elementData.elementAt(0); }

public void removeFirst () { elementData.removeElementAt(0); }

public Object findNth (int n) { return elementData.elementAt(n); }
```

Although finding the position into which a new element should be inserted requires only $O(\log n)$ steps, it is unfortunately the case that adding the element to the collection is more difficult. To see this, consider adding the value *Adam* to the following collection:

0	1	2	3	4	5
Abigail	Adela	Aiyana	Alex	Alice	Audrey

The binary search will tell us that the new element should go into position 1. But first, all the elements stored in positions 1 or larger must be shifted up:

0	1	2	3	4	5	6
Abigail		Adela	Aiyana	Alex	Alice	Audrey

It is only after a hole has been made for the new element that it can be inserted. Thus, insertion may require, in the worst case, $O(n)$ steps. Accessing the first element is a fast $O(1)$ operation. Unfortunately, removing the first element requires that all elements other than the first be moved down one position and is therefore also $O(n)$.

The `Bag` interface is the one most commonly used in conjunction with this data type. The `addElement` method is shared with the `FindMin` interface and does not need to be repeated. The others are implemented as follows:

```
  // Bag interface
public boolean containsElement (Object obj) {
  int index = binarySearch(obj);
  return index < elementData.size() &&
    elementData.elementAt(index).equals(obj);
}

public Object findElement (Object obj) {
  int index = binarySearch(obj);
  if (index < elementData.size() &&
    elementData.elementAt(index).equals(obj))
      return elementData.elementAt(index);
  else throw new NoSuchElementException(String.valueOf(obj));
}

public void removeElement (Object obj) {
  int index = binarySearch(obj);
  if (index < elementData.size() &&
    elementData.elementAt(index).equals(obj))
      elementData.removeElementAt(index);
  else throw new NoSuchElementException(String.valueOf(obj));
}
```

The `containsElement` and `findElement` methods are bounded by the execution time of the binary search and are thus $O(\log n)$. But the `removeElement` method may, like `removeFirst`, be forced to shift elements down one position in order to fill in the hole left after the removal of an element. Thus, this method is worst-case $O(n)$. We will subsequently find other data structures that provide a more efficient implementation of the `Bag` interface.

7.3 MERGE SORT

A useful feature of ordering is that two ordered collections can be *merged* into a third container very quickly. One simply walks through both collections in parallel, copying whichever value is the smallest in the two containers and placing it into the new structure. This insight is key to the creation of a unique sorting algorithm.

The merge sort algorithm (Figure 7.2) uses a somewhat specialized form of this merging operation. Within a vector, two subsections can be identified by three integer variables. We assume that the elements between index positions `low` and `mid` are ordered, as are the elements between `mid` and `high`. We make no assumptions about the elements with index positions less than `low` or greater than or equal to `high`:

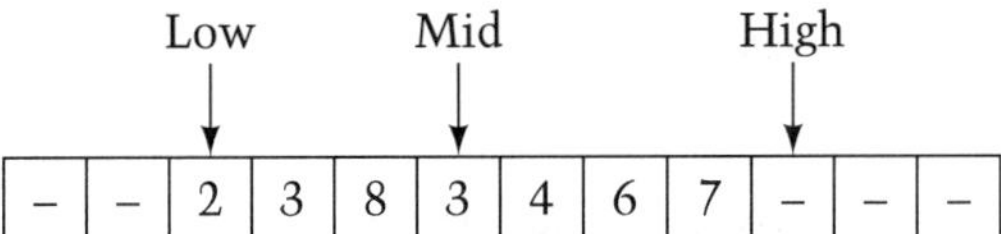

The goal is to combine just the elements between `low` and `high` into one sequence. This is accomplished by first merging the two collections into a new `Vector` and then copying the values from the vector back into the original locations.

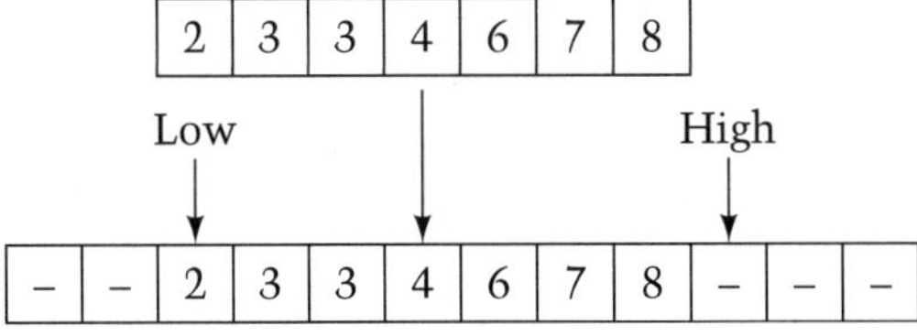

Although having two immediately adjacent ordered collections might at first seem unusual, it is exactly the situation that arises in the merge sort algorithm. The key idea is to start with an unordered collection of elements and then repeatedly break it into two roughly equal parts. Each

```
public class MergeSort implements SortAlgorithm {
  public MergeSort (Comparator t) { test = t; }
  private Comparator test;
  private Indexed data;
  private Vector stk = new Vector();

  public void sort (Indexed v) {
    data = v;
    stk.ensureCapacity(v.size());
    mergeSort(0, v.size());
  }

  private void mergeSort (int low, int high) {
    if (low+1 >= high) return;
    int mid = (low + high) / 2;
    mergeSort(low, mid);  // sort one part
    mergeSort(mid, high); // sort another
    merge(low, mid, high); // combine
  }

  private void merge (int low, int mid, int high) {
    stk.setSize(0);
    int i = low;
    int j = mid;
    while ((i < mid) || (j < high)) {
      if (i < mid)
        if ((j < high) &&
          (test.compare(data.elementAt(j),
            data.elementAt(i)) < 0))
          stk.addLast(data.elementAt(j++));
        else
          stk.addLast(data.elementAt(i++));
      else
        stk.addLast(data.elementAt(j++));
    }
    j = stk.size(); // copy stack back to original area
    for (i = 0; i < j; i++)
      data.setElementAt(stk.elementAt(i), low+i);
  }
}
```

FIGURE 7.2 The Merge Sort Algorithm

of these parts is then similarly broken in half. This continues until the portions consist of only a single element:

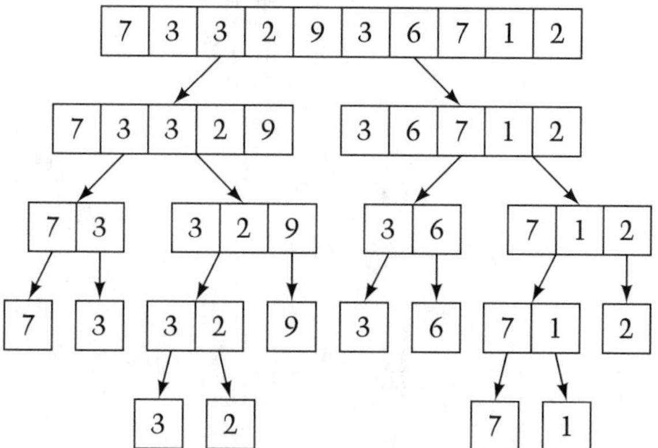

But a collection that consists of only one element is, indeed, ordered. So to produce a completely ordered sequence, all that is necessary is to merge the subportions into ever larger sequences as we return through the collection of calls. These two sequences will always be adjacent, satisfying the requirement we needed for the merge algorithm. When we reach the original vector, the entire collection has been ordered.

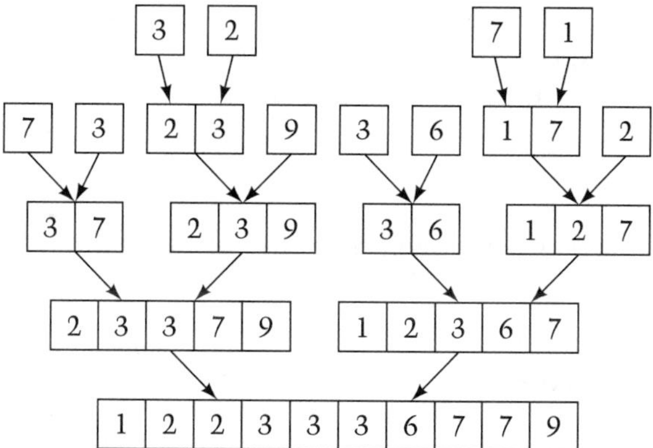

Figure 7.3 shows a snapshot of merge sort in the middle of execution. The left half of the vector has already been sorted, and various smaller groups have been created out of the right side. The right-side elements will subsequently be merged to form one unit, before being combined with the left half to form the final result.

How fast is merge sort? To determine the algorithmic complexity of a recursive procedure, we must determine the amount of work performed at each level of call, as well as the depth of the recursive call stack. Because

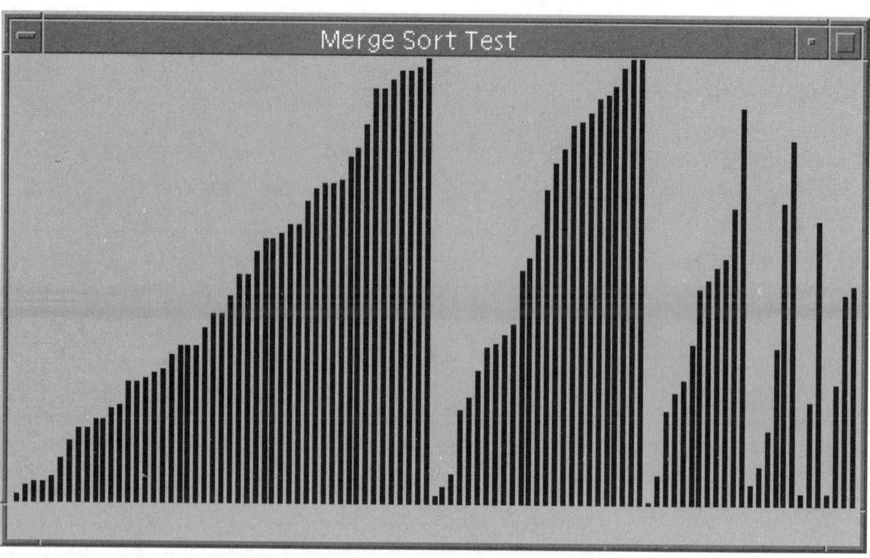

FIGURE 7.3 Merge Sort in Action

the merge step is a linear operation, it is easy to see that at each level of call, we are doing $O(n)$ work. To bound the recursive call depth, note that at each step, we are dividing the size of the input in half. Therefore, $\log n$ is an approximation to the depth of recursion.

We aren't quite finished, as *two* recursive calls are made at each level before the merge is used to combine the sequences back into one vector. What saves the running time of this algorithm is that each of these two

AN n LOG n LOWER BOUND FOR SORTING

It is possible to show that in certain circumstances, an $O(n \log n)$ sorting algorithm is the best we can do. Although the mathematics is more complicated than we are willing to present here, we can indicate the outlines of the argument. A key element in this argument—one that we will not try to justify here—is that by comparing two values, we can, at most, separate between two possible permutations as the correct result. To obtain a lower bound, we can simply count the number of permutations. But that is easy—there are $n!$ permutations for a collection of n elements. So $\log n!$ is a lower bound on sorting. An approximation to $n!$ is given by Sterling's formula, which states that $n! > (n/e)^n$. If we take the log of both sides and toss away a few constant terms, we have that $\log n! > n \log n$.

Of course, this applies only to sorting algorithms that achieve their result by comparing elements. In Chapter 16, we will encounter a series of sorting algorithms that work in an entirely different fashion and thereby can break the $n \log n$ barrier.

recursive calls is given a vector that is only half the size of the original. Thus, adding together the linear execution times of the merge operations on the immediately next-lower level results in an execution time that is still no larger than $O(n)$.

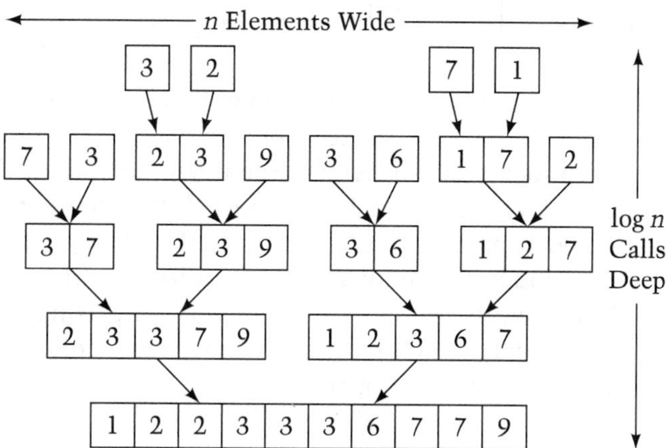

Putting everything together then yields a $O(\log n)$ depth of recursive function calls, each one of which is performing $O(n)$ work. The result is an $O(n \log n)$ sorting algorithm. This is a great improvement over the $O(n^2)$ algorithms we have seen earlier. However, in practice, merge sort suffers from a serious problem. It requires $O(n)$ additional memory, in the form of the vector that is allocated to hold the merged values. Management of this additional memory slows down the algorithm, so that it often may not even be as fast as Shell sort. In the next section, we will discover a different sorting algorithm that is normally much faster.

7.4 PARTITIONING

A number of interesting problems involve partitioning a vector into two sections, based on a comparison to an element in the collection. The element used in the comparison is termed the *pivot*, and thus this task is often termed *pivoting*. To illustrate the process of pivoting, consider the following unsorted vector:

2	97	17	37	12	46	10	55	80	42	39

Imagine that we want to pivot around the value 37. The result of the operation would be that the elements in the vector get rearranged as follows:

< Pivot   Pivot   > = Pivot

12	10	17	2	37	97	46	55	80	42	39

There are several features to note. First, note that the location of the element 37 has been shifted from the original. Furthermore, all the elements with index values less than the new location for the number 37 have values that are less than 37, whereas all the elements in locations larger than this position are larger than or equal to 37.

Although this may at first seem like a rather useless exercise, the idea of pivoting is the basis for two very surprising algorithms. The first is a technique for finding the *n*th element in a collection, and the second is an extremely fast sorting algorithm.

7.4.1 The Pivot Algorithm

The pivot algorithm is found in class `Partition`, part of which is shown in Figure 7.4. The data values will be stored in an internal indexed collection, in the variable named `elementData`. A method named `swap` will exchange two elements in this collection.

The first step in the pivot algorithm is to move the pivot to the beginning of the array by swapping the pivot position with the first element. Having moved this element out of the way, the partition can then be safely conducted by comparing against this value. As before, the partition algorithm will then divide the input into two groups: those that are known to be less than or equal to the pivot and those that are known to be greater than the pivot. (A proof of correctness is developed in exercise 9.) When the pivoting is finished, the result can be visualized as follows:

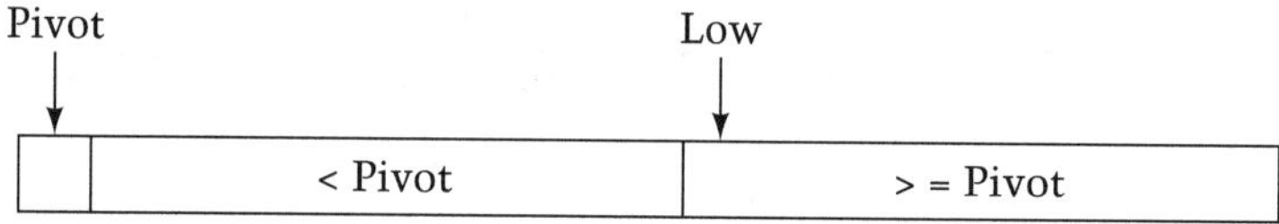

Note that the value returned by the partition step is the beginning of the larger group, whereas what we need is the previous value: the end of the smaller group. The partition value is decremented to obtain this position,

```
public class Partition implements FindNth, SortAlgorithm {
  Partition (Comparator c) { test = c; }
  Partition (Indexed v, Comparator c) { test = c; elementData = v; }
  protected Indexed elementData;
  protected Comparator test;
  .
  .
  .
    // the pivot algorithm
  private int pivot (int start, int stop, int position) {
    swap(start, position); // swap pivot into start position

    int low = start + 1;
    int high = stop;
    while (low < high) {
      if (test.compare(elementData.elementAt(low),
        elementData.elementAt(start)) < 0)
          low++;
      else if (test.compare(elementData.elementAt(--high),
        elementData.elementAt(start)) < 0)
          swap(low, high);
    }
    swap(start, --low); // swap pivot back into place
    return low;
  }

  private void swap (int i, int j) {
    if (i == j) return;
    Object temp = elementData.elementAt(i);
    elementData.setElementAt(elementData.elementAt(j), i);
    elementData.setElementAt(temp, j);
  }
}
```

FIGURE 7.4 The Pivot Algorithm from Class `Partition`

and the element stored there—which we know is less than or equal to the pivot—is swapped with the pivot.

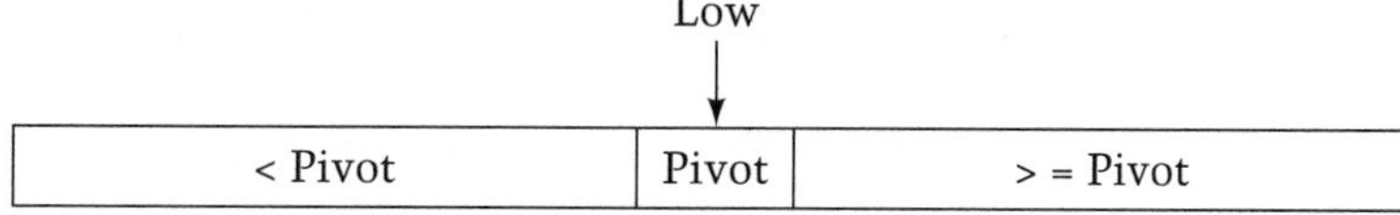

Each element in the vector is examined once. If the initial vector contains n elements, this is sufficient to show that the pivot algorithm is $O(n)$.

* 7.4.2 Finding the *n*th Element

Suppose that we wish to find the *n*th element in a collection. A common application is to find the median, or midpoint. This is the same as asking for the $n/2$ element, where n is the number of elements in the collection. One approach is to first sort the vector, as we do with the `SortedVector` collection. But sorting is doing much more work than is necessary. The sorted vector will tell us the position of each element in the ordered array, not simply the single value we are seeking. If we are interested in only *one* position (the median, for example), we might think that there is a better (that is, faster) algorithm that can be used.

The basic idea is to partition the vector. The resulting position yielded by the pivot algorithm either is or is not the index value we were seeking. If it is, we are finished. If it is not, it might at first appear that little information has been gained. But this is not necessarily the case. We have, in fact, divided the vector into two portions. Just as with binary search, we can in one step immediately rule out a large number of possible answers. By comparing the resulting index position for the pivot to the position we are seeking, we can recursively search either the lower or the upper portion of the transformed vector. The algorithm that results from this insight is as follows:

```
public Object findNth (int n) {
  if ((n < 0) || (n > elementData.size()))
    throw NoSuchElementException();
  return findNth(n, 0, elementData.size());
}

private Object findNth (int n, int low, int high) {
    // first partition
  int pivotIndex = pivot(low, high, (high + low)/2);
    // see if we are finished
  if (pivotIndex == n) return elementData.elementAt(n);
    // else try again
  if (n < pivotIndex) return findNth(n, low, pivotIndex);
  return findNth(n, pivotIndex+1, high);
}
```

How fast is this algorithm? It is relatively easy to see that the partition step will run in time proportional to the section of the vector it is processing. (To see this, note that each element in this section is examined only once.) The worst-case running time of the `findNth` algorithm, however, depends on how lucky one is in finding good pivot positions. The best case occurs if we just happen to stumble on the answer before we have recursed very many times. The next-best case occurs when the algorithm recursively calls itself until a partition consisting of just a single element is found, but the algorithm is fortunate in the selection of pivot elements. This happens when every pivot divides the vector roughly in half.

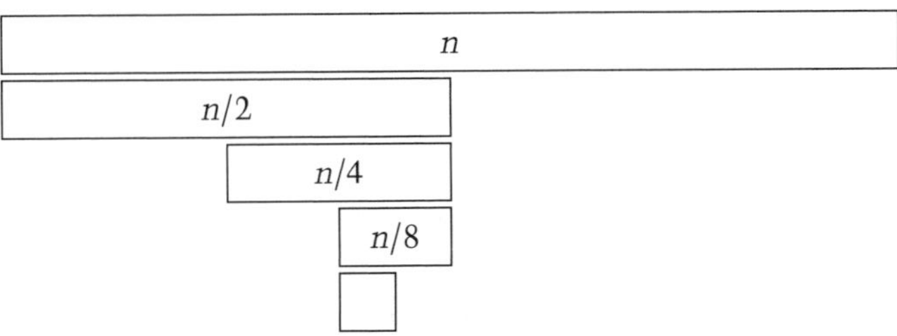

Execution time in this case is proportional to the sum $n + \frac{n}{2} + \frac{n}{4} + \cdots + 1$. If we factor out the common n term, the remaining sum can be expressed as $1 + \frac{1}{2} + \frac{1}{4} + \cdots$. The infinite series given by this pattern is bounded by 2, and thus any finite initial portion of the series must be similarly bounded. This is sufficient to show that in this case, the `findNth` algorithm will run in $O(n)$ steps.

But what if we make a series of bad choices for the pivot? The worst choice for a pivot would be one that represents either the largest or the smallest element in the collection. In this situation, one or the other of the vectors will be empty, and with $O(n)$ work at each step, we will have succeeded in eliminating only *one* element.

n

$n - 1$

$n - 2$

$n - 3$

...

3

2

1

The series that results from this string of poor choices is $n + (n - 1) + (n - 2) + \cdots + 1$. As we have seen in earlier chapters, this series characterizes an algorithm with $O(n^2)$ operations. This is even worse than our naive approach, which first sorted the vector.

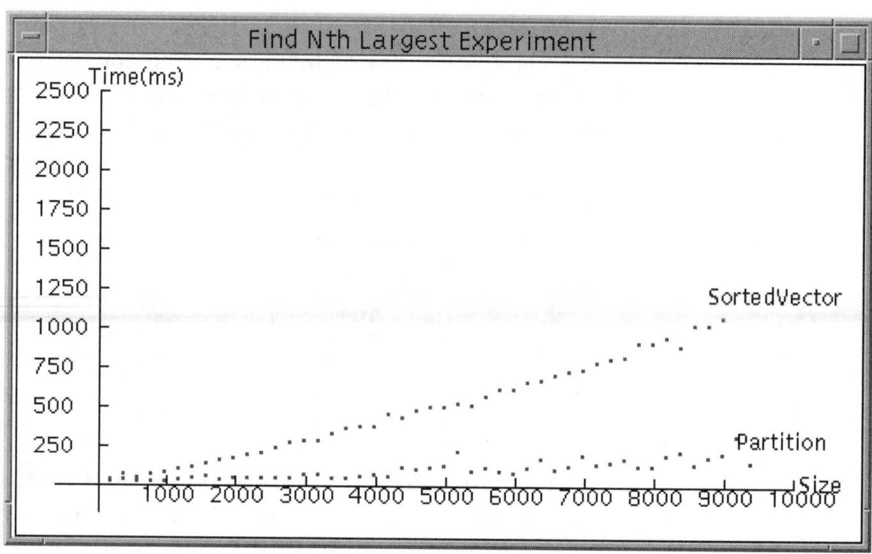

FIGURE 7.5 Experimental Timings of `FindN` Algorithms

So `findNth` is an algorithm that has terrific best-case performance and terrible worst-case performance. How does it perform in the "average" case? Can techniques be used to ensure that the worst-case performance is relatively rare? The answer to the first question is that on average, the `findNth` algorithm performs very quickly. It is possible to prove this analytically; however, the mathematics is complex.

Although a mathematical analysis is always preferable, when it is difficult to obtain, one can at least find some limited supporting evidence by conducting an experiment. One approach would be to randomly create a vector of n elements and then find their median. Timings for this test are shown in Figure 7.5. Note that the timings for the partition algorithm are not uniform, as execution time is heavily dependent on the input distribution, which is random. Nevertheless, they are uniformly better than

EXPERIMENT: EFFECT OF INPUT DISTRIBUTION ON EXECUTION TIME

The experiment reported in Figure 7.5 used an initially random distribution of values and searched for the median. If either of these factors were changed, would the results be similar? Test this by trying different distributions of inputs. If the input is initially sorted increasing and you seek the median, will the execution be fast? What if the input is sorted in decreasing order? How about if you are using the `FindNth` interface to find the *smallest* element in the collection? Does the distribution then make a difference?

the timings obtained from the `SortedVector`, as that data structure must spend the time to first sort the entire vector before it can find the median.

The key to positively ensuring fast performance of the partition algorithm is to try to intelligently select the pivot. Authors have proposed various strategies to do this, including the following.

- Simply use the first element as the pivot. This avoids the need for the initial swap but is a relatively poor choice if the vector is somewhat, but not completely, ordered.
- Select the pivot at random from the set of values.
- Select the pivot as the element in the midpoint of the range of elements (this is the option used in our version of the algorithm).
- Select three elements at random from the range and compute the median (middle) value from these three.

Readers interested in more complete analysis of these, and many other, possibilities can investigate the references cited at the end of this chapter.

7.4.3 Quick Sort

The pivoting algorithm shown in Figure 7.4 is at the heart of an extremely elegant and fast sorting algorithm. The algorithm was named *quick sort* by its originator, C. A. R. Hoare, now of Oxford University. The idea behind quick sort is simple. After one partition step, we have not entirely sorted a vector, but we have made some progress. For example, following the partitioning of the 11-element vector we described in Section 7.4, the vector held the following elements:

< Pivot   Pivot   > = Pivot

2	17	12	10	37	97	46	55	80	42	39

EXPERIMENT: CHANGING THE PIVOT SELECTION

The quick sort algorithm shown here uses the middle element for the pivot. Section 7.4.2 describes various other techniques that can be used, such as selecting a random index position for the initial pivot. Create a variation of quick sort that uses one of these techniques, and compare the running time to the program given in the text. Are there particular input distributions (all equal elements, sorted increasing, sorted decreasing) where your technique is preferable to the original?

Although not sorted, elements are at least closer to their final destination. More important, no elements need be exchanged across the pivot, thus yielding two separate areas that can now be sorted independently of each other. To obtain a full sorting, we simply recursively call the quick sort procedure, in order to sort each of the two subvectors resulting from the partition. This divide and conquer algorithm can be given as follows:

```
private void quickSort (int low, int high) {
    // no need to sort zero or one elements
  if (low >= high) return;
    // select a pivot and partition
  int pivotIndex = (low + high) / 2;
  pivotIndex = pivot(low, high, pivotIndex);
    // then sort two subarrays
  quickSort(low, pivotIndex);
  quickSort(pivotIndex + 1, high);
}
```

To make an algorithm that satisfies the `SortAlgorithm` interface, we simply write a driver that sets the elements in place and calls `quickSort`:

```
public void sort (Indexed data) {
  elementData = data;
  quickSort(0, data.size());
}
```

Figure 7.6 shows a snapshot of the quick sort algorithm in the middle of execution. Note that although it is nowhere exactly sorted, the larger elements have, for the most part, been moved to the right and the smaller elements moved to the left.

As with the `findNth` algorithm, the asymptotic execution time of the `quickSort` algorithm depends in part on how lucky one is in selecting

COMPARING MERGE SORT AND QUICK SORT

It is interesting to compare the merge sort and quick sort algorithms. Both are recursive algorithms, and both operate by repeatedly dividing a vector into smaller and smaller units until a section one element long or less is reached. They differ in the fact that merge sort does very little work before breaking the vector apart and so must spend more time putting it together. Quick sort, on the other hand, does more work (in the pivot algorithm) before the vector is broken apart and thus must spend almost no time in putting it back together.

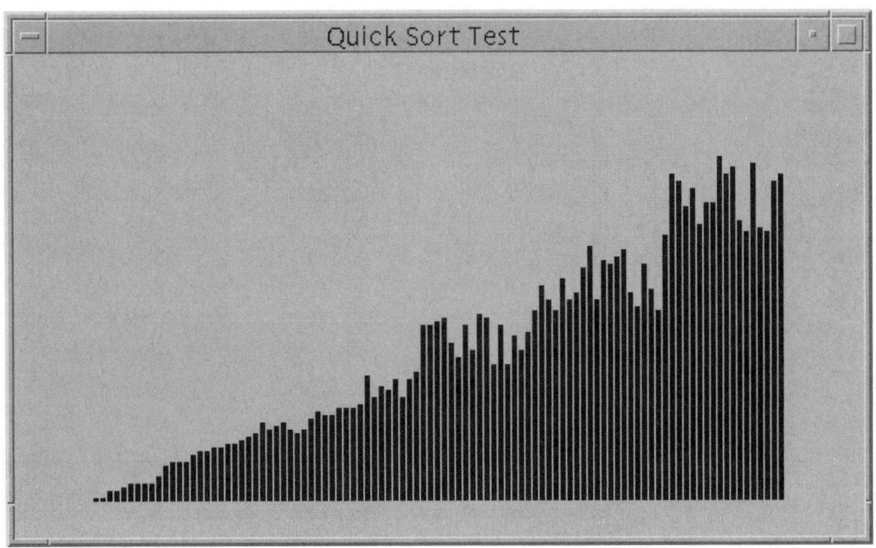

FIGURE 7.6 Quick Sort in Action

a pivot position. The best case occurs when the pivot breaks the vector exactly in half. The recursive calls then sort two arrays of approximately $n/2$ elements. Similarly, each of these is divided roughly in half, resulting in four arrays of approximately $n/4$ elements. The number of times one can divide a vector of size n in half is approximately $\log n$. Because each partition step executes in time proportional to the length of the array, the total time is $O(n \log n)$.

<table>
<tr><td colspan="16">n</td><td rowspan="5">$\log n$</td></tr>
<tr><td colspan="8">$n/2$</td><td colspan="8">$n/2$</td></tr>
<tr><td colspan="4">$n/4$</td><td colspan="4">$n/4$</td><td colspan="4">$n/4$</td><td colspan="4">$n/4$</td></tr>
<tr><td colspan="2">$n/8$</td><td colspan="2">$n/8$</td><td colspan="2">$n/8$</td><td colspan="2">$n/8$</td><td colspan="2">$n/8$</td><td colspan="2">$n/8$</td><td colspan="2">$n/8$</td><td colspan="2">$n/8$</td></tr>
<tr><td></td><td></td><td></td><td></td><td></td><td></td><td></td><td></td><td></td><td></td><td></td><td></td><td></td><td></td><td></td><td></td></tr>
</table>

The other extreme occurs when the pivot is always either the smallest or the largest element. One partition is then empty, and the other contains $n - 1$ elements. In this case, n recursive calls will be performed, and the

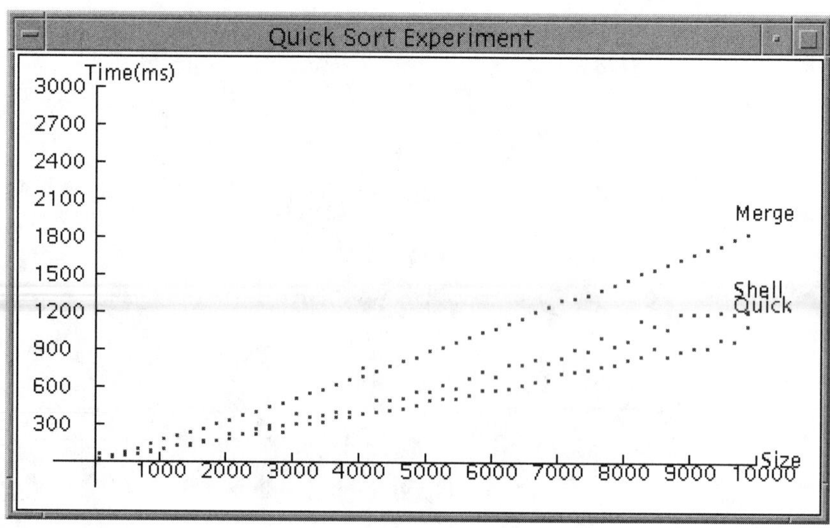

FIGURE 7.7 Experimental Timings of Quick Sort, Merge Sort, and Shell Sort

total execution time is proportional to $n + (n - 1) + (n - 2) + \cdots + 1$. As we have seen, this is $O(n^2)$.

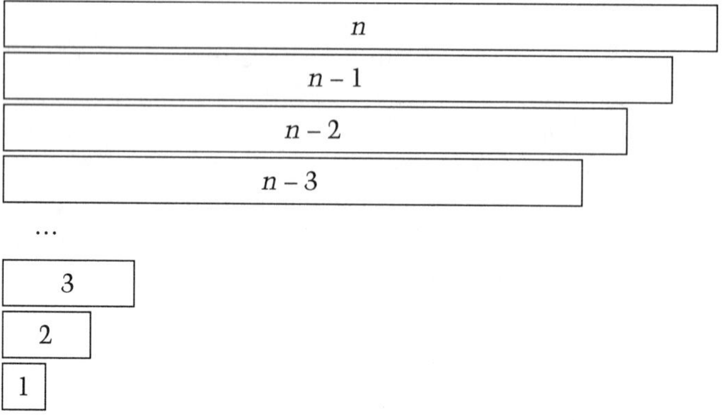

Once again we have vastly different best- and worst-case execution behavior. To determine the average execution time, we can either resort to sophisticated mathematics (see references at the end of this section) or perform empirical timings.[3] A comparison of Shell sort, heap sort, and quick sort on random vectors of length n yields the timings shown in Figure 7.7.

3. This sentence should not be taken to imply that empirical timings are ever a substitute for a rigorous mathematical analysis. Timings can always be skewed by a range of factors, from the input data distribution to the performance of the machine on which they are run. Their only advantage is that they are easy to do.

EXPERIMENT: IMPACT OF INPUT DISTRIBUTION

As we noted in the text, the execution time of quick sort can be very heavily influenced by the distribution of the input values. Will the relative ordering of execution times shown in Figure 7.7 still be observed if the input is an almost sorted vector? What about if it is almost reverse sorted?

Although Shell sort performs surprisingly well, quick sort is generally the fastest algorithm.

7.5 CHAPTER SUMMARY

KEY CONCEPTS

- Divide and conquer
- Binary search
- Sorted vector
- Merge sort
- Partition
- `FindNth`
- Quick sort

Maintaining the elements of a vector in order permits many operations to be performed very quickly. For example, binary search can be used to see whether a particular element is held in the collection. Unfortunately, inserting or removing elements from an ordered vector may require, in the worst case, moving all the elements.

The observation that two ordered collections can be easily merged into one leads to the discovery of a very fast sorting algorithm, *merge sort*. A totally different idea, the technique of partitioning an unsorted vector into those elements smaller than a given value and those elements larger than or equal to the value, leads to an entirely different sorting algorithm, *quick sort*. Partitioning is also the key to finding the *n*th largest element in a collection without first sorting the collection.

Further Information

The binary search algorithm has a notorious reputation for being easy to understand and difficult to get exactly right. In one study [Pattis 88], Richard Pattis examined data structure textbooks and found correct solutions in only 5 of 20 books. In another study, Jon Bentley found that when he asked a group of professional programmers to code the binary search algorithm, 90 percent of them made at least one error [Bentley 86]. Knuth [Knuth 98b] points out that although the first binary search algorithm was published in 1946, the first published error-free reference did not appear until 1962.

The partition, `findNth`, and quick sort algorithms were first described by C. A. R. Hoare [Hoare 61, Hoare 62]. In his ACM Turing Award lecture, published in [Ashenhurst 87], Hoare recounts how the algorithm was first developed in a nonrecursive form, which was extremely difficult to code or to understand. It was only with the introduction of recursion in the language Algol-60 that the elegance of the algorithm became clear.

Sedgewick [Sedgewick 78] provides an extremely thorough analysis of the quick sort algorithm. A slightly more accessible discussion of the relative merits of various techniques for selecting the pivot element is provided by Weiss [Weiss 96]. Several variations are described by Gonnet and Baeza-Yates [Gonnet 91].

Study Questions

1. What does the principle of "divide and conquer" mean? Under what circumstances will it lead to an efficient problem solution?
2. How is binary search an example of the divide and conquer principle?
3. How many steps will it take to perform a binary search of n elements?
4. In what way is a `SortedVector` different from a `Vector`?
5. Could a `SortedVector` be substituted in a program that expected a value of type `Vector`?
6. Which interfaces are supported by the `SortedVector` data abstraction?
7. What are the asymptotic execution times for the four methods described by the `Bag` interface in the `SortedVector` implementation?
8. What is the key insight behind the merge sort algorithm?
9. What is the asymptotic complexity of the merge sort algorithm? Why is it not as fast in practice as one would predict from this figure?
10. What does it mean to partition a vector around a value?
11. Explain how partitioning can be used to quickly find the nth element in a collection. What is the best-case complexity of this algorithm? What is the worst-case complexity?
12. Who discovered the quick sort algorithm?
13. In what way does the quick sort algorithm illustrate the principle of divide and conquer?
14. What is the best-case asymptotic execution time of the quick sort algorithm? What is the worst-case execution time? Under what circumstances will the best time be achieved? Under what circumstances will the worst-case time be achieved?

Exercises

1. Trace the values of `low` and `high` in the binary search algorithm during the course of a search for element 7 in the following vector:

   2 4 5 7 8 12 24 37 40 41 42 43 50 68 67

2. How many elements will be examined in performing a binary search on a vector of 10,000 elements?
3. Suppose that an ordered vector contains two or more instances of the key. Which index will the binary search algorithm return?
4. Suppose that an ordered vector contains a list of numbers. Imagine that we want to find all the values between two endpoints: for example, elements larger than 12 and less than 25. Show how to use the binary search algorithm to do this.
5. Trace the series of recursive calls performed by merge sort during the process of sorting the following vector: 3, 1, 4, 1, 5, 9, 2, 6, 5, 3, 5.
6. A sorting algorithm is said to be stable if two equal elements have the same relative position to each other in the output that they had in the input. Is the merge sort algorithm stable? If so, give an argument why. If not, give an example to illustrate the instability.
7. Using invariants, develop a proof of correctness for the `merge` algorithm in the `MergeSort` abstraction.
8. Students sometimes think that the quick sort algorithm can be speeded up by selecting the first element as the pivot and thereby avoiding the initial swap. Explain why, if the initial data is already sorted or nearly sorted, this is a very bad idea.
9. A proof of the correctness of the `pivot` procedure described in Figure 7.4 rests on establishing the following invariants:

```
private int pivot (int start, int stop, int position) {
  swap(start, position); // swap pivot into start position

  int low = start + 1;
  int high = stop;
  while (low < high) {
    if (test.compare(elementData.elementAt(low),
      elementData.elementAt(start)) < 0)
        low++;
    else if (test.compare(elementData.elementAt(--high),
      elementData.elementAt(start)) < 0)
        swap(low, high);
    // inv: index positions start+1 to low-1 contain elements
    // smaller than the pivot, and index positions high to
    // stop-1 contain elements greater than or equal to pivot
  }
  // inv: position low is smaller than stop, and
  // elements in positions start to low-1 are smaller than pivot,
```

```
    // and elements in positions low to stop-1 are greater than or
    // equal to pivot
    swap(start, --low); // swap pivot back into place
    return low;
}
```

Show that the first invariant is true regardless of the outcomes of the two comparison tests in the loop. Using this, show that the second invariant is true. Remember to also verify the case in which the loop is never executed. Finally, explain why the second invariant is sufficient to prove the correct outcome of the final result.

10. Assuming that the pivot algorithm works correctly, give a simple proof of correctness for the quick sort algorithm.
11. Is the quick sort algorithm stable? If so, give an argument why. If not, give an example to illustrate the instability.
12. Trace the series of recursive calls performed by quick sort during the process of sorting the following vector: 3, 1, 4, 1, 5, 9, 2, 6, 5, 3, 5.
13. What is the execution time of the quick sort algorithm when all elements in a collection are equal? Compare this to the execution time for insertion sort in the same situation.
14. What is the execution time of the quick sort algorithm when the input is already sorted? How would this be different if, instead of the midpoint, we selected the first element as the pivot value?
15. Construct a ten-element vector that makes quick sort exhibit the worst-case $O(n^2)$ behavior when we use the pivot selection strategy presented in this chapter.
16. As described in the analysis of the binary search algorithm, to prove that a looping algorithm will terminate, it is sufficient to find an expression that is integer, positive, and decreases each iteration through the loop. What value can be used to show termination for the pivot algorithm in Figure 7.4?
17. Suppose that we want to find the k smallest elements from a collection of n items. Show how to modify the algorithm in the class `Partition` to do this. What is the expected complexity of your algorithm? For what value of k does it become faster to sort the elements?
18. Although finding the smallest element in a `SortedVector` is fast, removing the element is a relatively slow $O(n)$ operation. Explain why a `FindMax` interface, if we included one in our library, would be an improvement in this regard over `FindMin`.

Programming Projects

1. In many applications, it is useful to be able to set both a lower index bound and a higher index bound for a `Vector`. For example, if one were dealing with values tied to dates, it might be useful to be able to use a range of dates, such as from 1995 to 2003, as the index values rather than being forced to have all index values begin at zero. Create a data type, `BoundedVector`, that supports all the `Vector` operations but that permits the user to specify both a lower and an upper bound as arguments with the constructor.

2. Imagine that we are searching a 10,000-element sorted vector holding values uniformly distributed between 1 and 1,000. If we are seeking element 850, it makes little sense to start the search at the midpoint of the collection, as the binary search algorithm does. Instead, we will probably want to start the search near the index 850. This idea is called an *interpolation search* and in certain situations can be faster than a binary search.

   Like binary search, interpolation search works by reducing the area of search until only one element remains. If we let k_{low} be the key for the low end of the search and k_{high} be the key for the high end, we expect the value we seek to be found at a point roughly $(key - k_{low})/(k_{high} - k_{low})$ through the list. The index value for this element is $low + (high - low) * (key - k_{low})/(k_{high} - k_{low})$. Select this value as the test point; then proceed recursively as with binary search.

   Program an interpolation search algorithm, and test your algorithm on various distributions of values, comparing the running time to binary search.

3. Any ordered data structure naturally suggests a sorting algorithm: Copy the values from a vector into the data structure, then copy them back out. The process of adding them to the data structure will naturally sort them. Using the `SortedVector`, implement a sorting algorithm based on this idea. What is the asymptotic complexity of the `sort` operation for this algorithm? In practice, how does it compare to the sorting algorithms we have seen already?

4. Show how an ordered vector of n elements can be merged with another ordered vector of m elements by copying the values into a new vector of size $n + m$, using $O(n + m)$ operations. Use this idea to show how to support the `Set` interface in the `SortedVector` abstraction. Implement the other three operators in this interface in a similar fashion.

5. A nonrecursive form of quick sort can be written by stacking pairs of indices (lower and upper bounds) that represent sections of the vector

waiting to be sorted. Thus, after partitioning, both the lower and the upper ranges are placed on the stack. At each step of the algorithm, a range of values is removed from the stack and partitioned. Because the `Vector` data type supports the `Stack` interface, we can use a separate `Vector` to hold these values. Implement this algorithm; then compare the execution time to the recursive version.

6. Insertion sort is faster than quick sort for very small collections (say, fewer than 20) and for collections that are almost already sorted. Both of these observations can be used to speed quick sort. One approach is to use insertion sort when the size of the subvector being sorted is smaller than 20. Another approach is to not sort such subvectors at all. This will leave the result of calling quick sort as an array that is only slightly unsorted. A final call in insertion sort can then be used to place the elements into their final position. Code one or both of these alternatives, and experimentally evaluate the execution time in comparison to the quick sort algorithm described in the text.

7. It is sometimes necessary to sort a collection of values that is larger than will fit in memory. When this occurs, the technique known as *file sort* can be used. The file sort algorithm as follows:
   a. First, the original file is read in blocks that are small enough to fit in memory; for example, 1,000 elements each. These are sorted using a conventional algorithm and written out to a temporary file. Number the temporary files t_1, t_2, t_3, and so on, up to t_n.
   b. In this chapter, we have noted how two ordered collections can be easily merged to form a new ordered collection. Elements are read from each file, and the smaller is copied to the output. It is never necessary to have more than two values in memory at any time. Using this technique, show how to merge two temporary files to form a new ordered temporary file that contains their union.
   c. Finally, using the technique you discovered in part (b), create an algorithm that will merge temporary files t_1 and t_2 to get a new file t_{n+1}, then t_3 and t_4 to get t_{n+2}. This continues until there is only one final file, which will be the ultimate result.

   Implement the file sort algorithm sorting lines from a text file.

CHAPTER 8

LINKED LISTS

In Chapter 1, we introduced the idea of a linked list. As in a chain, each link is tied to the next. To get from the beginning of the chain to the end, you must traverse every link.

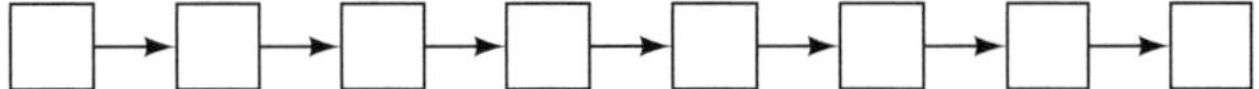

A linked list is often termed a *dynamic* data structure, as opposed to the more static array data type. The term denotes the observation that a linked list can grow and shrink as elements are added to and removed from the collection. An array, on the other hand, is a single fixed block of memory, and the number of elements is set when the array is created, and it cannot be changed. (This limitation is mitigated only slightly with the `Vector` data structure. With a `Vector`, it is still true that the size changes only infrequently as elements are added and removed.)

A linked list is also often called a *sequential* data structure. To access any item, we must move sequentially down the links from the start. An element cannot be randomly accessed from the middle of the collection, as we can do with an array or a `Vector`.

As we did with the vector, we will first examine a program that will use the linked-list abstraction and then proceed to consider various implementation techniques. Assume that we have a file that consists of student name and course name pairs on alternating lines:

```
Chris Smith
Art 250
```

```
Amy Grant
Bus 321
Amy Grant
Art 250
Chris Smith
CS 311
Randy Jones
CS 261
Randy Jones
Art 250
```

From this data, we want to generate two types of lists. First, we want to find the list of courses that each student is taking. Second, we want to find the list of students for each course.

```
students
  Chris Smith
    Art 250
    CS 311
  Amy Grant
    Bus 321
    Art 250
  Randy Jones
    CS 261
    Art 250
courses
  Art 250
    Chris Smith
    Amy Grant
    Randy Jones
  Bus 321
    Amy Grant
  CS 311
    Chris Smith
  CS 261
    Randy Jones
```

Recognizing the symmetry of the situation, we first create a data structure that will represent a name and a list. The name might be a course name and the list of students, or the name might be a student name and the list of courses. Methods are defined to add a new entry to the list and to print the list. Because both students and courses are represented by lists, the elements in each list will themselves be instances of `NameList`.

```
class NameList {
  NameList (String n) { name = n; }
```

```
  public final String name;
  public LinkedList list = new LinkedList();

  public void add (NameList newItem) {
    list.addElement(newItem);
  }

  public void print () {
    System.out.println("\t" + name);
    Enumeration e = list.elements();
    while (e.hasMoreElements()) {
      NameList nl = (NameList) e.nextElement();
      System.out.println("\t\t" + nl.name);
    }
  }
}
```

With the assistance of the NameList class, the program is very simple. As we did with the word frequency program in Chapter 6, lines will be read from the file by using a BufferedReader. As each student/course pair is read, we search the list of students and the list of courses to find the given element. The student is then entered in the course list, and the course is entered in the student list.

```
import java.util.Enumeration;
import java.io.*;
import jds.collection.LinkedList;

class ClassList {
  public static void main (String [ ] args) {
    try {
      LinkedList students = new LinkedList();
      LinkedList courses = new LinkedList();
        // step 1, read list of students and courses
        // add to lists
      FileReader fin = new FileReader(args[0]);
      BufferedReader in = new BufferedReader(fin);
      String studentName = in.readLine();
      while (studentName != null) {
        String courseName = in.readLine();
        NameList student = findEntry(students, studentName);
        NameList course = findEntry(courses, courseName);
        student.add(course);
        course.add(student);
```

```
          studentName = in.readLine();
        }
          // step 2, print the lists
        printList("students", students);
        printList("courses", courses);
      } catch (IOException e) {
        System.out.println("received IOException " + e);
      }

    }

  public static NameList findEntry (LinkedList list, String name) { ... }

  public static void printList (String heading, LinkedList list) { ... }
}
```

The method findEntry will find a named value in a given list, creating a new entry if no corresponding value is located:

```
public static NameList findEntry (LinkedList list, String name) {
  Enumeration e = list.elements();
  while (e.hasMoreElements()) {
    NameList nl = (NameList) e.nextElement();
    if (name.equals(nl.name))
      return nl;
  }
    // not found, make it now
  NameList nl = new NameList(name);
  list.addElement(nl);
  return nl;
}
```

The method printList will print a heading and then each value in a given list. The method is called once to print the list of students and then again to print the list of courses:

```
public static void printList (String heading, LinkedList list) {
  System.out.println(heading);
  Enumeration e = list.elements();
  while (e.hasMoreElements()) {
    NameList nl = (NameList) e.nextElement();
    nl.print();
  }
}
```

8.1 VARIETIES OF LINKED LISTS

Although the concept of linking is common to all linked lists, a number of other issues can affect a design in different ways. Figure 8.1 lists four of the most important design decisions. For each issue, we identify two solutions. These issues are independent of each other, yielding at least 16 designs that can all be called linked-list abstractions. Most of these 16 variations are, in the right circumstances, an appropriate solution to a given problem. The four issues noted in Figure 8.1 can be described as follows:

- **Header object**. Should the list have a special object that maintains the reference to the first link in the list? The advantage of this technique is that there is always an object that "represents" the list. Operations on the list are performed by sending messages to the list header. When a list header is not used, the list is simply represented by the first link. An

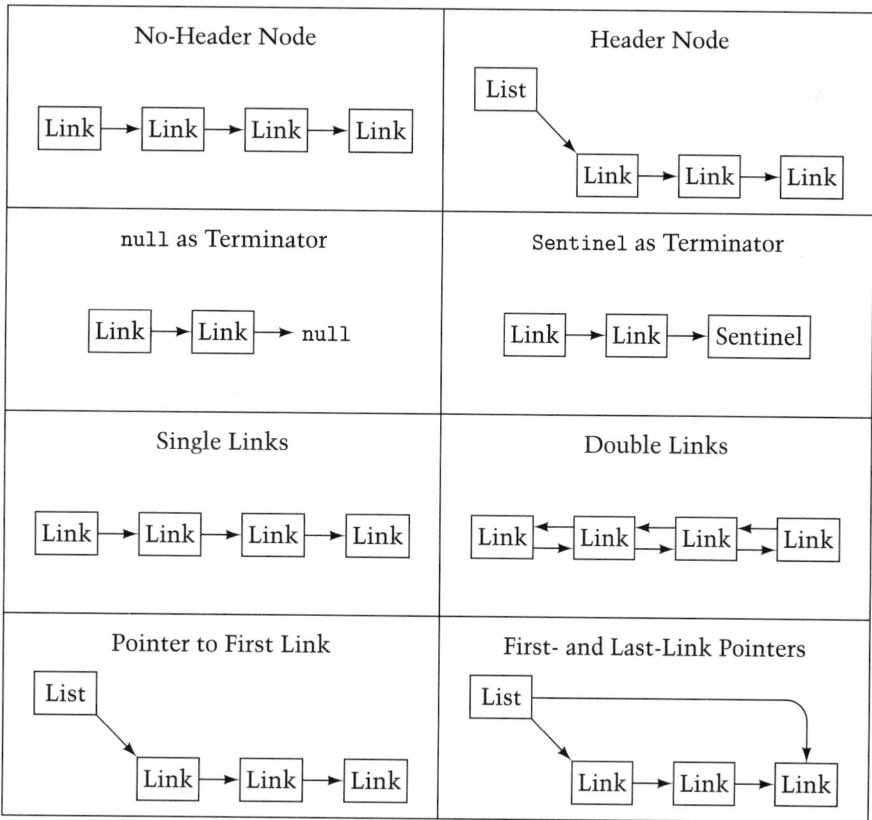

FIGURE 8.1 Design Issues in the Linked-List Abstraction

empty list is represented by a `null`. The disadvantage of having a header node is that there are two types of objects: the list header and the link field.

- **List termination**. How should the chain of links be terminated? One approach, the one we have been using in our discussion up to this point, is to simply use the special value `null` as the link in the last element. Another approach, one that we will see has certain advantages, is to use a designated element as a marker for the end of the list. An element used in this fashion is called a *sentinel*.
- **Single or double links**. Single links permit the list to be traversed in one direction only. It is sometimes useful to be able to move both forward and backward through a list. By maintaining links in both a forward and a backward fashion, we can more easily move through the list in either direction.
- **First- and last-link references**. A characteristic of the list is that efficient (constant-time) access to the elements is possible only at the ends of the list. To access an element in the middle requires traversing all the links in between and thus will vary in execution time, depending on the number of elements in the list. If we keep a reference only to the first link, accessing the last element in the list is slowest of all. By keeping references to both the first and the last links, we can have fast (constant-time) access to both the first and the last elements in the list.

EMBEDDING LINKS IN DATA

In older computer programs, you will often find a simple but not particularly elegant type of linked list. The idea was to simply place the link field inside a data object. For example, suppose that you are manipulating a list of `Card` objects. You could define these as follows:

```
public class Card {
  Card (int is, int ir) { // initialize a new Card
    suit = is; // suit
    rank = ir; // rank
  }

  public Card link; // next Card
  :
}
```

A card is then automatically a link in a linked list. The list consists of a reference to the first card, from which you can get to the next card, and so on. The final card will hold a `null` value in the link field.

Although this approach is easy to implement, it should be avoided, for several reasons. It makes your code very rigid; for example, you cannot move the `Card` abstraction to another program in which `Card`s are not on lists or need to be on more than one list. It confuses issues by combining the `Card`-specific operations with list operations. And finally, you end up duplicating code that you can more easily write once and reuse by using a standard linked-list container.

We will illustrate the range of possibilities by presenting two example implementations of the linked-list concept. The first corresponds roughly to the left column of Figure 8.1. This is a singly linked list, with no header node, using `null` to indicate the end of list. The second corresponds roughly to the right column. This is a doubly linked list with a header node, using a sentinel to mark the end of the list.

We should not give the mistaken impression that the 16 possibilities given by Figure 8.1 exhaust all the variations on the theme of lists. We will present other alternatives in the next chapter and in Chapter 12. Also, the programming exercises at the end of this chapter discuss a few more varieties of lists.

*8.2 LISP-STYLE LISTS

The first linked-list data type we will examine is also one of the oldest. The programming language *LISP*, which was developed in the 1950s, is based on the concept of singly linked lists as a fundamental data type. The language LISP has historically been associated with the computer science field of artificial intelligence, and many AI projects today are still written in LISP.

The fundamental unit in a LISP-style list is a *Cons-cell*, which we can write in Java as follows:

```
public class ConsCell {
  ConsCell (Object value, ConsCell link) { head = value; tail = link; }
  public Object head;
  public ConsCell tail;
  .
  .
  .
}
```

The term Cons is short for *constructor*. A Cons-cell has two parts: a value (the head) and a link to another Cons-cell (the tail). Of course, any recursive definition must always have a base case. In LISP, the base case is the empty list, which we will represent with a `null`.

Before we describe how operations on LISP-style expressions are performed, we should note that LISP is not an object-oriented language. Indeed, it was defined many years before the concepts of object-oriented languages were enunciated. Instead, LISP is what is called a *functional language*. One aspect of what we mean by that phrase is that operations are performed by *transformation* rather than by *modification*. An object-oriented language, such as Java, will consider adding an element to a collection class as something that modifies the collection. In LISP, on the other hand, adding an element to a list is an operation that results in a new list, one in which the new element has now appeared. A new Cons-cell is created and added to the front of the list. The original list will remain unchanged.

```
ConsCell oldList, newList;

  ... // somehow oldList is created

  // add new value to an old list
newList = new ConsCell(newValue, oldList);
```

Note how this technique creates and returns a new list. The functions to see whether a list contains a specific element or to construct the new list that results when an element is removed are perhaps even more characteristic of the functional style of programming:

```
public class ConsCell {
  ConsCell (Object value, ConsCell link) { head = value; tail = link; }
  public Object head;
  public ConsCell tail;

  public boolean contains (Object value) {
    if (head.equals(value)) return true;
    if (tail == null) return false;
    return tail.contains(value);
  }

  public ConsCell remove (Object value) {
    if (head.equals(value)) return tail;
    if (tail == null) return tail;
    return new ConsCell(head, tail.remove(value));
  }
}
```

The method `contains` checks to see whether the value held by the head of the list is the desired element. If so, we have found it and can return `true`. Otherwise, we must examine the rest of the list. If the rest of the list is the empty list, the element cannot be found. Otherwise, we recursively invoke the `contains` method. In the `remove` method, note how a new list is created, link by link, as the recursive calls return from execution. The new list will omit the argument but leave the original list intact.

Of course, a variable that is declared as holding a `ConsCell` may in fact be holding an empty list. For this reason, calls to such functions as contains or remove must always be checked before they can be invoked:

```
ConsCell aList;
.
.
.
if ((aList != null) && aList.contains(aValue))
  .
  .
  .
```

Although we will briefly use the ConsCell class once more in Chapter 18, we will not explore the use of this data structure any further here. The reason is not that the data type is uninteresting; LISP programmers have been exploring the use of this abstraction for decades. Rather, the functional approach to programming required by the use of this data type does not fit well with the Java model of computation. In general, most Java programs that require the use of lists will be better serviced by the data type we will consider next.

8.3 The LinkedList Abstraction

A major disadvantage of the LISP-style lists (besides the fact that they do not fit well into the object-oriented model of Java) is that although they permit constant-time addition and deletion of elements from the front of the list, they do not permit constant-time addition and deletion of elements from the end. We can solve this problem by using a combination of double links and a reference to the last element in the list.

Links in our new abstraction will be represented by the class DoubleLink, which is shown in Figure 8.2. A double link holds an element and a reference to both the next and the previous links:

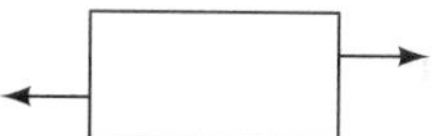

When we combine a series of DoubleLink objects, the result is a sequence of links chained in both directions:

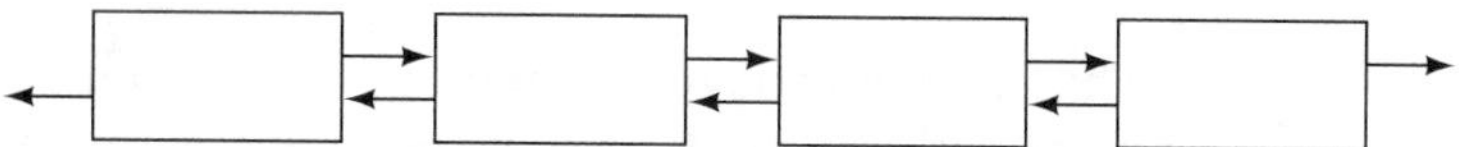

The class DoubleLink provides a number of useful operations. The method insert adds an element to a list so that it will appear immediately before a given link. It does this by creating a new link field, then invoking the method insertLink. The insertLink operation takes care

```
public class DoubleLink implements Serializable {
  public Object value;
  public DoubleLink next, prev;

  public DoubleLink (Object v, DoubleLink n, DoubleLink p)
    { value = v; next = n; prev = p; }

  public synchronized void insertLink (DoubleLink newLink) {
    newLink.next = this;
    newLink.prev = prev;
    if (prev != null) prev.next = newLink;
    prev = newLink;
  }

  public DoubleLink insert (Object newValue) {
    DoubleLink newLink = new DoubleLink(newValue, this, prev);
    insertLink (newLink);
    return newLink;
  }

  public synchronized void remove () {
    value = null;
    if (next != null) next.prev = prev;
    if (prev != null) prev.next = next;
    next = null;
    prev = null;
  }
}
```

FIGURE 8.2 The Class DoubleLink

of changing both the prev link in the current node and the next link in the previous node.

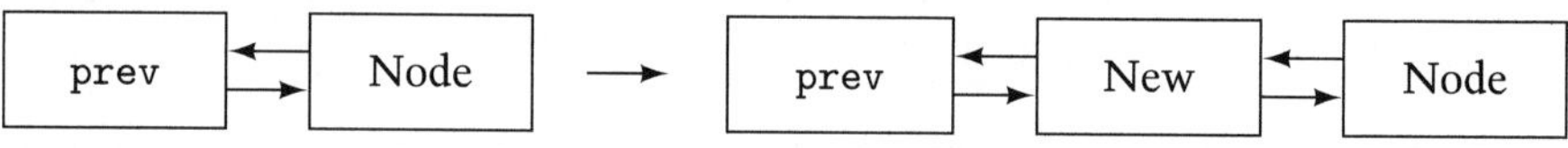

The method remove will remove a link from a linked list. This method changes both the next field in the previous link and the prev field in the next link:

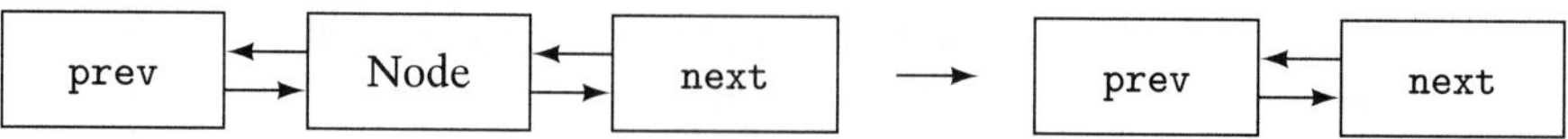

The DoubleLink class will be used not only in the LinkedList class but also in a number of other linked-list abstractions we will examine in subsequent chapters.

The LinkedList class is designed to support two of our abstract data type interfaces: the Deque and the Bag. We will explore how the class operates by examining the implementation of each of the interfaces in turn.

Instances of the class LinkedList serve as a header node, pointing to the first link. In addition, the class maintains a reference to the last link. These two values are held by the fields firstLink and sentinel, respectively.

```
public class LinkedList implements Deque, Bag {
    // constructor
  public LinkedList () { firstLink = sentinel; }

    // data areas
  protected DoubleLink firstLink;
  protected final DoubleLink sentinel = new Link(null);
  protected int elementCount = 0;

  .
  .
  .
}
```

Note that the sentinel field can be declared by using the final modifier, which indicates that once assigned, it will never be reassigned. The firstLink field, on the other hand, does not carry this modifier, as it will change frequently. Both links will be instances of the inner class Link, which will inherit from DoubleLink. We will examine the class Link in a moment. An instance of class Link, one with a null value, will be used as a sentinel to mark the end of the list. Among other consequences, this means that the fields firstLink and sentinel will never be null; as in an empty list, they will both refer to the sentinel:

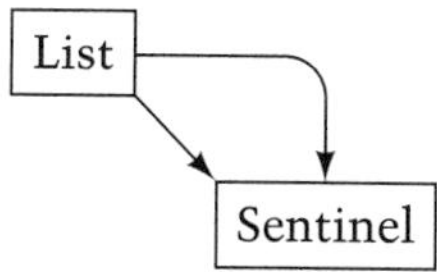

The Collection interface is the class from which both Bag and Deque inherit. Two of the three methods for this interface are isEmpty and size. As we have seen, an empty list is one in which both the first link and the last link point to the sentinel and hence are equal. To count the number of elements in a list, the insert and remove methods in class Link will

The Sentinel Design Pattern

name Sentinel (from the idea of "one that keeps guard").

forces A sentinel can be used whenever a sequence is of indefinite length and it is necessary to know when the end has been reached.

synopsis A sentinel is used to mark the end of a sequence. A simple example is reading values from an input file. A special value, for example −1, might be used to mark the end of the input. In Chapter 6, we used a blank word as a sentinel to mark the end of the vector in the word frequency example. Sentinels can also be used in recursive data structures, such as a linked list. Here, it is necessary to know when we have reached the last element. A special value, such as `null`, marks the last entry. The sentinel in this situation is acting as the base case for the recursive definition.

A list that uses a sentinel is never completely empty. This eliminates special code that would otherwise need to handle an empty-list situation. As we saw in the word frequency program in Chapter 6, sentinels can also make it easier to detect the end of a sequence and to ensure that all elements are processed.

counterforces Any traversal of the data structure must remember to check for the sentinel value. These explicit checks can sometimes be avoided by converting a passive sentinel into an active sentinel.

related patterns The term sentinel usually refers to a passive data value. In object-oriented languages, an alternative is the Active Sentinel (see page 359).

modify an integer variable `elementCount`, which will thus always have an accurate count of the number of elements in the collection.

```
public boolean isEmpty () { return firstLink == sentinel; }
public int size () { return elementCount; }
```

The `Deque` interface involves getting and setting the first and last values. To add an element to the front of the list, we simply `insert` the value in front of the first link. The `insert` method from the class `DoubleLink` would suffice, except that the newly placed element should now become the new first link:

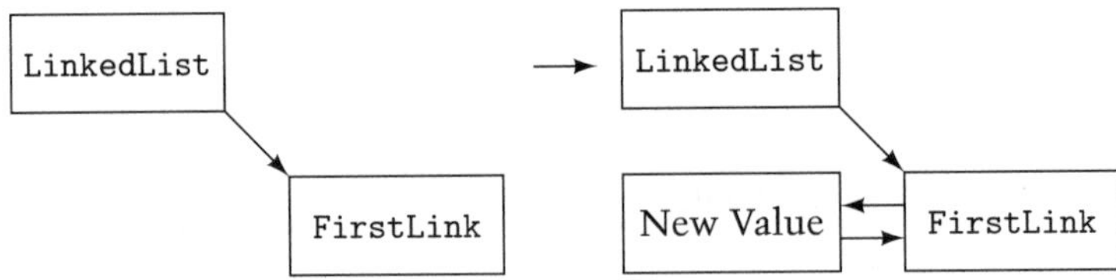

To solve this problem, the class `Link` overrides the methods `insert` and `remove` so that the first link field is always set appropriately:

```
protected class Link extends DoubleLink {

  public Link (Object v) { super(v, null, null); }
```

```
  public void insert (Object newValue) {
    elementCount++;
    Link newLink = new Link(newValue);
    insertLink(newLink);
    if (newLink.prev == null) firstLink = newLink;
  }

  public void remove () {
    if (this == sentinel)  // cannot remove sentinel element
      throw new NoSuchElementException();
    elementCount--;
    if (prev == null) firstLink = next;
    super.remove();
  }
}
```

To add an element to the end of the list, we simply insert it prior to the sentinel:

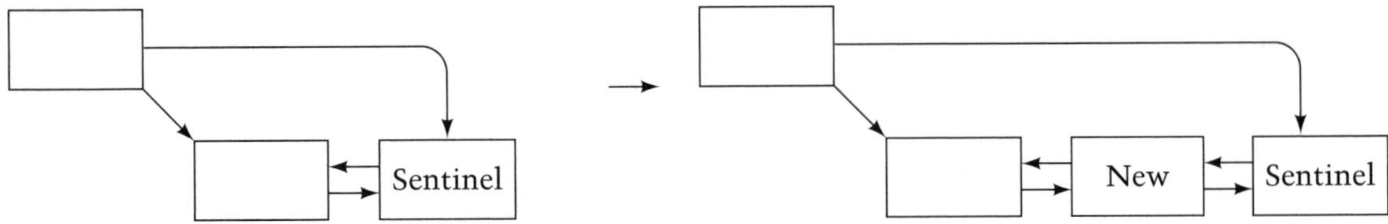

The methods to add an element to either the beginning or the end of a list can now be written using `insert`:

```
public void addFirst (Object newValue) { firstLink.insert(newValue); }

public void addLast (Object newValue) { sentinel.insert(newValue); }
```

To get the first element, we return the value held by the first link. To get the last element, we return the value held by the link immediately

REPLACEMENT AND REFINEMENT IN OVERRIDING

The two methods in class `Link` are an excellent example of the two ways that a method can override a similarly named method in a parent class. The method `insert` uses *replacement*, completely replacing whatever code appeared in the parent class. The method does so because we want to create here an instance of class `Link`, not the `DoubleLink` field created in the original method. The method `remove`, on the other hand, uses *refinement* semantics. As a final step, this method invokes the method in the parent class by using the pseudovariable `super`. Thus, the end result is a combination of the code from the child and the parent classes. Both replacement and refinement are valuable techniques in the correct circumstances.

preceding the last link. Both methods will throw an exception if the list is empty:

```
public Object getFirst () {
  if (isEmpty())
    throw new NoSuchElementException();
  return firstLink.value;
}

public Object getLast () {
  if (isEmpty())
    throw new NoSuchElementException();
  return sentinel.prev.value;
}
```

Removing the first and the last elements is handled by methods from the class `Link`:

```
public synchronized void removeFirst () {
  firstLink.remove();
}

public synchronized void removeLast () {
  if (isEmpty())
    throw new NoSuchElementException();
  sentinel.prev.remove();
}
```

Note that all methods used in implementing the `Deque` ADT are constant-time, or $O(1)$, operations.

The implementation of the `elements` methods uses an instance of an inner class named `ListEnumeration`. This class operates by maintaining a value, named `current`, which moves down the chain of links as elements are accessed. Because it is an inner class, `ListEnumeration` is allowed access to the data fields `firstLink` and `sentinel`. The current element is the value found in the node referenced by `current`:

```
public class LinkedList implements Bag, Deque {

  public Enumeration elements () {
    return new ListEnumeration();
  }
  .
  .
  .

  protected class ListEnumeration implements Enumeration {
    private DoubleLink current = firstLink;
```

```
      public boolean hasMoreElements () { return current != sentinel; }

      public Object nextElement () {
        Object result = current.value;
        current = current.next; // advance to next link
        return result;
      }
    }
  }
```

In an earlier chapter, we noted what problems can arise if one attempts to make changes to a vector while it is being enumerated. A similar problem can arise with lists, and indeed with most container classes. We explore this in more detail in exercise 7. The `LinkedList` abstraction also supports the `visit` method, which can be used to form a Visitor loop (see the earlier discussion in Chapter 6 on the Visitor design pattern.)

The `Bag` interface consists of four methods: `addElement`, `containsElement`, `findElement`, and `removeElement`. When added to a `LinkedList` by means of the method `addElement`, an element is placed at the end of the list, using the same code as for the method `addLast`:

THE ENUMERATION DESIGN PATTERN

name Enumerator (sometimes called an `Iterator`).

synopsis The problem addressed by the enumerator is how to provide access to the elements of a collection without exposing the implementation of the collection.

forces An enumerator is appropriate whenever it is necessary to provide access to a collection of values one at a time.

solution The enumerator is an object that provides a simple and fixed interface (for example, `java.util.Enumeration`) by means of which a client can gain access to the elements of a collection. The enumerator, provided by the developer of the collection, is indeed often an inner class defined inside the collection. Thus, the enumerator is permitted to have knowledge of the internal representation of the class, whereas the client need have no such knowledge.

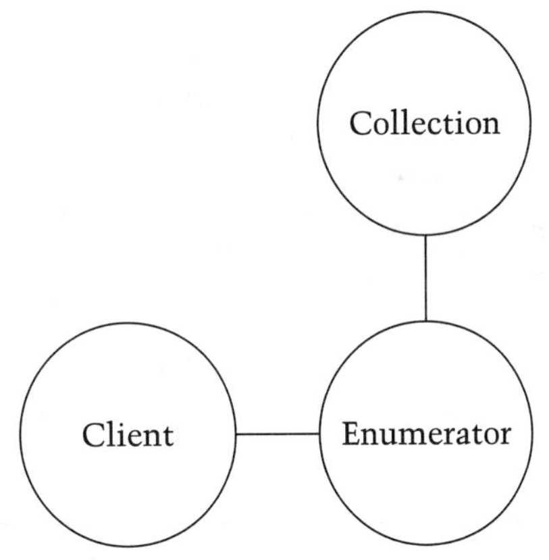

related patterns An alternative to Enumeration is the Visitor design pattern (see Chapter 6).

```
  // the Bag interface
public synchronized void addElement (Object newValue)
  { sentinel.insert(newValue); }
```

To determine whether a test value is held in a list, an `Enumeration` loop cycles over the elements and tests each one. The code for the `findElement` method is similar:

```
public boolean containsElement (Object test) {
  for (Enumeration e = elements(); e.hasMoreElements(); )
    if (test.equals(e.nextElement()))
      return true;
  return false;
}
```

The `Enumeration` loops for these methods can be contrasted with the loop in the method `removeElement`, which uses the link fields directly. This method searches for an element and if found, uses the `remove` method in the class `link` to delete it:

```
public synchronized void removeElement (Object newValue) {
  for (DoubleLink p = firstLink; p != sentinel; p = p.next)
    if (newValue.equals(p.value)) {
      p.remove();
      return;
    }
```

EXPERIMENT: THE COST OF BAG OPERATIONS

Both the `SortedVector` and the `LinkedList` implement the Bag interface; however, they optimize different operations in this interface. The `SortedVector` has a relatively slow addition method but a very fast containment test. A `LinkedList`, on the other hand, has a very fast insertion technique but a relatively slow test for inclusion:

	`SortedVector`	`LinkedList`
`addElement`	$O(n)$	$O(1)$
`containsElement`	$O(\log n)$	$O(n)$
`removeElement`	$O(n)$	$O(n)$

Suppose that we first create a collection of n integers randomly selected between 1 and n and then perform n tests to see whether the collection holds a value, also selected randomly between 1 and n. Using a `SortedVector`, the total time for additions would be $O(n^2)$, whereas the search time would be only $O(n \log n)$. Using a `LinkedList`, the total creation time would be $O(n)$, but the search time would be $O(n^2)$. Which do you think would end up being faster overall?

```
    throw new NoSuchElementException(newValue.toString());
}
```

Because all but the addElement method in the Bag interface require a loop that potentially could enumerate over the entire list, they are each $O(n)$ in the worst case, where n represents the number of elements in the list.

8.4 Application–Asteroids Game

The Asteroids game (Figure 8.3) is an example of a shooting-style video arcade game. The goal of the game is to protect a space station, represented by the line (the rocket launcher) in the lower center. Asteroids, represented here by circles, fall randomly from the top of the screen. The rocket launcher fires a rocket each time the space bar is pressed. When rockets hit an asteroid, it is reduced in size, eventually becoming space dust and disappearing. Each time an asteroid hits the space station, a count is incremented. The goal is to keep the count as low as possible for as long as possible.

Proof of Correctness: LinkedList.containsElement

Although the method containsElement in the class LinkedList may seem so simple that no proof of correctness is necessary, a formal treatment will, nevertheless, permit us to once again illustrate the use of invariants. Recall that an *invariant* is simply an assertion that we place in the body of a program. The invariant should state a property that we expect to be true when control reaches the point of the program where the invariant appears. The points where we place invariants represent important states in the program. By moving from invariant to invariant, we can then form a proof of correctness.

The method containsElement has three important points we can identify:

```
public boolean containsElement (Object test) {
  for (Enumeration e = elements();
                        e.hasMoreElements(); )
    // inv 1: no previous element has matched
    if (test.equals(e.nextElement()))
      // inv 2: current element has matched
      return true;
  // inv 3: no element in list matches
  return false;
}
```

Invariant 1 is encountered while we are iterating over the elements of a list. We may have already seen several elements. The enumerator e is pointing to the latest element:

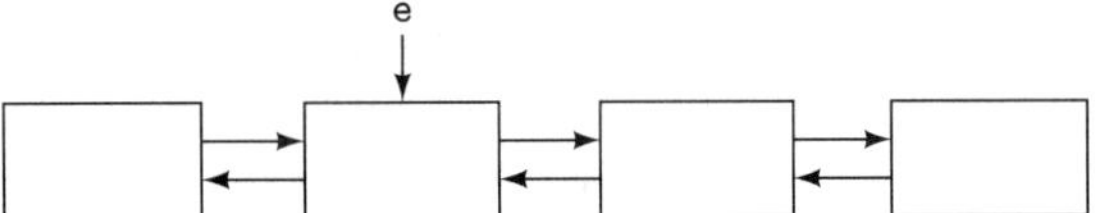

The invariant we want to assert at this point is that no element prior to the current element being referenced by e has matched the test value we are seeking. At invariant 2, we want to assert that we have found a list element that matches the value we seek, and thus we are justified in returning true. The invariant point 3 asserts that we have examined all the elements in the list and that none matches the value we seek. Thus, we are justified in returning false.

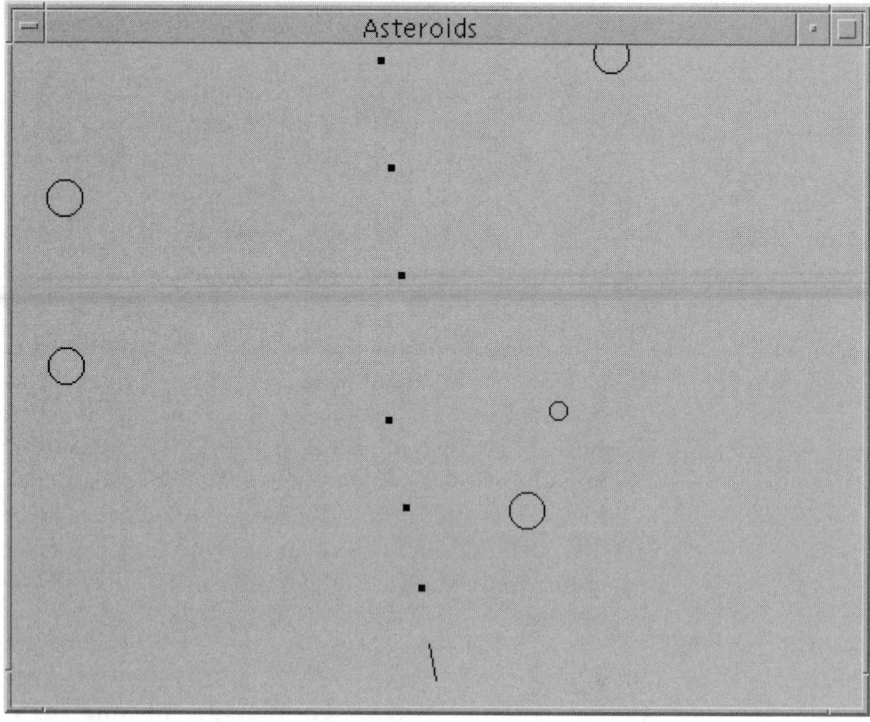

FIGURE 8.3 Screen Shot of Asteroids Game

We can use the implementation of this game as a vehicle to discuss object-oriented design, as well as to illustrate the use of linked lists. Recall from Chapter 1 that a feature of object-oriented systems is that they envision a program as a "universe" of interacting agents. The asteroids game has several obvious candidates for independent objects: the asteroids, the rockets, and the station itself. In addition, all Java programs will have the main class as an object. Because we wish to capture key presses, we will also require a listener to capture and to interpret the system-generated key events.

In the same way that an ADT characterizes a data type by its behavior and not its implementation, object-oriented design focuses on identifying the behavior of the various elements in a system. For example, what can we say is the behavior of an asteroid? Clearly, an asteroid should know its position, it should know how to display itself on the playing surface, it should know how to change when it has been hit, and it should know how to move slightly at each turn of the game. During the development of a program, it is often useful to describe each class on an index card, which will hold the name of the class and a list of responsibilities:

`Asteroid`
• Draw self.
• Respond to hit.
• Move.

This is termed a *CRC* card, for Class, Responsibility, and Collaborator. CRC cards are a useful way of recording design decisions. In addition, once a set of CRC cards has been developed, it is easy to simulate the execution of a program, even before the code has been written. Many logic errors can be caught in this fashion. During an initial design, you should always leave space for writing additional functionality as it becomes identified.

What are the responsibilities of a rocket? A rocket should also move slightly during each time step, perhaps checking to see whether it has then hit any asteroid. If so, it should notify the asteroid that it has been hit. A rocket must also know how to paint itself.

Responsibility-Driven Design

The object-oriented design technique described in this chapter is called *responsibility-driven* design. The idea is to always characterize objects by their responsibility, that is, their behavior. This technique is useful because we almost always know *what* we want to do before we understand *how* to do it. Responsibility-driven design works by simulating a typical example execution (called a *use case* or a *scenario*) and imagining that you already have a working system. You then ask a series of who/what questions. Each time you identify a specific behavior (a what), you ask who will perform the action (the who). In this way, the behavior of each object in the system is established.

Rocket
• Draw self.
• Move.
• See whether hit asteroids.

Finally, what should be the responsibility of a station? The station must know how to move the cannon left or right, fire, draw itself, and check to see whether an asteroid has hit the station.

Station
• Draw self.
• Move cannon left or right.
• Fire cannon.
• See whether hit by asteroid.

If we think about how a rocket will tell whether it hits an asteroid, we decide that we need a separate behavior to determine how close a rocket is to an asteroid. Should the responsibility be given to the rocket or to the asteroid? In symmeterical situations such as this, it can often be difficult to decide. However, we note that the station will also need to know how close it is to an asteroid. This tips the balance. If we put the behavior in the class `Asteroid` (by creating a method that asks "How close are you to (x, y)?"), the same code can be used by both rockets and the station.

Having determined the behavior for the major pieces of our game, we can then design the main application. The principal task of almost any object-oriented main program is to create the graphical display, create the initial elements in the object-oriented universe, and set things in motion. For this program, we need to create the station, create a container (a linked list, naturally) for the collection of asteroids and rockets, and create the listener for system-generated key presses.

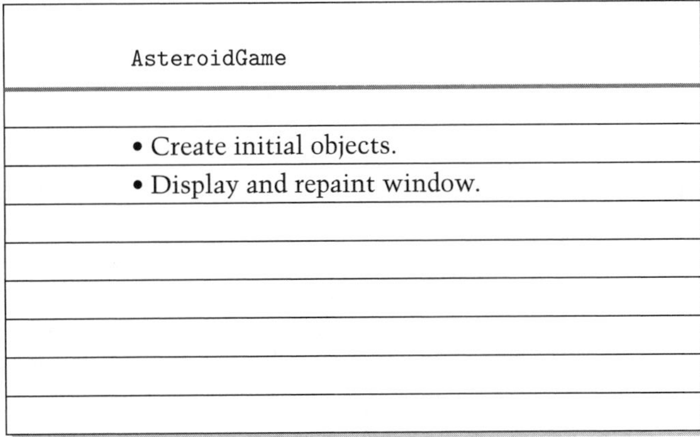

The listener will work closely with the main application class, waiting until a key is pressed. When the space bar is pressed, the listener will tell the station to fire. When a key is pressed that tells the cannon to move, the listener will pass this command on to the station.

WINDOW GEOMETRY

The Java windowing system, like many computer windowing systems, indexes positions starting from the top and moving down and to the right:

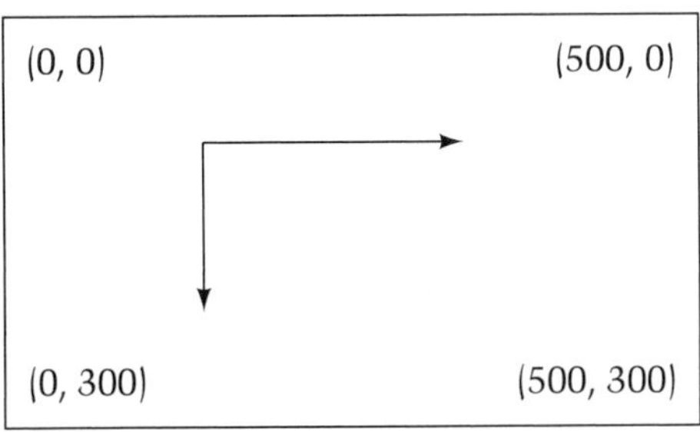

Note that the *y* coordinate is inverted from the way people often think about geometry, with the (0,0) position in the lower left. To move an object down the screen, the *y* coordinate must be made larger, not smaller.

KeyReader
• Listen for key presses.
• If *q*, quit game.
• If cannon move, tell station.
• If fire, tell station.

Having identified the behaviors for the various parts of our universe, we can now start programming. The `Asteroid` will maintain a location in a pair of x and y values and a pair of distances it will use to move each step. By maintaining these as double-precision numbers rather than as integers, we allow for small moves. The locations can be converted into integers when necessary for the printing operations:

```
class Asteroid {
  public Asteroid (double ix, double iy, double idx, double idy)
    { x = ix; y = iy; dx = idx; dy = idy; }

  public double x, y;
  public int size = 20;
  private double dx, dy;

  public void move () { x += dx; y += dy; }

  public void paint (Graphics g) {
    g.setColor(Color.black);
    g.drawOval((int) x, (int) y, size, size);
  }

  public void hit () { size = size - 4; }

  public boolean nearTo (double tx, double ty) {
    // use Pythagorean theorem to determine distance between points
    double distance = Math.sqrt((x-tx)*(x-tx)+(y-ty)*(y-ty));
    return distance < size;
  }
}
```

A rocket is slightly simpler. The rocket will be given the collection of asteroids each time it moves, so that it can check to see whether the asteroid has been hit. If so, the rocket will notify the asteroid. Note that the collection of asteroids is identified with the high-level ADT Bag rather than with the implementation type `LinkedList`. Wherever possible, code should refer to the interface types rather than to the implementation. This makes the code easier to understand (because the ADT definitions are shorter than the description of implementation types) and easier to modify (for example, to replace the data structure used to hold the asteroids with another type of container).

```
class Rocket {
  public Rocket (double ix, double iy, double idx, double idy)
    { x = ix; y = iy; dx = idx; dy = idy; }

  public double x, y;
  private double dx, dy;

  public void move (Bag asteroids) {
    x += dx; y += dy;
    Enumeration e = asteroids.elements();
    while (e.hasMoreElements()) {
      Asteroid rock = (Asteroid) e.nextElement();
      if (rock.nearTo(x, y))
        rock.hit();
    }
  }

  public void paint (Graphics g) {
    g.setColor(Color.black);
    g.fillOval((int) x, (int) y, 5, 5);
  }
}
```

The `Station` is concerned largely with moving the cannon and firing. Because the station does not move, we can save its location in a pair of values that have been declared `final`. A small amount of trigonometry is needed to draw the cannon and to determine the direction of a rocket when it leaves the cannon.

```
class Station {

  public Station (double ix, double iy) { x = ix; y = iy; }

  private double angle = Math.PI / 2.0;
  private int hits = 0;
```

```
 private final double x;
 private final double y;

 public void moveLeft () { angle = angle + 0.1; }
 public void moveRight () { angle = angle - 0.1; }

 public void fire (Bag rockets) {
   double cosAngle = Math.cos(angle);
   double sinAngle = Math.sin(angle);
     // rocket goes same direction as gun is pointing
   Rocket r = new Rocket(x + 15 * cosAngle, y - 15 * sinAngle,
     5 * cosAngle, - 5 * sinAngle);
   rockets.addElement(r);
 }

 public void checkHit (Asteroid rock) {
   if (rock.nearTo(x, y))
     hits += rock.size;
 }

 public void paint (Graphics g) {
   g.setColor (Color.black);
   double lv = 20 * Math.sin(angle); // gun is 20
   double lh = 20 * Math.cos(angle); // pixels long
   g.drawLine((int) x, (int) y, (int) (x + lh), (int) (y - lv));
   g.drawString("hits: " + hits, (int) (x + 10), (int) (y - 5));
 }
}
```

As we noted earlier, the main program is concerned largely with creating the initial object and displaying the output:

```
import java.awt.*;
import java.awt.event.*;
import java.util.Enumeration;
import jds.Bag;
import jds.collection.LinkedList;
import jds.util.CloseQuit;

class Asteroid {
public class AsteroidGame extends Frame {
  static public void main (String [ ] args)
  { AsteroidGame world = new AsteroidGame(); world.show(); world.run(); }

  public AsteroidGame () {
```

```
    setTitle("Asteroid Game");
    setSize(FrameWidth, FrameHeight);
    addKeyListener(new KeyReader());
    addWindowListener(new CloseQuit());
  }

  private int FrameWidth = 500;
  private int FrameHeight = 400;
  private Bag asteroids = new LinkedList();
  private Bag rockets = new LinkedList();
  private Station station = new Station(FrameWidth/2, FrameHeight-20);

  public void paint (Graphics g) {
    station.paint(g);
    Enumeration e = asteroids.elements();
    while (e.hasMoreElements()) {
      Asteroid rock = (Asteroid) e.nextElement();
      rock.paint(g);
    }
    e = rockets.elements();
    while (e.hasMoreElements()) {
      Rocket rock = (Rocket) e.nextElement();
      rock.paint(g);
    }
  }

  private class KeyReader extends KeyAdapter { ... }
}
```

Key presses are intercepted and interpreted by the inner class `KeyReader`. To perform the indicated action, the class passes commands on to the station:

```
private class KeyReader extends KeyAdapter { ... }
  public void keyPressed(KeyEvent e) {
    char key = e.getKeyChar();
    switch (key) {
      case 'j': station.moveLeft(); break;
      case 'k': station.moveRight(); break;
      case ' ': station.fire(rockets); break;
      case 'q': System.exit(0);
    }
  }
}
```

Starting the program, we discover that we have omitted an essential step. Although we have given the rockets and the asteroids the ability to move, nobody has the responsibility of telling them *when* to move. Similarly, we have no way to create new asteroids. We fix this by adding a new method to the main application class:

```
public class AsteroidGame extend Frame {
  .
  .
  .
  private void movePieces () {
      // create a random new asteroid
    if (Math.random() < 0.3) {
      Asteroid newRock = new Asteroid(
        FrameWidth * Math.random(), 20,
        10 * Math.random()-5, 3 + 3 * Math.random());
      asteroids.addElement(newRock);
    }
      // then move everything
    Enumeration e = asteroids.elements();
    while (e.hasMoreElements()) {
      Asteroid rock = (Asteroid) e.nextElement();
      rock.move();
      station.checkHit(rock);
    }
    e = rockets.elements();
    while (e.hasMoreElements()) {
      Rocket rock = (Rocket) e.nextElement();
      rock.move(asteroids);
    }
  }
}
```

We use a random-number generator in various places so that asteroids are not created every move but roughly three-tenths of the time and so that they begin with a random location and random direction.

But where should we call `movePieces`? The obvious place is in a loop after we have created the initial object and called the method `show`. However, if we simply loop, we find the game to be unresponsive: It does not respond to key presses. The reason is that the *system thread*, which is responsible for listening to key presses, is never given any time to execute. We solve this problem by having the main loop of the game move the pieces, schedule the window for repainting, and then *sleep* for a short period of time.

ALL JAVA PROGRAMS ARE MULTITHREADED

Even if the user does not create multiple threads, all Java programs are performing many tasks at the same time. For example, the system must be listening for user interactions (mouse or key presses), repainting the window, and performing memory management (garbage collection) at the same time the user's program is running. The use of the static `sleep` method from the class `Thread` allows the system time to perform these other actions and to catch up with the running program. The integer argument to this method is the number of milliseconds the process will wait before restarting. In Chapter 12, we will examine a program that explicitly creates multiple threads of control.

The key press commands will then be handled while the application is sleeping. (See sidebar on multithreading.)

```
public void run () {
  while (true) { // now move pieces
    movePieces();
    repaint();
    try {
      Thread.sleep(100);
    } catch (Exception e) { }
  }
}
```

With the addition of this loop, we have a reasonably realistic video game. A programming project at the end of the chapter will suggest various improvements that can be made.

8.5 APPLICATION—INFINITE-PRECISION INTEGERS

Some numerical applications, such as dealing with the national debt or factoring 200-digit numbers as part of a cryptographic package, require manipulating integer quantities that are larger than will fit in a normal Java `int`. For these we need a library that will represent infinite-precision integers. As our second application, we will present the beginning of such a library and outline how it can be extended.

The basic idea will be to represent a large integer as a list of smaller numbers, numbers that *can* be maintained in a simple `int` form. In our example, we will divide numbers by units of 1,000. Each link in our list will be a number that is less than 1,000. Because both addition and subtraction operate from the least-significant (smallest) digit to the largest, it will be convenient to store the numbers in our list in a backward fashion. A number such as 72,345,876, for example, will be held in a list of three nodes, as follows:

```
876 → 345 → 72
```

We will begin with a class that can hold large positive integers. The constructor for the class and the procedure to convert our value back into a string can be written as follows:

```
public class LargePositiveInteger implements Comparable {
  public LargePositiveInteger (int start) {
    while (start > 0) {
      digits.addLast(new Integer(start%1000));
      start = start / 1000;
    }
  }

  private LargePositiveInteger (LinkedList d) { digits = d; }

  private LinkedList digits = new LinkedList();

  public String toString () {
    if (digits.isEmpty()) return "0";
    String result = "";
    Enumeration e = digits.elements();
    while (e.hasMoreElements()) {
        // make each block exactly three digits long
      String block = "000" + e.nextElement();
      result = block.substring(block.length()-3) + result;
      }
    return result;
  }

  public LargePositiveInteger add (LargePositiveInteger right) { ... }

  public int compareTo (Object right) {  ... }

  public LargePositiveInteger sub (LargePositiveInteger right) { ... }
}
```

One interesting feature of this class is the inclusion of a private constructor. By declaring as `private` the constructor that takes a `LinkedList` as argument, we ensure that it can be used only from within the class, specifically from within the add method we will describe shortly. The other constructor, one that takes a normal integer as argument, is declared `public`.

We begin with the algorithm for adding two integers. The technique basically follows the approach you learned in grade school, except using units of 1,000 rather than units of 10. At each stage, we are summing two groups of numbers that are each less than 1,000 and are adding in a *carry*. The result is a number that may or may not be larger than 1,000. We divide the result by 1,000 to get the new carry that will be used in the next block, and the remainder after dividing by 1,000 is the result for this position.

0	1	0	Carry
242	476	342	Left
31	332	792	Right
273	809	134	Result
0	0	1	New carry

One complication comes from the problem that one list may be shorter than the second. This problem is easily addressed by appending zeros to one or the other until they are the same length.

```
private void makeSameSize (LargePositiveInteger right) {
  while (digits.size() < right.digits.size())
    digits.addLast(new Integer(0));
  while (right.digits.size() < digits.size())
    right.digits.addLast(new Integer(0));
}
```

The implementation of the addition algorithm is then straightforward:

```
public LargePositiveInteger add (LargePositiveInteger right) {
  makeSameSize(right);
  Enumeration le = digits.elements();
  Enumeration re = right.digits.elements();
  LinkedList result = new LinkedList();
  int sum = 0;
  int carry = 0;
  while (le.hasMoreElements() && re.hasMoreElements()) {
    Integer leftDigit = (Integer) le.nextElement();
    Integer rightDigit = (Integer) re.nextElement();
    sum = leftDigit.intValue() + rightDigit.intValue() + carry;
    carry = sum / 1000;
    result.addLast(new Integer(sum % 1000));
   }
  if (carry != 0)
    result.addLast(new Integer(carry));
  return new LargePositiveInteger(result);
}
```

To decide the relative order of two numbers is similar. We run down the two lists in parallel, comparing elements item by item. A flag named `test` will initially mark that the two values are equal and will be modified only when we find corresponding values that are not equal. When we are finished, the *last* value in which the comparison was changed will determine the result:

```
public int compareTo (Object r) {
  LargePositiveInteger right = (LargePositiveInteger) r;
  makeSameSize(right);
  int test = 0;
  Enumeration le = digits.elements();
  Enumeration re = right.digits.elements();
  while (le.hasMoreElements() && re.hasMoreElements()) {
    Integer leftDigit = (Integer) le.nextElement();
    Integer rightDigit = (Integer) re.nextElement();
    int ld = leftDigit.intValue();
    int rd = rightDigit.intValue();
    if (ld < rd) test = -1;
    if (ld > rd) test = 1;
  }
  return test;
}
```

The subtraction code handles only the case in which the right argument is less than the left, and hence the result is positive. The algorithm is similar to the addition algorithm:

```
public LargePositiveInteger sub (LargePositiveInteger right) {
    // pre: assumes that the argument is smaller than our value
  makeSameSize(right);
  Enumeration le = digits.elements();
  Enumeration re = right.digits.elements();
  LinkedList result = new LinkedList();
  int borrow = 0;
  while (le.hasMoreElements() && re.hasMoreElements()) {
    Integer leftDigit = (Integer) le.nextElement();
    Integer rightDigit = (Integer) re.nextElement();
    int ld = leftDigit.intValue();
    int rd = rightDigit.intValue();
    ld = ld - borrow;
    borrow = 0;
    if (ld < rd) {
      ld = ld + 1000;
      borrow = 1;
      }
```

```
        result.addLast(new Integer(ld - rd));
    }
    return new LargePositiveInteger(result);
}
```

What is surprising is that these three procedures are all that is necessary to implement addition and subtraction for all infinite-precision numbers. To create a number package, numbers will be represented by an instance of class `LargeInteger` in sign/magnitude form. An internal Boolean will keep track of the sign, whereas a `LargePositiveInteger` will hold the magnitude. We have seen the algorithm for the addition of two positive integers, as well as the technique used to subtract a smaller number from a larger one. Subtracting a larger positive number from a smaller one is the same as inverting the subtraction and changing the sign on the result. Adding a positive number to a negative one is the same as subtracting the second from the first, and so on. In this fashion, all the operations can be provided.

8.6 Chapter Summary

Key Concepts

- Linked list
- Link
- Sentinel
- Replacement overriding
- Refinement overriding
- Responsibility-driven design
- CRC cards

A linked list is a dynamic data structure that will grow and shrink as elements are added and removed. Values in a linked list are stored in links: small objects that each maintain one element and a reference to the next link.

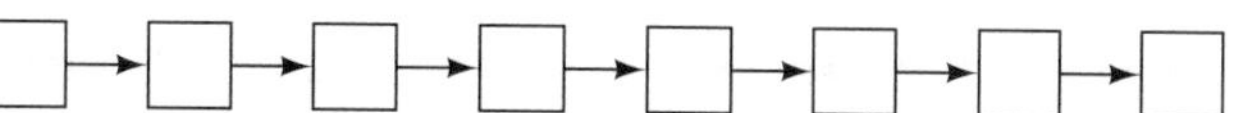

A linked list is also a sequential data structure. This means that to access any element, it is necessary to move down a chain of links, starting from the first. The `LinkedList` data structure implements two of our fundamental ADTs: the `Bag` and the `Deque`. This data structure provides rapid (constant-time) insertion into the collection, but search time is linear.

In this chapter, we also introduced a powerful design technique for creating object-oriented applications. This design technique is termed *responsibility-driven* design (RDD). Using RDD, objects are first characterized by their behavior, in the same way that an ADT specifies the behavior of a data structure. By simulating an imaginary application, the programmer uncovers the behavior of various parts of a system, recording the information on a CRC card. The CRC cards can then be used as a specification in the development of each object.

Further Information

The design technique described in Section 8.4, known as *responsibility-driven design*, was first described by Rebecca Wirfs-Brock [Wirfs-Brock 90]. CRC cards were developed by Kent Beck and Ward Cunningham [Beck 89]. A book-length treatment of CRC use is Bellin [Bellin 97].

Study Questions

1. Although sometimes used, why in general is it not a good idea to create a linked list by storing a link field directly in a data object?
2. What does it mean to say that a list uses a header object node?
3. What is a sentinel?
4. How does a doubly linked list differ from a singly linked list? What are the advantages of double links? What are the disadvantages?
5. What is the advantage of maintaining a reference to the last link in a linked list, as well as to the first link?
6. In what programming language are singly linked nodes called Cons-cells found?
7. What interfaces does the `LinkedList` class support?
8. What is the difference between overriding using replacement and overriding using refinement?
9. What special cases are avoided by the use of a sentinel in the `LinkedList` class?
10. The `LinkedList` method `containsElement` uses an enumeration loop, whereas the method `removeElement` references the links directly. What are the advantages and disadvantages of these two techniques?

Exercises

1. Show how to create a LISP-style list that contains the four numbers 3, 6, 2, and 7 in that order.
2. Having created the list in the previous exercise, show the sequence of recursive calls and their result that will occur when we create a new list in which the element 2 has been removed.
3. Imagine an instance of `DoubleLink` in the middle of a set of three similar links. Draw a picture that illustrates the state of all data fields

following each statement executed in the method `insertLink`. Do the same for the method `insert` in the class `LinkedList`.

4. Repeat the previous problem, this time using the method `remove`.
5. What will happen if you invoke the `removeFirst` operation on an empty list? Why must the `removeLast` method explicitly check for the empty list condition but not `removeFirst`?
6. Fill in the following table with the asymptotic execution time for the various operations in the `Bag` interface for the class `LinkedList`. For each entry, indicate whether the asymptotic time represents *all* cases, the *worst* case, or the *expected* (or average) case.

Operation	**Execution Time**
`addElement(v)`	$O(\_)$
`containsElement(v)`	$O(\_)$
`findElement(v)`	$O(\_)$
`removeElement(v)`	$O(\_)$

7. One should never make changes to a collection while it is being accessed by an `Enumeration`. To see what problems can occur, consider the following program, which will place nine items into a linked list, then loop over the list and print them out. Along the way, one item is deleted. Without executing the program, what do you expect will be the outcome? After you have made your prediction, execute the program and observe the result. Can you explain what has occurred?

```
public static void main (String [ ] args) {
  LinkedList lst = new LinkedList();
  for (int i = 1; i <= 9; i++)
    lst.addLast(new Integer(i));
  Enumeration e = lst.elements();
  while (e.hasMoreElements()) {
    Integer v = (Integer) e.nextElement();
    if (v.intValue() == 4)
      lst.removeElement(new Integer(5));
    System.out.println("Value is " + v);
  }
}
```

8. Could `removeElement` in the `Bag` interface for the class `LinkedList` be implemented by using an `Enumeration`? If so, show the code. If not, explain why not.

9. Using invariants, prove the correctness of the `removeElement` method in the class `LinkedList`.
10. Give an implementation of the `equals` method for class `LinkedList`. Two collections will be equal if they have the same elements, regardless of their ordering. What is the complexity of this task?
11. Is it possible to add methods to the `LinkedList` class so as to support the `Indexed` interface? What is the complexity of the method `elementAt`? How does this compare to the complexity of the same operation in class `Vector`?

Programming Projects

1. Although the LISP-style lists described in Section 8.2 are not particularly object-oriented, we can make them more so by adding a header node to surround the `ConsCell` values. Using this idea, create a class `SList` that satisfies the `Bag` interface and that internally will use the operations provided by the `ConsCell` class to implement the `Bag` operations. Include creating an enumerator for your data type.
2. Add methods to the data type you developed in the previous project so that it can be used like a stack.
3. Modify the data structure you created in project 1 so that it keeps a reference to the last link in the list. (So now the data type can be described as a list with a header node, `null` as terminator, single links, and a reference to the final link.) Can you now implement the `Deque` interface? Which operations are easy to implement? Which are difficult?
4. Try writing the `LinkedList`, using a `null` as the terminator for links. What special cases must now be handled that are not treated as special cases in the code given in the text?
5. Modify the `LinkedList` abstraction so that it will support the `FindMin` interface. What is the asymptotic complexity of the operations you must add?
6. A number of operations could be added to our `LinkedList` abstraction:
   a. Add a constructor that will take as argument a `Collection`, and initialize the list with the elements from the collection.
   b. Modify the class so that it will support the `Cloneable` interface, and produce a copy of a list in response to the method `clone`. Contrast this method with the code for the first part. What are the advantages and disadvantages of each?
   c. Add a method, `swap`, that will, in constant time, swap the contents of a `LinkedList` with an argument list.

d. Add a method, `append(LinkedList)`, that will, in constant time, append the elements of the argument linked list to the receiver list by reusing the `Link` fields in the argument. The argument list is then emptied, so that after the call, it will have no elements. Why is the latter condition necessary?

e. A shuffle-merge of two lists interleaves the elements, first one from the receiver list, then an element from the argument, then the second from the receiver, and so on. As with the `append` method, this can be done without creating any new link fields, as long as the argument list is emptied after completion of the operation. What should happen if the receiver has fewer elements than the argument list? What if it has more?

f. Suppose that the elements of a list are stored in ascending order. Write a method to merge with another such list so that the resulting list is also in ascending order.

g. Add a method, `unique`, that will replace repeated sequences of a single element by a single occurrence. For example, the list (2 3 3 1 1 1 5 5 2 2) would become (2 3 1 4 2).

h. Add a method that will reverse the elements in a linked list without creating any new `Link` nodes. What is the asymptotic complexity of your procedure?

7. Programming project 5 in Chapter 6 described the `Iterator` interface. Explain how the class `ListEnumerator` could be modified so as to support this interface. What problems are caused by the introduction of the `remove` method?

8. In our `LinkedList` abstraction, the `prev` reference in the first link is unused. Rather than use a sentinel, a *circular list* links the previous reference from the first link to the last node in the list and the next reference from the first link to the first node in the list. Show that we can then eliminate the reference to the last element and still have efficient (constant-time) methods to support the `Deque` interface. What operations become more difficult using this structure?

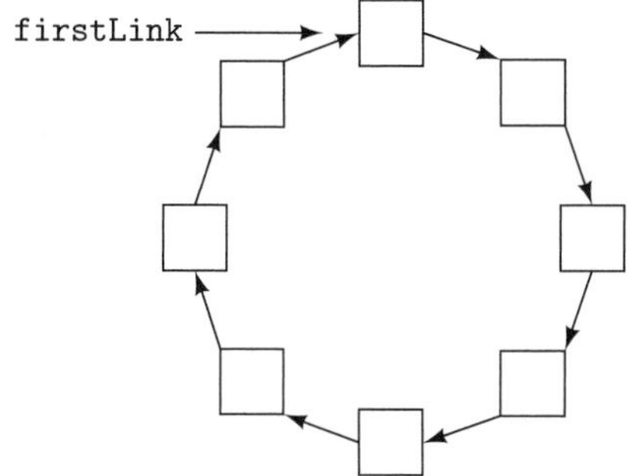

9. The asteroid game described in Section 8.4 can be improved by adding a number of features:
   a. Asteroids and rockets that move out of the playing window should be removed from their respective lists.
   b. The game should terminate rather than run forever. For example, the game can terminate when the hit count reaches a certain limit. Using the system timer (see the `TaskTimer` class in Section 4.5), you can discover the amount of time taken to reach the limit and award points for the longest time.
10. In a famous fable, a servant does a favor for the king. When the king asks what reward he would desire, the servant produces a chessboard and asks for one grain of rice to be placed on the first square. The second square should have twice as many as the first. The third square should have twice as many as the second one, and so on.

    If we try to use an `int` value to compute the number of grains of rice that the last (or sixty-fourth) square will contain, we quickly overflow the number size. However, using the fact that a number can be doubled by adding it to itself (that is, $2 \times x$ is the same as $x + x$), we can compute this value, using nothing more than the addition operator provided by `LargePositiveInteger`. Use this idea to determine how many grains of rice the servant will receive in the last square and how many grains he will receive in total.
11. Finish the infinite-precision number package described in Section 8.5 by writing the class `LargeInteger` as described. Your class should be able to handle arbitrary addition and subtraction of large integers. Multiplication of large integers can be handled in two steps. First, write a procedure to multiply a large positive integer by a primitive integer value (that is, less than 1,000). Multiplication of two infinite-precision integers is then performed as a series of multiplications by primitive `int`s and additions. The product $10{,}242 \times 3{,}673$, for example, can be computed as $(10{,}242 \times 3) \times 1{,}000 + 10{,}242 \times 673$. Note that to multiply an intermediate result by 1,000, it is necessary only to add a zero entry to the end of the list.
12. Chapter 4 described some of the objectives a good set of test cases should possess. How would you go about testing the infinite-precision number package? Write a harness program and execute the code, using your test values.

CHAPTER 9

LIST VARIATIONS

Just as Chapter 7 presented a number of variations on the `Vector` data type discussed in Chapter 6, this chapter discusses some of the more important variations on the theme of linked lists.

9.1 SORTED LISTS

In Section 7.2, we saw that maintaining the elements of a collection in sequence could yield a dramatic improvement in the execution time of certain operations. Ordering the elements of a vector, for example, enabled the use of the binary search algorithm to locate a value. This reduced the time to search for an element from $O(n)$ to $O(\log n)$.

Keeping the elements of a linked list in sequence is also a useful technique but for an entirely different reason. Ordering does not, by itself, change the fundamentally sequential nature of the list, so discovering whether a value appears in the list is still a task that requires $O(n)$ operations. (In Sections 9.2 and 9.3, we will discuss two approaches to improving the speed of searching a linked list.) But an important feature of a list is that elements can be added to the middle of the structure in constant time. When we combine this feature with ordering, we enable the creation of very fast algorithms for merging two collections. These will all be described in Section 9.1.1, after we have developed some of the basic features of the sorted list. Later, in Chapter 18, we will show how to extend this to other traditional set operations of union, intersection, and difference.

The class SortedList is built on top of a LinkedList, in much the same way that the SortedVector is built on top of the Vector data type:

```
public class SortedList implements Sorted, Bag, FindMin {

  public SortedList () { test = new DefaultComparator(); }

  public SortedList (Comparator t) { test = t; }

  private LinkedList elementData = new LinkedList();
  protected Comparator test;
  .
  .
  .
}
```

As with the SortedVector, the implementation of most of the methods will be handled by simply invoking the similar operation from the underlying list. An exception is the addElement operation, which must ensure that the new element is inserted in the correct location:

```
public void addElement (Object newElement) {
  DoubleLink ptr = elementData.firstLink;
  while (ptr != elementData.sentinel) {
      // skip over smaller elements
    if (test.compare(newElement, ptr.value) < 0) {
      ptr.insert(newElement);
      return;
    }
    ptr = ptr.next;
  }
  ptr.insert(newElement); // add to end
}
```

To perform an insertion, the method accesses the link fields of the underlying list directly. This is permitted, as the SortedList and the LinkedList data types exist in the same package, and the Link structures were declared as protected in the class LinkedList.[1] However, adding an element has now become much more costly. Whereas the addElement method was $O(1)$ in the LinkedList class, here we may iterate over almost the entire list before we locate the appropriate point for an insertion. Thus, the addElement operation is now $O(n)$ worst case.

1. Readers familiar with C++ will note the different meanings of the modifier protected. In C++, protected permits access only to child classes, and thus we would need to declare SortedList as a friend to get the effect we want here.

As was true with sorted vectors, supporting the `FindMin` interface is easy, as the minimum value is found at the front of the list. The `addElement` method we have already handled; the other two methods are as follows:

```
  // FindMin operations
public Object getFirst () { return elementData.getFirst(); }

public void removeFirst () { elementData.removeFirst(); }
```

9.1.1 Fast Merge

As we noted at the beginning of Section 9.1, a major reason for interest in the `SortedList` data structure is that it provides the ability to rapidly combine elements from two collections into one. For example, suppose that we are attempting to merge the elements of the following two lists:

2	4	6	8	10	12	15

1	1	3	7	9	13	14

To do this, we can simply walk down the two lists in parallel, for each element in the first list inserting the values that are smaller from the second list:

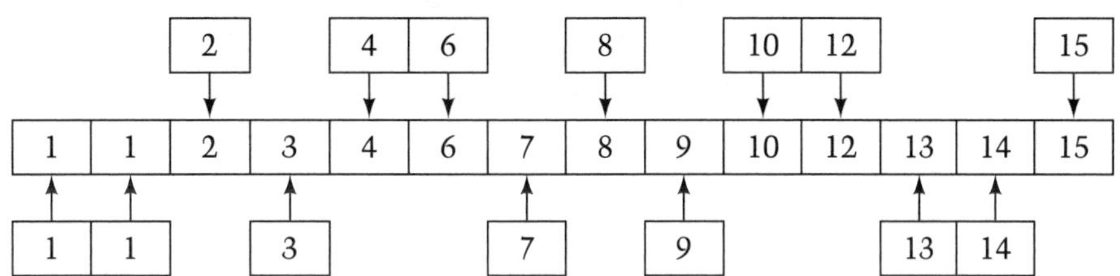

The method `mergeWith` implements this task:

```
public void mergeWith (Sorted newSet) {
  DoubleLink ptr = elementData.firstLink;
  for (Enumeration e = newSet.elements(); e.hasMoreElements(); ) {
    Object newElement = e.nextElement();
    while (true)
      if (ptr == elementData.sentinel)
        { ptr.insert(newElement); break; }
      else if (test.compare(ptr.value, newElement) < 0)
        { ptr = ptr.next; }
```

```
        else
          { ptr.insert(newElement); break; }
    }
}
```

Note that this algorithm makes a simple linear traversal of each list, one using the `Enumeration` interface and one using the link fields. If n elements are in one collection and m elements in the other, the entire merge operation is $O(n+m)$. We usually simplify this description by saying that the operation is $O(n)$, where n is the number of elements in the *resulting* collection. A proof of correctness for `mergeWith` is developed in exercise 2.

9.1.2 Execution Timings for Merge Operations

Although sorted vectors can also be used to rapidly merge two collections (see programming project 4 in Chapter 7), ordered lists generally have better performance. This is shown in Figure 9.1, which gives execution timings in an experiment in which two ordered collections of size n are first merged, and then the intersection of the second is formed with the first. As expected, both ordered vectors and ordered lists have linear time performance, but the list version is in practice slightly faster.

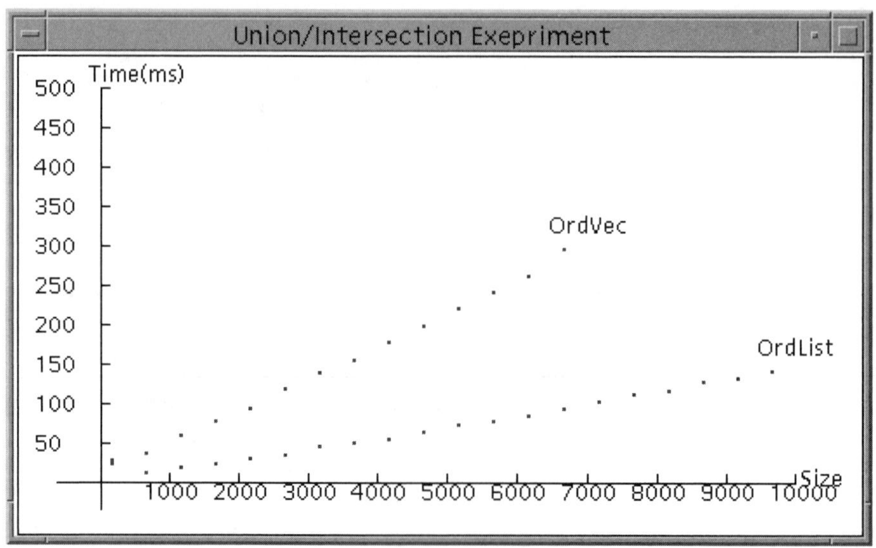

FIGURE 9.1 Execution Timings of Merge Operations

* 9.2 Self-Organizing Lists

In some situations that involve searching a list, the distribution of requests is not uniform, and some values will be sought much more frequently than others. Telephone companies use this principle, for example, when they place frequently referenced numbers, such as governmental offices, in a special section near the front of a telephone directory. In a similar fashion, a linked list can improve on the sequential nature of a search for an element by placing it near the front of a list.

But what if you know that searches will have this nonuniform property but you cannot predict which elements will be the most frequently requested? One common approach is to assume that when an element is requested, it has a high probability of subsequently being requested again. We can exploit this property by always moving an element to the front of a list on a successful search. A data structure that tries to improve *future* performance based on current usage is said to be *self-organizing*.

To implement the self-organizing principle, we need only create a subclass of `LinkedList` and override the `containsElement` method:

```
public class SelfOrgList extends LinkedList {

  public boolean containsElement (Object testElement) {
    for (DoubleLink ptr = firstLink; ptr != sentinel; ptr = ptr.next) {
      if (testElement.equals(ptr.value)) {
        ptr.remove(); // move to front
        addFirst(testElement);
        return true;
      }
    }
    return false;
  }
}
```

Use Inheritance or Not?

It is useful to consider why inheritance is the appropriate mechanism to use here, whereas we used composition for the earlier `SortedList` data type. Both mechanisms create a new data abstraction by leveraging from an earlier software component. But the key insight is that the self-organizing list does not reduce the number of operations provided by the underlying container; indeed, in this case, it does not change it at all. A `SortedList`, on the other hand, is needed to limit access to many of the `LinkedList` operations that were not appropriate for the new data abstraction.

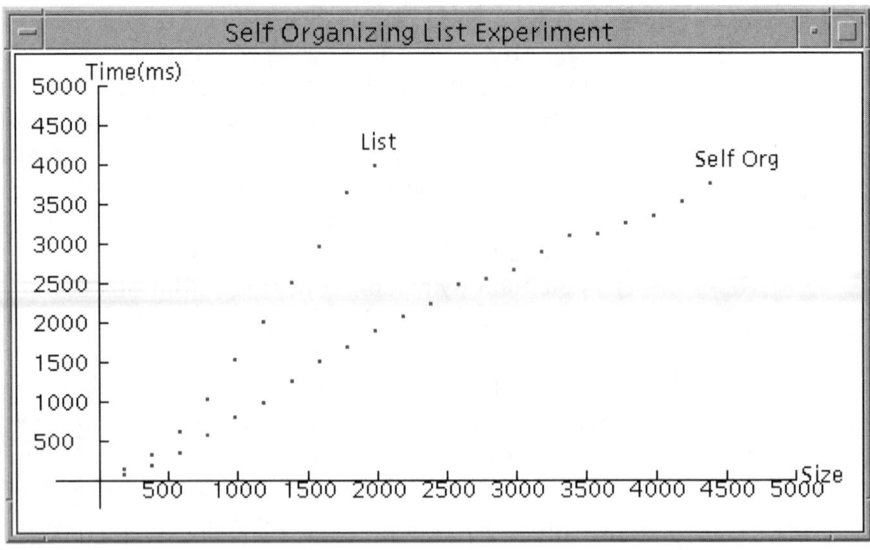

FIGURE 9.2 Search Timings for Self-Organizing Lists

To measure the effectiveness of this concept, we need to artificially create a series of requests in which certain elements will appear repeatedly. One approach is to create a list of *n* random elements and then perform *n* tests for inclusion but on every seventh test ask for the number 42. (These numbers were selected arbitrarily and have no intrinsic meaning.) If we compare the running time of the search process under these assumptions to the regular `LinkedList`, we get timing figures such as are shown in Figure 9.2.

Of course, the improvements obtained through the use of the self-organizing list are possible only when the series of requests fit a very particular pattern. In the next section, we will examine a different technique, one that will speed up the search for values in much more general situations.

EXPERIMENT: FINDING THE LIMITS OF SELF-ORGANIZATION

These experimental results seem to show that the principle of self-organization is useful when every seventh request repeats an earlier request. What happens if this ratio is changed? What would happen if, instead, we artificially made every thirtieth request match an earlier one? At what point does the overhead of moving the elements outweigh the benefits?

*9.3 Skip Lists

The major problem with the linked list as a data structure is the property of sequential access. To see whether an element is contained in a list requires starting from the beginning and examining every value until the element is found or the list is exhausted. Even keeping the list in order is seemingly of little help. Why? Why can't we perform something similar to binary search on a linked list?

To see why, note that to perform a binary search would require a link into the middle of a list, something we normally do not have:

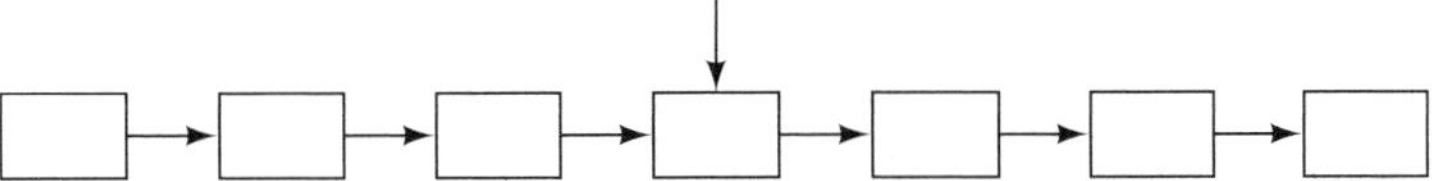

But such a link would give us only the first step in our search. To make the next step, we would need links into the middle of each subgroup:

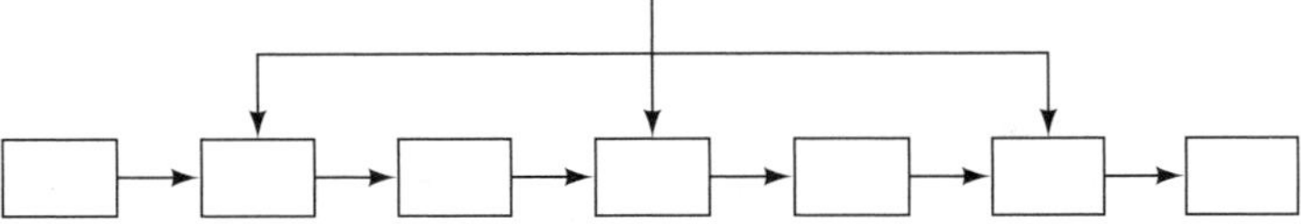

And so on until we reached links to individual elements:

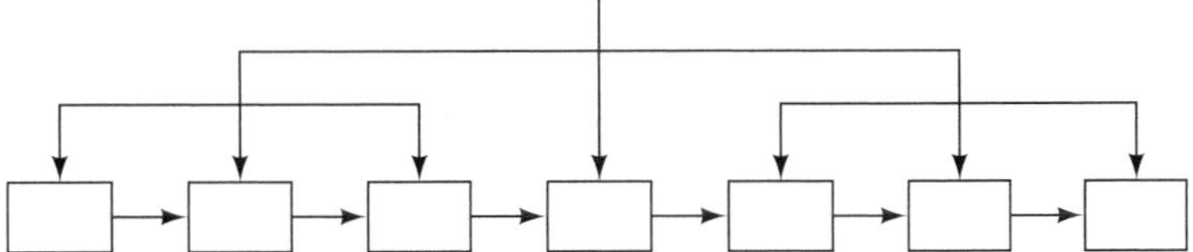

It would be possible to create such a hierarchy of links, but the work required to keep the links up-to-date as elements were added and removed would almost certainly overwhelm any benefits the links would provide. The `SkipList` data structure gets around this problem by *not* being precise and instead relying on randomization and chance.

The idea of the skip list is very simple. Elements are stored in an ordered list. Overlaying the list will be a hierarchy of other ordered lists. Nodes in these auxiliary lists will have an additional field that will point downward to a link in the next-level list or ultimately to a node in the lowest-level list that holds the element. These auxiliary lists will be arranged so that each level will have, on average, approximately half the number of elements of the list below it. As with the LinkedList abstraction, each list will have a right-hand sentinel. A typical list might be the following:

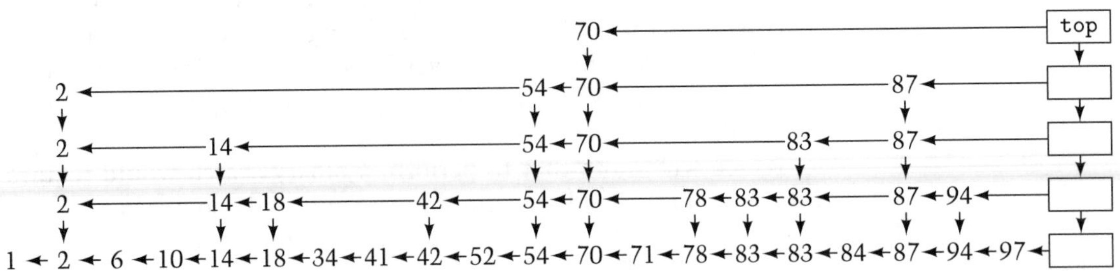

The SkipList data abstraction maintains two internal data fields. The field bottom points to the linked list in which the lowest-level elements are stored. Because we will use the LinkedList data abstraction for this collection, determining the size of the collection and iterating over the elements can be performed by using the methods in this class. The variable top will point to the right-hand sentinel for the highest-level list.

To see how the skip-list links are maintained, imagine that we want to add the element 38 to the preceding structure. We begin at the list referenced by top. The slideLeft operation traverses this list backward as long as the values in the list are greater than or equal to the new element. When this process stops, we have the location where 38 could be inserted into the top-level list without violating the ordering of elements:

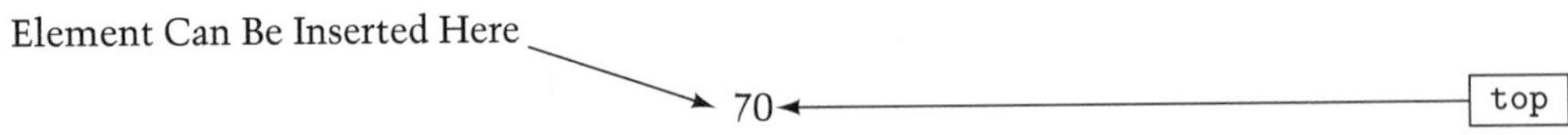

Because we are not at the bottom, we drop down one level. But although we know where the element should be inserted in the upper list, the node found in the down link may not be the valid location for the insertion in the next level down. So once again, we perform a slideLeft operation, to locate the proper location for insertion in the new level.

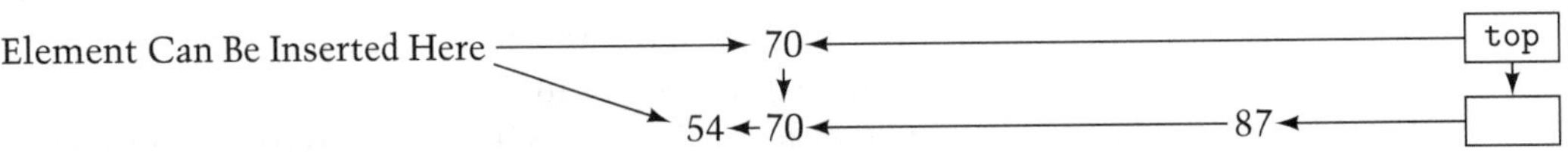

This process continues until we find the location to insert the element into the bottommost list:

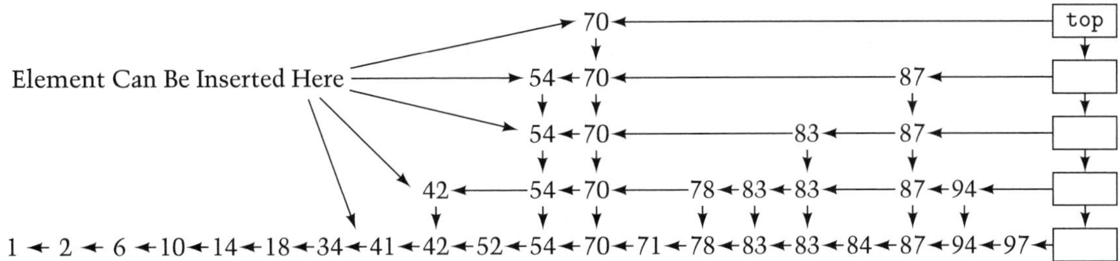

The new element is added to the bottommost list. The next step is where randomization comes into play. As we return to the level above the bottommost list, we flip a coin. If the coin is heads, we insert a new link into the list. This link will point downward to the link for the field we inserted into the bottom list. If the insertion is performed, we return the reference to the new link; otherwise, we return `null`.

38 42 54 70 78 83 83 87 94
1 2 6 10 14 18 34 38 41 42 52 54 70 71 78 83 83 84 87 94 97

The next level up, we also flip a coin but only if the insertion at the level below resulted in a new link. Because an insertion at this level requires that heads be tossed on two consecutive coin flips, the chance is only

The Role of Random Chance

It is easy to overlook the most important aspect of the `SkipList`, which is the role played by random chance in ensuring good execution-time performance. All the other data structures we have examined to this point are *deterministic*. This means that the same order of insertions and deletions will always result in exactly the same structure. This is not true of the `SkipList`. Because an essential step in the insertion of a new element into the skip list involves flipping a coin, the exact same sequence of insertions and deletions could, at two different times, result in very different internal structures.

The `SkipList` works because random events in large numbers are very predictable. Even if we cannot predict the outcome of any single coin toss, we can with confidence predict that in 100 coin tosses, about 50 will be heads and about 50 will be tails. The same reasoning allows us to say that if we flip a coin to determine whether to move up one level, each level will be about half the size of the previous, and hence the resulting structure will have approximately $O(\log n)$ levels.

25 percent that a link will be made. This process repeats all the way up the list. At the topmost level, if new nodes were generated all the way to the top, we again flip a coin. If heads, we create a new level of the hierarchy, consisting of one link to the newly added element.

Now let us examine the Java code that implements the SkipList abstraction. Like the SortedList, the constructor will take a Comparator to be used in comparing elements:

```
public class SkipList implements Sorted, Bag {
  private SkipLink top;
  private LinkedList bottom = new LinkedList();
  protected Comparator test;

  public SkipList (Comparator t) {
    test = t;
    top = new SkipLink(null, bottom.sentinel);
  }
```

The constructor creates a LinkedList named bottom. You will recall that the constructor for the LinkedList class created a single sentinel node to mark the end of the empty list. This node can be accessed as bottom.sentinel. So, to create a sentinel for the first skip list, we simply create a node with no value and point the node to the list sentinel:

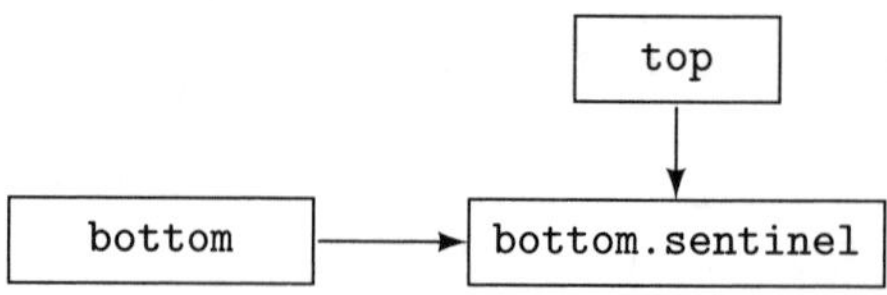

Because the SkipList stores the elements in an underlying LinkedList, the operations in the Collection interface can simply make use of the LinkedList methods:

```
public class SkipList implements Sorted, Bag {
  .
  .
  .
    // collection interface
  public boolean isEmpty () { return bottom.isEmpty(); }
  public int size () { return bottom.size(); }
  public Enumeration elements () { return bottom.elements(); }
  .
  .
  .
}
```

Now let us return to the issue of adding an element to the collection. The method in the class `SkipList` merely handles the manipulation of the variable `top`. The actual insertion is delegated to the link nodes:

```
public class SkipList implements Sorted, Bag {
  .
  .
  .
    // Bag interface
  public void addElement (Object newElement) {
    DoubleLink p = slideLeft(top, newElement);
    p = p.insert(newElement);
    if ((p != null) && flip()) {
      top = new SkipLink(null, top);
      top.insertLink(new SkipLink(newElement, p));
      }
  }

  private DoubleLink slideLeft (DoubleLink p, Object testElement) {
    while ((p.prev != null) &&
      (test.compare(p.prev.value, testElement) >= 0))
        p = p.prev;
    return p;
  }
  .
  .
  .
}
```

Flipping a coin can be simulated by any random test that has a 50 percent probability of being true:

```
private boolean flip () { return Math.random() < 0.5; }
```

With the exception of the lowest level, the links in our lists are instances of the class `SkipLink`. Like the links in the `LinkedList` class, these are built on top of the class `DoubleLink`:

```
public class SkipLink extends DoubleLink {
  public DoubleLink down;
  public Object value;
```

EXPERIMENT: EFFECT OF COIN FLIPPING

Would the operations of the `SkipList` be faster or slower if we added a new link one-third of the time rather than one-half of the time? What about if the probability were higher, say, two-thirds of the time? Design an experiment to discover the effect of this change.

```
  SkipLink (Object v, DoubleLink d) { super(v, null, null); down = d; }

  public DoubleLink insert (Object newElement) {
    DoubleLink p = slideLeft(down, newElement);
    DoubleLink d = p.insert(newElement);
    if ((d != null) && flip()) {
      SkipLink newLink = new SkipLink(newElement, d);
      super.insertLink(newLink);
      return newLink;
      }
    return null;
  }

  public void remove () { down.remove(); super.remove(); }
}
```

The insertion code in the link class handles the sliding for the next level down, then uses the method `insert` to place the element into the next lower-level list. Once placed, the coin is flipped to see whether a node should be entered into the current list. The result yielded by the `insert` method is either a new node, if the insertion was performed, or `null`, if it was not.

So how fast is an insertion using this scheme? The best scenario occurs when every other node in each list is mirrored by a node in the next-level list. In this case, because each list is exactly half the size of the next level down, there are $\lceil \log n \rceil$ levels in a list containing n elements. Furthermore, each slide-left operation examines at most two nodes. Therefore, the total time for insertion is $O(\log n)$, a considerable improvement over the $O(n)$ time required to insert an element into either a `SortedVector` or a `SortedList`.

Of course, not every path to insertion will be a perfect zig-zag from top to bottom. But again, if we assume that each level has about half the nodes of the level below, a long search on one level will always be compensated by a series of short searches on lower levels. In fact, it can be shown, although the details are more complex than we can go into here, that as long as our coin is true (that is, returns heads half the time), the *average* path followed to insert an element must always be $O(\log n)$.

To test the behavior of this data abstraction, we first compared the insertion time to that of an ordered list. To do this, we inserted n random integers into both collections, for increasing values of n. The results are shown in Figure 9.3. As each insertion into an ordered list may require $O(n)$ steps, inserting n elements will take $O(n^2)$ time. The experimental

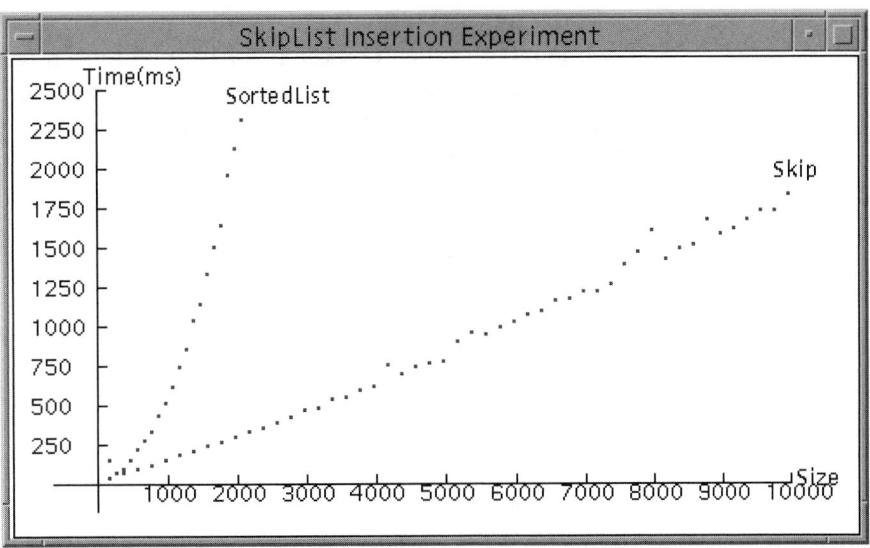

FIGURE 9.3 Insertion Timings for Skip Lists

timings bear this out, showing a nice parabolic curve. Our hypothesis is that under most circumstances, inserting an element into a skip list requires $O(\log n)$ steps, and so inserting n elements will take $O(n \log n)$ time. The experimental results seem to validate this; indeed, they appear to be almost linear.

As gratifying as a fast insertion time may be, that was not the motivation for creating the skip-list abstraction. Indeed, neither the ordered list nor the skip list can match the $O(1)$ insertion time for adding elements to the front of a simple linked list. At the beginning of this section, we noted the reason for developing the skip-list concept: to find a fast mechanism for searching a linked list. This is the task of the methods `containsElement` and `findElement`.

The implementation of the method `containsElement` is similar to `addElement`, only the loop to traverse down the hierarchy of lists is found

EXPERIMENT: EFFECT OF INSERTION ORDER

Does the order in which elements are inserted have any effect on the behavior of the `addElement` method? What if elements are inserted in increasing order? In decreasing order? Design an experiment to compare these alternatives to adding elements in random sequence.

in the method rather than distributed among the links. At each level, we slide left and then test the resulting element. If it is not the sentinel and is equal to the element we seek, we are finished. Otherwise, if possible, we drop down one level and seek again. If we cannot drop, the element is not in the collection:

```
public boolean containsElement (Object val) {
  DoubleLink p = top;
  while (p != null) {
    p = slideLeft(p, val);
    if ((p.value != null) && (val.equals(p.value))) return true;
    if (p instanceof SkipLink) p = ((SkipLink) p).down;
    else p = null;
  }
  return false;
}
```

The `findElement` method is similar, only it returns the element if it is found and throws a `NoSuchElementException` if not. The same argument used to justify the asymptotic complexity of the `addElement` procedure can be used to show that this method is also expected to be $O(\log n)$. Indeed, in practice, it may even be faster than the `addElement` method, because the search can halt as soon as we find the element in question rather than progressing all the way down to the bottommost list.

The `removeElement` method is also similar but invokes the `remove` method on the link if the element is found. The `remove` method in the class `SkipLink` will remove all the associated elements immediately referenced by `down` links from the deleted node.

So how fast is the `containsElement` method in comparison to other structures? This time, because we want to test only the comparison time, we create a list of n values in the initialization section of the task timer and then perform n random comparison tests in the timed portion. For this experiment, we have also included the `SortedVector` data abstraction in the test. The results are shown in Figure 9.4.

Overall, the best performance is the guaranteed $O(\log n)$ timing of the `SortedVector`. However, the expected $O(\log n)$ timing of the `SkipList` is very close, almost as good, and certainly much better than the $O(n)$ timing of the `SortedList`.

So why would one ever use a `SkipList` when it still cannot match the search-time performance of the `SortedVector`? To see why, you must remember that although the `SortedVector` has a very good search time, the complexity of adding and removing elements is not as good:

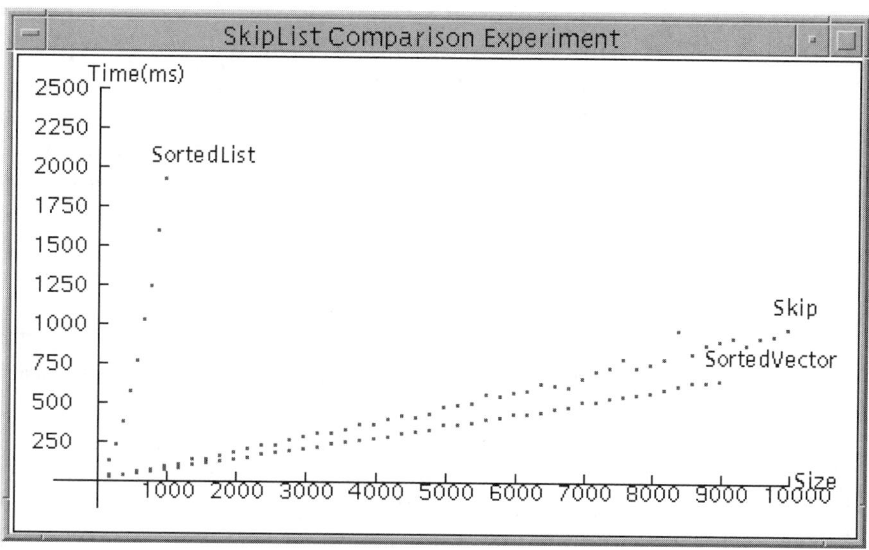

FIGURE 9.4 Comparison Timings for Skip Lists

Container	Addition	Search	Removal
`SkipList`	$O(\log n)$	$O(\log n)$	$O(\log n)$
`SortedVector`	$O(n)$	$O(\log n)$	$O(n)$
`SortedList`	$O(n)$	$O(n)$	$O(n)$
`LinkedList`	$O(1)$	$O(n)$	$O(n)$

To select the appropriate container, one must consider the entire mix of operations a task will require. For a combination of insertions, removals,

EXPERIMENT: SKIP LIST AS A BASIS FOR SORTING

Any data structure that supports the `Sorted` interface is naturally the basis for a sorting algorithm: Elements are copied from a vector into an instance of the data structure, then copied back into the vector. Because insertion into a `SkipList` is an $O(\log n)$ operation, this yields an $O(n \log n)$ sorting algorithm.

Modify the `SkipList` data abstraction so that it will implement this algorithm. Then compare the running time to that of `QuickSort`, the fastest sorting algorithm we have seen so far. Try your algorithm on various distributions of values (random, already sorted, sorted in reverse). Under what circumstances is your algorithm faster than `QuickSort`?

and inclusion tests, the `SkipList` is a good overall structure. If insertion tests are the dominant operation—for example, if a large number of elements are created all at once, followed by a long sequence of tests—the `SortedVector` may be the more appropriate choice. If addition is the dominant operation and inclusion tests and removals are less common, it may be that the simple `LinkedList`, with its constant-time insertion behavior, is the most appropriate choice.

9.4 CHAPTER SUMMARY

KEY CONCEPTS

- Sorted lists
- Linear time set operations
  - Set union
  - Set intersection
  - Set difference
- Self-organizing lists
- Inheritance versus composition
- Skip list
- Randomization

In this chapter, we have explored some of the more important variations on the idea of a linked list. A sorted list is a linked list that maintains elements in order. Sorted lists are important because they provide a very fast way to merge two lists. They can also be used to implement the `Bag` and `FindMin` ADTs. A self-organizing list tries to improve the speed of future searching operations, based on information derived from past uses.

A skip list improves on the linked list by providing much faster search and access to elements. The most interesting feature of the skip list is the way it achieves this result. The skip list makes use of random chance, a simulated tossing of a coin, in the creation of internal links. Although no single coin toss can be predicted, a sequence of coin tosses has an easily predictable pattern. Using this observation, the skip list provides very fast insertion and removal methods.

Further Information

Variations on linked-list structures are discussed by Knuth in Volume 1 of his three-volume set [Knuth 97]. A number of approaches to self-organizing data structures are discussed by Gonnet and Baeza-Yates [Gonnet 91]. Sleator and Tarjan show that the move-to-front rule for self-organizing lists is within a constant factor of the best possible self-organizing rule [Sleator 85].

William Pugh invented the skip-list abstraction [Pugh 90]. A slightly different presentation of the concept can be found in Shaffer [Shaffer 97] and in Wood [Wood 93].

The few examples in this chapter do not come close to exhausting the range of possible variations on the theme of linked lists. Some other abstractions will be examined later in this book; many others are discussed by other authors. For example, in Chapter 12, we will encounter the `RingBufferQueue`. In many ways, this is nothing more than a *circular* linked list:

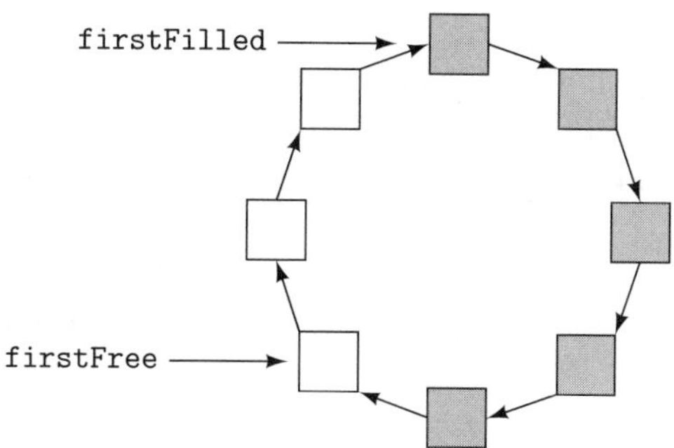

Study Questions

1. What operations are made faster by maintaining a list in order?
2. The `SortedList` data abstraction implemented four different interfaces. What are they, and what operations are required by each?
3. How is the `addElement` operation of a `SortedList` different from the similarly named operation in the class `LinkedList`?
4. Why is the `FindMin` interface so much easier to support in the class `SortedList` than in the class `LinkedList`?
5. Explain why finding the intersection of two lists is easier when the lists are ordered than when they are not. What is the complexity of the operation in each of these cases?
6. What do we mean when we say that a data abstraction is self-organizing?
7. Why is inheritance an appropriate mechanism for the implementation of the self-organizing list and not for the `SortedList` abstraction?
8. Under what circumstances will a self-organizing list perform better than an ordinary linked list?
9. In what way is the skip list different from an ordinary linked list? In what way are they the same?
10. In what way is the skip list different from an ordered list? In what way are they the same?
11. Explain the role that the random coin toss plays in the implementation of the skip list.
12. How are the links in a skip list different from the links in the linked-list abstraction?
13. Suppose that you need a container that supports the `Bag` interface. Under what circumstances is it most appropriate to use a `SkipList`? a `SortedVector`? a `LinkedList`?

Exercises

1. Exercise 11 in Chapter 8 showed that we could add the method elementAt(int) to the List data type, albeit with a slow $O(n)$ implementation. Suppose, however, that we added this method to the class SortedList and then tried to perform a binary search (see Section 7.1.1). What would be the complexity of searching a list of n elements? Would this be a very good way of finding whether an element occurs in a linked list?
2. In this exercise, we will develop a proof of correctness for the algorithm embodied by the mergeWith method in class SortedList. Begin by noting that the method contains two nested loops. The inner loop surrounds two conditional if statements and a third else block that will be executed if neither if condition is true. Begin by describing, in picture form, the state of execution when either of the two if test conditions is true and the state when both test conditions are false and the else block is executed. Based on these, can you find an invariant that will always be true following execution of the if statements, regardless of their outcome? How about an invariant that will always be true between the while statement and the start of the if statement? What about following execution of the while statement? Using these invariants, develop a proof of correctness.
3. Give an implementation of the equals method for class SortedList. Two collections will be equal if they have the same elements. What is the complexity of this task?
4. Suppose that you want to merge two collections of elements that do not have an ordering, such as collections of polygons. For a collection that supports the Bag interface, the obvious way to implement the merge operation is as follows:

   ```
   public void mergeWith(Collection newSet) {
     for (Enumeration e = newSet.elements(); e.hasMoreElements(); )
       addElement(e.nextElement());
   }
   ```

   What would be the complexity of this algorithm if implemented in the class LinkedList? What about the class SortedVector?
5. Can the mergeWith method in class SortedList be implemented using two enumerators rather than an enumerator and direct access to the links? If so, give the code. If not, explain why not.
6. Can the containsElement method be written using findElement?
7. Write implementations for the operations in the Set interface, and describe their performance.

8. At the end of Section 9.3, we described how any data abstraction that supports the `Sorted` interface naturally suggests a sorting algorithm: Copy the elements into the data structure, then copy them out. If we construct such an algorithm using a `SortedList`, what is the complexity of the resulting algorithm?
9. The chart of asymptotic execution timings for the various types of `Bag` presented only part of the picture. Complete the chart by indicating whether each time represents a time *always* possible, an *average* execution time, or a *worst-case* time.

Container	Addition	Search	Removal
`SkipList`	$O(\log n)$	$O(\log n)$	$O(\log n)$
`SortedVector`	$O(n)$	$O(\log n)$	$O(n)$
`SortedList`	$O(n)$	$O(n)$	$O(n)$
`LinkedList`	$O(1)$	$O(n)$	$O(n)$

10. Simulate adding ten random values into a `SkipList`, using a real coin to decide whether to create a new node. Repeat the operation three times with the same input values and compare the resulting structures.
11. One way to estimate the execution time of the `addElement` operation for a skip list is to count the number of arcs traversed in reaching each element in the list. For example, in the skip list shown in this chapter, seven arcs are traversed to reach element 52, whereas only five are traversed to reach element 97. Compute this arc count for each element in the list, and then determine the average arc length.

Programming Projects

1. Although we have discussed *sorted* lists in this chapter, we have not discussed *sorting* a list. Show how the insertion sort algorithm can be modified to work with a linked list. Then, using this algorithm, add to the `SortedList` class a constructor that will take an ordinary `LinkedList` as argument, then sort the list before placing it as the underlying data area in the `SortedList` class. Is the resulting operation faster than simply adding the elements one by one into an empty list? Why is it more difficult to modify the Shell sort algorithm for use with a linked list?
2. Implement for the `SortedList` abstraction a `Comparator` that uses the set-subset relationship for ordering. That is, one list is considered

to be less than another if the elements of the first are a subset of the second. If you assume that both arguments are `Sorted`, can you write an $O(n)$ algorithm for comparing two lists? What if they are not `Sorted`?

3. An alternative approach to the self-organizing list concept is termed the *transpose method*. When a successful search is found, the selected element is transposed with its neighbor, moving one location closer to the front of the list. In this fashion, elements move much more slowly to the front of the list; however, the results are more stable, as a series of requests for rare values cannot get in the way of a commonly accessed element moving to the front. Implement a self-organizing list by using the transpose method, and experimentally compare the running time of this technique to the mechanism studied in this chapter.
4. Modify the `SkipList` so that it will support the `FindMin` interface. Why is it not sufficient to simply invoke the method `bottom.removeFirst()` as we did with the `SortedList`?
5. Modify the `SkipList` so that it will support the `Set` interface, and then compare the execution time on these operations to that of the `SortedList`.
6. The use of randomization in the `SkipList` suggests another approach for improving the efficiency of operations in the `SortedList` data type. Imagine that the data abstraction is augmented with a *cursor*, a reference to a link. This value moves around as operations are performed.
   a. When an insertion is made using `addElement`, the search begins at the cursor location rather than at the start of the list. The cursor is advanced either forward or backward as necessary until the appropriate location is found. The cursor is left pointing to the newly inserted value.
   b. A search using `containsElement` or a removal using `removeElement` will begin at the current cursor location, which will again move either forward or backward as necessary.

   Implement a version of the `SortedList` data abstraction based on these ideas. Compare the execution of the result to the original. Can some distributions of values be more quickly inserted into the collection using the new scheme? Are some distributions much slower?
7. In programming project 5 in Chapter 6, we explored the concept of an `Iterator` as an alternative to the class `Enumeration`. Explain how the inclusion of the method `remove` would complicate the implementation of the iterator in the class `SkipList`. Implement an `Iterator` for this data type.

CHAPTER 10

STACKS

In the general Bag ADT, we abstracted away information about the order in which elements are (1) stored within the container and (2) inserted into the collection. However, there are many problems in which either one of these properties is important. In the next three chapters, we will explore data structures that are useful when the order of insertion must be maintained.

The *push-down stack*, or more simply the *stack*, represents a collection ADT in which elements are maintained in the order they were inserted. At any moment, only one element from a stack may be removed, and that element is the value that has been held by the stack for the shortest period of time.

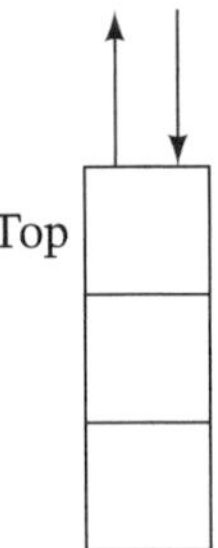

This style of use is sometimes termed last in first out, or LIFO. A stack of dinner plates is a good mental image of this abstraction. Plates on the bottom of the stack can be reached only after the plates on top have been removed.

Stacks, queues, and deques (the topics of Chapters 10–12) are often referred to as *linear* data abstractions. What this means is that elements are added only at the ends and retain the order in which they were inserted.

Stacks are used extensively in many computer systems, both in application programs and in the implementation of programming languages and operating systems. In later sections, we will describe the use of stacks in several types of applications. An example stack that you have probably seen is found in a Web browser. Almost all Web browsers have `Back` and `Forward` buttons the user can click to move through a series of Web pages. The `Back` button returns the browser to the previous Web page. Clicking the `Back` button again will return to the page before that, and so on. The browser uses a stack to maintain the list of Web pages in the order they were viewed.

Another example stack that the programmer has undoubtedly encountered is the *activation record stack*. Each time a method is invoked, space is set aside for the parameters and local variables in an area called the *activation record*. If we ignore multithreading, methods follow a very strict order of execution: If method `A` invokes method `B`, method `A` will temporarily halt when method `B` begins; method `B` will then run to completion and must finish before method `A` will restart.[1] This simple execution strategy permits a very efficient mechanism for memory management. Each time a method begins, an activation record containing enough space for local variables and parameters is placed on a stack.[2] Each time a method exits, the stack is popped, and the space is recovered. It is this technique that ensures, for example, that each invocation of a recursive method will receive its own space for local variables.

Stacks are also used in the processing of characters typed at a keyboard. Imagine that you enter several keys and then discover a mistake. You press the backspace key to move backward over a previously entered key. Several backspaces may be used in turn to erase more than one character. Suppose that you enter the following:

```
correcktw ←←←← ttw ← ext
```

---

1. Multiple threads complicate this picture but only slightly. Basically, each thread is given its own stack for local variables and parameters.

2. For technical reasons too complex to explain here, objects in Java also make use of an auxiliary area termed the *heap*. This is not to be confused with the `heap` data type described in Chapter 15. Nevertheless, activation records in Java implementations are still used for primitive data values and other information.

The computer will arrive at the correct text because it uses a stacklike structure to store the individual characters. Each backspace pops one character off the stack.

10.1 THE STACK ADT

As an abstract data type, the *stack* is defined in part by the `Stack` interface, shown in Figure 10.1. In addition to the methods inherited from `Collection`, this interface incorporates the ability to add elements to and remove elements from the collection.[3] To complete the specification of the ADT requires that we also include the LIFO requirement and the property that elements are maintained in the order they are inserted. Including the inherited operations, the interface and some of its properties can be described as follows:

`void addLast (Object)` Adds an element to the top (last end) of the stack. The relative position of all other elements in the collection remains unchanged. The inserted value will become the new topmost element.

`Object getLast ()` Returns the element that has been in the stack the shortest period of time. Because elements can be inserted at only one end of the stack, this will naturally be the element at the top. This method will throw `NoSuchElementException` if the stack is currently empty. Invoking this method will not change the state of the collection in any way.

`void removeLast ()` Removes the current top of the stack. This method will throw `NoSuchElementException` if the stack is currently empty.

`elements` Returns an `Enumeration` that can be used to access the elements held in the collection. Elements are enumerated from the bottom to the top of the stack, which is the same order in which they were inserted.

`isEmpty` Returns `true` if the collection is empty and returns `false` otherwise. This method will always return `true` when applied on a newly created collection. Invoking this method will not change the state of the collection in any way.

---

3. The Java standard library provides a `Stack` data type, which is slightly different from the interface described here. Details of the Java standard class can be found in Appendix C.

```
public interface Stack extends Collection {
  public void addLast (Object newElement);
  public Object getLast ();
  public void removeLast ();
}
```

FIGURE 10.1 The Stack Interface

WHAT'S IN A NAME?

We have broken with tradition in the naming of our stack operations. Traditionally, the name push is used for the operation of adding an element to the stack, the name pop is used to remove the element, and the name top is used to access the top element. We have used the names addLast, removeLast, and getLast for these operations, for two reasons. First, both the Vector and the LinkedList abstractions provide very efficient implementations of these operations. Second, this naming scheme will pave the way for the discussion of the Deque data type in Chapter 11. In Exercise 3, we suggest one way to change this naming convention.

Another common variation is to have the removal operations (removeLast or pop) both remove and return the topmost element. By separating these operations, we make the implementations slightly simpler and can more easily discuss the cost of individual operations.

size Returns an integer that indicates the number of elements held by the collection. This method will always return zero when applied on a newly created collection. Invoking this method will not change the state of the collection in any way.

10.2 CHECKING FOR BALANCED PARENTHESES

A simple application that will illustrate the use of the stack operations is a program to check for balanced parentheses and brackets. By balanced, we mean that every open parenthesis is matched with a corresponding close parenthesis and that parentheses are properly nested. We will make the program slightly more interesting by considering both parentheses and brackets. All other characters are simply ignored. So, for example, the inputs (x(y)(z)) and a({(b)}c) are balanced, whereas the inputs w)(x) and p({(q)r)} are not.

The program reads the input from the system input stream and writes to the system output. The stack is used to hold the value of the character we *expect* to see as an ending to balance a given starting character. For example, a closing parenthesis is stored as the expected match for an opening parenthesis, whereas a closing bracket is stored as the expected match for an opening parenthesis.

```
import java.io.*;
import jds.Stack;
import jds.collection.Vector;

public class ParenCheck {
  public static void main (String [ ] args) {
    try {
      ParenCheck world = new ParenCheck(System.in);
    } catch (IOException e) {
      System.out.println("Received IO Exception " + e);
    }
  }

  public ParenCheck (InputStream in) throws IOException {
    int i = in.read();
    while (i != -1) {
      if (i == '(') push(')');
      else if (i == '{') push('}');
      else if (i == ')') check(')');
      else if (i == '}') check('}');
      i = in.read();
    }
    if (stk.isEmpty())
      System.out.println("Parenthesis Balance");
    else reportError();
  }

  private Stack stk = new Vector();

  private void push (char c) { stk.addLast(new Character(c)); }

  private void check (char c) {
    if (stk.isEmpty())
      reportError();
    Character s = (Character) stk.getLast();
    stk.removeLast();
    if (c != s.charValue())
      reportError();
  }

  private void reportError () {
    System.out.println("Parentheses do not Balance");
    System.exit(1);
  }
}
```

The method push adds an element to the stack, whereas the method check both removes the topmost value from the stack and checks that it is the correct type. The method reportError will halt the program at the first reported error. Errors can occur if the stack contents do not match the expected value or if the stack becomes empty prematurely.

Note that the program does not recognize parentheses that occur as part of string or character literals. Thus, for example, the program will report an error if it is used to check itself! The solution to this problem is left as a programming exercise.

10.3 Towers of Hanoi, Revisited

One place we have already seen a use of stacks is in the Towers of Hanoi puzzle examined in Chapter 5. Disks were added to the poles by placing them on top of the existing disks, and only the topmost disk was ever removed from a pile. This is exactly like a stack of plates (the only difference being that the disks are not all the same size). Although the description of the algorithm used to solve the puzzle does not require the use of stacks, a visual display of the output is certainly simplified when we use a stack to hold the values being stored on the three poles. This is illustrated by the following program. Each disk will be represented by an Integer value held by one of the three stacks. The recursive program that solves the puzzle (found in the method solveHanoi) makes a single move, repaints the window, sleeps for a short period of time, and then goes on to the next move:

```
import java.awt.*;
import java.util.Enumeration;
import jds.Stack;
import jds.collection.LinkedList;
import jds.util.CloseQuit;

public class Hanoi extends Frame {
  static public void main (String [ ] args)
    { Hanoi world = new Hanoi(); world.show(); world.run(); }

  public Hanoi () {
    setSize(400, 200); setTitle("Towers of Hanoi");
    addWindowListener(new CloseQuit());
  }

  public void run () {
      // put initial disks on pole one
```

```
    int size = 10;
    for (int i = size; i > 0; i--)
      poleOne.addLast(new Integer(i));
        // now solve puzzle
    solveHanoi(size, poleOne, poleTwo, poleThree);
  }

  private Stack poleOne = new LinkedList();
  private Stack poleTwo = new LinkedList();
  private Stack poleThree = new LinkedList();

  public void paint (Graphics g) {
    paintStack(poleOne, g, 100, 180); // numbers are locations
    paintStack(poleTwo, g, 200, 180); // of base for
    paintStack(poleThree, g, 300, 180); // each stack
  }

  private void paintStack (Stack stk, Graphics g, int x, int y) {
    Enumeration e = stk.elements();
    while (e.hasMoreElements()) {
      Integer disk = (Integer) e.nextElement();
      int size = disk.intValue();
        // each disk is 10 pixels high, 4*size wide
      g.fillRect(x - 4 * size, y, 8 * size, 10);
      y = y - 10;
    }
  }

  private void solveHanoi (int n, Stack a, Stack b, Stack c) {
    if (n > 0) {
      solveHanoi(n-1, a, c, b); // first recursive call
        // move one disk
      Object disk = a.getLast();
      a.removeLast();
      b.addLast(disk);
        // then repaint
      repaint();
      try {
        Thread.sleep(200);
      } catch(Exception e) { }
      solveHanoi(n-1, c, b, a); // second recursive call
    }
  }
}
```

FIGURE 10.2 Screen Shot of Towers of Hanoi Puzzle

To paint the window, we simply paint each of the three stacks. This common task is factored out into a method `printStack`, which is then invoked using different locations for each of the three poles.

The recursive procedure `solveHanoi` should be compared to the version presented in Chapter 5. Figure 10.2 shows a screen shot of this program.

10.4 A Four-Function Calculator

The standard example illustrating the use of a stack is the implementation of a calculator. Many readers will have used a calculator that accepts input in the form termed *postfix notation*, sometimes called *reverse Polish notation*, or RPN. To add the values 12 and 42 in RPN style, the user would type the keys 1-2-Enter-4-2-Plus. Note how the addition was specified after the two operand values had already been entered. RPN has the property that expressions can be evaluated as they are processed, token by token. In the normal *infix* form, when evaluating an expression such as "12 + 42," it is necessary to remember the addition while reading the right argument (the 42). Using RPN, by the time the addition operator is encountered, both operands are immediately available.

The display for our calculator (Figure 10.3) is constructed out of two simple types of components: a text area for the output and a four-by-four grid of buttons. The latter can be easily created by declaring a `Panel` that is displayed using a `GridLayout`. The panel is then declared as the center of the display, whereas the text is the topmost (or "north") part of the display.

In earlier chapters, we discussed what features make a computer program object-oriented. The principal aspect we have identified is that an object-oriented program is viewed as a community of agents (objects) that

FIGURE 10.3 Screen Shot of Calculator Application

must interact in order to achieve their objective. If we imagine how we might design our calculator in this manner, we see that there are many candidate objects. As we have observed in previous programs, buttons in Java are always represented by a listener object, an object that will perform

---

WHY POLISH?

Why is Polish notation called Polish? The answer is that it was named for its inventor, the logician Jan Łukasiewicz, who lived in the early part of the twentieth century.[a] Łukasiewicz observed that by moving a binary operator from its normal position between its arguments and instead placing it before the two arguments, the need for parentheses in order to specify precedence was eliminated. An expression such as

$(3 + 4) \times 9$

could be written instead as $\times + 3\ 4\ 9$. The expression without the parentheses, in which the multiplication is performed before the addition, is written $+ 3 \times 4\ 9$.

Later, it was noted that writing the operators *after* the arguments would also work and had certain advantages. This form was termed *reverse Polish*, or *postfix, notation*. The reverse Polish representation of the preceding expression is $3\ 4 + 9 \times$, whereas the expression that performs the multiplication first is $3\ 4\ 9 \times +$.

[a] So why isn't Polish notation referred to as Łukasiewicz notation?

a certain task when clicked. Thus, we can imagine an operation button with the following description:

`OperationButton`
When clicked:
• Pop two values from stack.
• Do operation.
• Push result on stack.

A `Quit` button will clearly halt the application. The `Enter` button can easily be charged with placing a zero on the stack. What about the digit buttons? Imagine that the user clicks the buttons 4, 7, and 3 in succession. We expect the result to be 473. We can obtain this behavior if a digit button reads the current top of the stack, multiples it by 10, adds its particular value, and then places the result back in the stack.

`DigitButton`
When clicked:
• Pop value from stack.
• Multiply by 10, add value.
• Push back on stack.

The task of the main program is now clear. After creating the initial universe of objects, it must simply maintain the stack of values used by the buttons and display the current stack contents.

Omitting for the moment the code for the various buttons, the calculator application is as follows:

```
import java.awt.*;
import java.util.*;
import jds.Stack;
import jds.collection.Vector;
import jds.util.ButtonAdapter;
import jds.util.CloseQuit;

public class Calculator extends Frame {
  public static void main (String [ ] args)
    { Calculator world = new Calculator(); world.show(); }

  public Calculator () {
      // create the high-level display
    setSize(200, 300); setTitle("Calculator");
    addWindowListener(new CloseQuit());
    Panel p = new Panel();
    p.setLayout(new GridLayout(4,4,2,2));
    add("Center", p);
    add("North", display);
      // now create the buttons
    p.add(new DigitButton(1)); p.add(new DigitButton(2));
    p.add(new DigitButton(3)); p.add(new OpButton('+'));
    p.add(new DigitButton(4)); p.add(new DigitButton(5));
    p.add(new DigitButton(6)); p.add(new OpButton('-'));
    p.add(new DigitButton(7)); p.add(new DigitButton(8));
    p.add(new DigitButton(9)); p.add(new OpButton('*'));
    p.add(new QuitButton());   p.add(new DigitButton(0));
    p.add(new EnterButton());  p.add(new OpButton('/'));
      // initialize the data stack
    pushValue(0.0);
  }

  private Label display = new Label("0");
  private Stack data = new Vector();

  private double dataStackTop () {
      // return top of stack as a double
    Double dtop = (Double) data.getLast ();
    data.removeLast();
    return dtop.doubleValue();
  }

  private void pushValue (double d) {
      // push value onto stack and update display
```

```
      data.addLast(new Double(d));
      display.setText(String.valueOf(d));
      repaint();
    }

    private class DigitButton extends  ButtonAdapter { ... }

    private class OpButton extends ButtonAdapter { ... }

    private class EnterButton extends ButtonAdapter { ... }

    private class QuitButton extends ButtonAdapter { ... }
}
```

The stack will be used to hold the numeric intermediate results, stored as instances of the class Double. The method dataStackTop will remove and return the current top of stack, converting it to a primitive double in the process. The method pushValue does the reverse; it takes as argument a double and, because primitive types, such as double, cannot be stored in the Stack data structure, wraps it up in a Double object before inserting it onto the stack.

All the real work for the application occurs in response to button clicks. Four varieties of buttons are used in this application: one for digits, one for operators, one for the Enter button, and one for the Quit button. All are declared as instances of the class ButtonAdapter, which you have already encountered in Chapter 6. You will recall that the constructor for this class took as argument the label for the button. When the user clicks a button created using a ButtonAdapter, the method pressed will be invoked.

The simplest button is the Quit button. When clicked, it simply halts the application:

```
private class QuitButton extends ButtonAdapter {
  QuitButton () { super("Q"); }
  public void pressed () { System.exit(0); }
}
```

Only slightly more complicated is the EnterButton. When clicked, it pushes a new zero onto the stack:

```
private class EnterButton extends ButtonAdapter {
  EnterButton () { super("E"); }
  public void pressed () { pushValue(0.0); }
}
```

The digit keys are each represented by an instance of the class DigitButton. The constructor for this class requires the number the key is representing. This is converted into a string to be used as argument for the parent class constructor. When clicked, the current value in the display is multiplied by 10 and the digit added to the result. In this fashion, a number can be built out of individual keystrokes.

```
private class DigitButton extends  ButtonAdapter {
  DigitButton (int v) { super(String.valueOf(v)); digit = v; }

  private int digit;

  public void pressed ()
    { double d = dataStackTop(); d = d * 10 + digit; pushValue(d); }
}
```

All that remains is the implementation of the operator buttons. A variable in the class will hold the character that is used both for the label on the button and to determine which operation to perform. All operations require two arguments; if the user has entered only one argument, nothing will change. Otherwise, a `switch` statement selects the appropriate operation, and the updated result is placed back on the stack.

```
private class OpButton extends ButtonAdapter {
  OpButton (char o) { super(String.valueOf(o)); op = o; }

  private char op;

  public void pressed () {
    double right = dataStackTop();
    if (data.isEmpty()) { // only one operand
      pushValue(right); // push it back
      return;
    }
    double left = dataStackTop();
    switch (op) {
      case '+': left += right; break;
      case '-': left -= right; break;
      case '*': left *= right; break;
      case '/': left /= right; break;
    }
    pushValue(left);
  }
}
```

10.5 A Solitaire Program

Card games are another place where stacks are found. Here, the stack is used to hold a pile of playing cards. We will illustrate this application by describing a simple solitaire program named Frog.

The layout for Frog is shown in Figure 10.4. To play Frog, a deck of cards is shuffled. Thirteen cards are drawn from the deck and placed above the deck in what is called the *stock*. Next to the stock are the four *foundations*. As in most solitaire games, the objective is to build the foundations from ace to king. In Frog, however, unlike many other solitaire games, suit is unimportant; for example, a 4 of any suit can be played on top of a 3 of spades. Below the foundations are four *waste piles*. Any card in play can be moved to any waste pile, regardless of the number of cards already in the pile or their rank. However, there can be no more than four waste piles. Thus, at most six cards are available for play at any one time: the topmost card on the four waste piles, the topmost card on the deck, and the topmost card on the stock. Any one of these six can be moved onto a foundation. The game ends when no cards remain in the stock or the deck.

The first obvious abstraction is the playing card. We will provide a very simple playing card class and discuss improvements in the exercises:

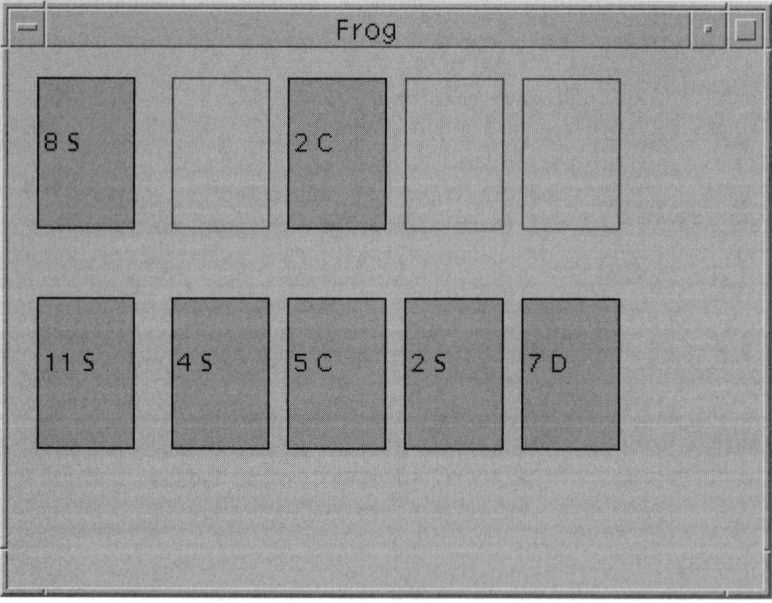

FIGURE 10.4 Screen Shot of Solitaire Game

```
public class Card {
  Card (int is, int ir) { suit = is;  rank = ir; }
  public final int suit;
  public final int rank;

  public static final int diamond = 1;
  public static final int club = 2;
  public static final int spade = 3;
  public static final int heart = 4;

  public Color color () {
    if ((suit == diamond) || (suit == heart))
      return Color.red;
    else
      return Color.black;
  }

  final public static int height = 75;
  final public static int width = 50;

  public void draw (Graphics g, int x, int y) {
    g.setColor(Color.yellow);
    g.fillRect(x, y, width, height);
    g.setColor(Color.black);
    g.drawRect(x, y, width, height);
    String body = String.valueOf(rank);
    if (suit == heart) body = body + " H";
    if (suit == club) body = body + " C";
    if (suit == diamond) body = body + " D";
    if (suit == spade) body = body + " S";
    g.drawString(body, x+3, y+height/2);
  }
}
```

A card has a suit and a rank, which are stored in a `final` data field, and so cannot be modified once set. Static fields are used to represent the height and width of a card. The method `draw` will draw the card image at a specified location.

The next abstraction is a pile of cards. The class `CardPile` will use a stack to hold the actual playing cards; other data fields represent the location of the card pile on the playing surface. Here, we make use of a `LinkedList` to represent our stack. Methods are defined for adding and removing cards to and from the deck. The method `draw` draws a picture of the card pile, which is a simple empty rectangle if the pile is empty or the

INHERITANCE FOR SPECIALIZATION

The creation of the various card piles in the `Frog` game marks the first time we have used inheritance as a tool within a program, as opposed to inheriting from library classes, such as `Frame` or `ButtonAdapter`. Inheritance is most commonly used as a technique for *specialization*, for taking a very general abstraction and making it fit a specific set of circumstances. An application specializes a `Frame`, for example, by changing the way a window is displayed. A button specializes a `ButtonAdapter` by changing the action performed when the button is clicked.

In the `Frog` game, we have created a very general abstraction representing a pile of playing cards, providing behavior common to many types of card piles. The various subclasses then alter the behavior to make it appropriate to a specific set of circumstances. You should think about using inheritance any time you create a number of types of objects that do not have identical behavior but share common features.

topmost card if it is not. The method `includes` tells whether a specific point in the playing surface is in the area of the card pile. The method `canTake` tells whether it is legal to add a specific card to this particular stack of cards.

```
public class CardPile {

  public CardPile (int ix, int iy) { x = ix; y = iy; }

  public void addCard (Card aCard) { cards.addLast(aCard); }

  public boolean isEmpty () { return cards.isEmpty(); }

  public boolean canTake (Card aCard) { return false; }

  public Card topCard () {
    Card result = (Card) cards.getLast();
    cards.removeLast();
    return result;
  }

  public boolean includes (int tx, int ty) {
    return ((tx > x) && (ty > y) &&
      (tx <= x + Card.width) && (ty <= y+Card.height));
  }

  public void draw (Graphics g) {
    g.setColor(Color.blue);
    if (cards.isEmpty())
```

```
      g.drawRect(x, y, Card.width, Card.height);
    else {
      Card aCard = (Card) cards.getLast();
      aCard.draw(g, x, y);
    }
  }

  private int x, y;
  protected Stack cards = new LinkedList();
}
```

In large part, the game logic consists of defining various categories of card piles, using inheritance and overriding to create specialized behavior. For example, a `WastePile` is permitted to take any a card in any situation:

```
class WastePile extends CardPile {
  public WastePile (int ix, int iy) { super(ix, iy); }

  public boolean canTake (Card aCard) { return true; }
}
```

A foundation pile, on the other hand, is permitted to take a card only if the pile is empty and the card is an ace or if the card is one higher than the current topmost card in the pile:

```
class FoundationPile extends CardPile {
  public FoundationPile (int ix, int iy) { super(ix, iy); }

  public boolean canTake (Card aCard) {
    if (isEmpty()) return aCard.rank == 1;
    Card tp = (Card) cards.getLast();
    if (aCard.rank == 1 + tp.rank) return true;
    return false;
  }
}
```

Note that methods in the class `FoundationPile` can access the data field `cards` because it has been declared as `protected` in the parent class `CardPile`. Had it been declared `private`, child classes would have been forbidden to access the field.

Simple card piles can be used for the deck and the stock. Complexity in the main application comes from two sources. The first is initialization of the application and the various data piles, and the second is the handling of the mouse events.

```
import java.awt.*;
import java.awt.event.*;
```

```
import jds.Stack;
import jds.collection.Vector;
import jds.util.CloseQuit;

public class Frog extends Frame {
  public static void main (String [ ] args)
    { Frog world = new Frog(); world.show(); }

  public Frog () {
      // frame initialization
    setSize(400, 300); setTitle("Frog");
    addMouseListener(new MouseKeeper());
    addWindowListener(new CloseQuit());
      // application initialization
    deck = new CardPile(20, 150);
      // now add the deck of cards
    Vector v = new Vector();
    for (int i = 1; i <= 13; i++) {
      v.addLast(new Card(Card.heart, i));
      v.addLast(new Card(Card.club, i));
      v.addLast(new Card(Card.diamond, i));
      v.addLast(new Card(Card.spade, i));
    }
      // now shuffle the cards
    while (! v.isEmpty()) {
      int i = (int) (v.size() * Math.random());
      Card c = (Card) v.elementAt(i);
      v.removeElementAt(i);
      deck.addCard(c);
    }
      // create the stock pile
    stock = new CardPile(20, 40);
    for (int i = 0; i < 13; i++)
      stock.addCard(deck.topCard());
      // and the other piles
    foundation = new CardPile[4];
    for (int i = 0; i < 4; i++)
      foundation[i] = new FoundationPile(90+60*i, 40);
    waste = new CardPile[4];
    for (int i = 0; i < 4; i++)
      waste[i] = new WastePile(90+60*i, 150);
  }
```

```
  CardPile deck;
  CardPile stock;
  CardPile [ ] foundation;
  CardPile [ ] waste;

  public void paint (Graphics g) {
    deck.draw(g);
    stock.draw(g);
    for (int i = 0; i < 4; i++) {
      foundation[i].draw(g);
      waste[i].draw(g);
      }
  }

  private class MouseKeeper extends MouseAdapter { ... }
}
```

Each of the various decks is assigned a specific location on the playing surface. A vector is used to shuffle the initial deck. First, the cards are placed into a vector, and then the cards are randomly drawn one by one from the vector and inserted into the deck. The result is not the most efficient algorithm (see exercises at the end of the chapter) but is easy to understand. To paint the application, it is sufficient to ask each of the card piles to paint itself.

To play the game, the user will press the mouse while over a specific deck, then drag the mouse to the deck where the card should be played, releasing the mouse in the new location. To accomplish this, you will recall, it is necessary to create a "listener" object that will "hear" mouse events and respond to them. We will call the class that defines the behavior for our listener object `MouseKeeper`. By making `MouseKeeper` extend

MOUSEADAPTER

The `MouseAdapter` in the Java standard library is a `MouseListener` (see Chapter 6 for a discussion of listeners) that automatically responds to mouse movements and then separates them into the various commands. Each command is handled by a separate method, which is given a null method body in the class:

```
class MouseAdapter implements MouseListener {
  public void mouseClicked (MouseEvent e) { }
  public void mouseEntered (MouseEvent e) { }
  public void mouseExited (MouseEvent e) { }
  public void mousePressed (MouseEvent e) { }
  public void mouseReleased (MouseEvent e) { }
}
```

By inheriting from the class `MouseAdapter`, we can override only the methods of interest—for example, mouse presses and mouse releases—and ignore the other types of mouse operations.

from MouseAdapter, we can concentrate on the mouse events of interest, ignoring the other types of events:

```
private class MouseKeeper extends MouseAdapter {
  CardPile sourceDeck = null;

  public void mousePressed (MouseEvent e)
    { sourceDeck = findDeck(e.getX(), e.getY()); }

  public void mouseReleased (MouseEvent e) {
    if (sourceDeck == null) return;
    if (sourceDeck.isEmpty()) return;
    CardPile toDeck = findDeck(e.getX(), e.getY());
    if (toDeck == null) return;
    Card playCard = sourceDeck.topCard();
    if (playCard == null) return;
    if (toDeck.canTake(playCard))
      toDeck.addCard(playCard);
    else
      sourceDeck.addCard(playCard);
    repaint();
  }
}
```

Two mouse events are of interest. When the mouse is pressed, we use the findDeck method to discover which deck is being specified. When the mouse is released, we once again use the findDeck method to find the destination deck. Assuming that both decks are legal and that the first contained at least one card, we try to move the card to the new deck. If the new deck cannot take the card in question, it is placed back on the original deck. The repaint method then specifies that the application window should be redrawn.

The method findDeck uses the ability of each deck to know whether it occupies a given location:

```
public CardPile findDeck (int x, int y) {
  if (deck.includes(x, y)) return deck;
  if (stock.includes(x, y)) return stock;
  for (int i = 0; i < 4; i++) {
    if (foundation[i].includes(x, y))
      return foundation[i];
    if (waste[i].includes(x, y))
      return waste[i];
  }
  return null; // no valid deck
}
```

In the exercises, we will explore some improvements to this game, as well as several alternative solitaire games.

10.6 Implementation of the Stack Abstraction

We have already encountered the `Vector` and the `LinkedList`, two data structures that implement the `Stack` interface. A third data structure that implements this interface is the `IndexedDeque`, which we will examine in more detail in Chapter 11.

Consider the use of a `Vector` as the container. A snapshot of the vector during execution might reveal the following. The capacity of the vector is given by the largest number of elements it has been asked to hold up to the current point, whereas the size represents the number of elements the vector currently holds. A `push` will simply increase the size, unless the size reaches the capacity, in which case a memory reallocation will be performed to create a larger buffer.

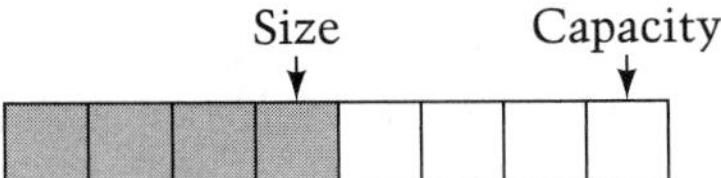

In the `LinkedList` implementation, on the other hand, only the elements currently in the collection are maintained. Each element added to the list causes a new memory allocation, and each element freed releases a list node.

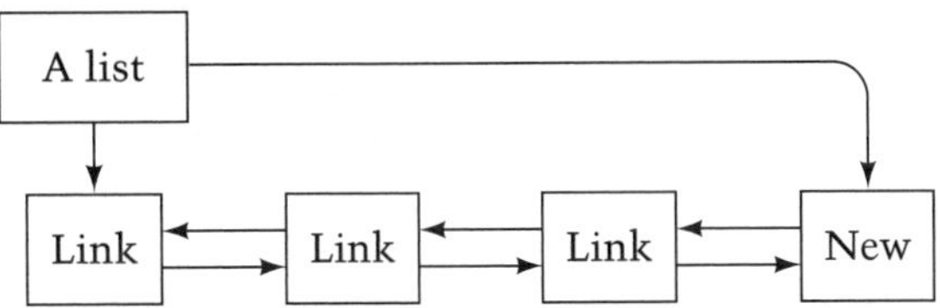

In both the `Vector` and the `LinkedList` implementations of the stack abstraction, both insertion and removal operations are constant time, or

Experiment: Which End Is Up?

Although we have used the methods `addLast` and `removeLast` to implement the `Stack` abstraction, as far as the `LinkedList` is concerned, we could have just as easily used `addFirst` and `removeFirst`. Design an experiment to compare the relative execution times for these two alternatives.

EXPERIMENT: EXPLORE THE EFFECT OF INCREASING STACK SIZES

Suppose that instead of keeping the size of the stack constant, for each value n, we insert n integers into the stack, then remove them all. Do you think that the `Vector` will still be faster than a `LinkedList`? Do you think that the difference will be more or less than for the experiment shown in Figure 10.6? Using the class `TaskTimer`, design an experiment to test your hypothesis.

$O(1)$. Thus, to gain an appreciation of the relative efficiency of these operations, we must perform experiments to compare actual running times. One experiment, for example, would be to insert and remove ten elements n times and to measure the execution time as n increases. Here, the size of the stack remains relatively small, and we are measuring only the time to perform insertions and removals.

A program to conduct this experiment is shown in Figure 10.5. If we execute this program, we obtain a timing similar to that shown in Figure 10.6. Here, we see that, at least for this distribution of values, the stack operations provided by a `Vector` are faster than those provided by the `LinkedList` abstraction. However, the differences are small, and in practice, either implementation should work. Deciding which data structure to use would then be based on other factors.

```
class StackTester extends TaskTimer {

  public StackTester (Reporter rep, Stack q)
    { super(rep); que = q; value = new Integer(42); }

  private Stack que; // stack being tested
  private Object value; // value inserted and removed from stack

  public void doTask (int n) {
    for (int i = 0; i < n; i++) {
      for (int j = 0; j < 10; j++)
        que.addLast(value);
      for (int j = 0; j < 10; j++)
        que.removeLast();
    }
  }
}
```

FIGURE 10.5 A Program to Compare the Running Times of Various Stack Implementations

```
public class StackExperiment extends Frame {

  public static void main (String [ ] args)
  { StackExperiment world = new StackExperiment(); world.show();
                                                    world.run(); }

  public StackExperiment () {
    setTitle("Stack Experiment"); setSize(500, 300);
    addWindowListener(new CloseQuit());
    add("Center", graph);
  }

  private GraphMaker graph = new GraphMaker(10000, 2500);

  public void run () {
    StackTester t1 = new StackTester(graph.getReporter("Vector"),
        new StackTester(new Vector()));
    t1.run(0, 10000, 200);
    StackTester t2 = new StackTester(graph.getReporter("List"),
        new LinkedList());
    t2.run(0, 10000, 200);
  }
}
```

FIGURE 10.5 *(Continued)*

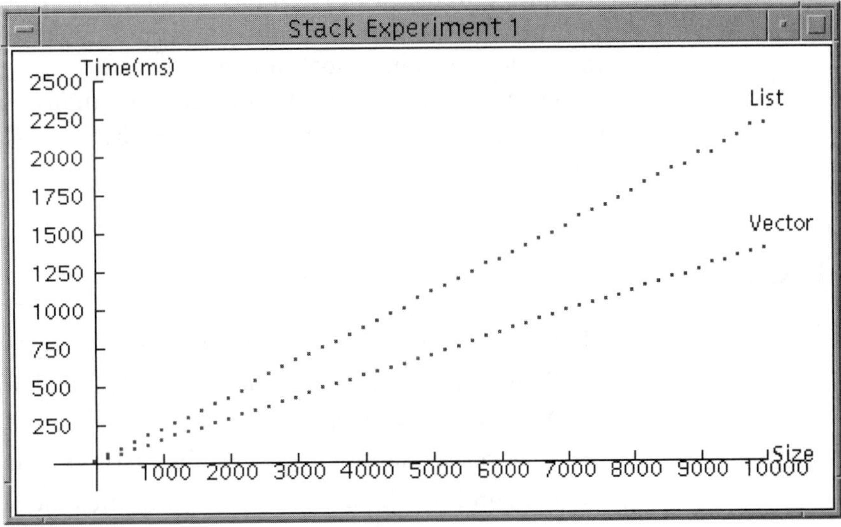

FIGURE 10.6 Timings of Stack Operations

10.7 Chapter Summary

Key Concepts

- Stack
- Traditional stack operations:
  - Push
  - Pop
  - Top
- LIFO
- Activation record stack
- Polish notation

The stack is a data abstraction in which elements can be placed and removed only from one end. This style of use is sometimes termed last in first out, or LIFO. Stacks are used extensively in applications and operating system utilities and are a basic feature of machine-level program execution.

Stacks can be efficiently implemented by using either a `Vector` or a `LinkedList`. Generally, the `Vector` implementation has slightly better execution time performance but can use more memory if the size of the stack grows and shrinks over a wide range.

Further Information

Stacks and queues are discussed extensively by Knuth [Knuth 97]. The terms LIFO and FIFO (FIFO being a term to describe the access of elements in a queue) were first used by accountants. The following hypothetical example illustrates the use of the terms in the accounting field. Suppose that in March, Mr. Jones purchases 10 shares of stock at $70 and in April purchases 20 more shares at $90. Now imagine that in July, Mr. Jones sells 10 shares of stock at $80. Should the shares be considered to be those purchased in March (first in first out), or should they be considered to be the ones purchased in April (last in first out). Under the one assumption, the investment will have shown a profit, whereas under the other, the investment will have lost money.

Because Polish notation simplifies so many notation problems, it is surprising that it was not discovered before 1929. The original source is [Lukasiewicz 29].

Study Questions

1. What are the defining characteristics of the stack abstraction?
2. Explain the meaning of the term LIFO. Explain why FILO might have been equally appropriate.
3. Give some examples of stack abstractions found in real life.
4. Explain how the use of a stack simplifies the allocation of memory for program variables.

5. Explain how the use of the activation record stack makes possible memory allocation for recursive procedures.
6. Evaluate the following two reverse Polish expressions:

$$2\;3 + 5\;9 - \times$$

$$2\;3\;5\;9 + - \times$$

Exercises

1. Describe the state of an initially empty stack after each of the following sequences of operations. Indicate the values held by any variables that are declared; also indicate any errors that may occur:

a.
```
stk.addLast(new Integer(3));
Object a = stk.getLast();
stk.addLast(new Integer(5));
stk.removeLast();
```

b.
```
stk.addLast(new Integer(3));
stk.addLast(new Integer(4));
stk.removeLast();
stk.removeLast();
Object a = stk.getLast();
```

2. Fill in the following chart with the execution times for each operation, using the indicated implementation technique. For each entry, indicate whether the execution time is *always*, *worst case*, or *expected*.

Operation	`Vector`	`LinkedList`
`addLast`	$O(\_)$	$O(\_)$
`getFirst`	$O(\_)$	$O(\_)$
`removeFirst`	$O(\_)$	$O(\_)$

3. Suppose that one really wanted to use the traditional names push, pop, and `top` for the stack operations. Describe an *adapter* that could be written to provide this functionality. The adapter should maintain a

stack abstraction as described in this chapter but simply change the name of the operations.

4. Suppose that you wanted to give a proof of correctness of the `mouseReleased` method in class `MouseKeeper`. Suggest invariants you could use with your proof, and indicate the locations in the method where the invariants must be `true`.
5. What is the Polish notation representation of the following expression?

$$(a * (b + c)) + (b/d) * a$$

6. One problem with Polish notation is that you cannot use the same symbol for both unary and binary operators. Illustrate this by assuming that the minus sign is used for both unary and binary negation, and explain the two alternative meanings for the following postfix Polish expression:

$$7\ 5\ -\ -$$

7. Write a procedure to translate a postfix Polish expression into an infix expression that uses parentheses only where necessary.
8. Using only the features provided by the four-function calculator described in Section 10.4, show how to obtain the negation of the value in the display.
9. In Chapter 6, we learned that to remove a value from a `Vector` requires, in the worst case, $O(n)$ operations, where n is the number of elements in the vector. Given this fact, what is the execution time of the shuffle algorithm described in Section 10.5?
10. The following algorithm can be used to shuffle a vector of n elements in $O(n)$ steps. A `for` loop will cycle an index value from 0 to n. At each iteration, compute a random number between 0 and n, which will be used as the second index. Then exchange the two values at these index positions. Show how to implement this algorithm in the Frog game described in Section 10.5.
11. Phil Parker runs a parking lot where cars are stored in six stacks holding at most three cars each. Patrons leave the keys in their cars so that they can be moved, if necessary.

Assuming that no other parking space is available, should Phil allow his parking lot to become entirely full? Assuming that Phil cannot predict the time at which patrons will return for their cars, how many spaces must he leave empty to ensure that he can reach any possible car?

12. Imagine a railroad switching circuit such as the following. Railroad cars are given unique numbers, from 1 onward. Cars come in from the right in a random order, and the goal is to assemble the cars in numeric order on the left.

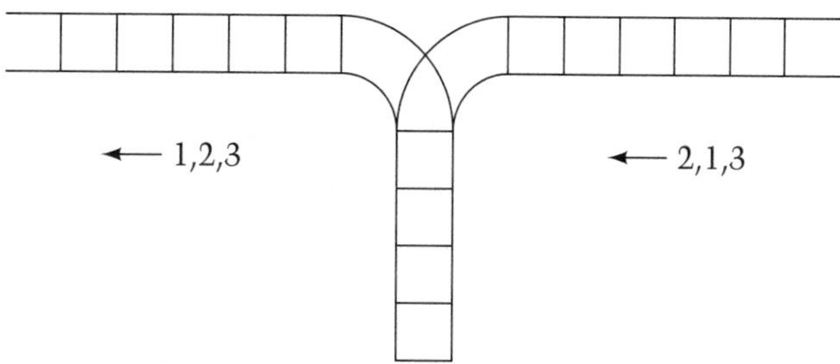

For example, to assemble the cars in the sequence shown (2, 1, 3), the car numbered 2 would be switched onto the siding. Then the car numbered 1 would be moved onto the siding and then to the left. Next, the car numbered 2 would be moved up from the siding and assembled behind car 1. Finally, the car numbered 3 would be moved from the right to the left, via the siding. Note that the cars in the siding work as a stack, because if a car is moved onto a nonempty siding, the existing cars cannot be accessed until the new car is removed.

Can you describe an algorithm that will rearrange the cars in sequential order regardless of the order in which they appear on the left? What is the complexity of your algorithm as a function of n, the number of cars entering on the right?

13. Suppose that your railroad switching circuit has the property that you can move cars onto the siding and from there move them to the left, but you cannot move cars back to the right once they have been moved to the siding. Can you now rearrange any sequence of cars into ascending order? Can you characterize what sequences can be ordered and what sequences cannot?

14. Some people prefer to define the `Stack` data type by means of a series of *axioms*. An example axiom might be that if an `addLast` operation is followed by a `getLast`, the value at the top of the stack will be the same as the value inserted. We can write this in a codelike fashion, as follows:

```
Object val = new Integer(7);
stk.push(val);
boolean test = (val == stk.getLast()); // test must always be true
```

Trace the `Vector` implementation of the stack and verify the following axioms:

a.
```
Stack stk = new Stack();
boolean test = stk.isEmpty(); // should always be true
```

b.
```
stk.addLast(new Integer(2));
boolean test = stk.isEmpty(); // should always be false
```

c.
```
Stack stk = new Stack();
boolean test = stk.getLast(); // should always raise error
```

15. Using a `LinkedList` as the implementation structure, do the same analysis as in the previous question.

Programming Projects

1. Modify the program presented in Section 10.2 so that it will ignore parentheses and brackets given in string or character literals. Also add the ability to check for brackets as well as the other two categories of values.

2. Here is a technique that uses two stacks in order to determine whether a phrase is a palindrome, that is, reads the same forward and backward—for example, the word "rotator" is a palindrome, as is the string "rats live on no evil star."
   a. Read the characters one by one and transfer them into a stack. The characters in the stack will then represent the reversed word.

b. Once all characters have been read, transfer half the characters from the first stack into a second stack. Thus, the order of the words will have been restored.

c. If there was an odd number of characters, remove one further character from the original stack.

d. Finally, test the two stacks for equality, element by element. If they are the same, the word is a palindrome.

Write a procedure that takes a `String` argument and test to see whether it is a palindrome, using this algorithm.

3. Modify the program from the previous question so that it can handle spaces (as in "race car") and upper- and lowercase differences. A further modification will strip out punctuation, as in "a man, a plan, a canal, panama."

4. Modify the Calculator program described in Section 10.4 to add the following four new buttons:

   a. `Clear`. This will clear the current display, setting it to zero.

   b. `Memory`. This will pop the current value from the stack.

   c. `Reverse`. This will reverse the top two elements in the stack.

   d. `Duplicate`. This will duplicate the current value in the stack, placing the same value on the top of the stack and one level down.

5. Using the Calculator program described in Section 10.4, if you enter the sequence 5 (Enter) 2 (divide), you will see 2.5, the expected result. If you now click a numeric key, such as 3, you will see the display changed to 23.5. That is, the numeric key has multiplied the display by 10 and added the value 3. This is correct when numbers are being entered but not following a processing of an operation. To correct this, modify the program so that it will keep track of whether the last button clicked was a digit button. If a digit button is clicked after an operation, it should do an implicit `enter` operation before performing the digit action.

6. Another classic application of stacks is the conversion of expressions written in infix notation, such as $(2 + 3) * 4$, into equivalent expressions written in postfix Polish. Here, the stack is used to hold intermediate operators while the right-hand operand is being discovered. Write a program that reads an infix value and produces the equivalent postfix Polish expression.

7. The playing card abstraction described in Section 10.5 is very simple. For example, it can display cards only in a face-up fashion. In many games, cards can be either face up or face down. Describe the changes that need to be made to the class `Card` to support the manipulation of cards that can be face down as well as face up.

8. The display for the card faces is very primitive. One improvement is to use the graphics capabilities provided by the class `Graphics` to draw simple forms, such as the following:

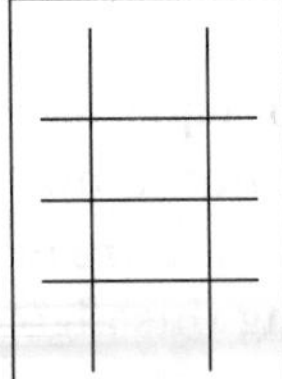
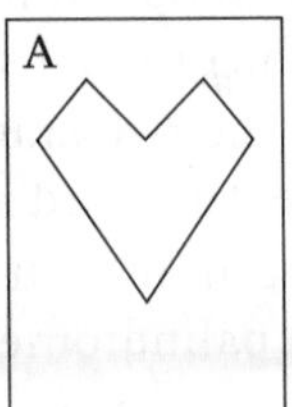

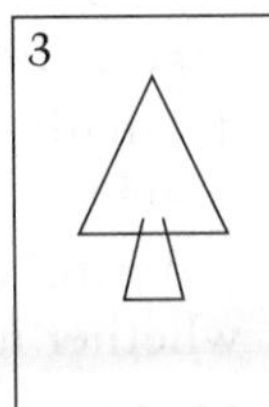

9. An even better display for the playing card abstraction uses the ability of `Graphics` to display a bit-mapped image. Many public domain images of playing cards can be found on the Web. Find such a collection and modify the `Card` abstraction so that it will display the image.
10. Investigate the `MouseMotionListener`, which permits the program to be informed as the mouse is moving, between the time it is pressed and released. Using this facility, you can redraw the topmost card from the source deck and show it moving across the screen to the destination deck.
11. Using the ability to load sound clips from a file, add some sounds to the solitaire game, such as a swish when cards are moved or a beep when a move cannot be made.
12. One rule of Frog that we did not include is that if any aces are uncovered as the 13 cards are being initially dealt into the stock, they can be immediately played on one of the waste piles. Modify the program to incorporate this feature.
13. Another simple solitaire game is Calculation. This game is similar to Frog, only the foundations are built up in an arithmetical progression. The first foundation builds by ones, as in Frog. The second foundation builds by twos, as in the sequence ace, 3, 5, 7, 9, jack, king, 2, 4, 6, 8, 10, queen. The third foundation builds by threes, and the last by fours.
14. More complicated solitaire games, such as Klondike (the "traditional" solitaire game), require both that cards have the ability to be both face up and face down (see programming project 7) and that card piles will display all the elements in the stack, with all cards other than the first showing only their top half. Describe such a card pile, and use it to implement one of these solitaire games.
15. Blackjack is another popular two- (or more) person card game. Using the playing card abstraction developed in this chapter, write a program that will permit the computer to play blackjack with the user. What data structure is most useful for storing the hand of cards?

CHAPTER 11

DEQUES

The *deque* ADT (pronounced "deck") is another abstraction in which the order that elements are inserted is not abstracted away but must be explicitly maintained. The deque is a combination of the stack and the queue. The term is short for *double-ended queue,* although *doubled-ended staque* might be equally appropriate. The deque corresponds to a linear collection that permits elements to be inserted or removed from either end:

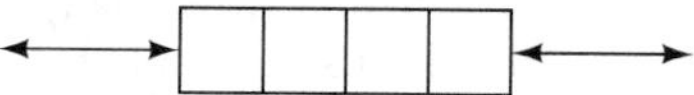

In our library, the deque ADT is represented by the `Deque` interface. This interface inherits from both the `Stack` and `Queue` interfaces and, for the sake of completeness, adds the method `addFirst`, thereby providing all the facilities needed to access, add, and remove values from either end:

```
public interface Deque extends Stack, Queue {
  public void addFirst(Object newElement);
};
```

An interface that inherits from two or more parent interfaces is sometimes said to be exhibiting *multiple inheritance*. This topic, controversial in some languages, is one that we explore in more detail in the sidebar. If we add to the interface the methods inherited (through both `Stack` and `Queue`) from `Collection`, we get the following list:

`void addFirst (Object)` Inserts a new element by placing it at the front of the deque. The relative positions of all other elements in the deque remain unchanged.

`void addLast (Object)` Inserts a new element by placing it at the back of the deque. The relative positions of all other elements in the deque remain unchanged.

`Object getFirst ()` Returns the element at the front of the deque. This method will throw `NoSuchElementException` if the deque is currently empty. Invoking this method will not change the state of the collection in any way.

`Object getLast ()` Returns the element at the back of the deque. This method will throw `NoSuchElementException` if the deque is currently empty. Invoking this method will not change the state of the collection in any way.

`void removeFirst ()` Removes the current front of the deque. This method will throw `NoSuchElementException` if the deque is currently empty.

`void removeLast ()` Removes the current end of the deque. This method will throw `NoSuchElementException` if the deque is currently empty.

MULTIPLE INHERITANCE IN INTERFACES: NO DIAMOND OF DEATH

A class that has two or more parent classes is said to be using *multiple inheritance*. Java restricts multiple inheritance to interfaces, whereas some other languages, such as C++, permit classes to use the mechanism as well. There is nothing inherently wrong with the technique; indeed, it can often be a very useful and powerful programming tool. There are, nevertheless, some subtle dangers the programmer can stumble over. What will happen, for example, if the two parent classes turn out to have a common ancestor?

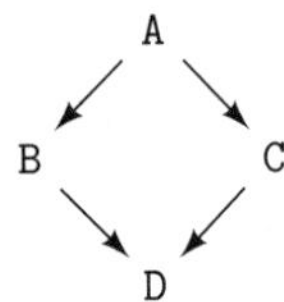

What happens if the classes `B` and `C` use the same method name for different operations? Which method should be the one used by `D`? Another problem occurs if class `A` declares any data fields. How many copies of these fields should instances of class `D` possess? One or two? These difficulties have led some authors, such as Scott Meyers [Meyers 98] writing about C++, to label this the "diamond of death" and to suggest that it be avoided at all costs.

In Java, however, multiple inheritance is restricted to interfaces. You cannot create a class that has more than one parent. Thus, the problems inherent in the diamond of death do not arise. An interface cannot declare a data field, and thus there is no need to decide how many data fields a child should be given. Similarly, interfaces provide only descriptions of methods, not the code itself. If the same description is found in two parent interfaces, they are simply combined in the description of the child class. Thus, using multiple inheritance in interfaces is perfectly safe.

`Enumeration elements ()` Returns an `Enumeration` that can be used to access the elements held in the collection. Elements are enumerated from the front to the back of the deque.

`boolean isEmpty ()` Returns `true` if the collection is empty, and returns `false` otherwise. This method will always return `true` when applied on a newly created collection. Invoking this method will not change the state of the collection in any way.

`int size ()` Returns an integer value that indicates the number of elements held by the collection. This method will always return zero when applied on a newly created collection. Invoking this method will not change the state of the collection in any way.

It might seem more natural to postpone our discussion of the deque ADT until after Chapter 12, which discusses queues. However, if a deque can be viewed as a generalization of a queue, a queue can also be viewed as a restriction of a deque. The *implementation* of the queue ADT is almost always accomplished by using a data structure that implements the more general `Deque` interface.

We have already encountered one data type that supports the `Deque` interface: `LinkedList`. However, we have seen in Chapter 10 that a vectorlike structure can, in some situations, have faster execution times than can a linked list. We will see this again when we investigate the `IndexedDeque` data type later in this chapter. First, however, let us explore some typical uses for the deque data abstraction.

* 11.1 A Fractal Snowflake

Both stacks and queues are frequently used as "work lists," as holders for tasks waiting to be performed. In these cases, selecting a stacklike access strategy will result in tasks being performed in a different order from that resulting from a queuelike access strategy. We will illustrate this with a simple, but nicely visual, example program.

We can use the idea of *fractals* (see sidebar) to create a snowflake pattern. We start with a triangle, which is composed of three lines. Selecting each line in turn, we divide the line into thirds. Removing the middle third, we replace it with two new lines that form a smaller triangle. In this fashion, one line has been replaced by four.

FRACTALS AND BROCCOLI

The fundamental idea behind a *fractal* is to repeat the same pattern over and over at ever smaller levels of resolution.

One time, I started to explain fractals to my ten-year-old daughter, and she stopped me by saying, "Oh, I know all about fractals. They are just like broccoli." She was right. If you look at a broccoli stem, it looks just like the entire broccoli clump. And if you look at a smaller piece of the stem, it looks like the stem itself, and so on. So fractals are nothing new; nature has been using them for a very long time.

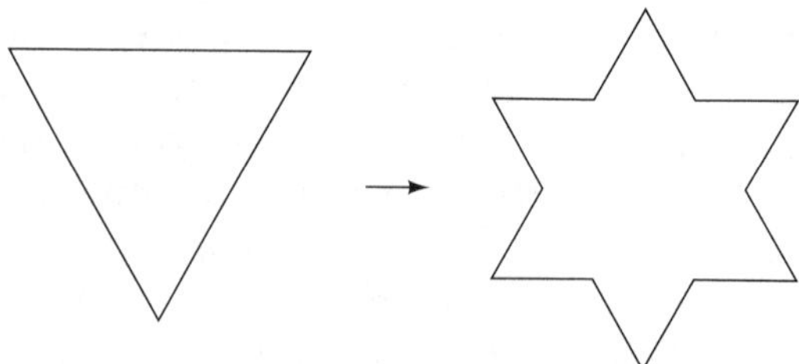

Each of these four is then given a similar treatment, and so on. Of course, we cannot continue indefinitely, and so we will halt when the lines become sufficiently small. An example output is shown in Figure 11.1.

Our fractal snowflake program makes use of a class `Line`, which is defined as follows:

```
class Line {
  public Line (Point s, Point e) { start = s; stop = e; }
  public Point start, stop;

  public void draw (Graphics g)
    { g.drawLine(start.x, start.y, stop.x, stop.y); }
}
```

WHAT'S THE POINT?

The class `Point` used in `Snowflake` is another useful class provided by the Java standard library. A `Point` represents a location in two-dimensional space and contains two public integer data fields, represented by the names `x` and `y`. Points can be used whenever it is necessary to manipulate integer coordinates.

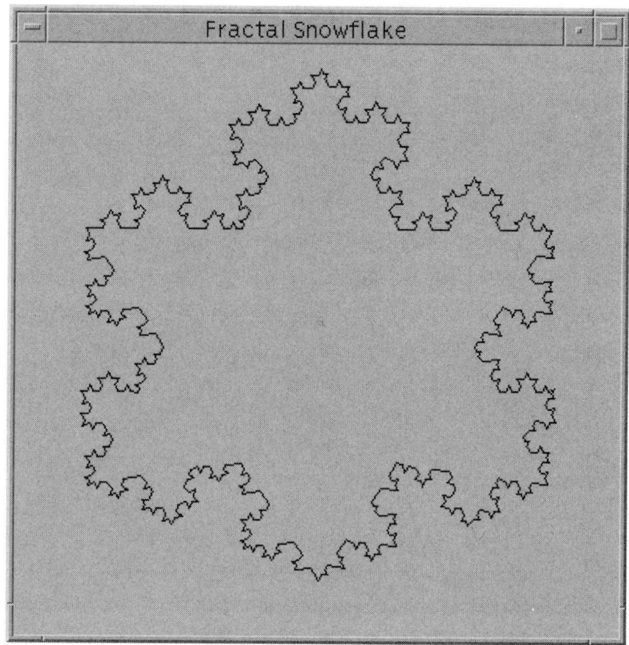

FIGURE 11.1 Screen Shot of Fractal Snowflake Application

A line is defined by two endpoints, which are represented as pairs of coordinates. To transform a line, we first compute the difference in x and y coordinates. Because we are dividing the line into thirds, it is easier to let dx represent one-third of the x coordinate difference and dy one-third of the y coordinate difference. Using these values, the positions of the new endpoints can then be determined as offsets:

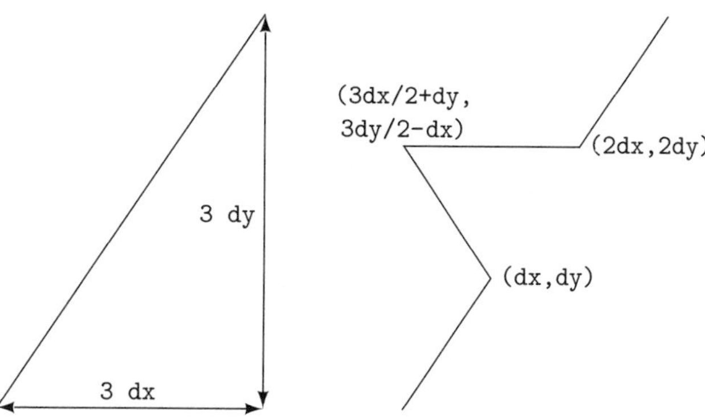

The program to produce a fractal snowflake is as follows. Two collections are being used. The working set of lines is held in the variable `lines`. When a line becomes sufficiently small, it is moved to the container held by the variable done. Printing the image therefore consists of simply printing the values from both of these collections. The `sleep` command is used to slow the program, so that the results are produced in the fashion of an animation.

```
import java.awt.*;
import java.util.Enumeration;
import jds.Deque;
import jds.collection.LinkedList;
import jds.collection.IndexedDeque;
import jds.util.CloseQuit;

public class Snowflake extends Frame {
  public static void main (String [ ] args)
  { Snowflake world = new Snowflake(); world.show(); world.run(); }

  public Snowflake () {
    setTitle("Fractal Snowflake"); setSize(400, 400);
    addWindowListener(new CloseQuit());
      // insert first lines into snowflake
    Point a = new Point(50, 140);
    Point b = new Point(350, 140);
    Point c = new Point(200, 360);
    lines.addFirst(new Line(a, b));
    lines.addFirst(new Line(b, c));
    lines.addFirst(new Line(c, a));
  }

  private Deque lines = new IndexedDeque();
  private Deque done = new IndexedDeque();

  public void run () { // now make the snowflake
    while (! lines.isEmpty()) {
      Line aLine = (Line) lines.getFirst();
      lines.removeFirst();
      processLine(aLine);
      try { Thread.sleep(100); } catch(Exception e) { }
      repaint();
    }
  }
```

```
  private void processLine (Line aLine) {
      // first compute line lengths
    int dx = (aLine.stopx - aLine.startx)/3;
    int dy = (aLine.stopy - aLine.starty)/3;
    if ((dx * dx + dy * dy) < 10) {
      done.addFirst(aLine); // line is too small
    } else { // divide the line into four smaller lines
      Point a = new Point(lne.start.x + dx, lne.start.y+dy);
      Point b = new Point(lne.start.x + 3*dx/2 + dy,
          lne.start.y + 3*dy/2 - dx);
      Point c = new Point(lne.start.x+2*dx, lne.start.y+2*dy);
      lines.addFirst(new Line(lne.start, a));
      lines.addFirst(new Line(a, b));
      lines.addFirst(new Line(b, c));
      lines.addFirst(new Line(c, lne.stop));
    }
  }

  public void paint (Graphics g) {
    Enumeration e = lines.elements();
    while (e.hasMoreElements()) {
      Line lne = (Line) e.nextElement();
      lne.draw(g);
    }
    e = done.elements();
    while (e.hasMoreElements()) {
      Line lne = (Line) e.nextElement();
      lne.draw(g);
    }
  }
}
```

The order in which lines are processed is relatively unimportant, and so either stacklike commands (inserting the elements into the list using `addFirst`) or queuelike commands (inserting the elements into the list using `addLast`) can be used. In the exercises at the end of this chapter, we explore some of the implications of this difference.

11.2 Depth- and Breadth-First Search

Many problems involve a searching process, but any search that includes a step requiring choosing between two or more alternatives may require the ability to back up and start again from an earlier location. This process is termed *backtracking*.

In one sense, backtracking is simply a technique that uses a collection like a work list, just as in the fractal snowflake program. That is, the container can be used to hold the places we have visited but not yet completely searched, which are simply in one sense jobs waiting to be performed—namely, pressing onward from a location we know we can reach.

The problem we will explore in this section is a classic backtracking puzzle: finding a path through a maze. Our main purpose in this presentation is to illustrate how a stack and a queue each provide very different types of solutions to this problem. These two approaches are given names. The style of solution we get using a stack is called a *depth-first search*, whereas the style of solution we get from a queue is termed a *breadth-first search*.

A typical maze is as follows. We will assume that the starting point for the search is always in the lower-right corner of the maze and that the goal is the upper-left corner.

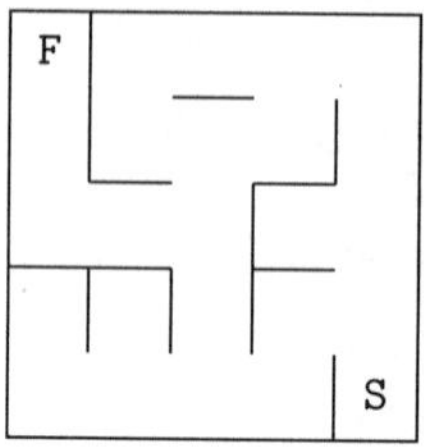

We want the maze-searching program to be general, able to solve any two-dimensional maze and not simply the example maze shown here. We therefore design a scheme so that the description of the maze can be read from an input file. Different files can be used to test the program on a variety of mazes. To see how to do this, note that a maze can be described as a sequence of squares, or *cells*. The maze shown here, for example, is a 5-by-5 square of 25 cells. Each cell can be characterized by a number, which describes the surrounding walls. Sixteen numbers are sufficient. In this fashion, we have the following vocabulary for describing cells:

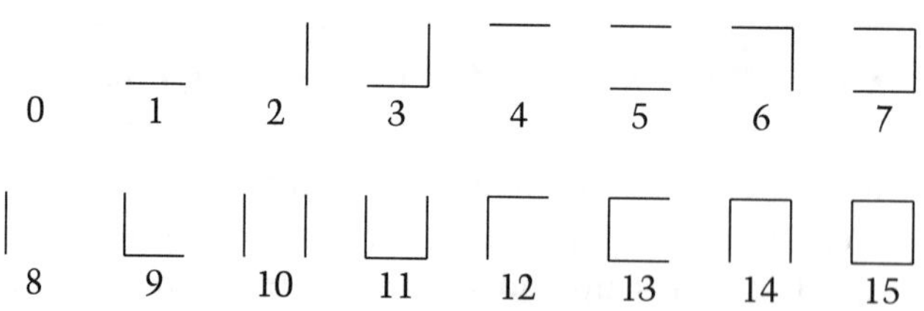

The pattern of the numeric values becomes apparent if one considers the number not as a decimal value but as a binary pattern. The 1's position indicates the presence or absence of a south wall, the 2's position the east wall, the 4's position the north wall, and the 8's position the west wall. A value such as 13 is written in binary as 1101. This indicates that there are walls to the north, west, and south but not the east.

Using this scheme, the example maze could be described by 25 integer values. In the following, we have superimposed these values on the maze to better illustrate their relationship to the original structure.

14	12	5	4	6
10	9	4	3	10
9	5	2	13	2
14	14	10	12	2
9	1	1	3	11

Our first version of the program will initialize the maze data as literal values. In the programming projects, we will suggest various improvements to this representation. The program then will display the maze. The integer array `visited` will mark the order in which cells are visited. We use this for two purposes; first, it will give us a way to tell whether a cell has been already visited. Second, it will provide a graphical representation of the order in which the search progresses.

Using Integers as Bitwise Values

Normally, we think of integers as representing arithmetic quantities, and the operations we use are addition, subtraction, multiplication, and division. But viewed in another light, an integer is nothing more than a packed array of 32 Boolean values:

01100100110011101011001010100110

In the maze program, we use only the last four Boolean positions. The *bitwise* integer operations can be used to access or to set individual bits. For example, by performing an AND operation with the constant value 4, a number we know has only 1 binary digit set, we can determine whether the corresponding bit is set in the argument:

`walls[x][y]`	0110
& 4	0100
result	0100

```
import java.awt.*;
import java.io.*;
import jds.Deque;
import jds.collection.LinkedList;
import jds.util.CloseQuit;

public class Maze extends Frame {
  public static void main (String [ ] args)
  { Maze world = new Maze("mazedata"); world.show(); world.solveMaze(); }

  public Maze (String file) {
    setSize(200, 230); setTitle("Maze Puzzle");
    addWindowListener(new CloseQuit());
  }

  private int mazeWidth = 5;
  private int mazeHeight = 5;
  private int [ ] [ ] walls = { {14, 12, 5, 4, 6}, {10, 9, 4, 3, 10},
    {9, 5, 2, 13, 2}, {14, 14, 10, 12, 2}, {9, 1, 1, 3, 11}};
  private int [ ] [ ] visited = new int[5][5];

  private void solveMaze () { ... }

  public void paint (Graphics g) {
    int y = 50;
    for (int i = 0; i < mazeHeight; i++) {
      int x = 50;
      for (int j = 0; j < mazeWidth; j++) {
        if ((walls[i][j] & 1) != 0) g.drawLine(x, y+50, x+50, y+50);
        if ((walls[i][j] & 2) != 0) g.drawLine(x+50, y, x+50, y+50);
        if ((walls[i][j] & 4) != 0) g.drawLine(x, y, x+50, y);
        if ((walls[i][j] & 8) != 0) g.drawLine(x, y, x, y+50);
        if (visited[i][j] != 0)
          g.drawString(String.valueOf(visited[i][j]), x+5, y+30);
        x += 50;
      }
      y += 50;
    }
  }
}
```

The strategy for solving the maze is found in the method `solveMaze`:

```
private void solveMaze () {
    // initialize deque with starting location
```

```
  LinkedList que = new LinkedList();
  que.addLast(new Point(mazeWidth-1, mazeHeight-1));
  int visitCount = 0;
  while (! que.isEmpty()) { // now do search
    Point p = (Point) que.getLast();
    que.removeLast();
    if (visited[p.x][p.y] == 0) { // new cell
      visited[p.x][p.y] = ++visitCount;
      repaint();
      if ((p.x == 0) && (p.y == 0))
        return; // success, we're done
      putNeighbors(p.x, p.y, que);
      try {Thread.sleep(200);} catch (Exception e) { }
    }
  }
  System.err.println("no solution");
}
```

A deque, here represented by a linked list, is used to hold the cells waiting to be investigated. The deque is initialized with the start cell, which is the lower-right corner of the maze. Two-dimensional values are here represented by instances of class `Point`, a useful class from the Java standard library. Because the deque is not empty, we remove the current element, and if it is one we have not already seen, we mark it as having been visited. The screen of the display is repainted to show the current step as having been made. Then all the neighbors for the current cell will be placed into the collection. The `sleep` method is again simply used to slow the program down, giving the appearance of an animation.

The method `putNeighbors` searches for valid neighboring cells. To do this, the variable `walls` is checked to determine which sides are walls and which are open.

```
private void putNeighbors(int x, int y, LinkedList que) {
  if ((walls[x][y] & 1) == 0) que.addLast(new Point(x+1, y));
  if ((walls[x][y] & 2) == 0) que.addLast(new Point(x, y+1));
  if ((walls[x][y] & 4) == 0) que.addLast(new Point(x-1, y));
  if ((walls[x][y] & 8) == 0) que.addLast(new Point(x, y-1));
}
```

Describing the first few steps in the process will illustrate how the search through the maze proceeds. Only one cell is reachable from the starting position, and thus the deque initially contains only one element.

Front	(3,4)	Back

This value is pulled from the deque and the neighbors of the cell inserted back into the deque. This time, there are three neighbors, so the deque will have three entries. Note that we do not check to see whether a cell has been visited at the time it is inserted into the deque, only when it is removed. Thus, the cell (4,4) will be found in the deque, even though it has already been explored.

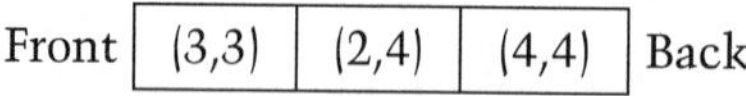

Only one value can be explored at any time. So the first element is removed from the deque and its neighbors inserted, and so on repeatedly. Two steps later, we again have a choice, and both neighbors are inserted into the deque. At this point, the deque has the following contents:

Front	(4,1)	(3,2)	(4,3)	(3,3)	(2,4)	(4,4)	Back

The next cell to be explored will be (4,1), but cells (3,2) and (2,4) and the others are also known to be reachable and are waiting to be considered should the current path not prove to be a solution. This in fact occurs when we reach cell (3,0), at which point the deque looks as follows:

Front	(3,0)	(4,1)	(3,1)	(4,2)	(3,2)	(4,3)	(3,3)	(2,4)	(4,4)	Back

Because cell (3,0) adds no new values to the deque (having no unvisited neighbors), the next entry is automatically popped from the deque. In this fashion, we start pursuing the path from (4,1), which turns out to be already visited. Position (3,1) is new but immediately dead-ends. Finally, the entry (3,2) is popped from the deque, and the search continues. The solution is ultimately found in 15 steps. The following shows the path to the solution, with the cells numbered in the order in which they were considered.

The strategy embodied in this code doggedly pursues a single path until either it reaches a dead-end or the solution is found. When a dead-end is encountered, the most recent alternative path is reactivated, and the search continues. This approach is called *depth-first search*, as it moves deeply into the structure before examining alternatives. Depth-first search is the type of search a single individual might perform in walking through a maze.

Suppose, on the other hand, that a group of people are walking through the maze. When a choice of alternative directions is encountered, the group may decide to split itself into two smaller groups and pursue both paths simultaneously. When another choice is reached, the group again splits, and so on. In this manner, all potential paths are investigated at the same time. Such a strategy is known as *breadth-first search*.

What is intriguing about the maze-searching procedure is that the code for breadth-first search is almost identical to the code for depth-first search. In fact, all that is necessary is to change the `getLast` and `removeLast` commands in `solveMaze` to `getFirst` and `removeFirst`:

```
private void solveMaze() {
  .
  .
  .
  while (! que.isEmpty()) {
    Point p = (Point) que.getFirst();
    que.removeFirst();
    .
    .
    .
  }
}
```

In doing so, we change our use of the deque from being stacklike to being queuelike. This can be illustrated by once more describing the state of the deque at various points during execution. For example, after the first step, the deque has the following values. Note how the elements are in the opposite order from the one they held in the depth-first searching version.

Front	(2,4)	(3,3)	Back

The pair (2,4) is pulled from the deque, but its neighbors—the cells (1,4) and (2,3)—are placed on the *back* of the queue. The next node to be investigated will therefore not be one of the immediate neighbors of the most recent node but an entirely different path altogether.

Front	(3,3)	(1,4)	(2,3)	Back

A few steps later, the search has been split several times, and the deque contains the following values:

Front	(3,1)	(4,0)	(0,1)	(1,2)	(1,2)	(2,1)	Back

As one might expect, a breadth-first search is more thorough but may require more time than a depth-first search. Recall that the depth-first search was able to discover the solution in 15 steps. The depth-first search is still looking after 20 steps. The following describes the search at this point.

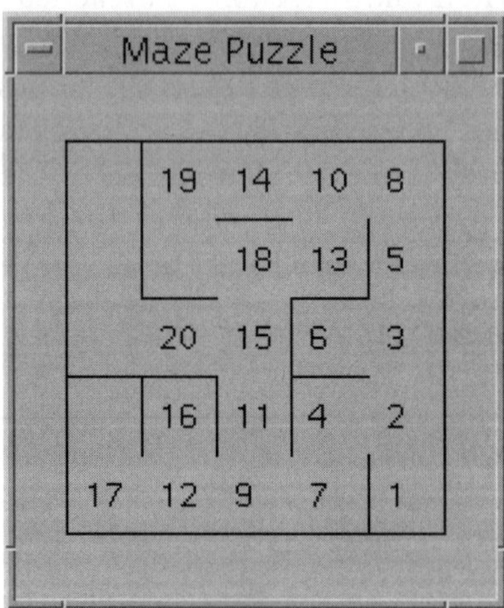

Trace carefully the sequence of the last few cells that were visited. Note how the search has jumped around all over the maze, exploring a number of alternatives at the same time. Another way to imagine breadth-first search is that it describes what would happen if one were to pour ink into the maze at the starting location, as the ink slowly permeated every path until the solution was reached.

Depth first and breadth first are both valuable techniques in a variety of searching problems and arise in a number of forms and contexts. The following differences can be noted in comparing breadth-first and depth-first searching.

- Because all paths of length 1 are investigated before examining paths of length 2, and all paths of length 2 before examining paths of length 3, a breadth-first search is guaranteed to always discover a path containing the fewest steps from start to goal, whenever such a path exists.
- Because one path is investigated before any alternatives are examined, a depth-first search *may*, if it is lucky, discover a solution more quickly than the equivalent breadth-first search. This occurs here, where the goal is encountered after examining only 15 locations in the depth-first version, whereas the goal is reached only after 25 iterations in the breadth-first version. But this benefit is not certain, and a bad selection of alternatives to pursue can lead to many dead-end searches before the proper path to the goal is revealed.
- In particular, suppose that for a particular problem, some but not all paths are infinite and there exists at least one finite path from start to goal. Breadth-first search is guaranteed to find the shortest solution. Depth-first search may have the unfortunate luck to pursue a never-ending path and can hence fail to find a solution.

11.3 An Implementation: The IndexedDeque

In Chapter 10, we noted how the `Vector` data abstraction could, in the right situation, be preferable to a `LinkedList` as an implementation of the `Stack` ADT. One would expect that a similar array-based technique might be applicable for implementing the deque. However, the `Vector` suffered from an inability to remove or insert values at the front.

In this section, we will describe a new data type, the `IndexedDeque`. Like the `Vector`, the `IndexedDeque` will maintain data values in an array. The key difference is that in the `Vector`, the first position, the bottom, is always location zero, whereas the `IndexedVector` allows this position to move as values are added to and removed from the collection. An internal data field, named `firstFilled`, points to the location that contains values.

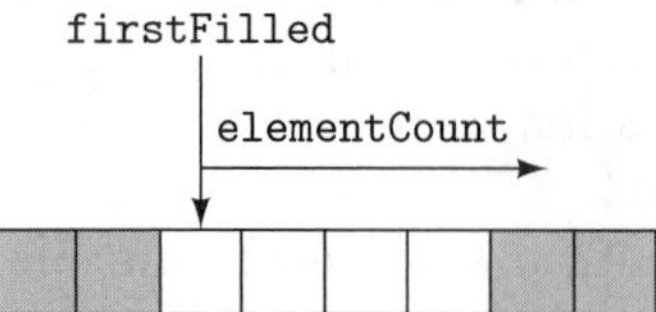

In some cases, the values held in the array can wrap around from top to bottom, so that the first empty position has an index value smaller than the first filled:

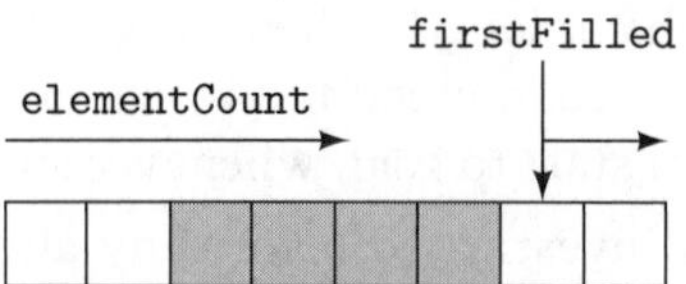

It is easy, and useful, to permit this data structure to be indexed, in the same fashion as the `Vector`. The methods in the class IndexedDeque that implement the Indexed interface are as follows:

```
public class IndexedDeque implements Indexed, Deque {

  private int firstFilled = 0;
  private int elementCount = 0;
  private Object [ ] elementData = new Object [5];

    // the Collection interface
  public boolean isEmpty () { return elementCount == 0; }
  public int size () { return elementCount; }
  public Enumeration elements () { return new IndexedEnumeration(this); }

    // the Indexed interface
  public Object elementAt (int index) {
    if ((index < 0) || (index >= elementCount))
      throw new ArrayIndexOutOfBoundsException(index);
    return elementData[(firstFilled+index) % elementData.length];
  }

  public void setElementAt (Object val, int index) {
    if ((index < 0) || (index >= elementCount))
      throw new ArrayIndexOutOfBoundsException(index);
    elementData[(firstFilled+index) % elementData.length] = val;
  }

  public void setSize (int newSize) {
    while (newSize > elementData.length)
```

```
      ensureCapacity(2 * elementData.length);
    elementCount = newSize;
  }

  public synchronized void ensureCapacity (int newCapacity) {
    if (newCapacity <= elementData.length) return;
    Object [ ] newArray = new Object [newCapacity];
    int count = 0;
    if (firstFilled + elementCount <= elementData.length) {
      for (int i = firstFilled; count < elementCount; i++)
        newArray[count++] = elementData[i];
    } else {
      for (int i = firstFilled; i < elementData.length; i++)
        newArray[count++] = elementData[i];
      for (int i = 0; count < elementCount; i++)
        newArray[count++] = elementData[i];
    }
    firstFilled = 0;
    elementData = newArray;
  }

  public synchronized void addElementAt (int index, Object val) {
    if ((index < 0) || (index > elementCount))
      throw new ArrayIndexOutOfBoundsException(index);
    setSize(elementCount+1);
    for (int i = elementCount-1; i > index; i--)
      setElementAt(elementAt(i-1), i);
    setElementAt(val, index);
  }

  public synchronized void removeElementAt (int index) {
    if ((index < 0) || (index >= elementCount))
      throw new ArrayIndexOutOfBoundsException(index);
    while (++index < elementCount)
      setElementAt(elementAt(index), index-1);
    setElementAt(null, index-1);
    elementCount--;
  }
  .
  .
  .
}
```

There is no constructor for the class; however, when first created, the data fields `firstFilled` and `elementCount` will be initialized to zero, and the elementData will be set aside large enough to hold five values. Both the size and the capacity of the collection can be modified by the methods setSize and ensureCapacity. Exercise 6 has a series of questions that lead you through the analysis of this code.

To support the Deque interface, we must incorporate methods to add, access, and remove values from the front and the back of the collection. These methods can be written as follows:

```
public class IndexedDeque implements Indexed, Deque {

  public Object getFirst () { return elementAt(0); }

  public Object getLast () { return elementAt(elementCount-1); }

  public void addLast (Object val) { addElementAt(val, elementCount); }

  public synchronized void addFirst (Object val) {
    if (++elementCount >= elementData.length)
      ensureCapacity (2 * elementData.length);
    if (--firstFilled < 0) firstFilled = elementData.length-1;
    setElementAt(val, 0);
  }

  public void removeLast () { removeElementAt(elementCount-1); }

  public synchronized void removeFirst() {
    if (elementCount == 0) throw new NoSuchElementException();
    elementData[firstFilled] = null;
    if (++firstFilled == elementData.length) firstFilled = 0;
    elementCount--;
  }
}
```

The series of questions in exercise 8 will lead you through an exploration of this code.

We know from Chapter 12 that the IndexedDeque is faster than the LinkedList when used as a Queue (and much faster than the Vector when used as a Queue), but how does the IndexedDeque compare to the Vector when used as a Stack (Figure 11.2)? If we repeat the experiment from Section 10.6 that measured the execution time of the Stack abstraction, substituting an IndexedDeque for the LinkedList, we observe the timings shown in Figure 11.3. The result indicates a small performance gain for the Vector over the IndexedDeque.

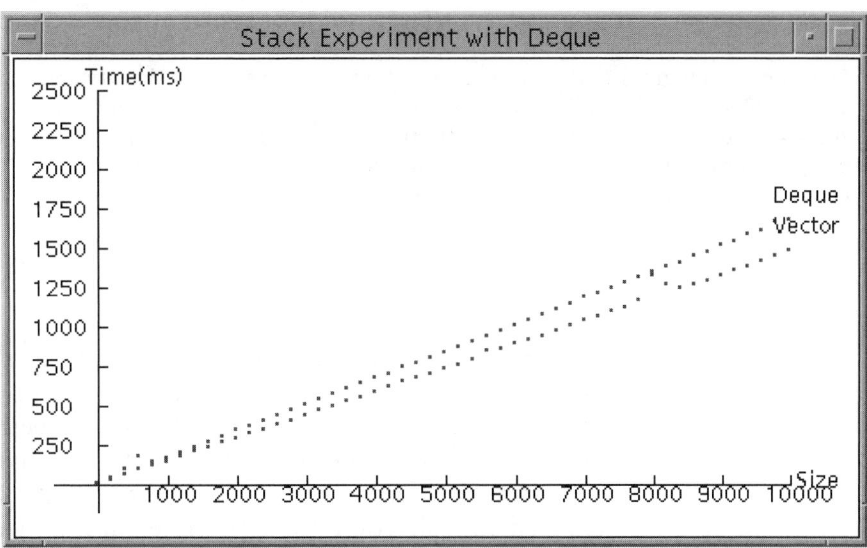

FIGURE 11.2 Comparison of `Vector` and `IndexedDeque` as `Stack`

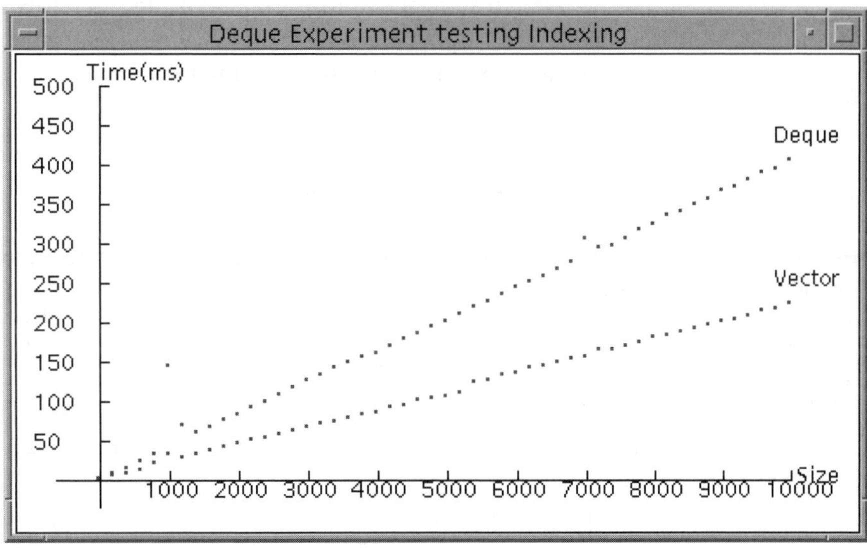

FIGURE 11.3 Comparison of `Vector` and `IndexedDeque` as `Indexed`

EXPERIMENT: USING THE INDEXEDDEQUE AS A STACK

Develop the program that tests the use of an `IndexedDeque` as a `Stack`, and verify the results shown. In Chapter 10, two distributions of operations were described: One distribution performed N sets of insertions and removals on a stack of size 10, and the other performed insertions and removals on a stack of size N. Do you observe similar relative execution times with both distributions?

Suppose that instead of keeping the size of the stack constant, we compare a `Vector` and an `IndexedDeque` on the speed of their indexing operations. The `IndexedDeque`, you will recall, performs an addition modular division on each element access. We can investigate this by writing a program that repeats, N times, accessing and setting each element in a ten-element collection. Here, the differences between the `Vector` and the `IndexedDeque` become more pronounced. This experiment suggests that when the queuelike features, that is, the ability to set and to access elements from the front of the collection, are unimportant, the `Vector` should be used in preference to the `IndexedDeque`. However, when deque operations are important, the `IndexedDeque` is almost always faster than the `LinkedList` performing the same task.

EXPERIMENT: WHICH END IS UP?

Because the `Deque` interface permits values to be added or removed from either end, there are two ways to use this structure as a stack. Either the pair `addLast`, `removeLast` or the pair `addFirst`, `removeFirst` will work. For either implementation of this abstraction (the `LinkedList` or the `IndexedDeque`), is there a measurable difference in the execution times between these two alternatives? The same experiment can be performed with regard to `Queue` operations.

EXPERIMENT: USING AN INDEXEDDEQUE AS A VECTOR

Develop the program to compare the execution time of the `IndexedDeque` when used as an indexed structure to the execution time of the `Vector`. In this experiment, the size of the collection has been limited to ten elements. Would the results be different if we were dealing with a collection of N elements?

11.4 Chapter Summary

Key Concepts

- Deque
- Multiple inheritance
- Depth-first search
- Breadth-first search
- Backtracking
- `IndexedDeque`

A deque is an abstraction that represents a linear collection permitting insertion or removal from either end. A deque can be seen as a generalization of both stack and queue. Alternatively, stacks and queues can be seen as limited forms of a deque.

We have used the deque as a vehicle to explore two important approaches to searching: depth-first search and breadth-first search. The first stores the intermediate states in a stack and as a consequence will follow a single path as far as possible. A breadth-first search, on the other hand, stores the intermediate states in a queue and so pushes each path out a little farther until one path eventually reaches the goal.

Finally, we have explored a new data structure that supports the `Deque` ADT. The `IndexedDeque` is implemented in a fashion similar to the `Vector`, holding elements in an underlying array of objects. Unlike the `Vector`, the `IndexedDeque` keeps a reference to both the starting position and the number of elements in the collection. This permits rapid insertion and removal from the front of the container.

Further Information

If we simply combined the `Stack` and `Queue` interfaces but did not add any new methods, we would have a data abstraction that permitted insertions at either end but removals from only one side. Such a structure is sometimes termed a *scroll* [Nyhoff 99]. Other authors term this an output-restricted doubled-ended queue [Knuth 97, Weiss 96].

The reference for Scott Meyers's discussion of multiple inheritance is [Meyers 98].

Study Questions

1. What is the term *deque* short for?
2. What are the defining characteristics of the deque data abstraction?
3. What does it mean to say that the class `Deque` exhibits multiple inheritance?
4. What methods does the `Deque` class inherit from `Stack`? What methods from `Queue`? What methods from both?
5. What data structure defined in earlier chapters supports the `Deque` interface?
6. Why is multiple inheritance of classes more difficult than multiple inheritance of interfaces?

7. What does it mean to say that a deque is being used in a "stacklike" fashion or a "queuelike" fashion?
8. What are the characteristics of a depth-first search? A breadth-first search?
9. Explain the relationship between the numbers 0 to 15 and the walls and halls in the maze puzzle.
10. Give the integer encoding of the following simple six-cell maze:

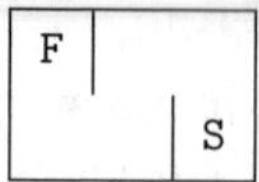

11. Explain the seemingly paradoxical statement that a breadth-first search is guaranteed to find a shortest path through a maze, although it may take longer than a depth-first search to find it.
12. What is the fundamental difference between the `Vector` data type and an `IndexedDeque`?

Exercises

1. How might you use a single deque to determine whether a string is a palindrome? (See programming project 2, Chapter 10).
2. Fill in the following chart with the execution times for each operation, using the indicated implementation technique. For each entry, indicate whether the execution time is *always, worst case,* or *expected*.

Operation	`LinkedList`	`IndexedDeque`
`addFirst`	*O*(_)	*O*(_)
`addLast`	*O*(_)	*O*(_)
`getFirst`	*O*(_)	*O*(_)
`getLast`	*O*(_)	*O*(_)
`removeFirst`	*O*(_)	*O*(_)
`removeLast`	*O*(_)	*O*(_)

3. Compare the abstraction of the `IndexedDeque` to the `RingBufferQueue` described in Section 12.4.2. In what ways are they similar? In what ways are they different?

4. Execute the fractal snowflake program, first using stack commands and then using queue commands. Describe the difference you see. Can you explain how this difference comes about?
5. Consider the following diagram. Starting from node A, list the vertices as they might be visited in a breadth-first search and as they might be visited in a depth-first search. Note that there are many different sequences for both forms of search.

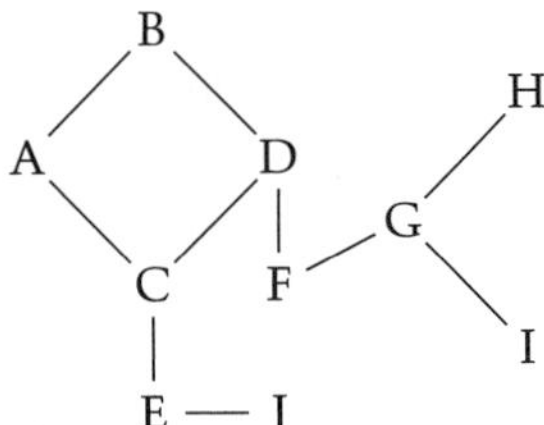

6. The following questions will lead you through an analysis of the `IndexedDeque` methods that support the `Indexed` interface.
   a. Which methods in the `IndexedDeque` class are $O(1)$? Which are $O(n)$?
   b. Explain the purpose of the modular division operator in the method `elementAt`. Consider an array with six positions, holding four values that begin at location 3. Show the actual positions in the buffer for each deque index value, and verify the calculation used to translate the deque index into a buffer index.
   c. Describe with a picture the result of calling `setSize` under each of the following conditions.
      (i) The new size is smaller than the current size.
      (ii) The new size is larger than the current size but smaller than the current capacity.
      (iii) The new size is larger than the current capacity.
   d. What happens if a call to `ensureCapacity` is made with a new capacity smaller than the current capacity?
   e. Assume that a call to `ensureCapacity` is made on an indexed queue with characteristics as described in part (b). The new capacity is set at 8. Draw a picture of the resulting queue.
   f. To see why the method `ensureCapacity` must be synchronized, explain what will happen if it were not and two threads each tried to perform the actions described in part (e). Assume that the first thread was suspended immediately after allocating the new buffer, whereas the second ran to completion.

g. What is the worst-case complexity of the method `addElementAt`? What situation does the worst case represent? Does the result differ depending on whether reallocation of the inner buffer occurs in the method `ensureCapacity`? (Be careful here; part (f) should make you think more carefully about the first two.)

h. Whereas the other methods check that the index value is not greater than or equal to `elementCount`, the `addElement` method checks only greater than. Why? Verify that the correct result is produced if an element is added to position zero of an empty collection. Imagine a collection of three elements; there are four positions where one could add a new element. Describe these four positions, identify the call that would be made to add an element in each position, and verify that the correct result is produced in each case.

i. What is the worst-case complexity of the method `removeElementAt`? What situation does the worst case represent?

j. Write a scenario similar to question (f) to illustrate why the `addElementAt` and `removeElementAt` methods must be synchronized.

7. Why does the method `setSize` double the size of the current buffer rather than simply setting it equal to the value passed as argument? *Hint:* Consider the total execution time of a long series of `addLast` operations.

8. The following questions will lead you through an analysis of the `IndexedDeque` methods that support the `Deque` interface:

   a. Verify that the method `addLast` produces the correct result in each of the following situations:

      (i) An initially empty collection

      (ii) A collection that is not yet at capacity

      (iii) A completely full collection, that is, one for which the size is the same as the capacity

   b. Why is it not necessary to synchronize the method `addLast`?

   c. Assuming that a reallocation of the buffer does not take place, what is the complexity of the method `addFirst`? Could `addFirst` have been implemented using `addElementAt`? Why would this not have been a good idea?

   d. What is the complexity of the method `removeFirst`? Could `removeFirst` have been implemented using `removeElementAt`? Why would this not have been a good idea?

9. Describe a situation in which a call on `nextElement` in a vector enumeration will throw a `NoSuchElementException`. *Hint:* What can happen if a value is removed from a vector between the invocations of `hasMoreElements` and `nextElement`?

Programming Projects

1. At the beginning of Chapter 10, we explained how a `Stack` would be used to facilitate the processing of backspace keys when handling keyboard input. But in fact, character values are read from both sides: from the front to access the character values and from the back to remove characters in response to a backspace. Create an application that will simulate this use. Your application will display a text box, which will be updated every time the programmer types a key. On some platforms, you may not be able to trap the backspace as a key value, so you can substitute another key, such as the `@` key, for this purpose.
2. Replace the `LinkedList` in the fractal snowflake program with an instance of `IndexedDeque`. Then, using the ability to index this data structure, write a loop that randomly selects a line to process rather than selecting the line from the beginning or the end. Describe how the graphical display of this program differs from either the stack or the queue versions of the program.
3. What happens if the triangle that begins the fractal snowflake program is replaced by a square? What happens if the original figure is a set of nested triangles?
4. In exercise 8(d), you explored the difference in execution time between `removeFirst()` and `removeElementAt(0)`. Would it be possible to rewrite `removeElementAt` so that removals of the first position would be as fast as `removeFirst`? What about removal of the second position if the size of the array is very large? Rewrite the `removeElementAt` so that removals anywhere in the first half of the collection are speeded up.
5. Modify the `Maze` puzzle so that it will read the maze description from a file. First, read two integer values that represent the height and the width of the maze and then the values that describe the maze. Adjust the size of the window according to the height and the width of the maze.
6. In the implementation of the `IndexedDeque`, an alternative to maintain an explicit count of the number of elements is to maintain the index of the first free position, as well as the first filled position. Implement a version of the `IndexedDeque` using this approach. Which methods become easier? Which become more difficult? Design and conduct experiments to compare the execution times of the two implementations.
7. Here is another classic searching puzzle: A farmer on the south side of the Thames River is holding a wolf, a goat, and a cabbage and somehow

must transport all four to the north side of the river. Unfortunately, he has only one very small boat—so small, in fact, that in addition to himself, it can hold only one other occupant. (It is a very large cabbage.) Only the farmer can row the boat. He cannot leave the goat alone with the cabbage; nor can he leave the wolf alone with the goat. The wolf, fortunately, will not eat the cabbage. What are the crossings the farmer must perform to carry all four to the north side of the Thames?

Explain how to characterize this problem using backtracking; then write a program to solve the puzzle. Is it faster to use depth-first or breadth-first searching?

8. Construct a program to automatically create maze descriptions, in the format of Section 11.2. The mazes must not have openings along the outside edges and must be solvable.

CHAPTER 12

QUEUES

Like the stack, the queue represents a linear collection. You will recall that a linear data abstraction is one that remembers the order in which values were placed into the collection. In the case of the queue, elements are added to one end and removed from the other:

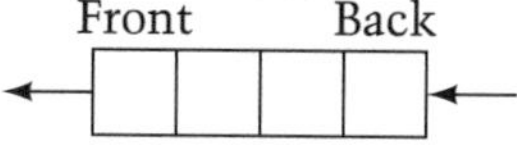

This style of use is sometimes termed first in first out, or FIFO. Queues occur frequently in everyday life, such as a queue of people waiting for a checkout clerk at a grocery store or waiting to enter a theater.

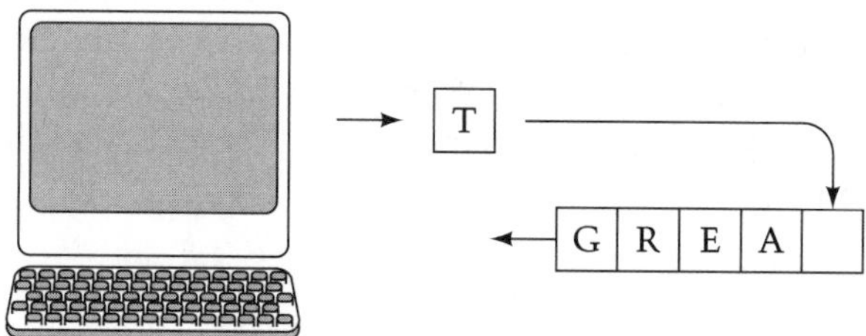

Queues are used extensively in the implementation of many computer applications, such as operating systems. A good example is the processing of characters in response to the user's pressing a key on a keyboard. Typically, the hardware associated with a keyboard will store in a buffer one character wide the binary representation of the key that was pressed and then notify the operating system (by raising an interrupt) that a keyboard event has taken place. It is important that the operating system respond to this interrupt very quickly, before the user has time to strike another key and overwrite the one-character buffer. But because the operating system must act very quickly, it does not have time to perform many tasks. In particular, the application program that is reading the keyboard may not yet be ready to receive the value. Thus, the operating system copies the character from the one-character buffer onto a queue of waiting characters. At a later point, the application program reads these values, removing them from the character queue. By the time the application program performs the `read` operation, several characters may have already been processed by the operating system and placed into the queue. Because the characters are stored in a queue, they will be processed by the application program in the same order that they were entered at the keyboard.

12.1 THE QUEUE ADT

As an abstract data type, the queue is defined in part by the `Queue` interface, shown in Figure 12.1. This interface inherits directly from `Collection` and incorporates the ability to add elements to and remove elements from the collection. Including the inherited operations and the properties that must also be included as part of the queue ADT, the interface can be described as follows:

`void addLast (Object)` Inserts a new element by placing it at the back of the queue. The relative positions of all other elements in the queue remain unchanged.

`Object getFirst ()` Returns the element that has been in the queue the longest period of time. Because elements can be inserted only at the end of the queue, this will naturally be the element at the front. This method will throw `NoSuchElementException` if the queue is currently empty. Invoking this method will not change the state of the collection in any way.

```
public interface Queue extends Collection {
  public void addLast (Object newElement);
  public Object getFirst ();
  public void removeFirst ();
};
```

FIGURE 12.1 The Queue Interface

`void removeFirst ()` Removes the current front of the queue. This method will throw `NoSuchElementException` if the queue is currently empty.

`Enumeration elements ()` This method returns an `Enumeration` that can be used to access the elements held in the collection. Elements are enumerated from the front to the back of the queue, which is the same order in which they were inserted.

`boolean isEmpty ()` Returns `true` if the collection is empty and returns `false` otherwise. This method will always return `true` when applied on a newly created collection. Invoking this method will not change the state of the collection in any way.

`int size ()` Returns an integer that indicates the number of elements held by the collection. This method will always return zero when applied on a newly created collection. Invoking this method will not change the state of the collection in any way.

We have again broken with tradition in the naming of the operations, for the same reason we outlined in Chapter 10. Historically, the name *enqueue* is used for the operation of adding an element to a queue, the name *dequeue* for the operation of removal, and the name *front* for accessing the first element without removal.

Two operations can potentially give rise to exception conditions. If an attempt is made to access the first element in an empty queue, by either the method `getFirst` or the method `removeFirst`, the exception `NoSuchElementException` can be thrown. In some versions of the queue abstraction, although not any we will discuss here, a limit is imposed on the number of elements the container can hold. In such situations, it is also possible for the method `addLast` to generate an exception.

12.2 The Caterpillar Game

A good illustration of the use of queues is provided by the video game Caterpillar. In this game, players manipulate a caterpillar, moving the animal left, right, up, or down in order to avoid walls and other obstacles, such as other players. The body of the caterpillar is represented by a series of segments, which we can draw as simple filled circles (Figure 12.2). The queue is an ideal data structure to represent the body of the animal because the process of "slithering" can be implemented by removing a segment from one end of the caterpillar and adding a new segment to the other—exactly the operations provided by a queue.

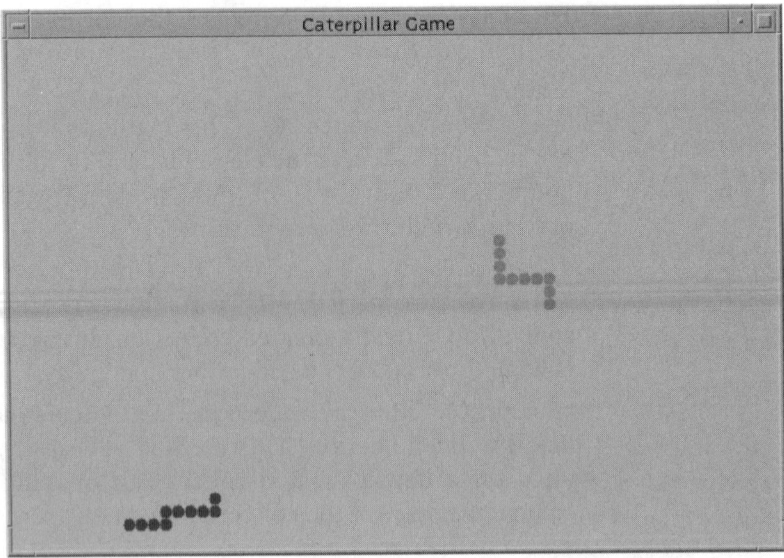

FIGURE 12.2 Screen Shot of Caterpillar Game

We will give only the beginning of the implementation of the game, sufficient to illustrate the use of the queue and to show the overall structure. Filling in the remaining details to create the final game will be left as an exercise.

Although the Caterpillar game is a two-player video game, it will have much in common with the Asteroids game we developed in Chapter 8. Both games will be designed in an object-oriented style, as a universe of interacting agents. In both programs, the object that represents the game will wait and listen for user-generated keystrokes, whereas a separate thread moves the caterpillar bodies.

We start by imagining that a caterpillar is an object that knows how to paint itself and how to make a single move:

`Caterpillar`
• Draw self.
• Move.

The main program will create the universe of objects (two caterpillars and a key press listener) and set them in motion.

CaterpillarGame
• Create universe of objects.
• Repaint window.
• Move caterpillars.

KeyReader
• Listen for key press.
• Tell caterpillar.

We next refine the design, filling in more details. If we ask ourselves how the key press reader will communicate with a caterpillar, we can see our first problem. We have no way of controlling the speed with which the player will enter commands. If the user enters commands too quickly, they may be lost before the caterpillar can respond. The solution to this problem is to use a `Queue`. Each caterpillar will maintain a queue of commands. The key press reader will place a command into the queue, and the caterpillar will remove commands from the queue has as it moves.

Moving next to the caterpillar itself, we must ask how the caterpillar will know the location of each of its segments. To solve this problem, a simple technique is to imagine the board for the Caterpillar game as a 60-by-40 grid of cells, each 10 pixels square. We can use the class `Point` (which we encountered in Chapter 11) to represent a location in two-dimensional space. The body of the caterpillar can be represented by a `Queue` of points. The queue is useful in this case because to move the caterpillar forward, one segment is removed from the tail and a new segment is added to the head.

Having made these design decisions, we can write the first version of the Caterpillar game:

```
import java.awt.*;
import java.awt.event.*;
import java.util.Enumeration;
import jds.Queue;
import jds.collection.LinkedList;
import jds.util.CloseQuit;

public class CaterpillarGame extends Frame {
  public static void main (String [ ] args)
  {CaterpillarGame world = new CaterpillarGame();world.show();world.run();}
```

```
  public CaterpillarGame () {
    setSize((BoardWidth+2)*SegmentSize, BoardHeight*SegmentSize+30);
    setTitle("Caterpillar Game");
    addKeyListener(new KeyReader());
    addWindowListener(new CloseQuit());
  }

  private Caterpillar playerOne =
    new Caterpillar(Color.blue, new Point(20, 10));
  private Caterpillar playerTwo =
    new Caterpillar(Color.red, new Point(20, 30));
  final static int BoardWidth = 60;
  final static int BoardHeight = 40;
  final static int SegmentSize = 10;

  public void run () {
    while (true) {
      movePieces();
      repaint();
      try { sleep(100); } catch (Exception e) { }
    }
  }

  public void paint (Graphics g)
    { playerOne.paint(g); playerTwo.paint(g); }

  public void movePieces ()
    { playerOne.move(this); playerTwo.move(this); }

  private class KeyReader extends KeyAdapter { ... }
}
```

The main game object creates two instances of class `Caterpillar` and a key press reader (as in the Asteroids game). Different characters are used to control the two caterpillars. The keyboard values *a*, *d*, *w*, and *s* control the first caterpillar, and the keyboard values *j*, *k*, *l*, and *i* control the second. The method `keyPressed` reads a keyboard value and communicates the command to the appropriate caterpillar. Within the class `Caterpillar`, the method `setDirection` places a value into the queue of pending commands:

```
private class KeyReader extends KeyAdapter {
  public void keyPressed (KeyEvent e) {
    char c = e.getKeyChar();
    switch (c) {
```

```
      case 'a': playerOne.setDirection('W'); break;
      case 'd': playerOne.setDirection('E'); break;
      case 'w': playerOne.setDirection('N'); break;
      case 's': playerOne.setDirection('S'); break;
      case 'j': playerTwo.setDirection('W'); break;
      case 'k': playerTwo.setDirection('S'); break;
      case 'l': playerTwo.setDirection('E'); break;
      case 'i': playerTwo.setDirection('N'); break;
    }
  }
}
```

Adding such features as a color and an initial location, our first version of class `Caterpillar` is the following:

```
class Caterpillar {
  public Caterpillar (Color c, Point sp) {
    color = c;
    for (int i = 0; i < 10; i++) {
       position = new Point(sp.x+i, sp.y);
       body.addLast(position);
    }
  }

  private Color color;
  private Point position;
  private char direction = 'W';
  private Queue body = new LinkedList();
  private Queue commands = new LinkedList();

  public void setDirection (char d)
    { commands.addLast(new Character(d)); }

  public void move (CaterpillarGame game) {
      // first see if we should change direction
    if (commands.size() > 0) {
      Character c = (Character) commands.getFirst();
      commands.removeFirst();
      direction = c.charValue();
    }
      // then find new position
    Point np = newPosition();
      // erase one segment, add another
    body.removeFirst();
```

```
    body.addLast(np);
    position = np;
  }

  private Point newPosition() {
    int x = position.x;
    int y = position.y;
    if (direction == 'E') x++;
    else if (direction == 'W') x--;
    else if (direction == 'N') y--;
    else if (direction == 'S') y++;
    return new Point(x, y);
    }

  public void paint(Graphics g) {
    g.setColor(color);
    Enumeration e = body.elements();
    while (e.hasMoreElements()) {
      Point p = (Point) e.nextElement();
      g.fillOval(5 + CaterpillarGame.SegmentSize * p.x,
        10 + CaterpillarGame.SegmentSize * p.y,
        CaterpillarGame.SegmentSize, CaterpillarGame.SegmentSize);
    }
  }
}
```

The calculation of a new position is somewhat complex. Rather than complicate the `move` method with this code, we have abstracted the behavior and placed it in a separate method. New methods should be created whenever a part of a larger operation seems overly complex.

If we start the game, we immediately see a problem. Nothing prevents a caterpillar from running off the edge of the screen. Worse yet, nothing prevents a caterpillar from running into another caterpillar. The first problem is easy to solve, but the second is more difficult. The class `Caterpillar` does not know that there are two instances; indeed, as far as it is concerned, there might be many more instances of the class. Only the main game object knows how many instances of the `Caterpillar` class have been created. Thus, to solve the move problem requires a coordinated effort between the two objects. A caterpillar will ask the game object whether it is safe to move into a new square. The game object, in turn, will ask each of the caterpillars if it currently occupies the square. Only if no object occupies the square will the move be accepted.

```
class Caterpillar {
    .
    .
    .
  public void move (CaterpillarGame game) {
      .
      .
      .
    Point np = newPosition();
      // erase one segment, add another
    if (game.canMove(np)) {
      body.removeFirst();
      body.addLast(np);
      position = np;
    }
  }

  public boolean inPosition (Point np) {
    Enumeration e = body.elements();
    while (e.hasMoreElements()) {
      Point location = (Point) e.nextElement();
      if (np.equals(location)) return true;
    }
    return false;
  }
}

class CaterpillarGame extends Frame {
    .
    .
    .
  public boolean canMove (Point np) {
      // test playing board
    if ((np.x <= 0) || (np.y <= 0)) return false;
    if ((x >= BoardWidth) || (y >= BoardHeight)) return false;
      // test caterpillars
    if (playerOne.inPosition(np)) return false;
    if (playerTwo.inPosition(np)) return false;
      // ok, safe square
    return true;
  }
}
```

This completes the description of the minimal game. So far, the only abilities we have included permit two players to control their respective animals. The following describes a sequence of steps that you can pursue to make a more interesting game.

1. First, we need to make an objective for the game. In the real game, numbers appear in random locations. The first player to occupy the square in which a number appears gets the points specified by the number. The following steps will add this feature:
   a. In the game class, add data fields that will hold the position of the number square and its value. The value should start at 1 and increment every time a caterpillar catches it.
   b. Modify the `paint` method in `CaterpillarGame` to display the number square, as well as the two caterpillars.
   c. Create a method `newNumberSquare` to create a new, randomly distributed number value. Use the `inPosition` method provided by the two caterpillars to ensure that the number is not placed in a square already occupied by a caterpillar.
   d. Add a `score` data field to each caterpillar, to hold its current score. As part of advancing to a new position, have the caterpillar test the new position to see whether it is a scoring position. This can be most easily accomplished by adding a method `squareScore` to the class `CaterpillarGame`. This method will take as argument the new position offered by a caterpillar. If the new position is not a scoring position, it will return zero. If it is a scoring position, it will return the score and call `newNumberSquare` to create a new scoring position.
   e. Add labels to the game window to display the two caterpillar scores.
2. The two-player game now has scores but no simple way to end. In the original game, each caterpillar segment has a lifetime. This can be simulated by having each `Caterpillar` maintain a counter—say, one that starts at 20 and counts down at each step. Each time a score is made, the counter is reset to 20, and a new segment is added to the caterpillar. If the counter reaches 0, an extra segment is removed from the caterpillar, and the counter is reset to 20. When one of the caterpillars loses all its segments, the game is over.

* 12.3 A Pastry Factory Simulation

One of the more important uses for queues is as a synchronization tool for multiple processes. Many problems can be described abstractly as interactions between producers and consumers. We described one example of this problem at the beginning of the chapter. A user produces a character by pressing a key, and the system consumes the character by issuing a read operation. The producers (there may be one or many) generate some objects, whereas the consumers (again there may be one or many) process the values. If producers and consumers are independent, how can they communicate? What will happen if the producers generate a value and no consumer is ready or if a consumer is ready to use a value but no producer has yet created one?

A queue solves this problem nicely. Producers can place items on the queue and not worry about whether a consumer is available. A consumer can remove items from the same queue and does not need to be concerned with the operations of the producer.

A mental image of this process looks somewhat like a factory assembly line. Packages enter at one end, move down the line, and are removed at the other.

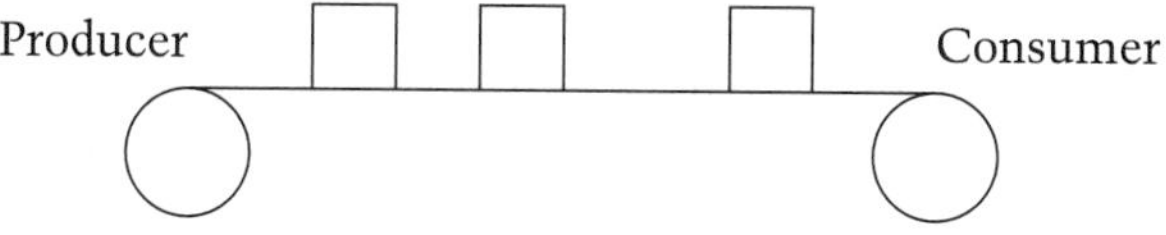

We take this association as the starting point for our next example program. Imagine that you want to simulate a pastry factory. The factory has three types of machines: one that produces cookies, one that produces donuts, and one that produces eclairs. All three machines feed their results onto a common queue; at the other end, a packaging machine removes items from the queue and places them into boxes. Eclairs and donuts, of course, take longer to produce than cookies, and all three machines have a certain variability built in, so that the precise amount of time necessary to create a pastry is slightly random.

Creating the simulation begins with a pair of utility classes: one for pastries and one for boxes. The characteristics of a pastry are, for our purposes, a name and a weight (boxes are sold by weight). These values will be set by the constructor for the class. By declaring the data fields as `final`, we can be assured that the values, once set by the constructor, can

THE PRODUCER/CONSUMER PATTERN

name Producer/Consumer

synopsis How do you synchronize one or more producers, who generate values, with one or more consumers, who process values?

solution Have both producers and consumers operate by manipulating a queue rather than by dealing directly with each other. In this fashion, the synchronization can be very loose. Neither the producer nor the consumer need have explicit knowledge of how fast the other is working.

counterforces Not all interactions can be ignored; the producer should ensure that the queue does not become overly large.

never be changed, and hence we will permit other portions of the program to have direct access to the fields.

```
class Pastry {
  public Pastry (double w, String n) { weight = w; name = n; }

  public final double weight;
  public final String name;
}
```

A box contains a collection of pastries, which we will hold in a `Vector`. The box has a weight, which can be accessed by means of the method `weight`. By hiding the data field in a `private` variable and accessing it only through an *accessor method*, we ensure that the weight cannot be unintentionally set by means outside the class. A box is also given the means to produce a printable representation of its contents, by means of the method `print`.

```
class Box {
  public Box () { w = 0; pastries = new Vector(); }

  private double w; // weight of pastries
  private Vector pastries; // pastries

  public void addPastry (Pastry p) {
    pastries.addLast(p);
    w += p.weight;
  }

  public double weight () { return w; }

  public void print () {
    String result = "Box with ";
    Enumeration e = pastries.elements();
    while (e.hasMoreElements() ) {
      Pastry p = (Pastry) e.nextElement();
      result = result + " " + p.name;
      }
    System.out.println(result);
  }
}
```

Each of the three pastry machines will be represented by an instance of the class `PastryProducer`. The constructor for the class provides the queue onto which the output will be placed, an example pastry, and a random-number generator that will be used to represent the time it takes to create an instance of the pastry. To allow the three machines to run independently of one another, each is declared as its own thread.

```
class PastryProducer extends Thread {
  public PastryProducer (Queue q, Pastry p, RandomInteger r)
    { que = q; example = p; rand = r; }

  private Queue que;
  private Pastry example;
  private RandomInteger rand;

  public void run () {
    while (true) {
        // produce pastry
      que.addLast(example);
        // and sleep
      while (rand.intValue() != 1)
        try { sleep(20); } catch(Exception e) { }
    }
  }
}
```

The execution of the pastry producer is described by the method `run`. In this method, a pastry is added to the output queue, and then the program sleeps for a period of time, presumably making the next pastry. We randomize the amount of time the machine sleeps, using an instance of `RandomInteger`. Each time we request a result from this class, a new integer from a fixed range is produced. We can control the range of these values in the constructor for the class. The machine sleeps until this random-number generator produces a 1.

MULTIPLE THREADS OF EXECUTION

Although we have mentioned the possibility of multiple threads of execution, the pastry factory simulation is the first program we have examined that makes use of this facility. A thread is declared by creating a subclass of Thread and begins execution when this object is given the message `start`. Thereafter, the thread will run independently of the main application program.

In reality, most computers have only a single processor, and so execution moves between the currently active threads, giving each a small slice of execution time. In general, one cannot predict when a thread will be *suspended* and the next thread started. This is why it is important to use the `synchronized` modifier when you do not want two or more threads executing the same code at the same time. Threads will always be suspended when they `sleep`, giving other threads time to execute while the sleeping thread is inactive.

```
class RandomInteger {
  RandomInteger (int m) { max = m; }
  private int max;

  public int intValue () { return (int) (max * Math.random()); }
}
```

Meanwhile, the pastry consumer is pulling pastries from the queue and placing them into boxes. Boxes are sold by weight. As soon as the weight of the box exceeds a given threshold, the box is sealed and a new box is started. Here, we simply print out the box (recall that this will print the box contents) and start a new box:

```
class PastryBoxer extends Thread {
  public PastryBoxer (Queue q) { que = q; }

  private Queue que;

  public void run () {
    Box currentBox = new Box();
    while (true)
```

SYNCHRONIZING REMOVAL: MORE DIFFICULT THAN INSERTION

The three pastry machines in this simulation can use the same queue because the addLast operation for queues is synchronized. This means that no more than one method can ever be executing the method at the same time. Removal, however, is more subtle. In the program, we avoid this problem by having only one machine that removes elements, so contention can never occur. In an exercise at the end of the chapter, we suggest adding a second machine.

The reason removal is more difficult is that the actions are spread over three statements:

```
if (! que.isEmpty) {
  Object value = que.getFirst();
  que.removeFirst();
  .
  .
  .
```

Erroneous results can occur if two threads are executing this code with a queue that contains only one element and the first is suspended at any point between the call on isEmpty and removeFirst. This problem is more difficult to solve. It is not sufficient to simply place the code shown inside a synchronized method, as the removal operations will likely be in different objects. Instead, these operations must synchronize themselves, using another object. Java provides this ability, using the synchronized statement. In this case, we can synchronize on the queue itself, as in the following:

```
synchronized(que) {
  if (! que.isEmpty() {
    Object value = que.getFirst();
    que.removeFirst();
    .
    .
    .
  }
}
```

The result will be that no two threads will be allowed to execute the statements within the block (or any other synchronized methods in the queue object) at the same time.

```
      if (! que.isEmpty()) {
        Pastry p = (Pastry) que.getFirst();
        que.removeFirst();
        currentBox.addPastry(p);
          // boxes are 12 ounces
        if (currentBox.weight() > 12) {
          currentBox.print();
          currentBox = new Box();
        }
      }
  }
}
```

All that is now needed to start the simulation is to create the various objects, link them, and start the independent threads for the various components:

```
class PastryFactorySimulation {
  public static void main (String [ ] args) {
      // create the queue
    Queue que = new LinkedList();
      // create the machines
    PastryProducer m1 = new PastryProducer(que,
      new Pastry(0.25, "cookie"), new RandomInteger(3));
    PastryProducer m2 = new PastryProducer(que,
      new Pastry(1.25, "donut"), new RandomInteger(7));
    PastryProducer m3 = new PastryProducer(que,
      new Pastry(2.0, "eclair"), new RandomInteger(15));
    PastryBoxer c = new PastryBoxer(que);
      // start the threads
    m1.start(); m2.start(); m3.start(); c.start();
  }
}
```

An example execution of the program might produce the following:

```
Box with  cookie donut eclair cookie cookie eclair donut
  cookie eclair cookie cookie cookie cookie eclair
Box with  donut donut cookie eclair cookie cookie donut
  eclair cookie cookie cookie cookie cookie cookie
  cookie cookie cookie cookie cookie cookie eclair
Box with  donut donut donut donut donut donut cookie donut
  eclair cookie cookie cookie cookie donut
Box with  cookie donut donut donut cookie cookie donut cookie
  eclair cookie cookie cookie eclair cookie cookie eclair
Box with  cookie cookie cookie cookie cookie cookie cookie
  donut donut cookie cookie cookie cookie donut donut
```

```
  cookie cookie cookie cookie cookie cookie cookie cookie
  cookie cookie eclair
Box with  eclair donut donut donut eclair cookie cookie
  eclair eclair
```

12.4 IMPLEMENTATION OF THE QUEUE ABSTRACTION

We will describe several implementations of the Queue data type. The first three are formed by using existing data structures, and a fourth is new.

We have already seen two data structures that support the Queue interface: the LinkedList and the IndexedDeque. The LinkedList simply adds elements to one end of the list and removes them from the other:

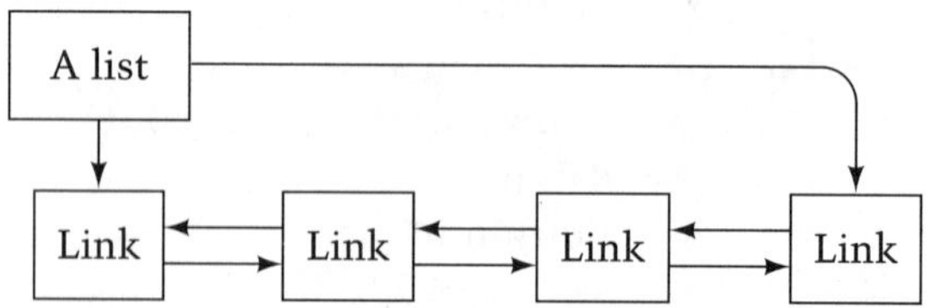

Insertion and removal are each constant-time, or $O(1)$, operations. However, you will recall that insertion involves allocation of a new link, which is subsequently recovered when the element is removed.

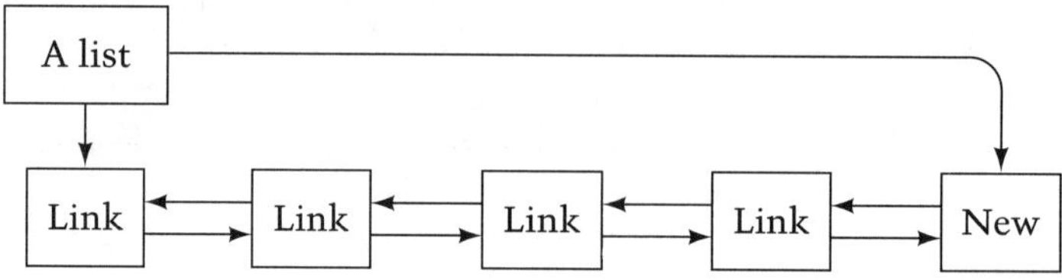

Overhead costs in both space and time are not found in the alternative, the IndexedDeque. Additional space is required for the two link fields that are part of each node. Additional time is required for the memory allocation of a new node each time an element is added to the collection and ultimately the recovery of the node memory when an element is removed.

An alternative data structure is the IndexedDeque, which we developed in Chapter 11. This structure, you will recall, maintained values in an array structure, similar to a vector. Two variables in the Deque referred to the index position of the first position used and the number of elements currently being held by the data structure.

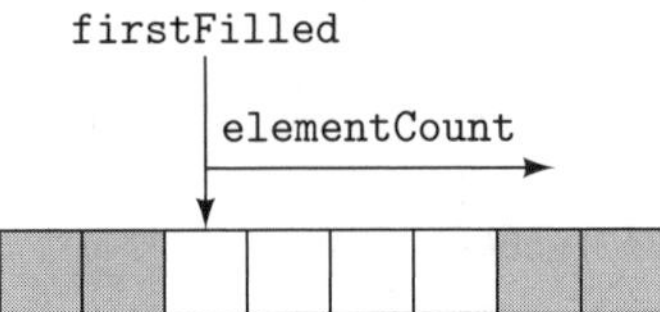

Values could be inserted at the top of the IndexedDeque and removed from the bottom, normally in a very fast ($O(1)$) manner. However, should the underlying array become full, the capacity is automatically increased. This property means that the IndexedDeque can hold an arbitrary number of elements, which is a desirable trait. However, it comes at a cost. Should the buffer need to be reallocated, insertion suddenly becomes an $O(n)$ time operation. We describe this situation by saying that insertion and removal from the IndexedDeque are each $O(1)$ average (or expected) operations.

Asymptotically, the execution times for insertion and removal operations are $O(1)$ in both implementations. However, that does not imply that they are identical. Addition to a linked list involves the creation of a new link node, and removal requires that memory for this node be recovered. No such allocation is required for insertion or removal from a deque, which normally involves manipulation of only the index values. On the other hand, the linked list can never "overflow," as space is allocated for each node as necessary. When insertion of an element into the deque causes the number of elements to exceed the capacity of the array, an entire new array is created, and the values are copied from the old array into the new one. Although we hope that this process will occur very rarely, it nevertheless can be quite costly. Thus, it is not initially obvious which technique will be most efficient, particularly under various types of use.

We can compare the running time of the two techniques by performing simple experiments, using various distributions of operations. Consider first a program that loops n times, on each iteration adding ten elements to a queue, then removing ten elements. The maximum size of the collection remains relatively constant, and so we would expect that over time, as n increases, the memory management efficiency of the IndexedDeque over the LinkedList would manifest itself as improved execution times. We can test this hypothesis by creating an application that makes use of the GraphMaker and TaskTimer components that were introduced in Chapter 4. This application is shown in Figure 12.3. Executing this program, we observe the distribution of execution times shown in Figure 12.4. From these timings, we note that indeed, the IndexedDeque has a small advantage in execution time over the LinkedList.

```
class QueueTester extends TaskTimer {

  public QueueTester (Reporter rep, Queue q) {
    super(rep);
    que = q; value = new Integer(42);
  }

  private Queue que; // queue being tested
  private Object value; // value inserted and removed from queue

  public void doTask(int n) {
    for (int i = 0; i < n; i++) {
      for (int j = 0; j < 10; j++)
        que.addLast(value);
      for (int j = 0; j < 10; j++)
        que.removeFirst();
    }
  }
}

public class QueueExperiment extends Frame {

  public static void main (String [ ] args)
  { QueueExperiment world = new QueueExperiment(); world.show();
                                                   world.run(); }

  public QueueExperiment () {
    setTitle("Queue Experiment 1"); setSize(500, 300);
    add("Center", graph);
  }

  private GraphMaker graph = new GraphMaker(10000, 2500);

  public void run () {
    QueueTester t1 = new QueueTester(graph.getReporter("Deque"),
        new Deque());
    t1.run(0, 10000, 200);
    QueueTester t2 = new QueueTester(graph.getReporter("List"),
        new LinkedList());
    t2.run(0, 10000, 200);
  }
}
```

FIGURE 12.3 A Program to Compare the Running Times of Various Queue Implementations

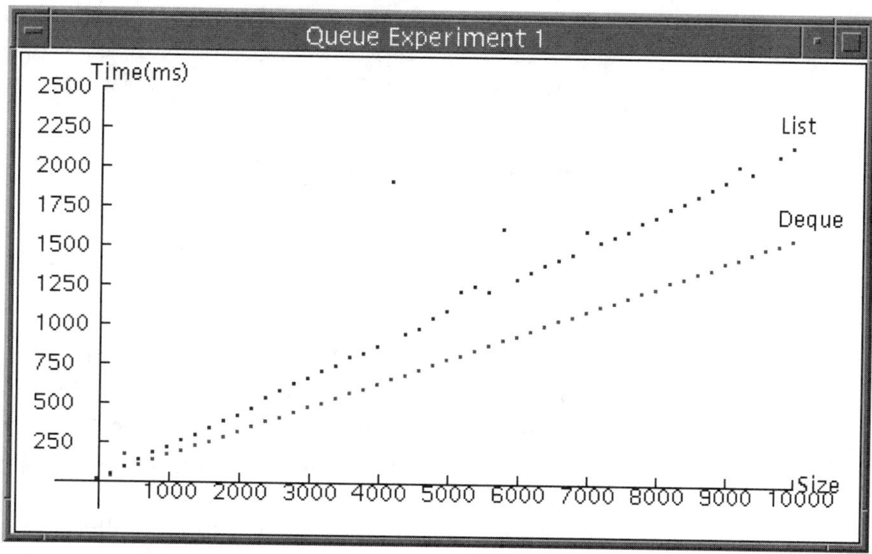

FIGURE 12.4 Output of Queue-Timing Experiment

The outcome of a second experiment is more difficult to predict. Imagine a different program that loops n times, on each iteration adding n elements to a queue, and then removing n elements. Here, the size of the queue is continually increasing. In time, we might expect that the cost to copy the array of values into a new array when the capacity is exceeded would be more than the cost of allocating nodes in the linked list. We leave the exploration of this possibility as an exercise.

EXPERIMENT: EXPLORE THE COST OF INCREASING QUEUES

Modify the `QueueTester` so that it performs the distribution of operations just described; that is, it inserts n values into the queue and then removes n values. Compare the running times of the linked-list-based queue with the deque-based queue as n increases.

EXPERIMENT: WHICH END IS FRONT?

This experiment is similar to one described in the previous chapter. Although we have used the methods `addLast` and `removeFirst` to implement the `Queue` abstraction, as far as the `LinkedList` is concerned, we could have just as easily used `addFirst` and `removeLast`. Design an experiment to compare the relative execution times for these two alternatives.

```
public class VectorQueue extends Vector implements Queue {
  public Object getFirst () { return elementAt(0); }
  public void removeFirst () { removeElementAt(0); }
}
```

FIGURE 12.5 A Vector-Based Implementation of a Queue

12.4.1 A Vector-Based Queue

The analysis presented in this section will illustrate the point that it is important to remember not only the operations provided by various data structures but also their asymptotic execution times. Recall that the difference between the `Vector` and the `IndexedDeque` data structures is that the `Vector` does not provide constant-time insertion and removal operations from the front (or bottom) of the collection. By not supporting these operations, the `Vector` can make other operations slightly faster than they are in the `IndexedDeque`, which provides similar functionality. Nevertheless, the `Vector` *does* provide the ability to remove the element stored at an arbitrary location, using the operation `removeElementAt`. Using this, we can construct a new data structure that satisfies the `Queue` interface. This data structure is shown in Figure 12.5. However, unlike the $O(1)$ removal operation for the `Deque`, the cost of removing the first element will be $O(n)$, where n is the number of elements in the collection.

Because removing an element from the front of a queue is an $O(n)$ operation, removing all elements from a queue of size n will require roughly $O(n^2)$ operations. If we redo the second experiment described in the previous section, we will observe this behavior (Figure 12.6). Note that the dimensions of both the x and y coordinates have been changed from the earlier plot, in order to make the graph fill the space provided. The execution time of the `Deque`-based queue is repeated in order to make it easier to compare the two graphs.

EXPERIMENT: MEASURING THE VECTOR IMPLEMENTATION UNDER VARIOUS LOADS

Will we observe such a dramatic difference in execution times if we use the distribution of operations specified in the first experiment in Section 12.4? Using the `GraphMaker`, illustrate the difference in execution time between the implementation based on the `Deque` and the one based on the `Vector`.

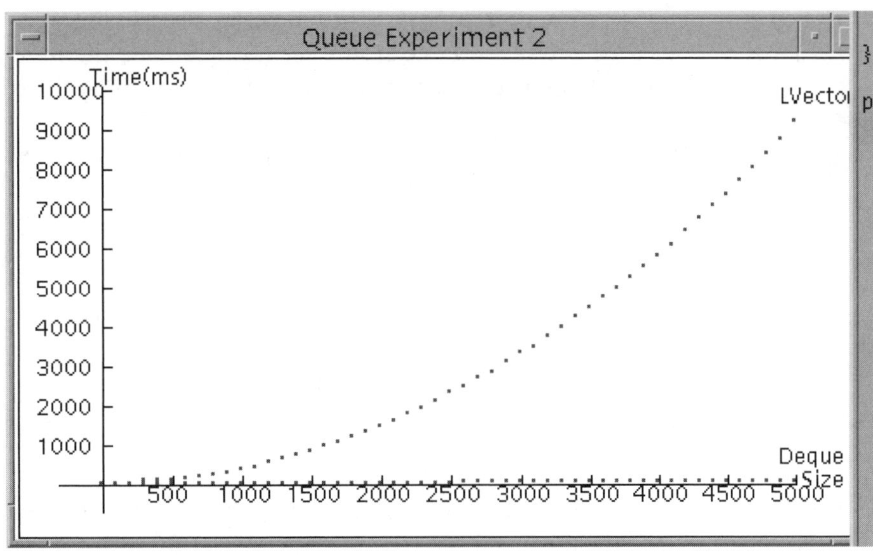

FIGURE 12.6 The Cost of Increasing Queues (Revised)

* 12.4.2 The Ring Buffer Queue

Another implementation technique for the Queue abstraction is frequently encountered, particularly in the design of operating systems, which might use a queue to hold a sequence of jobs waiting to be serviced by a printer, for example. This technique is termed a *ring buffer queue*, or sometimes simply a *circular queue*. This basic idea is similar to the linked-list implementation of a queue, only the list is circular and so has no beginning and no end. As the list is traversed in only one direction, only single links are necessary in the linked list. And, unlike the linked-list abstraction, nodes in the list are not recovered when elements are removed. Instead, they remain in the list and are reused as new values are inserted.

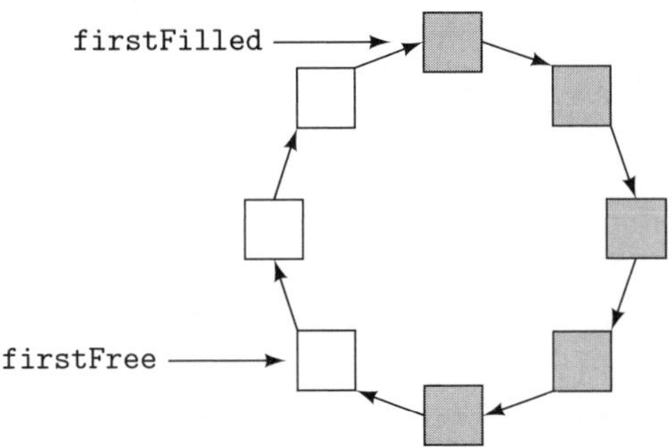

Two references point into the list of elements. One reference denotes the first available empty location and one the first filled location. When an element is inserted, the first available empty position is advanced:

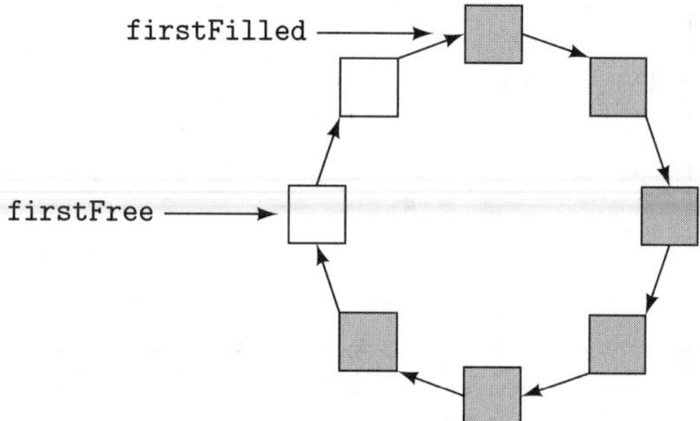

Similarly, when a value is removed, the reference to the first filled location is advanced:

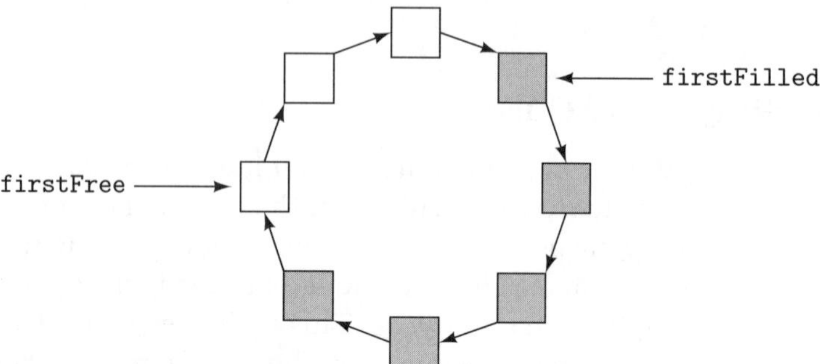

As with all queue abstractions, an exception will be thrown if an attempt is made to remove an element from an empty queue (that is, when the two references point to the same element). The other extreme occurs if an attempt is made to insert an element into a completely full queue. For reasons we will explore in the following sequence, at least one unused node must always be in the ring buffer elements. As we noted with the previous implementations of the queue data type, two courses of action are possible. One is to throw an exception in this case. The other is to simply expand the queue through the addition of a new node.

Figure 12.7 gives an implementation of a queue that illustrates the ring buffer technique. We have here chosen to expand the queue when full rather than to throw an exception. The following series of exercises is intended to help you better understand the ring buffer implementation and to provide an informal proof of correctness.

```
public class RingBufferQueue implements Queue {

  RingBufferQueue () {
    firstFilled = firstFree = new RingBufferNode(null);
    firstFree.next = firstFree;
    }

  private RingBufferNode firstFree, firstFilled;

  public boolean isEmpty () { return firstFilled == firstFree; }

  public int size () {
    int count = 0;
    RingBufferNode p = firstFilled;
    for (; p != firstFree; p = p.next) count++;
    return count;
  }

  public synchronized void addLast (Object val) {
    if (firstFree.next == firstFilled)
      firstFree.next = new RingBufferNode(firstFree.next);
    firstFree.value = val;
    firstFree = firstFree.next;
  }

  public Object getFirst () {
    if (firstFilled == firstFree) throw new NoSuchElementException();
    return firstFilled.value; }

  public synchronized void removeFirst ()
  {
    if (firstFilled == firstFree) throw new NoSuchElementException();
    firstFilled = firstFilled.next;
  }
}

class RingBufferNode {
  public Object value;
  public RingBufferNode next;
  public RingBufferNode (RingBufferNode n) { next = n; }
}
```

FIGURE 12.7 Implementation of the Class `RingBufferQueue`

1. Draw a representation of the ring buffer as it is first created by the constructor. Verify that the method `isEmpty` will return `true`.
2. Trace the execution of the method `addLast` and verify that if we ignore the execution-time cost of allocating the new node, the cost of all other operations is bounded by a constant; therefore, addition of a new value is $O(1)$. Then draw a representation of the ring buffer after one element has been inserted. Verify that the method `isEmpty` will now return `false`.
3. Add a second element and once more draw a representation of the resulting structure.
4. To understand why it is necessary to always maintain an unused node in the ring buffer, imagine changing the test in the method `addList` to the following:

   ```
   if (firstFree == firstFilled)
   ```

   This would have the effect of forcing the addition of a new node when the structure was completely filled rather than when it was almost filled. Simulate the addition of another new element. Now simulate the execution of the method `isEmpty`. What do you observe? For an alternative solution to this problem, see exercise 10 in this series.
5. The preceding exercises have examined the validity of the method `addLast` when the queue was entirely empty and when it was almost full. One more test is necessary. Imagine that several elements have been added and removed, so that the buffer contains six nodes, three filled. Simulate the addition of a fourth value, and draw the representation of the state of the queue before and after the insertion.
6. Simulate the method `size` on the structure left at the end of the previous exercise, and verify that it returns the correct value.
7. Simulate the execution of the methods `getFirst` and `removeFirst` on the queue left after the previous exercise. What value is yielded? What is the resulting structure of the ring buffer queue? Verify that in all situations, the execution time of the method will be bounded, and thus removal is an $O(1)$ time operation.
8. What will happen if an attempt is made to access the first value in an empty queue?
9. Consider a ring buffer with five nodes, only one of which is filled. Simulate the execution of the method `removeFirst`. Draw a represen-

tation of the structure both before and after the removal, and verify that the method `isEmpty` will return `true`.

10. To understand why the `addLast` must be `synchronized`, simulate the following sequence of events that could potentially occur were two threads permitted to execute the method at the same time. Draw a picture of the state of the buffer after each step. Explain why the ring buffer queue is left in an invalid state.
    a. Two calls on `addLast` are made on the same almost full queue. The first invocation of the method gets as far as allocating a new node before it is suspended.
    b. The second invocation completes the `if` statement, including allocating a new node and assigning the value to `firstFree.next`, before it is suspended.
    c. The first method then runs to completion.
    d. The second method runs to completion.

* 12.4.3 Piped Input/Output Streams

An example ring buffer is found in the Java standard library in the implementation of the classes `PipedInputStream` and `PipedOutputStream`. These two classes provide a convenient mechanism for organizing producer/consumer problems, such as the one we described earlier in this chapter. Producers simply write values into a `PipedOutputStream`, using the same protocol as they would write to an external file. Consumers read from a matched `PipedInputStream`, again using the same stream protocol used for other stream-based tasks, such as reading from a file.

Because the values being stored are bytes rather than objects, the ring buffer can be more efficiently represented by a simple byte array rather than as a linked list of nodes. This is similar to the `Deque`-based implementation of a `Queue` described earlier. Two integer indices refer to locations in the byte array. The value in `out` refers to the first filled location, whereas

EXPERIMENT: EVALUATE RING BUFFER EXECUTION TIMES

Under what conditions is the ring buffer implementation more efficient than the other two implementation techniques that have been described? Test the ring buffer implementation using the two different distributions of operations described in Section 12.4.1, and compare the running time to that of the `Deque`- and `LinkedList`-based queues.

the value in `in` refers to the first empty location. As with the `Deque`, these values can wrap around the end of the byte array:

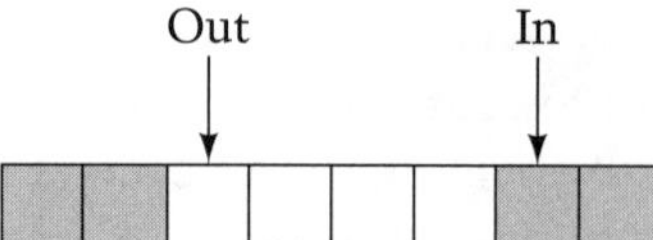

A `read` operation from a piped input stream will suspend if the buffer is empty and will be restarted when a value is placed into the queue. Similarly, a `write` to a piped output stream will suspend if the queue is full and will wait for a reader to remove an element and thereby free up some space. The key to the power of the abstraction is that the user of these components does not need to think about these synchronization issues and can simply structure a program as if it were reading from or writing to a file.

12.5 Chapter Summary

Key Concepts

- Queue
- FIFO
- Traditional queue operations
  - Enqueue
  - Dequeue
  - Front
- Ring buffer
- Thread
- Synchronization

The queue is a data abstraction that permits elements to be added at one end of a linear container and removed from the other end. Elements are maintained in the order they are inserted, and so when an element is removed, it will be the value that has been in the container the longest.

In earlier chapters, we explored two data structures that support the queue ADT: the `LinkedList` and the `IndexedDeque`. In this chapter, we have developed a third useful data structure: the `RingBufferQueue`.

In this chapter, we have seen for the first time how the user can explicitly create multiple threads of execution. When we need to prevent more than one thread at a time from accessing the data fields, the methods used to access the data must be declared as `synchronized`.

Further Information

In addition to the term FIFO, queues are also sometimes described as FCFS (first come first served).

We will see another use of queues in the radix sort algorithm described in Chapter 16.

Study Questions

1. Explain why the term FIFO is appropriate in describing the queue abstraction.

2. What will happen if an attempt is made to remove a value from an empty queue?
3. In what way is a queue similar to a factory assembly line?
4. What is the purpose of the `final` modifier in the declaration of the `weight` and `name` fields in the `Pastry` class?
5. Why is the `weight` data field in the class `Box` handled differently from the `weight` data field in `Pastry`?
6. What purpose is served by providing access to data fields through an *accesser function*?
7. Each instance of the class `Caterpillar` maintains two queues. What do these represent?
8. What might happen if the command values were maintained in a one-character buffer rather than in a queue?

Exercises

1. Describe the state of an initially empty queue after each of the following sequences of operations. Indicate the values held by any variables that are declared, and also indicate any errors that may occur:

   a.
   ```
   que.addLast(new Integer(2));
   Integer a = que.getFirst();
   que.addLast(new Integer(3));
   que.removeFirst();
   ```

   b.
   ```
   que.addLast(new Integer(2));
   Integer a = que.getFirst();
   que.addLast(new Integer(4));
   que.removeFirst();
   que.addLast(new Integer(6));
   que.removeFirst();
   ```

   c.
   ```
   que.addLast(new Integer(2));
   que.getFirst();
   que.addLast(new Integer(3));
   que.removeFirst();
   que.removeFirst();
   Integer a = que.getFirst();
   ```

2. Fill in the following chart with the execution times for each operation, using the indicated implementation technique. For each entry, indicate whether the execution time is *always*, *worst case*, or *expected*.

Operation	LinkedList	IndexedDeque	RingBuffer
addLast	O(_)	O(_)	O(_)
getFirst	O(_)	O(_)	O(_)
removeFirst	O(_)	O(_)	O(_)

3. What are the objects found in the pastry factory simulation program? Create a CRC card that describes the behavior of each class of object.
4. Using only the operations provided by a queue and a stack, describe an algorithm to reverse the elements in a queue.
5. By using both a stack and a queue of character values, show how to determine whether a string is a palindrome. (A palindrome is a string that reads the same both forward and backward. An example is the word "rotator.")
6. Explain why removal of the first element of a vector-based queue is an $O(n)$ operation rather than $O(1)$. What tasks are being performed during this time?
7. Section 12.4.1 described the problem of removing all elements from a vector-based queue that initially held n values. Note that as the size of the queue is reduced, the time required to perform the removal operation becomes smaller. Argue why despite this the overall time to remove all elements is still $O(n^2)$.
8. Implement the method `elements` for the ring buffer queue described in Section 12.4.2. This is most easily accomplished by creating a new inner class of type `Enumeration`. Give an informal argument to demonstrate the correct functioning of your implementation.
9. Experimentally compare the running time of the ring buffer queue to the other two queue implementations described in this chapter. Under what types of distributions of operations will it provide better performance than the other two techniques?
10. Rewrite the `RingBufferQueue` class so that it maintains a data member `count` that stores the number of elements in the queue. Show that the requirement that the ring buffer queue always maintain an empty position can now be removed.
11. By performing a large number of insertions and removals, experimentally evaluate the effect on execution time of the modification described in the previous exercise. Does the cost of keeping track of the queue size substantially alter the time to perform these operations?

12. Yet another alternative solution to the problem explored in exercise 10 is to maintain a Boolean data member named `full`. This value will be `false` except when the queue is entirely full. Implement a version of the `RingBufferQueue` using this approach. Show how this approach permits the queue to be completely full without encountering the problem described in Section 12.4.2. What is the new implementation of the member function `isEmpty`?
13. Experimentally compare the execution time of the queue modification described in the previous question to the original ring buffer queue described in Section 12.4.2.
14. Imitating the idea of the ring buffer queue, show how to create a circular double-ended queue: a queue that permits elements to be inserted or removed from either end.
15. Using character values to represent the various types of pastry, rewrite the pastry shop simulation described in Section 12.3 to use classes `PipedInputStream` and `PipedOutputStream`.

Programming Projects

1. The following are several possible improvements to the pastry factory simulation described in Section 12.3.
   a. Change the `print` method in class `Box` so that the weight of each box is printed when the contents of the box are displayed.
   b. Continually compute the average box weight. Display this value each time a box is displayed.
   c. Continually compute the average number of cookies, donuts, and eclairs placed into each box, and display this value each time a box is displayed.
   d. Add a second packaging machine. The second machine will package 24-ounce boxes instead of the 12-ounce boxes produced by the first.
2. The following projects will complete the unfinished Caterpillar game described in Section 12.2.
   a. Complete the modification of the Caterpillar game so that it will maintain and display a score value.
   b. Complete the modification of the Caterpillar game so that caterpillars will lose segments if they do not score.
3. Many computer applications present practice drills on a subject, such as arithmetic addition. Many such systems will present the user with a series of problems and keep track of those the user answered incorrectly. At the end of the session, the incorrect problems will then be

presented to the user a second time. Implement a practice drill system for addition problems having this behavior.

4. By placing all knowledge of the application domain (that is, addition problems) in a class `Problem`, modify the system you developed in the previous project so that it represents a general-purpose practice drill system. Test your design by implementing a drill from a totally different area, such as taking English verbs in present tense and having the user enter the corresponding verb in past tense.
5. `FollowMe` is a popular video game. The computer displays a sequence of values and then asks the player to reproduce the same sequence. Points are scored if the entire sequence can be reproduced in order. In implementing this game, we can use a queue to store the sequence for the period of time between generation by the computer and response by the player. We will describe two variations of this game.
   a. The textual version displays characters or numbers. Remember, these must be placed on top of each other and must be erased when the sequence is finished. In response, the player uses the keyboard to describe the pattern.
   b. The graphical version uses a grid of colored squares and highlights (by enlarging or temporarily brightening) the current square. The player then uses mouse clicks to reproduce the sequence.
6. In text formatting, endnotes are similar to footnotes but are printed at the end of a document. However, for an author, it is more convenient to write an endnote at the point in the text where it is referenced. Write an application that will read and print a textual file. However, any text between braces (that is, { and }) should be replaced by the expression "(endnote *n*)," where the value *n* is replaced by a number that increases with each endnote. At the end of the document, print each endnote in order, preceded by its numeric tag.
7. A bank wishes to know how many tellers it should have working on the average day. Bank customers stand in a common queue and then go to the first free teller. Create a simulation for the bank, making some reasonable assumptions about the arrival time for customers, the average time it takes to service a customer, and so on. Then run your simulation and compute the average time a customer is waiting in line.
8. Simulate the flow of traffic at a four-way intersection. Each of the four roads (heading north, south, east, and west) will maintain a queue of waiting cars, created by a separate thread for each road, that will create new cars according to a distribution (say, entering every 10 seconds, with a random factor added to make the simulation more interesting). The traffic signal itself will run in another thread that interacts with

the other four by means of their shared queues. When the traffic light is green in the north-south direction, it can let only a limited number of cars pass through. Assume, for example, that the light remains green for 15 seconds and that it takes 4 seconds for each car to clear the intersection. Thus, no more than four cars can pass during any one change in light. Compute the average time a car will wait at the intersection.

9. Many additions can be made to the game described in the previous project.
   a. Add buses and trucks and other types of vehicles. A bus will take longer to clear the intersection than will a car.
   b. Add the ability for a car or truck to turn left. A left-turning vehicle will block the intersection until either the traffic is clear in the opposite direction or the light is about to change.
   c. A demand light will turn green only when cars are waiting; otherwise, it will remain green in the direction that has the greatest traffic flow. Measure the average traffic flow both with and without the demand-light feature.
10. Implement the double-ended ring buffer queue described in exercise 14, and experimentally compare its running time to that of the `Deque`.

CHAPTER 13

TREES

Trees, especially binary trees, are ubiquitous in computer algorithms. For this reason, it is important to understand a few basic properties of trees. In this chapter, we will present some of their more important characteristics.

Just as the intuitive concepts of a stack or a queue can be based on everyday experience with similar structures, so too is the idea of a tree—and not just the arboreal variety—found frequently in everyday life. For example, sports events are often organized using trees, where each node represents a pairing of contestants, the winner of each pairing advancing to the next level. The winner of the last pairing is the winner of the tournament.

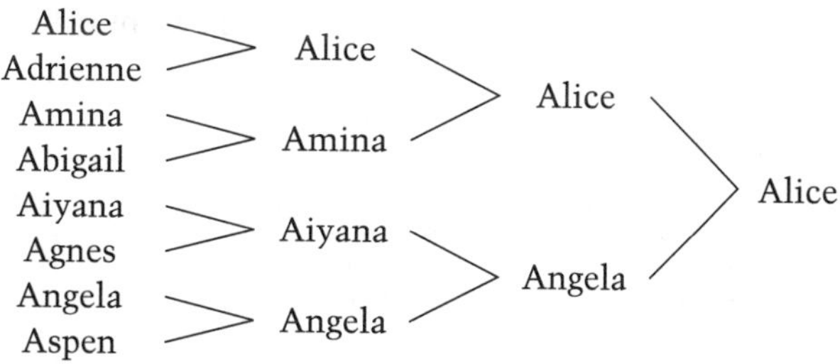

Similarly, information about ancestors and descendants is often organized into a tree structure. A typical family tree is shown in Figure 13.1. An arrow indicates the parent/child relationship. For example, Persephone is a daughter of Demeter, and Zeus and Poseidon are both children of Cronus. As we will see, much of the terminology used in computer science to

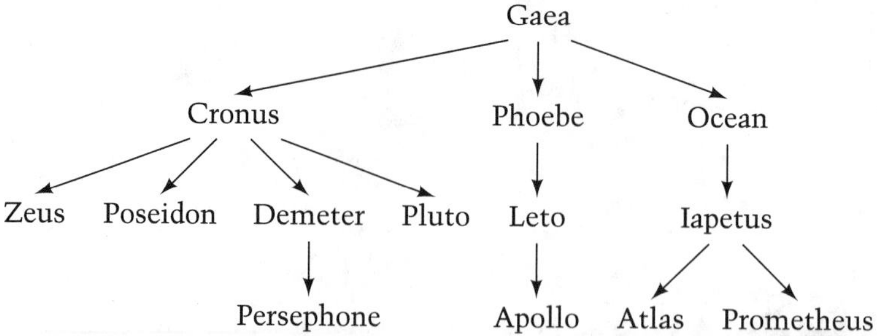

FIGURE 13.1 A Typical Family Tree

discuss trees is derived from such usage. For example, "child nodes" correspond to children in the family tree.

The inverse, in a sense, of a family tree is an ancestor tree. Whereas a family tree traces the descendants from a single individual, an ancestor tree records the ancestors of an individual. An example ancestor tree is shown in Figure 13.2. We could infer from this tree, for example, that Iphigenia is the child of Clytemnestra and Agamemnon, and Clytemnestra is in turn the child of Leda and Tyndareus. We will shortly have more to say about the characteristics of trees typified by these two forms.

After vectors and lists, trees are perhaps the data structure most frequently encountered in computer programs. The manipulation of trees illustrates many of the most important concepts in data structures and the analysis of algorithms. For example, a tree is a natural representation for information that is organized in a hierarchical fashion. The table of contents of this book provides a good example of a hierarchical structure.

The general characteristics of trees can be illustrated using Figure 13.1. A tree consists of a collection of *nodes* connected by directed arcs. A tree is headed by a single *root*, which contrary to nature, appears at the top of the

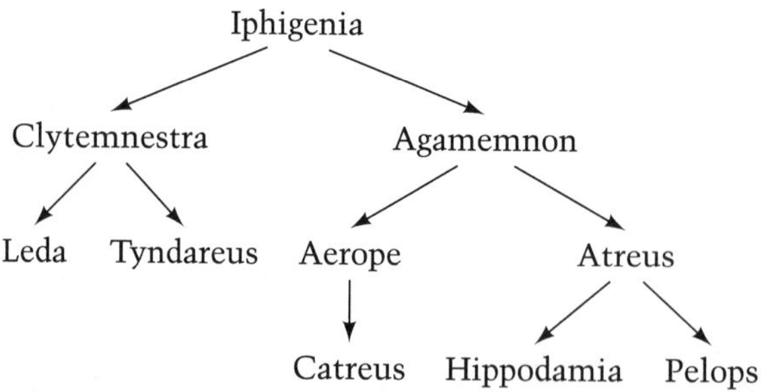

FIGURE 13.2 A Typical Ancestor Tree

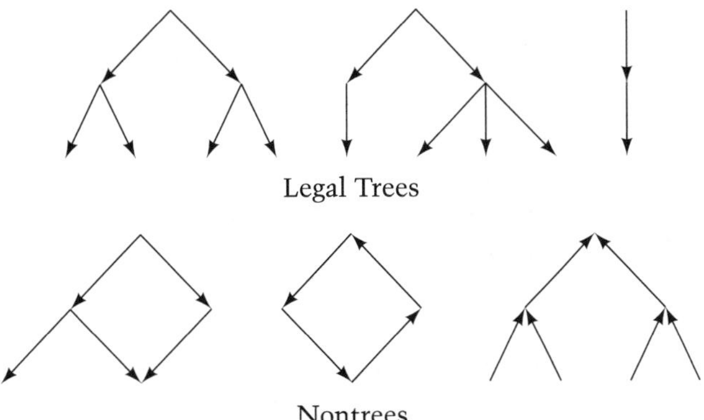

FIGURE 13.3 Various Trees and Nontrees

structure.[1] A node that points to other nodes is said to be the *parent* of the nodes pointed to, which in turn are referred to as the *children* of the first node. Continuing the familial metaphor, the term *descendants* is used to describe the children of a node, and the children of those nodes, and their children, and so on. A characterization of the root node is, therefore, that the root in a structure is the single node that does not possess a parent and from which all other nodes are descended. At the other end, nodes that do not have children are called *leaf nodes*. A node that does possess children is often called an *interior node*. Information is associated with both leaf and interior nodes.

An important characteristic of trees is that there is a single unique path along arcs from the root to any particular node. That is, arcs do not join together. Figure 13.3 illustrates various trees and nontrees. The largest number of arcs traversed in moving from the root to any leaf is known as the *height* of the tree.

Note that in a valid tree, any node can itself be considered to be a root of the tree formed by considering only the descendants of the node (Figure 13.4). We call this second tree the *subtree* rooted at the node. This recursive nature of trees leads naturally to a recursive characterization of trees.

- A node with no children is a tree. Such a node is called a *leaf*. A leaf node has *height* 0.

1. Donald Knuth claims that the convention of writing the root of the tree at the top stems from handwritten drawings, where naturally it is easier to begin with the fixed root and to proceed down the page.

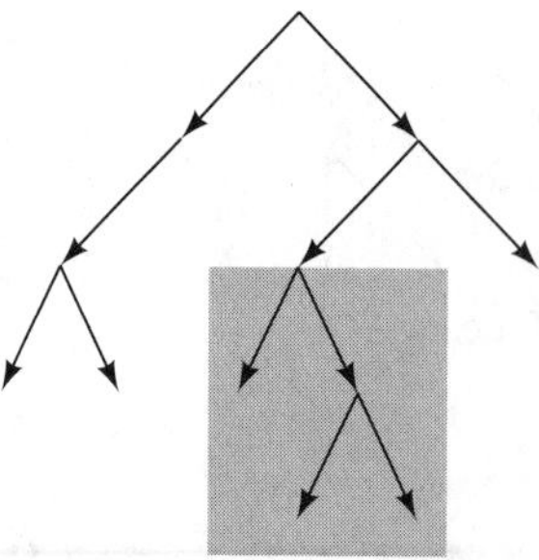

FIGURE 13.4 A Subtree Is Also a Tree

- A node with a nonempty collection of children is a tree. The node so constructed is in turn called the *parent* to the children trees. A node with a nonempty set of children is called an *interior* node. The height of an interior node is one greater than the maximum height of any child.
- The single node with no parent is called the *root* of the tree.

Trees appear in computer science in a surprisingly large number of varieties and forms. A common example is the *parse tree*. Computer languages are defined in part by using a grammar. Grammars provide rules that explain how the tokens in the language can be put together. We saw a simple grammar in the silly-sentence-generation program described in Chapter 6. In the silly-sentence example, the categories *subject*, *verb*, and *object* each described a part of speech and could be replaced with various values. The concept of a part of speech is generalized in a grammar to the idea of a *nonterminal*. Rules specify how a nonterminal can be rewritten in a more specialized form.[2] A portion of a grammar for a programming language could be given as follows:

<statement>	::= <select-statement> | <expr>
<select-statement>	::= `if` (<expr>) <statement> `else` <statement>
<expr>	::= <relational-expr> | <assign-expr> | `identifier`
<relational-expr>	::= <expr> < <expr>
<assign-expr>	::= <expr> = <expr>

A statement, such as the following, is analyzed by constructing a tree (Figure 13.5).

```
if (a < b) max = b else max = a
```

---

2. When viewed in this light, grammar is thus another example of the abstraction principle of division into specialization that we examined in Chapter 1.

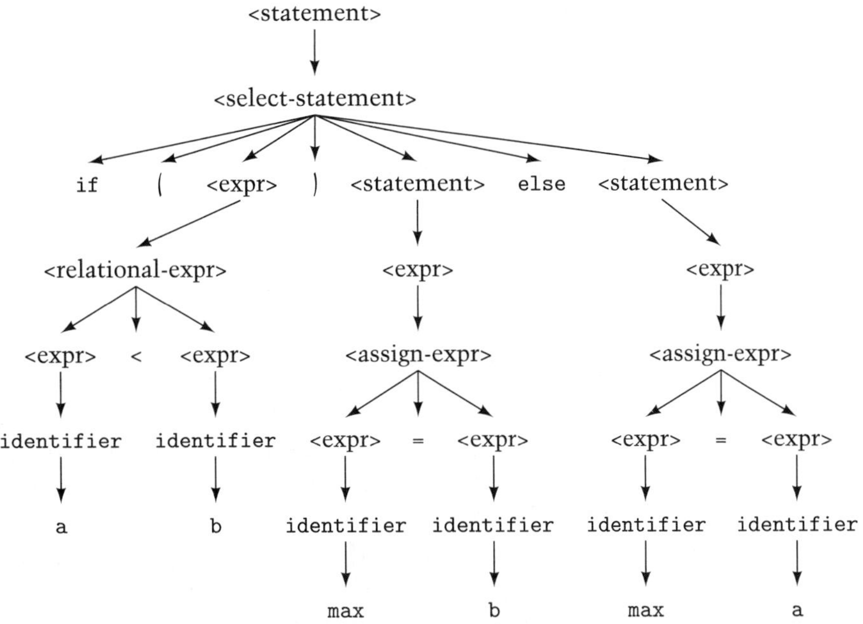

FIGURE 13.5 A Typical Parse Tree

Leaf nodes represent the tokens, or symbols, used in the statement. Interior nodes represent syntactic categories. A major task of a compiler is to construct a parse tree for an input program and then to associate information, such as types, with every node in the tree. As a last step in the compilation process, code is produced for the program by traversing the tree, that is, visiting each node in the tree in sequence. At each node encountered during this traversal, code is generated that will, when executed, perform the operation being described.

A slightly different form of a tree is an *expression tree*. As the name suggests, an expression tree (sometimes called an *abstract syntax tree*) is used to describe expressions. The two-dimensional nature of the tree eliminates the need for such features as parentheses or precedence. An expression tree for $A + (B + C) * D$ is shown in Figure 13.6.

There is an important relationship between expression trees and the prefix and postfix notations we encountered in Chapter 10. Try "walking" over the expression in Figure 13.6 by placing your finger at the root (the topmost addition node) and moving to child nodes, left to right, returning to parent nodes when you cannot move downward to any further children.

- If you write down the value of a node *before* you visit the children, you will generate the corresponding *prefix* value of the expression. In this example, the prefix representation is $+ A * + B\ C\ D$.

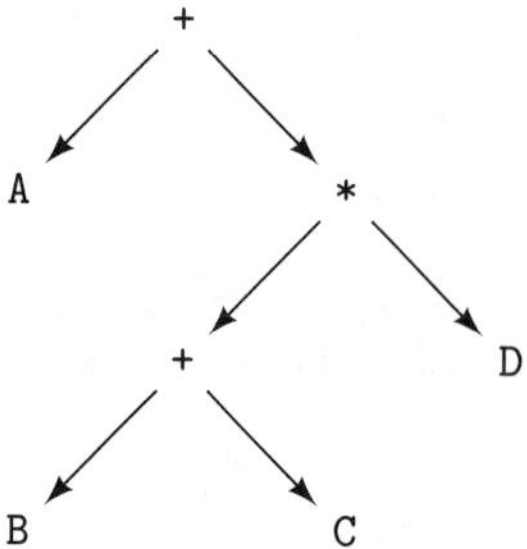

FIGURE 13.6 A Typical Expression Tree

- If you write down the value of a node after you have visited its left child and before you have visited its right child, you will generate the *infix* value of the expression (but without the parentheses that may be necessary to indicate the precedence of operations). The infix traversal of this tree will produce $A + B + C * D$.
- If you write down the value of a node after you have visited both children, you will generate the *postfix* value of the expression. In this example, the postfix representation is $A\ B\ C + D * +$.

Given our characterization of trees, there is an obvious implementation in which a tree is defined as a recursive structure, or tree node. Each tree node maintains some information and a list of references to children tree nodes. It turns out, however, that almost all trees used in computer programs are of a specialized form, called a binary tree. For this form, we can develop much more efficient algorithms:

```
public class treeNode {
  public treeNode(Object v) { value = v; }

  private Object value;
  private Bag children = new LinkedList(); // list of child nodes
  .
  .
  .
}
```

13.1 BINARY TREES

The defining characteristics of a binary tree can be illustrated by comparing the trees shown in Figures 13.1 and 13.2. An important characteristic of the tree shown in Figure 13.2 is that no node has more than two children. Furthermore, we have ordered the nodes; the mother is always represented by the left child arc and the father by the right child arc. Because no individual can have more than two parents,[3] every node can be thought of as possessing exactly two child fields. In some situations, the field may be empty, indicating, in this example, that the information is not known. A node can have only one subtree, indicating that only one of the parents is known, but it must be made clear whether the subtree represents a left or a right child. For example, the information that Catreus is the father of Aerope is conveyed by the fact that the node Catreus is the right subtree of the node Aerope, not the left subtree. A tree with these characteristics is known as a *binary tree*. The importance of binary trees stems from their frequency; they occur often in algorithms and from the fact that they can be very efficiently manipulated.

The most important properties of trees, especially binary trees, are related to the ratio of the number of nodes to the height of the tree. Thus, we first investigate this value.

Height: 0
Nodes: 1
Leaf: 1

Height: 1
Nodes: 3
Leaves: 2

Height: 2
Nodes: 7
Leaves: 4

A binary tree with height 0 can hold one node, which must be a leaf. The largest possible binary tree with height 1 holds three nodes, two of which are leaves. A full binary tree of height 2 holds seven nodes, including four leaves. It is not difficult to see that at each new level, the number of leaves will be twice the number of leaves of the preceding level.

→ **Theorem 1** A full binary tree of height n will have 2^n leaves.

The proof is by induction. The base cases for 0, 1, and 2 can be proved by inspection. Assume that a tree of height n has 2^n leaves. To form a full tree of height n, we create a new root with subtrees of height $n-1$. The number of leaf nodes is thus $2 \times 2^{n-1}$, or 2^n.

→ **Theorem 2** The number of nodes in a full binary tree of height n is $2^{n+1}-1$.

This theorem is validated by noting that the number of nodes in a full binary tree is $1+2+\cdots+2^n$. That this sum is $2^{n+1}-1$ can be easily verified by induction.

3. At least prior to the advent of modern surrogate techniques.

An Alternative Proof

An alternative verification that the sum $1 + 2 + 2^2 + 2^3 + \cdots + 2^n$ is $2^{n+1} - 1$ should be obvious to any computer scientist. The binary representation of 2^k is a 1 followed by k zeros. Thus, this sum can be represented in a tabular fashion as follows:

1	1
$+2$	10
$+2^2$	100
$+2^3$	1000
$+2^4$	10000
Sum	11111

The sum $1 + 2 + 2^2 + 2^3 + \cdots + 2^n$ is represented as a sequence of $n + 1$ one bits. Adding 1 will force a carry in each position, yielding as a result a 1 followed by $n + 1$ zeros, or 2^{n+1}.

We have been careful in the preceding discussion to describe the trees as "full" binary trees. Without this property, the results do not hold. Consider a tree with four nodes, all linked down the right child arc (Figure 13.7). The tree has height 3 yet only four nodes instead of the fifteen nodes predicted by the theorem. The reason is obvious: The tree is "thin," as most of the nodes have only one child. Most of the algorithms associated with trees possess a running time proportional to the height of the tree. Thus, attaining good performance will require ensuring that long, thin trees do not occur. One approach is to require trees to maintain a certain form. A common requirement is that every node have exactly two children, except on the bottommost two levels. A binary tree that is completely filled, with the possible exception of the bottom level, which is filled from left to right, is known as a *complete binary tree*. Figure 13.8 gives an example of such a tree.

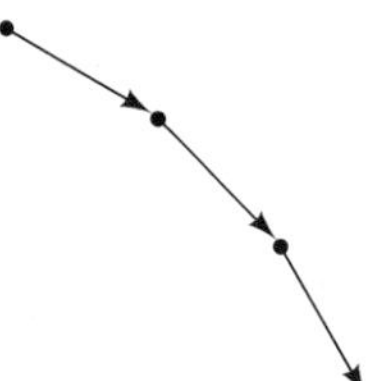

Figure 13.7 A Thin, Unbalanced Tree

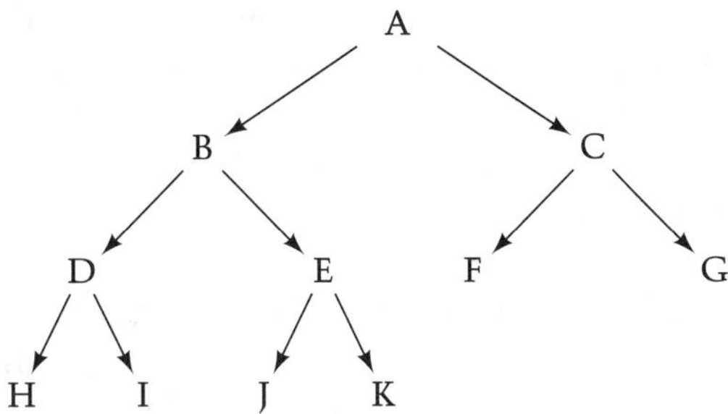

FIGURE 13.8 A Complete Binary Tree

A complete binary tree of height h is somewhere between a full binary tree of height $h - 1$ and a full binary tree of height h. As we know the number of nodes in a full binary tree, we see that a complete binary tree of height h has between 2^h and $2^{h+1} - 1$ nodes. Inverting this shows that a complete binary tree containing n nodes must have a height greater than or equal to $\lfloor \log n \rfloor$ and less than $\lceil \log n \rceil$. From this, we see that the longest path from root to leaf in a complete binary tree is $O(\log n)$.

Complete binary trees provide the maximal number of leaves with the minimal path length. This observation is behind a pair of theorems we will use to obtain lower-bound values in later chapters.

→ **Theorem 3** A binary tree containing n nodes must have at least one path from root to leaf with a length greater than or equal to $\lfloor \log n \rfloor$.

→ **Theorem 4** In a complete binary tree containing n nodes, the longest path from root to leaf traverses no more than $\lceil \log n \rceil$ nodes.

We have only touched the surface in describing the known properties of binary trees. Many other interesting characteristics are described in the literature. However, these few properties will be sufficient for our purposes for the remainder of the book.

13.2 Vector Implementation

Because a complete binary tree possesses such a regular structure, the data values can easily be maintained in a vector. Just as the vector implementations of stacks and queues were more efficient than the linked-list versions because they avoided the necessity of dynamic memory allocation, so too is the vector implementation of a tree very efficient.

To represent a tree in a vector, we will store the root of the tree in position 0. The children of the node stored at position i will be stored in position $2 \times i + 1$ and $2 \times i + 2$. In this manner, the complete binary tree shown in Figure 13.8 would be stored as follows:

0	1	2	3	4	5	6	7	8	9	10
A	B	C	D	E	F	G	H	I	J	K

Accessing the parents is easy. The parents of the node stored at position i will be found at position $\lfloor (i-1)/2 \rfloor$ (integer division, truncating any remainder). Thus, not only is the storage for references not required in this representation, but also the operations used to move up and down the tree are simple arithmetic functions and can be performed very rapidly.

The difficulty with this representation, of course, is the requirement that the trees be complete. To represent the thin, unbalanced tree in Figure 13.7 would require a vector of 15 elements, the same as for the complete binary tree of height 3. Yet most of these would be "unused." Some indication would need to be maintained in order to know which elements in the vector are valid and which represent "holes." Such a scheme is occasionally encountered, but in most cases where the complete binary tree structural property cannot be easily maintained, the more general dynamic memory implementation described in the next section will be used to implement operations on trees.

0	1	2	3	4	5	6	7	8	9	10	11	12	13	14
A		B				C								D

13.3 DYNAMIC MEMORY IMPLEMENTATION

The obvious representation for a node in a binary tree is a structure containing a value field and references to right and left children. (We omit for the moment a description of the `visit` method, which is used to implement the Visitor design pattern on a collection of binary nodes.)

```
public class BinaryNode implements java.io.Serializable {
  BinaryNode () { value = null; }
  BinaryNode (Object v) { value = v; }

  public Object value;
  public BinaryNode leftChild = null;
  public BinaryNode rightChild = null;

  public void visit (Visitor v) { ... }
}
```

The `BinaryNode` plays the same role in a tree that `Link` played in a linked list. We will use this class in many of the data structures we will develop in subsequent chapters.

13.3.1 Application—Guess the Animal Game

We will illustrate the use of binary trees with a program that plays a simple interactive game, Guess the Animal. The player thinks of an animal. The computer then poses a number of questions, attempting to discover the animal the player has in mind. An example session might look as follows:

```
Does it live in water?
no
Does it bark?
no
I know.  Is it a cat?
yes
I won!
Try again?
```

The database of animal facts is stored in a binary tree of strings. Interior nodes represent questions, and leaf nodes represent answers (animals). Initially, the game database has very little information. In our game, we start with simply one answer, namely, the animal "cat." When the computer fails to match the animal the player has in mind, it "learns" by asking for the name of the user's animal and by asking a distinguishing question to differentiate the animal from a known animal. An example session might look as follows:

```
Does it live in water?
yes
I know.  Is it a fish?
no
What is the animal you had in mind?
a duck
What is a yes/no question that I can use to tell a fish from a duck?
Does it have webbed feet?
For a duck is the answer yes or no?
yes
Try again?
```

The main program stores the database of animal facts in the tree held by the variable `root`, although this is used only during reinitialization of the game. The current node is referred to by the variable `current`, which travels down the tree, asking questions.

Streams and Readers

The Java I/O library implements two similar systems: `Stream` classes, which work with 8-bit bytes, and `Reader` classes, which work with 16-bit international characters. The 16-bit character is used to represent a number of nonroman alphabets, such as Japanese. As internationalization of programs becomes more important, you should always try to use the `Reader` and `Writer` classes rather than the lower-level `Stream` version.

Nevertheless, the programmer is likely to encounter `Streams` in two common situations. The first occurs in this program. Standard input that the user types at a console is accessed through `System.in`, which is declared as a stream. Here, we immediately convert the stream into a `Reader`, using the class `InputStreamReader`. The `Reader` is then converted into a `BufferedReader`, which allows us to read an entire line with one instruction. The second place that streams are commonly found is in conjunction with writing object values to a file, using the class `ObjectOutputStream`. We will see an example of this in Chapter 17.

```
import java.io.*;
import jds.util.BinaryNode;

class AnimalGame {
  public static void main (String [ ] args) {
    System.out.println("Lets play guess the animal");
    AnimalGame world = new AnimalGame();
    world.play();
  }

  private BinaryNode root = new BinaryNode("Cat");
  private BufferedReader din = new BufferedReader(
      new InputStreamReader(System.in));

  public void play () {
    BinaryNode current = root;
    while (current != null) {
        // if node has children it is a question
      if (current.leftChild != null) {
        System.out.println(current.value);
        if (answer())
          current = current.leftChild;
        else
          current = current.rightChild;
      } else { // no children, it is an answer
        System.out.println("I know.  Is it a " +
          current.value + "?");
```

```
        if (answer())
          System.out.println("I won");
        else // time to learn something
          learnNewAnimal (current);
        current = null;
      }
    }
    System.out.println("Try again?");
    if (answer()) play();
  }

  private boolean answer () { ... }

  private void learnNewAnimal (BinaryNode current) { ... }
}
```

The majority of questions are designed to have simple yes/no answers. The decoding of the user responses is performed by the routine named `answer`, as follows:

```
private boolean answer () { // read yes, no answer
  String line;
  try {
    line = din.readLine();
  } catch (IOException e) { line = " "; }
  char c = line.charAt(0);
  if ((c == 'y') || (c == 'Y')) return true;
  if ((c == 'n') || (c == 'N')) return false;
  System.out.println("Please answer yes or no");
  return answer();
}
```

The only other procedure is the code used to learn about a new animal when the computer makes a wrong guess. This is performed by the procedure `learnNewAnimal`. The procedure asks for the name of the new animal and the distinguishing question. The current node, which must be a leaf node, is then changed into a question node, and the two animals are installed as child nodes.

```
private void learnNewAnimal (BinaryNode current) {
  String currentAnimal = (String) current.value;
  System.out.println("What is your animal?");
  try {
    String newAnimal = din.readLine();
    System.out.println("what is a yes/no question that " +
      "I can use to tell a " + currentAnimal + " from a " +
      newAnimal);
```

```
        String question = din.readLine();
        BinaryNode node1 = new BinaryNode(currentAnimal);
        BinaryNode node2 = new BinaryNode(newAnimal);
        System.out.println("For a " + newAnimal +
          " is the answer yes or no?");
        current.value = question;
        if (answer()) {
          current.leftChild = node2;
          current.rightChild = node1;
        } else {
          current.leftChild = node1;
          current.rightChild = node2;
        }
      } catch (IOException e) { } // no nothing
    }
```

13.4 Tree Traversals

Just as it is often necessary to examine each node of a linked list in sequence, it is frequently necessary to examine every node in a binary tree. But whereas a list has an obvious linear ordering, no single ordering is the obvious "correct" way to iterate over the elements of a tree. If we consider each of the n nodes of a binary tree as independent, there are $n!$ different orderings, or sequences, in which one could visit every node ($n!$ is n factorial, or $n \times (n-1) \times \ldots \times 1$). Of course, most of these sequences have little regularity and are thus of dubious use in practice. Generally, traversal algorithms are defined recursively out of three steps.

1. Process a node.
2. Recursively visit and process the left child subtree.
3. Recursively visit and process the right child subtree.

But even within this framework, these tasks can be arranged in six possible ways.

1. Process value, then left child subtree, then right child subtree.
2. Process left child subtree, then value, then right child subtree.
3. Process left child subtree, then right child subtree, then value.
4. Process value, then right child subtree, then left child subtree.
5. Process right child subtree, then value, then left child subtree.
6. Process right child subtree, then left child subtree, then value.

In almost all cases of interest, the subtrees are analyzed left to right. Thus, the six possibilities are reduced to the first three. As we noted earlier, these three are given names. Visiting the node first, the left child second, and the right child third is called *preorder traversal*. Visiting the left child first, processing the node, and then visiting the right child is called *in-order traversal*. Finally, visiting the left child first and then the right child, followed by processing the node is known as *postorder traversal*.

Just as the "post" in postfix Polish notation implied that we viewed the arguments before encountering the operator in an arithmetic expression, here the "post" means that we will process the child nodes prior to processing the parent. In fact, we earlier noted the simple relationship between these tree traversals and pre- and postfix Polish notation. Consider a tree traversal of the expression tree shown in Figure 13.6, printing out the value of each node when it is processed. A prefix traversal will result in the following output:

$$+ a * + b c d$$

This is simply the prefix Polish form of the tree, where operators are written first, followed by their operands. An in-order traversal results in the following:

$$a + b + c * d$$

This is the infix form of the expression, minus parentheses (see exercise 6). A postfix traversal, as you might expect, produces the postfix Polish expression:

$$a b c + d * +$$

The translation of these into recursive functions that operate on instances of class `node` is relatively simple. Because the children fields of a binary node are accessible, such a function can be defined either outside the `BinaryNode` class or within the class. The following example function defined outside the class illustrates a preorder traversal of a tree:

```
// preorder processing of tree rooted at current
void preorder (BinaryNode current)
{  // visit node, left child, right child
  if (current != null) {
    process(current.value); // process current
    // then visit children
    preorder(current.leftChild);
    preorder(current.rightChild);
    }
}
```

The method visit in the class BinaryNode implements the Visitor design pattern on a binary tree by performing a recursive in-order traversal of the tree structure:

```
class BinaryNode {
   .
   .
   .
    // perform task on every element in collection
  public void visit (Visitor task) {
      // visit all nodes in left subtree
    if (leftChild != null)
      leftChild.visit(task);
     task.apply(value); // do task on our value
      // visit all nodes in right subtree
    if (rightChild != null)
      rightChild.visit(task);
  }
}
```

Outside of the recursive calls, each of these functions is performing only a constant amount of work at every node. Thus, iterating over all n elements in a tree can be performed in $O(n)$ steps, regardless of the order used.

Unfortunately, these functions suffer from a serious problem. With the Visitor design pattern, the visitor must be rewritten for each new task to be performed. For the external function, the function itself must be rewritten, but the writing of the method exposes the internal representation details of the structure. To avoid this, we define a family of enumerator classes for traversing trees. By doing so, a normal enumerator loop can be used to access each element of the tree.

13.4.1 Postorder Tree Traversal

The first traversal algorithm we examine is the postorder traversal, which examines the left child first and then the right child and, finally, processes a node. The following diagram numbers the nodes in the order they would be processed by a postorder traversal.

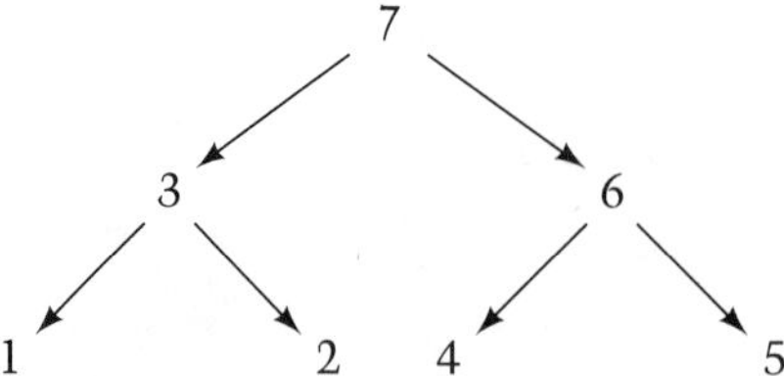

The first node we want to return in this traversal is the leftmost descendant of the root. Each of the traversal algorithms we will examine will use a stack to remember a path from root to leaf. The constructor finds the first element by using a method named `slideLeft`. This method first moves left as far as possible, then recursively examines the descendants of the right child, if any, at the end of the path.

```
class PostorderTreeTraversal implements Enumeration {
  public PostorderTreeTraversal (BinaryNode root) { slideLeft(root); }

  private Stack stk = new Vector();

  private void slideLeft (BinaryNode current) {
    while (current != null) {
      stk.addLast(current);
      current = current.leftChild;
    }
    if (stk.isEmpty()) return;
    current = stk.getLast();
    slideLeft(current.rightChild);
  }

  public boolean hasMoreElements () { return ! stk.isEmpty(); }

  public Object nextElement() {
    BinaryNode current = (BinaryNode) stk.getLast();
    stk.removeLast();
    if (! stk.isEmpty()) {
      BinaryNode parent = (BinaryNode) stk.getLast();
      if (parent.rightChild != current)
        slideLeft (parent.rightChild);
    }
    return current.value;
  }
}
```

The loop will continue as long as the stack is not empty. The method `nextElement` both returns the current element and sets the stack up for the next value. In the case of postorder traversal, this involves removing the current value, then examining the next value in the stack, which could be the parent for the current value. If it is a parent and the child is the right child, it means that both left and right children have been examined. Otherwise, if the child is not the right child, it means that the right child has not yet been examined and must be done now.

We would like to claim that a complete traversal of a binary tree with n nodes could be performed in $O(n)$ steps. One way to ensure this would be if the increment operation required only a constant number of steps. However, clearly this is not so. The `while` loop performing the left slide in the increment (as well as in the constructor) can, in the worst case, traverse a complete path from root to leaf, potentially requiring $O(n)$ steps (in a very badly skewed tree). It would seem, therefore, that the best bound we could make for n invocations of the `nextElement` method would be $O(n^2)$.

However, this worst-case behavior for the method does not occur in every case and, in fact, does not occur in most cases. A more careful accounting of how time is spent in traversing a tree will suffice to show that, although we cannot bound the time for each iteration operation, the total time for a tree traversal is still satisfactory.

To see how this could be so, we first note that every node is eventually selected as the current node, and no node is selected more than once. If every node is "assigned" a constant amount of time, the total time to perform a complete iteration must be no larger than n times this constant, or $O(n)$. This is true even if some nodes "borrow" time from other nodes, as long as the records are kept even.

We next argue that no node is ever passed over more than once in a left slide. The left slide is used simply to find the leftmost descendant of a node; once found, the next sequence of iterations will slowly move back up a tree.

The secret, then, is for the increment operation that is performing a left slide to "borrow" the time from those nodes it is sliding over. The nodes

EXECUTION TIMES: BEST, WORST, AND AVERAGE

In the various algorithms we have seen, we have encountered a number of slightly different interpretations for the characterization of algorithmic execution time. Some algorithms, such as bubble sort, perform $O(n^2)$ operations no matter what input values they are given. In contrast, some algorithms, such as insertion sort, are $O(n)$ for some inputs and $O(n^2)$ for others. In the absence of a more complete characterization, we describe this by saying that insertion sort is $O(n^2)$ *worst case*.

The time to perform a call on `nextElement` for the tree traversal algorithm is yet a third possibility. We cannot bound the execution time for any single call with anything better than $O(n)$. Yet we aren't usually interested in a single invocation of this method. Instead, the method is used as part of a loop, and we wish to bound the execution time of the loop. When we consider iterating over the entire tree, we see that the total amount of work is proportional to the number of nodes in the tree, and therefore the average amount of effort expended for each node must be constant.

An argument of this sort, that bounds a sequence of events without bounding the time for any single event, is called an *amortized analysis*. We say that the execution time for each step in an enumeration is $O(1)$ *average* time.

passed over will never themselves perform a left slide and so must always produce their results in constant time.

13.4.2 Preorder Tree Traversal

A preorder traversal visits first the current node, then nodes associated with the left child, and finally nodes associated with the right child. The following diagram indicates the sequence in which nodes would be visited using a preorder traversal.

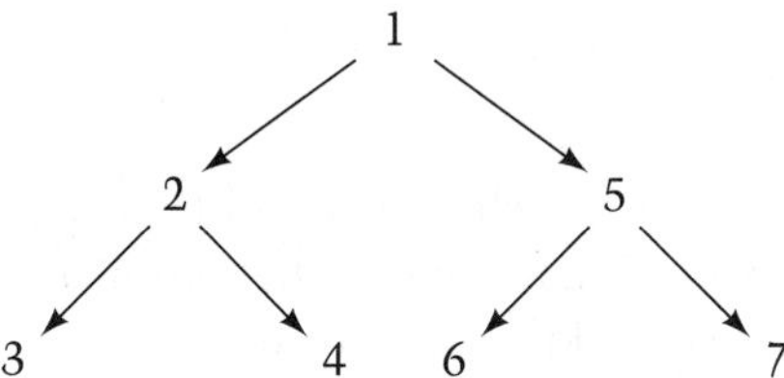

The preorder tree traversal starts at the root of the tree, so the constructor simply sets the current node to the argument value. The enumeration will loop as long as the stack is not empty.

```
class PreorderTreeTraversal implements Enumeration {
  public PreorderTreeTraversal (BinaryNode root) { stk.addLast(root); }

  private Stack stk = new Vector();

  public boolean hasMoreElements () { return ! stk.isEmpty(); }

  public Object nextElement () {
    BinaryNode current = (BinaryNode) stk.getLast();
    if (current.leftChild != null)
      stk.addLast(current.leftChild);
    else {
      BinaryNode parent = (BinaryNode) stk.getLast();
      stk.removeLast();
      while (parent.rightChild == null) {
        if (stk.isEmpty())
          return current.value;
        parent = (BinaryNode) stk.getLast();
        stk.removeLast();
      }
      stk.addLast(parent.rightChild);
    }
    return current.value;
  }
}
```

The increment operation divides into several cases. If the current node has a left child, it becomes the current node. If there is no left child, we move back up the tree until we find a node that has a right child that has not yet been processed. The right child then becomes the next node.

An amortized analysis similar to that presented for postorder traversal shows that the total execution time of an iteration is $O(n)$, despite the fact that we cannot bound the time for any individual increment step. Thus, on average, the execution time for each call on `nextElement` is a constant $O(1)$.

13.4.3 In-Order Tree Traversal

An in-order traversal visits the left child first, then the current node, and finally the right child. The following diagram illustrates the order in which nodes would be processed using an in-order traversal.

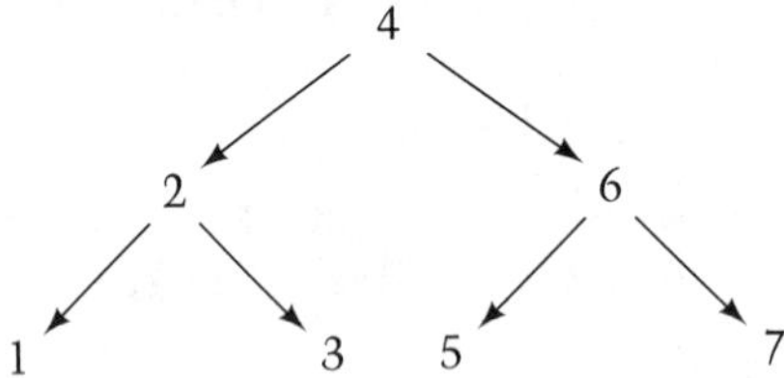

To initialize the traversal, we slide left to find the leftmost child node. The time required to perform this step is proportional to the length of the associated path, but we will argue in a moment that over time, this cost can be ignored.

```
public class InorderTreeTraversal implements Enumeration {
  public InorderTreeTraversal (BinaryNode root) { slideLeft(root); }

  private Stack stk = new Vector();

  public boolean hasMoreElements () { return ! stk.isEmpty(); }

  public Object nextElement () {
    BinaryNode current = (BinaryNode) stk.getLast();
    stk.removeLast();
    slideLeft(current.rightChild);
    return current.value;
  }

  private void slideLeft (BinaryNode p) {
    while ((p != null) && ! p.isEmpty()) {
```

```
        stk.addLast(p);
        p = p.leftChild;
      }
    }
  }
```

To advance to the next node, we examine the right child of the current node, then slide left as far as possible. The analysis of the running time for the `nextElement` method is slightly more subtle than for pre- and postorder traversals but is similar in structure and result. We "charge" the cost of the traversal not to the loop in which it occurs but to the step in which it is eventually returned as a value. Therefore, a constant amount of processing time is assigned to each node. This is sufficient to show that in total, the amount of time performed by an in-order tree-traversal iteration loop is $O(n)$, despite the fact that we cannot bound the execution of any single instance of the `nextElement` method.

13.4.4 Level-Order Tree Traversal

A fourth type of tree traversal is encountered occasionally, although less frequently than the previous three. It does, however, provide a good example of the use of the `Queue` data type. A *level-order* traversal of a tree examines all nodes at level 1 (namely, the root) before examining nodes at level 2. Next, all nodes of level 2 are examined. In general, all nodes of level i are examined before any node of level $i+1$. A level-order traversal would visit nodes of a complete binary tree of height 3 in the following order:

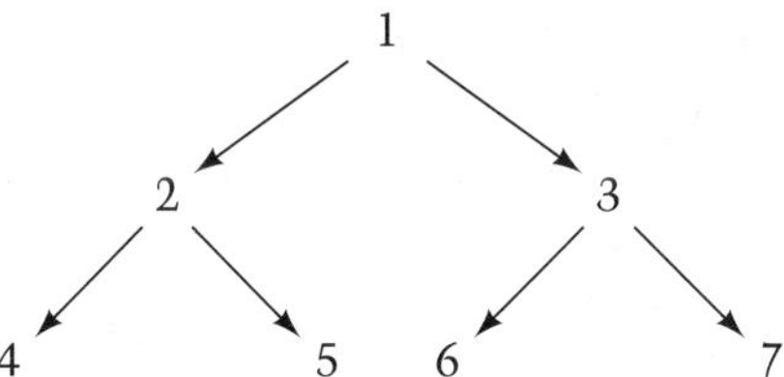

To initialize the level-order traversal, the root node is inserted into an empty queue. To increment each step, a node is removed from the front of the queue, and the children of the removed node are inserted into the end of the queue. The nature of the queue will ensure the level-order property.

```
class LevelorderTreeTraversal implements Enumeration {
  public LevelorderTreeTraversal (BinaryNode root)
    { que.addLast(root); }

  private Queue que = new LinkedList();
```

```
  public boolean hasMoreElements () { return ! que.isEmpty(); }

  public Object nextElement () {
    BinaryNode current = (BinaryNode) que.getFirst();
    que.removeFirst();
    if (current.leftChild != null)
      que.addLast(current.leftChild);
    if (current.rightChild != null)
      que.addLast(current.rightChild);
    return current.value;
  }
}
```

The execution time of the nextElement method can be bounded by a constant, and thus the total execution time is $O(n)$. The maximum number of elements in the queue is bounded by the maximum number of elements at any one level. Unfortunately, as an examination of a complete binary tree will show, this value can be as large as $n/2$.

* 13.5 Euler Tours

The three common tree-traversal algorithms—preorder, in-order, and post-order traversal—can be unified into a single algorithm by assuming that we will visit every node three times. A node will be visited before its left children (if any) are explored, after all its left children have been explored but before any right children have been explored, and after all right children have been explored. This traversal of a tree is termed an *Euler tour*.

An Euler tour is like a walk around the perimiter of a binary tree. In the following diagram, for example, note how each node is touched once on the left, once in the middle, and once on the right. For leaf nodes, these three "touchings" happen one right after the other, whereas for interior nodes, a period of time may pass between being touched on the left and being touched in the middle or on the right.

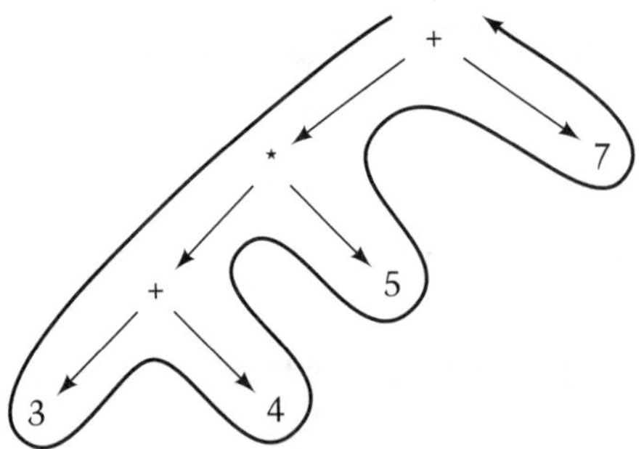

Often, the purpose of a tour is to compute a value. We can facilitate this process by starting the tour with an initial value, which is then updated as the tour progresses. This idea is captured in the code for the `EulerTour`:

```
public class EulerTour {
  public final Object traverse (BinaryNode n, Object info) {
    info = beforeLeft(n, info);
    if (n.leftChild != null)
      info = traverse(n.leftChild, info);
    info = inBetween(n.value, info);
    if (n.rightChild != null)
      info = traverse(n.rightChild, info);
    info = afterRight(n.value, info);
    return info;
  }

  public Object beforeLeft (BinaryNode nd, Object info)
    { return info; }

  public Object inBetween (BinaryNode nd, Object info)
    { return info; }

  public Object afterRight (BinaryNode nd, Object info)
    { return info; }
}
```

The method `traverse` is declared as `final`, which means that it cannot be overridden. However, the methods `beforeLeft`, `inBetween`, and `afterRight` are each expected to be overridden.

Suppose, for example, that we have formed a collection of binary nodes that represent the expression tree described in the earlier diagram. Numbers will be represented by a node holding a value of type `Integer`, whereas the interior nodes will hold a value of type `Character`. If we simply wanted to print the tree, we could do so by defining the following subclass of `EulerTour`:

```
class PrintExpression extends EulerTour {

  public Object beforeLeft (BinaryNode nd, Object info)
    { System.out.print("("); return null; }

  public Object inBetween (BinaryNode nd, Object info)
    { System.out.print(nd.value); return null; }

  public Object afterRight (BinaryNode nd, Object info)
    { System.out.print(")"); return null; }
}
```

The tour will print a left parenthesis before every node, print the value of each node, and print a right parenthesis after each node. If instead of printing the expression directly, we wanted to form the result as a string, we could use the information arguments:

```
class StrExpression extends EulerTour {

  public Object beforeLeft (BinaryNode nd, Object info) {
    String res = (String) info;
    return res + "(";
  }

  public Object inBetween (BinaryNode nd, Object info)  {
    String res = (String) info;
    return res + val;
  }

  public Object afterRight (BinaryNode nd, Object info)  {
    String res = (String) info;
    return result + ")";
  }
}
```

To invoke this tour, it would be necessary to pass an empty string as the initial value:

```
BinaryNode anExpr; // ... build the expression
EulerTour strMaker = new StrExpression();
System.out.println(strMaker.traverse(anExpr, ""));
```

A more complicated task would be to evaluate the expression tree. Here, it is useful to pass a `Stack` as the intermediate result. Values are pushed on the stack as they are encountered. Operators pop the top two items from the stack and push back their result. When all finished, the final value will be the topmost item in the stack. Because operators can be performed only after both arguments are known, it is necessary to redefine only the method `afterRight`:

```
class EvalExpression extends EulerTour {
  public Object afterRight (BinaryNode nd, Object info) {
    Stack stk = (Stack) info;
    if (nd.value instanceof Integer)
      stk.addLast(nd.value);
    else { // must be an operation
      Character Operation = (Character) nd.value;
      char c = Operation.charValue();
      Integer right = (Integer) stk.getLast();
```

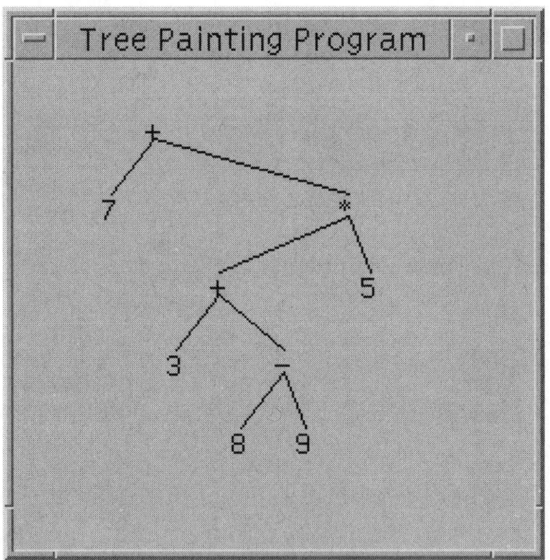

FIGURE 13.9 Screen Shot of Binary Tree Printing Application

```
         stk.removeLast();
         Integer left = (Integer) stk.getLast();
         int newValue = 0;
         if (c == '+') newValue = left.intValue() + right.intValue();
         if (c == '-') newValue = left.intValue() - right.intValue();
         if (c == '*') newValue = left.intValue() * right.intValue();
         if (c == '/') newValue = left.intValue() / right.intValue();
         stk.addLast(new Integer(newValue));
      }
      return info;
   }
}
```

We can use the Euler tour procedure to create a program that will display a binary tree. A screen shot of this application is shown in Figure 13.9. Like the evaluation procedure, the information variable will use a stack to hold intermediate values. Items held by the stack will be instances of the class `Point`. Internal to the tree printing routine will be a pair of private x and y values. As we move down the tree, the y values increase (remember that window geometry puts the 0,0 coordinate at the upper-left corner). As we display new values, the x value will increase.

```
class PaintTree extends EulerTour {

   public PaintTree (Graphics pg, BinaryNode nd) {
      g = pg;
```

```
    traverse(nd, new LinkedList());
  }

  private Graphics g;
  private int x = 50;
  private int y = 50;

  public Object beforeLeft (BinaryNode nd, Object info) { ... }

  public Object inBetween (BinaryNode nd, Object info) { ... }

  public Object afterRight (BinaryNode nd, Object info) { ... }
}
```

The `beforeLeft` method pushes our best guess for the position of the current node on the stack, then increments the y position so that the child nodes will appear below:

```
public Object beforeLeft (BinaryNode nd, Object info) {
  Stack stk = (Stack) info;
  stk.addLast (new Point(x, y));
  y += 35;
  return info;
}
```

The `inBetween` method has two cases, depending on whether there is a left child. If there is, its position is topmost on the stack, and under it is an estimate of the current position of our node. This estimate will have an incorrect x value, as we could not until now know how wide the left subtree would be. We fix the x value, then draw a line from our position to the child:

```
public Object inBetween (BinaryNode nd, Object info) {
  Stack stk = (Stack) info;
  Point myPos;
  if (nd.leftChild != null) {
    Point childPos = (Point) stk.getLast();
    stk.removeLast();
    myPos = (Point) stk.getLast();
    stk.removeLast();
    x += 10;
    myPos.x = x;
    g.drawLine(myPos.x, myPos.y+10, childPos.x, childPos.y);
  } else {
    myPos = (Point) stk.getLast();
```

```
    stk.removeLast();
  }
  g.drawString(nd.value.toString(), myPos.x-5, myPos.y+12);
  stk.addLast(myPos);
  x += 10;
  y = myPos.y + 35;
  return stk;
}
```

If there was no left child, the top of the stack contains the position of the current node. We print the string representation of the node value, then reset the y coordinate that will be used by the right subtree.

After the right subtree has been processed, we need to print the line from the current node to the child node. Both values are on the stack. If there was no right child, we leave our position on the stack:

```
public Object afterRight (BinaryNode nd, Object info) {
  Stack stk = (Stack) info;
  if (nd.rightChild != null) {
    Point childPos = (Point) stk.getLast();
    stk.removeLast();
    Point myPos = (Point) stk.getLast();
    stk.removeLast();
    g.drawLine(myPos.x, myPos.y+10, childPos.x, childPos.y);
    stk.addLast(myPos);
  }
  return stk;
}
```

* 13.6 BINARY TREE REPRESENTATION OF GENERAL TREES

It is interesting to note that the binary tree abstract data type is sufficient to represent any tree structure. To illustrate this, consider the following example tree:

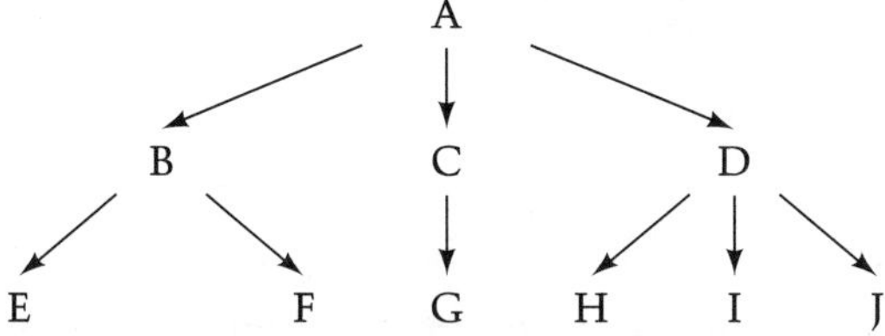

In the general case, the concept of an in-order traversal is not well defined. However, preorder, postorder, and level-order traversals can be described. For this example, preorder and postorder traversal algorithms would visit the nodes in the following sequence:

Preorder: A B E F C G D H I J

Postorder: E F B G C H I J D A

To represent this tree using binary nodes, let us use the left reference on each node to indicate the first child of the current node. Let us use the right reference to indicate a "sibling," a child with the same parents as the current node. The tree would thus be represented as follows:

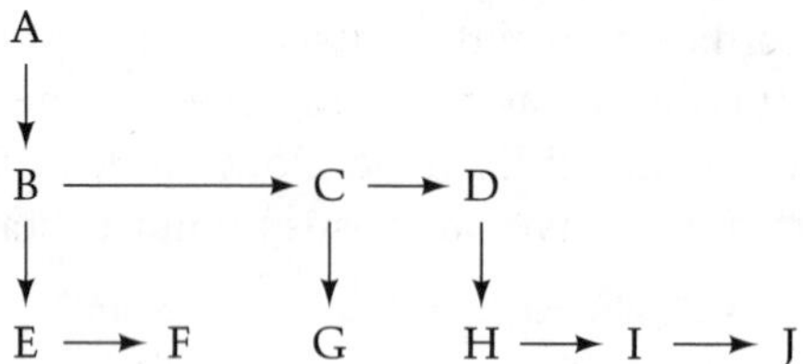

Turning the tree 45 degrees makes the representation look more like the binary trees we have been examining in earlier parts of this chapter.

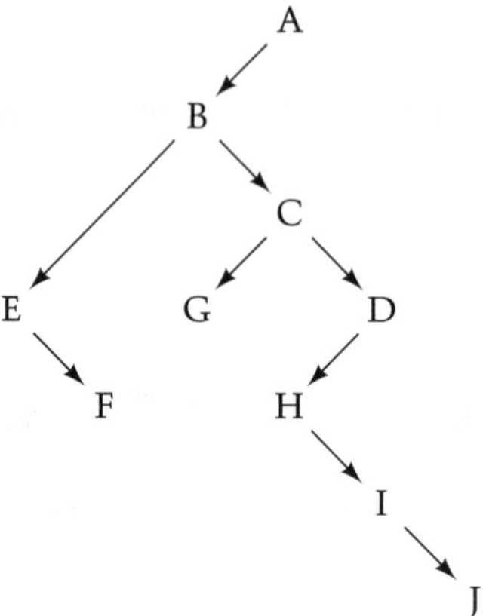

Now let us note the order in which nodes would be examined in the various traversal strategies:

Preorder: A B E F C G D H I J

In-order: E F B G C H I J D A

Postorder: F E G J I H D C B A

An interesting fact to observe is that a preorder traversal of the binary tree representation corresponds to the preorder traversal of the original tree. Even more surprising, a postorder traversal of the original tree corresponds to an in-order traversal of the binary tree representation.

13.7 Chapter Summary

Key Concepts

- Tree
  - Node
  - Root
  - Arc
  - Parent
  - Child
  - Leaf
  - Interior node
  - Subtree
  - Height
- Binary tree
- Vector implementation of complete binary tree
- Tree traversals
  - Preorder
  - In-order
  - Postorder
  - Level-order
- Euler tour

In this chapter, we have introduced the concept of a binary tree. Along with vectors and lists, trees are a fundamental building block for many important data structures. The importance of trees stems from the fact that they can hold a great deal of information and yet access the information very quickly; in a balanced tree, the longest path from root to any node is approximately proportional to the logarithm of the number of elements held by the tree.

In a binary tree, each node has at most two children. The children of a tree are themselves trees. We have examined two implementation techniques for binary trees: an encoding that packs elements of a binary tree into a vector and a more general technique that uses references and dynamically allocated nodes.

There is no obvious linear order for the elements in a tree. We have examined four traversal strategies for a binary tree. The differences are characterized by the order in which each node is processed relative to the processing of the nodes in the subtrees associated with the left and right children.

- A preorder traversal visits each node, followed by a preorder traversal of the left child, and, finally, a preorder traversal of the right child.
- An in-order traversal performs an in-order traversal of the left child, followed by visiting the node, and, finally, an in-order traversal of the right child.
- A postorder traversal performs a postorder traversal of the left and right children, then visits the node.
- A level-order traversal visits all nodes of a specific depth or path length from the root before considering any nodes of a further distance.

The analysis of execution time for the traversal algorithms presented an interesting challenge. The worst-case execution time for any single operation could often be given no better than an $O(n)$ characterization. Yet we could show that this worst-case behavior was very rare. The solution to this problem was to not characterize just one execution but instead to examine all n executions of the algorithm that would be involved in a complete traversal of a collection. If we could show that all n executions could be performed in $O(n)$ time, the *amortized* cost of any single operation would be $O(1)$. The term amortized comes from accounting, in which a costly investment, such as a new piece of equipment, might be spread over many years' budgets.

An Euler tour unifies the preorder, in-order, and postorder tours by visiting each node three times: once before any subtrees have been examined, once between the examination of the left and right subtrees, and once after the right subtree has been examined.

Finally, we noted how arbitrary trees with any number of children per node can be encoded by using binary trees. Because algorithms making use of binary trees are common and easy to use, this encoding makes it easy to extend these processes to general tree structures.

Further Information

The idea of an Euler tour is adapted from Goodrich [Goodrich 98].

Study Questions

1. What is the root of a tree? What is a leaf node? What is an ancestor node?
2. When referring to trees, what is the definition of the term height? How is the height related to the number of arcs traversed when moving from root to leaf?
3. How is the structure of a family tree different from the structure of an ancestor tree?
4. What is a complete binary tree?
5. Why are vectors generally used only to maintain complete binary trees?
6. Give an example that illustrates each of the four types of tree traversals.

Exercises

1. What are some of the ways that trees are used as descriptive devices in non–computer science applications?
2. Write the expression tree for $(a + b) * (c + d * e)$.
3. Write the prefix and postfix representations of the expression given in the previous exercise.
4. Using the grammar described in this chapter, draw the parse tree for the statement

```
if (x < y) then a = x else if (y < z) then a = z else z = y
```

5. The following is a complete binary tree of height 3:

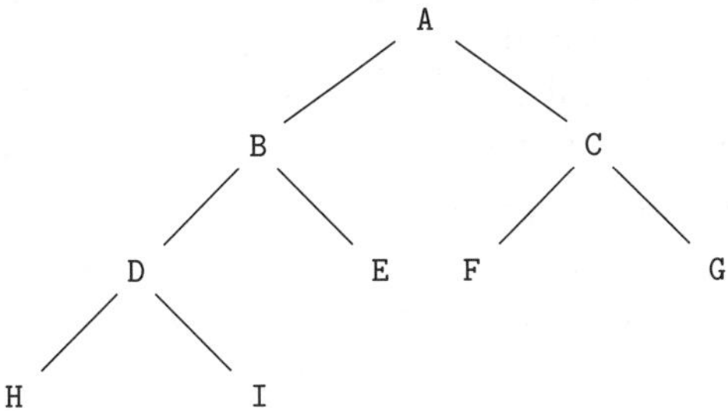

For each of the traversal algorithms we have described (preorder, in-order, postorder, and level-order), list the sequence in which nodes would be processed.

6. Recall that the in-order traversal of an expression tree did not yield the original expression, as parentheses grouping was lost. One possible solution to this problem is to print out an opening parenthesis prior to visiting every child node and a closing parenthesis after visiting each child. This, however, results in far too many parentheses. For the expression tree shown in Figure 13.6, the result would be $((a) + (((b) + (c)) * (d)))$. Describe a recursive algorithm that prints out the minimal number of parentheses necessary. This example expression tree should produce the original expression $a + (b + c) * d$.

7. Rewrite the family tree shown in Figure 13.1, using the binary tree representation of general trees described in Section 13.6 (page 351). What is the height of the resulting tree?

8. When trees are represented in the format described in Section 13.6, the right child of the root node will never be used. Explain why. Explain how we can use this fact to represent a collection of trees. A collection of trees is often called a *forest*.

Programming Projects

1. In the beginning of the chapter, we noted how trees could be constructed out of instances of `treeNode`. Each node contained a value and a collection of child nodes. Complete the implementation of this data type. What operations should a tree node provide? Can you describe a traversal algorithm for a tree represented by this data type?

2. In Section 13.6, we described how general trees could be represented as binary trees; however, we did not produce working code for the data abstraction. Create a class definition that implements this technique for representing general tree structures. What methods should your class provide?

3. Using the `TaskTimer` facility, investigate empirically the relative execution speeds of the various iteration techniques. Do this by constructing a somewhat large tree, then iterating over the nodes several times. Make several timings of the program execution, using the various iteration techniques.
4. It is sometimes useful to have each node in a binary tree maintain a reference to its parent, in addition to references to each of its children. This increases the space required to hold each node but will simplify many algorithms. For example, a postorder tree traversal can be performed without needing to maintain a complete stack. At each step of a postorder traversal, the next node either is the parent of the current node or is found along the right subtree of the parent node. Verify that the following algorithm will perform a postorder traversal, and implement it in the form of an `Enumeration`.
   a. Is there a parent node? If not, we are finished.
   b. If there is a parent node, was the current node the right child? If so, the next node to be processed should be the parent.
   c. Finally, if there is a parent node, and if the current node was the left child of the parent node, *and* if there is a right child for the parent, the next node will be found down the subtree of the right child. Examine the right child of the parent, and then find the leftmost descendant of this child.
5. Using the representation described in the previous projects, verify that the following algorithm will produce a preorder traversal, and implement it in the form of an `Enumeration`.
   a. The initial current node is the root.
   b. If there is a left child, it becomes the current node.
   c. If there is no left child but there is a right child, it becomes the current node.
   d. If there is neither a left nor a right child, move back up the tree. When you find a node with a right child that has not been processed, it becomes the current node.
6. Create subclasses of `EulerTour` that will perform each of the following tasks.
   a. Generate an integer value that represents the number of nodes in a tree.
   b. Generate an integer value that represents the height of a tree.
   c. Generate a string that represents the postfix form of an expression tree.
   d. Generate a string that represents the prefix form of an expression tree.

CHAPTER 14

BINARY SEARCH TREES

One of the most important applications of binary trees is in the creation of a data structure that is both *ordered* and *efficient*. Recall that in the abstract Bag ADT, all information about the order in which elements were inserted and held by the collection was lost. In the stack and queue abstractions, we discussed data structures that removed the first limitation by remembering the order in which elements were inserted into a collection.

The requirement that elements be stored in order by their value is a characteristic of the `Sorted` ADT. Recall that unlike the `Stack` or `Queue` interfaces, the `Sorted` interface did not add any new methods but merely changed the property we associated with the `elements` method, insisting that the values be enumerated in order smallest to largest.

We have already encountered data structures that satisfied the `Sorted` interface. In earlier chapters, we have seen both a sorted vector and a sorted list. However, inserting new values into or deleting values from either of these data structures was a relatively costly ($O(n)$) task. By carefully managing a binary tree, we can create a new data structure that also satisfies the `Sorted` requirments but permits much more efficient insertion and removal operations.

A *binary search tree* is a binary tree with the additional property that at each node, all the values associated with the descendants to the left are less than or equal to the value held by the node, and all the values associated with descendants to the right are greater than or equal to the value of the node. An example binary search tree, holding a set of names, is shown in

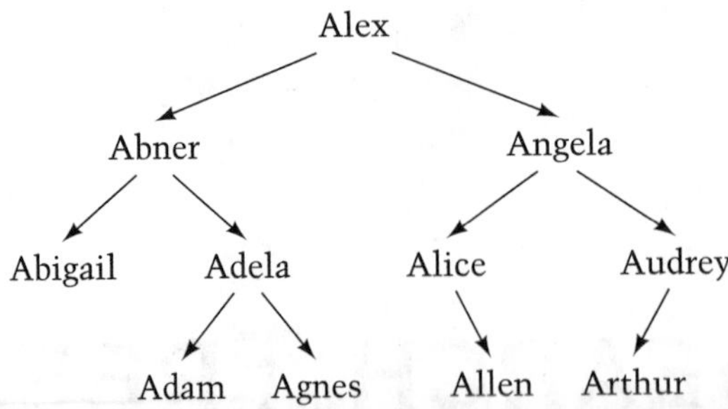

FIGURE 14.1 A Binary Search Tree

Figure 14.1. Note that a useful consequence of this property is that an in-order traversal of the tree will enumerate the names in alphabetical order.

The advantage of maintaining the elements of a collection in a binary search tree is that most operations on trees require nothing more than traversing a path from the root of the tree to a leaf. If the tree is reasonably full, the length of this path is $O(\log n)$. The tree in Figure 14.1 contains 11 elements, yet the longest path has only three arcs.

For example, determining whether a node is present in a binary search tree is relatively easy. All that is necessary is to follow a single path from the root to the leaf, checking at each node to determine whether the links of the right or the left child should be recursively pursued. Because only one path needs to be traversed, the running time of the procedure is proportional to the length of the path, not the number of nodes in the tree. This is once more an example of the principle *divide and conquer*, which we first encountered in Chapter 1.

To illustrate, suppose that we wish to discover whether the name *Agnes* is stored in the tree shown in Figure 14.1. We first compare the test element, *Agnes*, to the root of the tree, *Alex*. Because *Agnes* is (lexicographically) smaller than *Alex*, we can ignore the subtree to the right of the root and be assured that if in the tree at all, *Agnes* must be in the left subtree. Moving left, we compare *Agnes* to *Abner*. Finding *Abner* smaller, we move right and compare *Agnes* to *Adela*. Moving right again, we finally come to a node with value *Agnes*, and so we know that it is present in the collection.

We will call the data structure we implement based on this idea a `BinarySearchTree`. The nodes in the tree will be derived from the class `BinaryNode` we described in Chapter 13; however, we will find it useful to use inheritance to create a specialized version of this class. We will find it convenient to also use another technique we first discussed in Chapter 8: the concept of a *sentinel*. You will recall that a sentinel is simply a special marker, which we used in Chapter 8 to mark the end of a linked list. Here, we will use a sentinel to mark the empty-leaf positions in a binary tree. We can distinguish the sentinel by having it respond `true` to the method `isEmpty`, whereas normal nodes will respond with a `false` value. If we represent sentinels with squares, a typical binary tree might look as follows:

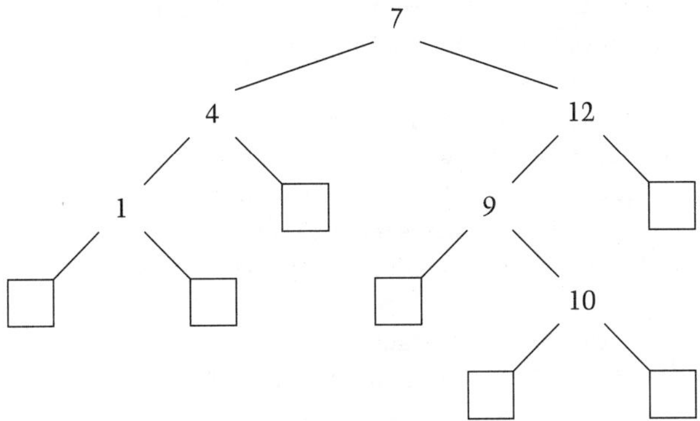

Although it is convenient to think that there are as many sentinels as necessary, in fact there is only one, and each of the squares in the diagram will refer to the same object.

One advantage of the use of a sentinel is that we never have a truly empty tree. This means that most of the binary search tree operations can be implemented by passing messages on to the root node, which must be either a node in the tree or the sentinel (Figure 14.2).

THE ACTIVE SENTINEL DESIGN PATTERN

name ActiveSentinel (a Sentinel that also responds to messages).

synopsis A sentinel marks the end of a sequence of indefinite length. If the sequence is formed using objects and messages are being sent to each object in the sequence in turn, we can distinguish the sentinal value from the other values by changing the way it responds to messages.

forces The idea of an active sentinel can be used whenever a recursive data structure is formed using objects.

solution A fundamental principle of object-oriented programming is that objects can be characterized by the messages they respond to. Assume that we have a recursive data structure formed out of objects of a class *node*. We can make an active sentinel by creating a new class that inherits from `node` and overriding the behavior of the parent:

```
class node { ... }
class sentinel extends node { ... }
```

Because the sentinel marks the end of the recursive definition, care must be taken to ensure that the sentinel does not attempt to pass messages on to any further nodes in the sequence.

counterforces Requires a new class definition for the sentinel. This will add one more class name to the current scope.

related patterns Active Sentinel is based on the simpler Sentinel design pattern (page 192).

```
public class BinarySearchTree implements Bag, Sorted, FindMin {
  public BinarySearchTree (Comparator t) { test = t; }
  public BinarySearchTree () { test = new DefaultComparator(); }

  protected final Comparator test;
  protected BSTNode root = new BSTSentinel();
  protected int elementCount = 0;

    // the Collection interface
  public boolean isEmpty () { return root.isEmpty(); }
  public int size () { return elementCount; }
  public Enumeration elements ()
    { return new InorderTreeTraversal(root); }

    // the Bag interface
  public boolean containsElement (Object val)
    { return root.contains(val); }
  public Object findElement (Object val)
    { return root.find(val); }
  public synchronized void addElement (Object val)
    { root = root.add(val); elementCount++; }
  public synchronized void removeElement (Object val)
    { root = root.remove(val); elementCount--; }

    // the FindMin interface
  public Object getFirst () { return root.getFirst(); }
  public void removeFirst ()
    { root = root.removeFirst(); elementCount--; }

    // internal node class
  private class BSTNode extends BinaryNode {
    public boolean isEmpty () { return false; }
    public BSTNode add (Object newElement) { ... }
    public boolean contains (Object val) { ... }
    public Object find (Object val) { ... }
    public Object getFirst () { ... }
    public BSTNode removeFirst () { ... }
    public BSTNode remove (Object oldElement) { ... }
  }

    // internal sentinel class
  private class BSTSentinel extends BSTNode { ... }
}
```

FIGURE 14.2 The Class BinarySearchTree

A simple example is the method contains. This is implemented in the node class by one method that will perform a recursive search and in the sentinel class by another method that reports that the element is absent:

```
private class BSTNode extends BinaryNode {
.
.
.
  public BSTNode left () { return (BSTNode) leftChild; }
  public BSTNode right () { return (BSTNode) rightChild; }

  public boolean contains (Object newElement) {
    int testResult = test.compare(newElement, value);
    if (testResult == 0) return true; // found it
    if (testResult < 0)
      return left().contains(newElement);
    return right().contains(newElement);
  }
}

private class BSTSentinel extends BSTNode {
.
.
.
  public boolean contains (Object newElement) { return false; }
}
```

The methods left and right are necessary because the data fields leftChild and rightChild inherited from class BinaryNode are references to a BinaryNode structure and must be cast before we can use them as references to a BSTNode value. The findElement method, which uses a method named find in the node class, is similar.

New values are always added to a binary search tree at the leaves. The add method in class BSTNode simply traverses the path from root to leaf. The add method in the sentinel creates a new node. Note how the sentinel sets the left and right child references in the new node to point to the sentinel. This is how all leaf nodes end up pointing to the same sentinel node.

```
private class BSTNode extends BinaryNode {
.
.
.
  public BSTNode add (Object newElement) {
    if (test.compare(newElement, value) < 0)
      leftChild = left().add(newElement);
    else
      rightChild = right().add(newElement);
```

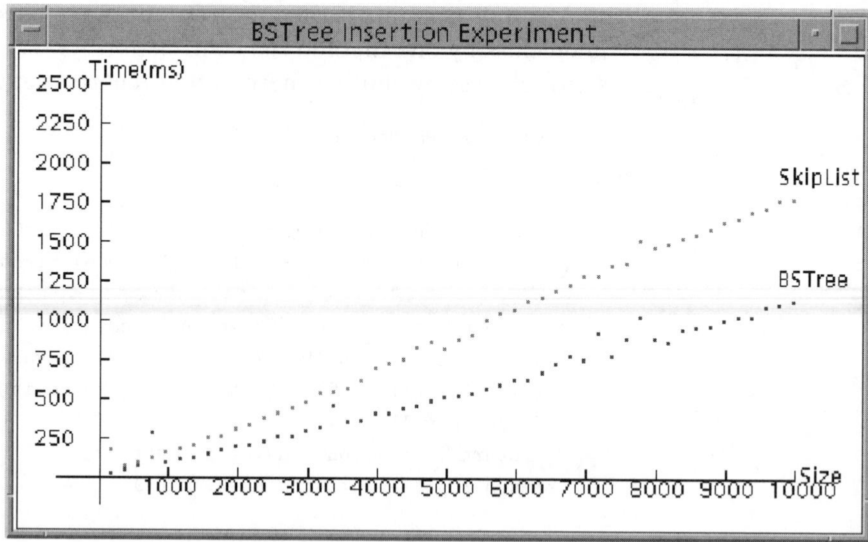

FIGURE 14.3 Execution Timings for Addition of Random Values

```
      return this;
    }
  }

  private class BSTSentinel extends BSTNode {
  .
  .
  .
    public BSTNode add (Object newElement) {
      BSTNode newNode = new BSTNode(newElement);
      newNode.leftChild = this; // both children
      newNode.rightChild = this; // are sentinels
      return newNode;
    }
  }
```

As long as the tree remains relatively well balanced, the addition of values to a binary search tree is very fast. This can be seen in the execution timings shown in Figure 14.3. Here, we compare the time required to place n random values into a collection, comparing the binary search tree to the `SkipList`, which had the fastest execution times for this operation we have seen up to this point. However, the requirement that the tree remain well balanced is important, a topic we will return to in Section 14.1.

The `BinarySearchTree` also supports the `FindMin` interface. In addition to the method `addElement`, this interface consists of two methods:

EXPERIMENT: SEARCH-TIME PERFORMANCE OF A BINARY SEARCH TREE

In many problems, execution time is dominated by searching a collection, using either the method `containsElement` or the method `findElement`. Here, too, the best execution time we have seen up to this point was provided by the `SkipList` data abstraction. Create a collection of n random values; then record the execution time required to perform n search operations for random values. Compare the execution time of the binary search tree to that of a `SkipList`.

`getFirst` and `removeFirst`. Note that the smallest element in a binary search tree is found by traversing the left-child links. This is performed by a recursive method in the node class:

```
class BSTNode extends BinaryNode {
  public Object getFirst () {
    if (leftChild.isEmpty()) return this;
    return left().getFirst();
  }
}
```

Removing the smallest element is similar. The traversal follows the same path as `getFirst`.

```
class BSTNode extends BinaryNode {
  public BSTNode removeFirst () {
    if (leftChild.isEmpty()) return right();
    leftChild = left().removeFirst();
    return this;
  }
}
```

When the node containing the smallest element is found, the right child is returned. Either the right child is empty (the sentinel value), or it is not.

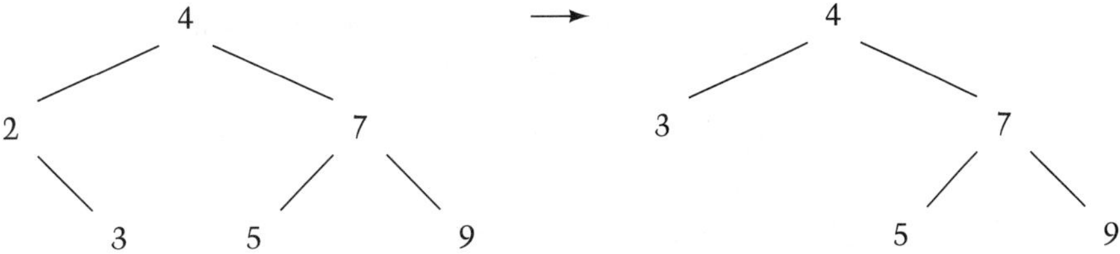

The removal of items other than the smallest is more complex. Finding the value to be removed is not difficult; we simply traverse the path from root to the element, throwing an exception if we get to a sentinel without finding the value in question:

```
private class BSTNode extends BinaryNode {
.
.
.
  public BSTNode remove (Object oldElement) {
    int testResult = test.compare(oldElement, value);
    if (testResult == 0) { // found item to be removed
      .
      .
      .
    } else if (testResult < 0)
      leftChild = left().remove(oldElement);
    else
      rightChild = right().remove(oldElement);
    return this;
  }

}

private class BSTSentinel extends BSTNode {
.
.
.
  public BSTNode remove(Object oldElement)
    { throw new NoSuchElementException(oldElement.toString()); }
}
```

However, having found the element, we then face a problem. If we remove the element, we leave a "hole." The hole cannot be left in the tree, and so it must be filled. But what element should we use to fill the hole? Filling it with either the immediate left or right child may destroy the binary search tree property.

Two elements *can* be used to fill the hole: the largest value in the left subtree or the smallest value in the right subtree. You should verify that if either of these values is used, the binary search tree property will be maintained and that if any other value is used, the binary search tree property will be lost. Because we already have a method to find and to remove the smallest element in a subtree, we will manipulate the right subtree.

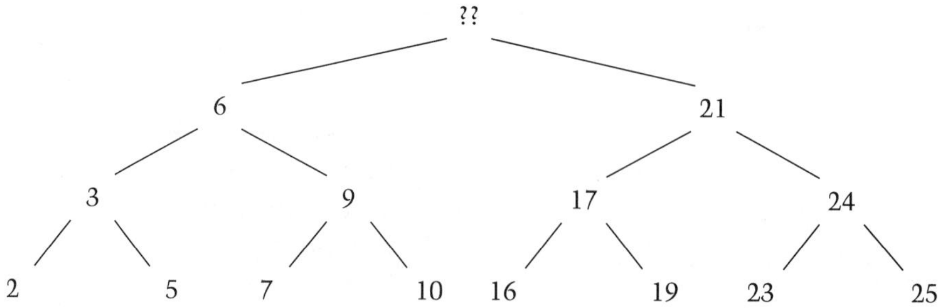

But what if there is no right child? In this special case, the left child can simply be returned, as each subtree in a binary search tree preserves the search tree property. (Cover up the tree rooted at 21 in the preceding diagram to see this possibility.) In the general case, we copy the value from the smallest right descendant into the current node, then remove the value from the right subtree. The code to perform a removal is as follows:

```
public BSTNode remove (Object oldElement) {
  int testResult = test.compare(oldElement, value);
  if (testResult == 0) { // found it
    if (right().isEmpty())
      return left();
    value = right().getFirst(); // copy smallest descendant
    rightChild = right().removeFirst(); // and delete original
  } else if (testResult < 0)
    leftChild = left().remove(oldElement);
  else
    rightChild = right().remove(oldElement);
  return this;
}
```

14.1 THE IMPORTANCE OF BALANCE

We have been careful to note that the complexity of each of the operations performed on a search tree is proportional to the length of the path from root to the node being manipulated. In a well-balanced tree, such as that shown in Figure 14.1, the length of the longest path is roughly $\log n$. A well-balanced tree could have a million entries, for example, and still maintain a maximum path length no larger than 20.

On the other hand, if we happen to insert elements into the tree in order, we can easily create the tree shown in Figure 14.4. This is still a binary search tree, but the expected time to perform an operation will be $O(n)$, or linear in the number of nodes. This is simply a very expensive way to implement a linked list.

We can see this effect by altering the sequence in which elements are added to a tree. Rather than generating random value, as we did in Figure 14.3, we instead add the values 1 to n in order. In this case, the execution time of the `BinarySearchTree` rapidly deteriorates, as shown in Figure 14.5.

In order to avoid this difficulty, we require a method to ensure that our search trees remain balanced. In this section, we will investigate one simple technique to preserve this property. It should be noted that the technique we will describe is not the only known approach for creating

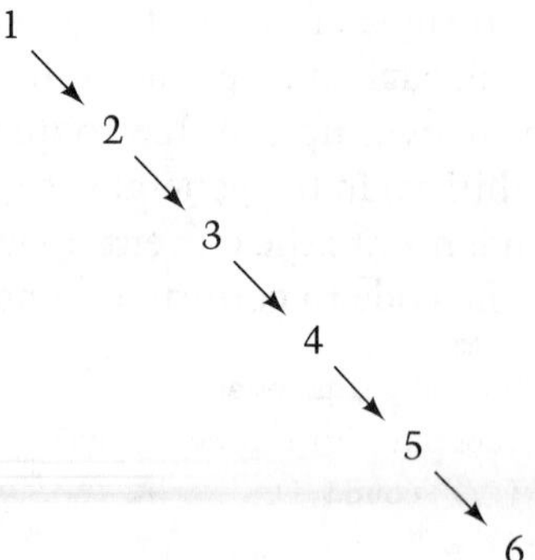

FIGURE 14.4 A Very Unbalanced Search Tree

balanced search trees. In the section Further Information at the end of the chapter, we will point to references that discuss various other techniques.

First, let us examine one idea that will not work. In Chapter 13, we introduced the idea of a *complete binary tree* and noted that this form had the shortest overall path length for any binary tree. A path from root to leaf in a complete binary tree with n elements is guaranteed to have no more than $\lceil \log n \rceil$ nodes. So it makes sense that if we could keep our binary search tree in the form of a complete binary tree, we would then have very fast search time. But although search times for such a tree will be very

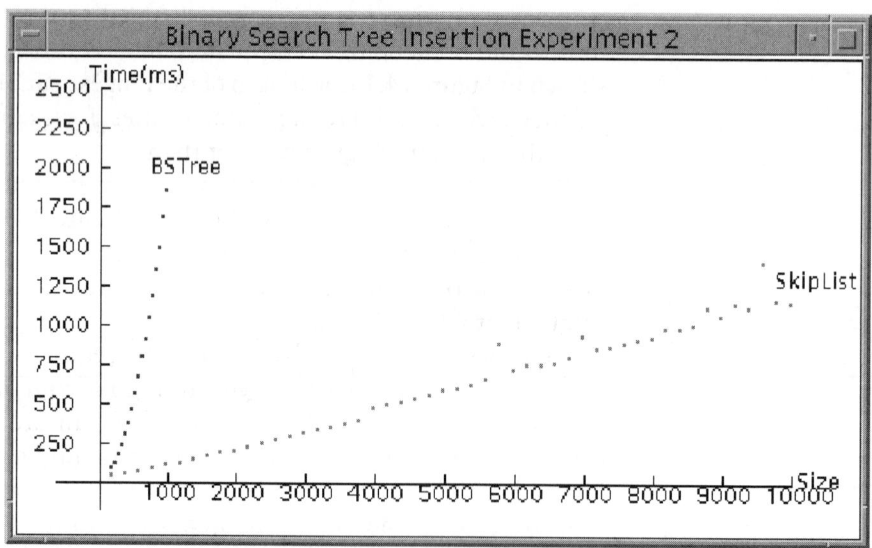

FIGURE 14.5 Execution Timings for Addition of Values in Order

fast, it is unfortunate that the time to add an element to such a tree must be relatively slow. This can be seen in the following, where we have taken the tree on the left and added the element 1, resulting in the tree on the right.

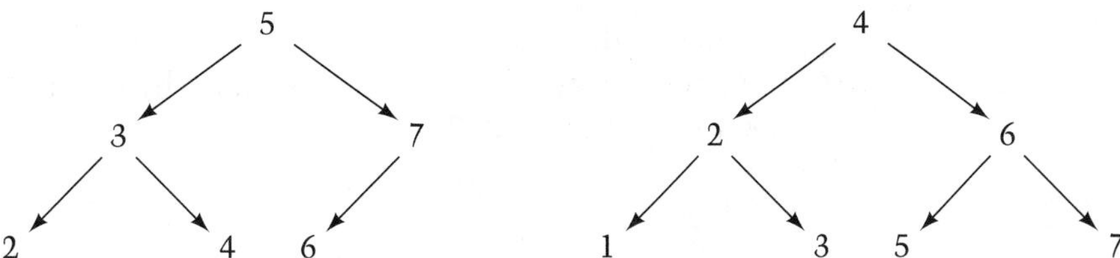

Note that *every* element has moved to a different position. We would therefore need to at least touch every node in the tree, and this would require at least $O(n)$ effort. Thus, demanding that the trees maintain complete balance is simply too costly.

Fortunately, we can still get a dramatic improvement in the execution time for all operations by slightly relaxing our objectives. Rather than seeking the absolute shortest overall tree structure, let us seek one that is still relatively well balanced, even if it is not the absolute best. A *height-balanced* binary tree has the property that for each node, the *difference* in heights of the right child and the left child is no larger than 1. This property ensures that locally, at each node, the balance is roughly maintained, although globally, over the entire tree, differences in path lengths can be somewhat larger. Figure 14.6 shows an example height-balanced binary tree.

Clearly, a complete binary tree is also height balanced. Thus, the *largest* number of nodes in a balanced binary tree of height h is $2^{h+1} - 1$. An interesting question is to discover the *smallest* number of nodes in a height-

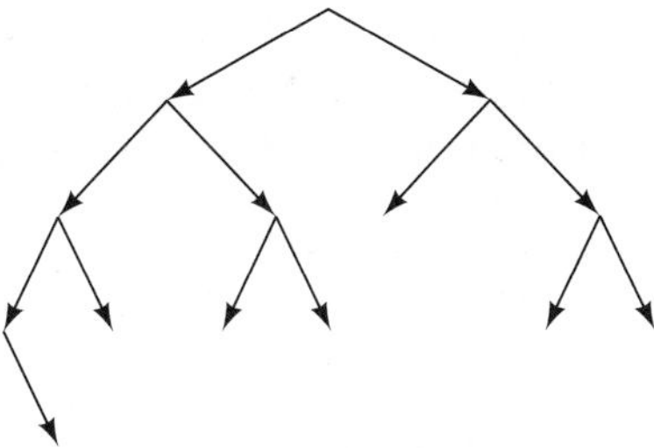

FIGURE 14.6 A Height-Balanced Binary Tree

balanced binary tree. For height 0, there is only one tree. For height 1, there are three trees:

The smallest of these has two nodes. In general, for a tree of height h, the smallest number of nodes is found by connecting the smallest tree of height $h-1$ and $h-2$.

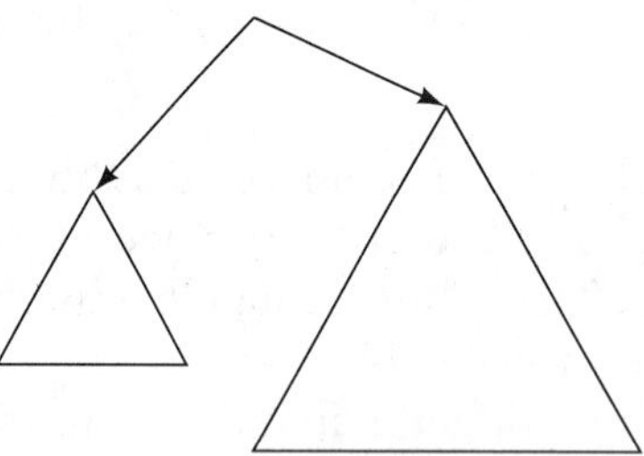

If we let M_h represent the function yielding the minimum number of nodes for a height-balanced tree of height h, we obtain the following equations:

$$M_0 = 1$$

$$M_1 = 2$$

$$M_{h+1} = M_{h-1} + M_h + 1$$

These equations are very similar to the famous *Fibonacci numbers* defined by the formula $f_0 = 0$, $f_1 = 1$, $f_{n+1} = f_{n-1} + f_n$. An induction argument (exercise 8) can be used to show that $M_h = f_{h+3} - 1$. Using induction, it is easy to show that we can bound the Fibonacci numbers by 2^n. In fact, it is possible to establish an even tighter bounding value. Although the details need not concern us here, the Fibonacci numbers have a closed-form solution, that is, a solution defined without using recursion (see exercise 11). The value F_h is approximately $\frac{\Phi^i}{\sqrt{5}}$, where Φ is the golden mean value $(1+\sqrt{5})/2$, or approximately 1.618. Using this information, we can show that the function M also has an approximate closed-form solution:

$$M_h \approx \frac{\Phi^{h+3}}{\sqrt{5}} - 1$$

By taking the logarithm of both sides and discarding all but the most significant terms, we obtain the result that $h \approx 1.44 \log M_h$. This tells us that the longest path in a height-balanced binary tree with n nodes is at worst only 44 percent larger than the $\log n$ minimum length. Hence, algorithms on height-balanced binary trees that run in time proportional to the length of the path are still $O(\log n)$.

14.2 AVL Trees

An *AVL tree* attempts to guarantee efficient performance by maintaining the binary search tree property while at the same time guaranteeing the height-balanced characteristic. That is, for each node, we ensure that the difference in heights between the left and right subtrees is no larger than 1. The method for doing this was first described in 1962 by two Russian mathematicians, Georgii M. Adel'son-Vel'skiĭ and Evgeniĭ Mikhaĭlovich Landis, and the resulting binary search trees are named in their honor.

The class `AVLTree` is almost identical to the class `BinarySearchTree` described in Figure 14.2. Differences are that the root will be declared an instance of class `AVLNode` rather than `BSTNode` and that the class also supports the `SortAlgorithm` interface. The sorting algorithm associated with this class will be described in Section 14.3.

The class `AVLNode` (Figure 14.7) adds an integer `height` data field but in other respects is very similar to the class `BSTNode`. The methods `contains` and `find` are exactly the same. The methods `add` and `remove` are similar but rather than returning a new node, they instead invoke a method `setHeight` that will both set the `height` field in the node and restore balance to the tree.

Before we present the implementation of the `setHeight` method, we will consider the problem posed by the addition of a new node to an AVL tree and how transformations must be applied to maintain the height-balanced property. We will do so by working through a simple example and then abstracting the general algorithm from the specific problems we encounter. Consider inserting the integer values 1 to 7 in order into an empty tree. Inserting 1 into an empty tree, of course, causes no difficulty. An insertion of 2 yields the following structure. The value preceding the colon is the element, and the value following the colon is the height.

As with the earlier binary search trees, we first walk down the path until we discover a leaf node or interior node with only one child, where the value can be inserted. The insertion is either along a left link or along a

```
protected class AVLNode extends BinaryNode {
  AVLNode (Object v) { super(v); }
  protected int height = 0;

  private AVLNode left () { return (AVLNode) leftChild; }
  private AVLNode right () { return (AVLNode) rightChild; }

  public AVLNode add (Object newElement) {
    if (test.compare(newElement, value) < 0)
      leftChild = left().add(newElement);
    else
      rightChild = right().add(newElement);
    return setHeight();
  }

  public boolean contains (Object newElement) { ... }

  public Object find (Object newElement) { ... }

  public AVLNode remove (Object oldElement) {
    .
    .
    .
    return setHeight();
  }

  public AVLNode removeFirst () {
    if (leftChild.isEmpty()) return right();
    leftChild = left().removeFirst();
    return setHeight();
  }

  private AVLNode setHeight () { ... }
}
```

FIGURE 14.7 The AVLNode Class

right link. In the case of the addition of 2, the insertion is along the right link.

We continue the addition of ascending numbers. When we try to insert the value 3, we run into our first problem. The sentinel will always report a height of -1. As a consequence, the root will note that it has one child node with a height of 1 and another child node with a height of -1. Because this difference is greater than 1, we have lost the height-balance property.

To rectify this, we perform a *rotation* to the left, making the node 2 into the new root.

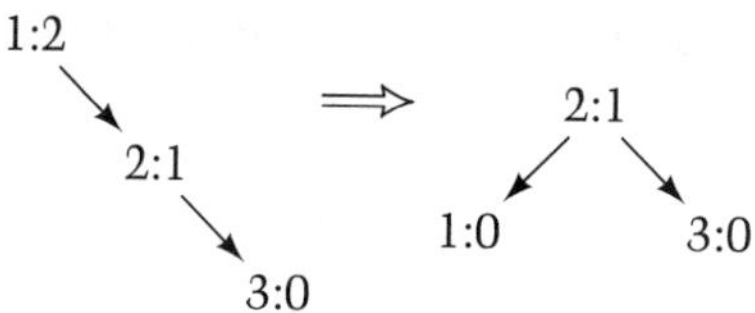

The code used to perform a left rotation is the following. The code for the right rotation is similar.

```
class AVLNode {
  ⋮

  private AVLNode rotateLeft () {
    AVLNode newTop = right();
    rightChild = newTop.leftChild;
    newTop.leftChild = setHeight();
    return newTop.setHeight();
  }
}
```

Returning to our example, the insertion of the value 4 causes no difficulty. The insertion of the value 5 forces another left rotation, this time rooted at the right child node.

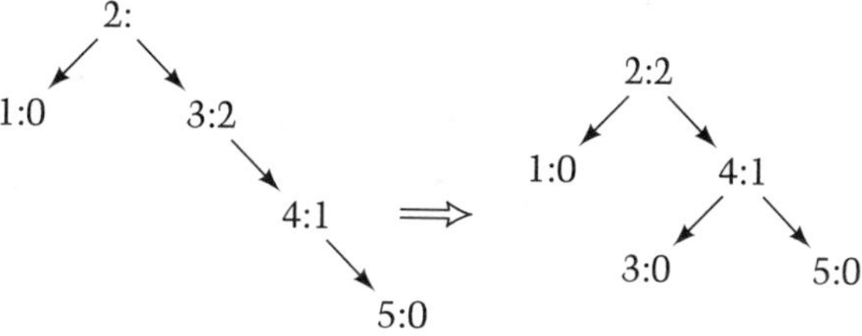

The insertion of 6 does not cause a balance problem for the child subtrees but does generate a problem for the root, as the left subtree has height 0 but the right subtree would have height 2. A single rotation restores the correct balance by making the previous root, 2, a child of the new root 4. The insertion of 7 causes one last rotation, leaving us with a balanced tree.

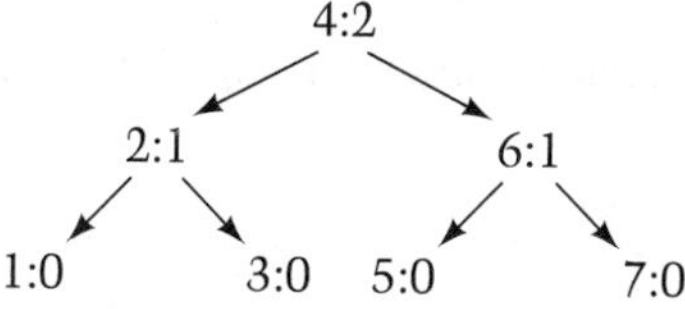

Occasionally, single rotations are not sufficient. To see this, let us try inserting the values 15 and 16 in reverse order. The insertion of 16 is simple; however, the insertion of 15 causes a height imbalance. Unlike the earlier cases, a single rotation is not sufficient to restore the height-balance property.

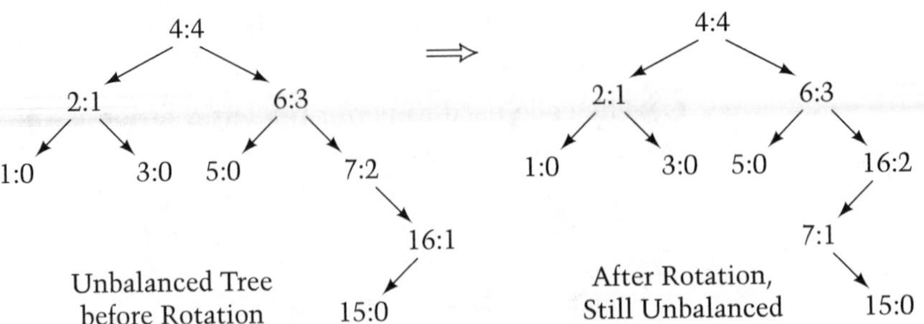

The problem arises when an insertion is made into the left child—causing it to become heavy—of a node that is itself a heavy right child. It can be shown (exercise 12) that these are the only two instances when a single rotation will produce a value that is not balanced. Fortunately, this situation is easy to both recognize and handle. The solution is a combination of *two* single rotations and is thus called a *double* rotation. First, we perform a right rotation on the right child. This is followed by a left rotation at the point of the earlier imbalance.

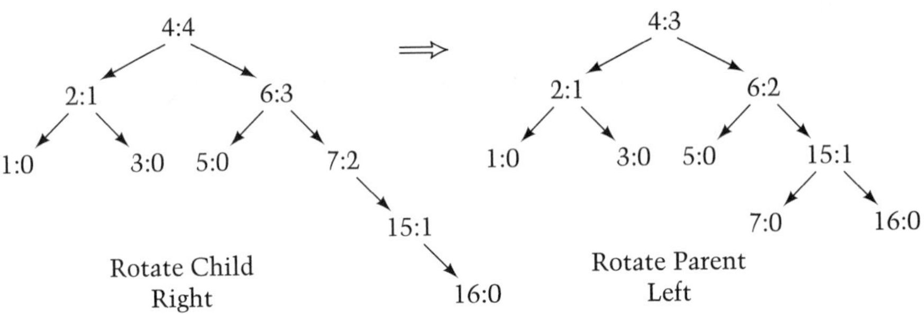

The following procedure is used to rebalance a subtree, selecting either a single or a double rotation as necessary. The method bf computes the *balance factor*, the difference between the left and right subtrees. If this value is negative, the left subtree is larger than the right; if positive, the right subtree is larger than the left; if zero, they are the same height.

```
private int bf () { return right().height - left().height; }

private AVLNode balance () {
  if (bf() < 0) {
    if (left().bf() > 0) // double rotation
```

```
      leftChild = left().rotateLeft();
    return rotateRight(); // single rotation
  }
  if (right().bf() < 0)
    rightChild = right().rotateRight();
  return rotateLeft();
}
```

We are finally in a position to present the code that both sets the `height` field in a node and, if necessary, rebalances the tree:

```
private AVLNode setHeight () {
  int lh = left().height;
  int rh = right().height;
  int nbf = rh - lh; // balance factor
  if ((nbf < -1) || (nbf > 1))
    return balance(); // restore balance
  height = 1 + ((lh < rh)?rh:lh);
  return this;
}
```

We can see the effect of rebalancing by repeating the experiment described in Figure 14.5, in which elements were placed into the collection in order. This time, as shown in Figure 14.8, the AVL tree continues to perform well, still surpassing the time for a `SkipList` and thus becoming the fastest data structure we have yet seen for these operations.

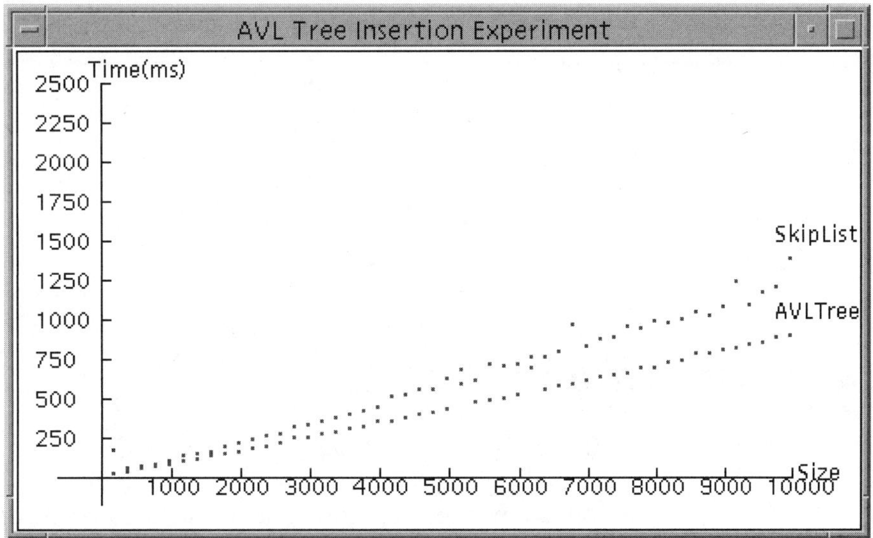

FIGURE 14.8 Execution Timings for AVL Insertion of Sorted Values

EXPERIMENT: REMOVAL-TIME PERFORMANCE OF AN AVL TREE

The removal of elements in both an AVL tree and a SkipList is predicted to have $O(\log n)$ performance, so asymptotic execution figures are no help in deciding which will have the faster execution times. Perform the following experiment to measure the actual execution time of the removal operation. First, create a collection of n random values between 1 and n. Then time the process of first testing and then, if present, removing n values from the collection. Compare the running time of the AVL tree to that of the SkipList.

The removal of a value from an AVL tree simply requires invoking `setHeight` at the end of the `removeFirst` and the more general `remove` methods, as shown in Figure 14.7. For example, consider removing the root value, 4, from the tree we have just constructed. The first step will be to replace the value 4 with the smallest element in the right subtree, which is the value 5. As we return from the `removeFirst` method, we will discover an imbalance at the node with value 6:

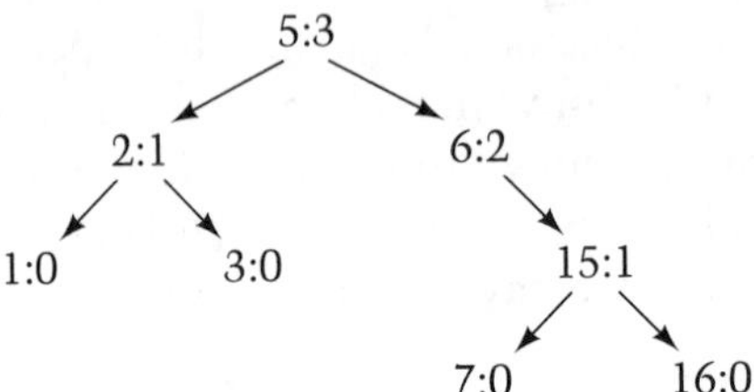

A single left rotation is performed, and the tree is once again balanced.

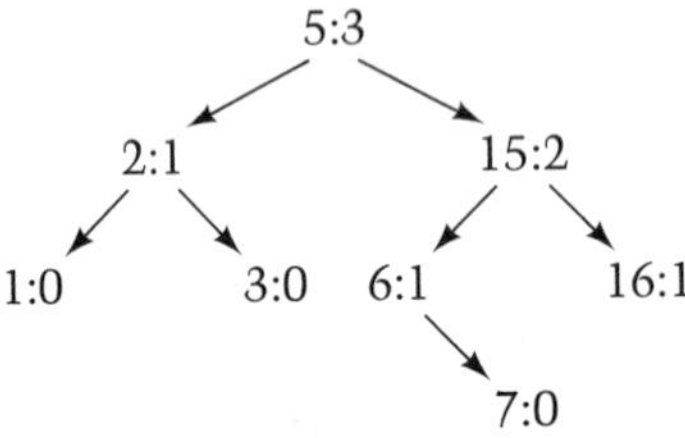

14.3 APPLICATION—TREE SORT

As we noted in Chapter 7, any class that supports the `Sorted` interface naturally suggests a sorting algorithm: Simply copy the values into the collection, then copy them back out. Because inserting the values will, as a side effect, place them in sequence, the result is a sorting algorithm.

```
public class AVLTree implements Bag, Sorted, FindMin, SortAlgorithm {
:
:
    // the SortAlgorithm interface
  public void sort (Indexed data) {
    AVLTree t = new AVLTree(test);
    int n = data.size();
        // copy them in
    for (int i = 0; i < n; i++)
      t.addElement(data.elementAt(i));
        // copy them out
    Enumeration e = t.elements();
    int i = 0;
    while (e.hasMoreElements())
      data.setElementAt(e.nextElement(), i++);
  }
}
```

In practice, the execution time for the tree sort algorithm on random values (Figure 14.9) matches almost exactly the execution time for the quick sort algorithm from Chapter 7. Quick sort is one of the fastest sorting algorithms we have seen so far. Even better, the tree sort algorithm is not troubled by input that is sorted or almost sorted. Recall that these values could make the quick sort algorithm exhibit its worst-case $O(n^2)$

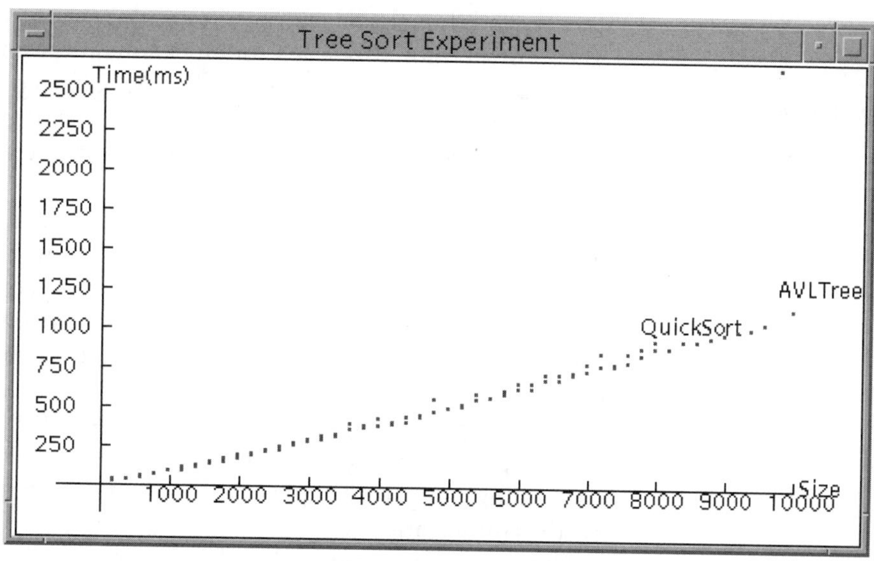

FIGURE 14.9 Execution Timings for Tree Sort on Random Values

EXPERIMENT: TREE SORT EXECUTION TIME ON NONUNIFORM DISTRIBUTIONS

Compare the execution time of the tree sort algorithm to that of quick sort and heap sort on collections of values that are almost sorted.

performance. On the negative side, the tree sort algorithm requires the additional space to store both the vector and the binary search tree, in effect doubling the memory requirements for the sorting operation. The quick sort algorithm operated in place and did not require any additional memory.

14.4 CHAPTER SUMMARY

KEY CONCEPTS

- Binary search tree
- Algorithms for binary search tree
  - Insertion
  - Test for element
  - Removal
- Height-balanced binary tree
- AVL tree
- Tree sort algorithm

In this chapter, we have investigated the *binary search tree*. A binary search tree is a binary tree in which for each node, elements held by descendants in the left child subtree are smaller than or equal to the value of the node, and elements held by descendants in the right child subtree are larger than or equal to the value of the node.

Binary search trees have several important properties. Two key features are that an in-order traversal of the tree will enumerate elements in sequence, and thus the data structure satifies the requirements of the `Sorted` ADT. Furthermore, to seach for any element requires only a linear traversal from root to leaf along one path. In a balanced binary search tree, this means that search, insertion, and removal operations can be performed in $O(\log n)$. However, in an unbalanced tree, these same operations can be $O(n)$.

In order to guarantee good performance, it is necessary to ensure that trees remain close to balanced. It is easy to show that we cannot insist on absolute balance. However, a slightly weaker requirement, called *height balanced*, is almost as good. In a height-balanced tree, the difference in heights between the left and the right subtrees in any node is no larger than 1.

We have presented one data structure, the `AVLTree`, that maintains this height-balanced property. Many other varieties of trees achieve the same goal, using other techniques. Some of these are described in the section Further Information.

Finally, we concluded the chapter by presenting yet another sorting algorithm that could be constructed by using a height-balanced binary tree.

Further Information

Searching large quantities of data was one of the first applications for modern digital computers. Thus, trees and search trees have been extensively studied and have a large associated literature. Most of the classic algorithms are examined in Volumes 1 and 3 of Knuth [Knuth 97, Knuth 98b]. The book by Weiss [Weiss 96] also provides an extensive bibliography.

AVL trees were first proposed by Adel'son-Vel'skiĭ and Landis in 1962 [Velskii 62]. A slightly more accessible discussion is found in Weiss [Weiss 96]. Many presentations of the AVL algorithms prefer to maintain the balance factor, that is, the difference between the left and the right subtree height rather than the height itself. This may be because the balance factor is never larger than 2 in absolute value and so in theory could be stored in only a few bits. However, the height is never very large either, and in practice, allocating an integer is just as efficient as allocating a few bits. The algorithms are also somewhat easier to explain and faster when the actual heights are stored rather than the balance factors. For readers interested in the alternative, I have presented a version of the algorithm based on balance factors in [Budd 94].

Readers concerned with space will note that we could have stored the height as a `short` or even a `byte` rather than as an `int`. (Even a `byte` would permit us to represent a tree with approximately 2^{128} elements, which is far more than one is likely to encounter in practice.) I have not done so, because using a shorter representation would necessarily require adding casts to convert various results from `integer` to `short`, and these tend to obscure the intent of the code. In practice, however, this might be a useful alternative.

There are many other types of height-balanced binary search trees. Popular alternatives to the AVL tree include red-black trees and splay trees. A splay tree is a self-organizing binary search tree, one that tries to improve future search behavior based on a past sequence of searches, similar to the technique used in the self-organizing list described in Chapter 9. All of these are discussed by Weiss [Weiss 96].

The tree sort algorithm was first described by Robert Floyd in 1964 [Floyd 64].

Study Questions

1. What is the primary characteristic of a binary search tree?
2. How is the search for an element in a binary search tree representative of the idea *divide and conquer*?

3. How is the sentinel used in the class `BinarySearchTree`? How is this different from the sentinel in the class `LinkedList`?
4. Suppose that we have a complete binary search tree with 15 elements and we add one new element. What will be the length of the path from the root to the new element?
5. Why is removal from a binary search tree complicated?
6. Why is it important that a binary search tree remain reasonably balanced? What can happen if a binary search tree becomes unbalanced?
7. Why can we not insist that a binary search tree remain in the form of a complete binary tree?
8. What is the definition of a height-balanced binary tree?
9. What is the equation for the smallest number of elements in a height-balanced binary tree of height h? From this, what can we discover about the longest path in a height-balanced binary tree with n nodes?
10. What do the letters AVL stand for in the name AVL tree?
11. What additional information is maintained by the nodes in an AVL tree?
12. How does a left rotation change a binary tree? A right rotation?
13. What is a double-left rotation? Draw a picture of a binary tree before and after a double left rotation is applied.
14. Describe informally the tree sort algorithm.

Exercises

1. What is the maximum height of a binary search tree that contains 100 elements? What is the minimum height?
2. Show the result after inserting the values 1, 3, 1, 4, 1, 5, 9 into an initially empty binary search tree. Then show the result after deleting the root node.
3. Show all the binary search trees that could result after inserting the values 1, 2, 3, and 4 in various permutations. How many different trees are there?
4. What is the complexity of determining whether two binary search trees are the same, that is, the same size and have the same elements?
5. In Section 14.2, an AVL tree is constructed by a series of insertions and a single removal. Continue removing the values 1 to 3 and show the AVL tree that will result after each rebalancing.

6. Show all the AVL trees that could result after inserting the values 1, 2, 3, and 4 in various permutations. How many different trees are there?
7. What permutation of the values 1, 2, ..., n will, when inserted into an AVL tree, result in the tree with the longest possible path?
8. Use an induction argument to show the link between the minimum height of a height-balanced binary tree (Section 14.1) and the Fibonacci numbers.
   a. Show that $M_h = f_{h+3} - 1$ is true for $h = 0$ and $h = 1$.
   b. Assume that $M_h = f_{h+3} - 1$ is true for all values of h smaller than n. Using the fact that $M_{n+1} = M_n + M_{n-1} + 1$ and that $F_{n+1} = F_{n-1} + F_n$, show that $M_{h+1} = f_{h+4} - 1$. This proves the desired result.
9. Use an induction argument to show that the ith Fibonacci number is smaller than 2^i.
10. Using the result you proved in exercise 9, we know that the smallest number of nodes in a height-balanced binary tree of height h must be less that 2^{h+3}. Starting from the equation $M_h < 2^{h+3}$, solve for h. This result shows that h is within a constant factor of $\log M_h$.
11. Prove that the following formula describes the Fibonacci numbers.

$$Fib_n = \frac{1}{\sqrt{5}}\left[\left(\frac{1+\sqrt{5}}{2}\right)^n - \left(\frac{1-\sqrt{5}}{2}\right)^n\right]$$

   a. Verify that the formula works for values 0, 1, and 2.
   b. Show that $(\frac{1+\sqrt{5}}{2})^2$ is the same as $1 + \frac{1+\sqrt{5}}{2}$ and, similarly, that $(\frac{1-\sqrt{5}}{2})^2$ is the same as $1 + \frac{1-\sqrt{5}}{2}$.
   c. By substituting the formula, verify that $Fib_{n+1} = Fib_{n-1} + Fib_n$. (*Hint:* Rewrite $(\frac{1+\sqrt{5}}{2})^{n+1}$ as $(\frac{1+\sqrt{5}}{2})^{n-1} \times (\frac{1+\sqrt{5}}{2})^2$; then use the property you verified in the previous step.)
   d. Argue why as n gets larger, the second term in the subtraction contributes less and less to the result. (*Hint:* consider the values of the second term as n increases.)
   e. We know from (d) that, for large values of n, the value of Fib_n is approximately $\frac{1}{\sqrt{5}}\left(\frac{1+\sqrt{5}}{2}\right)^n$. Let c represent the constant value $\frac{1+\sqrt{5}}{2}$. Compute the decimal approximation to c, giving at least two digits to the right of the decimal point.
   f. Taking the logarithm of both sides, we have that $\log Fib_n \approx \log \frac{1}{\sqrt{5}} + n \log c$. We can ignore as insignificant the left argument to the addition. Compute the value of $\log c$.

g. Dividing both sides by $\log c$, we obtain the final result, which is that $n \approx \frac{1}{\log c} \log Fib_n$. Compute the value of $\frac{1}{\log c}$.

12. Letting triangles represent subtrees, we can represent a left rotation as follows:

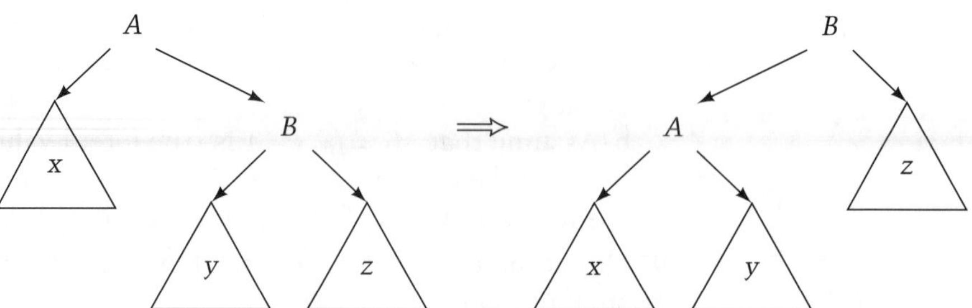

We perform a left rotation because the height of the right node has become two larger than the height of the left node, that is, $h(B) = h(x) + 2$. We also know, however, that the node B is balanced, and thus there are only three possibilities: $h(y) = h(z)$, $h(y) + 1 = h(z)$, or $h(y) = h(z) + 1$.

a. By working out the heights of the final trees after rotation, show that the height-balanced property has been restored in the first two cases but not in the third.

b. By refining the representation of y (breaking it into its two subtrees) and performing further case analysis, depending on which of these two subtrees is larger, show that a double rotation will always restore balance.

13. Is the tree sort algorithm stable? To determine this, simulate the execution of the algorithm on the four-element vector $2_1, 1, 3, 2_2$. Track carefully the relative positions of the two 2 values and note whether it is possible for them to change places during the sorting process.

Programming Projects

1. Finding the largest value in a binary search tree is no more difficult than finding the smallest. Create an interface `FindMax` that is similar to `FindMin`. Then modify the `AVLTree` data structure so that it supports this interface.
2. The Java standard library class `TreeSet` provides the following operations. Show how they could also be implemented in the binary search tree class.

a. `Bag subSet(Object start, Object stop)` returns a set that contains all the elements larger than or equal to the first and smaller than the second.
b. `Bag headSet(Object stop)` returns a set that contains all the elements smaller than the given element.
c. `Bag tailSet(Object stop)` returns a set that contains all the elements larger than or equal to the given element.

3. Add two new constructors to the class `AVLTree`. The first takes a comparator and a collection as argument and initializes the tree with the values from the collection. The second takes a comparator and an enumeration as argument and does the same. Given these, can you then simplify the tree sort algorithm?
4. If we add an integer `count` data field to the class `BSTNode` and modify the addition and removal algorithms to set these values, we can quickly (in constant time) discover the number of elements in any subtree. Show how to use this information to implement the `Indexed` interface. (You can ignore the method `setSize`.)
5. Following programming project 1, rewrite the AVL tree removal algorithm so that it uses the largest value in the left subtree rather than the smallest value in the right subtree. Try timing the two algorithms under various conditions. Are the differences in execution time notable?
6. The fact that *either* the largest value in the left subtree *or* the smallest value in the right subtree can be used to fill a hole being left by a deleted value is the basis for an alternative balanced binary search tree algorithm. As in the AVL tree, nodes in a `RemovalTree` will maintain a height field. When performing a removal, select the element from the largest subtree. This will never have the effect of making the tree unbalanced and may, in fact, make the tree more balanced.

   As in the AVL tree, nodes in the `RemovalTree` will call a method `setHeight` to both set the height field and rebalance the tree. If the tree is discovered to be unbalanced, the root is deleted and then reinserted into the tree. Because deletions have the effect of restoring balance, this will ultimately lead to a balanced tree. Although this technique works and is relatively simple, in practice, a `RemovalTree` does not have as consistently good performance as the `AVLTree` class.
7. Another approach to maintaining balance is to exploit randomness, as was done with the `SkipList` data type. In this approach, it is not necessary to maintain either heights or balance factors in the nodes. Instead, when a new element is inserted, at each level coming out of the sequence of recursive calls, a coin is tossed. If it is tails, nothing

more is done. If it is heads, either a right or a left rotation is performed. To decide which, the coin can be tossed again. If it is heads and a right rotation can be performed, it is done. If tails, a left rotation is attempted. Implement a search tree based on this idea. How does the performance compare to the AVL tree?

CHAPTER 15

PRIORITY QUEUES

A *priority queue* is a data structure useful when it is important to be able to rapidly and repeatedly find and remove the smallest value from a collection of elements. We have already seen at least one data structure that does exactly that: namely, the `SortedVector` described in Chapter 7. However, although accessing the first element in a sorted vector is extremely fast, both insertions and removals are a relatively poor $O(n)$. In this chapter, we will present two priority queue implementations that have much better performance. The first technique uses an abstraction called a *heap*. The heap is constructed as an adapter built on top of an indexed collection, typically a vector. Many people consider the heap to be one of the most elegant of the classic data structures. Among other applications, the heap data structure is used as a basis for yet another approach to sorting.

The second implementation we will examine is the *skew heap*. The skew heap is notable in that both insertion and removal are treated as specific instances of a more general operation, merging two heaps. Although this operation is fundamental to skew heaps, such a merging of heaps is very difficult to perform using the `Heap` data type. Another interesting feature of the `SkewHeap` is that it does not provide guaranteed performance bounds for any single operation, but it can be shown that if a number of operations are performed over time, the average execution time of each operation will be small. As a demonstration of one of the more common uses of heap, the chapter concludes with a discussion of discrete event–driven simulation.

15.1 The Priority Queue ADT

An everyday example of a priority queue is the "to do" list of tasks waiting to be performed that most of us maintain to keep ourselves organized. Some jobs, such as "clean house," are not imperative and can be postponed arbitrarily. Other tasks, such as "finish report by Monday" or "buy flowers for Sally's birthday," are time crucial and must be addressed more rapidly. Therefore, we sort the tasks waiting to be accomplished in order of their importance (or perhaps based on a combination of their critical importance, how much time they require to complete, their long-term benefit, and how much fun they are to do) and choose the most pressing.

For a more computer-related example, an operating system will use a priority queue to maintain a collection of currently active processes, where the priority associated with each element in the queue represents the urgency of the task. It may be necessary to respond rapidly to a key pressed at a workstation, for example, before the data is lost when the next key is pressed. Other tasks can be temporarily postponed in order to handle those that are time critical. For this reason, a priority queue is used so that the most urgent task can be quickly determined and processed.

Another example might be files waiting to be output on a computer printer. It would be a reasonable policy to print several one-page listings before a one-hundred-page job, even if the larger task was submitted earlier than the smaller ones. For this reason, a queue would maintain files to be printed in order of size or a combination of size and other factors and not simply on time of submission.

A simulation, such as the one we will describe in Section 15.4, will use a priority queue of "future events," where each event is marked with a time at which the event is to take place. In this collection, the element with the closest following time is the next event that will be simulated. As each event is executed, it may spawn new events to be added to the queue. These are only a few instances of the types of problems for which a priority queue is a useful tool.

A priority queue is an abstract data type that supports the `FindMin` interface, shown in Figure 15.1, and satisfies the properties we have outlined in Chapter 2. Recall that these were described as follows:

`void addElement (Object)` *Pre:* It is assumed that the argument is comparable with any elements currently in the collection. *Post:* Adds an element to a collection. The size of the collection is increased by 1. The location of the element in relation to existing elements (as, for example, revealed by an enumeration) is undefined.

```
public interface FindMin extends Collection {
  public void addElement (Object newElement);
  public Object getFirst ();
  public void removeFirst ();
}
```

FIGURE 15.1 The FindMin Interface

`Object getFirst ()` Returns the smallest element in the collection. Will throw `NoSuchElementException` if the collection is empty. Invoking this method will not change the state of the collection in any way.

`void removeFirst ()` Removes the smallest element from the collection. Will throw `NoSuchElementException` if the collection is empty. The size of the collection is decreased by 1.

Note that the name priority *queue* is a misnomer in that the data structure is not a queue in the sense we used the term in Chapter 12, as it does not return elements in a strict first in first out (FIFO) sequence. Nevertheless, the name is now firmly associated with this particular data abstraction.

A priority queue can be implemented in at least three obvious but inefficient ways. One approach would be to insert new elements at the front of a `LinkedList`, thus requiring only constant time for addition. The list could then be searched to discover the smallest element, but this would require $O(n)$ steps, which is prohibitively expensive.

Another approach to implementing a priority queue is to take a collection of items and sort them. From the sorted collection, we could obtain not only the smallest element but also the next smallest, and the next, and so on. But as we have seen, sorting is a relatively expensive operation. Furthermore, it is difficult to insert new elements into a sorted collection. Because we are interested in finding only the smallest element in the collection, we can use techniques that are much more efficient. In particular,

DOES "FIRST" MEAN MINIMUM OR MAXIMUM?

Although the definition speaks of removing the smallest element, the value of interest in many problems is the largest item. Some authors use the term *min-heap* to refer to the abstraction we described here and *max-heap* to refer to a priority queue that finds the largest value. It is easy, however, to change one into the other by simply inverting the sense of the comparison test used by the `Comparable` object. The `jds` library provides a comparison object, `InvertComparable`, for just this purpose.

we will develop data structures in which we can find the smallest element in a collection of n elements in constant time, and we can find and remove the smallest element in time proportional to $\log n$.

One more method is obvious and not obviously inefficient. In Chapter 14, we examined the AVL tree and noted that this data structure satisfied the `FindMin` interface. (This was due largely to the fact that finding the smallest element in a subtree was an essential step in the removal algorithm.) As we observed in Chapter 14, elements can be added to or removed from an AVL tree in $O(\log n)$ steps. The reason for rejecting this approach is not asymptotic inefficiency but practical realistic inefficiency. An AVL tree is maintaining more information than we need. We can develop alternative data structures that, although they have no better asymptotic efficiency (they are still $O(\log n)$), generally yield execution times much better than would be possible using AVL trees.

We will investigate two data structures that can be used to implement priority queues. The classic data structure for this purpose is termed a *heap* and maintains the elements of the collection in an array. The operations to add or to remove an element to or from the heap are relatively efficient; however, the heap suffers from the problem common to many array-based algorithms. This is that the array will be expanded as necessary to the maximum size but will not be made smaller as the heap is reduced.

The second data structure, a *skew heap*, avoids the maximum-size difficulty by maintaining the heap elements in a binary tree. But solving one problem comes only at the cost of introducing another, namely, the difficulty of keeping the tree relatively well balanced. Skew heaps are interesting in that the worst-case cost for insertions and deletions is a relatively slow $O(n)$, but one can show that this worst-case behavior does not occur frequently and cannot be sustained. In particular, the occurrence of a worst-case situation must necessarily be followed by several insertions and deletions that are much faster. Thus, amortized over a number of insertions and deletions, the average cost of an operation is still relatively good. Another advantage of the skew heap will be that it provides a fast implementation for the operation of merging two priority-queue heaps to form a new queue.

15.2 HEAPS

A *heap* is a complete binary tree in which every node possesses the property that its value is less than or equal to the value associated with either child node. This is referred to as the *heap-order property*. A simple induction argument establishes that the value at each node in a heap must be

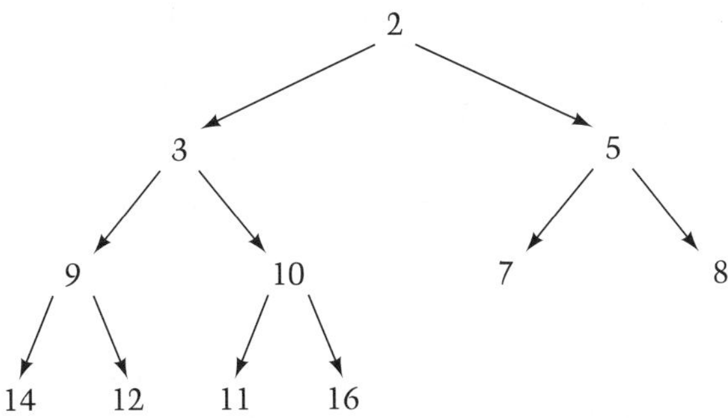

FIGURE 15.2 A Complete Binary Tree in Heap Form

the smallest value held in the subtree rooted at the node. It follows from this that the smallest element in a heap will always be found at root node.

As we noted in Chapter 13, a *complete binary tree* is a binary tree that is entirely filled (in which every node has two children), with the exception of the bottom level, which is filled from left to right. Figure 15.2 shows a complete binary tree that is also a heap. Because the number of elements doubles at each level of a binary tree, the path from root to leaf of a complete binary tree is never larger than $\lceil \log(n+1) \rceil$, where n is the number of nodes in the tree.

The key insight behind the heap data structure is the observation that a complete binary tree can be represented efficiently in an array. The root of the tree will be maintained in position 0 of the array. The left child of node n will be found at position $2n+1$ and the right child at position $2n+2$. The array corresponding to the tree in Figure 15.2 is the following:

0	1	2	3	4	5	6	7	8	9	10
2	3	5	9	10	7	8	14	12	11	16

A sorted vector is also a heap, but as this example illustrates, the reverse is not true. That is, a vector can maintain a heap and still not be ordered.

HEAPS AND HEAPS

The term *heap* is used for two very different concepts in computer science. The heap *data structure* is an abstract data type used to implement priority queues, as well as being used in a sorting algorithm we will discuss shortly. The terms *heap*, *heap memory*, *heap allocation*, and so on, are also frequently used to describe memory that is allocated directly by the user, using the `new` operator. You should not confuse the two uses of the same term.

Given the index to a node, discovering either the parent or the children of that node is a simple matter of division or multiplication. No explicit child references need be maintained in the array structure, and traversals of the heap can be performed very efficiently. Note that the property of completeness is important to ensure that no "gaps" are in the array representation. Recall from Chapter 13 that the length of the longest path from root to leaf in a complete binary tree can be bounded by $\lceil \log n \rceil$.

The following is the class definition for the `Heap` data type. As with all ordered collections, a `Comparator` object can be provided with the constructor to define the comparison relationship between elements.

```
public class Heap implements FindMin, SortAlgorithm {

    // constructors
  public Heap (Comparator t) { test = t; elementData = new Vector(); }
  public Heap (Comparator t, Indexed data)
    { test = t; buildHeap(data); elementData = data; }

  private Indexed elementData;
  private Comparator test;

    // implementation of the Collection interface
  public Enumeration elements () { return elementData.elements(); }
  public boolean isEmpty () { return elementData.isEmpty(); }
  public int size () { return elementData.size(); }

    // implementation of the FindMin interface
  public synchronized void addElement (Object val) {  ... }
  public Object getFirst () { return elementData.elementAt(0); }
  public synchronized void removeFirst () {  ... }

    // implementation of the SortAlgorithm interface
  public void sort (Indexed data) { ... }

    // internal methods
  private void buildHeap (Indexed data) {  ... }
}
```

The `Collection` interface simply uses methods from the underlying indexed container. With the exception of `getFirst`, the methods for the `FindMin` interface are more complex and will be discussed shortly. As we noted earlier, the `Heap` also provides an interesting sorting algorithm, and thus the container supports the `SortAlgorithm` interface and the method `sort`.

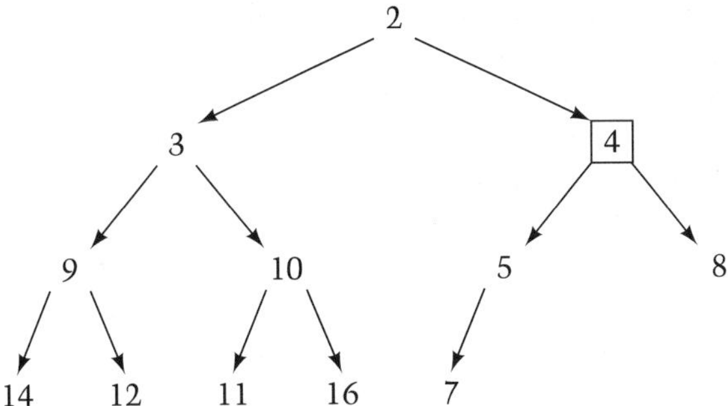

FIGURE 15.3 An Element Percolating up into Position

Two of the operations we have omitted from the class listing are insertion (the method `addElement`) and deletion (the method `removeFirst`). We will deal with insertion first. When a new element is added to a heap, it is obvious that *some* value must be moved to the end of the array, to maintain the complete binary tree property. However, it is likely that the new element cannot be placed in this position without violating the heap-order property. This violation will occur if the new element is smaller than the parent element for the location. A solution is to place the new element in the last location, then move it into place by repeatedly exchanging the node with its parent node until the heap-order property is restored (that is, until either the new node rises to the top or we find a parent node that is smaller than the new node). Because the new element rises until it finds a correct location, this process is sometimes known as a *percolate up*.

Figure 15.3 shows the value 4 being inserted into the Figure 15.2 heap. Originally, the element was inserted at the end of the heap, as the left child of the 7 node. But because 4 was smaller than 7, the value was exchanged with the parent. Similarly, the 4 was exchanged with the 5. Because 4 is larger than the value 2, the percolating will stop here, and the 4 will have found its proper location.

The insertion method for percolating an element into place follows. We have added the invariants required to establish the correctness of the procedure. Because the `while` loop moves up one level of the tree each cycle, it is obvious it can iterate no more than $\log n$ times. The running time of the insertion procedure is therefore $O(\log n)$.

```
public synchronized void addElement (Object val) {
    // inv: assume elementData is a valid heap
    // we will add new element to the end
  int position = elementData.size();
```

```
    elementData.addElementAt(val, position);
    int parentPosition = (position-1)/2;
      // inv: tree rooted at position is a heap
      // tree rooted at parentPosition may not be
    Object parentValue = null;
    if (parentPosition >= 0)
      parentValue = elementData.elementAt(parentPosition);
    while ((position > 0) && (test.compare(val, parentValue) < 0)) {
      elementData.setElementAt(parentValue, position);
      position = parentPosition;
      parentPosition = (position-1)/2;
        // inv: tree rooted at position is now a heap
        // tree rooted at parentPosition may not be
      if (parentPosition >= 0)
        parentValue = elementData.elementAt(parentPosition);
    }
    elementData.setElementAt(val, position);
      // tree rooted at position is heap
      // therefore entire structure is now a valid heap
}
```

The proof of correctness for the method addElement begins with the assumption that the collection represents a valid heap, with the possible exception of the very last element, which may be out of order. The sole task of the algorithm is to move this one element into place. Throughout the process, the variable position will maintain the index position of this value, and the variable parentPosition will maintain the index position of the parent node.

The while loop at the heart of the procedure has two test conditions. Both must be true for the loop to execute. Together, the two conditions assert that the position has a parent (that is, the position is not yet the root node) and that the parent value is larger than the position, in contradiction to the heap-order property. The following illustrates this situation.

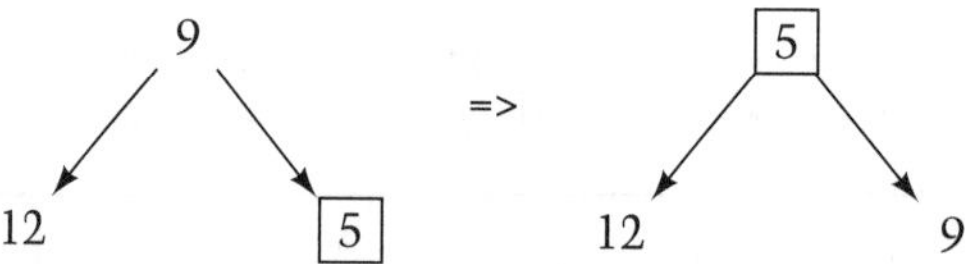

The invariant at the top of the loop body asserts that the subtree rooted at position represents a heap. This will trivially be true the first time the while loop is executed, as the subtree represents only a leaf. Because the parent node is already smaller than the other child (if the parent has two children), simply swapping the position with the parent is sufficient to locally reestablish the heap-order property. (To see why, note that any children of node position must have originally been children of node parent and must therefore be larger than the parent.) Following the swap, the tree rooted at the index value parent will therefore be a heap. This value becomes the new position, and we determine the new parent index.

The while loop terminates either when the element percolates all the way to the top of the heap or when a node is encountered that is smaller than the new element. In the first case, the final loop invariant is asserting that the entire structure represents a heap. If, on the other hand, the loop terminates because of the second case, we know that the subtree rooted at parent has the heap-order property. But because this subtree holds the only element that could have been out of order, we therefore can conclude that the entire structure must have the heap-order property.

The deletion procedure is handled in a manner similar to insertion. We want to remove the root element but cannot leave a hole in the tree. To fill the hole, we swap the last element into the first location. Because this may destroy the heap-order property, the element must *percolate down* to its proper position by exchanging places with the smaller of its children. For reasons that will shortly become clear, we invoke another routine, named adjustHeap, to perform this task.

```
public synchronized void removeFirst () {
  int lastPosition = elementData.size()-1;
    // copy last element to first position
  if (lastPosition != 0) {
    Object lastElement = elementData.elementAt(lastPosition);
    elementData.setElementAt(lastElement, 0);
  }
    // remove last element
  elementData.removeElementAt(lastPosition);
    // rebuild heap property
  adjustHeap(elementData, elementData.size(), 0);
}
```

Figure 15.4 shows an intermediate step in the adjustHeap process. The value 3 has been promoted to the root position, where it now represents the smallest element. The hole has moved down to the position formerly occupied by the element 3. The temporary variable is holding the former last element in the heap, 7. As this value is smaller than the smallest child of the hole position (9, in this case), the value will be moved into the hole. Otherwise, the smallest child would have been promoted to the hole position, and the hole would have moved down one level. If the hole reaches the bottom level without finding a location for the value, the element is simply copied to the hole location.

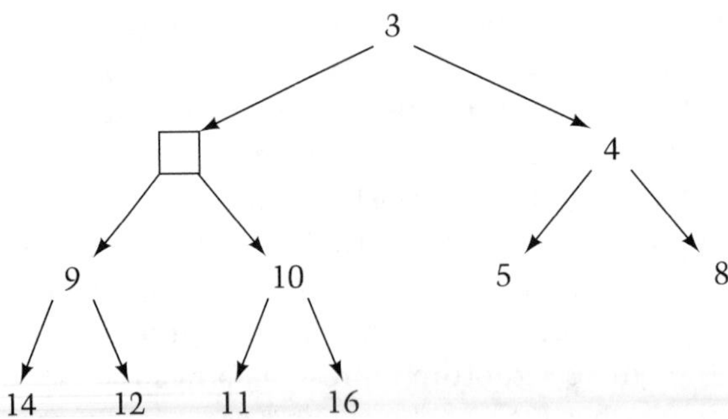

FIGURE 15.4 Filling a Hole Left by Deletion of the Smallest Element

As at most three comparisons of data values are performed at each level and the `while` loop traces out a path from the root of the tree to the leaf, the complexity of the deletion procedure is also $O(\log n)$. (This observation requires noting that the call on `removeElementAt` will always operate in constant time. Can you see why this is so?)

The routine to restore the heap-order property is as follows:

```
private synchronized void adjustHeap
    (Indexed data, int max, int index) {
  Object value = data.elementAt(index);
  while (index < max) {
    int childpos = index * 2 + 1;
    if (childpos < max) {
        // make childpos index of smallest child
      if (((childpos+1) < max) &&
        (test.compare(data.elementAt(childpos+1),
          data.elementAt(childpos)) < 0))
            childpos++;
      if (test.compare(value, data.elementAt(childpos)) < 0) {
        data.setElementAt(value, index);
        return;
      } else {
        Object v = data.elementAt(childpos);
        data.setElementAt(v, index);
        index = childpos;
      }
    } else {
      data.setElementAt(value, index);
      return;
    }
  }
}
```

The `adjustHeap` method is in some ways the opposite of the `addElement` procedure. Here, the invariant is that although the structure rooted at `position` may not be a heap, its two children are. The task, therefore, is to restore the heap-order property by making only local transformations.

To reestablish the heap-order property, the two children of node `position` are examined. The element indexed by `childpos` is set to the smaller of the two children. If this element is larger than the value in question, the heap-order property does in fact hold, and therefore the entire structure must be a heap. If, on the other hand, the smaller child is also smaller than the element in question, they must be swapped. This is illustrated in the following diagram:

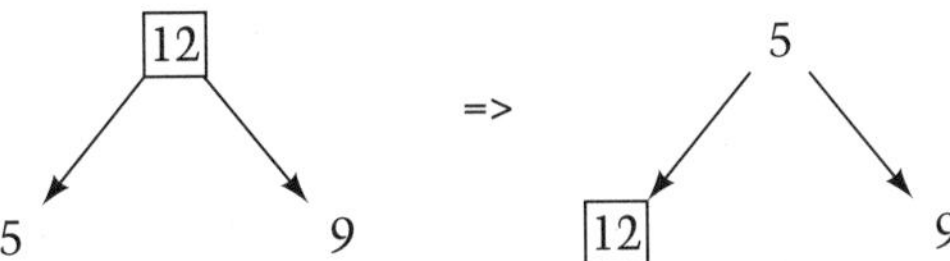

Note that because the element was swapped with the smaller of the two children, the new root must therefore be smaller than not only the element in question but also the larger child. Thus, we need not consider the subtree rooted at the larger child. But it is now necessary to continue to examine the subtree rooted at the position into which the value in question was swapped. The smaller child position becomes the new value held by the variable `position`, and the `while` loop continues. The process terminates when either the value in question finds its location (being smaller than both children) or it reaches a point where it has no children.

One case we have not considered occurs when the programmer provides a vector of data values to be used in the construction of the initial heap. Because the sequence of elements in the collection may not satisfy the heap-order property, it is necessary to convert the collection into a heap. This is the responsibility of the method `buildHeap`:

```
private void buildHeap (Indexed data) {
  int max = data.size();
  for (int i = max/2; i >= 0; i--) {
    adjustHeap(data, max, i);
    // inv: tree rooted at i is a heap
    }
  // entire structure is a heap
}
```

To prove that this algorithm creates a heap, it is necessary to understand the task being performed by the loop at the heart of the procedure. At

WHY USE BUILDHEAP?

Why do we need the procedure `buildHeap`? The same result could be achieved by simply inserting the initial values one by one, which would require no more than $O(n \log n)$. This would still be sufficient to show, for example, that the heap sort algorithm we will describe shortly is $O(n \log n)$.

The answer is that the `buildHeap` procedure is $O(n)$, although demonstrating this is not easy. First, note that the execution time of `adjustHeap` is, in the worst case, proportional to the length of the path the method will follow from its initial node to the root. The `buildHeap` procedure will call this routine, starting from each interior node. We must therefore derive a formula for the sum of the lengths of the paths in a tree. Note that there are two paths of length 1, four paths of length 2, and, in general, 2^k paths of length k. In a complete binary tree, the length of the path associated with an interior node is at worst $\lfloor \log n \rfloor$, so the summation we seek is

$$\sum_{k=1}^{\lfloor \log n \rfloor} k\, 2^k$$

This sum can be shown to be $O(n)$.

each step, the assumption is that the subtrees representing the children of node `i` are proper heaps, and the task to be performed is to make the subtree rooted at node `i` into a heap.

Note that the variable `i` is initialized to the value `heapSize/2` and moves downward. Observe that because we are dealing with a complete binary tree, all subtrees with index positions larger than `heapSize/2` represent leaf nodes. Leaf nodes possess the heap-order property, as they have no children. Thus, the first time execution moves from the start of the procedure to the assertion in the body of the loop, the assertions must be `true`. We have already proved the `adjustHeap` procedure, and therefore the invariant following the procedure call must be `true`.

Now consider the case in which we perform the `adjustHeap` action at the beginning of the loop body, after having executed some previous iterations of the loop. In this case, the children of node `i` either must be leaves, or they must have been previously processed. In either case, the subtrees rooted at the child nodes must be heaps, and therefore following execution of the body of the loop, the subtree rooted at node `i` must be a heap.

To establish the final condition, we simply note that either the loop was executed, in which case the final condition matches one of the loop invariants we previously established, or the loop was never executed, which can happen only if the heap contains only a single leaf. In the latter case, we have already noted that a leaf node is a heap.

The heap data structure provides an elegant technique for sorting an array. The idea is to first form the array into a heap. To sort the array, the

EXPERIMENT: BUILDING AN INITIAL HEAP

In many applications, such as the one we will examine in Section 15.4, several elements are placed into the heap at the start of execution, before any `removeFirst` operations are performed. In this situation, two alternative techniques could be used. One approach would be to simply use `addElement` to insert the elements into the heap one by one. The alternative is to place the elements into a vector and then to use the `buildHeap` operation to convert the vector into a heap. Is there a measurable difference in execution time between these two approaches? Does the difference depend on the initial order of elements? Suppose, as in Section 15.4, that the initial elements are already sorted smallest to largest. Does this improve the execution time? Suppose, on the other hand, that they are already sorted largest to smallest; does this make a difference?

top of the heap (the smallest element) is swapped with the last element of the array, and the size of the heap is reduced by 1. The effect of the swap, however, may be to destroy the heap property. But this is exactly the same condition we encountered in deleting an element from the heap. And, not surprisingly, we can use the same solution. Heap order is restored by invoking the `adjustHeap` procedure. This algorithm is exhibited in the following procedure:

```
public void sort (Indexed data) {
    // build the initial heap
  buildHeap(data);
    // then find values, one by one
  for (int i = data.size()-1; i > 0; i--) {
      // swap into last position
    Object temp = data.elementAt(i);
    data.setElementAt(data.elementAt(0), i);
    data.setElementAt(temp, 0);
      // and rebuild heap
    adjustHeap(data, i, 0);
  }
}
```

Figure 15.5 shows a snapshot in the middle of a heap sort, captured here using the `VisualVector` data type described in Chapter 6. The elements on the right-hand side of the figure have already been sorted, whereas the left-hand side is the current heap. Note that the heap elements are not ordered, although the smallest elements do tend to congregate on the left and the largest values on the right (with the current smallest, of course, being the very first element).

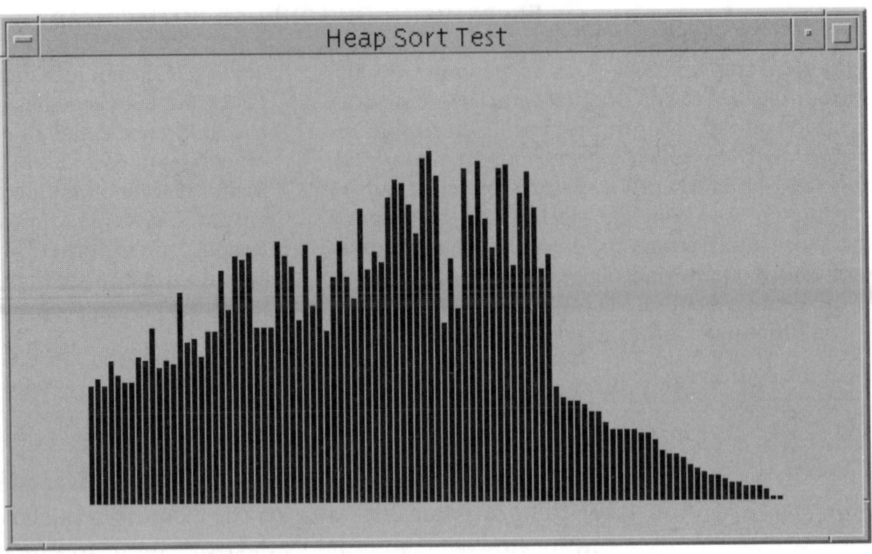

FIGURE 15.5 A Snapshot of Heap Sort

To derive the asymptotic running time for this algorithm, recall that the `adjustHeap` procedure requires $O(\log n)$ steps. There are n executions of `adjustHeap` to generate the initial heap and n further executions to reheap values during the sorting operation. Combining these tells us that the total running time is $O(n \log n)$, which matches that of the merge sort algorithm and the average execution time of the quick sort algorithm (both Chapter 7) and is better than the $O(n^2)$ bubble and insertion sort algorithms (Chapter 4).

Of a more practical benefit, note that the heap sort algorithm does not require any additional space, as the algorithm constructs the heap directly in the vector input value. This was not true of some of the previous sorting algorithms we have seen. Merge sort, for example, must pay the cost of not

EXPERIMENT: PERFORMANCE OF HEAP SORT

Empirically compare the execution-time performance of heap sort to that of merge sort and quick sort. Try various input distributions. Is the heap sort algorithm influenced by different input distributions in the same fashion as quick sort?

only the sorting itself but also the allocation and deallocation of the data structures formed during the process of ordering the elements.

* 15.3 SKEW HEAPS

The obvious method to avoid the bounded-size problem of heaps is to use a tree representation. This is not, however, quite as simple as it might seem. The key to obtaining logarithmic performance in the heap data structure is the fact that at each step, we were able to guarantee that the tree was balanced. Finding the next location to be filled in an array representation of a balanced binary tree is trivial; it is simply the next location following the current top of the array. In a tree form, this is not quite as easy. Consider the tree shown in Figure 15.2. Knowing the location of the last element (the value 16) is of little help in discovering where the next element should be inserted in order to maintain the balanced binary tree property. In fact, the next element is part of a subtree entirely different from that containing the current last element.

A *skew heap* avoids this problem by making no attempt to maintain the heap as a balanced binary tree. As we saw in Chapter 13, this means that a tree can potentially become almost linear, and we can place no guarantee on logarithmic performance for any individual operation. But we can make another critical observation about heaps: The order of the left and right children for any node is essentially arbitrary. We can exchange the left and right children of any node in a heap without destroying the heap-order property. We can make use of this observation by systematically swapping the left and right children of a node as we perform insertions and deletions. A badly unbalanced tree can affect the performance of one operation, but it can be shown that subsequent insertions and deletions must as a consequence be very rapid. In fact, if m insertions or deletions are performed, it can be shown (although the details are beyond the discussion here) that the total time to perform all m operations is bounded by $O(m \log n)$. Thus, *amortized* over time, each operation is no worse than $O(\log n)$.

The second observation critical to the implementation of skew heaps is that both insertions and deletions can be considered as special cases of merging two trees into a single heap. This is obvious in the case of the deletion process. Removing the root of the tree results in two subtrees. The new heap can be constructed by simply merging these two child trees. Similarly, insertion can be considered a merge of the existing heap and a new heap containing a single element. The `skewHeap` data structure makes use of this observation by implementing both insertions and deletions, using an internal method merge:

```
public class SkewHeap implements FindMin {

    // constructor
  public SkewHeap (Comparator t) { test = t; }
  private Comparator test;
  private elementCount = 0;
  private BinaryNode root = null;

    // Collection interface
  public boolean isEmpty () { return root == null; }
  public Enumeration elements () { return new InorderTreeTraversal(root);
}
  public int size () { return elementCount; }

    // FindMin interface
  public void addElement (Object val)
    { elementCount++; root = merge(root, new BinaryNode(val)); }

  public Object getFirst () {
    if (root == null) throw new NoSuchElementException();
    return root.value;
  }

  public void removeFirst () {
    if (root == null) throw new NoSuchElementException();
    elementCount--;
    root = merge(root.leftChild, root.rightChild);
  }

    // merge method
  public void mergeWith (SkewHeap right) {
    root = merge(root, right.root);
    elementCount += right.elementCount;
    right.root = null; right.elementCount = 0;
  }

    // internal method
  private synchronized BinaryNode merge
      (BinaryNode left, BinaryNode right) {
    .
    .
    .
  }
}
```

The class BinaryNode is one we presented in Chapter 13. The recursive merge operation follows. If either argument is empty, the result of a merge is simply the other tree. Otherwise, we compare the roots of the two trees. If the left is smaller, it becomes the new root, and we exchange its children and merge with its left child. Otherwise, if the right is smaller, the exchange is symmetric.

```
private synchronized BinaryNode merge (BinaryNode left, BinaryNode right)
{
  if (left == null) return right;
  if (right == null) return left;

  Object leftValue = left.value;
  Object rightValue = right.value;

  if (test.compare(leftValue, rightValue) < 0) {
    BinaryNode swap = left.leftChild;
    left.leftChild = merge(left.rightChild, right);
    left.rightChild = swap;
    return left;
  } else {
    BinaryNode swap = right.rightChild;
    right.rightChild = merge(right.leftChild, left);
    right.leftChild = swap;
    return right;
  }
}
```

The fact that skew heaps operate by merging two heaps to form a new heap means that it is relatively easy to combine two instances of the data structure. We have taken advantage of this by providing a mergeWith method that takes another instance of skew heap as argument. The merge procedure used is the same as the merge used in implementing the addition and removal methods and can thus be expected to run very rapidly, in time proportional to the longest path in the largest heap, not the number of elements in the argument heap, as would be the case if the values were simply added one by one.

An important feature to note, however, is that this operation empties the argument heap, by setting its root to zero. If we did not do this, we would have the same nodes appearing in two different trees. Manipulations of one of the trees would then change the other, potentially resulting in disastrous consequences.

We will illustrate the execution of the skew heap data abstraction with the following example. Suppose that we are merging a heap containing the elements 2, 5, and 7 with a heap containing the two elements 4 and 6. As the element at the top of the left heap, 2, is smaller, it becomes the new root. At the same time, the old left child of the root becomes the new right child. To form the new right child, we recursively merge the old right child and the original right argument:

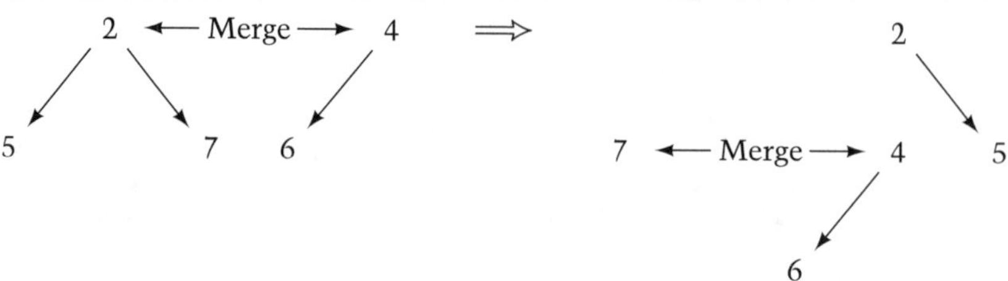

The first step in the recursive call is to flip the arguments so that the smallest element is held in the first argument. The top element of this heap then becomes the new root. As before, the old left child of this node becomes the new right child. A recursive call is made to insert the right argument, 7, into the now empty former right child of the node 4. This results in the node 7 being returned and the final result produced.

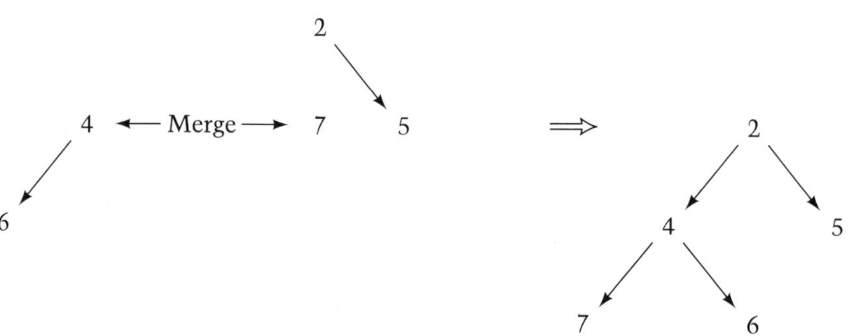

To illustrate why the amortized analysis of skew heaps can be so good, note that the worst-case situation occurs when the left subtree contains a long path along the right child links. For example, consider merging the singleton 10 into such a tree:

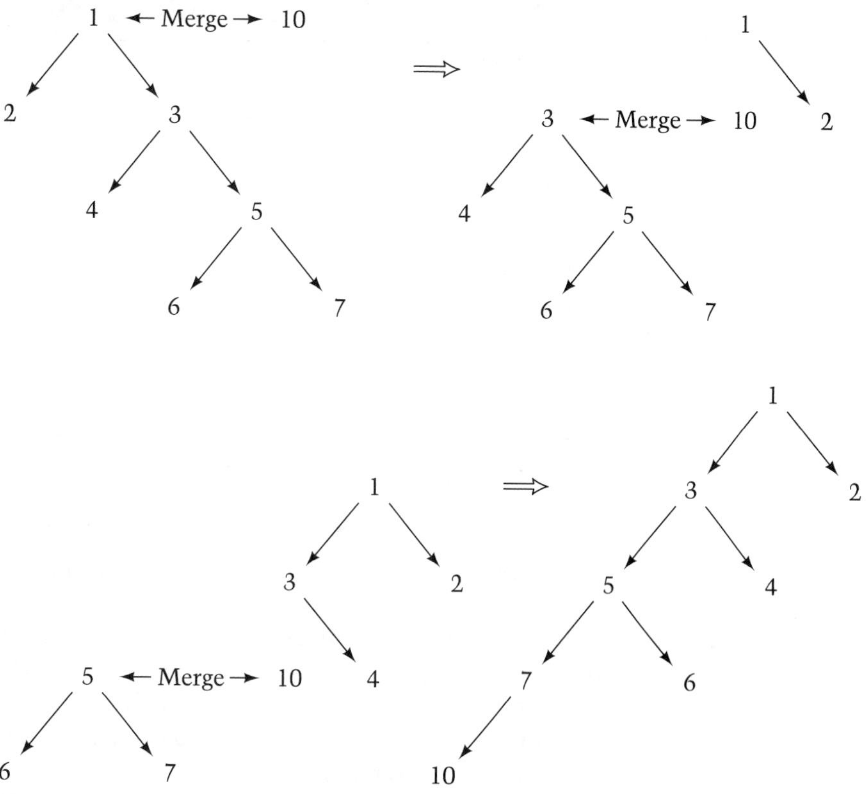

The merge requires four steps. However, note that the long right path has now been converted into a long left path. Thus, the next insertion will be relatively quick. Assume, for example, that we now insert the single element 11:

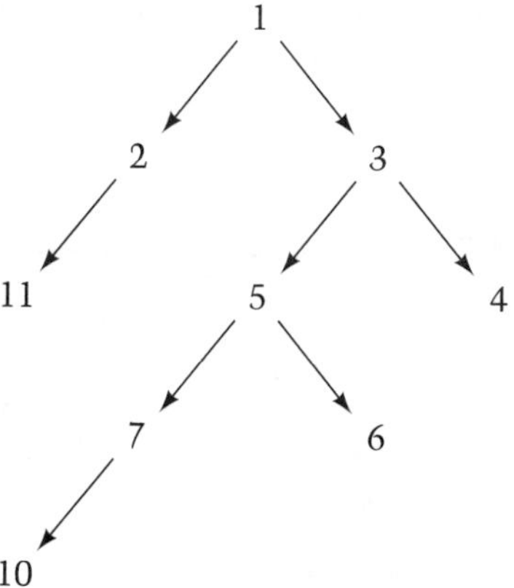

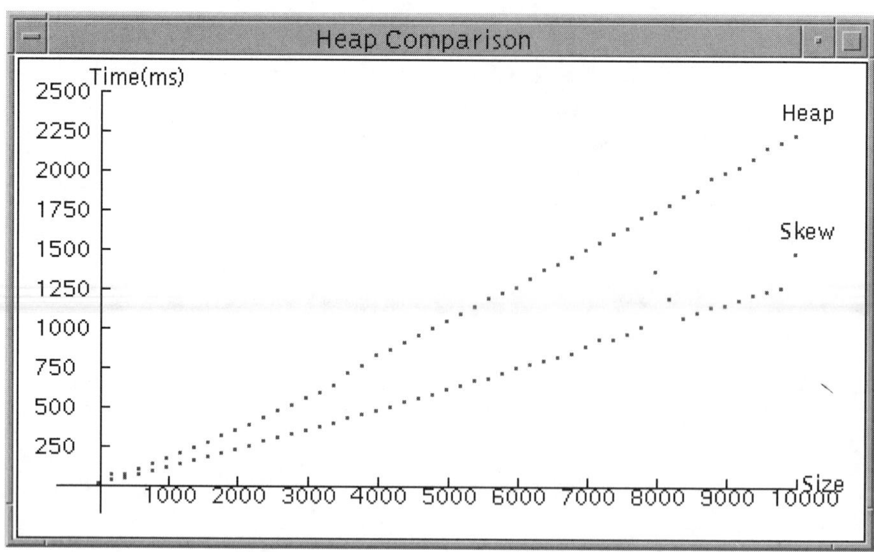

FIGURE 15.6 Comparison of Execution Times for Heap and SkewHeap

It is tempting to conjecture that after two insertions, we would be back to the original poor configuration. But note that this has not occurred. The longest path is still a left path, although it is now on the right side. It will be quite a few steps before the situation can arise such that a long right path can slow insertions.

To measure the relative performance of the `Heap` and the `SkewHeap` abstractions, we conducted an experiment in which we inserted n random integers between 0 and 100 into a heap and then removed them. A plot of the execution times for various values of n is shown in Figure 15.6. The result indicates that even though the `SkewHeap` is performing many more memory allocations than the `Heap`, the overall execution time is still faster. Nevertheless, the nonuniform nature of the `SkewHeap` timings most likely reflects the increased memory use, as garbage collection interrupts other tasks.

EXPERIMENT: MEASURING THE IMPACT OF INPUT VALUE DISTRIBUTIONS

Whereas the running time of the `Heap` seems to be relatively unaffected by the distribution of input values, the same cannot be said of the `SkewHeap`. To see this, repeat the experiment described here with two different sets of inputs. In the first experiment, insert the integers from 1 to n in order. In the second experiment, insert the integers from n to 1 in decreasing order. What differences do you observe? Can you explain this change in behavior?

15.4 Application—Discrete Event—Driven Simulation

The most common application for a priority queue is in the creation of simulations. A *discrete event–driven simulation* is one popular simulation technique. Objects in the simulation model objects in the real world and are programmed to react as much as possible as the real objects would react. A priority queue is used to store a representation of "events" waiting to happen. This queue is ordered based on the time the event should occur, so the smallest element will always be the next event to be modeled. As an event occurs, it can spawn other events. These subsequent events are placed into the queue as well. Execution continues until all events have occurred or until a preset time for the simulation is exceeded.

Imagine that you are thinking about opening an ice cream store on a popular beach location. You need to decide how large the store should be, how many seats you should have, and so on. If you plan too small, customers will be turned away when there is insufficient space, and you will lose profits. On the other hand, if you plan too large, most of the seats will be unused, and you will be paying useless rent on the space and hence losing profits. So you need to choose approximately the right number, but how do you decide?

To create a simulation, you first examine similar operations in comparable locations and form a model that includes, among other factors, an estimation of the number of customers you can expect to arrive in any period of time, the length of time they will take to decide on an order, and the length of time they will stay after having been served. Based on this, you can design a simulation.

To see how we might create a simulation of our ice cream store, consider a typical scenario. A group of customers arrive at the ice cream store. From our measurements of similar stores, we derive a probability that indicates how frequently this occurs. For example, suppose that we assume that groups will consist of from one to five people, selected uniformly over that range. (In actual simulations, the distribution would seldom be uniform. For example, groups of size two and three might predominate, with groups of one and groups larger than three being relatively less frequent. The mathematics involved in forming nonuniform distributions is subtle and not particularly relevant to our discussion. We will therefore use uniform distributions throughout.) These groups will arrive at times spaced from 1 to 10 minutes apart, again selected uniformly. Once they arrive, a group will either be seated or, seeing that there are no seats, leave. If seated, they will take from 2 to 10 minutes to order and then will remain from 15 to 35 minutes in the store. We know that every customer will order from one to three scoops of ice cream and that the store makes a profit of $0.35 on each scoop.

The primary object in the simulation is the store itself. It might seem odd to provide "behavior" for this inanimate object, but we can think of the store as a useful abstraction for the servers and managers who work in the store. The store manages two data items: the number of available seats and the amount of profit generated. The behavior of the store can be described by the following list.

- When a customer group arrives, the size of the group is compared to the number of seats. If insufficient seats are available, the group leaves. Otherwise, the group is seated and the number of seats decreased.
- When a customer orders and is served, the amount of profit is computed.
- When a customer group leaves, the seats are released for another customer group.

A class description for `IceCreamStore` is as follows:

```
public class IceCreamStore {
  public static void main (String [ ] args)
    { IceCreamStore world = new IceCreamStore(); }

  IceCreamStore () { ... }

  private int freeChairs = 35;
  private double profit = 0.0;
  private SimulationFramework simulation = new SimulationFramework();

  private int randBetween (int low, int high) {
    return low + (int) ((high - low + 1) * Math.Random());
  }

  public boolean canSeat (int numberOfPeople) {
    System.out.println("Group of " + numberOfPeople +
      " customers arrives at time" + simulation.time());
    if (numberOfPeople < freeChairs) {
      System.out.println("Group is seated");
      freeChairs -= numberOfPeople;
      return true;
    } else
      System.out.println("No Room, Group Leaves");
    return false;
  }
```

```
  private void order (int numberOfScoops) {
    System.out.println("Serviced order for " + numberOfScoops +
      " at time " + simulation.time());
    profit += 0.35 * numberOfScoops;
  }

  private void leave (int numberOfPeople) {
    System.out.println("Group of size " + numberOfPeople +
      " leaves at time " + simulation.time());
    freeChairs += numberOfPeople;
  }

  private class ArriveEvent extends Event { ... }

  private class OrderEvent extends Event { ... }

  private class LeaveEvent extends Event { ... }
}
```

The method `randBetween` returns a random integer between the two endpoints. The methods `canSeat`, `order`, and `leave` manipulate the profits and the number of chairs. The execution of the simulation is controlled by the simulation framework and the inner classes `ArriveEvent`, `OrderEvent`, and `LeaveEvent`, which are described next.

15.4.1 A Framework for Simulations

Rather than simply code a simulation of this one problem, we will generalize the problem and first produce a generic *framework* for simulations. At the heart of a simulation is the concept of an *event*. An event will be represented by an instance of class `Event`. The only value held by the class will be the time the event is to occur. The method `processEvent` will be invoked to "execute" the event when the appropriate time is reached.

```
public abstract class Event implements Comparable {
  public Event (int t) { time = t; }
  public abstract void processEvent ();
  public final int time;

  public int compareTo (Object o) {
    Event right = (Event) o;
    if (time < right.time) return -1;
    if (time == right.time) return 0;
    return 1;
  }
}
```

An Abstract Idea

The class `Event` is the first time we have seen a class declared as `abstract`. Note that the modifier is used both on the class and on the method `processEvent`. An `abstract` method is like an interface; it describes a behavior without giving an implementation. An `abstract` class must have at least one `abstract` method.

An `abstract` class is similar to an interface in another regard. The presence of an `abstract` method means that it is not possible to create instances of the class directly. Instead, it is first necessary to write a subclass of the `abstract` class and to override any `abstract` methods. It is only when a child class provides concrete implementations of all `abstract` methods that the creation of an instance is possible.

The simulation queue will need to maintain a collection of various types of events. Each form of event will be represented by different derived classes of class `Event`. Not all events will have the same type, although they will all be derived from class `Event`. (This is sometimes called a *heterogeneous* collection, and the value that points to an event is sometimes called a *polymorphic* variable.)

Because a heap is a container that orders the elements it holds, we provide a basis for comparisons by having the class `Event` implement the `Comparable` interface. This interface consists of only one method, `compareTo`. This method returns an integer result, which is −1 if the current value is less than the argument, 0 if they are equal, and 1 if the current value is larger than the argument.

We are now ready to define the class `SimulationFramework`, which provides the basic structure for the simulation activities. The class `SimulationFramework` provides three basic functions. The first is used to insert a new event into the queue, the second runs the simulation, and the third returns the current simulation time, which is being held in a private data field:

The Polymorphic Variable

Although we have seen inheritance previously, as in the solitaire game described in Chapter 10, the ice cream store simulation is the first place we have made extensive use of inheritance combined with the *polymorphic variable.* A rough translation of polymorphic is the phrase "many forms." A polymorphic variable is one that is *declared* as one type but in *reality* is another type. In Java, polymorphic variables can be created using either interfaces or inheritance. Here, a variable is declared as holding an `Event`, but in reality it will hold one of the various subclasses for `Event`.

```
import jds.FindMin;
import jds.collection.Heap;
import jds.util.DefaultComparator;

public class SimulationFramework {

  public void scheduleEvent (Event newEvent)
    { eventQueue.addElement(newEvent); }

  public void run () {
    while (! eventQueue.isEmpty()) {
      Event nextEvent = (Event) eventQueue.getFirst();
      eventQueue.removeFirst();
      currentTime = nextEvent.time;
      nextEvent.processEvent();
    }
  }

  public int time() { return currentTime; }

  private int currentTime = 0;
  private FindMin eventQueue = new Heap(new DefaultComparator());
}
```

The heart of the simulation is the member function `run`, which defines the event loop.

FRAMEWORKS

A framework is like the skeleton of an application. It provides the structure for a solution but none of the application-specific behavior. Our framework for simulations describes the features common to all discrete event–driven simulations, namely, the concept of a priority queue of pending events and a loop that repeatedly removes the next event from the queue and executes it. But note that the framework has no knowledge of the specific simulation being constructed.

To create a working application, certain key classes provided by the framework are used to create subclasses. These subclasses can provide the application-specific behavior. In our simulation framework, the key class is `Event`. Three new types of events are created, corresponding to people arriving at the ice cream store, people ordering, and people leaving.

Another framework we have seen already but not identified as such is the AWT. To create a new application, the programmer uses inheritance to subclass from `Frame`, adding application-specific behavior. Frameworks can be created for any task that is repeated with a wide range of variations but that has a core of common functionality.

15.4.2 Ice Cream Store Simulation

Having created a framework for simulations in general, we now return to the specific simulation in hand, the ice cream store. An instance of class `SimulationFramework` is defined in our main class as a data field named `simulation`.

As we have noted, each activity is matched by a derived class of `Event`. Each derived class of `Event` includes an integer data field, which represents the size of a group of customers. The arrival event occurs when a group enters. When executed, the arrival event creates and installs a new order event:

```
private class ArriveEvent extends Event {
  ArriveEvent (int time, int gs) { super(time); groupSize = gs; }
  private int groupSize;

  public void processEvent () {
    if (canSeat(groupSize)) {
      simulation.scheduleEvent (
        new OrderEvent(time + randBetween(2,10), groupSize));
    }
  }
}
```

An order event similarly spawns a leave event:

```
private class OrderEvent extends Event {
  OrderEvent (int time, int gs) { super(time); groupSize = gs; }
  private int groupSize;

  public void processEvent () {
    for (int i = 0; i < groupSize; i++)
      order(1 + randBetween(1, 3));
    simulation.scheduleEvent(
      new LeaveEvent(time + randBetween(15, 35), groupSize));
  }
}
```

Finally, leave events free up chairs but do not spawn any new events:

```
private class LeaveEvent extends Event {
  LeaveEvent (int time, int gs) { super(time); groupSize = gs; }
  private int groupSize;

  public void processEvent () { leave(groupSize); }
}
```

The main program simply creates a certain number of initial events and then sets the simulation in motion. In our case, we will simulate 2 hours

(120 minutes) of operation, with groups arriving with random distribution between 2 and 5 minutes apart:

```
IceCreamStore () {
  int t = 0;
  while (t < 120) {
    t += randBetween(2, 5);
    simulation.scheduleEvent(new ArriveEvent(t, randBetween(1,5)));
  }
  simulation.run();
  System.out.println("Total profits " + profit);
}
```

An example execution might produce the following log:

```
Group of 1 customers arrives at time 5
Group is seated
Group of 4 customers arrives at time 9
Group is seated
Group of 2 customers arrives at time 14
Group is seated
Serviced order for 4 at time 15
Group of 5 customers arrives at time 16
Group is seated
Serviced order for 2 at time 17
  .
  .
  .
Group of size 4 leaves at time 147
Group of size 2 leaves at time 151
Group of size 4 leaves at time 158
Total profits 109.90
```

15.5 Chapter Summary

Key Concepts

- Priority queue
- Heap
- Heap-order property
- Heap sort
- Skew heap
- Discrete event-driven simulation

A priority queue is not a queue at all but rather a data structure designed to permit rapid access and removal of the smallest element in a collection. The vector or deque version of a priority queue is called a heap. The heap structure forms the basis of a very efficient sorting algorithm.

A form of heap is a skew heap, which does not have the fixed-size characteristic of the heap. The skew heap data structure is interesting in that it can potentially have a very poor worst-case performance. However, it can be shown that the worst-case performance cannot be maintained, and following any occurrence, the next several operations of insertion or removal must be very rapid. Thus, when measured over several operations, the performance of a skew heap is very impressive.

A common problem addressed using priority queues is the idea of discrete event–driven simulation. We have illustrated the use of heaps in an example simulation of an ice cream store. In Chapter 20, we will once more use a priority queue in the development of an algorithm for computing the shortest path between pairs of points in a graph.

Further Information

The binary heap was first proposed by John Williams in conjunction with the heap sort algorithm [Williams 64]. Although heap sort is now considered to be one of the standard classic algorithms, a thorough theoretical analysis of the algorithm has proved to be surprisingly difficult. It was only in 1991 that the best-case and average-case execution-time analysis of heap sort was reported [Schaffer 91].

Properties of complete binary trees are discussed by Knuth in Volume 1 of his series [Knuth 97], and several alternative priority queue data structures are discussed in Volume 3 [Knuth 98b]. Weiss [Weiss 96] also describes a number of alternative data structures.

Skew heaps were first described by Donald Sleator and Robert Tarjan in [Sleator 86]. An explanation of the amortized analysis of skew heaps is presented in [Weiss 96]. Aho et al. [Aho 83] call a heap structure that supports the *merge* operation, such as the `SkewHeap`, a *mergeable heap*.

The ice cream store simulation is derived from a similar simulation in my book on Smalltalk [Budd 87]. A version written in C++ can be found in [Budd 98].

Gonnet and Baeza-Yates [Gonnet 91] summarize several alternative techniques for implementing priority queues and include an extremely through bibliography of the relevant literature.

Study Questions

1. What is the primary characterization of a priority queue?
2. What is the main drawback to the use of a `SortedVector` as a priority queue?
3. Why is a priority queue not a true queue?
4. How could a priority queue be constructed using a list?
5. What is the heap data structure?
6. What are the two most common uses of the term heap in computer science?
7. What is the heap-order property?

8. What is a complete binary tree?
9. What is the length of a path from root to leaf in a complete binary tree containing n elements?
10. In what position will the children of node i be found in the vector representation of a heap?
11. Where is the second-smallest item in a heap? The third smallest?
12. Give a vector of ten elements ordered smallest to largest; then show the corresponding complete binary tree. Why will the tree always be a heap?
13. In comparison to other sorting algorithms we have seen, what is different about the ordering of elements in the output following a call on `Heap.sort`?
14. In the skew heap data structure, what is similar about the `addElement` and `removeFirst` routines?
15. What is a discrete event–driven simulation?
16. What is a heterogeneous collection?

Exercises

1. Complete the design of a priority queue constructed using lists. That is, develop a data structure with the same interface as the `Heap` data type but that uses lists as the underlying container and implements the interface using list operations.
2. Give an example of a priority queue that occurs in a noncomputer science situation.
3. The following tasks are intended to help you get a better feel for the implementation of the operations in the `Heap` data type.
   a. Create an initially empty heap, and verify that the method `isEmpty` will return `true`.
   b. Add the element 4 to the heap. Verify that `isEmpty` will now return `false`.
   c. Add the value 7. Show the structure of the new heap.
   d. Add the value 3. Show the structure of the new heap once the new value has been moved into place.
   e. Add the values 8, 9, 6, and 5, and show the structure of the final heap.
   f. Remove the value 3, and show the heap after it has been rebuilt.
   g. Remove each of the remaining values one by one, and show the heap after each operation.

4. The FindMin ADT requires that an attempt to access or to remove a value from an empty heap will throw NoSuchElementException. How is this requirement being met in the Heap data structure?
5. Imagine a heap that contains 2^n values. This will naturally represent a complete binary tree. Note that the heap property is retained if the left and right subtrees of any node are exchanged. How many different equivalent heaps can be produced using only such swappings?
6. Consider the following alternative implementation of addElement:

```
public synchronized void addElement (Object val) {
  int heapSize = elementData.size();
  int position = heapSize;
  elementData.addElementAt(val, position);

  // now restore the possibly lost heap property
  while (position > 0) {
    // reheap the subtree
    adjustHeap(elementData, heapSize, position);
    // move up the tree
    position = (position-1)/2;
  }
}
```

   a. Prove that this algorithm will in fact successfully add a new element to the heap.
   b. Explain why, as a practical matter, this algorithm is less desirable than the algorithm presented in the text.
7. Describe an algorithm for merging two Heap structures. What is the complexity of your algorithm? How does this compare to the complexity of merging two SkewHeap collections?
8. Suppose that two equal elements are inserted into a Heap. Will they necessarily be removed in the same order they were inserted? If you wanted to modify the Heap algorithm to ensure a first in first out (FIFO) property, how might you do this?
9. A sorting algorithm is said to be *stable* if, when two elements in the original vector are equal, their relative ordering in the output is the same as their relative ordering in the input. Is the heap sort algorithm stable?
10. Perform the operations described in exercise 3, using a SkewHeap rather than a heap.
11. Another heap-based sorting algorithm can be constructed using skew heaps. The idea is to simply copy the values from a vector into a skew

heap, then copy the values one by one back out of the heap. Write a procedure to do this. How does the execution time of your procedure compare to the heap sort algorithm?

12. Perform empirical timings on the algorithm you wrote for the previous exercise. For input, use vectors of various sizes containing random numbers. Compare the running time of this algorithm to that of the tree sort and the heap sort.
13. Show that unless other information is maintained, finding the maximum value in a `Heap` must be an $O(n)$ operation. *Hint:* How many elements in the collection could potentially be the maximum value?
14. An operation we have not discussed is the ability to change the value of an item already in the heap. This is frequently required when heaps are used, as their name suggests, as priority queues and we wish to increase or to decrease the priority of a specific task. Describe an algorithm to change the priority of a specific element stored in a `Heap`. What is the complexity of your algorithm?
15. Multithreaded systems frequently allow the user to set a task priority. For example, the Java `Thread` class provides the method `setPriority(int)`. In such a system, it would not be a good idea to always select the highest-priority task, as low-priority tasks would never get executed. This is termed *starvation*. Instead, low-priority tasks should occasionally be given control, although not as often as high-priority tasks. Describe a system that avoids starvation but still gives high-priority tasks more access to the computer than low-priority tasks.

Programming Projects

1. A queue can be implemented using a priority queue and a counter. Each time an element is added to the collection, the counter is incremented and stored along with the element value. Items in the priority queue are ordered using their counter value. Implement a class that supports the `Queue` interface and uses this idea. Using the experiment described in Section 12.4, compare your code to other `Queue` implementations. Can you implement a `Stack` using the same approach?
2. Design a simulation of an airport. The airport has two runways. Planes arrive and request permission to land, and, independently, planes on the ground request permission to take off.
3. One alternative to the use of uniform distributions is the idea of a weighted discrete probability. Suppose that we observe a real store

and note that 65 percent of the time, customers will order one scoop; 25 percent of the time, they will order two scoops; and 10 percent of the time, they will order three scoops. This is certainly a far different distribution from the uniform distribution we used in the simulation. In order to simulate this behavior, we can add a new method to our class `random`.

a. Add a method named `weightedDiscrete` to the class `Simulation-Framework`. This method will take as argument a vector of unsigned integer values. For example, to generate the preceding distribution, the programmer would pass the method a vector of three elements, containing 65, 25, and 10.
b. The method first sums the values in the array, resulting in a maximum value. In this case, the value would be 100. A random number between 1 and this maximum value is then generated.
c. The method then decides in which category the number belongs. This can be discovered by looping through the values. In our example, if the number is less than 65, the method should return 0 (remember, index values start at 0); if less than or equal to 90, return 1; and otherwise, return 2.

4. Modify the ice cream store simulation so it uses the weighted discrete random number–generated function implemented in the previous exercise. Select reasonable numbers for the weights. Compare a run of the resulting program to a run of the program using the uniform distribution.

5. A *keyed priority queue* is an ADT that implements both the `Map` and the priority queue (or `FindMin`) interface. Like a map, elements are inserted as a key/value pair. Like a priority queue, the smallest element can be quickly accessed and removed. However, unlike the priority queues we have seen previously, the object returned as a result of `FindMin` will be the value associated with the smallest key. Similarly, the `removeMin` operation will remove the key/value pair associated with the smallest key.

   Show how to implement this ADT by building on top of an existing data type that supports the `FindMin` interface. *Hint:* Create a helper class `Association` to maintain a key/value pair. You might sneak a peek at Chapter 17 for some suggestions on how to do this.

6. A *ternary heap* is similar to a binary heap, but each node has three children.
   a. Devise a technique for storing a ternary heap in a vector. What are the index values for the children of node `i`?
   b. Rewrite the heap data type to make use of a ternary heap.

c. Compare the execution time of your ternary heap algorithm to the binary heap algorithm.

7. Program a discrete event–driven simulation of a hospital emergency room. A triage doctor assigns each arriving patient a number based on the severity of his or her condition. The room has a fixed number of beds. As each bed is freed, the next most urgent patient is handled. Patients take varying amounts of time to handle, depending on their condition. Collect statistics on the length of time each patient will have to wait.

8. An alternative approach to the skew heap is a *leftist heap*. In a leftist heap, the height of the left child is always larger than or equal to the height of the right child. As two children in a heap can always be swapped without violating the heap-order property, this is an easy condition to impose. To construct a leftist heap, nodes are modified so as to remember their height. (We saw how to do this in the AVL tree described in Chapter 14.) As with the skew heap, all operations on a leftist heap are implemented using the single task of merging two heaps. The following steps are then used to merge heaps T1 and T2.
   a. If the value in T2 is less than the value in T1, merge in the opposite order.
   b. The root of T1 is therefore the root for the new heap. The right child of T1 is recursively merged with T2.
   c. If the resulting height of the right child is larger than the left child, the two children are reversed.
   d. The height of the result is set as one larger than the height of the left child.

   Because a merge is always performed with a right child, which is always smaller than the tree rooted at the left child, the result can be produced very quickly. Provide an implementation of a heap data structure based on this principle.

CHAPTER 16

HASH TABLES

In several places, we have seen the power of the idea *divide and conquer*. We encountered this as a tool of abstraction (Chapter 1) and then as a guide to program development in the binary search algorithm (Chapter 7). The principle also lay behind the development of the heap (Chapter 15) and of binary trees in general (Chapter 13). For most operations on a binary tree, the tree is divided into two roughly equal parts at each step, thereby reducing the complexity of the task by half. But what if one could reduce the problem by a factor larger than 2? Suppose that in a single constant-time operation, one could reduce a problem by a factor of 10 or by 1,000. Intuitively, it would seem that this would offer even greater benefits than those provided by binary trees.

In a certain sense, this benefit is exactly what is happening when we use a vector. When an index is used with a vector, a single constant-time operation allows us to access any element. We move from thinking about the vector as an entire collection to thinking about just a single element. But implicit in the use of vectors are two primary problems. The first is that a vector must be indexed using an integer value, and the second is that each position of a vector can hold only a single element. The *hash table* is a data structure that overcomes both of these difficulties.[1] The first problem

1. It is unfortunate that the Java standard library uses the name `Hashtable` to describe a data structure that does not use the traditional `Set` interface but instead is something more appropriately described as a `Map` in the sense of Chapter 17. The standard library does include a `HashSet` abstraction that is closer in spirit to the traditional data abstraction.

is addressed through the use of a *hash function*, which maps values into integer locations. This allows the programmer to think of a problem in terms of values instead of indices. The second difficulty is more subtle and is addressed using two different techniques.

The next two sections will describe in detail these two features of hash tables. We will then illustrate the use of hash tables by considering a pair of sorting algorithms, differing from each other but similar in their use of the concept of hashing. Finally, we will conclude the chapter by developing hash tables as a series of general-purpose container classes.

16.1 Hash Functions

Suppose that six friends—*Alfred, Alessia, Amina, Amy, Andy,* and *Anne*—have started a club and wish to maintain a database containing the amount of club dues they each have paid. Dues are paid each time a member attends a meeting, but not all members attend all meetings; nor do they pay the same amount each time they meet. The club programmer, Amy, is in charge of writing programs to do the bookkeeping.

Initially, Amy uses the integer indices 0 to 5 to represent each of the members. One day, however, Amy discovers an interesting fact. If she takes the third letter of each member's name, treats the letter as representing an integer by letting *a* represent the value 0, *b* represent the value 1, and so on, up to *z* for the value 25, and then computes the remainder yielded after dividing each value by 6, each returns a different integer value between 0 and 5.

	Name		Value	Remainder
Al	f	red	5	5
Al	e	ssia	4	4
Am	i	na	8	2
Am	y		24	0
An	d	y	3	3
An	n	e	13	1

Amy has just discovered what is called a perfect hash function. A *hash function* is a function that takes as input an element from a set of values and returns an integer result. The term "to hash" evokes an image of random mixing and shuffling. This is appropriate, as hash functions are permitted wide latitude in the manner of transformations they may use. We will have much more to say about hash functions in our subsequent discussion. A *perfect hash function* is a hash function that in addition yields a one-to-one mapping from the keys onto the integers starting at

0 and extending to the number of elements in the set, so that each element maps onto a *different* integer value.

Using her hash function, Amy writes the simple program shown in Figure 16.1 to manage her club finances. Input consists of a series of names and amounts, such as the following:

```
Alfred  2.32
Alessia  1.76
Amina  4.87
Alfred  3.71
Amy  0.51
Andy  7.59
Alessia  2.63
Anne  3.62
```

The output of the program is a summary of the amount each member has paid. The program makes use of a `StreamTokenizer`, which will automatically convert a stream of characters into words and numbers.

StreamTokenizer

The class `StreamTokenizer` used in Amy's program is part of the Java I/O system. This tool is used to divide input, which consists of nothing more than a sequence of characters, into more abstract units, such as words and numbers. The key features of the class can be described as follows:

```
class StreamTokenizer {
  StreamTokenizer (Reader);
  int nextToken (); // read next token,
                    // return type or
                    // next character
    final static int TT_EOF; // end of file
                             // encountered
    final static int TT_EOL; // end of line
    final static int TT_NUMBER; // found a
                                // number
    final static int TT_WORD; // found a word
  public String sval; // value of word token
  public double nval; // value of number
                      // token
  public void lowerCaseMode (boolean);
                    // convert word to
                    // lowercase?
  public void ordinaryChar (char);
                    // don't consider char
                    // part of word
}
```

The constructor takes as argument a `Reader`, used to obtain the character values. Each call on `NextToken` reads in one new token. The result returned by this function is either one of the four named static constant values or a single-character value if the next nonspace character is neither part of a word nor a number. Word values can be subsequently accessed via the variable `sval`, numbers via `nval`.

A variety of methods can be used to modify the processing of characters. We have shown only two, although there are many more. Setting the `lowerCaseMode` to `true` will automatically convert text to lowercase as it is processed. By means of `ordinaryChar`, the user can change the processing of character values. In Chapter 18, for example, we will use this method to change the categorization of the period, which is by default considered part of the word-making characters, into an ordinary (and hence single-character symbol) character.

```
//
//  Amy's program to compute club finances
//

import java.io.*;

class AmyClub {
  public static void main (String [ ] args) {
    double [ ] funds = new double[6];
    try {
      Reader rin = new FileReader("data");
      StreamTokenizer tok = new StreamTokenizer(rin);
      int c = tok.nextToken();
      while (c != StreamTokenizer.TT_EOF) {
        String name = tok.sval;
        tok.nextToken();
        double amount = tok.nval;
          // now update amount
        funds[nameHash(name)] += amount;
        c = tok.nextToken();
      }
    } catch (IOException e) { System.err.println("IO Err " + e); }
      // now print updated records
    System.out.println("Alfred paid " + funds[nameHash("Alfred")]);
    System.out.println("Alessia paid " + funds[nameHash("Alessia")]);
    System.out.println("Amina paid " + funds[nameHash("Amina")]);
    System.out.println("Amy paid " + funds[nameHash("Amy")]);
    System.out.println("Andy paid " + funds[nameHash("Andy")]);
    System.out.println("Anne paid " + funds[nameHash("Anne")]);
  }

  public static int nameHash (String name) {
    return (int) (name.charAt(2) - 'a') % 6;
  }
}
```

FIGURE 16.1 Amy's Program to Compute Club Finances

Of course, Amy's carefully worked-out system falls apart when the set of keys changes. Suppose, for example, that *Alan* wishes to join the club. The nameHash calculation for Alan will yield 0, the same value as for Amy. Two elements that have the same hash value are said to have *collided*.[2]

---

2. Therefore, another definition of a perfect hash function is a hash function that operates on a set of n elements, generating result indices between 0 and $n - 1$ and for which no two elements cause a collision.

Although it would seem that collisions would preempt the use of the hashing technique, we will see in Section 16.2 how this difficulty can be overcome.

It might appear at this point that the discovery of a hash function, and in particular a perfect hash function, is simply a matter of blind luck. This is in part true and in part not true. It is true in that no known systematic procedure can be used to generate a perfect hash function from an arbitrary set of elements. However, techniques can be used in the majority of cases of practical interest. The section Further Information at the end of this chapter will point the interested reader to some of the related literature.

16.1.1 Hash Functions

The application of a hash function is almost always a two-step process of

1. Transforming the key into an integer value
2. Mapping the resulting integer into a valid index for the hash table

A number of well-known methods accomplish the first task. Often, these are used in combination: mapping, folding, shifting, and casts.

- **Mapping.** Integer values that occur in the key can be transformed, or mapped, into other integer values. This is the technique Amy used in her hash function. The character `a` was mapped onto 0, the character `b` onto 1, and so on. Another example might be a hash function for playing cards, mapping each card onto a value from 0 to 3 by its suit (see exercise 3 for an even better alternative). Often, more complex maps are defined using an array. The elements of the array are specified ahead of time, when the program is compiled. To hash a value is simply a matter of indexing into the array. This idea is the basis for the most commonly used algorithm for generating a perfect hash function from a known set of identifiers.
- **Folding.** With folding, the key is partitioned into several parts, and the (perhaps hashed) integer values for the individual parts are combined. The combination is usually accomplished using an efficient operation, such as addition, multiplication, shifting, or the logical exclusive `OR` operation. For example, the following loop converts a string into an integer value by summing the integers corresponding to each character.

```
int hashval = 0;
int i = str.length();
while (i > 0)
  hashval += (int) str.charAt(--i);
```

Care must be taken to ensure that folding does not distort the range of hash values. Consider using a logical `OR` to combine values. We will illustrate the problem with 2-bit quantities, although the problem is still present in larger numbers. Here are all the combinations for a pair of 2-bit values:

	00	01	10	11
00	00	01	10	11
01	01	01	11	11
10	10	11	10	11
11	11	11	11	11

Note that the resulting values are hardly uniform. The value 00 appears only once, 01 and 10 appear three times each, and 11 appears nine times!

- **Shifting.** The application of these techniques often results in values for which the low-order bits are not random. For example, printable character values are only a small range of the total integer values. In these situations, a shift operation can be used to eliminate the undesirable portions of the number.

  Shifting can also be used to avoid a problem that occurs when folding is performed using a commutative operator, such as addition. The problem is that a commutative operator will produce the same hash value for permutations of the arguments. Thus, the loop just given will produce the same hash value for the strings `apt`, `tap`, and `pat`. By shifting the results of the previous calculation before performing the addition, we can eliminate this difficulty.

```
int hashval = 0;
int i = str.length();
while (i > 0)
  hashval = (hashval << 1) + (int) str.charAt(--i);
```

- **Casts.** A cast can be used to convert a numeric type into an integer. An example of this is found in the class `Character`, which converts the ASCII value for a character into an integer and uses the resulting value as the hash index.

The second step—transforming the hashed key value into a legal index—is almost always accomplished by taking the remainder (or mod) after dividing by the table size. Although this is easy, it is not the only possibility. Sometimes, a right shift can be used. Shift instructions have a speed advantage over divisions, but they can be used only in situations where the number of indices is a power of 2. Another alternative is to use bitwise operations to select just a few binary digits from an integer key.

Special care must be taken to guarantee that the value returned by the modular division operation is a legal index. In particular, a negative value for the left argument could result in a negative (and, hence, out of range) index. The safest approach is to use only positive arithmetic in computing hash values.

If division is used, the only source of variation is the size of the table. Let us consider the effect of a computation to take the remainder by dividing by n, the hash table size:

$$index = key \bmod n$$

Some values of n are much better than others in shuffling the original hash values. If n is even, for example, the index will be even for even key values and odd for odd key values. In many cases, this is unacceptable. For example, on most machines, object addresses are always even, often always multiples of 4. If the key is simply an address, this would result in the odd-numbered indices being totally unused. If n is a power of 2, the mod is simply the low-order bits of the key value. Not only is the mod instruction an inefficient way to obtain this value, but also these bits are usually not as random as we would like. Empirical evidence suggests that better scattering is achieved when n is a prime number. Thus, if one wants a hash table of "about" 1,000 elements, a size of 997 or 1,009 is preferable.

16.1.2 Hash Functions in the Java Standard Library

All Java objects have the ability to be used with a hash table. The reason is that the method `hashCode` is defined in the class `Object`, which is parent to every other class in the language. This method is then overridden by many other classes. The following are some examples:

- `Character`: the character value cast to an `int`
- `Date`: a value associated with the current time
- `Double`: a value generated by the bitwise representation
- `Integer`: the `int` value itself
- `String`: a folded sum of the character values
- `URL`: the hash code of the host name

Generally speaking, if the `equals` operator is overridden, the `hashCode` method should be overridden as well to ensure that if two objects are equal, they have the same hash value. Note that the reverse is, of course, not necessarily true.

16.2 Collision Resolution

It is possible—indeed likely—that more than one value will hash into the same location. Generally speaking, there are two broad approaches to solving this problem, yielding two very different types of data structure.

The first approach is termed *open-address hashing*. Here, all elements are stored in the hash table itself. When two elements collide, we *probe* for a free location in which to store the second value. A number of techniques are commonly used to search for a new position to examine. The easiest probing algorithm is termed *linear probing*; you simply move forward, position by position, until an empty location is found.[3]

For example, assume that we want to add the name *Alan* to an eight-element hash table, using Amy's hashing function. The hash value for *Alan* is 1, which is not yet taken. Unfortunately, both *Amina* and *Amy* have hash value 0, and so the entry for *Amy* has been pushed into location 1. (For *Amina*, $i = 8$, which has remainder 0 after division by 8. For *Amy*, $y = 24$, which also has remainder 0 after division by 8.) Because we cannot therefore store *Alan* at location 1, we move forward and discover that the next free space is found at location 2. It is in this location that we store the information for *Alan*.

Amina	Amy		Andy	Alessia	Alfred	Anne	

If Albert wishes to join the club, we will find that the location corresponding to his hash value, position 2, is already filled. Also, the next free location will not occur until position 7.

If we assume that the distribution of insertions is uniformly random, filling one location—for example, position 0—doubles the likelihood that the next position will be filled. The reason is that there are now two hash values, 0 and 1, which will cause this position to be filled. Having filled two adjacent locations makes it three times more likely that the next location will be filled, as an element with any of three different hash values can occupy this slot.

The following chart illustrates this problem. Assume that we have a ten-entry table into which five elements have already been placed. Assume that the next placement will have a uniform probability of hashing to each of the ten locations. The numbers shown in the free locations indicate the probabilities that each will be the next slot filled. The first position has a 1 in 10 chance of being filled, as only the values that hash into this location

3. Some of the other probing techniques are explored in the exercises.

THE BIRTHDAY PARADOX

The frequency of collisions when performing hashing is related to a well-known mathematical puzzle. How many randomly chosen people need be in a room before it becomes likely that two people will have the same birth date? Most people would guess hundreds, as there are 365 possible birthdays (excluding leap years). In fact, the answer is only 24 people.

To see why, consider the opposite question. With n randomly chosen people in a room, what is the probability that no two have the same birth date? If we take a calendar and mark off each individual's birth date in turn, the probability that the second person has a birthday different from the first is 364/365, as 364 different possibilities are not already marked. Similarly, the probability that the third person has a birthday different from the first two is 363/365. These two probabilities are independent of each other, so the probability that they are *both* true is their product. Continuing in this fashion, if we have $n - 1$ people all with different birthdays, the probability that individual n has a different birthday is

$$\frac{364}{365} \times \frac{363}{365} \times \frac{362}{365} \times \cdots \times \frac{365 - n + 1}{365}$$

When $n \geq 24$, this expression becomes less than 0.5. This means that if 24 or more people are gathered in a room, the odds are better than even that two individuals have the same birthday.

The implication of the birthday paradox for hashing is to tell us that for any problem of reasonable size, we are almost certain to have some collisions. Functions that avoid duplicate indices are surprisingly rare, even with a relatively large table.

can occupy the space. The position after the two adjacent elements, on the other hand, has a 3 in 10 chance of being filled, as values that hash into either of the two previous positions will also end up in this space. As a series of adjacent filled locations becomes larger, it raises the probability that the group will grow even more.

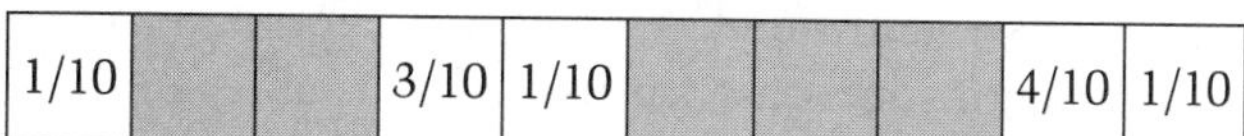

Therefore, as the hash table becomes more filled, rather than seeing a uniform density of elements throughout the table, we instead observe many large clumps of elements, as shown in Figure 16.2. This phenomenon is termed *clustering*.

An entirely different approach comes from letting each element in the hash table be a collection, such as a linked list. The idea is to separate the elements to be maintained into one of several *buckets*. Each bucket can hold an arbitrary number of elements. Thus, for example, the addition of a new element is a two-step process: First choose the bucket into which the element is to be inserted, and then place the element into the bucket. The inclusion test and the removal of an element from the collection are handled similarly. Because buckets can hold multiple elements, the

FIGURE 16.2 Open Hash Table Cluster

problem of collisions goes away. This process is termed *chaining*, or simply *hashing using buckets*.

Generally, the bucket is formed using one of the data structures we have previously examined, such as a `Vector` or a `LinkedList`.

A major incentive for using hash tables is the speed with which operations can be performed. To illustrate this, let us consider the asymptotic complexity of determining whether a value is contained in a hash table constructed using buckets.

An analysis of the asymptotic running time of hash table operations is complicated by the uncertainty involved in the hash function. The worst-case hash function would be one that always returned a single value, such as 0. Although this behavior is certainly permissible under our definition of a hash function, the effect would be to place all elements into a single bucket. This does imply, however, that our worst-case complexity can be no better, but also no worse, than the execution behavior of the underlying data structure used to represent the buckets. If we were to use an `AVLTree` for the buckets, for example, the worst-case asymptotic complexity of lookup would be $O(\log n)$.

The best-possible hash function would be one that uniformly distributes elements over the range of hash values: a function that has the effect of maintaining approximately the same number of elements in each bucket. Discovering such a function is not always easy but is the key to obtaining the best performance from a hash table. We will present the asymptotic runtime analysis of our hash table assuming this case.

If we let m represent the size of our hash table, approximately n/m elements are in each bucket. This value is termed the *load factor* and is usually written using the Greek letter λ. For open-address hashing, the load factor will be between 0 and 1; for hashing using buckets, the load factor can be larger than 1.

If we assume that the time to compute the hash function itself is constant, as is the time to discover which bucket an element corresponds to, the time to access an element is the search time for an underlying container of size λ. Searching for an element in an `AVLTree` of size k can be performed in $O(\log k)$ steps; this means that testing whether an element occurs in a well-balanced hash table can be performed in $O(\log \lambda)$ steps.

In addition to having a good hash function, a key to obtaining the best performance from a hash table is to declare the table large enough that the load factor remains small. For example, we might assume that the number of hash table buckets is roughly *proportional* to the total number of elements. That is, the number of elements in the table will never exceed, say, $m * 10$. Thus, n/m is no larger than $\frac{10m}{m}$, or 10. Hence, $O(\log \lambda)$ can be no larger than $O(\log 10)$. The logarithm of any constant is itself a constant, so we can simply say that the asymptotic complexity of search is $O(1)$.

Hence, we see that the worst-case performance for a hash table is essentially the worst-case performance of the underlying bucket data structure. The best-case performance permits operations to be performed in constant time. But this best-case time was predicated on some key requirements: namely, that the hash function distribute elements over all the buckets and that the load factor not become overly large. Analysis of the "average" case is complicated, in part because of the uncertainty involved in defining the meaning of the term "average" for various hash functions and distributions of key values. Nevertheless, in practice, when used with a reasonable hash function, the performance of hash tables can be quite good.

16.3 Hash Table Sorting Algorithms

We will illustrate the use of hash tables by describing two very different sorting algorithms that use the same idea, hashing into buckets, in different ways. Although both of the following techniques use the concept of

FAST SEARCHING USING BUCKETS

In Chapter 7, we noted that hash tables would, in theory, provide us with a means to perform searches for elements in faster than $O(\log n)$ time but only under certain conditions. Having described the hash table technique, the idea is obvious. To tell whether a certain element is contained in a collection, it is necessary only to select the appropriate bucket to which the element would be assigned if it were present and to search just the one bucket. The hash operation is typically fast; if the element is present, it must be in only one bucket. Thus, the time to search for a single element is the time to search just a single bucket, which is potentially much faster than the time to search the entire collection.

For this to be a nontrivial gain in execution time, we must carefully monitor the load factor. That is, we must maintain the requirement that the number of buckets be a significant percentage of the number of elements (so that each bucket contains only a few elements) and that the hash function distribute elements from the collection relatively uniformly to each of the buckets. Because it is frequently difficult to discover a hash function having these characteristics, using an asymptotically less efficient data structure, such as a `SkipList`, will nevertheless often be more practical.

hashing to create fast programs, neither can really be termed a general-purpose sorting algorithm. Rather, both are applicable only to the problem of sorting positive integers. In the programming projects at the end of the chapter, we will suggest other approaches, some of which are more generally applicable than the two algorithms presented here, to sorting based on hash tables.

16.3.1 Counting Sort

The first algorithm is used to sort positive integers from a limited range. For example, suppose that you need to sort 1,000 elements but know that the elements are each between 0 and 19. One approach would be to simply count the number of zeros, the number of ones, and so on. In the end, you might come up with a table such as the following:

0 : 47	5 : 114	10 : 36	15 : 93
1 : 92	6 : 16	11 : 92	16 : 12
2 : 12	7 : 37	12 : 43	17 : 15
3 : 14	8 : 41	13 : 17	18 : 63
4 : 32	9 : 3	14 : 132	19 : 89

This would tell you that in the sorted array, there would be 47 zeros, followed by 92 ones, then 12 twos, and so on. Simply stated, there is no need to manipulate the elements themselves, simply their count.

```
public class CountingSort {

  public void sort (int [ ] data, int m) {
  // sort the array of integers, each element no larger than m
    int [ ] counts = new int[m];

      // count the occurrences of each value
    for (int i = 0; i < data.length; i++)
      counts[data[i]]++;

      // now put integers back into the array
    int i = 0;
    for (int j = 0; j < m; j++)
      for (int k = counts[j]; k > 0; k--)
        data[i++] = j;
  }
}
```

FIGURE 16.3 The Counting Sort Algorithm

The procedure that embodies this idea is shown in Figure 16.3. The input is an array of integers and an integer that represents the largest value in the array. The hash table in this case is simply an array of integers, initially 0. The program loops through the input array, incrementing the counts. Once the counts have all been determined, the program loops through the counts array and overwrites the original data array. (A set of such counts is sometimes called a *histogram*. If the input sequence is letters, for example, the histogram will indicate the frequency of occurrence of different letters. The intent of gathering such information might not be sorting, but the techniques are similar.)

To determine the asymptotic execution-time efficiency of this algorithm, we need to consider both the quantity n (the number of data elements) and m (the largest data value). The first loop, the loop that copies counts into the data array, is clearly $O(n)$. The analysis of the nested loops that end the algorithm is more subtle. Clearly, the outer loop will execute m times. In the worst case, the inner loop could execute n times. This might lead us to suspect that the execution time is $O(m \times n)$; however, this is not the case. Indeed, you can easily convince yourself that the assignment statement will be executed exactly n times. Thus, the total execution time is the *maximum* of n and m, often written as $O(n + m)$. This is extremely fast in comparison to the other sorting algorithms we have seen.

EXPERIMENT: HOW LARGE CAN M BE?

How large can m get before the execution time of the counting sort algorithm is worse than that of an $O(n \log n)$ algorithm, such as quick sort? Try answering the question first on the asymptotic analysis figures. Then try the following experiment. Fix the size of an array at, say, 5,000 elements. Then try varying the value of m from, say, 10 to 10,000. For each value of m, compute a vector of size n containing integers randomly distributed between 0 and m, and compare the running time of the counting sort algorithm to that of quick sort.

This simple algorithm has been rediscovered many times and is often cited as a counterexample to the assertion that sorting requires $O(n \log n)$ operations. However, it is important to point out that this technique can be used in only a narrow set of circumstances. In particular, the elements must be integers and must be drawn from a small range.

16.3.2 Radix Sorting

An entirely different way of using hash tables and buckets is illustrated by the radix sort algorithm. Like counting sort, *radix sorting* is a technique for ordering a list of positive integers. The elements are successively ordered on digit positions, from right to left. This is accomplished by copying the elements into buckets, where the index for the bucket is given by the position of the digit being sorted. Once all digit positions have been examined, the collection must be sorted.

The list to be sorted is as follows:

624 762 852 426 197 987 269 146 415 301 730 78 593

The following table shows the sequences of elements found in each bucket during the four steps involved in sorting the list. During pass 1, the one's-place digits are ordered. Each value that ends in 2 is placed into the same bucket, as are all elements that end in 3, and so on. During pass 2, the ten's-place digits are ordered, retaining the relative positions of elements set by the earlier pass. Again, all elements that have 2 in the ten's position are placed into the same container, as are all values that have 3 in the ten's position, and so on. On pass 3, the hundred's-place digits are ordered, again retaining the previous relative ordering. After three passes, the result is an ordered collection.

Bucket	Pass 1	Pass 2	Pass 3
0	730	301	78
1	301	415	146, 197
2	762, 852	624, 426	269
3	593	730	301
4	624	146	415, 426
5	415	852	593
6	426, 146	762, 269	624
7	197, 987	78	730, 762
8	78	987	852
9	269	593, 197	987

Sorting Punchcards

Although less common today than they once were, computer punchcards were once commonly used to store information both for computer use and for other business applications. A punchcard was made out of stiff paper, and holes in the card indicated a specific letter. A card could typically hold 80 columns of information.

Because it was far too easy to drop a tray of cards and get them out of order, a convention developed to place a sequencing number somewhere on the card, often in the last eight columns. A common task was to order a collection of cards according to their sequencing number. Radix sort was a perfect way to do this. A machine called a *sorter* would divide a deck of cards into buckets, based on their value in a specific column.

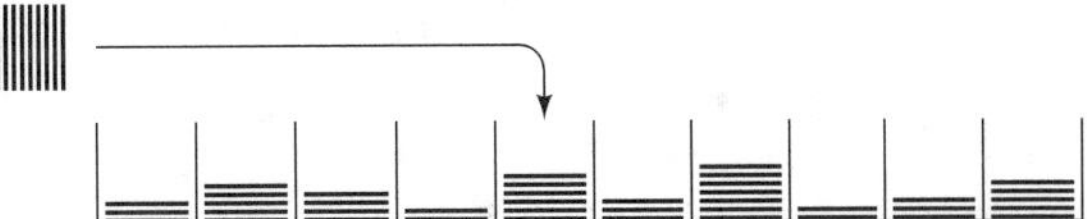

The person doing the sorting would make several passes over the deck. Suppose, for example, that the sequencing numbers appeared in columns 78, 79, and 80. The deck would first be sorted on column 80. The user would then, by hand, gather the resulting decks together and sort once again, this time on column 79. Gathering together for a third time, the deck would be sorted on column 78. After the third sort, the deck would be completely ordered.

```
import jds.Queue;
import jds.collection.LinkedList;

public class RadixSort {

  public void radixSort (int [ ] data) {
    boolean flag = true;
    int divisor = 1;
    Queue [ ] buckets = new Queue[10];
    for (int i = 0; i < 10; i++)
      buckets[i] = new LinkedList();

    while (flag) {
      flag = false;
        // first copy the elements into buckets
      for (int i = 0; i < data.length; i++) {
        int hashIndex = (data[i] / divisor) % 10;
        if (hashIndex > 0) flag = true;
        buckets[hashIndex].addLast(new Integer(data[i]));
      }
        // then copy the elements back into array
      divisor *= 10;
      int i = 0;
      for (int j = 0; j < 10; j++) {
        while (! buckets[j].isEmpty()) {
          Integer ival = (Integer) buckets[j].getFirst();
          buckets[j].removeFirst();
          data[i++] = ival.intValue();
        }
      }
    }
  }
}
```

FIGURE 16.4 The Radix Sort Algorithm

In this case, because the relative order of the elements is vitally important, we are using a `Queue` implemented by means of a `LinkedList` as the data type for the underlying bucket. Each pass must preserve the relative order of the elements established by the previous pass.

The radix sorting algorithm, shown in Figure 16.4, has a slightly more complex structure than the counting sort algorithm. A `while` loop is used to cycle through the various passes. The value of the variable `divisor` indicates which digit is currently being examined. A Boolean flag is used

EXPERIMENT: COMPARING RADIX SORT TO QUICK SORT

This experiment is similar to the one proposed for the counting sort algorithm. As with counting sort, the execution time of radix sort is determined in part by the range of integers being sorted, as the number of iterations is determined by the number of decimals in the largest integer value. Fix a value n, the number of elements, and then vary the range of elements. Compare sorting integers randomly selected between 0 and 10 to sorting integers randomly selected between 0 and 10,000. At what point does a conventional sorting algorithm, such as quick sort, become faster?

to determine when execution should halt. Each time the `while` loop is executed, an array of lists is initialized. Note that new lists are created on each iteration. Each time the loop is executed, the elements in the input are copied into the appropriate bucket. Once distributed into the buckets, the elements are gathered back into the input. As long as more than one bucket is used, the program must continue. The flag is finally set to `false`, and execution halted, when all elements map into the first bucket.

An examination of the radix sort algorithm will show that the nested loops are proportional to the number of elements in the data array, whereas the number of executions of the surrounding loop is controlled by the maximum number of digits in the largest data value. Thus, the execution-time performance of radix sort is, like counting sort, tied to the range of integers being sorted.

* 16.4 OPEN-ADDRESS HASHING

Open-address hashing will be the basis for the first data abstraction we will examine. You will recall that in this technique, all elements are stored in the hash table directly rather than in buckets. The data structure shown in Figure 16.5, which supports the `Bag` interface, is a simple example of this idea. A `Vector` is used to hold the table. The size of this table may be initially set by the user, or we will simply use the size of the supplied `Vector`. A value will track the number of elements that have been inserted into the collection.

The collision-resolution algorithm is found in the method `addElement`. We first test to see whether the container has sufficient room for the new element, readjusting the size if not. This is similar to the way that a `Vector` will automatically grow if new elements are added to the container. Note that the test will always ensure that there is one free location, even after the new element has been inserted. This fact is used by the methods

```
public class OpenHashtable implements Bag {
    // constructors
  public OpenHashtable (int size)
    { elementData = new Vector(); elementData.setSize(size); }
  public OpenHashtable (Indexed ed)
    { elementData = ed; }
  private Indexed elementData;
  private int elementCount = 0;

    // the Collection interface
  public boolean isEmpty () { return elementCount == 0; }
  public int size () { return elementCount; }
  public Enumeration elements ()
    { return new OpenHashtableEnumerator(); }

    // the Bag interface
  public void addElement (Object val) {
      // make certain we have room for element
    if (elementCount + 1 >= elementData.size()) reAdjustTable();
      // then add to table
    int index = Math.abs(val.hashCode()) % elementData.size();
    while (elementData.elementAt(index) != null)
      if (++index >= elementData.size()) index = 0;
    elementData.setElementAt(val, index);
    elementCount++;
  }

  public boolean containsElement (Object val) { ... }

  public Object findElement (Object val) { ... }

  public void removeElement (Object val)
    { throw new NoSuchElementException(val.toString()); }

  private void reAdjustTable () { ... }

  private class OpenHashtableEnumerator implements Enumeration {
    .
    .
    .
  }
}
```

FIGURE 16.5 The OpenHashtable Data Type

containsElement and findElement, which terminate once they find an empty space.

Some variations on the hash table abstraction will expand the table before it becomes too full. Recall that the term *load factor* describes the percentage of the table that has already been filled. Hash table abstractions sometimes allow the user to specify the largest permitted load factor—for example, expanding the table when it becomes more than 75 percent full rather than waiting for it to become completely full. A lower maximum load factor will decrease search and insertion time but will, of course, increase the amount of memory being used.

Once we are assured that there is space, the initial hash value is computed. To find the location for the free element, we simply march forward from the location until we find an empty space. Because we have already checked that the table has room for the new element, the loop must eventually terminate, although it may test almost every position before it finds an empty location.

As was true with the Vector, readjustment of the hash table occurs if there is insufficient space. To add more space, we double the size of the hash table and then simply reinsert each value into the new collection:

```
private void reAdjustTable () {
  Indexed oldTable = elementData;
  elementData = new Vector();
  elementData.setSize(oldTable.size() * 2);
  elementCount = 0;
  for (int i = 0; i < oldTable.size(); i++) {
    Object val = oldTable.elementAt(i);
    if (val != null) addElement(val);
  }
}
```

The method containsElement does not need to check the size of the container but otherwise performs a search similar to that conducted by the addElement method:

```
public boolean containsElement (Object val) {
  int index = Math.abs(val.hashCode()) % element.Data.size();
  while (elementData.elementAt(index) != null) {
    if (val.equals(elementData.elementAt(index)))
      return true;
    if (++index >= elementData.size()) index = 0;
    }
  return false;
}
```

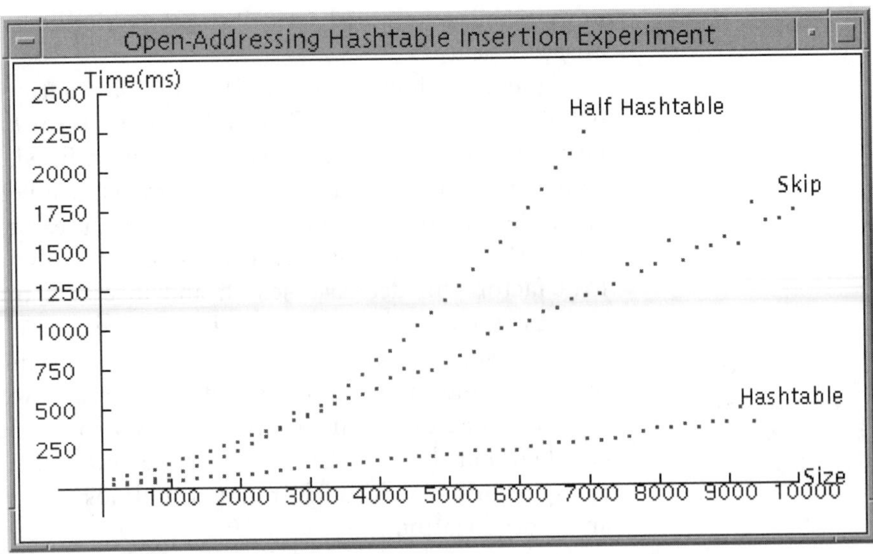

FIGURE 16.6 Execution Timings for Open-Addressing Hash Table Insertion

A fundamental problem with open-address hashing is the difficulty in dealing with the removal of a value. The reason is that the `searchElement` operation uses an empty location to signal that the search can be halted and that the element cannot be found in a container. If the `removeElement` method simply placed a `null` value into the table, certain elements might become inaccessible (see exercise 17). This problem can be solved in two ways. One approach is to simply disallow removal of elements, as we have done here. The second approach is to create a special marker to indicate a space that is free following a removal. The `addElement` method can then reuse this space, whereas the `containsElement` and `removeElement` algorithms must not terminate their loops when they encounter such a value. (This special marker is sometimes called a *tombstone*.)

The efficiency of hash table operations using the open-addressing scheme depends strongly on the range of elements being manipulated and the hash function being used. This can be seen in the timings shown in Figure 16.6. We first add N integers randomly distributed between 0 and N to a `SkipList` and to an `OpenHashtable` declared with table size $N + 13$. Under these circumstances, where collisions are relatively rare, the running time of the hash table is better than that of the list. But next, we change the distribution of integers from being randomly distributed from 0 to N to being randomly distributed between 0 and $N/2$. This has the effect of roughly doubling the number of collisions, as all elements will hash into locations in the first half of the array. The execution time in this case rapidly deteriorates.

EXPERIMENT: EFFECT OF THE PROBING ALGORITHM ON OPEN-ADDRESS HASHING

To what extent is the running time of open-address hashing impacted by the selection of the probing algorithm? Here are some of the probing algorithms that have been proposed:

- *Linear probing* by a constant amount larger than 1—for example, adding 7 to each index position to find the next location. Note that this will require using a modular division operator to find the appropriate location when the values wrap around the end of the container and not simply using 0 as the new location as we do here. (Many authors suggest using a constant that is relatively prime to the size of the table. We explore why in exercise 15.)
- *Quadratic probing* advances the index by squares, as in $n+1$, $n+4$, $n+9$, $n+16$, and so on.
- *Double hashing* hashes the original index value (before we divide by the table size) using a different function. For example, if K is the original hash value (the key) and m the table size, the first hash function can be written as $K \bmod m$. The second hash function might be $(7k \bmod (m-1)) + 1$. Note that this function does not hash into location 0 but will reach all other buckets.
- *Random probing* advances the index by a random number. Because the result must be reproducible, a random-number generator that can be reset to a specific location must be used. In Java, this can be accomplished by using the `setSeed` method in an instance of class `Random`.

Try modifying the probing algorithm and compare the running time to that of the data structure given in the text. Will any of these techniques help with the problem illustrated in the experimental timings when all elements are initially hashed into the first half of the table?

16.5 THE HASHTABLE DATA TYPE

The `Hashtable` data type (Figure 16.7) is built around the idea of buckets and is much simpler than the open-addressing abstraction. As we did with the open-addressing data type, we will implement the `Bag` interface. One question that must be decided in creating a hash table is the type of collection to use for the buckets; in particular, should one use an ordered container or not? An ordered container will permit much faster removal and inclusion tests but is restricted to use with elements that themselves can be ordered. An unordered bucket is more general, but some operations may be slower. We have provided for both ordered and unordered possibilities here. If the user provides a `Comparator` object in the constructor, an ordered collection (a `SkipList`) will be used for the buckets. If no comparator is provided, a simple unordered `LinkedList` will be used.

With the exception of computing the size of the collection and enumeration, the implementation of the `Bag` interface is very simple. Each argument is hashed, using the internal method `bucket`, and the operation passed to the appropriate bucket.

```
public class Hashtable implements Bag {
  protected Bag [ ] buckets;

    // constructors
  public Hashtable (int n) {
    buckets = new Bag[n];
    for (int i = 0; i < n; i++) buckets[i] = new LinkedList();
  }

  public Hashtable (int n, Comparator test) {
    buckets = new Bag[n];
    for (int i = 0; i < n; i++) buckets[i] = new SkipList(test);
  }

    // the Collection interface
  public boolean isEmpty () { return 0 == size(); }

  public int size () {
    int count = 0;
    for (int i = 0; i < buckets.length; i++)
      count += buckets[i].size();
    return count;
  }

  public Enumeration elements () { return new HashtableEnumerator(); }

    // the Bag interface
  public void addElement (Object val)
    { bucket(val).addElement(val); }
  public boolean containsElement (Object val)
    { return bucket(val).containsElement(val); }
  public Object findElement (Object val)
    { return bucket(val).findElement(val); }
  public void removeElement (Object val)
    { bucket(val).removeElement(val); }

    // internal method
  protected Bag bucket (Object val)
    { return buckets[Math.abs(val.hashCode()) % buckets.length];}

  protected class HashtableEnumerator implements Enumeration { ... }
}
```

FIGURE 16.7 Implementation of the Hashtable Data Type

The implementation of the enumeration is slightly tricky. The enumerators from each of the underlying buckets must be merged to form a single new enumeration. An internal variable maintains the index for the bucket being examined, as well as the enumeration associated with that bucket. When the enumeration becomes exhausted, we must first search to see whether any other buckets have a nonempty enumeration.

```
protected class HashtableEnumerator implements Enumeration {
  Enumeration currentEnumeration;
  int index = 0;

  public HashtableEnumerator ()
    { currentEnumeration = buckets[0].elements(); }

  public boolean hasMoreElements () {
    if (currentEnumeration.hasMoreElements()) return true;
    while (++index < buckets.length) {
      currentEnumeration = buckets[index].elements();
      if (currentEnumeration.hasMoreElements()) return true;
    }
    return false;
  }

  public Object nextElement () {
    return currentEnumeration.nextElement(); }
}
```

To evaluate the performance of the hash table abstraction, we again inserted N elements into a container, for increasing values of N. We compared the timings for both `LinkedList` and `SkipList` hash tables with the performance of the simple containers. For both hashing structures, we created a table of size 37. The elements were randomly generated between 0 and 1,000. As can be seen in Figure 16.8, the execution time of the linked-list hash table is close to that of the simple `LinkedList` itself. The execution of the hash table formed using the ordered structure fares slightly better, showing an improvement over the execution time of the

EXPERIMENT: HOW MANY BUCKETS ARE SUFFICIENT?

To what extent is the performance of the sorted hash table dependent on the number of buckets? Try fixing the value N, the number of elements to be inserted, and changing the value B, the number of buckets. Try performing insertions for values of B ranging from 10 up to N. Does the overall time to perform N insertions change in relation to B?

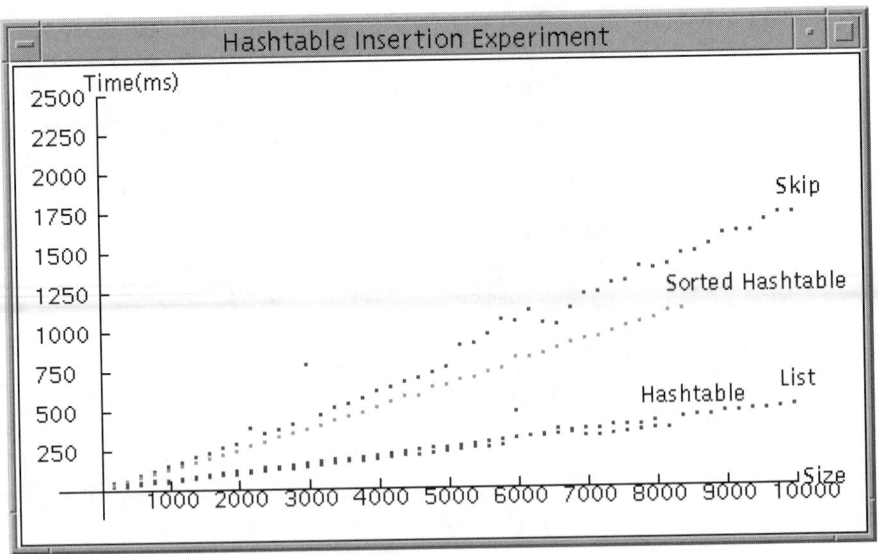

FIGURE 16.8 Execution Timings for Hashtable Insertion

simple `SkipList`. But as with open-address hashing, performance of the `Hashtable` abstraction depends strongly on finding an efficient hashing function that will distribute the elements of a collection uniformly over the set of buckets.

16.6 APPLICATION—RANKING POKER HANDS

A good application of hash tables is a tool to store and to rank a hand of cards in the game of poker. As a first step, we will give the `Card` abstraction a hash function with the property that in a hash table of size 4, cards of the same suit will hash into the same bucket (see exercise 3). Furthermore, we assume that cards implement the `Comparable` interface and that when compared, are ordered based on their rank.

Because we will subsequently want access to the individual buckets, we will make our abstraction, `CardTable`, a subclass of `HashTable`. (Ultimately, we would probably want to hide the `HashTable` interface, exposing only the card-related operations. This could be accomplished by nesting `CardTable` within another class.) For reasons we will describe shortly, as cards are added to a `CardTable`, we will maintain an array that simply keeps track of the ranks of the individual cards:

```
class CardTable extends HashTable {
  private int counts [ ];
```

```
  private Card highCard;

  CardTable () {
    super(new CardComparison()); // order buckets by ranks
    counts = new int[13];
  }

  public void addCard (Card aCard) { // add a card to hand
    counts[aCard.rank()]++; // increment count
    addElement(aCard); // add to hash table
  }
}
```

A poker hand consists of five cards. The *value* of a hand is determined by one of the following combinations, which are listed in order most valuable to least valuable:

- *Straight flush*, the highest possible hand. All five cards are of the same suit and are in sequence. To test for this combination, first test to see whether any bucket has size 5. If any does, then test to see whether the cards are in order. Two straight flushes are compared based on the ranks of their highest cards; for this reason, if a straight flush is found, the high card will be stored in the variable `highCard`.
- *Four of a kind*, or four cards of the same rank. This is easily determined by testing to see whether the `counts` array has value 4 in any location. Once more, two instances of this combination are ordered based on the rank value, so an instance of one of the cards will be stored in the variable `highCard`.
- *Full house*, or three cards of one rank and two cards of another. This can easily be determined by examining the `counts` array, looking for both a 3 and a 2. The high card is an instance of the triple.
- *Flush*, or five cards of the same suit but not all in sequence. A flush will be indicated by any bucket with five cards. The highest card in the flush is stored as the `highCard`.
- *Straight*, or five cards in sequence but not all of the same suit. This can be determined by five consecutive nonzero values in the `counts` array. The high card is the highest card in the straight.
- *Three of a kind* rank under a straight. This can be determined by simply looking for the value 3 in the `counts` array.
- *Two pairs* rank next under three of a kind. The high card is from the highest pair.

- *One pair* beats any hand containing no combination but is lower than any other combination.
- *No-combination hands*, ranked by their highest card.

An algorithm for ordering poker hands can be constructed by first writing a function that tests for each of the named combinations, returning a Boolean `true` value and setting the `highCard` variable if found and a `false` otherwise. Using this, we can encode the `value` of a hand as an integer variable from 0 to 8, with higher hands having the larger integer value:

```
  // return numeric value of a hand
int value() {
  if (straightFlush()) return 8;
  if (fourOfAKind()) return 7;
  .
  .
  .
  if (onePair()) return 1;
  if (findHighest()) return 0;
}
```

We will continue the development of this abstraction and of a poker game based on it as a programming project.

16.7 Chapter Summary

Key Concepts

- Hashing
- Hash functions
- Collisions
- Hash tables
- Buckets
- Asymptotic analysis of hash tables
- Counting sort
- Bucket sorting
- Radix sorting

To *hash* a value means simply to apply a function that transforms a possibly noninteger key into an integer index. This simple idea is the basis for a powerful data structuring technique. If it is possible to discover a function that transforms a set of keys via a one-to-one mapping onto a set of integer indices, it is possible to construct a vector using noninteger keys. More commonly, several keys will map into the same integer index. Two keys that map into the same value are said to have *collided*.

The problem of collisions is handled in one of two ways. Using *open-address hashing,* we probe, or search, for another unused location in the table. The alternative is *hashing using buckets*. Here, we maintain a *bucket* for each possible index. The bucket will hold all elements with the same hash value.

The state of a hash table can be described in part by the *load factor*, which is the number of elements in the table (n) divided by the size of the hash table (m). For open-address hashing, the load factor will always be less than 1, as there can be no more elements than the table size. For hashing using buckets, the load factor can be larger than 1.

The process of hashing permits access and testing operations that potentially are the fastest of any data structure we have considered. Unfortunately, this potential depends on the wise choice of a hash function, maintaining a reasonable load factor, and luck with the key set. A good hash function must uniformly distribute keys over each of the different buckets. Discovering a good hash function is often the most difficult part of using the hash table technique.

For open hash tables, the observed execution times can often be quite good, but as the load factor increases, the execution time deteriorates quickly, becoming $O(n)$ in the worst case. Execution time for hashing using buckets also depends on the load factor. If we assume that elements are uniformly distributed over the buckets and the load factor remains bounded by a constant, the expected performance of insertion and removal operations is constant, or $O(1)$. If any of the many assumptions are unsatisfied, the execution time reduces in the worst case to the execution time of a single individual bucket and will depend on what data structures are used to implement the buckets.

In addition to describing the implementation of a pair of general-purpose data structures, we illustrated the use of hash tables by describing two sorting algorithms. Both of these algorithms use the idea of distributing elements into different buckets, but each uses the buckets for a different purpose.

Further Information

Almost all authors follow Knuth [Knuth 98b] in using the name *open-address hashing*. One exception is Aho et al. [Aho 83], who use the term *closed hashing*. That term is in many ways more descriptive, as the elements are *enclosed* within a single table; nonetheless, the alternative term has never caught on. Aho also uses the term *open hashing* for what we here term hash tables using buckets; again, the alternative name is not found elsewhere.

A novel approach to a spelling checker uses a `BitSet` as a hash table. First, a large dictionary of correctly spelled words is processed, and each word is converted by a hash function into an integer value. The associated bit is then set in the `BitSet`. The resulting bit set is then stored and forms the basis for the spelling checker. To check a document, each word is hashed, using the same hash function, and the bit set is tested. If the associated bit is 0, the word is definitely not in the dictionary and must be misspelled. Of course, if the bit is 1, it may still be misspelled, but at least we have filtered out some of the words.

A topic we do not address is *extendible hashing*, which occurs when the hash table is maintained in memory, but the data items themselves are maintained on disk. Here, the main consideration is to reduce the number of disk accesses.

As with most data structures, the exposition by Knuth [Knuth 98b] provides a wealth of information on hashing. Good analysis of the average-time complexity of hashing is found in Cormen et al. [Cormen 90] and in Gonnet et al. [Gonnet 91]. Other explanations can be found in Aho et al. [Aho 83] and Weiss [Weiss 96]. The merits of various hash functions in a practical setting (namely, compiler symbol tables) is discussed in Aho et al. [Aho 86]. Drozdek [Drozdek 96] describes a number of hashing algorithms written in C++. Langsam [Langsam 96] discusses a variety of techniques that can be used to find a perfect hash function.

Study Questions

1. In what ways does indexing a vector illustrate the principle of *divide and conquer*? In what ways is it different?
2. What is a hash function?
3. What is a hash function collision?
4. What is a perfect hash function?
5. What two steps are generally taken in converting a value into an index for a hash table?
6. What are some techniques commonly used to come up with a hash function? Give an example of each.
7. What are the two general approaches to collision resolution?
8. Under what circumstances does one need to *probe* for a free location when using open-address hashing?
9. What are hash table buckets?
10. Section 16.1.2 suggested that if the `equals` method is overloaded, the `hashCode` method should be as well, to ensure that if two elements are equal, they have the same hash code. What problems could ensue if this is not done?
11. What properties must be satisfied for a hash table to permit constant-time insertion, access, and removal of elements? What is the worst-case time for these operations?
12. Give a short English-language description of the counting sort algorithm.
13. What is the asymptotic complexity of the counting sort algorithm?

14. Why is the counting sort algorithm not considered to be a general-purpose sorting algorithm?
15. Give a short English-language description of the radix sort algorithm.
16. For what type of inputs would it be appropriate to use the radix sorting algorithm?
17. What properties must the buckets have in the radix sort algorithm? What other data structures could be used in place of a `LinkedList`?
18. What is the complexity of the worst-case insertion time for an `OpenHashtable`? Does the result depend on whether a readjustment is performed? What is the complexity of the search for an element?
19. What is the advantage of using buckets in a hash table as opposed to open-address hashing?
20. What are some of the advantages of using a `SkipList` for the buckets in a hash table? What are some disadvantages?
21. Because a hash table requires merely that the underlying buckets satisfy the `Set` interface, we could, in theory, use hash tables themselves for buckets. Would this be a good idea? Explain your answer.

Exercises

1. When Alan wishes to join the circle of six friends, why can't Amy simply increase the size of the vector to 7?
2. Amy's club has grown and now includes the following members:

Abel	Abigail	Abraham	Ada
Aspen	Adrian	Adrienne	Agnes
Albert	Alastair	Angelique	Amina
Amanda	Alexis	Andrew	Alaric
Angela	Anita	Anne	Antonia
Andreas	Arthur	Audrey	

   a. Find what value would be computed by Amy's hash function for each member of the group.
   b. Assume that we use Amy's hash function and assign each member to a bucket by simply dividing the hash value by the number of buckets. Determine how many elements would be assigned to each bucket for a hash table of size 5. Do the same for a hash table of size 11.
3. A playing card is described by two integer quantities: the suit, which can be represented by a number between 0 and 3; and the rank, which

can be represented by a number between 1 and 13. Using these two values, devise a hashing function that has the property that every card hashes to a different numeric value, yet when we take the remainder of this value mod 4, we get back the suit value. (Thus, in a hash table of size 4 using buckets, all cards of the same suit would hash into the same bucket.)

4. In searching for a good hash function over the set of integer elements, one student thought he could use the following:

```
int index = (int) Math.sin(value);
```

   What was wrong with this choice?

5. Can you come up with a perfect hash function for the days of the week? The names of the months? The names of the planets?
6. Examine a set of 12 or more telephone numbers—for example, the numbers belonging to your friends. Suppose that we want to hash into seven different buckets. What would be a good hash function for your set of telephone numbers? Will your function continue to work for new telephone numbers?
7. Experimentally test the birthday paradox. Gather a group of 24 or more people and see whether any two have the same birthday.
8. Most people find the birthday paradox surprising because they confuse it with the following: If n people are in a room, what is the probability that somebody else shares *your* birthday? Ignoring leap years, give the formula for this expression, and evaluate this when n is 24.
9. The counting sort algorithm need not be restricted to integers between 0 and m or even to only positive integers. Explain how to modify the counting sort algorithm so that it takes as argument two integer quantities that represent the largest and smallest values in the set of elements.
10. Building on the previous exercise, write an algorithm that will, in $O(n)$ time, discover both the largest and the smallest value in an array of integer elements. Using this, write a version of `CountingSort` that takes only a single argument, namely, an array of integers.
11. Is the radix sort algorithm shown in Figure 16.4 stable?
12. Explain why the doubly nested loop near the end of the `radixSort` algorithm (Figure 16.4) need not be performed on the final iteration, when the value of `flag` is `false`.
13. When an `OpenHashtable` readjusts its size, why must all elements be reinserted? Why can we not simply move elements to the same index positions in the new table?

14. Suppose that we permitted an `OpenHashtable` to become completely full. Can you think of another technique we could use to avoid an infinite search in the `containsElement` in this case?
15. In the variation on probing in which we advance the index by a constant value *C* that is larger than 1, what is the advantage of selecting a value *C* that is relatively prime with the size of the table? Try experimenting with a table of size 7, and use 3 as the value *C*. Starting from any position, how many elements will be examined before you return to the same position?
16. Show that probing by any constant amount will not reduce the problem caused by clustering, although it may make it more difficult to observe, as clusters are not adjacent. To do this, assume that elements are uniformly inserted into a seven-element hash table, with a linear probe value of 3. Having inserted one element, compute the probability that any of the remaining empty slots will be filled. (You can do this by simply testing the integers 0 to 6 and observing which locations they will hash into. If only one element will hash into a location, the probability is 1/7; if two, the probability is 2/7, and so on.) Explain why the empty locations do not all have equal probability. Place a value in the location with highest probability, and again compute the likelihood that any of the remaining empty slots will be filled. Extrapolate from these observations and explain how clustering will manifest itself in a hash table formed using this technique.
17. This exercise will help explain why we cannot simply place a `null` value into a hash table when an element is removed. Suppose that we create a hash table of four elements and, using Amy's hash function, insert the names *Alfred*, *Alex*, and *Anne*, in that order. Now we remove the name *Alex* and replace it with a `null` value. If we now search for the name *Anne*, what will be the result?
18. It is only if a hash function has certain important characteristics that it would make sense to create a `HashTable` that used instances of `OpenHashTable` as buckets. Explain what features the hash function must have and what problems can arise if the sizes of the two tables are not selected carefully. (*Hint:* What can happen if both tables have the same size? Can this problem develop even if they have different sizes?)

Programming Projects

1. A technique that is a compromise between open-address hashing and chaining is *fixed-sized bucketing*. Using this approach, each hash location is allotted a fixed number of elements, such as five locations.

When the number of locations becomes full, probing is used to find a free cell in the next bucket. Implement a hash table based on this abstraction, and compare the running time to that of the separate chaining algorithm.

2. The only reason for converting the integer values into instances of class `Integer` in the `radixSort` algorithm (Figure 16.4) is that the data structures we have developed cannot hold primitive values, such as integers. Create an implementation of the `Queue` data type that will hold integers (and only integers) directly. Then measure how much this changes the execution speed of the radix sort algorithm.
3. Implement an enumerator for the `OpenHashtable` data abstraction. Remember, your enumerator must skip empty locations and still yield every value found in the container.
4. The conventional way to add the ability to remove elements from an `OpenHashtable` is to create a special element to represent a formerly filled but now emptied location. (This value is sometimes called a *tombstone*.) An `addElement` operation can fill such a position, but the loop in `containsElement` must not be prematurely halted when this value is encountered. Modify the implementation of `OpenHashtable` to incorporate these changes.
5. An alternative algorithm for handling removals from an open-addressing hash table is the following. When a value is to be removed, all elements following the element up to the next `null` location are examined. If any of them would hash into the location being vacated, they are then moved (and the algorithm is applied recursively). Otherwise, a `null` value is inserted. Explain why this avoids the problem described in exercise 17. Why can we stop the search when we encounter a subsequent `null` value? Would this be true if we used a different probing strategy?
6. As we described in Section 16.2, efficient performance of the hash table data structure requires not only a good hash function but also a small load factor. The `Hashtable` data structure in the Java standard library permits the user to specify a maximum load factor and will automatically increase the table size when the number of elements causes this limit to be exceeded. Modify the `Hashtable` data structure to incorporate this feature.
7. One technique for creating a general-purpose sorting algorithm based on hash tables can be described as follows. Given a vector of elements and a `Comparator` algorithm, create an ordered hash table using the comparator, and insert each of the elements into the hash table. The result will be a series of sorted `SkipLists`, but there is no particular

relationship among the various lists. However, using the fact that a `SortedList` can be efficiently merged with another ordered data structure, merge each bucket in turn into one `SortedList`. As a final step, copy the `SortedList` back into the vector. Implement this algorithm, and compare the running time to various other sorting algorithms.

8. Another sorting algorithm is possible if we can find a hashing function that has the properties that all elements that hash into location 0 are strictly smaller than those elements that hash into location 1, which are smaller in turn than those elements that hash into location 2, and so on. For example, if our elements are numbers between 0 and 10,000, dividing an element by 1,000 will have this property. If we can find such a hash table, to order a list of elements, it is sufficient to copy them into an ordered hash table and copy them back out.

   Create an alternative to the wrapper class `Integer`, and change the `hashCode` method as suggested here; then compare the running time of this `BucketSort` algorithm to various other sorting algorithms, such as quick sort.

9. If you have access to a large online dictionary of English words, you can perform the following experiment. Create an `OpenHashtable` that has 50 percent more positions than the number of entries in the dictionary. Insert every element into the dictionary, and modify the `OpenHashtable` algorithm so as to count the number of linear probes that are performed when a word cannot be placed in the initial location. What is the average probe length over all words? Why is this not the same as the average probe length that will be observed when searching for random words?

10. In this project, we will complete the development of the poker hand abstraction begun in Section 16.6 and continue with it to create a simple poker game.

    a. Extend the `CardTable` abstraction so that it satisfies the `Comparable` interface. Two abstractions should be ranked first on their combination value and then, if they represent equal combinations (such as two full houses), on their highest card.
    b. Using the graphical capabilities of the `Card` abstraction, modify the `CardTable` class so that it can display itself on a graphical output.
    c. Using this as a basis, you can then create a simple poker game in which the player competes against the computer. The computer and the player each draw five cards. Only the human player's cards are displayed. The human can designate up to four cards to be replaced, and they are drawn again. The computer will randomly draw between zero and four new cards as well. When this is done, the two hands are displayed, and the winner is shown.

The improvements to this game are obvious and numerous. There are hundreds of different poker games. More difficult is trying to come up with good strategies for the computer player rather than having the computer simply play randomly.

CHAPTER 17

MAPS

In all the containers we have examined up to now, the primary emphasis has been on the values themselves. A Bag, for example, can be used to hold a collection of values and to tell whether a specific value is part of the collection. But for many applications, a value may be the means we use to get hold of other information.

Consider, for example, a dictionary. As we have noted in earlier chapters, the words in a dictionary are sorted, thereby permitting very fast access. But we seldom use a dictionary in the fashion of a Bag. We don't simply ask, Is the word *ptisan* found in this collection? Instead, we use the word as a key to access the further information, namely, a definition (*ptisan:* a medical infusion, such as barley water).

A *map*—sometimes called a *table, search table, dictionary, associative array*, or *associative container*—is a data abstraction optimized for a very specific type of search. Elements are placed in pairs into a map. Each pair consists of a *key* and a *value.* To do a retrieval, the user supplies a key, and the container returns the associated value. Each key identifies one entry; therefore, each key must be unique. However, nothing prevents two different keys from being associated with the same value.

A keyed container can be contrasted with an indexed container, such as an array or a `Vector`. Index values are a form of key; however, they are restricted to being integers and must be drawn from a limited range: usually zero to one less than the number of elements. Because of this restriction and because elements in an array or a `Vector` are stored in a contiguous block, the index can simply be used as part of an array offset calculation. The index need not be stored explicitly as part of the container.

```
public interface Map extends Collection {
  public boolean containsKey (Object key);
  public Object get (Object key);
  public void removeKey (Object key);
  public void set (Object key, Object value);
}
```

FIGURE 17.1 The Map Interface

A key, on the other hand, can be any type of object. For this reason, the container must maintain both the key and its associated value. Like a `LinkedList` or a `Bag`, a `Map` does not limit the number of elements that can be held in the structure.

We are defining a `Map` as an ADT: a container that implements the `Map` interface, shown in Figure 17.1, and that satisfies the properties we associate with the data type.[1] Combining with the methods inherited from the `Collection` interface yields the following list of operations and their properties:

`void set (key, value)` *Pre:* Assumes that the key is comparable with keys already contained in the collection. *Post:* Creates an association between the key and the value. A subsequent retrieval using the same key will yield the value. Overwrites any previous associations that used the same key.

`Object get (key)` *Pre:* Assumes that the key is comparable with keys already contained in the collection. *Post:* If the container currently maintains an association with the given key, the value portion is returned. Otherwise, the method will throw `NoSuchElementException`.

`void removeKey (key)` *Pre:* Assumes that the key is comparable with keys already contained in the collection. *Post:* If the container currently maintains an association with the given key, the association is deleted. If the key does not denote a currently valid association, the method will throw `NoSuchElementException`.

`boolean isEmpty ()` Returns `true` if no associations are currently being maintained by the collection. Does not change the collection.

`int size ()` Returns the number of associations currently being held by the collection. Does not change the collection.

---

1. Our `Map` interface is similar to the `Dictionary` interface in the Java standard library. See Appendix C for further discussion of the differences between our library and the Java standard library.

`boolean containsKey (key)` Indicates whether the collection is currently maintaining an association with the given key. Does not change the collection.

`Enumeration elements ()` Returns an `Enumeration` of the keys being held in the collection. The order in which elements appear is undefined. Does not change the collection.

17.1 Example Programs

We will present three example programs that illustrate the use of the `Map` data type.

17.1.1 Silly-Sentence Generation, Revisited

In Chapter 6, we presented a program that would generate a sequence of nonsense English sentences. By using a map to represent a more complex grammar, we can greatly improve the power of this program. A typical context-free grammar is shown in Figure 17.2. The left column is a syntactic category, whereas the right column is a list of possible rewritings that match the category. We can encode a grammar as a `Map`, using the category as the key and a `Vector` containing a `LinkedList` of words as the value.[2]

Let us see how this grammar can generate the sentence "my sister loves eating with the man next door." A graphical representation, called a *parse tree*, is shown in Figure 17.3. Our beginning symbol for the grammar is the syntactic category SENTENCE. One of the four possible sentence rewritings is selected randomly. In this case, it is the sentence of the form PERSON DOES SOMETHING. Each of the terms in this line will be recursively tested in turn. For PERSON, our grammar selects (again, choosing randomly) the text "my sister." For DOES, the text "loves" is chosen, and for SOMETHING, the text "ACTIVITY with PERSON" is chosen. One of the possibilities for ACTIVITY is the text "eating," whereas for PERSON, the string "the man next door" can be used.

We will read the grammar from an input file. Each line of the file begins with one word representing the category; the rest of the line is the remainder of the grammar rule. Internally, the grammar will be stored in a map. The key to the map will be the category, whereas the value will, as we have

2. We use a `Vector` for the value so that we can have multiple entries in our collection under the same category. In effect, we are creating a *multimap*, a data abstraction we develop in more detail in the next section and in programming project 8.

SENTENCE	PERSON DOES SOMETHING PERSON thinks that I am PROPERTY I DO SOMETHING you think that I am PROPERTY
ACTIVITY	dancing eating sleeping
OBJECT	PERSON life my computer my friends
DO	hate am jealous of love
DOES	hates loves
PERSON	my sister my father my girl friend the man next door
PROPERTY	creative intelligent
SOMETHING	ACTIVITY ACTIVITY with PERSON OBJECT

FIGURE 17.2 Grammar for Silly Sentences

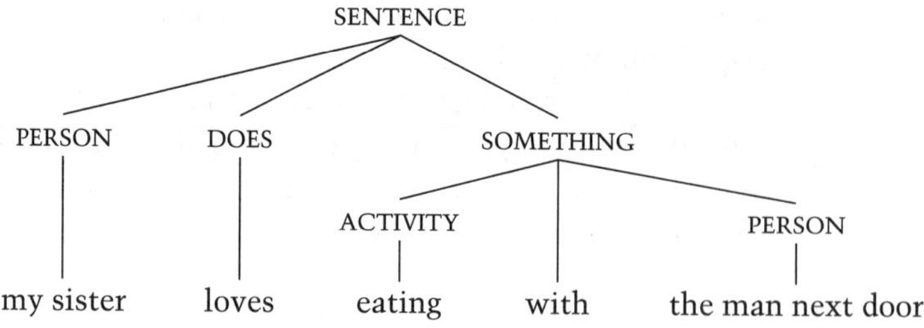

FIGURE 17.3 A Typical Parse Tree

noted already, be a `Vector` of `LinkedLists`. Each entry in the `Vector` will be a different rule, and each rule is represented as a list of words.

The procedure that reads this input grammar and translates it into the internal form is found in the constructor for the class `SillySentence2`:

```
import java.io.*;
import java.util.*;
import jds.Map;
import jds.collection.Vector;
import jds.collection.MapAdapter;
import jds.collection.LinkedList;

class SillySentence2 {
  public SillySentence2 (BufferedReader input) throws IOException {
    while (true) {
      String text = input.readLine();
      if (text == null) return;
      Enumeration e = new StringTokenizer(text);
      LinkedList rule = new LinkedList();
      while (e.hasMoreElements())
        rule.addLast(e.nextElement());
      String category = (String) rule.getFirst();
      rule.removeFirst();
      if (! rules.containsKey(category))
        rules.set(category, new Vector());
      Vector v = (Vector) rules.get(category);
      v.addLast(rule);
    }
  }

  protected Map rules = new MapAdapter(new LinkedList());
  .
  .
  .
}
```

StringTokenizer

The Java library class `StringTokenizer` is the string version of the I/O class `StreamTokenizer` that we encountered in Chapter 16. A `String-Tokenizer` reads from a string and creates an `Enumeration`. Each entry in the enumeration is an individual word from the string. Words are defined as any run of characters separated by *delimiter characters*, such as spaces and tabs.

The input is read from a `BufferedReader`, which is passed as argument to the constructor. This abstraction can read a file line by line, returning `null` on end of input. Each line is assumed to be a different grammar rule. The rule is broken into parts, using a `StringTokenizer`. Each word in the rule is then placed into a linked list. The first word in this list is taken to be the category for the rule. If this is the first rule with the given category, a new entry is made in the map; otherwise, a `Vector` already exists under this category. The rule is added as a new entry in the `Vector`.

The heart of the generation of sentences is a simple recursive procedure that takes as input a word and returns a silly sentence generated from the word. The procedure checks to see whether the given word is a category name. If not, it is simply returned, padded with a little extra space. If it is a category name, a randomly selected element of the `Vector` is chosen. Each part of the selected grammar rule is then independently processed, as it could potentially expand further:

```
public String generateString (String start) {
  if (rules.containsKey(start)) {
    Vector v = (Vector) rules.get(start);
    int i = (int) (v.size() * Math.random());
    LinkedList rule = (LinkedList) v.elementAt(i);
    String result = "";
```

A Collection of Containers

Although it is a short program, the silly-sentence generator uses many of the data structures we have explored in earlier chapters. The following drawing captures the most significant:

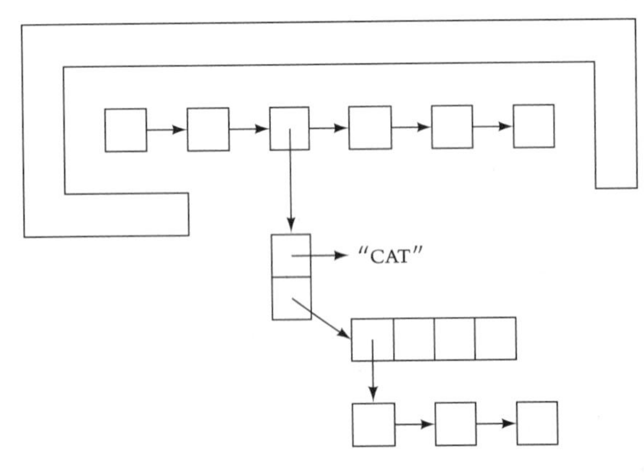

The `Map`, implemented as a `MapAdapter`, is a wrapper that surrounds a `LinkedList`. As we will see, the elements held by the `LinkedList` are each instances of `Association`, which is a small class used to hold a key/value pair. The key, in this case, is a string. The value is a `Vector`, each element of which is another `LinkedList` of words.

```
    Enumeration e = rule.elements();
    while (e.hasMoreElements())
      result = result + generateString((String) e.nextElement());
    return result;

  }
  return start + " "; // add padding at end
}
```

A main method to test our program is written as follows:

```
public static void main (String [ ] args) {
  try {
    FileReader f1 = new FileReader(args[0]);
    SillySentence2 grammar = new SillySentence2(
      new BufferedReader(f1));
    System.out.println(grammar.generateString("SENTENCE"));
  } catch (Exception e) { System.err.println("got exception" + e); }
}
```

The following table illustrates the sequence of recursive calls invoked in producing the sentence "my sister loves eating with the man next door." The first column represents the argument to the procedure `generateString`. The second column is the level of recursive call. The final column is the item randomly selected as matching the key, if the first argument is an index into the table; if the item in the first column is not an index into the table, it is simply printed.

Word	**Level**	**Selection**
SENTENCE	1	PERSON DOES SOMETHING
PERSON	2	my sister
my sister	3	*not in table, return:* my sister
DOES	2	loves
loves	3	*not in table, return:* loves
SOMETHING	2	ACTIVITY with PERSON
ACTIVITY	3	eating
eating	4	*not in table, return:* eating
with	4	*not in table, return:* with
PERSON	4	the man next door
the man . . .	5	*not in table, return:* the man next door

The following illustrates some of the sentences that can be generated in this fashion:

my father hates dancing with my father
my sister loves eating with the man next door
I love my computer
I hate life
my sister thinks that I am intelligent
the man next door thinks that I am creative
my father thinks that I am intelligent
the man next door loves dancing
I love sleeping with my girl friend
you think that I am creative

17.1.2 An Address Database

Our second example program is a simple address database. Figure 17.4 is a screen shot for this application. The main panel is divided into two text areas: a small one-line text box at the top, used for entering the keys under which a database entry is stored, and a larger multiline text area below that is used to enter the information stored with the key. To the right is a bank of four buttons. One button is used to search the database for an existing entry that matches the key. Another button is used to enter a new key/value pair into the database. A third button will save the database on disk, and the last button is used to quit the application.

As with most of the graphical applications we have developed in this book, the majority of the code creates the graphical components and sets

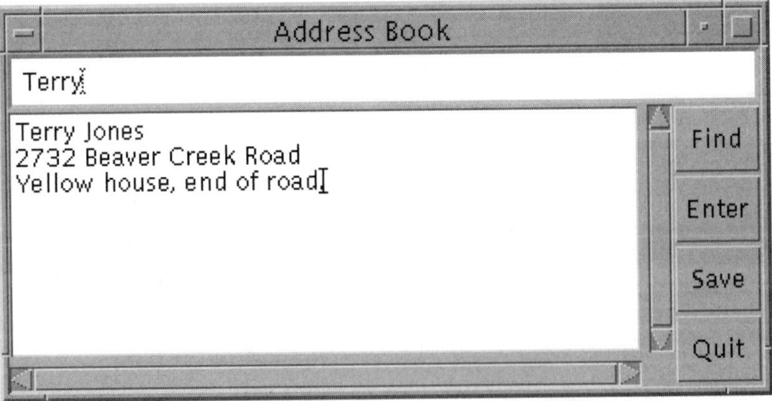

FIGURE 17.4 Screen Shot of the Address Database Application

them in place. The constructor for the class AddressBook places the two text areas in the north and center parts of the window; on the east side, a new panel with four positions is created and filled with the button objects:

```
class AddressBook extends Frame {
  public static void main (String [ ] args)
    { AddressBook world = new AddressBook(); world.show(); }

  public AddressBook () {
      // set window characteristics
    setSize(400, 200);
    setTitle("Address Book");
      // create our GUI
    add("North", keyBox);
    add("Center", valueBox);
    Panel buttonPanel = new Panel();
    buttonPanel.setLayout(new GridLayout(4, 1));
    add("East", buttonPanel);
    buttonPanel.add(new FindButton());
    buttonPanel.add(new EnterButton());
    buttonPanel.add(new SaveButton());
    buttonPanel.add(new QuitButton());
      // initialize the database
    try {
      FileInputStream fs = new FileInputStream("addresses");
      ObjectInputStream fi = new ObjectInputStream(fs);
      database = (Map) fi.readObject();
    } catch(IOException e) {
      // do nothing
    } catch (ClassNotFoundException e) {
      valueBox.setText("received file conversion error"+ e);
    }
  }

  private TextField keyBox = new TextField();
  private TextArea valueBox = new TextArea();
  private Map database = new MapAdapter(new LinkedList());

  private class FindButton extends ButtonAdapter { ... }
  private class EnterButton extends ButtonAdapter { ... }
  private class SaveButton extends ButtonAdapter { ... }
  private class QuitButton extends ButtonAdapter { ... }
}
```

The information for the database will be kept in a variable of type Map named database. As with the silly-sentence-generation program, a MapAdapter built on top of a LinkedList is being used as the implementation of the Map interface. (We will examine the MapAdapter in more detail in Section 17.2.)

Before we discuss the buttons, let us deal with the last part of the initialization performed by the constructor. This section tries to read entries from a file named addresses. If this file does not exist, an IOException will be raised and will be caught by the try block. Because the catch section of the try block has no action, the program will continue with an empty database. If the file is opened, it is converted first into a FileInputStream and then into an ObjectInputStream. The class ObjectInputStream permits objects to be saved and restored. In this fashion, the entire database can be read in from the file with a single invocation of the method readObject.

The four buttons are each created by subclassing from ButtonAdapter. The Find button, when clicked, reads the current contents of the key text box and searches the database. If an entry is found, it is printed in the value text box; otherwise, an error message is produced:

```
private class FindButton extends ButtonAdapter {
  public FindButton () { super("Find"); }
  public void pressed () {
    String key = keyBox.getText();
    if (database.containsKey(key))
      valueBox.setText((String) database.get(key));
```

SAVING AND RESTORING CONTAINER CONTENTS

Because the effort to save and to restore the contents of our address database from a file requires only a few lines of code, it is easy to overlook their significance. From the very beginning, we have been careful to declare all our container abstractions as subclasses of the Java library class Serializable. Any serializable object—and that includes our *entire* address database—can be written to an ObjectOutputStream with just a single command:

```
fo.writeObject(database);
```

The only restriction is that the contents of the containers—both keys and values—must themselves be serializable. All the standard Java objects have this property.

Similarly, to read a serializable object from an ObjectInputStream requires only a single command:

```
database = (Map) fi.readObject();
```

Note that a *cast* must be used to convert the result into the appropriate type. All the containers we have developed can be stored using this technique.

```
      else
        valueBox.setText("no entry");
    }
}
```

The Enter button is simpler. It merely reads the contents of the two text boxes and enters them into the database. The key field is then erased, so as to give the user a visual cue that the task has been completed:

```
private class EnterButton extends ButtonAdapter {
  public EnterButton () { super("Enter"); }
  public void pressed () {
    database.set(keyBox.getText(), valueBox.getText());
    keyBox.setText("");
  }
}
```

The Save button creates the file that will subsequently be read by the constructor the next time the application is started. A FileOutputStream is opened and converted into an ObjectOutputStream. The content of the database is then written to the object output stream and a visual cue provided to reassure the user that the task has been performed:

```
private class SaveButton extends ButtonAdapter {
  public SaveButton () { super("Save"); }
  public void pressed () {
    try {
      FileOutputStream fs = new FileOutputStream("addresses");
      ObjectOutputStream fo = new ObjectOutputStream(fs);
      fo.writeObject(database);
      valueBox.setText("database saved");
    } catch (IOException e) { valueBox.setText("got IO Error " + e); }
  }
}
```

The Quit button simply halts the application:

```
private class QuitButton extends ButtonAdapter {
  public QuitButton () { super("Quit"); }
  public void pressed () { System.exit(0); }
}
```

17.1.3 A Concordance

Our final example program to illustrate the use of the Map data type will be a concordance. A concordance lists the words in a text alphabetically and indicates the line numbers on which each word occurs. The data elements are maintained in the concordance by a MultiMap, a data structure described by programming project 8 at the end of the chapter. A `MultiMap` is similar to a `Map` but permits multiple entries using the same key. This data structure is used for this problem because the same word will often appear on multiple lines; indeed, discovering such connections is one of the primary purposes of a concordance.

Our implementation of a concordance is as follows:

```
class Concordance {
  private MultiMap dict = new MultiMap(new StringCompare());

  public void readLines (BufferedReader input) throws IOException {
    String delims = " \t\n.,!?;:";
    for (int line = 1; true; line++ ) {
      String text = input.readLine();
      Integer iline = new Integer(line);
      if (text == null) return;
      text = text.toLowerCase();
      Enumeration e = new StringTokenizer(text, delims);
      while (e.hasMoreElements()) {
         String word = (String) e.nextElement();
         if (! dict.contains(word, iline))
          dict.set(word, iline);
      }
    }
  }

  public void generateOutput (PrintStream output) {
    Enumeration e = dict.elements();
    while (e.hasMoreElements() ) {
      String word = (String) e.nextElement();
      Enumeration f = (Enumeration) dict.get(word);
      output.print(word + ": ");
      while (f.hasMoreElements())
        output.print(f.nextElement() + " ");
      output.println(" ");
    }
  }
}
```

The concordance has two methods: one to read lines from an input and to create the concordance and the other to print the concordance entries.

As with the silly-sentence program, the method `readLines` uses a `BufferedReader` as the input source. An integer variable counts the line numbers as they are read. Once a line is read, it is converted to lowercase by the `String` method `toLowerCase`. Then the line is split into individual words, using a `StringTokenizer`. Each word is then inserted into the dictionary.

Output is produced by using the method `generateOutput`. An outer loop iterates over the dictionary keys, which are the individual words. An inner loop iterates over entries associated with the word: the line numbers on which the word was found.

To test our concordance, we create a buffered reader from the standard input stream, as follows:

```
public static void main (String [ ] args) {
  Concordance cd = new Concordance();
  try {
    cd.readLines(new  BufferedReader(new InputStreamReader(System.in)));
  } catch(IOException e) { System.err.println("received IO error " + e);}
  cd.generateOutput(System.out);
}
```

Suppose, for example, that the input was the text

```
It was the best of times,
it was the worst of times.
```

The output, from best to worst, would be

```
best: 1
it: 1 2
of: 1 2
the: 1 2
times: 1 2
was: 1 2
worst: 2
```

17.2 An Implementation

We will present one implementation of the `Map` interface and will discuss various others in the programming exercises at the end of the chapter. The implementation we will discuss is an *adapter* built on top of a container that supports the `Bag` interface. A variety of effects can be produced by using different data structures as the underlying container.

The fundamental idea of the `MapAdapter` is that a `Map` can be managed as a set of key/value pairs, which will be held as instances of an inner class named `Association`. An `Association` holds a key and a value in data fields declared simply as class `Object`. The hash code for an association is determined entirely by the hash code for the key (to more easily permit maps to be constructed using the hash table techniques of Chapter 16). Similarly, equality and comparison between two associations are determined entirely by the keys, not by the associated values. The comparison test in the latter is determined by a `Comparator` object, named `test`, held in the outer class:

```
public class MapAdapter implements Map {
  protected Bag elementData;
  protected Comparator test;
.
.
.
  protected class Association implements Comparable {
    public Object key;
    public Object value;

    Association (Object k, Object v) {key = k; value = v; }

    public int hashCode () { return key.hashCode(); }

    public boolean equals (Object testElement) {
      Association pair = (Association) testElement;
      return key.equals(pair.key);
    }

    public int compareTo (Object testElement) {
      Association pair = (Association) testElement;
      return test.compare(key, pair.key);
    }
  }
}
```

After defining the class `Association`, the implementation of the `MapAdapter` is relatively easy. The constructor for the class takes an underlying set and, optionally, a comparator to be used in ordering the keys:

```
public class MapAdapter implements Map {
  protected Bag elementData;
  protected Comparator test;

    // constructors
  public MapAdapter (Bag aCollection)
    { elementData = aCollection; test = new DefaultComparator(); }
  public MapAdapter (Bag aCollection, Comparator t)
    { elementData = aCollection; test = t; }
  .
  .
  .
}
```

Specifying the Comparator

A subtle feature of the MapAdapter is the observation that the comparator for elements must be specified as part of the declaration of the Map, not as part of the declaration of the underlying Bag. Suppose, for example, that we want to use an AVLTree as the container and have defined a comparator named KeyCompare for ordering the keys. We do not declare the map as follows:

```
Map newMap = new MapAdapter
  (new AVLTree(new KeyCompare())); // error
```

Rather, the comparator is given directly to the Map:

```
Map newMap = new MapAdapter(new AVLTree(),
                  new KeyCompare());//right
```

The reason is that the AVLTree will be maintaining a collection of Association values, not the elements in the map. The comparator for the AVLTree will be the one specified for associations, which in turn will make use of the comparator for the keys. Of course, if the underlying Bag is unordered, there is no need to specify a comparator.

With the exception of enumeration, the Collection interface is easily built out of the methods provided by the underlying Bag:

```
  // Collection interface
public boolean isEmpty () { return elementData.isEmpty(); }
public int size () { return elementData.size(); }
public Enumeration elements ()
  { return new MapEnumerator(elementData.elements()); }
```

The containsKey method, get, and removeKey are all implemented by simply forming a new Association and then invoking commands on the underlying container:

```
public boolean containsKey (Object key) {
  Association dummy = new Association(key, null);
  return elementData.containsElement(dummy);
}

public Object get (Object key) {
  Association dummy = new Association(key, null);
  Association pair = (Association) elementData.findElement(dummy);
  return pair.value;
}

public void removeKey (Object key) {
  Association dummy = new Association(key, null);
  elementData.removeElement(dummy);
}
```

It is here that the curious implementation of the equals and compareTo methods for class Association becomes relevant. Take, for example, the removal method. For a Bag, the removeElement method will remove any element that tests equal to the argument, whether or not they are the same object. (This is the distinction between object *equality* and object *identity* that we discussed back in Chapter 2.) Because two Associations are equal if they have the same key, the effect of forming a new Association with a null value and then trying to remove this element will be to remove any Association with the same key.

The set method is slightly more subtle. Keys must be unique; that is, two entries can never have the same key. There are, accordingly, two cases to consider in the set method: The key may already exist, or it may not. As we did with the get operator, we can use the method containsElement to search for an existing association with the given key. If one exists, we use findElement to retrieve it, and we modify the value field. If no association with the given key exists, a new entry is inserted into the collection:

```
public void set (Object key, Object newValue) {
  Association dummy = new Association(key, newValue);
  if (elementData.containsElement(dummy)) {
    Association pair = (Association) elementData.findElement(dummy);
    pair.value = newValue;
  } else
    elementData.addElement(dummy);
}
```

The enumerator for the MapAdapter is constructed on top of the enumerator provided for the underlying Bag. Only the nextElement method is changed, so as to return the key portion of the association:

```
protected class MapEnumerator implements Enumeration {
  private Enumeration elementEnumeration;

  MapEnumerator (Enumeration ed) { elementEnumeration = ed; }

  public boolean hasMoreElements ()
    { return elementEnumeration.hasMoreElements(); }

  public Object nextElement () {
    Association pair = (Association) elementEnumeration.nextElement();
    return pair.key;
  }
}
```

The MapAdapter can be built on top of any container that supports the Bag interface. In earlier chapters, we examined several containers that satisfy this constraint. The running time for the various operations specified by the Map interface is determined by the running time of the underlying container. The following chart summarizes the containers we have seen that can be used with a MapAdapter and their associated asymptotic execution times.

	get	set	containsKey	removeKey
LinkedList	$O(n)$	$O(n)$	$O(n)$	$O(n)$
SortedVector	$O(\log n)$	$O(n)$	$O(\log n)$	$O(n)$
SortedList	$O(n)$	$O(n)$	$O(n)$	$O(n)$
SkipList	$O(\log n)$	$O(\log n)$	$O(\log n)$	$O(\log n)$
AVLTree	$O(\log n)$	$O(\log n)$	$O(\log n)$	$O(\log n)$
OpenHashtable	$O(1)$	$O(1)$	$O(1)$	*NA*
Hashtable	$O(1)$	$O(1)$	$O(1)$	$O(1)$

The simplest container supporting the Bag interface is the LinkedList. However, the performance of a LinkedList on all operations is linear. The SortedVector can improve the speed of those operations that do not involve adding or removing an element; however, this container is applicable only if the elements can be ordered. The MapAdapter itself does not require ordering and can be used with unordered elements as long as an unordered container, such as a LinkedList or a Hashtable, is used. The SortedList is generally no faster than a simple LinkedList; however, a SkipList or an AVLTree is considerably faster. But this speed is once again purchased at the cost of requiring elements to be ordered. The two hash table–based collections are potentially the fastest and do not require ordered elements. However, their effectiveness is very much influenced by the quality of the hash function used on the keys, the size of the hash table, and the load factor.

This table permits us to once again emphasize that it is important to understand the mix of operations required for any particular application and to select a data structure appropriately. For example, suppose that one application involves creating a large collection all at one time and that thereafter, the program will test to see whether elements are in the collection, but no new elements will be added. Both a SortedVector and a SkipList will provide a good $O(\log n)$ search mechanism, but in practice, the SortedVector is slightly faster (see Figure 17.5). However, if the problem involves removing elements from the container, the $O(n)$ removal operation from the SortedVector starts to dominate the execution time, and the SkipList performance is preferable (Figure 17.6).

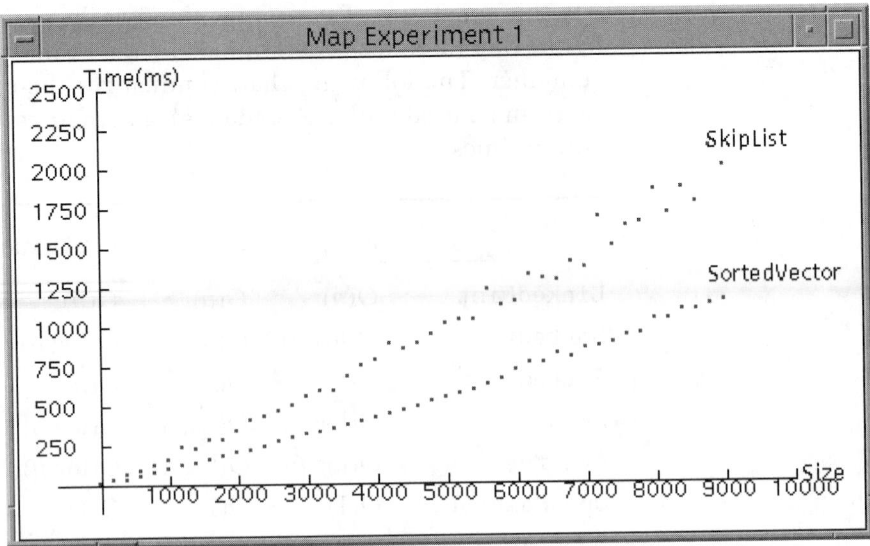

FIGURE 17.5 Comparison of Execution Times for `containsKey` Test

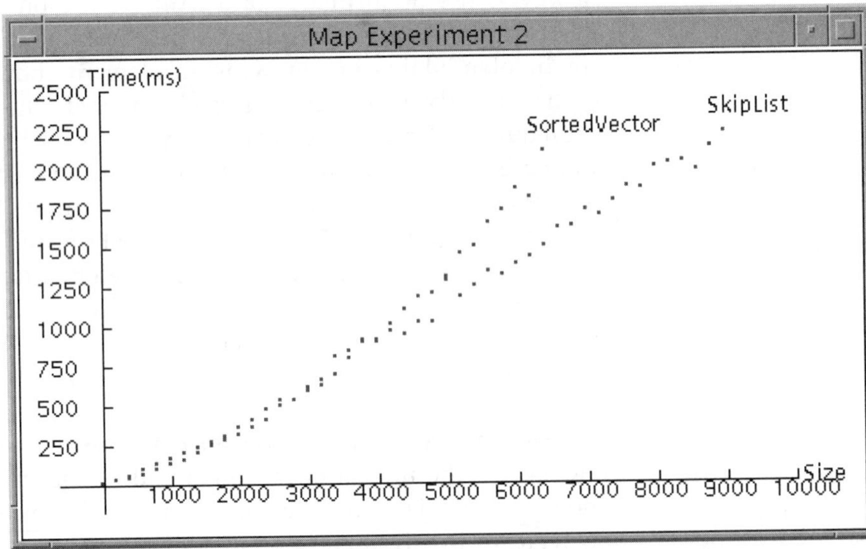

FIGURE 17.6 Execution Times for `containsKey` and `removeKey` Combined

EXPERIMENT: VERIFY EXECUTION TIMINGS

Verify that the asymptotic runtimes described in the table match the execution times. Do this by designing an experiment that will insert into a map new elements with keys randomly generated between 0 and n, for ever larger values of n. Compare the execution timings for a linked list, a skip list, and a hash table. Do the results match your expectations? What happens if the size of the hash table is reduced? Try making it $n/2$, then $n/10$. What if the size of the hash table is held constant? Try the experiment with a table size of 100. What happens if n becomes much larger than this value?

17.3 SEARCHING PROBLEMS AND MAPS

The map concept has many important variations. We will explain here only a few of the more significant ones. We have already discussed the concept of a *multimap*, a maplike structure that permits more than one entry for each key. We will explore the implementation of this data type in one of the programming projects at the end of this chapter.

In a later chapter, we describe the `SparseVector` data type. This structure is implemented in the same manner as the `MapAdapter` but uses integer keys and implements the `Indexed` interface. Unlike a `Vector`, the `SparseVector` maintains only those index positions that have a nonempty value. Thus, this structure is useful when relatively few nonempty values are scattered over a large range.

One way to view a map is as a tool to reduce the work needed to perform a search over a collection of keys. For example, we could easily have developed the address database abstraction using earlier data structures, by including a feature to search for a given name or address. However, searching for the name would have potentially required accessing every entry in the database. Using a map eliminates the need to explicitly iterate through the collection to perform a search. (The search may still be performed, but it is hidden behind the `Map` interface.) However, this is true only because we have forced the user to access the records using the key terms. If the user needs to search in another fashion, such as finding the name of the person who lives on Beaver Creek Road, we are back to performing a record-by-record search.

We can, however, use the fact that a map is a type of index into the records as a key insight to speed up several forms of search. For example, consider the concordance application described in Section 17.1.3. Suppose that we have not one but three different words and we want to find the lines on which all three words appear. To discover this, we can simply take the three lists of lines given by the map, using as the key each individual word, and then form the *intersection* of these three lists. (Forming the intersection of lists was discussed in Chapter 9.) The list that results from the intersection is the list of lines on which all the selected words appear.

Let us apply this idea to another problem domain. Suppose that you want to maintain a database of recipes used in cooking and wish to permit users to search the database for recipes that use specific ingredients. One technique would be to have each ingredient serve as a key in a `MultiMap` and to store all the recipes that use that ingredient in the list associated with the key. Each recipe will, of course, be found in as many lists as the number of different ingredients.

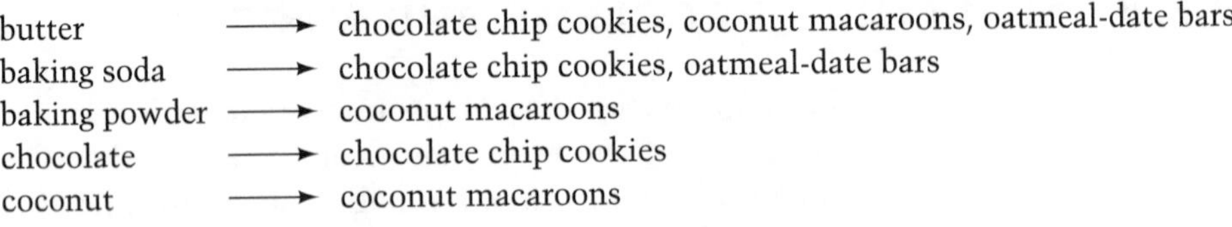

When a new recipe is added to the collection, the database should be updated so that the recipe is listed under each different ingredient. Now, to provide the searching capability we desire, we can use the same technique as we did with the concordance. We consider the lists of recipes for each ingredient in turn and form the intersection of each of these lists. The result will be the list of all recipes that contain all the given ingredients.

Oftentimes, it is useful to have one database of information organized in two or more different ways. For example, a catalog for a collection of books might be organized by both author and title. This could be accomplished by having two separate maps for the same set of records. One map would be indexed by author, the second by words in the title.

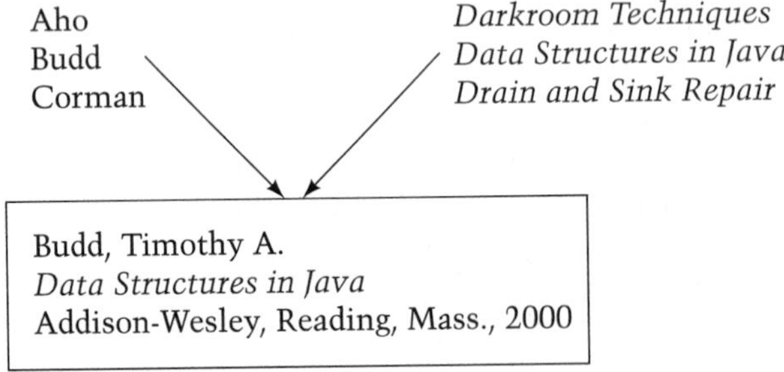

Up to this point, we have discussed searching for an exact match. However, combining a map with various other types of searchable data structures provides even more flexibility. For example, one advantage of a list of numbers stored in an ordered vector is that a binary search algorithm can find all the entries in a given range, not simply whether an exact match occurs (see exercise 4 in Chapter 7).

Imagine, for example, that we have a database of U.S. cities. Each record stores the city and state and the population. It might be reasonable to maintain three different index structures, all pointing to the same records: one map keyed by the city name, one map keyed by the state name, and an ordered vector keyed by the population. Using this, one could then quickly ask combined queries, such as What are all the cities in Oregon with populations between 12,000 and 25,000? The range query is answered by searching the ordered vector, using binary search, then intersecting the results with the list obtained by means of the state name.

17.4 Chapter Summary

Key Concepts

- Map and multimap
- Association
- `MapAdapter`

Whereas `Bags`, `Stacks`, `Queues`, and the other data types we have examined up to this point all emphasize a collection of individual values, a `Map` is an ADT designed to maintain pairs consisting of a key and a value. Entries are placed into a map as a key and an associated value. To recover a value, the user provides the key.

In this chapter, we have explored one implementation technique that can be used in the realization of the `Map` abstraction, although there are many others. By using an `Association` as an intermediary value, a `Map` can be constructed using any of the many types of data structures that are realizations of the `Bag` ADT. The characteristics of the various `Bag` implementations then lead naturally to different types of `Maps`. For example, a sorted `Bag`, such as a `SkipList` or an `AVLTree`, can have very fast insertion and removal times but requires the ability to compare keys against one another. A `HashTable` need not require comparisons but does require a hash function that will distribute keys uniformly over a range of integer values. If neither requirement can be satisfied, a `Map` can be constructed using a simple `LinkedList`, which imposes no requirements other than the ability to compare elements for equality, but it also yields a relatively slow $O(n)$ performance for most operations.

Further Information

Many textbooks (for example, Berman [Berman 97]) use the term *table* to describe the data abstraction we have examined in this chapter. However, that term is easily confused with the `Hashtable` abstraction described in Chapter 16. Although they are a common tool used to implement maps, hash tables are by no means the only technique. By separating the two concepts, we make it easier for you to understand the range of possibilities.

The `Hashtable` data abstraction in the Java standard library is a form of `Map` implemented using a hash table.

Compilers and other system software often use a map to create a *symbol table.* A symbol table will link the names of identifiers to various attributes associated with the identifier, such as type and location. Further information on this particular use can be found in [Aho 86].

Dictionaries and tables, found in a number of other programming languages, are one of the fundamental data structures in the string processing language SNOBOL [Griswold 71] and in the more recent language, Icon, by the same author [Griswold 90]. The dictionary type is a basic part of the Smalltalk standard library [Goldberg 83].

The silly-sentence generators are adapted from an example *ABC* program written by Steven Pemberton [Geurts 85]. A version written in C++ can be found in my C++ data structures textbook [Budd 98].

Study Questions

1. What are the characteristics of a `Map`?
2. How is a `Map` similar to a `Vector`? How is it different?
3. In the silly-sentence program, what do the map keys represent? What data structures are used to store the value associated with each key?
4. What ability is provided by the class `BufferedReader` that is not provided by a simple `InputStream` or a `Reader`?
5. What task is being performed by a `StringTokenizer`?
6. Explain how the example grammar will generate the sentence "the man next door hates my computer."
7. Give three more example sentences that could be generated by the grammar in Figure 17.2.
8. A map is used as data repository for the address database application. Where do the keys for this map come from?
9. What facility is provided by an `ObjectStream`? How are objects written to an `ObjectStream`? How are they read?
10. What is the purpose of a concordance?
11. Why is it more appropriate to use a `MultiMap` with a concordance than a simple `Map`?
12. How is the example implementation of the `Map` data type tied to the implementation of the `Bag` data type?
13. What is an `Association`?

14. Why is it important that comparisons between two objects of type Association be based only on their keys?
15. How does the MapAdapter ensure that no two entries have the same key?
16. What would be a reason for using a Bag abstraction with a relatively slow access time, such as a LinkedList, as a basis for a MapAdapter?
17. Why might you want to have a collection of records indexed by two or more different Maps?

Exercises

1. Explain how a Map could be used to solve Amy's club database problem described in Section 16.1.
2. The method containsKey can be used to determine whether a map has an entry with a given key. How would you determine whether any entry has a given value? What is the complexity of your procedure?
3. Extend the grammar for the silly-sentence-generation program so that it generates questions as well as statements.
4. Draw parse trees for the following sentences.
   a. I am jealous of my computer
   b. the man next door thinks that I am intelligent
   c. I am jealous of my girl friend with my sister
   d. my sister loves my father
5. Assuming that the random-number generator selects all possibilities with equal probability, what is the probability of the program on any one run producing the sentence "I love my computer"?
6. Complete the following table by indicating which times are *always* achieved, are *worst-case* figures, or are *expected* bounds.

	get	set	containsKey	removeKey
LinkedList	$O(n)$	$O(n)$	$O(n)$	$O(n)$
SortedVector	$O(\log n)$	$O(n)$	$O(\log n)$	$O(n)$
SortedList	$O(n)$	$O(n)$	$O(n)$	$O(n)$
SkipList	$O(\log n)$	$O(\log n)$	$O(\log n)$	$O(\log n)$
AVLTree	$O(\log n)$	$O(\log n)$	$O(\log n)$	$O(\log n)$
OpenHashtable	$O(1)$	$O(1)$	$O(1)$	*NA*
Hashtable	$O(1)$	$O(1)$	$O(1)$	$O(1)$

7. Assume that the `MapAdapter` for the address database application has only the one entry shown in Figure 17.4. Draw a representation of the internal structure for the `Map`, including nodes in the underlying linked list, and all other data values.
8. Repeat the previous problem, assuming that a `SortedVector` is used for the underlying set.
9. Modify the concordance class by adding a method that will print the entries in the concordance in order of their frequency of use, with words used most frequently first and words used least frequently last. Show how you can use a specially built `Comparison` object in conjunction with a different `Map` data abstraction to make this task easier.
10. Concordances often filter out common words, such as "the" or "and." Suppose that you have a file of common words, which is then read into a `set`. Modify the concordance program so that it checks words from this set and if found does not enter them into the database.

Programming Projects

1. Rewrite the silly-sentence program so that it will generate ten example sentences instead of just one sentence.
2. Create a class that takes a `Map` as argument to the constructor, satisfies the `Enumeration` protocol, and returns as each entry in the enumeration a *value* (not a key) from the map.
3. In programming project 5 in Chapter 6, we described the `Iterator` interface. Explain how the class `MapIterator` would need to be changed so as to support this interface. What problems are caused by the introduction of the `remove` method?
4. Here are some improvements we could make to the address database program.
   a. Add a button that, when clicked, will display in the lower text box a list of all the keys stored in the database.
   b. Add the ability to save and to restore from multiple databases. Do this by changing the effect of the `Save` button so that if the key text box is nonempty, the text found there is used as the name of the file under which the contents will be saved. Then add a new button, `Load`, that will read the key text box and load the database from the file stored under the given name.
5. Write an application that scans an input file and produces an alphabetized list of the words in the input along with their frequency of

occurrence. This can be accomplished by using a map in which the word is a key and stores the number of occurrences as a value.

6. One way to reduce the size of a dictionary used by a spell checker is to store only root words and to maintain with each word information that indicates how the word can be modified. For example, a simple one-word bitmap can encode the following types of transformations:

Bit Position	Modification
1	prefix *un*
2	prefix *in*
3	suffix *s*
4	suffix *ies*
5	ending *y* becomes *ies*

   There are, of course, many other common prefix and suffix rules. A `Map` can store the root word as the key and the bitmap as the value. Create two applications. The first creates the dictionary file, permitting the user to enter new words and their valid forms. The second application then reads the dictionary file and a file containing the source text and looks for words in the source that are not found in the dictionary.

7. Another approach to implementing the `Map` interface is to use a pair of parallel arrays. One array will maintain the keys, and one will maintain the values, which are stored in corresponding positions.

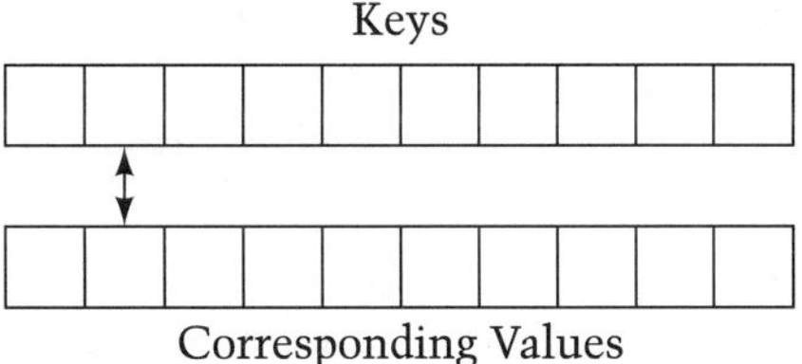

   The key array is sorted, in the fashion of the `SortedVector`. Binary search can then be used to quickly locate an index position in the key array. Develop a data structure based on these ideas.

8. A `MultiMap` is a map abstraction that permits more than one value to be stored using the same key. The key insight is similar to the idea of using buckets in a hash table. Instead of a single value, each entry in the `MultiMap` stores all the values for the given key in a container, such as a `LinkedList`. Values are inserted into this container as the

user enters them into the map. Create this data structure by building on top of the existing `MapAdapter`. Your `MultiMap` data type should implement the `Map` interface with the following modifications:

- `size`: This method must return the total number of elements stored in the collection, not simply the number of keys.
- `set`: This method must first check to see whether an entry using the given key already exists. If so, the value is simply inserted into the existing list of values associated with the key. Otherwise, a new `LinkedList` is created as the value associated with the key, and the value provided by the user is entered as the first element in the list.
- `contains`: This method is in addition to the `containsKey` method required by the `Map` interface. The `contains` method will take two arguments, both a key and a value, and return `true` only if an entry exists in the container that matches both.
- `get`: This method returns an `Enumeration` that will yield all the elements stored under the given key.
- `removeKey`: This method removes all the values stored under the given key. In addition, you should provide a method `remove` that takes both a key and a value argument and removes the value from the list associated with the key. If removing a value results in an empty list, the association for the key should be removed as well.

We illustrate one use of the `MultiMap` data type in the concordance program described in Section 17.1.3.

9. A *keyed priority queue* is an ADT that implements both the `Map` and the priority queue (or `FindMin`) interface. As with a map, elements are inserted as a key/value pair. As with a priority queue, the smallest element can be quickly accessed and removed. However, the object returned as a result of `FindMin` will be the value associated with the smallest key. Similarly, the `removeMin` operation will remove the key/value pair associated with the smallest key.

   Give an implementation of this ADT as an adapter. What interfaces must your underlying container support?

10. Another approach to silly-sentence generation is the following. An existing text is analyzed, and a `MultiMap` is formed by using each word as the key and storing with each word the set of all words that *followed* the key in the original text. To generate new sentences, an arbitrary first word is selected as the starting point. A random word in the successor list is then selected and printed. This is then used as the key, and the next word is randomly selected. The process is continued as long as desired.

11. The idea for this problem is described in Section 17.3. Suppose that you want to maintain a database of recipes used in cooking and wish to permit users to search the database for recipes that use specific ingredients. One technique would be to have each ingredient serve as a key in a `MultiMap` and to store all the recipes that use that ingredient in the list associated with the key. Each recipe will, of course, be found in as many lists as the number of different ingredients.

    Define a data structure for the `Recipe` data type. Then design a data structure for the `RecipeDatabase` abstraction. When a new recipe is added to the collection, the database should be updated so that the recipe is listed under each ingredient. Then write a method that will take a list of different ingredients and, by taking the intersection of each ingredient list, will return an enumeration of all the recipes that contain all items on the first list.

12. Individuals unfamiliar with a foreign language will often translate a sentence from one language to another by using a dictionary and word-for-word substitution. Although this does not produce the most elegant translation, it is usually adequate for short sentences, such as "Where is the train station?" Write a program that will read from two files. The first file contains a series of word-for-word pairs for a pair of languages. The second file contains text written in the first language. Examine each word in the text, and output the corresponding value of the dictionary entry. Words not in the dictionary can be printed in the output surrounded by brackets, as are [these] [words].

13. The department of motor vehicles maintains a database that typically includes the following fields:

    a. The name of the person who registered the car
    b. The address of the person who registered the car
    c. The driver's license number of the person who registered the car
    d. The serial number of the car
    e. The license plate number of the car

    Design an indexed data structure for this database. Assume that you want to search using name (assumed unique), serial number of car, or license plate number. A search on any one should yield the other fields. Design for your application a graphical interface that will permit both searching and the insertion or removal of records.

CHAPTER 18

SETS

In Chapter 2, we noted that a `Set` ADT contains methods with the same type signatures as the Bag but changes one important property.[1] Elements in a `Set` must be unique; the same element cannot appear more than once. Because this restriction was not part of the Bag abstraction, we must change the properties associated with the method used to add an element to the collection:

`void addElement(newElement)` *Pre:* The argument must at least be comparable for equality with the existing values in the collection. Some implementations also require the ability to order elements. *Post:* Ensures that the argument value is contained in the collection. If the argument value is already present in the collection prior to the invocation, the collection is unchanged; otherwise, it is added to the collection.

In addition, the `Set` interface adds methods for combining or comparing entire collections in one operation. These will be described in Section 18.2 when we consider the relationship between this data type and the concept of set in mathematics.

In addition to exploring the `Set` as a data type, we will investigate a number of other problems related to the difficulty of distributing elements

1. We here refer to the traditional definition of the set abstraction. Version 1.2 of the Sun data structure library includes the name `Set` as an interface but does not insist on the unique-element property.

into a collection of categories. Finally, we will examine a useful data structure, called the `BitSet`, for representing sets of positive integers.

18.1 CHANGING A BAG INTO A SET

Any data abstraction that supports the Bag interface can be made into a `Set`. In Table 18.1, we summarize the data types we have seen that implement the Bag interface. In selecting an appropriate tool for holding the underlying elements, the user must consider more than simply the asymptotic execution times. For example, both `SortedVector` and `SkipList` have very fast asymptotic runtimes but require that elements have an ordering that can be determined by a `Comparator` object. If elements have no natural ordering, these data structures cannot be used. The hash table abstractions do not require an ordering, but the stated asymptotic figures are realized only when the elements possess a hash function that distributes the values uniformly and the load factor does not become unreasonably large.

To convert a Bag into a `Set`, we must do two things. First, we must disallow the repeated insertion of any element already in the container. Second, we must provide an implementation for the additional `Set` operations not specified as part of the Bag interface. The following shows how we can create an *adapter* that will wrap around any implementation of the Bag data type and will filter out duplicate elements:

TABLE 18.1 DATA ABSTRACTIONS THAT SUPPORT THE Bag ADT

	`addElement`	`containsElement`	`findElement`	`removeElement`
`LinkedList`	$O(1)$	$O(n)$	$O(n)$	$O(n)$
`SortedVector`	$O(n)$	$O(\log n)$	$O(\log n)$	$O(n)$
`SortedList`	$O(n)$	$O(n)$	$O(n)$	$O(n)$
`SkipList`	$O(\log n)$	$O(\log n)$	$O(\log n)$	$O(\log n)$
`AVLTree`	$O(\log n)$	$O(\log n)$	$O(\log n)$	$O(\log n)$
`OpenHashtable`	$O(1)$	$O(1)$	$O(1)$	*NA*
`Hashtable`	$O(1)$	$O(1)$	$O(1)$	$O(1)$

```
public class SetAdapter implements Set {
  public SetAdapter (Bag s) { elementData = s; }
  private Bag elementData;

    // the Collection interface
  public boolean isEmpty () { return elementData.isEmpty(); }
  public int size () { return elementData.size(); }
  public Enumeration elements () { return elementData.elements(); }

    // the Bag interface
  public void addElement (Object val)  // add only if not there
  { if (! elementData.containsElement(val))
                                    elementData.addElement(val); }

  public boolean containsElement (Object val)
    { return elementData.containsElement(val); }

  public Object findElement (Object val)
    { return elementData.findElement(val); }

  public void removeElement (Object val)
    { elementData.removeElement(val); }

    // the Set interface
  public void unionWith (Set aSet) { ... }
  public void intersectWith (Set aSet) { ... }
  public void differenceWith (Set aSet) { ... }
  public boolean subsetOf (Set aSet) { ... }
}
```

This approach has one small problem, however. Adding an element to a set now performs both a test for inclusion and the insertion. In a `LinkedList`, for example, the insertion operation was a fast $O(1)$ task, whereas testing to see whether the element is already in the set requires $O(n)$ steps. Thus, our set adapter can change the asymptotic runtime performance of some set implementations.

Clearly, wrapping a `SetAdapter` around a `LinkedList` will dramatically change the execution-time performance, as the cost of an addition will go from $O(1)$ to $O(n)$. But what is the impact when an adapter is used with an `AVLTree`, where the costs of insertion and test are both $O(\log n)$? To measure this, we insert n randomly generated elements into

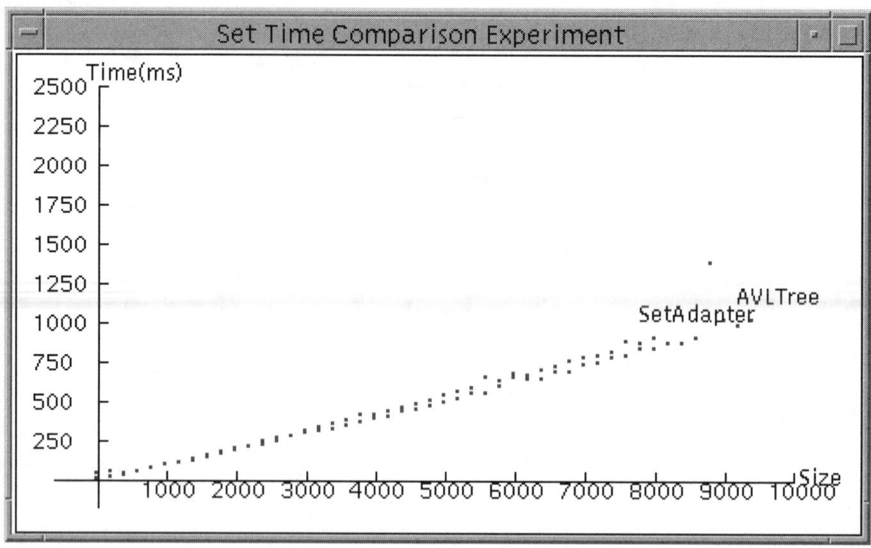

FIGURE 18.1 Measuring Cost of Insertion in a SetAdapter

EXPERIMENT: THE COST OF BAG OPERATIONS

Reducing the range of elements formed by the random-number generator will increase the likelihood of the same number's being repeated more than once. Does this have any impact on the execution timings? Repeat the same experiment using a `SkipList` or a hash table abstraction.

an `AVLTree` and compare the execution time to the same task performed using an `AVLTree` wrapped in a `SetAdapter`. As can be seen in Figure 18.1, the cost of the addition test in the insertion method is almost unnoticeable.

18.2 SET UNION, INTERSECTION, AND DIFFERENCES

A characteristic feature of the concept of sets from mathematics is the inclusion of operations that act on entire collections. These operations can be defined for sets that permit multiple copies of values but are normally encountered only in situations having elements that are unique. Although the mathematical definitions are symmetric, they lose their symmetry when we convert them into methods. Thus, instead of forming a set union as a new set, we speak of creating the union by adding elements from the argument set into the current set. In the following, we give both the conventional mathematical characterization and a description of the properties we expect from the corresponding operation in the `Set` interface.

- A *union* of two sets is the set of values that are present in either set. (When multiple copies of elements are permitted, we normally speak of a *merge* rather than a *union*.)

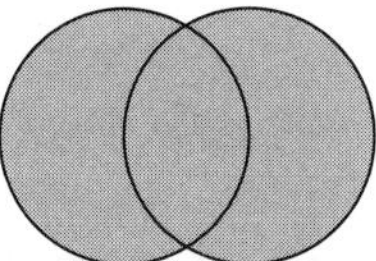

`void unionWith(Set aSet)` *Pre:* Assumes that all values in the argument set are comparable with elements in the collection. *Post:* This method forms the union of the current set with the argument set. In the argument set, all values that are not already members of the current set are added. The argument set is not modified.

- The *intersection* of two sets is the collection of elements that appear in both sets.

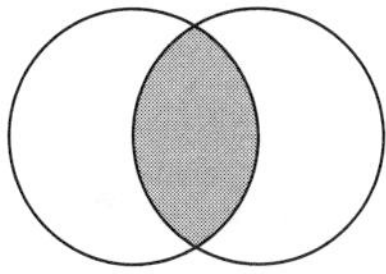

`void intersectWith(Set aSet)` *Pre:* Assumes that all values in the argument set are comparable with elements in the collection. *Post:* This method forms the intersection of the current set with the argument set. In the current set, all elements that are not members of the argument set are deleted. The argument set is not modified.

- The *difference* of two sets is the set of first-set elements that do not appear in the second set.

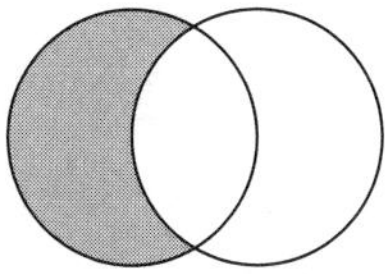

`void differenceWith(Set aSet)` *Pre:* Assumes that all values in the argument set are comparable with elements in the collection. *Post:* This method forms the difference between the current set and the argument set. In the current set, all elements that are members of the argument set are deleted. The argument set is not modified.

- A set is said to be a *subset* of another set if all elements from the first set appear in the second set.

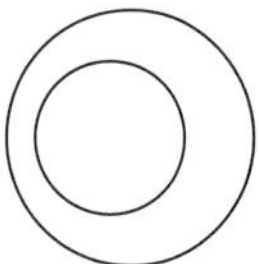

`boolean subsetOf(Set aSet)` *Pre:* Assumes that all values in the argument set are comparable with elements in the collection. *Post:* This method returns `true` if all members of the current set are members of the argument set, returning `false` otherwise. The argument set may include additional elements that are not members of the current set. The argument set is not modified.

The class `SetAdapter` implements the obvious naive algorithm for these operations. Here, for example, is the implementation of the `unionWith` method:

```
public void unionWith (Set aSet) {
  for (Enumeration e = aSet.elements(); e.hasMoreElements(); )
    addElement(e.nextElement());
}
```

The intersection and difference methods are slightly more complex because modifications to collections performed in the middle of an enumeration can yield unpredictable results. We first construct a set of elements to be removed from the collection; then, in a second pass, we remove them:

```
public void intersectWith (Set aSet) {
  Bag removedItems = new LinkedList();
    // find elements to be removed
  Enumeration e;
  for (e = elements(); e.hasMoreElements(); ) {
```

Proof of Correctness: intersectWith

A proof of correctness for the `intersectWith` procedure involves establishing the following invariants at the points indicated by comments in the code.

Invariant 1 When execution reaches this point in the procedure, the set held by `removedItems` contains all elements that appear in the current set and are not in the argument set. These elements must be removed in order to yield the intersection.

Invariant 2 When execution reaches this point in the procedure, all the values that were present in the set originally and do not appear in the argument set have been removed, leaving the intersection.

```
      Object val = e.nextElement();
      if (! aSet.containsElement(val))
        removedItems.addElement(val);
    }
      // now remove them (invariant 1)
    for (e = removedItems.elements(); e.hasMoreElements(); )
      removeElement(e.nextElement());
      // invariant 2
}
```

To see whether a set is a subset of another, we simply iterate over the elements, testing each against the argument set:

```
public boolean subsetOf (Set aSet) {
  for (Enumeration e = elements(); e.hasMoreElements(); )
    if (! aSet.containsElement(e.nextElement()))
      return false;
  return true;
}
```

All these procedures operate by iterating over one collection while performing operations on the other. If we are merging a collection of m elements into another with n elements, forming the union with a `LinkedList` would be $O(n \times m)$, whereas with a `SkipList`, the same task would be $O(m \log n)$. In exercise 3, you will compute the asymptotic running time for each operation with each of the various data structures.

18.3 Sorted List Sets

In Chapter 9, we hinted that the `SortedList` abstraction could be used to provide a faster $O(n + m)$ implementation of the `Set` operations—at least when used with an argument set that is also `Sorted`. We exploit this by creating a new data structure, the `SortedSet`, that inherits from the class `SortedList`:

```
public class SortedSet extends SortedList implements Set {

  public SortedSet (Comparator t) { super(t); }

    // override the add method so elements are unique
  public void addElement (Object newElement) {
    if (! containsElement(newElement))
      super.addElement(newElement);
  }
.
.
.
}
```

The SortedSet overrides the addElement method in the same fashion as the SetAdapter. The remaining methods in the Bag portion of the Set interface can be inherited from SortedList with no additional code whatsoever. There remain only the set-specific operations. We consider union first:

```
public void unionWith (Set newSet) { // assumes newSet is Sorted
  DoubleLink ptr = elementData.firstLink;
  Sorted argSet = (Sorted) newSet;
  for (Enumeration e = argSet.elements(); e.hasMoreElements(); ) {
    Object newElement = e.nextElement();
    while (true)
      if (ptr == elementData.sentinel)
        { ptr.insert(newElement); break; } // invariant 1
      else if (test.compare(ptr.value, newElement) < 0)
        ptr = ptr.next; // invariant 2
      else {
        if (test.compare(newElement, ptr.value) < 0)
          ptr.insert(newElement); // invariant 3
        // invariant 4
        break;
      }
  }
}
```

As with the mergeWith method in SortedList, the union algorithm runs down both its own collection and the argument collection in parallel. The assumption that the argument set is sorted is important because both sets must maintain their elements in a monotonically increasing sequence. At each point, two values are being compared: the element referenced by the link named ptr and the current enumeration from the argument set. A proof that the code is correct can be obtained by identifying four critical points in execution and arguing that the correct task is performed at each

VARIETIES OF INHERITANCE

Although class inheritance is a single mechanism, it can be used for a range of purposes. We note that the form of inheritance being used by SortedSet is very different from that used by the subclasses of Event in Chapter 15. The Chapter 15 inheritance is often termed *subclassing for specialization*, because the child class is a more specialized form of the parent. The type of inheritance used here is termed *subclassing for construction*. The idea is that we are using the parent class, SortedList, because it provides a large number of operations that we want to inherit and pass on to our children.

of these points. The four locations have been marked by comments in the code shown. The proof is easier to follow if we consider the locations out of order.

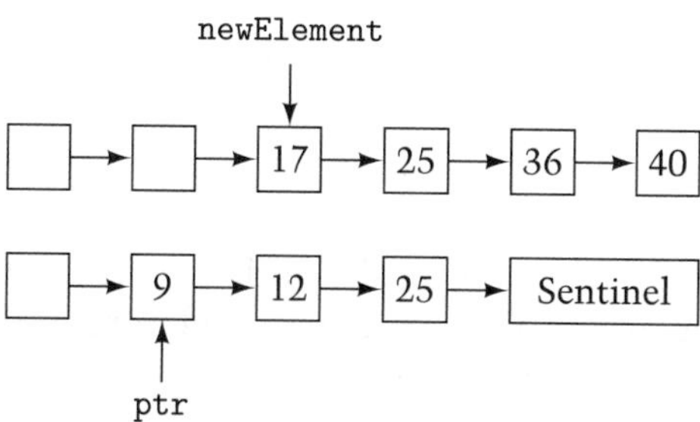

Invariant 2: Execution reaches this point when the link `ptr` references a value that is smaller than the value most recently produced by the argument enumeration (the value referenced by `newElement`). Because the argument is assumed to be sorted, this means that the `ptr` reference does not appear in the argument but should appear in the union. Because no other element in the argument set can be equal to the `ptr` value, we can safely advance `ptr` to the next link. The new value (held in the next link) should then be compared to the most recent value from the argument. The inner `while` loop takes care of this, allowing us to compare the new values without advancing the argument enumeration.

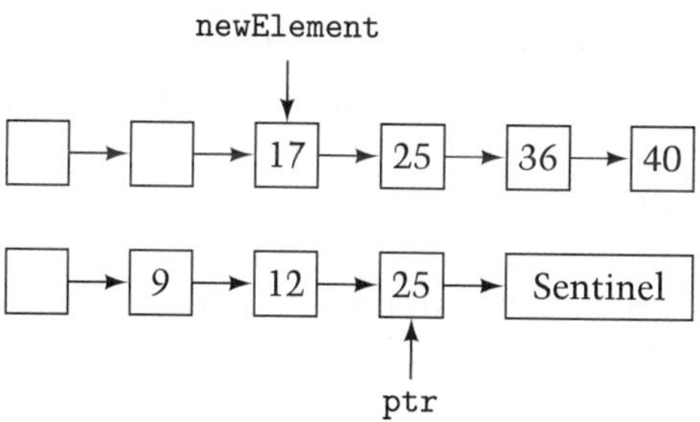

Invariant 3: Execution reaches this point when the argument value is smaller than the current value being referenced by `ptr`. Had the argument been equal to any earlier value in the current list, we would have detected this condition in a previous iteration of the `while` loop; this therefore means that the argument value does not appear in the current set and must be inserted.

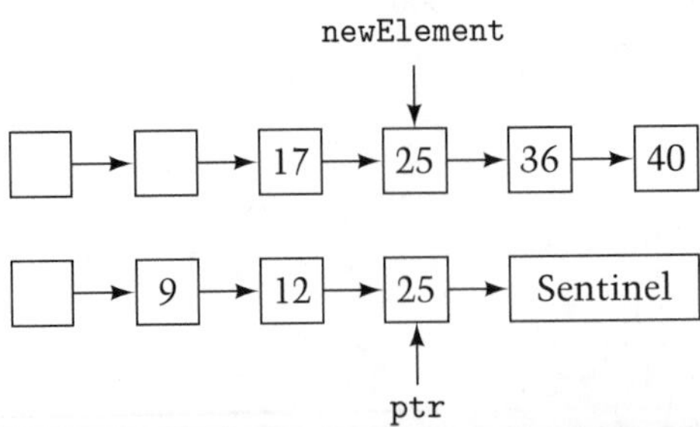

Invariant 4: Execution reaches this point when the argument value is less than or equal to the value being referenced by `ptr`. If the argument is strictly less than the value referred to by `ptr`, the argument will have been inserted into the list (at invariant 3). If these two quantities are equal, we want to advance to the next value in the argument enumeration. So in either case, we want to `break` out of the `while` loop and continue with the outer `for` loop.

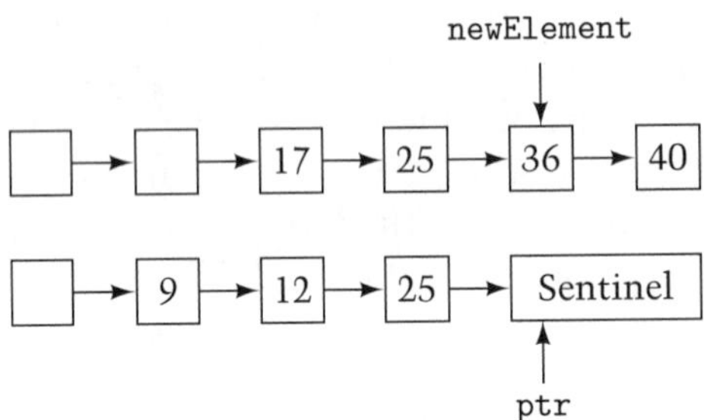

Invariant 1: If execution reaches this point (inside the compound statement), it is only because the link `ptr` has reached the end of the current set, yet the argument set still has values. Because all of these must be larger than any value in the current set (otherwise, they would have been detected before `ptr` reached the end of the list), they should all be inserted into the list. The `break` statement will force continuation of the outer `for` statement, and execution will continue until all values from the argument list have been inserted.

The procedure for `differenceWith` is similar. A proof of correctness for this algorithm is left as an exercise.

```
public void differenceWith (Set newSet) { // assumes newSet is sorted
  DoubleLink ptr = elementData.firstLink;
  Sorted argSet = (Sorted) newSet;
  for (Enumeration e = argSet.elements(); e.hasMoreElements(); ) {
    Object newElement = e.nextElement();
    while (true)
```

```
      if (ptr == elementData.sentinel)
        break;
      else if (test.compare(ptr.value, newElement) < 0)
        ptr = ptr.next;
      else {
        if (test.compare(newElement, ptr.value) < 0)
          break;
        DoubleLink rptr = ptr;
        ptr = ptr.next;
        rptr.remove();
      }
  }
}
```

The `intersectWith` algorithm is different. It forms the intersection of the two sets in a temporary local variable as it moves along in parallel, then at the end, changes the value of the current set to the newly constructed intersection. Again, a proof of correctness for this algorithm is left as an exercise, as is the implementation of the `subsetOf` operation.

```
public void intersectWith (Set newSet) { // assumes newSet is sorted
  DoubleLink ptr = elementData.firstLink;
  Sorted argSet = (Sorted) newSet;
  LinkedList intersect = new LinkedList();
  for (Enumeration e = argSet.elements(); e.hasMoreElements(); ) {
    Object newElement = e.nextElement();
      // skip smaller elements
    while ((ptr != elementData.sentinel) &&
      (test.compare(ptr.value, newElement) < 0))
        ptr = ptr.next;
      // save if in both sets
    if ((ptr != elementData.sentinel) &&
      ptr.value.equals(newElement))
        intersect.addLast(ptr.value);
  }
    // change elements to intersection
  elementData = intersect;
}
```

All these procedures work by looping over the two lists. A careful analysis shows that although there are nested loops, each iteration of the inner loop advances the `ptr`, whereas each iteration of the `for` loop advances the enumeration of the argument values. In total, the inner `while` loop cannot execute more than n times, whereas the outer loop executes m times. Therefore, their execution behavior is $O(n + m)$, where n and m represent the size of the receiver and argument lists, respectively.

18.4 APPLICATION—A SPELLING CHECKER

We can illustrate the utility of the Set operations by developing a spelling checker, such as might be found in a word processor. The basic idea of a spelling checker is to generate from a document a set of words that may be misspelled. We say "may be" because even the best spelling checkers cannot handle names or technical terms, so all one can do is indicate to the user a potential source of problems.

The spelling checker we will describe uses two different sets of words. The first set contains all the words found in the input document. The second is a set of words known to be correctly spelled. By forming the difference between these two sets, we can then generate the set of words that are found in the document but not known to be correctly spelled.

Both the dictionary and the set of words in the document are formed by calling a method named readWords. This function takes an input stream and breaks it apart, using a StreamTokenizer, a class we have already encountered in an application in Chapter 16. By setting the lowerCaseMode, the StreamTokenizer will even convert the input to all lowercase for us:

```
import java.io.*;
import java.util.Enumeration;
import jds.Set;
import jds.collection.SortedSet;
import jds.util.StringCompare;

class SpellCheck {

  private static Set readWords (Reader in) throws IOException {
    Set result = new SortedSet(new StringCompare());
    StreamTokenizer tok = new StreamTokenizer(in);
    tok.ordinaryChar('.'); // don't attach periods to words
    tok.lowerCaseMode(true);
    int c = tok.nextToken();
    while (c != StreamTokenizer.TT_EOF) {
      if (c == StreamTokenizer.TT_WORD)
        result.addElement(tok.sval);
      c = tok.nextToken();
    }
    return result;
  }

  static public void main (String [ ] args) {
    try {
      // read the two sets of words
    Set dict = readWords(new FileReader("words"));
```

```
    Set doc = readWords(new FileReader("input"));

      // remove the correctly spelled words
    doc.differenceWith(dict);

      // now print the misspellings
    Enumeration e = doc.elements();
    while (e.hasMoreElements())
      System.out.println(e.nextElement());
    } catch (IOException e) { System.err.println("exception:"+e); }
  }
}
```

Once the two sets have been formed, we simply take the difference between the document set and the dictionary set. Any words in the document that are not in the dictionary are then printed. We will explore various improvements to this program in the exercises and programming projects at the end of this chapter.

* 18.5 The Union-Find Problem

The following description is typical of a large class of similar problems. Recently, merger mania has hit the owners of the ten pizza restaurants in town. First, Peter, of Peters Pizza, purchased Pizza World. Then Pizza Fillup and Pizza Planet combined. Next was Perfect Pizza and Precision Pizza. Norm's bought Stellar Pizza, and the owner of Pizza World bought out the APizza franchise. Finally, Precision Pizza decided that it would combine with the company that owned Peters Pizza. After all these mergers, we want to know whether the owner of Norm's is the same as the owner of Peters Pizza.

A. Perfect Pizza
B. Precision Pizza
C. Pizza Pizzazz
D. Peters Pizza
E. APizza
F. Pizza Fillup
G. Pizza World
H. Pizza Planet
I. Stellar Pizza
J. Norm's

This type of problem is known as a *union-find* problem. The task is to divide a group of elements (the pizza restaurants) into a *collection* of sets. These collections are sometimes called a *partition*. There are two basic operations. The first, called `find`, is to find the set in which an element is held. The second, termed `merge`, is to merge two partitions. Performing the `merge` operations described in the scenario leads to the following partitions:

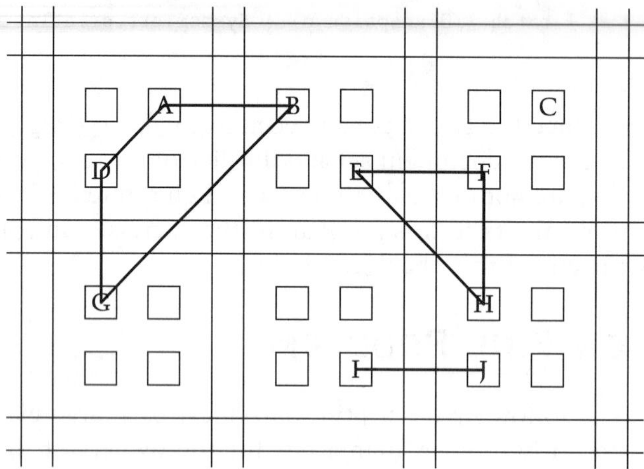

So the answer is no, Norms is owned by a different company than Peters. A data structure that can solve this type of problem is the following:

```
public class UnionFind {
  private Map map = new MapAdapter(new LinkedList());

  public void addElement (Object val) {
    LinkedList lst = new LinkedList();
    lst.addElement(val);
    add(val, new SetAdapter(lst));
  }

  public void add (Object val, Set set) { map.set(val, set); }

  public Set find (Object val) { return (Set) map.get(val); }

  public void union (Object left, Object right) {
    Set leftSet = find(left);
    Set rightSet = find(right);
      // first set all right elements to left set
    for (Enumeration e = rightSet.elements(); e.hasMoreElements(); )
```

```
      map.set(e.nextElement(), leftSet);
      // then merge the two sets
    leftSet.unionWith(rightSet);
  }
}
```

Internally, the `UnionFind` data abstraction will maintain a `Map` that will link elements to sets. Elements can be added, using the method `addElement`, in which case a set adapter built on top of a linked list will be used for the underlying set, or they can supply the set explicitly, using the method `add`. The `find` operation simply uses the map to obtain the set associated with a specific element. The time it takes to perform this operation depends on the type of `Map` being used. A hash table could provide constant time, whereas a `LinkedList` could require $O(n)$.

The key operation is `union`. This method takes two elements and merges the sets associated with each element. This is accomplished by first changing the map entries for the second argument to point to the first set, then merging the elements in the second set into the first. As we have seen, the asymptotic runtime for the `unionWith` operation can range from $O(n)$ (for a `SortedSet`) to $O(n^2)$ (for an ordinary `LinkedList`).

If it is not necessary to generate the partition sets but only to tell whether two elements are in the same set, an even simpler data structure can be used. The basic idea is similar. Each element will be used as a key in a `Map` that will hold a single `ConsCell`, where `ConsCell` is the single-link data abstraction we introduced in Chapter 8. Partitions will be formed by combining links to point to one another. Two elements are in the same partition if they ultimately have the same root link:

```
public class UnionFind2 {
  Map map = new MapAdapter(new LinkedList());

  public void addElement (Object val)
    { map.set(val, new ConsCell(val, null)); }

  public void merge (Object left, Object right) {
    ConsCell sleft = findRoot(left);
    sleft.link = findRoot(right);
  }

  public boolean sameSet (Object left, Object right)
    { return findRoot(left) == findRoot(right); }

  private ConsCell findRoot (Object val) {
    ConsCell root = (ConsCell) map.get(val);
```

```
    while (root.link != null) root = root.link;
    return root;
  }
}
```

Let us apply this abstraction to the original problem. Initially, each restaurant is placed in its own link. After the first few merge operations, we have the following situation:

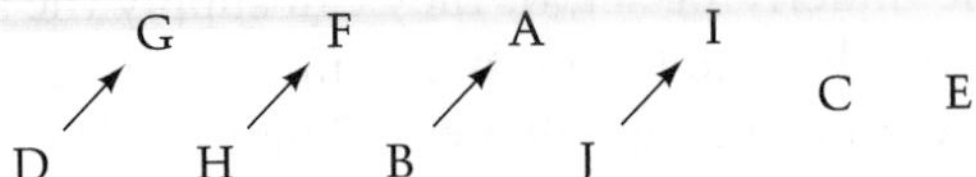

Next, Pizza Planet is merged with the APizza franchise. But because Pizza Planet (node H) is not a root, we travel up to the root node, which is F (Pizza Fillup). Node F is then linked to node E (APizza):

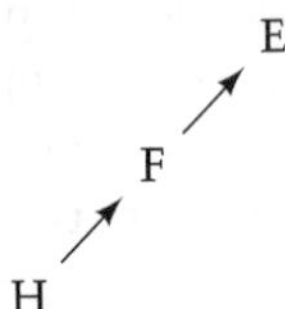

In the final merge, the partition that holds Precision Pizza (node B) is merged with the class that holds Peters Pizza (node D). Our final set of partitions is the following:

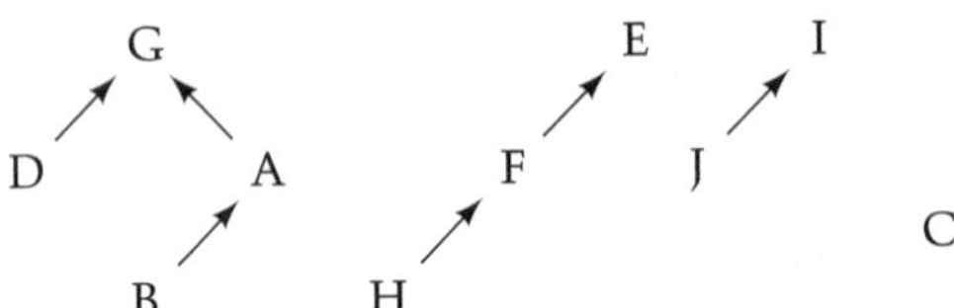

EXPERIMENT: EVALUATE MERGE-EXECUTION TIME

Experimentally evaluate the time it takes to perform the `merge` operation. You can do this by first constructing a `UnionFind` structure with values from 1 to n. Then measure the time it takes to randomly select n pairs of values and merge their two sets. Does your result change depending on the type of structure used for the `Map`? Are there restrictions on what types of implementations we can use for the `Map`?

* 18.6 The BitSet Abstraction

A `BitSet` is designed to represent a set of positive integers from a small range, such as a set drawn from the values between 0 and 75. Unlike with the other `Set` abstractions, we don't need to save the elements, as one integer is indistinguishable from another of the same magnitude. Instead, we can simply mark which elements have been inserted into the set and use these marks to test whether a value is found in the collection. The advantage of marking is that several marks can be efficiently packed into a single integer. A 64-bit `long` integer, for example, can hold the marks that represent 64 elements. If the set has more than this number, two `long` integers can be used, and so on.

The `BitSet` data structure built on this idea stores its marks in an array of `long` integers:

1101110...101	1001001...010	0011000...011

To access a particular element, an integer key must be converted into two separate integer quantities. The first is the index of the element in the array in which the mark is stored. This can be determined by simply dividing an integer by 64. The second is a position within the word. This is formed by creating a *mask*, a `long` integer in which only one binary position is set. This mask is created by shifting an integer 1 left by the appropriate number of elements. Figure 18.2 shows an implementation of the `BitSet` abstraction.[2]

To turn a bit on (member function `set`), we first require that the indicated bit will be found in the collection. The method `ensureCapacity` will expand the array as necessary so that the given index is a valid location.[3] Then, to mark the element as present in the set, we simply mask the corresponding integer. This is illustrated by the following (we use 8-bit quantities for illustration instead of the 64 bits used in the implementation).

Data: 10011001
Mask: 00100000
Result: 10111001

---

2. This version is slightly simpler than the one provided in the standard library distributed by Sun; however, it uses the same interface.

3. An alternative would have been to throw an exception for index values that are out of bound. We are here following the lead of the Java standard library. Unfortunately, it does not say why Sun elected to expand the set rather than to throw an exception.

```
public class BitSet implements Serializable {
    // constructor
  public BitSet (int size) { ensureCapacity(size); }

    // data area
  private long [ ] bits = new long[1];

    // operations
  public void clear (int indx) {
    if (index(indx) < bits.length) bits[index(indx)] &= ~ mask(indx);
  }

  public boolean get (int indx) {
    if (index(indx) < bits.length)
      return 0 != (bits[index(indx)] & mask(indx));
    return false; //  not set
  }

  public void set (int indx) {
    ensureCapacity(indx);
    bits[index(indx)] |= mask(indx);
  }

  public void and (BitSet set) { ... }
  public void or (BitSet set) { ... }

    // private operations
  private int index (int i) { return i / 64; }

  private long mask (int i) { return 1L << (i % 64); }

  private synchronized void ensureCapacity (int size) {
    int required = 1 + index(size);
    if (required > bits.length) {
      // must make larger
      long [ ] newArray = new long[required];
      for (int i = 0; i < bits.length; i++)
        newArray[i] = bits[i];
      bits = newArray;
    }
  }
}
```

FIGURE 18.2 An Implementation of the BitSet Abstraction

BITWISE OR, LOGICAL OR, AND UNION

There are important differences between the bitwise operators & and | and the logical operators && and ||. The bitwise operators take two *integer* arguments and operate on each of the corresponding bits in the two values. The logical operators require two *Boolean* arguments and use *short-circuit* evaluation. This means that if the truth of the entire expression can be determined after evaluating only the left argument, the right argument is not considered. (This occurs with logical && if the left argument is `false` and with logical || if the left argument is `true`.)

There is a further relationship between the bitwise operations on a `BitSet` and the set operations we discussed at the beginning of this chapter. A bitwise `or` corresponds to forming a *union* of the two sets, whereas a bitwise `and` corresponds to forming the *intersection*.

The method `get` is used to test the mark stored for a given element. To test a bit position, the vector data element is `and`ed with the mask. If the result is nonzero, the data byte must have had a 1 in the selected position. If the result is zero, the data type must have contained a zero bit. If a test key is larger than the current set, the element need not be tested, and we will simply report that the element is not in the collection:

Data: 10011001
Mask: 00100000
Result: 00000000

To clear an element, a logical `and` is performed with the corresponding word and the bitwise inverse of the mask. The member function with no arguments resets all bit positions. As index values larger than the current array are assumed to be clear in any case, there is no need to change them.

Data: 10111001
Mask: 00100000
Inverted mask: 11011111
Result: 10011001

Note that the running times of these operations are related to the size of the set but are independent of the number of elements in the set, that is, the number of bits that hold a 1 value. This is not true of sets maintained by, for example, a linked list.

In addition to the ability to set and to test individual bits, the `BitSet` abstraction provides methods for forming the intersection and unions of bit sets. The union of two bit sets can be formed using the method or, which is defined as follows:

```
public void or (BitSet set) {
  for (int i = 0; i < bits.length; i++)
    if (i < set.bits.length) bits[i] |= set.bits[i];
}
```

It is necessary to consider only index positions that are common to both the sets, and we therefore need determine only the shorter of the two arrays. The and operation, used in forming the intersection of two sets, is more complex. If the set is smaller than the argument set, all the larger positions should be zeroed:

```
public void and (BitSet set) {
  for (int i = 0; i < bits.length; i++)
    if (i < set.bits.length) bits[i] &= set.bits[i];
    else bits[i] = 0;
}
```

18.7 APPLICATION—PRIME NUMBER SIEVE

Discovering prime numbers is a classic problem that can be solved using a bit vector. The technique was described by the Greek mathematician/philosopher Erastosthenes in the third century B.C. and is commonly referred to as the *sieve of Erastosthenes.*

The basic idea behind the algorithm is to take a list of all the positive integers and to strike out those that cannot possibly be prime numbers. When all those that cannot be prime are removed, the remaining elements must therefore be prime. Suppose that we wish to discover the prime numbers less than 20. We can visualize the collection of elements as follows:

2	3	4	5	6	7	8	9	10	11	12	13	14	15	16	17	18	19	20

As the set of elements we are interested in begins with 2, we will simply ignore the index positions 0 and 1.

The algorithm can be described as follows. A finger, or index, will move through the collection, starting from the beginning. At each step, we advance this counter to the next element that has not been eliminated. The first time we do this, we will discover the first element, namely, 2. We know at this point that 2 is in the final collection, that is, that 2 is a prime

PROOF BY CONTRADICTION

The argument for the correctness of the sieve algorithm uses a technique termed *proof by contradiction*. In a proof by contradiction, we assume that the *opposite* of the conjecture we wish to establish is true and then show that a contradiction must necessarily ensue. Proof by contradiction is often useful when programs manipulate discrete items, such as integers.

In this case, the conjecture we wish to establish is that all nonprimes must be crossed out. Because we are dealing with discrete integers, we can assert that there must be a *first* nonprime integer. But a simple argument then shows that this value must clearly have been eliminated. Because there therefore cannot be a first nonprime integer that survives being crossed out, all nonprimes must be crossed out.

number. Starting from *this* position, we delete all multiples of this number. Deleting all multiples of 2 yields the following collection.

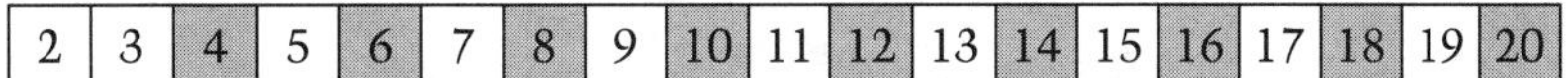

2	3	4	5	6	7	8	9	10	11	12	13	14	15	16	17	18	19	20

We next advance the finger, or counter, to the next position that has not been eliminated. In this example, it is the next element, namely, 3. Once again, we eliminate multiples of 3. Note that some of these elements may have already been eliminated by the previous step. The resulting collection can be visualized as follows:

2	3	4	5	6	7	8	9	10	11	12	13	14	15	16	17	18	19	20

Next, we consider the element 5, crossing out the multiples 10, 15, and 20. We continue in this fashion until all elements have been examined. Any remaining elements *must* be prime.

To see why, assume that in the final list, there exists at least one element that is not prime. Let n be the first such element. If it is not prime, n must have at least one prime factor. Let m be a prime factor of n. Because n was the first nonprime in the list, m must be on the list. But then n would have been eliminated when we deleted the multiples of m. Therefore, n will not be on the final list.

The program that follows from this reasoning takes as input an integer `n` and returns a `BitSet` in which all the prime numbers less than or equal to `n` have been marked. One simplification to the algorithm previously described has been made. We can, in fact, cease examining numbers when we reach the square root of the maximum, as any nonprime less than n

must have at least one factor smaller than or equal to the square root. Rather than compute the square root of n, we simply cease when the square of the current value is larger than n:

```
import jds.collection.BitSet;

class Sieve {
  public BitSet sieve (int n) {
    BitSet values = new BitSet(n);
      // mark all values as on
    for (int i = 2; i < n; i++)
      values.set(i);

      // now search for nonzero cells
    for (int i = 2; i*i <= n; i++) {
      if (values.get(i)) {
        // inv: i has no factors
        for (int j = i + i; j < n; j+= i)
          values.clear(j);
        // inv: multiples of i have been cleared
      }
      // inv: all marked values smaller than i are prime
    }
    // inv: all marked values are prime
    return values;
  }
}
```

18.8 CHAPTER SUMMARY

KEY CONCEPTS

- Set
- Set operations
  - Union
  - Intersection
  - Difference
  - Subset
- Union find
- BitSet

A Set is a collection in which every element is unique. In addition, the historical definition of a set from mathematics includes a number of operations for combining or comparing entire sets. These operations include set union, set intersection, set difference, and set subset.

A set can easily be constructed by using an adapter around any container that supports the Bag interface. The asymptotic execution-time performance of the resulting structure depends on the behavior of the underlying Bag.

A variation on the merge algorithm for SortedLists provides the key to create an implementation of the Set abstraction that permits union, intersection, and difference to be computed in $O(n + m)$ operations.

Union-find problems entail dividing up a collection of values into partitions and subsequently asking whether two values end up in the same partition.

A BitSet is a special form of set used for storing small positive integer values. These can be held in a very efficient representation by using bitwise operations on integer values.

Further Information

The data abstraction represented by the BitSet is sometimes termed a *characteristic vector*.

Study Questions

1. What data structures yield the fastest time to test to see whether an element is in a set? What restrictions are there on the use of this container? What is the fastest container without any restrictions?
2. How is the Bag data type different from the Set data type?
3. For what data structures will using a Bag as a tool to implement a Set asymptotically increase the runtime for inserting elements?
4. The intersection algorithm in Set uses two loops. Why do we not want to remove the elements directly in the first loop?
5. What are the characteristics of the union-find problem?
6. What type of elements are stored in a bit set?

Exercises

1. What invariants might you use to prove that the SetAdapter procedures unionWith and subsetOf are correct?
2. Complete the implementation of the SetAdapter by providing the implementation of the differenceWith method. Give invariants and a simple proof of correctness.
3. A SetAdapter can be built by using any container that supports the Bag interface. The asymptotic runtimes will differ, depending on the underlying container. For each of the following containers, describe the asymptotic times for the following set operations:

	addElement	unionWith	intersectionWith	differenceWith	subsetOf
LinkedList					
SortedVector					
SortedList					
SkipList					
AVLTree					
OpenHashtable					
Hashtable					

4. Describe the union, intersection, and differences for the following two sets:

   Set A: $1, 2, 5, 7, 12$

   Set B: $1, 5, 12, 36, 52$

5. The *symmetric difference* is the union of two sets minus the intersection.

   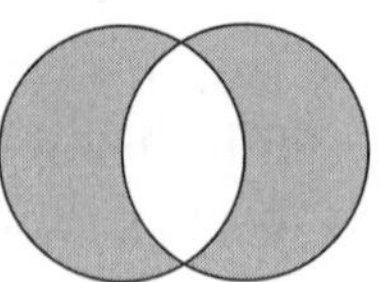

   Show how to compute the symmetric difference as a combination of union, intersection, and difference.

6. Prove that a set A is a subset of a set B if and only if the intersection of A and B is equal to A. Would this be a very good way to implement the subset test? Why or why not?
7. Using invariants, provide a proof that the `differenceWith` algorithm in the class `SortedSet` is correct.
8. Using invariants, provide a proof that the `intersectWith` algorithm in the class `SortedSet` is correct.
9. Complete the implementation of the `SortedSet` data structure by giving an implementation of the `subset` relationship, and provide a proof of correctness for your algorithm.

10. Explain why it would probably not be a good idea to define a `Comparator` object to order sets using the subset relation. *Hint:* consider all the possible orderings.
11. Prove that a set A is a subset of a set B if and only if the union of A and B is equal to B. Would this be a very good way to implement the subset test? Why or why not?
12. Prove that two sets are equal if and only if they are both subsets of each other.
13. Is there an advantage to using a `SkipList` and a `MapAdapter` to create the `Map` in the `UnionFind` data structure? Why might you not want to do this?
14. In the second `UnionFind` data abstraction, show that it is not necessary to perform the `findRoot` operation on the right argument in the method `merge`. Will this change speed up or slow down subsequent `merge` operations?
15. Assume that n `Set` operations have been performed to set n different bit values in a `BitSet`. What is the complexity of the `or` operation with another similarly sized `BitSet`?
16. A student proposes that the hash value computed for a `BitSet` be computed by adding the values of the `long` integers that make up the set and then converting the result into an integer. Do you think that this is a good idea? Why or why not?
17. Explain why it is not possible (or, at least, not easy) to generate a multiset version of a set that is implemented using bit vectors.

Programming Projects

1. The spelling checker described in the text reads an entire document before it begins checking for misspelled words. An alternative is to test each word from the document as it is read. What are some of the advantages and disadvantages of the two techniques? Develop a program that uses the second approach. As each misspelled word is encountered, display the word for the user. A more complex feature would permit the user to enter a replacement, which would be entered into the document in place of the misspelled word. The latter feature can be combined with the next project.
2. Our spelling checker can be improved by adding the ability to suggest alternatives for a misspelled word. Although there are no guaranteed algorithms for correcting English spelling, various heuristics can be used to discover alternatives. The basic idea is to use one or more of

these techniques to create a list of possible replacements. The dictionary is then used to filter out the replacements that are not correctly spelled, and the remainder are presented to the user as possible alternatives. Heuristics include the following:

a. *Removing a letter.* This generates as many alternatives as there are letters in the word.
b. *Adding a letter.* This can generate a large number of alternatives if each letter is tried in each location. In this case, it is better to filter the list by examining the dictionary as each alternative word is constructed.
c. *Swapping two adjacent letters.*

3. In the second implementation of the `UnionFind` algorithm, the `merge` operation is symmetric; we can make either the first argument parent to the second or the second parent to the first. You might have noticed in the example problem that if we had linked APizza to Pizza Fillup rather than the other way around, changing the order might have resulted in a slightly shorter tree:

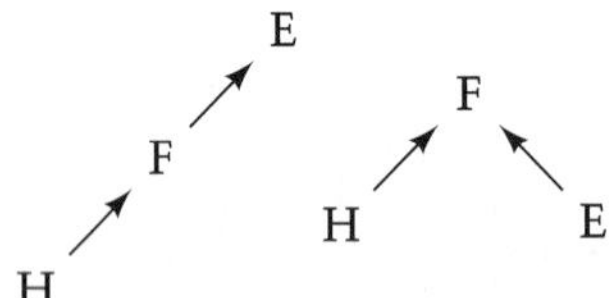

Unfortunately, the data structure shown does not have enough information to make an informed decision. To permit this, we need to maintain along with each node an integer that is the *height* of the tree rooted at each node. When a merge is performed, the shorter tree is merged into the larger or, if they are the same height, one is selected randomly, and the height of the new root is adjusted. Show how to modify the `UnionFind2` data abstraction to incorporate this feature.

4. A completely different technique for creating a spelling checker is based on using a `BitSet` in the fashion of a hash table. Begin with a `BitSet` large enough to hold t elements. We first take the dictionary of correctly spelled words, hash each word to yield a value h, and then set the position $h\%t$. After processing all the words, we will have a large hash table of 0/1 values. Now to test any particular word, we perform the same process: Hash the word, take the remainder after dividing by the table size, and test the entry. If the value in the bit set is 0, the word is misspelled. Unfortunately, if the value in the table is 1, it may *still* be misspelled, as two words can easily hash into the same location.

To correct this problem, we can enlarge our bit set and try using more than one hash function. An easy way to do this is to select a table size t and to select some number of prime numbers, for example, five, that are larger than t. Call these p_1, p_2, p_3, p_4, and p_5. Now, rather than just using the hash value of the word as our starting point, we first take the remainder of the hash value when divided by each of the prime numbers, yielding five different values. Then we map each of these into the table. Thus, each word may set five different bits. The following illustrates this with a table of size 21, using the values 113, 181, 211, 229, and 283 as our prime numbers:

word	hashcode	h%113	h%181	h%211	h%229	h%283
this	6022124	15(15)	73(10)	184(16)	111(6)	167(20)
text	6018573	80(17)	142(16)	9(9)	224(14)	12(12)
example	1359142016	51(9)	165(18)	75(12)	223(13)	273(0)

this							1				1					1	1				1
text										1			1		1		1	1			
example	1									1			1	1					1		
	1	0	0	0	0	0	1	0	0	1	1	0	1	1	1	1	1	1	1	0	1

The key assumption is that different words may map into the same locations for one or two positions but not all five. Thus, we reduce considerably the chances that a misspelled word will score a false positive hit.

Analysis shows that this is a very reliable technique as long as the final bit vector has roughly the same number of zeros as ones. Performance can be improved by using more prime numbers. Implement a version of the spell checker based on these ideas, and compare its running time to that of the spell checker given in the text.

5. In earlier chapters, we proposed that our `Card` abstraction yield a unique hash value between 0 and 51. Given this, show how to create, using a `BitSet`, a data abstraction that will maintain a hand of cards. Add the ability to add or to remove cards from your hand. Measure the time required to do these operations, and compare to the execution time for an implementation that keeps the cards themselves in a `Set` data structure.

CHAPTER 19

MATRICES

A *matrix* is a two-dimensional array of elements. Matrices occur frequently in a variety of mathematical and financial problems. Matrices are related to arrays and vectors. Just as it is useful to create the `Vector` data type on top of the underlying Java array, so too it is useful to create a variety of matrix data abstractions.

In this chapter, we will first examine matrices as primitive data types in Java. We then describe some of the problems implicit in this representation and examine a number of alternative implementation techniques for two-dimensional structures.

19.1 JAVA MATRICES

A simple matrix in Java is created by declaring the extent of each dimension. Consider the following statement:

```
double [ ][ ] d = new double[3][4];
```

The value `d` is a 3-by-4 matrix of double-precision elements. It consists of three rows and four columns. The space set aside by the compiler for this data type will constitute 12 double-precision elements. These will be placed end to end in memory, as follows:

[0][0]	[0][1]	[0][2]	[1][0]	...	[2][2]	[2][3]

Normally, however, we think of a matrix in a two-dimensional form, something like the following:

d[0][0]	d[0][1]	d[0][2]	d[0][3]
d[1][0]	d[1][1]	d[1][2]	d[1][3]
d[2][0]	d[2][1]	d[2][2]	d[2][3]

Because elements are placed in memory in order, with the second subscript changing more quickly than the first, it is possible to view this as an array of arrays. That is, a singly subscripted value, such as `d[1]`, is a quantity of type "array of double." You can see this by assigning the value `d[1]` to a variable that is declared as a simple array:

```
double [ ] d1 = d[1];
```

The variable `d1` can be used as a one-dimensional array and references exactly the same elements as the middle row of the matrix d.

Like arrays, matrices can be initialized by the declaration statement in which they are created, by placing the initial values in a list of quantities, surrounded by braces. Each row of elements is given a separate set of braces. The following initializes a 3-by-4 matrix of elements:

```
double [ ][ ] prices =
      { { 1.25, 1.09, 0.58, 0.25 },
      { 1.35, 0.98, 0.62, 0.35 },
      { 1.40, 1.12, 0.43, 0.19 } };
```

Individual elements of a matrix are accessed by using two applications of the subscript operator. This is illustrated by Figure 19.1, which describes the conventional matrix multiplication operation. You will recall that when multiplying two matrices, each row of the first matrix is combined with each column of the second, multiplying paired values and summing the results.

To illustrate the use of the matrix data type, consider the following problem. The matrix named `prices`, described previously, is an encoding of the following table of prices for various items from three grocery stores:

Price per Unit	Hamburger	Chicken	Tomatoes	Lettuce
Store A	\$1.25	\$1.09	\$0.58	\$0.25
Store B	\$1.35	\$0.98	\$0.62	\$0.35
Store C	\$1.40	\$1.12	\$0.43	\$0.19

```
void matrixMultiply (double [ ][ ] a, double [ ] [ ] b, double [ ] [ ] c)
{
  int n = a.length();
  for (int i = 0; i < n; i++) {
    for (int j = 0; j < n; j++) {
      c [i][j] = 0.0;
      for (int k = 0; k < n; k++) {
        c[i][j] += a[i][k] * b[k][j];
      }
    }
  }
}
```

FIGURE 19.1 A Matrix Multiplication Algorithm

In a typical week, three families consume different quantities of these items, represented by the following table:

	Family:		
Item	**Smith**	**Brown**	**Jones**
Hamburger	5	2	0
Chicken	4	5	0
Tomatoes	2	1	6
Lettuce	1	2	4

We can discover which store would be least expensive for each family by solving a matrix multiplication problem. The matrix of stores by items is multiplied by the matrix of items by family, resulting in a new matrix of stores by family. This process could be performed by the following short program:

```
class PriceCompare {
  public static void main (String [ ] args) {
    double [ ][ ] prices = { ... as above };
    double [ ][ ] quantity = { ... };
    double [ ][ ] cost = new double[3][3];

      // perform the matrix multiplication
    matrixMultiply(prices, quantity, cost);

      // output the result
    System.out.println("cost per family, Smith Brown, Jones");
    matrixOutput(cost);
  }
  .
  .
  .
}
```

The results would indicate that family Smith would be better off shopping at store A, family Brown at store B, and family Jones at store C. The routine `matrixOutput` is a simple procedure we can use to print a two-dimensional matrix.

19.2 Application—Rain Game

Matrices can be found in many games that use a two-dimensional playing surface. Examples include board games, such as chess or checkers, or arcade games. We present a simple example of the latter. As we did with the Caterpillar game in Chapter 12, we will describe only the heart of this application, sufficient for illustrating the use of a matrix. We leave the completion of the game as a programming exercise.

In the Rain Game, Figure 19.2, colored pieces fall like rain from the sky, settling on the ground. By means of keyboard commands, the user can move the pieces left or right as they fall. If the user manages to make four pieces of the same color in any row, column, or diagonal, the pieces are removed, and those pieces above the removed elements move down.

FIGURE 19.2 Screen Shot of the Rain Game

Players receive one point for every piece entered into play. The goal is to achieve the highest score.

The main data structure is a rectangular grid of `Colors`. This grid is used to draw the graphical display. The grid is also used to determine whether a piece can be moved left, right, or down. The initialization and the drawing of the grid are performed by the following:

```
import java.awt.*;
import java.awt.event.*;
import jds.Queue;
import jds.collection.LinkedList;
import jds.util.CloseQuit;

class Rain extends Frame {
  public static void main (String [ ] args)
    { Rain world = new Rain(); world.show(); world.run(); }

  public Rain () {
      // window initialization
    setSize(FrameWidth, FrameHeight); setTitle("Rain Game");

      // application-specific initialization
    for (int i = 0; i < BoardHeight; i++)
      for (int j = 0; j < BoardWidth; j++)
        grid[i][j] = Color.white;
    addKeyListener(new keyDown());
    addWindowListener(new CloseQuit());
  }

  private Color [ ] [ ] grid = new Color[BoardHeight][BoardWidth];
  private Queue commandQueue = new LinkedList();
  private Piece piece = new Piece(3, 3, BoardHeight-1);
  final static int FrameWidth = 150;
  final static int FrameHeight = 330;
  final static int BlockSize = 20;
  final static int BoardHeight = 15;
  final static int BoardWidth = 5;

  public void paint (Graphics g) {
    for (int i = 0; i < BoardHeight; i++)
      for (int j = 0; j < BoardWidth; j++) {
        g.setColor(grid[i][j]);
        g.fillRect(PieceWidth*j,
          FrameHeight-PieceWidth*(i+1),
```

```
          PieceWidth, PieceWidth);
        }
  }

  public void run () { ... }
  private class keyDown extends KeyAdapter { ... }
  private class Piece { ... }
}
```

As with the Caterpillar game, the game object and the pieces will communicate by passing commands through a `Queue`. You recall that key presses in Java are caught by a key press listener. Our listener is an instance of the class `keyDown`. When it detects that a key has been pressed, the listener places a value into the command queue (or quits, if the user presses the letter q):

```
private class keyDown extends KeyAdapter {
  public void keyPressed (KeyEvent e) {
    char key = e.getKeyChar();
    switch (key) {
      case 'a': commandQueue.addLast(new Character('l')); break;
      case 'd': commandQueue.addLast(new Character('r')); break;
      case 'q': System.exit(0);
    }
  }
}
```

The class `Piece` represents a piece in play. A piece has a color and a location. Pieces move in response to the method `move`, which returns `true` if the piece was able to move and `false` if not:

```
private class Piece {
  public Piece (int v, int ix, int iy) {
    switch (v) { // set color
      case 0: color = Color.red; break;
      case 1: color = Color.blue; break;
      case 2: color = Color.green; break;
      default: color = Color.yellow; break;
    }
    y = iy; // set position
    x = ix;
    grid[y][x] = color;
  }

  private Color color;
  private int x, y;
```

```
  public boolean move () {
    if (! commandQueue.isEmpty()) {
      Character command = (Character) commandQueue.getFirst();
      commandQueue.removeFirst();
      if (command.charValue() == 'r')
        moveRight();
      else moveLeft();
    } else {
      if ((y > 0) && grid[y-1][x].equals(Color.white)) {
        grid[y][x] = Color.white;
        y = y - 1;
        grid[y][x] = color;
      } else return false;
    }
    return true;
  }

  private void moveRight () {
    if ((x < (BoardWidth-1)) && grid[y][x+1].equals(Color.white)) {
      grid[y][x] = Color.white;
      x = x + 1;
      grid[y][x] = color;
    }
  }

  private void moveLeft () {
    if ((x > 0) && grid[y][x-1].equals(Color.white)) {
      grid[y][x] = Color.white;
      x = x - 1;
      grid[y][x] = color;
    }
  }
}
```

To finish the application, we need only define the method run, which puts the pieces into play. Pieces are added as long as they can be placed at the top of the board without hitting an existing piece. The game is over when attempting to place a piece into the top row results in a collision:

```
public void run () {
  boolean loop = true;
  while (loop) {
    if (! piece.move()) {
        // create a new playing piece
      int ic = (int) (4 * Math.random());
```

```
      int iy = BoardHeight-1;
      int ix =  (int) (BoardWidth * Math.random());
      if (grid[iy][ix].equals(Color.white)) {
        piece = new Piece(ic, ix, iy);
        }
      else loop = false;
      }
    repaint();
    try { Thread.sleep(100); } catch(Exception e) { }
  }
  // game over
  System.out.println("game over");
}
```

The additional functionality necessary to detect rows of colors and to calculate the game score is left as an exercise.

* 19.3 Binary Matrices

In many applications, a matrix need hold only 0/1 (true/false or yes/no) values. A matrix of this form is called a binary matrix, or bit matrix. As we saw in the examination of the `BitSet` (Chapter 18), using an entire integer, or even a character, to store each value in such a collection uses far too much memory. Instead, many bits can be efficiently packed into a single integer.

The class `BitMatrix` is built on top of the `BitSet` abstraction and uses the same method names for operations on the elements. The difference is that operations on a `BitMatrix` require a row and column pair rather than a single index. The number of rows and columns is set in the constructor:

```
public class BitMatrix {
    // constructor
  public BitMatrix (int numRows, int numColumns) {
    rows = new BitSet[numRows];
    for (int i = 0; i < numRows; i++)
      rows[i] = new  BitSet(numColumns);
  }

    // data field
  private BitSet [ ] rows;

    // operations
  public void clear (int i, int j) { rows[i].clear(j); }
  public boolean get (int i, int j) { return rows[i].get(j); }
  public void set (int i, int j) { rows[i].set(j); }
}
```

The `BitMatrix` creates a two-dimensional structure as an array of `BitSets`. In effect, it is making a matrix out of an array of vectors:

We will later see a similar technique applied to ordinary elements when we examine the implementation of sparse matrices.

19.4 Application—The Game of Life

The Game of Life is not a game but rather a simulation. It was first described by the British mathematician John Conway in 1970 and was popularized by Martin Gardner in a series of articles on recreational mathematics in *Scientific American*.

The simulation uses a rectangular grid of elements called *cells*. Each cell is either *alive* or *dead*. We can therefore use a binary matrix to represent the state of the simulation. Cells grow in a series of discrete *generations*, according to the following rules:

1. The neighbors of a given cell are the eight cells that touch it vertically, horizontally, or diagonally. Cells on the edge of the playing surface can have fewer neighbors. (In principle, this could be avoided by having an infinite grid, but a grid of such size is difficult to display.)
2. If a cell is alive but has either no neighboring cells alive or only one alive, the cell dies of loneliness in the next generation.
3. If a cell is alive and has four or more neighboring cells also alive, the cell dies of overcrowding in the next generation. However, a cell with either two or three living neighbors remains alive in the next generation.
4. If a cell is dead, it will become alive if it has exactly three neighboring cells in the next generation. All other dead cells remain dead in the next generation.

For example, consider the following initial configuration. The first step is to determine the number of neighbors, both alive and dead, for each cell.

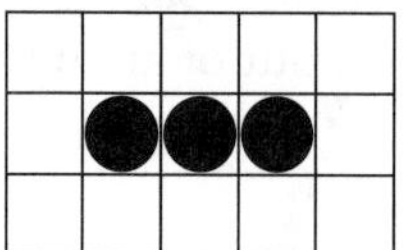

1	2	3	2	1
1	(1)	(2)	(1)	1
1	2	3	2	1

Live cells with two or three neighbors remain live, and dead cells with three neighbors become live. This leads to the following configuration. Can you tell what the subsequent generation will look like?

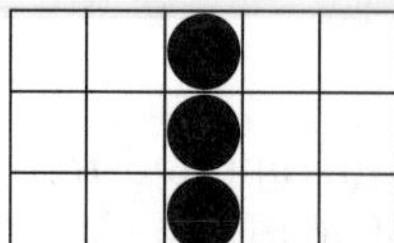

0	2	(1)	2	0
0	3	(2)	3	0
0	2	(1)	2	0

The following program will run the Game of Life simulation. The initial configuration, including the number of rows and columns and the values of the initial live cells, will be read from an input file specified by a command line argument. To paint the display, the program iterates over the `BitMatrix`, which indicates the live cells and draws a filled oval for each cell:

```
class Life extends Frame {
  public static void main (String [ ] args) {
    try {
      FileReader fin = new FileReader(args[0]);
      Life world = new Life(fin);
      world.show();
      while (true) {
        world.nextGeneration();
        world.repaint();
        Thread.sleep(500);
      }
    } catch (Exception e) {
      System.err.println("unable to initialize");
    }
  }

  public Life (Reader fin) throws IOException {
      // window initialization
    setSize(FrameWidth, FrameHeight); setTitle("Game of Life");
    addWindowListener(new CloseQuit());
      // application-specific initialization
    .
    .
    .
    }
}
```

```
  private int numRows, numColumns;
  private BitMatrix cells;
  final static int FrameWidth = 300;
  final static int FrameHeight = 300;

  public void paint (Graphics g) {
    int cellHeight = FrameHeight / numRows;
    int cellWidth = FrameWidth / numColumns;
    for (int i = 0; i < numRows; i++)
      for (int j = 0; j < numColumns; j++)
        if (cells.get(i, j))
          g.fillOval(i * cellHeight,
            j * cellWidth, cellHeight, cellWidth);
      // now sleep for a while, then draw again
    try { Thread.sleep(1000); } catch (Exception e) { }
    nextGeneration();
  }

  private void nextGeneration () { ... }
}
```

Determining the next generation is a two-step process. First, the neighbor count for each cell is computed. Second, each cell is examined and is either killed or revived, depending on the neighbor count:

```
private int [ ] [ ] neighborCount;

private void nextGeneration () {
    // first count neighbors
  for (int i = 0; i < numRows; i++)
    for (int j = 0; j < numColumns; j++)
      neighborCount[i][j] = countNeighbors(i,j);
    // then make new generation of cells
  for (int i = 0; i < numRows; i++)
    for (int j = 0; j < numColumns; j++)
      if (cells.get(i,j)) {
        if ((neighborCount[i][j] < 2) || (neighborCount[i][j] > 3))
          cells.clear(i,j);
      } else if (neighborCount[i][j] == 3)
        cells.set(i,j);
}

private int countNeighbors (int i,int j) {
  return living(i-1, j-1) + living(i-1, j) +
  living(i-1,j+1) + living(i, j-1) + living(i,j+1) +
  living(i+1, j-1) + living(i+1, j) + living(i+1, j+1);
}
```

```
private int living (int i, int j) {
  if ((i < 0) || (i >= numRows)) return 0;
  if ((j < 0) || (j >= numColumns)) return 0;
  if (cells.get(i, j)) return 1;
  return 0;
}
```

All that remains is the code to read the initial configuration. We use a `StreamTokenizer`, which is a version of the `StringTokenizer` (see Chapter 16) designed for working with files. The `StringTokenizer` will automatically convert the input into a sequence of numbers, which are used to determine the initial cell settings:

```
public Life (Reader fin) throws IOException {
    // window initialization
  setSize(FrameWidth, FrameHeight); setTitle("Game of Life");
    // application-specific initialization
  StreamTokenizer tok = new StreamTokenizer(fin);
  tok.nextToken(); numRows = (int) tok.nval;
  tok.nextToken(); numColumns = (int) tok.nval;
  cells = new BitMatrix(numRows, numColumns);
  neighborCount = new int [numRows][numColumns];
  while (tok.nextToken() != StreamTokenizer.TT_EOF) {
    int i = (int) tok.nval;
    tok.nextToken();
    int j = (int) tok.nval;
    cells.set(i, j);
  }
}
```

Figure 19.3 shows a screen shot taken from this application. People are often surprised and amused at the patterns that can arise from these simple rules. Can you tell what will happen given each of the following initial configurations?

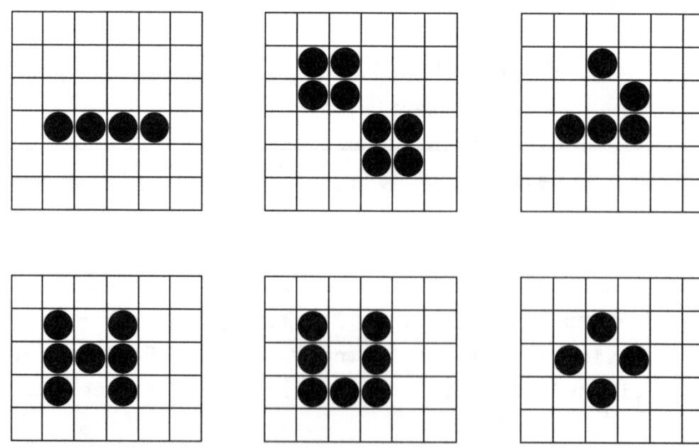

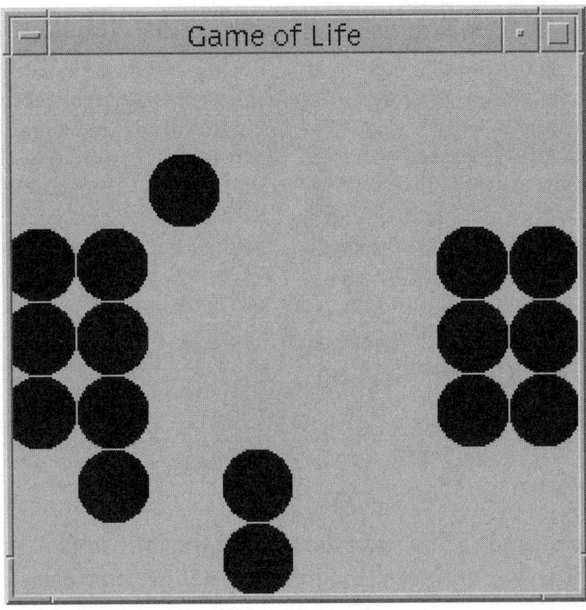

FIGURE 19.3 Screen Shot from Game of Life

* 19.5 SPARSE VECTORS

In preparation for discussing the concept of a *sparse matrix*, we first develop a slightly simpler abstraction, the `SparseVector`. A sparse vector is a data type that satisfies the same `Indexed` interface used by the class `Vector`. This means that elements can be accessed using an integer key. Instead of storing the elements of the collection in a single large array, however, only those elements that have explicitly been assigned a value

ANOTHER TIME/SPACE TRADEOFF

A characteristic of the `Vector` data type is that access to any element can be performed in constant time. For the `SparseVector`, however, as with the `Map`, the time to access an element is determined by the underlying data structure. In the example shown here, we use a `SkipList` for the set, which gives us a worst-case $O(\log n)$ execution bound for accessing each element. Sparse vectors therefore represent yet another example of a time/space tradeoff.

A sparse vector is used when too many elements in the conventional representation would be uninitialized. Thus, the conventional representation uses too much space in relation to the amount of information being stored. The sparse vector uses less memory but requires greater time to access each element. Deciding which representation to select for any particular problem requires balancing the competing requirements for these two resources.

EXPERIMENT: RUNNING TIME OF VECTOR OPERATIONS

A comparison of the running times for indexing operations using the `Vector` and the `SparseVector` data types is reasonable only in the particular situation in which the `SparseVector` data structure is an appropriate tool. In most problems, the $O(1)$ access time for elements held in a `Vector` data structure will totally dominate the $O(\log n)$ element access time for the `SparseVector`. To be fair, the `SparseVector` must be examined in situations in which the number of elements stored in the structure is small in relation to the size of the vector.

One experiment would measure the time required to create a vector of size n and then assign values to a small number of randomly selected elements. Try these two experiments. First, assign values for only a constant number of positions in the vector, for example, only 100 positions. For what vector size n does the running time of the `Vector` exceed that of the `SparseVector`? Then try assigning some percentage of the cells, for example, $n/100$. For what percentage does the running time of the `SparseVector` then exceed that of the `Vector`?

are stored. Thus, this data type is useful when the number of index positions that are set is relatively small in comparison to the entire range of possible index values. Such a collection is said to be *sparse*.

The `SparseVector` is implemented using the `Map` data type described in Chapter 17. Elements in the collection are stored using the index (suitably wrapped in an `Integer`) as the key.

The illusion being maintained is that the collection represents a very large vector in which most index positions remain uninitialized. For this reason, the size of the collection, as set by the `setSize` method in the `Indexed` interface, has very little relation to the number of elements being held by the container. Instead, the size is simply stored in an integer variable, used to ensure that index operations are valid. By default, the size is the largest legal integer, so subscript checking is disabled. The constructor also permits the user to specify an optional default value, to be returned when an attempt is made to access an element that has not yet been set.

The methods `setElementAt` and `elementAt` search for an element with the given integer key. The methods `addElementAt` and `removeElementAt` are more complex because like their `Vector` counterparts, they must reduce by 1 the index values for all entries at larger index positions. We leave the implementation of these methods as programming exercises.

```
public class SparseVector implements Indexed {

    // constructors
  public SparseVector () { }
  public SparseVector (Object d) { defaultValue = d; }
```

```
    // data fields
  protected int elementSize = Integer.MAX_VALUE;
  protected Bag elementData = new Map(new SkipList(), new IntegerCompare();
  protected Object defaultValue = null;

    // Collection interface
  public boolean isEmpty () { return elementSize == 0; }
  public int size () { return elementSize; }
  public Enumeration elements () { new IndexedEnumeration(this); }

    // Indexed interface
  public void setSize (int size) { elementSize = size; }

  public Object elementAt (int index) {
    if ((index < 0) || (index > elementSize))
      throw new ArrayIndexOutOfBoundsException(index);
    Integer key = new Integer(index);
    if (elementData.containsKey(key))
      return elementData.get(key);
    return defaultValue;
  }

  public void setElementAt (Object v, int index) {
    if ((index < 0) || (index > elementSize))
      throw new ArrayIndexOutOfBoundsException(index);
    Integer key = new Integer(key);
    elementData.set(key, v);
    }
  }

  public void addElementAt (Object val, int index) { ... }

  public void removeElementAt (int index) { ... }
}
```

19.6 An Application—(Almost) Infinitely Large Hash Tables

We will illustrate one application of the sparse vector by considering a variation on the DNA searching problem we presented in Chapter 4. Instead of DNA, let us consider a search of a simple text string. The task is to see whether any substring of length n is repeated two or more times.

Our approach will be as follows. We will form each possible substring of length 5 in turn and will hash each one. We use the hash value as an index and place the word into a vector. If we let n be 5, the first few entries formed using this paragraph as text would be as follows:

Word	Hash Value
`Our a`	154142467
`ur ap`	225098788
`r app`	215412299
`appr`	65044079
`appro`	187624410
`pproa`	215739438
`proac`	215836121
`roach`	219413397
`oach`	213084623
`ach w`	186951943

To see whether any word is repeated, we could merely test the element stored at the given position before inserting. If we see that a word is there already, we have a match. Or do we? What if two or more words hash to the same integer location? Because we have no control over the hashing function used by the `String` data type, this may be possible; indeed, it may be likely. But this is exactly the problem we considered when we developed the `OpenHashtable` data type. We solved the problem by introducing the idea of *probing*: storing an element in a location other than the original key position.

If we examine the `OpenHashtable` data structure, we see that it requires only that the underlying table satisfy the `Indexed` interface. Thus, nothing prevents us from creating an `OpenHashtable` on top of a `SparseVector`:

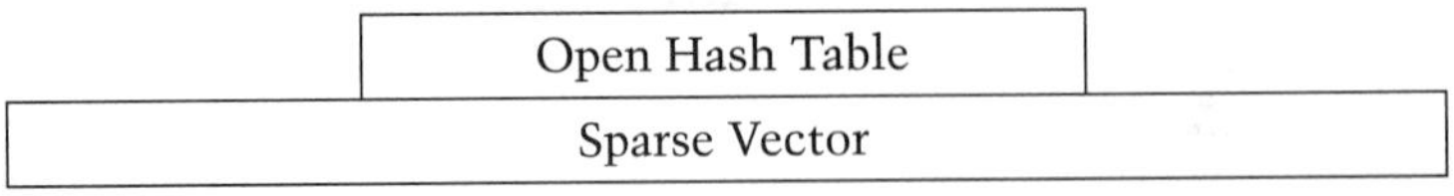

Open Hash Table
Sparse Vector

In effect, we are acting as if we have an extremely large hash table. But because the sparse vector stores only those elements that are *used,* the memory requirements are kept in check. The string search procedure can act as if it were using a simple Bag:

```
public void findRepeats (String str, int n) {
  int max = str.length() - n;
  Bag words = new OpenHashtable(new SparseVector());
  for (int i = 0; i < max; i++) {
    String sub = str.substring(i, i+n);
    if (words.containsElement(sub))
      System.out.println("found a repeat " + sub);
    else
      words.addElement(sub);
  }
}
```

19.7 SPARSE MATRICES

In practice, sparse matrices are even more common than sparse vectors, particularly in numerical problems. However, instead of having `null` in the uninitialized fields, they often have a specific numeric value, such as 0. Figure 19.4 shows one such example matrix. Just as with the sparse vector, storing all the elements in a sparse matrix may be unnecessarily costly. Instead, one could simply store information that indicates which elements are indeed nonzero, and return zero for all other elements.

By building on top of the `SparseVector`, the technique for doing this is surprisingly easy. The `SparseMatrix` will maintain a `SparseVector` of

```
0 0 0 0 0 0 0 0 0 0 0 0 0 0 0
0 2 0 0 0 0 0 0 0 0 0 0 0 0 0
0 0 0 0 0 0 0 0 0 0 0 0 0 0 0
0 0 0 0 0 0 7 0 0 0 0 0 0 0 0
0 0 0 0 0 0 0 0 0 0 0 0 0 0 0
0 0 0 0 9 0 0 0 0 0 0 4 0 0 0
0 0 0 0 0 0 0 0 0 0 0 0 0 0 0
0 0 0 0 0 0 0 0 0 0 0 0 0 0 0
0 0 0 0 0 0 0 0 3 0 0 0 0 0 0
0 0 1 0 0 0 0 0 0 0 0 0 0 0 0
```

FIGURE 19.4 An Example Sparse Matrix

rows. Thus, each row will maintain a SparseVector of elements. New rows or elements are created only when necessary:

```
public class SparseMatrix implements Matrix {
    // constructors
  public SparseMatrix () { }
  public SparseMatrix (Object d) { defaultValue = d; }

    // data fields
  protected Object defaultValue = null;
  protected SparseVector rows = new SparseVector();

    // get and set operations
  public Object elementAt (int i, int j) {
    Object r = rows.elementAt(i);
    if (r == null) return defaultValue;
    SparseVector row = (SparseVector) r;
    return row.elementAt(j);
  }

  public void setElementAt (int i, int j, Object v) {
    Object r = rows.elementAt(i);
    if (r == null) {
      r = new SparseVector(defaultValue);
      rows.setElementAt(r, i);
    }
    SparseVector row = (SparseVector) r;
    row.setElementAt(v, j);
  }
.
.
.
}
```

Although this implementation is workable, is does have a few unsatisfactory properties. For example, if we apply the matrix multiplication algorithm to this structure, we will end up putting an entry into every location, even when most of these match the default value. An improvement, therefore, would be to modify the put method so as to remove the association when assigning the default value.

* 19.8 NONINTEGER KEYS

The Map data type was designed to address the problem in which we needed an indexed data type, but the index quantities were not integer. In a similar fashion, the need sometimes arises for a two-dimensional collection in which neither index value is numeric. Just as the SparseMatrix was easily constructed on top of the SparseVector, a two-dimensional MapMatrix can be easily formed using the existing Map data abstraction:

```
public class MapMatrix {
    // constructors
  public MapMatrix () { }
  public MapMatrix (Object d) { defaultValue = d; }

  protected Object defaultValue = null;
  protected Map rows = new MapAdapter(new LinkedList());

    // get and set operations
  public Object get (Object key1, Object key2) {
    if (rows.containsKey(key1)) {
      Map row = (Map) rows.get(key1);
      if (row.containsKey(key2))
        return row.get(key2);
    }
    return defaultValue;
  }

  public void set (Object key1, Object key2, Object v) {
    Map row;
    if (rows.containsKey(key1))
      row = (Map) rows.get(key1);
    else {
      row = new MapAdapter(new LinkedList());
      rows.set(key1, row);
    }
    row.set(key2, v);
  }

}
```

For example, suppose that we want to represent the following table of average temperature (degrees Fahrenheit) for various cities:

City	January	April	July	October
Bismark	9.9	43.5	71.7	46.7
Denver	28.5	46.4	72.9	51.4
Wichita	32.0	56.7	80.9	59.9
San Francisco	50.7	55.7	58.8	61.4

One approach would be to declare a MapMatrix and index this by using the string names. To create a chart, we simply declare a new variable, then initialize the variable with a sequence of assignment statements:

```
MapMatrix temps = new MapMatrix();
temps.set("Bismark", "January", new Double(9.9));
temps.set("Bismark", "April", new Double(43.5));
.
.
.
temps.set("San Francisco", "January", new Double(50.7));
temps.set("San Francisco", "April", new Double(55.7));
temps.set("San Francisco", "July", new Double(58.8));
```

19.9 CHAPTER SUMMARY

KEY CONCEPTS

- Matrix
- Matrix multiplication
- Sparse matrix
- Matrix with non-integer keys

A matrix is a two-dimensional array of elements. Matrices occur in a number of mathematical and financial problems. The Java language provides a primitive matrix facility; however, this data type suffers from problems similar to those for the array data type.

We can construct more general matrix abstractions in a variety of ways. A simple form of matrix is a vector of vectors. By using a map in place of a vector, we can implement the idea of a sparse matrix: a matrix that stores only the elements that are being used. Finally, a map of maps provides a means of implementing a two-dimensional matrix structure in which the index values are not integers.

Further Information

Various alternative data structures for the Game of Life are discussed by Kruse [Kruse 99].

The string-matching problem examined in Section 19.6 is related to a classic technique known as the *Rabin-Karp search algorithm*. The key difference is that the Rabin-Karp algorithm creates the hash values slightly differently. Rather than recomputing each new hash value from scratch, the hash value for each substring is formed based on the hash value for the previous substring and the one new character. This permits the hash values for each string to be formed very quickly, giving an overall improvement in performance. A good analysis of the Rabin-Karp algorithm is presented in Cormen [Cormen 90].

Study Questions

1. What is a matrix?
2. How many elements will be contained in a matrix with four rows and six columns?
3. What is the asymptotic execution time of the matrix multiplication procedure shown in Figure 19.1?
4. What is a sparse matrix?
5. What are the two ways in which a matrix element is used?
6. What property of a `map` makes it useful in implementing the sparse matrix class? What property makes it useful in implementing the data type `chartType` in Section 19.8?

Exercises

1. Assume that two-dimensional matrices are laid out in memory as shown on page 508. Write a formula that will determine the memory offset for location i, j relative to the start of the matrix, assuming that the matrix has n rows of m elements. (For example, for the given 3-by-4 matrix, element `d[1][2]` is found at offset 6, whereas element `d[2][1]` has offset 9.)
2. In the `vector` data type, the member function `resize()` changes the number of elements that can be stored in the container. We used this member function, for example, in the constructor for the class `matrix`. Implement a variation on `resize()` for two-dimensional matrices. Your function should take two integer arguments and alter both the number of rows and the number of columns.
3. Using the chart representation described in Section 19.8, write short programs to perform the following.
   a. Compute the mean temperature for all cities and all months.
   b. For each month, compute the mean temperature across all cities.
   c. Find the cities with the highest and the lowest average temperatures.
   d. Find the city with the greatest temperature variation.
4. A two-dimensional matrix is said to be *symmetric* if the element held at index position i, j is the same as that held at position j, i. Given such a structure, it is not necessary to store both elements. Instead, we might store only those elements corresponding to positions i, j, where $i <= j$. A request for j, i, where $j < i$, would then be turned around and the element i, j returned. Show how to modify the `sparse_matrix`

data type so as to represent symmetric matrices in this fashion. (*Hint:* The sparse matrix element type will need to store a reference to the entire array, not simply one row.)

5. Two-Dimensional Binary Search: Imagine a matrix n by m ordered along each row and each column. The following is an example:

0	2	3	5	7
3	6	7	8	12
7	8	9	12	20
11	13	14	18	22

   Your task is to discover whether a specific element t is contained in the collection. Can you devise a binary search variation that will find the result more quickly than simply comparing every element? What is the algorithmic complexity of your procedure?

Programming Projects

1. A number of features must be added to the Rain game described in Section 19.2 before it becomes a truly interesting arcade game. These include the following.
   a. Add a counter to keep track of the number of pieces that have been generated. This is the current score. Display the score in a `Label` at the bottom of the window.
   b. We have not provided the code to check for four or more blocks of the same color in a row or a diagonal. Add this check as a method that will be invoked by the main `run` method when it detects that a piece is no longer moving. If such a set of blocks is discovered, they are erased, and the blocks in the grid above the erased blocks are moved down.
   c. Permit the user to enter another key command, for example, `x`. When this key is pressed, the block immediately drops to the bottom.
   d. As the score grows higher, the sleep time for the game piece can be reduced, thereby increasing the speed of the game.
   e. Maintain a file of the top ten scores. Display this list at the end of the game. When the game is finished, see whether the current score is sufficient to place the user on this list. (See the address book application in Chapter 17 for an example of how to save containers in a file.)
2. Program the game Columns. This is similar to Rain, only pieces come down in a group of three. The colors of the three pieces of the columns

are selected randomly. A group of three can be rotated so as to be either a vertical or a horizontal block.

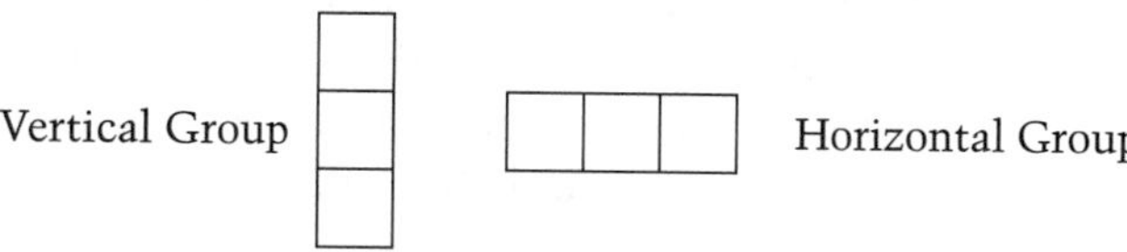

In the simple version of the game, the pieces are independent, so that the pieces of a horizontal block will come apart when they reach the bottom. A more complex version keeps the pieces rigid, so that gaps can form in the pile at the bottom of the window when a horizontal block becomes caught.

3. The game Tetris is similar to Columns, only the pieces have more complex shapes.

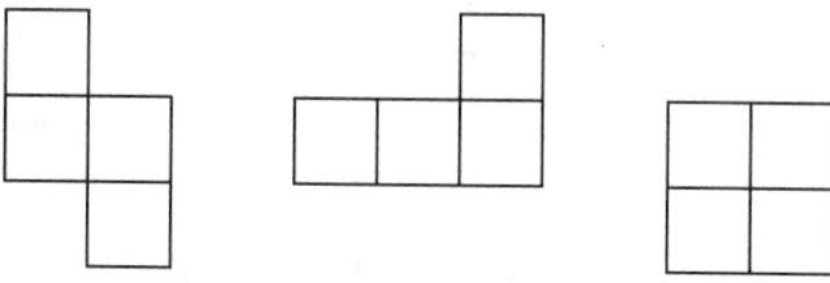

The goal in Tetris is not to form a row with the same color but to simply fill a row.

4. The following steps are needed to finish the implementation of the `SparseVector` data type and to add certain new features.
   a. Complete the body of the `addElementAt` and `removeElementAt` methods.
   b. If a position is assigned and subsequently reassigned to the default value, using the method `setElementAt`, the association for the element can be removed from the underlying `Map`, as access will return the default value anyway.
5. Modify the implementation of the `SparseMatrix` to correctly handle the situation in which the default value is assigned, using the method `set`. In this situation, no new entry should be inserted into the collection; if any entry already exists using the given keys, it should be removed.
6. Another approach to implementing the `SparseMatrix` data type would be to use a simple `Map` indexed by a `Pair` of row/column coordinates. Develop an abstraction based on these ideas, and compare the running time to that of the implementation given in the text.

7. The traditional, albeit slightly more complex, implementation of sparse matrices is termed the *orthogonally linked-list* representation. Two arrays are used to represent the rows and columns of the matrix. Each array refers to the first element in a collection of `BinaryNodes`, the same as we used in the binary tree representations studied in Chapter 13. The left field in each node points to the next element in the same column, and the right field points to the next element in the same row.

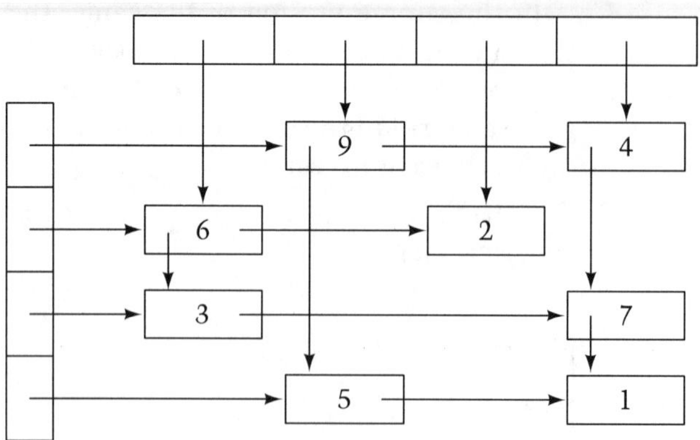

The advantage of the orthogonally linked-list representation is that it is easy to traverse the matrix by either rows or columns, something that is important in many numerical algorithms.

Develop the data structure based on this principle. How does the complexity of the insertion algorithm compare to that of the techniques examined in this chapter? How does the execution time compare?

CHAPTER 20

GRAPHS

Graphs occur in a variety of applications in computer science. In this chapter, we provide a brief introduction to the concept, illustrating the two major data structures used to represent this abstraction. Example problems are then solved, illustrating both the benefits and the limitations of each of these representations. Our purpose is not to summarize the field of graph theory, which is a rich and complex cross between mathematics and computer science but rather to illustrate the use of many of the data structures we have been developing in earlier chapters in the solution of realistic nontrivial problems.

A graph, such as the one shown in Figure 20.1, is composed of *vertices* and *edges*. Either may carry additional information. If the graph is being used to model real-world objects, such as a roadmap, the value of a vertex might represent the name of a city, whereas an edge could represent a road from one city to another.

Graphs are of various types. A graph is said to be *directed* if the edges have a designated beginning and ending point; otherwise, a graph is said to be undirected. We will restrict our discussion in this chapter to directed graphs. This is, in fact, no restriction at all, as an undirected graph can always be simulated by a directed graph, in which each edge is represented by two arcs traveling in opposite directions:

A second source of variation in the idea of a graph is the distinction between a *weighted*, or *labeled*, graph and an *unweighted* graph. In a

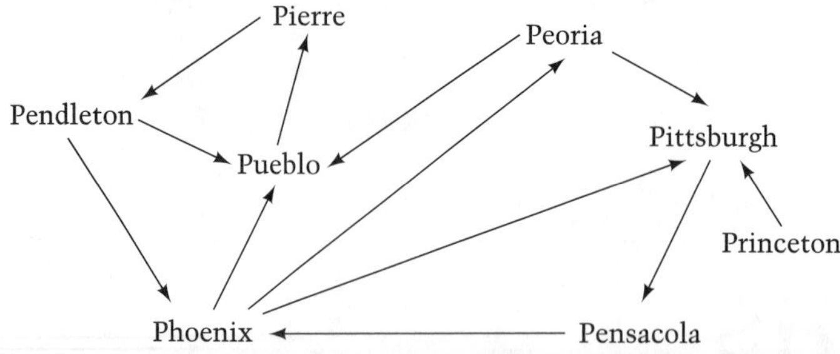

FIGURE 20.1 A Typical Graph

weighted graph, each edge is given a numerical value. For example, the value might represent the distance of the highway connecting two cities or the cost of the airfare between two airports. An unweighted graph carries no such information. We will begin by considering algorithms for unweighted graphs. This discussion will then be followed by a pair of algorithms that operate on the weighted forms.

The two most common data representations for a graph are an adjacency matrix and an edge list. The *adjacency matrix* represents the graph as a two-dimensional matrix, similar to those studied in Chapter 19. The vertices in the graph are used as index values for the matrix. This means that either the vertices must be numbered in the original graph, or a mechanism must be provided to associate each vertex with an integer value. To represent the graph shown in Figure 20.1, we could simply list the cities in alphabetical order and number the list. A 1 value in the position indexed by *i* and *j* in the matrix indicates that there is an edge from vertices *i* to *j*; a 0 value indicates that there is no such connection. By convention, a node is always considered to be connected to itself; thus, all positions in the major diagonal (that is, positions with the same row and column index value) are 1. The adjacency-matrix representation for the graph in Figure 20.1 is as follows:

City	0.	1.	2.	3.	4.	5.	6.	7.
0. Pendleton	1	0	0	1	0	0	0	1
1. Pensacola	0	1	0	1	0	0	0	0
2. Peoria	0	0	1	0	0	1	0	1
3. Phoenix	0	0	1	1	0	1	0	1
4. Pierre	1	0	0	0	1	0	0	0
5. Pittsburgh	0	1	0	0	0	1	0	0
6. Princeton	0	0	0	0	0	1	1	0
7. Pueblo	0	0	0	0	1	0	0	1

The adjacency-matrix representation has the disadvantage that it always requires $O(V^2)$ space to store a matrix with V vertices, regardless of the number of edges—unless, of course, the graph has few edges and a sparse matrix representation, such as the one presented in Chapter 19, is used to hold the adjacency values. An alternative representation, the *edge list*, stores only the edges and is thus advantageous if the graph is relatively sparse. The basic idea is that each vertix will hold a set of adjacent edges:

Pendleton:	{ Pueblo, Phoenix }
Pensacola:	{ Phoenix }
Peoria:	{ Pueblo, Pittsburgh }
Phoenix:	{ Pueblo, Peoria, Pittsburgh }
Pierre:	{ Pendleton }
Pittsburgh:	{ Pensacola }
Princeton:	{ Pittsburgh }
Pueblo:	{ Pierre }

In a weighted graph, each set can be replaced by a `Map` (Chapter 17) in which the map key is the vertex and the map value is the weight. The size of this representation is dominated by V, the number of vertices, and E, the number of edges. We say that this representation uses $O(V + E)$ space. In the following sections, we will examine each of these representations in more detail and will present several of the more famous algorithms used in the manipulation of graphs.

20.1 Adjacency-Matrix Representation

As we noted earlier, an adjacency matrix is simply a two-dimensional array that indicates which vertices have connections. One could define the adjacency matrix as an array in the following fashion:

```
int [ ] [ ] adjacency = { { 1, 0, 0, 1, 0, 0, 0, 1},
        { 0, 1, 0, 1, 0, 0, 0, 0},
        { 0, 0, 1, 0, 0, 1, 0, 1},
        { 0, 0, 1, 1, 0, 1, 0, 1},
        { 1, 0, 0, 0, 1, 0, 0, 0},
        { 0, 1, 0, 0, 0, 1, 0, 0},
        { 0, 0, 0, 0, 0, 1, 1, 0},
        { 0, 0, 0, 0, 1, 0, 0, 1} };
```

One could ask a number of questions about any particular graph. One of the fundamental problems is the question of *reachability*. That is, what is the set of vertices that can be reached by starting from a particular vertex and moving only along the given edges in the graph? Conversely, are there any vertices that cannot be reached by traveling in such a fashion?

This question has two basic variations. The *single-source* question poses a specific initial starting vertex and requests the set of vertices reachable from this vertex. The *all-pairs* question seeks to generate this information simultaneously for all possible vertices. Of course, a solution to the all-pairs question will answer the single-source question as well. For this reason, we would expect that an algorithm that solves the all-pairs problem will require at least as much effort as any algorithm for the single-source problem. Next, we will present a solution to the all-pairs reachability problem. A solution to the single-source reachability problem will be presented in Section 20.2.

The algorithm we will describe to illustrate the use of the adjacency-matrix representation of graphs is known as Warshall's algorithm, after the computer scientist credited with its discovery. Warshall's algorithm is designed to generate a *reachability* matrix. A reachability matrix is similar to an adjacency matrix; a 1 value in location `i,j` indicates that vertex `j` can be reached by some path starting from vertex `i`, even if the two vertices are not directly connected. The heart of Warshall's algorithm (Figure 20.2) is a trio of loops that operate very much like the loops in the algorithm for matrix multiplication presented in Figure 19.1. The key idea is that at each iteration through the outermost loop (index `k`), we add to the graph any path of length 2 that has node `k` as its center.

The process of adding information to the graph is performed through a combination of bitwise integer operations. The expression `a[i][k] & a[k][j]` is `true` if there is a path from node `i` to node `k`, and if there is a path from node `k` to node `j`. This tells us that there is therefore a path from node `i` to node `j`. By using the bitwise `or` assignment operator, we add this information to position `a[i][j]`. The use of bitwise `or` ensures that if a 1 bit was already in the position, indicating we had already discovered a previous path, the earlier information will not be erased. Figure 20.3 gives the intermediate values of the matrix `a` as we execute Warshall's algorithm on the adjacency matrix from the graph of Figure 20.1.

The easiest way to understand Warshall's algorithm is to simulate a few iterations through the outer loop. In the first iteration, we are looking for paths that flow through node 0, which represents Pendleton. Because Pierre has the only edge flowing into Pendleton, Pierre is the source of the only possible new paths. In this case, two new paths are discovered: one that links Pierre with Phoenix and another that links Pierre with Pueblo.

In the second iteration, we investigate paths that travel through node 1, Pensacola. We discover one new edge, which links Pittsburgh with

```
class Warshall {
//
// warshall
//  solve the all-pairs reachability problem
//  using the adjacency-matrix representation of a graph
//  converts adjacency matrix into a reachability matrix
//
  static void warshall (int [ ] [ ] a) {
    int n = a.length;
    for (int k = 0; k < n; k++) {
      for (int i = 0; i < n; i++)
        for (int j = 0; j < n; j++)
          a[i][j] |= a[i][k] & a[k][j];
    // inv: if there is a path from vertex i to vertex j
    // that does not go through any vertex higher than k
    // then a[i][j] is 1.
    }
  }

  static public void main(String [ ] args) {
    int [ ] [ ] adjacency = { ... };
    warshall(adjacency);
      // ... print result
  }
}
```

FIGURE 20.2 Warshall's Algorithm

Phoenix. It turns out in the next step that no new paths flow through Peoria, and thus we have omitted this table from Figure 20.3.

The next step is to discover paths through Phoenix, and it is here that we can see how Warshall's algorithm really operates. From the original graph, we can derive the edges from Pendleton to Peoria, and Pendleton to Pittsburgh, just as we did in the earlier steps. But now we can do more. From the previous steps, we now know that one can travel from Pierre to Phoenix and from Pueblo to Phoenix. Thus, by extending paths we have earlier encountered, we can now say that it is possible to travel from Pierre to Peoria and Pittsburgh, and from Pueblo to the same two destinations. Even though at each step we consider only paths of length 2, the algorithm discovers paths of any length by repeatedly extending existing edges.

It is easy to see that Warshall's algorithm is $O(n^3)$, where n is the number of nodes in the graph. In the sidebar, we provide a proof of correctness for the algorithm.

```
1 0 0 1 0 0 0 1
0 1 0 1 0 0 0 0
0 0 1 0 0 1 0 1
0 0 1 1 0 1 0 1
1 0 0 0 1 0 0 0
0 1 0 0 0 1 0 0
0 0 0 0 0 1 1 0
0 0 0 0 1 0 0 1
```
Initial Matrix

```
1 0 0 1 0 0 0 1
0 1 0 1 0 0 0 0
0 0 1 0 0 1 0 1
0 0 1 1 0 1 0 1
1 0 0 1 1 0 0 1
0 1 0 0 0 1 0 0
0 0 0 0 0 1 1 0
0 0 0 0 1 0 0 1
```
Matrix after Iteration 0

```
1 0 0 1 0 0 0 1
0 1 0 1 0 0 0 0
0 0 1 0 0 1 0 1
0 0 1 1 0 1 0 1
1 0 0 1 1 0 0 1
0 1 0 1 0 1 0 0
0 0 0 0 0 1 1 0
0 0 0 0 1 0 0 1
```
Matrix after Iteration 1

```
1 0 1 1 0 1 0 1
0 1 1 1 0 1 0 1
0 0 1 0 0 1 0 1
0 0 1 1 0 1 0 1
1 0 1 1 1 1 0 1
0 1 1 1 0 1 0 1
0 0 0 0 0 1 1 0
0 0 0 0 1 0 0 1
```
Matrix after Iteration 3

```
1 0 1 1 0 1 0 1
0 1 1 1 0 1 0 1
0 0 1 0 0 1 0 1
0 0 1 1 0 1 0 1
1 0 1 1 1 1 0 1
0 1 1 1 0 1 0 1
0 0 0 0 0 1 1 0
1 0 1 1 1 1 0 1
```
Matrix after Iteration 4

```
1 1 1 1 0 1 0 1
0 1 1 1 0 1 0 1
0 1 1 1 0 1 0 1
0 1 1 1 0 1 0 1
1 1 1 1 1 1 0 1
0 1 1 1 0 1 0 1
0 1 1 1 0 1 1 1
1 1 1 1 1 1 0 1
```
Matrix after Iteration 5

```
1 1 1 1 0 1 0 1
0 1 1 1 0 1 0 1
0 1 1 1 0 1 0 1
0 1 1 1 0 1 0 1
1 1 1 1 1 1 0 1
0 1 1 1 0 1 0 1
0 1 1 1 0 1 1 1
1 1 1 1 1 1 0 1
```
Matrix after Iteration 6

```
1 1 1 1 1 1 0 1
1 1 1 1 1 1 0 1
1 1 1 1 1 1 0 1
1 1 1 1 1 1 0 1
1 1 1 1 1 1 0 1
1 1 1 1 1 1 0 1
1 1 1 1 1 1 1 1
1 1 1 1 1 1 0 1
```
Matrix after Iteration 7

FIGURE 20.3 Some Intermediate Graphs while Executing Warshall's Algorithm

PROOF OF CORRECTNESS: WARSHALL'S ALGORITHM

To prove the correctness of Warshall's algorithm, we first note that if there is a path from vertex `i` to vertex `j`, there is a path that never travels through any vertex more than once. (Simply remove such loops, resulting in a shorter path.)

The heart of the algorithm then involves establishing the invariant shown at the end of the outermost loop in Figure 20.2. We will use a technique similar to mathematical induction.

To establish the base case, note that any path that goes through vertex zero and uses no vertices with labels larger than zero will be marked at the end of the first iteration through the loop. Such a path must consist of only two legs: vertex `i` to vertex zero, then vertex zero to vertex `j`. Each of the legs must be present as edges in the initial graph. But they will therefore be recognized when the index values match the given vertex numbers, and we have that `a[i][j]` must be set to 1.

Next, we consider the induction step. Assume that we are on the `k`th iteration and that all paths that traverse only vertices labeled `k` or less have been marked. Assume that a path from vertex `i` to vertex `j` goes through vertex `k` and uses no vertices numbered larger than `k`. But this means that there is a path from vertex `i` to vertex `k` that does not go through any vertices larger than `k`. Therefore, by our induction hypothesis, `a[i][k]` must be 1. Similarly, there must be a path from vertex `k` to vertex `j`, which also cannot use vertex `k`. Therefore, `a[k][j]` must be 1. But at the point the index values match the vertex numbers, the value `a[i][j]` will therefore be set to 1. So the invariant remains true at the end of the loop.

Therefore, once the variable `k` finishes cycling through all vertices, we know that for all `i, j` pairs, if there is a path from vertex `i` to vertex `j` that goes through vertices labeled `n` or less (that is, all vertices), `a[i][j]` will be 1. But this implies that all possible paths will have been discovered.

20.2 EDGE-LIST REPRESENTATION

As we noted earlier, the adjacency-matrix representation has the disadvantage that it always requires $O(V^2)$ space to store a matrix with V vertices, regardless of the number of edges. The edge-list representation stores only the edges and in some cases may therefore be much smaller. The basic idea is for each vertex to maintain a set of references to vertices to which it is connected. This is accomplished by the following class declaration:

```
public class Vertex {
    // constructors
  public Vertex () { name = null; }
  public Vertex (Object init) { name = n; }

    // data fields
  public final Object name;
  protected Bag edges = new LinkedList();
```

```
    // operations
  public void addEdge (Vertex v) { edges.addElement(v); }
  public void removeEdge (Vertex v) { edges.removeElement(v); }
  public String toString () { return name.toString(); }
  public Bag findReachable () { ... }
}
```

The method named addEdge is used to create a new edge that originates at the vertex. If necessary, a graph can then be represented as a Bag of Vertex values:

```
class Graph {
    // data areas
  protected Bag vertices = new LinkedList();

    // operations
  public void addVertex (Vertex v) { vertices.addElement(v); }
  public void removeVertex (Vertex v) { vertices.removeElement(v); }
}
```

The graph in Figure 20.1 could be created by the following sequence of statements:

```
//  make the initial vertices
Graph g = new Graph();
Vertex pendleton = new Vertex("pendleton"); g.addVertex(pendleton);
Vertex pensacola = new Vertex("pensacola"); g.addVertex(pensacola);
Vertex peoria = new Vertex("peoria"); g.addVertex(peoria);
Vertex phoenix = new Vertex("phoenix"); g.addVertex(phoenix);
Vertex pierre = new Vertex("pierre"); g.addVertex(pierre);
Vertex pittsburgh = new Vertex("pittsburgh"); g.addVertex(pittsburgh);
Vertex princeton = new Vertex("princeton"); g.addVertex(princeton);
Vertex pueblo = new Vertex("pueblo"); g.addVertex(pueblo);

// create the initial links
pendleton.addEdge(phoenix); pendleton.addEdge(pueblo);
pensacola.addEdge(phoenix);
peoria.addEdge(pittsburgh); peoria.addEdge(pueblo);
phoenix.addEdge(peoria); phoenix.addEdge(pittsburgh);
phoenix.addEdge(pueblo);
pierre.addEdge(pendleton);
pittsburgh.addEdge(pensacola);
princeton.addEdge(pittsburgh);
pueblo.addEdge(pierre);
```

We will illustrate the use of the vertex data type by presenting an algorithm for the single-source reachability problem. That is, we will explore

```
class Vertex {
  .
  .
  .
  public Bag findReachable () {
    Stack pendingVertices = new LinkedList();
    pendingVertices.addLast(this); // add ourselves as source
    Bag reachable = new OpenHashtable(17);

      // pull vertices from stack one by one
    while (! pendingVertices.isEmpty()) {
      Vertex vertx = (Vertex) pendingVertices.getLast();
      pendingVertices.removeLast();
        // if we haven't visited it yet, then do so now
      if (! reachable.containsElement(vertx)) {
        reachable.addElement(vertx);
          // add vertices that are now reachable
        Enumeration e = vertx.edges.elements();
        while (e.hasMoreElements())
          pendingVertices.addLast(e.nextElement());
      }
    }
    return reachable;
  }
}
```

FIGURE 20.4 Single-Source Reachability Algorithm

a procedure to discover which vertices may be reached by a sequence of edges, starting from a single-source vertex.

The procedure used to compute this is shown in Figure 20.4. The algorithm uses depth-first search, a technique we encountered in Chapter 11. You will recall that the depth-first search algorithm uses a stack. In this case, the stack holds vertices that are known to be reachable and through which other vertices may be reachable. The stack is constructed using a `LinkedList` for the underlying container and initially contains only the source vertex.

DEPTH- AND BREADTH-FIRST SEARCH

In the `findReachable` algorithm, simply changing the declaration of the `Stack` to a `Queue` and changing the methods `getLast` and `removeLast` to `getFirst` and `removeFirst` changes the search technique from a depth-first search to a breadth-first search. You should try simulating the program with this change, and note the difference in the order that vertices are visited.

One node is removed from the stack at each step of processing. If it is a node that has not previously been reported as reachable, it is added to the set of reachable vertices, and the neighbors of the node are pushed onto the stack. When the stack is finally empty, all nodes that can be reached will have been investigated.

For example, executing the following instructions will reveal that in our example graph, it is possible to get from Pierre to any city except Princeton:

```
public static void main (String [ ] args) {
  // create the initial graph(given earlier)
  Bag reachable = pierre.findReachable();
  System.out.println("Cities reachable from Pierre");
  Enumeration e = reachable.elements();
  while (e.hasMoreElements())
    System.out.println(e.nextElement());
  }
}
```

PROOF OF CORRECTNESS: REACHABILITY ALGORITHM

The proof of correctness of the reachability algorithm is an inductive argument, where the induction quantity is the length of the smallest path from the source vertex to the vertex in question. A trivial base case is provided by the starting vertex itself. There is a path of length 0 from the source vertex to itself, and thus the source is reachable. If we examine the code, we will see that the starting vertex is placed into the queue immediately after the queue is created. The queue is therefore not empty, and the `while` loop must execute at least once.

As the starting node is the only value in the queue, it must be the value first pulled from the queue. Because the set of values in `reachable` is empty (an assumption, not part of the code), the count will be 0 and the source vertex placed into the set. Thus, we have traced the execution to the point where we can assert that the source vertex must always be placed into the set of reachable vertices.

The induction step assumes that all vertices that are reachable along a path of length n or less will eventually be placed into the queue and subsequently pulled from the queue. (Note that we have just established this for $n = 0$.) The first time such a vertex is removed from the queue, the vertex will be not be found in the set of reachable vertices, and hence the `if` statement will be executed. But the body of the `if` statement places back into the queue all vertices reachable in one step from the vertex just pulled from the queue. Thus, vertices that are reachable along a path of length $n+1$ must eventually be placed into the queue (as a path of length $n+1$ is simply one step more than a path of length n).

It is simple to observe that all vertices placed into the queue must eventually be removed from the queue (as the `while` loop executes until the queue becomes empty). Together, these two prove that all vertices reachable along a path of length $n+1$ must eventually be pulled from the queue.

By induction, we have therefore proved that all vertices reachable along a path of any length will eventually be pulled from the queue. Because the first time this happens, the vertex will be added to the set of reachable vertices, all reachable vertices will eventually be added to the set.

To obtain a running time for this algorithm, observe that each entry placed into the stack corresponds to an edge and that no edge will be placed into the stack more than once. Therefore, the `while` loop will execute no more than E times, where E represents the number of edges. The `containsElement` test can return `true` no more than V times. Although it would seem as if the nested `while` loop would have an $O(E)$ upper bound, leading us to suspect a total running time of $O(V \times E)$ for the code within the `if` statement, further reflection tells us that the *total* number of times the nested `while` loop can execute cannot exceed the number of edges. Because with an appropriately sized open hash table, the set operations are $O(1)$ in the worst case, the total worst-case execution time is $O(E)$. An upper bound on E is V^2, where V is the number of vertices, although graphs frequently have far fewer edges. However, this shows that even in the worst case, the single-source reachability algorithm is faster than Warshall's algorithm.

20.3 Weighted-Graph Representation

Just as important as the question of what cities can be reached by starting at a given location is the question of how much the trip will cost. But to determine this, we must somehow encode the "cost" of traversing an edge. To accommodate this, we have the notion of a *weighted graph*, in which every edge has an associated value. For example, we might weight the edges in Figure 20.1, producing a graph such as that shown in Figure 20.5.

Just as there were two major representations of unweighted graphs, so, too, are there two primary techniques of encoding weighted graphs. These are the weighted-adjacency matrix and the labeled-edge-list representation. We will explore each of these in turn.

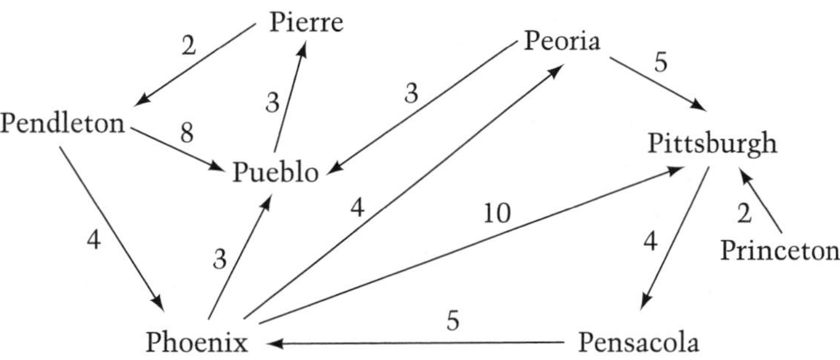

Figure 20.5 A Weighted Graph

20.3.1 Weighted-Adjacency Matrix

The weighted-adjacency matrix is a two-dimensional matrix, just like the unweighted form. Instead of simply using 0/1 values, the value in each position is the cost of moving from the vertex associated with the row to the vertex associated with the column. There are two special cases. The cost to move from any vertex to itself is 0. And the cost to move from any vertex to a vertex to which it is not connected is infinity (by convention, written ∞). In Java, we can use the value `Double.POSITIVE_INFINITY` to represent infinity. The weighted-adjacency-matrix representation of the graph shown in Figure 20.5 is as follows:

City	0.	1.	2.	3.	4.	5.	6.	7.
0. Pendleton	0	∞	∞	4	∞	∞	∞	8
1. Pensacola	∞	0	∞	5	∞	∞	∞	∞
2. Peoria	∞	∞	0	∞	∞	5	∞	3
3. Phoenix	∞	∞	4	0	∞	10	∞	3
4. Pierre	2	∞	∞	∞	0	∞	∞	∞
5. Pittsburgh	∞	4	∞	∞	∞	0	∞	∞
6. Princeton	∞	∞	∞	∞	∞	2	0	∞
7. Pueblo	∞	∞	∞	∞	3	∞	∞	0

20.3.2 Floyd's Algorithm

The weighted-adjacency-matrix version of Warshall's algorithm is called Floyd's algorithm, named for the computer scientist credited with the discovery of the algorithm (the same Robert Floyd who first described the tree sort algorithm we presented in Chapter 14). The procedure is shown in Figure 20.6. In place of the bitwise and operation in Warshall's algorithm, an addition is used in Floyd's; in place of the bitwise or used to update the path matrix, Floyd's algorithm uses a minimum-value calculation.

If we apply this algorithm to the data in our sample graph, we obtain the intermediate values shown in Figure 20.7. These can be contrasted with the similar output from Warshall's algorithm. Note that each time a value was changed in Warshall's matrix, the same value is being modified here. Now, however, the value held in the matrix is not simply an indication that there is a path but is the lowest known cost of the path.

```
class Floyd {
//
// floyd
//    Floyd's algorithm for finding the shortest
//    path between all pairs of vertices
//
  public static void floyd (double [ ] [ ] a) {
    int n = a.length;
    for (int k = 0; k < n; k++)
      for (int i = 0; i < n; i++)
        for (int j = 0; j < n; j++) {
          double m = a[i][k] + a[k][j];
          if (m < a[i][j]) a[i][j] = m;
        }
}
```

FIGURE 20.6 Floyd's Algorithm

20.3.3 Weighted-Edge-List Representation

As we noted earlier, the edge-list representation of a weighted graph can be formed by replacing the Bag in our previous `Vertex` class with a `Map`:

```
class WVertex {
    // constructors
  WVertex () { edges = new MapAdapter(new LinkedList()); }
  WVertex (Object n) { name = n; edges = new MapAdapter
                                        (new LinkedList()); }

    // data fields
  public Object name = null;
  protected Map edges;

    // operations
  public void addEdge (WVertex v, int w) { edges.set(v, new
                                                   Integer(w)); }
  public void removeEdge (WVertex v, int w) { edges.removeKey(v); }
  public String toString () { return name.toString(); }

  public Map dijkstra () {  ... }
}
```

The addEdge method has also been modified so as to set both the vertex and the weight.

$$\begin{matrix} 0 & \infty & \infty & 4 & \infty & \infty & \infty & 8 \\ \infty & 0 & \infty & 5 & \infty & \infty & \infty & \infty \\ \infty & \infty & 0 & \infty & \infty & 5 & \infty & 3 \\ \infty & \infty & 4 & 0 & \infty & 10 & \infty & 3 \\ 2 & \infty & \infty & \infty & 0 & \infty & \infty & \infty \\ \infty & 4 & \infty & \infty & \infty & 0 & \infty & \infty \\ \infty & \infty & \infty & \infty & \infty & 2 & 0 & \infty \\ \infty & \infty & \infty & \infty & 3 & \infty & \infty & 0 \end{matrix}$$

Initial Matrix

$$\begin{matrix} 0 & \infty & \infty & 4 & \infty & \infty & \infty & 8 \\ \infty & 0 & \infty & 5 & \infty & \infty & \infty & \infty \\ \infty & \infty & 0 & \infty & \infty & 5 & \infty & 3 \\ \infty & \infty & 4 & 0 & \infty & 10 & \infty & 3 \\ 2 & \infty & \infty & 6 & 0 & \infty & \infty & 10 \\ \infty & 4 & \infty & \infty & \infty & 0 & \infty & \infty \\ \infty & \infty & \infty & \infty & \infty & 2 & 0 & \infty \\ \infty & \infty & \infty & \infty & 3 & \infty & \infty & 0 \end{matrix}$$

Matrix after Iteration 0

$$\begin{matrix} 0 & \infty & \infty & 4 & \infty & \infty & \infty & 8 \\ \infty & 0 & \infty & 5 & \infty & \infty & \infty & \infty \\ \infty & \infty & 0 & \infty & \infty & 5 & \infty & 3 \\ \infty & \infty & 4 & 0 & \infty & 10 & \infty & 3 \\ 2 & \infty & \infty & 6 & 0 & \infty & \infty & 10 \\ \infty & 4 & \infty & 9 & \infty & 0 & \infty & \infty \\ \infty & \infty & \infty & \infty & \infty & 2 & 0 & \infty \\ \infty & \infty & \infty & \infty & 3 & \infty & \infty & 0 \end{matrix}$$

Matrix after Iteration 1

$$\begin{matrix} 0 & \infty & 8 & 4 & \infty & 13 & \infty & 7 \\ \infty & 0 & 9 & 5 & \infty & 14 & \infty & 8 \\ \infty & \infty & 0 & \infty & \infty & 5 & \infty & 3 \\ \infty & \infty & 4 & 0 & \infty & 9 & \infty & 3 \\ 2 & \infty & 10 & 6 & 0 & 15 & \infty & 9 \\ \infty & 4 & 13 & 9 & \infty & 0 & \infty & 12 \\ \infty & \infty & \infty & \infty & \infty & 2 & 0 & \infty \\ \infty & \infty & \infty & \infty & 3 & \infty & \infty & 0 \end{matrix}$$

Matrix after Iteration 3

$$\begin{matrix} 0 & \infty & 8 & 4 & \infty & 13 & \infty & 7 \\ \infty & 0 & 9 & 5 & \infty & 14 & \infty & 8 \\ \infty & \infty & 0 & \infty & \infty & 5 & \infty & 3 \\ \infty & \infty & 4 & 0 & \infty & 9 & \infty & 3 \\ 2 & \infty & 10 & 6 & 0 & 15 & \infty & 9 \\ \infty & 4 & 13 & 9 & \infty & 0 & \infty & 12 \\ \infty & \infty & \infty & \infty & \infty & 2 & 0 & \infty \\ 5 & \infty & 13 & 9 & 3 & 18 & \infty & 0 \end{matrix}$$

Matrix after Iteration 4

$$\begin{matrix} 0 & 17 & 8 & 4 & \infty & 13 & \infty & 7 \\ \infty & 0 & 9 & 5 & \infty & 14 & \infty & 8 \\ \infty & 9 & 0 & 14 & \infty & 5 & \infty & 3 \\ \infty & 13 & 4 & 0 & \infty & 9 & \infty & 3 \\ 2 & 19 & 10 & 6 & 0 & 15 & \infty & 9 \\ \infty & 4 & 13 & 9 & \infty & 0 & \infty & 12 \\ \infty & 6 & 15 & 11 & \infty & 2 & 0 & 14 \\ 5 & 22 & 13 & 9 & 3 & 18 & \infty & 0 \end{matrix}$$

Matrix after Iteration 5

$$\begin{matrix} 0 & 17 & 8 & 4 & \infty & 13 & \infty & 7 \\ \infty & 0 & 9 & 5 & \infty & 14 & \infty & 8 \\ \infty & 9 & 0 & 14 & \infty & 5 & \infty & 3 \\ \infty & 13 & 4 & 0 & \infty & 9 & \infty & 3 \\ 2 & 19 & 10 & 6 & 0 & 15 & \infty & 9 \\ \infty & 4 & 13 & 9 & \infty & 0 & \infty & 12 \\ \infty & 6 & 15 & 11 & \infty & 2 & 0 & 14 \\ 5 & 22 & 13 & 9 & 3 & 18 & \infty & 0 \end{matrix}$$

Matrix after Iteration 6

$$\begin{matrix} 0 & 17 & 8 & 4 & 10 & 13 & \infty & 7 \\ 13 & 0 & 9 & 5 & 11 & 14 & \infty & 8 \\ 8 & 9 & 0 & 12 & 6 & 5 & \infty & 3 \\ 8 & 13 & 4 & 0 & 6 & 9 & \infty & 3 \\ 2 & 19 & 10 & 6 & 0 & 15 & \infty & 9 \\ 17 & 4 & 13 & 9 & 15 & 0 & \infty & 12 \\ 19 & 6 & 15 & 11 & 17 & 2 & 0 & 14 \\ 5 & 22 & 13 & 9 & 3 & 18 & \infty & 0 \end{matrix}$$

Matrix after Iteration 7

FIGURE 20.7 Intermediate Steps in Floyd's Algorithm

20.3.4 Dijkstra's Algorithm

We illustrate the use of the weighted-edge-list representation of a graph by describing a solution to the *single-source shortest-path* problem. As the name suggests, the problem consists of discovering the shortest distance

```
class WVertex {
.
.
.
//
// dijkstra
//   Dijkstra's algorithm for finding the length of
//   the shortest path to each reachable destination
//   starting from a given source
//

public Map dijkstra () {
  Map distances = new MapAdapter(new LinkedList());
    // initialize queue with ourselves
  FindMin que = new SkewHeap(new DefaultComparator());
  que.addElement(new Distance(this, 0));
    // pull elements from queue one by one
  while (! que.isEmpty()) {
    Distance top = (Distance) que.getFirst();
    que.removeFirst();
    WVertex newcity = top.destination;
    if (! distances.containsKey(newcity)) {
      distances.set(newcity, new Integer(top.distance));
      Enumeration e = newcity.edges.elements();
      while (e.hasMoreElements()) {
        WVertex newCity = (WVertex) e.nextElement();
        Integer leg = (Integer) newcity.edges.get(newCity);
        que.addElement(new Distance(newCity,
          top.distance + leg.intValue()));
      }
    }
  }
  return distances;
}
.
.
.
}
```

FIGURE 20.8 Dijkstra's Single-Source Shortest-Path Algorithm

from a specific starting vertex to all other reachable nodes in a graph. The program, named `dijkstra` in honor of Edsger Dijkstra, the computer scientist credited with discovering the algorithm, is shown in Figure 20.8. Just as Floyd's algorithm has obvious similarities with Warshall's algorithm, so too do Dijkstra's algorithm and the single-source reachability algorithm presented in Figure 20.4. The most obvious difference is that the reachability algorithm stores the collection of vertices waiting to be analyzed in a stack, whereas Dijkstra's algorithm stores the vertices in a priority queue.

The use of a priority queue rather than a stack means that the items being maintained must be ordered in some fashion. In the case of Dijkstra's algorithm, the ordering will be based on the distance to a city that we already know is reachable. Removing the smallest value from this collection, Dijkstra's will then tell us the next city that can be reached with the least amount of effort. In order to more easily manage the pair of values representing a city and a distance, the following simple class is used:

```
private class Distance implements Comparable {
  Distance (WVertex to, int d) { destination = to; distance = d;}
  public WVertex destination;
  public int distance;

  public int compareTo (Object to) {
    Distance dto = (Distance) to;
    if (distance < dto.distance) return -1;
    if (distance == dto.distance) return 0;
    return 1;
  }
}
```

A `DistancePair` records a distance and a destination. Two instances of the class can be compared and are ordered on their distance values.

Table 20.1 illustrates the changes to both the priority queue and the resulting dictionary of distances as the program is executed on our example graph. Initially, the distance collection is empty, and the queue contains the starting vertex, Pierre. At each step, the smallest element in the pri-

GREEDY ALGORITHMS

Many problems, particularly search problems, can be phrased in a form so that at each step, there is a choice of many alternatives for the next move. The *greedy method* is a heuristic that provides guidance in how to construct an algorithm in these situations. The greedy technique says simply to take the next step that seems best from the current choices (that is, without resorting to any long-term planning). Dijkstra's algorithm is a classic greedy technique. At each step, we simply select the move that gets us to a new destination with the least amount of work. The priority queue is essential in ordering the possible moves, so that we can easily discover the move that gives us the best potential return.

TABLE 20.1 TRACE OF EXECUTION OF DIJKSTRA'S ALGORITHM

Distance	Priority Queue
	Pierre: 0
Pierre: 0	Pendleton: 2
Pendleton: 2	Phoenix: 6, Pueblo: 10
Phoenix: 6	Pueblo: 9, Peoria : 10, Pueblo: 10, Pittsburgh: 16
Pueblo: 9	Peoria: 10, Pueblo: 10, Pierre: 12, Pittsburgh: 16
Peoria: 10	Pueblo: 10, Pierre: 12, Pueblo: 13, Pittsburgh: 15, Pittsburgh: 16
	Pierre: 12, Pueblo: 13, Pittsburgh: 15, Pittsburgh: 16
	Pueblo: 13, Pittsburgh: 15, Pittsburgh: 16
	Pittsburgh: 15, Pittsburgh: 16
Pittsburgh: 15	Pittsburgh: 16, Pensacola: 19
	Pensacola: 19
Pensacola: 19	Phoenix: 24
	Empty

ority queue is removed. If the vertex removed from the queue is not yet present in the distances collection, we have found the length of the shortest path to a new node. The newly discovered node is added to the distances collection. Knowing the shortest distance to this node and knowing the distance to each neighbor of the node, we can compute the distances to each of the neighbor nodes.

In the first step, we discover that the distance to the starting node is 0. The distance to its only neighbor, namely, the city Pendleton, is 2. This value is computed and placed into the queue.

Next, the destination Pendleton is removed. We consider the distance from Pendleton to each of its adjacent neighbors, adding to this value the distance from our source to Pendelton. These combined distances are placed into the priority queue. Note that the queue maintains values in order based on their distance, so the entry representing Phoenix will be in front of the entry representing Pueblo.

The processing of the entry for Phoenix illustrates the importance for this algorithm of the use of a priority queue rather than a stack, as in depth-first search, or a simple queue, as in breadth-first search. From Phoenix, we discover paths to Peoria, Pittsburgh, and Pueblo. The latter is, in fact, a shorter path than the entry placed earlier into the queue that represented the edge from Pendleton. Because the priority queue maintains values in order of their least cost, it will be the shortest path to Pueblo, the path through Phoenix, that will be removed first from the queue. Subsequent deletion from the queue of cities that have already been processed will simply be ignored. In this manner, the shortest distance to each city will be discovered.

The proof that with Dijkstra's algorithm, all vertices that are reachable will eventually be pulled from the priority queue is similar to the induction proof presented for the reachability algorithm. The proof that the paths so uncovered are indeed the shortest paths is slightly more difficult and is

PROOF OF CORRECTNESS: DIJKSTRA'S ALGORITHM

The proof that Dijkstra's algorithm discovers the shortest paths from the source to each reachable vertex uses a technique we encountered in Chapter 18: *proof by contradiction*. We first make the following simple observation. The values pulled from the priority queue are each larger than or equal to their immediately preceding value. Note that this property is not inherent, simply because we are using a priority queue. In the middle of execution, it might be possible, for example, to insert a value into the queue that was smaller than values previously removed from the queue. But this cannot happen in Dijkstra's algorithm, because the values represent positive distances between vertices. Values inserted into the queue must be strictly larger than the value removed in the step in which they are created.

To prove that the distances discovered by Dijkstra's algorithm are indeed the shortest, we assume the opposite and prove a contradiction. That is, assume that the distance to at least one vertex is not the shortest. Let x be the *first* vertex that is so mislabeled. This means that Dijkstra's algorithm discovers a path of length c from the source to vertex x, but there is an alternative path with shorter distance. Let v be the next-to-last node in this alternative path. That is, there is a path of length w_1 from the source to v and an edge of length w_2 from v to x, and the sum $w_1 + w_2$ is less than c.

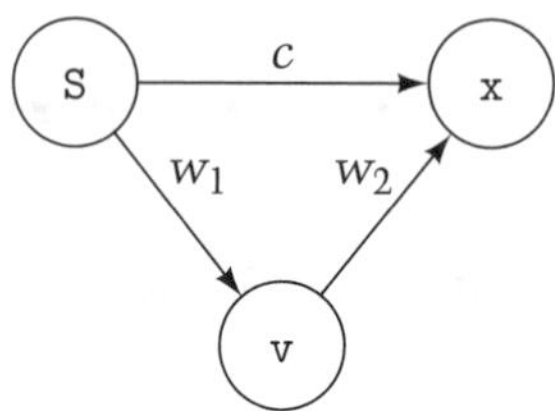

Because v is reachable, it will be discovered by Dijkstra's algorithm. Because w_1 is less than c, the analysis of v will occur prior to the analysis of x (otherwise, x would not be the *first* vertex mislabeled). But at the point v was considered, the path to x with cost $w_1 + w_2$ would have been inserted into the queue, and therefore the path to x with cost $w_1 + w_2$ would of necessity have been discovered before the path with cost c was even considered.

But this contradicts the assertion that the first time we removed vertex x from the queue, it had a path of length c. Therefore, there cannot exist a *first* vertex that is mislabeled, and therefore all vertices must be correctly labeled with their shortest distance.

presented in a sidebar. An analysis similar to the reachability algorithm shows that the running time of this algorithm is $O(E \log E)$.

20.4 Other Graph Problems

In this section, we will examine a few other classic graph problems and their solutions, using the representations we have examined in this chapter.

20.4.1 Topological Sorting

Oftentimes, a graph represents a sequence of tasks, where the link between one task and the next indicates that the first task must be completed before the second. The following, for example, might represent a prerequisite chain in a series of courses at a university:

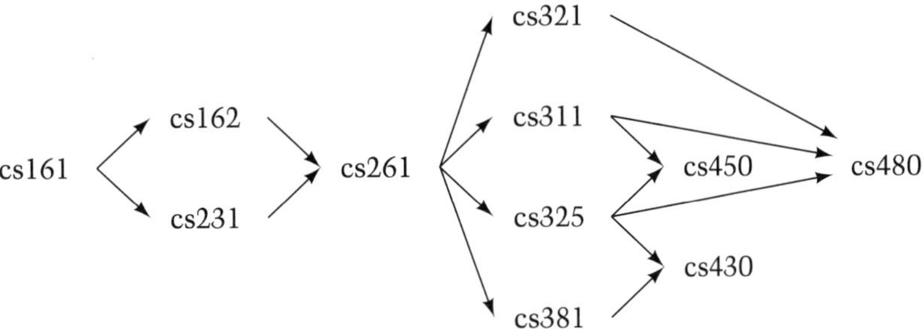

A *topological ordering* is a listing of vertices having the property that if b is a successor to a, b occurs later in the ordering than a. In effect, the topological ordering imposes a linear order on a graph. In our graph of courses, the topological sort ensures that the student does not take any course before taking its prerequisites. Of course, the topological ordering may not be unique; many orderings may satisfy the sequencing property. One topological ordering for this graph is the following: cs161, cs162, cs231, cs261, cs381, cs325, cs430, cs311, cs450, cs321, cs480.

An algorithm to determine a topological ordering is shown in Figure 20.9. Here, we have placed the code inside of class `Graph`. The algorithm first copies the vertices from the graph into a working set so as to not destroy the original graph. The algorithm then searches the set to find a vertex that has no successor in the set. Assuming that the graph has no cycles, such a vertex must exist. (See exercise 15.) Once found, the vertex is added to the front of the list and removed from the working set, and we continue to search for the next element.

```
class Graph {
    // data areas
  public Bag vertices = new LinkedList();;

    // operations
  public void addVertex (Vertex v) { vertices.addElement(v); }

  public LinkedList topologicalSort () {
    LinkedList result = new LinkedList();
      // first copy vertices, so we don't destroy graph
    Bag copy = new LinkedList();
    for (Enumeration e = vertices.elements(); e.hasMoreElements(); )
      copy.addElement(e.nextElement());
      // now perform sort
    while (! copy.isEmpty()) {
      Enumeration e = copy.elements();
      while (e.hasMoreElements()) {
        Vertex v = (Vertex) e.nextElement();
          // see if v has successor in set
        boolean flag = true;
        Enumeration f = v.edges.elements();
        while (f.hasMoreElements())
          if (copy.containsElement(f.nextElement()))
            flag = false;
        if (flag) { // found vertex with no successor
          result.addFirst(v);
          copy.removeElement(v);
          break;
        }
      }
    }
    return result;
  }
}
```

FIGURE 20.9 An Algorithm for Topological Sort of a Graph

20.4.2 Depth-First Search Spanning Tree

A tree, such as those we examined in Chapter 13, is a form of graph. Although all trees are graphs, not all graphs are trees. Trees have no cycles, and no vertex in a tree is pointed to by more than one other vertex. A *spanning tree* of a graph is a subset of the edges that form a tree and that include all the vertices. A spanning tree that starts at vertex `Princeton` for the Figure 20.1 graph is the following:

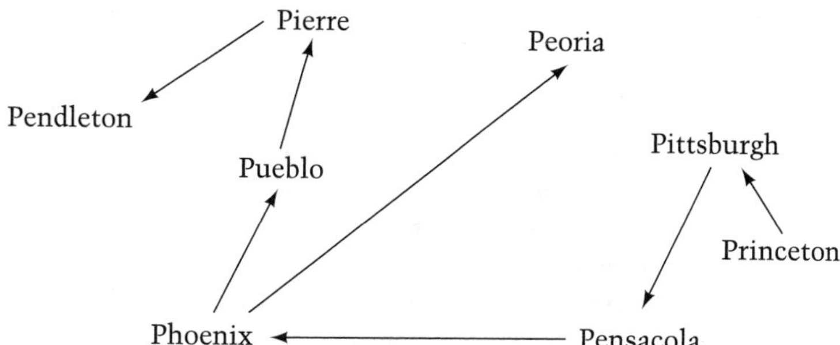

An algorithm to construct a spanning tree is shown in Figure 20.10. Once more, we have made the algorithm a method in class `Graph`. This algorithm performs a depth-first search on the graph, starting from a given starting node and, if possible, constructs a spanning tree, placing the result in a new graph. Several data structures are used in this algorithm. The map `visited` serves two purposes: It marks which nodes have been visited, and it gives the mapping between vertices in the original graph (which we do not wish to destroy) and vertices in the new graph. The stack `pendingVertices` holds vertices that we have yet to explore.

The search algorithm itself is very similar to the `findReachable` and `dijkstra` algorithms presented earlier. As long as the stack is not empty, we remove an element and consider all the edges from this element. If any edge leads to a new vertex—one that we have not yet explored—we add the new vertex to the spanning tree graph and place it into the stack.

Variations on depth-first search trees include breadth-first search trees and minimum-cost spanning trees. These are explored in the exercises and programming projects at the end of the chapter.

20.4.3 Problem–The Traveling Salesman

Another graph problem that is of both theoretical and practical interest is that of the *traveling salesman*. In this problem, a weighted graph represents the cost to travel between cities. The task is to find a path that touches every city, crosses no city more than once, and has least total cost.

This problem is interesting in that there is no known polynomial time algorithm to find a solution. The problem belongs to a large class of problems called *NP*, which stands for *nondeterministic polynomial*. The nondeterministic characterization comes from the fact that one can guess a

```
class Graph {
.
.
.
  public Graph DFSspanningTree (Vertex start) {
      // initialize the data structures
    Graph g = new Graph();
    Map visited = new MapAdapter(new LinkedList());
    Stack pendingVertices = new LinkedList();
    Vertex nv = new Vertex(start.name);
    visited.set(start, nv);
    g.addVertex(nv);
    pendingVertices.addLast(start);
      // now do the search
    while (! pendingVertices.isEmpty()) {
      Vertex v = (Vertex) pendingVertices.getLast();
      pendingVertices.removeLast();
      nv = (Vertex) visited.get(v);
        // add all cities not yet visited
      Enumeration e = v.edges.elements();
      while (e.hasMoreElements()) {
        Vertex dest = (Vertex) e.nextElement();
        if (! visited.containsKey(dest)) {
          Vertex ndest = new Vertex(dest.name);
          g.addVertex(ndest);
          nv.addEdge(ndest);
          visited.set(dest, ndest);
          pendingVertices.addLast(dest);
        }
      }
    }
    return g;
  }
}
```

FIGURE 20.10 An Algorithm to Determine a Spanning Tree

solution and in polynomial time check to determine whether it is the correct solution.

But the nature of NP problems gets even more curious. The traveling-salesman problem is what is known as *NP-complete*. This large collection of problems has the property that if any of them could be solved in polynomial time, they all could. Unfortunately, nobody has ever been able to find a fast algorithm for any of these; nor has anybody been able to prove that such an algorithm cannot exist.

20.5 Chapter Summary

Key Concepts

- Graphs, vertices, and edges
- Adjacency-matrix representation, weighted and unweighted
- Edge-list representation, unweighted and weighted (or labeled)
- Warshall's algorithm: all-pairs reachability
- Depth-first search used to compute single-source reachability
- Floyd's algorithm: all-pairs shortest distance
- Dijkstra's algorithm: single-source shortest distance

The major theme of this chapter has been to demonstrate the use of many of the data structures we have described in this text in the solution of realistic problems. Graphs are ubiquitous and the processing of graphs a common occurrence. By making use of some of the data structures that we have developed here, algorithms on graphs can be succinctly and elegantly described.

Consider the data structures used in Dijkstra's algorithm (Figure 20.8).

- The starting location for the search is encoded as a `WVertex`.
- The set of reachable vertices is returned as a value of type `Map`. But this is in fact being implemented by a `MapAdapter`, which is built on top of a `LinkedList`. The key for this map will be a city (represented by a `String`) and a distance (an integer wrapped in an `Integer`). These two values are combined into an `Association` by the map.
- The graph is implicitly represented by having each `WVertex` maintain another `Map` of destinations (represented by another `WVertex`) and distances.
- The algorithm makes use of a *priority queue*, which is an ADT that implements the `FindMin` interface. This is being implemented by an instance of `SkewHeap`.
- The comparison operator for the priority queue is constructed using the `DefaultComparator` object, which generates a less-than comparison test for comparing two `Distance` objects.

In total, more than a dozen data types are used in the execution of this one algorithm.

Further Information

Algorithms on graphs are described in a number of books dealing with algorithms. Examples include [Aho 83], [Cormen 90], [Sedgewick 92], and [Weiss 96]. Further information on graph theory as a discipline in itself can be found in the book by Hartsfield and Ringel [Hartsfield 90].

Dijkstra's algorithm was first described in 1959 [Dijkstra 59]. Floyd's and Warshall's algorithms both appeared in 1962 [Floyd 62, Warshall 62].

Study Questions

1. What are the two components of a graph?
2. What is the difference between a directed and an undirected graph?

3. How can directed graphs simulate undirected graphs?
4. What is the difference between a weighted (or labeled) and an unweighted graph?
5. What is an adjacency matrix?
6. For a graph with V vertices, how much space will an adjacency matrix require?
7. What are the features of an edge-list representation of a graph?
8. How much space does the edge-list representation of a graph require?
9. What are the two varieties of reachability questions for graphs?
10. What is the difference between Floyd's algorithm and Warshall's algorithm? What is the asymptotic complexity of these algorithms?
11. What is the execution-time complexity of the `findReachable` algorithm?
12. In what way is the `findReachable` algorithm characteristic of a depth-first search?
13. What problem is solved using Dijkstra's algorithm?
14. Why is it important that Dijkstra's algorithm stores the intermediate results in a priority queue rather than in an ordinary stack or a queue?
15. What is a topological ordering for a graph?
16. What is a spanning tree?

Exercises

1. Assuming that a graph is connected, what is the lower bound on the space requirements for a graph stored using the edge-list representation?
2. What is the complexity of finding out whether there is a direct link between two vertices if a graph is represented as an adjacency matrix? As an edge list? As an adjacency matrix using one of the sparse matrix techniques examined in Chapter 19?
3. At the beginning of the chapter, we noted how an undirected graph could be simulated by a directed graph. Construct the adjacency-matrix representation for the following graph:

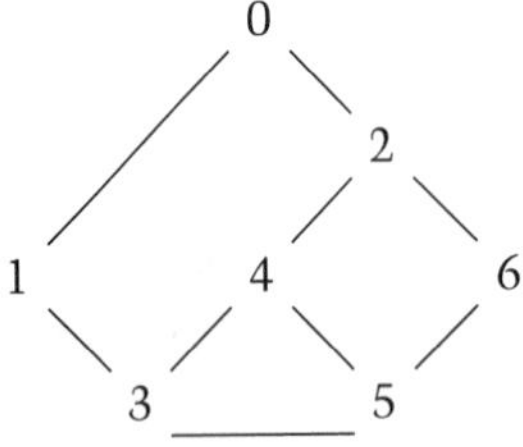

4. Construct the edge-list representation for the graph described in the previous exercise.
5. Suppose that Warshall's algorithm is implemented using a sparse matrix representation described in Chapter 19. What is the time complexity of the algorithm? How much space does it use? Can any changes be made to the algorithm to improve efficiency?
6. Suppose that there is a path from vertex v_i to vertex v_j in a graph. Argue why there must then be a path that never travels through any vertex more than once. (*Hint:* Assume that a path does travel through a vertex two or more times; show how the path can be shortened to eliminate one of the visits.)
7. Trace the depth-first search path followed by the algorithm given in Figure 20.4 through the graph given in Figure 20.1, numbering the vertices in the order they are visited by the algorithm.
8. What assumptions have we made in asserting that the execution time of the `findReachable` algorithm is $O(E)$? What is the complexity if we use a `LinkedList` for the set named `reachable`?
9. Starting from `Princeton`, show the order that cities will be found to be reachable using the `findReachable` algorithm. Suppose that we changed the algorithm to use a breadth-first search, as described in the text. Show another order that cities would be encountered using the modified algorithm.
10. An induction proof of correctness for Floyd's algorithm is very similar to the induction proof of correctness for Warshall's algorithm. Following the steps outlined in the sidebar proving Warshall's algorithm, provide a proof of correctness for Floyd's algorithm.
11. Redraw the graph shown in Figure 20.5, and number the vertices in the order they are visited by Dijkstra's algorithm.
12. Does the execution-time complexity of Dijkstra's algorithm depend on what implementation is used for the `distances` map? What are some of the possibilities?
13. Using the following graph as an illustration, argue why Dijkstra's algorithm requires the input graph to have nonnegative edge weights.

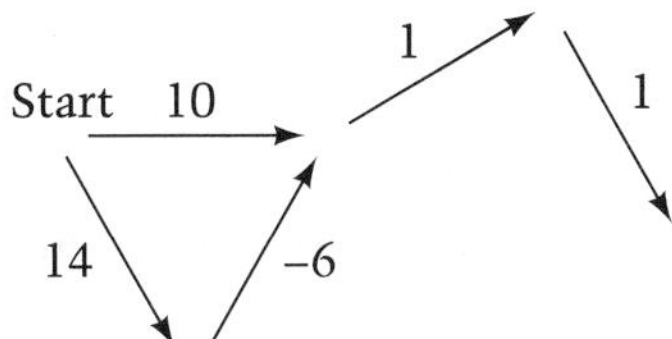

14. Give two different topological orderings for the graph described in Section 20.4.1.
15. Prove that a graph that contains no cycles must have at least one vertex that does not have a successor. (This can be done either by contradiction or as a counting argument.) Use this result to argue that the `topologicalSort` algorithm must always terminate.
16. What is the asymptotic execution time for the `topologicalSort` algorithm?
17. In what order were nodes visited in order to form the depth-first search spanning tree described in Section 20.4.2? How do we know that `Peoria` had to have been visited after `Pueblo`? What might the tree have looked like had `Peoria` been visited first?

Programming Projects

1. For class `Graph`, write a method that takes as input an adjacency-matrix representation for a graph and produces the equivalent graph represented in edge-list form.
2. A graph is said to have a *cycle* if, starting from a given vertex, a path with more than one arc leads back to the same vertex. One way to tell whether a vertex is part of a cycle is to modify the `findReachable` algorithm so that it will see whether a vertex is reachable from itself. Add the method `testCycle` to the class `Vertex` to test for this condition. The method should return `true` if the given vertix is part of a cycle and `false` otherwise.
3. A *path* can be described by a list of vertices, where each vertex in the list has an edge to the following. First, describe an algorithm to catenate two paths, forming a new path that combines the two end to end. What is the execution-time complexity of your algorithm? Using this representation of a path, we can modify Floyd's algorithm so that in addition to returning the length of the shortest path from point to point, it will also return the path. Do this by maintaining a separate V-by-V matrix of paths, and each time an entry is changed in the distance matrix, make the equivalent change in the path matrix. What is the execution-time complexity of the revised algorithm?
4. An alternative to the depth-first spanning tree is the breadth-first spanning tree, formed using a breadth-first search rather than a depth-first search. Describe one tree that might have been produced using this technique on the graph in Figure 20.1. For weighted graphs, an interesting technique is the *minimum-cost spanning tree*. This is the spanning

tree with the smallest total minimum cost. The technique to produce the minimum-cost spanning tree is similar to Dijkstra's algorithm. A priority queue is used to hold vertices known to be reachable, ordered by their smallest cost. Vertices are pulled from the queue in sequence and, if not yet visited, are added to the spanning tree. When a node is added to the spanning tree, all its neighbors are then added to the priority queue. This is known as *Prim's algorithm*. Program an implementation of Prim's algorithm.

5. Many graph problems can be solved using *backtracking*, a technique we encountered in Chapter 10. A good example is the *graph-coloring* problem: Can the vertices in a graph be colored with N colors in such a way that no two adjacent vertices have the same color? A backtracking framework (see Chapter 10) can be used to solve the graph-coloring problem as follows: A given start node is colored with the first color, and an arbitrary adjacent node is selected as the next node and colored with a different color. As each node is encountered, a test is made to see whether it can be colored any value different from all of its already colored adjacent neighbors. If so, a currently uncolored neighbor is selected as the next node. If not, the framework backtracks to an earlier node and tries to find another color. If no color is possible, the vertex is marked as uncolored, and the framework backs up even further. The result is either a completely colored graph or the assertion that it cannot be colored with just the given number of values. (A famous theorem asserts that all graphs that can be drawn on a plane without overlapping lines require no more than four colors.)

6. Adventure is a game based on an imaginary world that can be envisioned as a series of connected rooms. These rooms can be thought of as vertices in a large graph. In this text-based game, when you enter each room, the computer produces a description, such as the following:

```
You are standing in a large dinning hall.  In front of you is
a table on which there sits a candelabra.  Next to the candelabra
is a key resting on top of a folded piece of paper.  To the left
is an open window.  To the right is a wooden door.  Across from
you, behind the table, hangs a large curtain.
```

Users are allowed to enter simple commands, such as "pick up key," "read paper," or "exit through window." In response, the computer will tell you the contents of the next room, the contents of your pockets, or various other bits of information. Design an adventure game that has at least ten rooms and seven types of objects.

APPENDIX 

JAVA SYNTAX

This appendix gives an overview of the Java language as it is used in this book. The method of description is informal and is not intended to replace a reference manual for the language. For example, statements that are legal in Java but not used in the book are not described.

The presentation of the language is divided into three major sections:

1. *Program structure*, which defines the overall organization of a Java program: packages, interfaces, classes, and methods
2. *Statements*, focusing on declaration statements, assignment statements, and statements that control the flow of execution within a method
3. *Expressions*, in which individual values are computed

A.1 PROGRAM STRUCTURE

A Java program is written as a collection of files. Each file can contain an optional package name, an optional sequence of `import` declarations, and, finally, a sequence of class or interface declarations.

A.1.1 Packages

The package is a mechanism used to create a library of classes and interfaces. By using the `public` keyword, the developer of a package can select which names can be used outside of the package. Names that are not public are purely internal to a package and therefore cannot be confused with similar names in other packages.

The jds library distributed with this book is an example of a package. Every file in the jds library begins with the name of the package in which it is placed:

```
package jds.util;
.
.
.
public class ButtonAdapter ...
```

Unless they are creating a library, most programmars can just leave their code in the default (unnamed) package. All the application programs described in this book have used the default package.

A.1.2 Import Declaration

An import declaration names an item from another package that will be used in the subsequent class or interface declarations. An asterisk can be used to include all the items in a package.

```
import java.util.Date;
import java.net.*;
import java.io.*;
```

A.1.3 Class Declaration

A class declaration consists of an optional sequence of modifiers, the keyword class, the class name, an optional parent class name, an optional sequence of interfaces, and the class body. The class body is a sequence of class member or constructor declarations, surrounded by a pair of braces:

```
public class FirstProgram {

   public static void main (String [ ] args ) {
      System.out.println ( "My first Java program!" );
   }
}
```

The modifiers discussed in this book are public, abstract, and final. A public class can be used outside of the package in which it is declared. An abstract class is one that cannot be instantiated, one that must be subclassed before instances can be created. A final class is one that cannot be subclassed:

```
public abstract class ButtonAdapter {
        .
        .
        .
}
```

The optional parent class name is used to denote that this class is being constructed using inheritance from an existing class. The keyword `extends` indicates that inheritance is being performed:

```
public class ButtonAdapter extends Button {
        .
        .
        .
}
```

The optional sequence of interfaces is used to indicate that the class being defined implements all the methods described in an interface declaration. Note that a class can satisfy many different interfaces but can have only one parent class:

```
public class ButtonAdapter extends Button implements ActionListener {
        .
        .
        .
}
```

A.1.4 Interface Declaration

An interface declaration substitutes the keyword `interface` for the keyword `class`. The body of an interface contains methods but no data fields. In addition, the methods specify only the function and argument names but do not have a function body. In place of the method body, a semicolon is used to mark the end of a method declaration:

```
public interface Bag extends Collection {
  public void addElement (Object newElement);
  public boolean containsElement (Object testElement);
  public Object findElement (Object testElement);
  public void removeElement (Object oldElement);
}
```

A.1.5 Method Declaration

A method declaration consists of an optional series of modifiers, a return type, a method name, an optional `throws` part, a list of arguments, and (in class declarations) a method body. A method body is a sequence of statements surrounded by a pair of braces:

```
public class Vector {

   public boolean isEmpty() {
      return elementCount == 0;
   }
}
```

The following modifiers have been used in the book:

`public` The method can be invoked by messages sent to instances of this class. (Many examples occur, starting in Chapter 10.)

`protected` The method can be invoked only within other methods associated with the class of the object, within other classes in the same package, or in methods defined as part of subclasses.

`private` The method can be invoked only within other methods associated with this class.

`final` The method cannot be overridden in subclasses.

`abstract` The method must be overridden in subclasses. (A semicolon replaces the method body when this modifier is used.)

`static` The method can be invoked without first creating an instance of the class. The `main` method must always be declared `static`.

`synchronized` At any time, only one thread can be executing this method.

The return type for a method can be a primitive type, a class type, or `void`. The type `void` is used to indicate that the method does not return a value as a result.

A `throws` part, indicated by the keyword `throws`, identifies the exceptions this method might potentially throw, followed by a list of exception names, separated by commas:

```
class DataInputStream extends FilterInputStream {

   public byte readByte () throws IOException {
      .
      .
      .
   }
}
```

Certain exceptions, such as `ArrayIndexOutOfBoundsException` or `NoSuchElementException`, do not need to be declared in a `throws` clause. (Indeed, they cannot.)

The optional sequence of formal arguments is a list of zero or more formal argument declarations, separated by commas. Each formal argument is a type (either a primitive type or a class name) followed by a variable name:

```
private void enterWord (String word, Integer line) {
    .
    .
    .
}
```

A.1.6 Constructors

A syntax of a *constructor* is similar to a method but eliminates the return type, and the method name must match the class name. A constructor is invoked automatically when an instance of the class is created:

```
public class SkipList implements Sorted, Bag {
  private SkipLink top;
  private LinkedList bottom = new LinkedList();
  protected Comparator test;

  public SkipList (Comparator t) {  // constructor
    test = t;
    top = new SkipLink(null, bottom.sentinel);
  }
```

A.1.7 Data Field Declaration

A data field declaration has an optional modifier part, a type, a variable name, and an optional initialization. An initialization, if present, consists of an equals sign followed by a value:

```
public class SkipList implements Sorted, Bag {
  private SkipLink top;
  private LinkedList bottom = new LinkedList();
  protected Comparator test;
```

A `static` data field is shared by all instances of a class. Static data fields are often used to create symbolic constant names:

```
public class Card {
.
.
.
  public static final int diamond = 1;
  public static final int club = 2;
  public static final int spade = 3;
  public static final int heart = 4;
}
```

A data field that is `final` (whether `static` or not) cannot be reassigned a new value. A `public` data field can be read and set outside by class. A `protected` data field can be set only by other objects declared within the same package, and a `private` data field can be set only within the class in which the declaration appears. It is good programming practice to only declare a data field `public` if it is also `final`.

A.2 STATEMENTS

The following describes only those statements that we have used in the book. The Java language also permits other statement forms that we will not describe.

A.2.1 Declaration Statement

A declaration statement consists of a type (either a primitive or a class type) and a variable name. This statement can have an optional initialization part, which provides an initial value for the variable:

```
int size;
double pi = 3.14159;
Ball aBall;
```

A.2.2 Assignment Statement

An assignment statement is used to modify the value of a variable. The target variable (the value to the left of the equals sign) can be a simple variable, an array expresssion, or a field name. The right side can be any legal expression:

```
size = 3 + 4;
```

Binary operators can also be combined with an assignment statement. The effect is as if the target variable were used as the left argument with the binary operator and the result assigned to the target:

```
i += 3; // same as i = i + 3
```

A.2.3 Procedure Calls

A method can be invoked as a statement. A method that is declared as `void` can be executed only in this fashion. If the method returns a non-`void` result, the value will be ignored:

```
aBall.move(12, 13);
```

The expression to the left of the period is known as the *receiver*. The class of the receiver will determine which method will be executed. If no receiver is specified, a method in the current class will be executed.

A.2.4 if Statement

Together, `if` statements and `switch` statements are sometimes termed *conditional statements*. They allow the programmer to select one alternative out of many. The `if` statement makes a decision based on a Boolean-valued expression: If the expression is `true`, a statement is selected. The `else` portion of the statement is optional; if present and if the expression is `false`, the `else` statement will be executed:

```
if (a < b)
  smallest = a;
else
  smallest = b;
```

Braces can be used to group a series of statements to form a *compound statement*. These statements will then be executed as a unit, either all together or (if the condition is not satisfied) not at all:

```
public void Hanoi (int n, char a, char b, char c) {
  if (n == 1) {
    System.out.println("move disk from tower " + a + " to " + b);
    }
  else {
    Hanoi (n-1, a, c, b);
    System.out.println("move disk from tower " + a + " to " + b);
    Hanoi (n-1, c, b, a);
    }
}
```

A.2.5 switch Statement

A `switch` statement selects one alternative out of many. The selection is determined by the value of an expression. The result of the expression is compared against a list of constants; when a match is found, the associated statement is executed. One statement can be labeled as `default` and will be executed if no other match is successful:

```
switch (op) {
  case '+': left += right; break;
  case '-': left -= right; break;
  case '*': left *= right; break;
  case '/': left / = right; break;
}
```

The `break` statement is necessary in order to break out of the switch. If the `break` is omitted, control will, after execution of the `case` statements, drop into the next `case` statement. This is useful in rare situations; however, the normal situation is to `break` after each `case` statement.

A.2.6 while Statement

The `while` and the `for` statements are often termed *looping statements*, as they have the effect of executing a statement repeatedly until a condition is satisfied. The statement can be executed zero times if the condition is `false` the first time the statement is encountered:

```
while (theBall.y() < FrameHeight) {
   theBall.move ();
      .
      .
      .
}
```

A `break` statement can be used in the body of a `while` loop. When executed, the `break` will immediately cause the loop to terminate, continuing execution with the next statement following the loop.

A.2.7 for Statement

A `for` statement consists of an initialization part, a test for completion, an update statement, and the body of the loop. The `for` statement is just a convenient shorthand for a `while` loop. Consider the following:

```
for (int i = 0; i < 10; i++) {
   a[i] = 3 * i;
}
```

That statment can be rewritten, and has the same effect, as the following:

```
int i = 0;
while (i < 10) {
   a[i] = 3 * i;
   i++;
}
```

As with a `while` loop, a `break` statement can be used to terminate a `for` from within the body of the loop.

A.2.8 return Statement

A `return` statement is used to indicate the end of execution for a method. If an expression is provided, it will be the value returned as the result of the method execution. Otherwise, if no value is given in the result statement, the method must be declared as `void`:

```
return 3 + 4;
```

A.2.9 throw Statement

A `throw` statement is used to raise an exception. Control will immediately halt in the current procedure, and the most recent matching `catch` block from a calling procedure will be invoked:

```
throw new StackUnderflowException();
```

A.2.10 try Statement

Any code that can generate an exception should be invoked in a `try` block. The `try` statement is followed by an optional sequence of `catch` clauses. Each `catch` block specifies the type of exception it can handle. If the associated exception is thrown during the course of executing the statements in the `try` block, the code in the matching `catch` statement will be executed. An optional `finally` block is executed at the end of the statement, whether or not an exception has occurred.

```
try {
   URL address = new URL(args[0]);
   .
   .
   .
} catch (MalformedURLException e) {
   System.out.println("URL exception " + e);
} catch (IOException e) {
   System.out.println("I/O exception " + e);
}
```

A.3 Expressions

An expression is a programming construct that, when executed, will cause a value to be computed. Expressions are found in various types of statements, such as assignment statements, the conditional test in a `while` loop, or the selecting expression in a `switch` statement.

An expression can be placed in parentheses to form a new expression. This is often used to indicate grouping or when the precedence of operators does not provide the desired value. For example, $2 + 3 * 4$ will be evaluated and produce the result 14, but $(2 + 3) * 4$ will yield the value 20.

A.3.1 Literal

The simplest type of expression is a literal. A literal (sometimes called a *constant*) has a self-evident type and value:

```
7 // integer literal
3.14159 // floating-point literal
true // Boolean literal
'a' // character literal
"name" // string literal
null // object literal
```

The value `null` is a literal value that is used with variables of the class type. This value is the initial value of all variables before they are assigned. Thus, the value `null` can be thought of as asserting that the variable does not refer to any object.

The following escape characters can be used in a character or string literal:

```
\b  Backspace
\n  Newline
\r  Carrage return
\t  Tab stop
```

For example, consider the following statement:

```
System.out.println("Hello\\n\\n\\tWorld\!");
```

That statement will produce the following output:

```
Hello

    World\!
```

A.3.2 Variables

A variable is a storage location that has been declared in a declaration statement. When used as an expression, the value currently stored in the variable is the value returned.

The name `this` is sometimes called a *pseudovariable*, a variable that does not have to be declared. When used as an expression inside a method, a pseudovariable denotes the object executing the method (the object that was targeted as the *receiver* in the message expression that caused the method to be executed).

Data fields and methods declared within the class in which an expression occurs and `protected` or `public` data fields or methods declared in parent classes can be accessed simply by naming them as a variable. The meaning is the same as a data field access using `this` as the base expression; however, the more complete form is seldom written:

```
public class SkipList implements Sorted, Bag {
  private SkipLink top;
  private LinkedList bottom = new LinkedList();
  protected Comparator test;

  public SkipList (Comparator t) {
    test = t; // same as this.test = t
    top = new SkipLink(null, bottom.sentinel);
  }
```

The name `super` is another pseudovariable, one that can be used only as a receiver for a message or in a constructor. In a constructor, this receiver is used to indicate the parameters to be passed to the parent class:

```
private class QuitButton extends ButtonAdapter {
  QuitButton () { super("Quit"); }
  public void pressed () { System.exit(0); }
}
```

When used as a receiver for a message, `super` indicates that the method should be taken from the parent class rather than from the current class:

```
public class SkipLink extends DoubleLink {
  public DoubleLink down;
  public Object value;

  SkipLink (Object v, DoubleLink d) { super(v, null, null); down = d; }

  public void remove () {
    down.remove();
    super.remove();  // execute DoubleLink.remove
  }
}
```

A.3.3 Data Field and Method Access

Public fields within an object can be accessed by naming the object, followed by a period, followed by the field name:

```
aBall.location
```

Static fields can be accessed using a class name to the left of the period. As we noted earlier, data fields declared within the same class can be accessed without any base expression.

A method invocation uses the same notation as a data field access but is followed by a parenthesis, an optional list of comma-separated parameter values, and a closing parenthesis:

```
aBall.setColor (ballColor);
```

A.3.4 Operators

A unary operator takes one expression as an argument. An example is the increment operator, ++, which is used to increment an integer variable. A binary operator takes two expressions as arguments. An example is the addition operator, +, which adds two numeric values. (The addition operator can also be used with `String` values, in which case it means string catenation.) The following list gives the set of binary operators recognized by Java. They are shown in precedence order, with higher-precedence operators appearing before lower-precedence operators. Higher-precedence operators will be performed before lower-precedence operators; thus, $2 + 3 * 4 + 3$ will yield 17, not 23.

Postfix operator	`expr++ expr--`
Unary operator	`++expr --expr +expr -expr`
Creation or cast	`new` (type) `expr`
Multiplicative	`* / %`
Additive	`+ -`
Shift	`<< >> <<<`
Relational	`< > <= >= instanceof`
Equality	`== !=`
Bitwise and	`&`
Bitwise or	`|`
Logical and	`&&`
Logical or	`||`
Assignment	`= += -=` etc.

A.3.5 Object Creation

An object is created using the new operator. As part of the creation process, a constructor may be executed to initialize the object. If any arguments are supplied with the call, they are passed to the constructor for the class, to be used in initializing the object:

```
aCard = new Card (Card.diamond,1);
```

A.3.6 Arrays

An array is a homogeneous (same-typed) collection of values that is declared using a pair of brackets, without indicating the size:

```
Card [ ] cards;
```

The number of elements in the array is determined when the array value is allocated, using a `new` statement:

```
cards = new Card[52]; // create an array of 52 cards
```

An element in the array is accessed by an index position, which must be an integer value larger than or equal to zero and smaller than the number of values in the array:

```
card[8].rank();
```

A.4 FILES

Files in Java are based on the idea of a *stream*, which is simply a sequence of bytes accessed one after the other. In the UNIX tradition, three streams are always given to any program: the standard input (`System.in`), the standard output (`System.out`), and the error output (`System.err`). In Java, the first is an `InputStream`, and the latter two are instances of `OuputStream`. Non-UNIX platforms will often associate these abstractions with a specific window, sometimes termed the console window.

In addition to the standard streams, users can construct their own stream abstractions. Opening a `FileStream`, for example, creates a stream that can be used to access the values held by a file.

The standard library generally adds new functionality by creating subclasses of `InputStream`. A `DataInputStream`, for example, formats primitive values, such as integers and floating-point values, by reading a sequence of byte values and constructing a larger object. An `ObjectInputStream` does largely the same, allowing user-defined objects to be written to and read from a file. A `StreamTokenizer` can be used to break a stream into the typical token values found in textual input, such as numbers and words.

The `Stream` abstractions are intended to be very close to the physical representations, as they work with 8-bit byte values. On top of this physical layer is constructed a set of `Reader` and `Writer` abstractions. These manipulate 16-bit Unicode characters, which can be used to represent character values from most of the world's languages. As with streams, new functionality is generally provided in the standard library by classes that are subclasses of `Reader` and `Writer`. The one example we have used extensively in this text is a `BufferedReader`, which adds the ability to read an entire line of text at one time.

APPENDIX B

IMPORT LIBRARIES

In the interest of saving space, I have frequently omitted `import` directives from the example programs presented in this text. This could, in some cases, lead to confusion about which classes are found in the standard Java library as distributed by Sun and which are found in the library created specifically for this book. To settle all such questions, the following table lists the location for every data type used in this book:

Data Type	Location
`ActionListener`	`java.awt.event.ActionListener`
`BinaryNode`	`jds.util.BinaryNode`
`BitSet`	`java.util.BitSet`
`BitSet`	also `jds.collection.BitSet`
`BubbleSort`	`jds.sort.BubbleSort`
`BufferedReader`	`java.io.BufferedReader`
`ButtonAdapter`	`jds.util.ButtonAdapter`
`CloseQuit`	`jds.util.CloseQuit`
`Collection`	`jds.Collection`
`Comparable`	`jds.util.Comparable`
`Comparator`	`jds.util.Comparator`

(Continued)

Data Type	Location
ConsCell	jds.util.ConsCell
DefaultComparator	jds.util.DefaultComparator
DoubleLink	jds.util.DoubleLink
Enumeration	java.util.Enumeration
FileReader	java.io.FileReader
FindMin	jds.FindMin
FindNth	jds.FindNth
Frame	java.awt.Frame
GridLayout	java.awt.GridLayout
Indexed	jds.Indexed
InputStreamReader	java.io.InputStreamReader
InsertionSort	jds.sort.InsertionSort
Integer	java.lang.Integer
IntegerCompare	jds.util.IntegerCompare
KeyAdapter	java.awt.event.KeyAdapter
LinkedList	jds.LinkedList
Map	jds.Map
Matrix	jds.Matrix
MergeSort	jds.sort.MergeSort
MouseAdapter	java.awt.event.MouseAdapter
MouseListener	java.awt.event.MouseListener
MouseMotionListener	java.awt.event.MouseMotionListener
Panel	java.awt.Panel
Partition	jds.sort.Partition
Reporter	jds.util.Reporter
Serializable	java.util.Serializable
Set	jds.Set
SetUnion	jds.SetUnion
ShellSort	jds.sort.ShellSort
SortAlgorithm	jds.SortAlgorithm

(Continued)

Data Type	Location
Sorted	jds.Sorted
SortedVector	jds.SortedVector
StreamTokenizer	java.io.StreamTokenizer
StringCompare	jds.util.StringCompare
StringTokenizer	java.util.StringTokenizer
TaskTimer	jds.util.TaskTimer
Vector	jds.Vector
VisualVector	jds.util.VisualVector
WindowAdapter	java.awt.event.WindowAdapter
WindowListener	java.awt.event.WindowListener

APPENDIX C

DATA STRUCTURES IN THE JAVA STANDARD LIBRARY

When writing this book, I decided, for reasons I discuss in the preface, that the library of data structures provided by Sun in the standard Java distribution was not a suitable vehicle for *teaching* data structures. Nevertheless, I assume that for various reasons, most students will end up *using* the Sun standard library. Therefore, in this appendix, I discuss the standard library and how it fits into the categories of data structures outlined in the book.

C.1 COLLECTION

The Java standard library does provide a `Collection` interface, which serves much the same purpose as the `Collection` interface defined for this book. However, the Java version is very large, whereas our interface is intentionally minimal. Also, the Java standard library interface proposes that many of the operations are optional and need not be recognized by all subclasses. In my opinion, this is not an idea to be widely emulated.

The Java standard library `Collection` interface can be described as follows:

```
public interface Collection {
    // basic operations
  int size ();
  boolean isEmpty ();
```

```
  boolean contains (Object value);
  boolean add (Object value); // optional
  boolean remove (Object value); // optional
  Iterator iterator ();
    // group operations
  boolean containsAll (Collection c);
  boolean addAll (Collection c); // optional
  boolean removeAll (Collection c); // optional
  boolean retainAll (Collection c); // optional
  void clear (); // optional
    // misc operations
  Object [ ] toArray ();
}
```

C.2 ENUMERATORS AND ITERATORS

The earlier versions of the Java standard library provided only the class `Enumerator` that we have used in this text. Java versions 1.2 and later have added the concept of an `Iterator`, which permits the removal of elements and the creation of a loop.

```
public interface Iterator {
  public boolean hasNext ();
  public Object next ();
  public void remove ();
}
```

Various subclasses extend iterators with new methods. For example, a `ListIterator` allows enumeration to move both forward and backward.

C.3 VECTORS

The Java standard library includes a class named `Vector` that is similar to the class discussed in Chapter 6. However, the standard library `Vector` has a much larger interface, as it supports all the `Collection` interfaces and a variety of ways to add and to remove elements:

```
public class Vector {
  Vector ();
  Vector (int initialCapacity);
  Vector (Collection c);
  ...// collection interface omitted
  boolean add (Object value)
  void add (int index, Object value);
  void addElement (Object value);
```

```
  int capacity ();
  boolean contains ();
  Object elementAt ();
  Enumeration elements ();
  Object firstElement ();
  Object get (int index);
  int indexOf (Object value);
  void insertElementAt (Object obj, int index);
  boolean isEmpty ();
  Iterator iterator ();
  Object lastElement ();
  int lastIndexOf (Object value);
  Object remove (int index);
  boolean remove (Object value);
  void removeElementAt (int index);
  void removeRange (int low, int high);
  Object set (int index, Object value);
  void setElementAt (Object value, int index);
  void setSize ();
  int size ();
  void trimToSize ();
}
```

C.4 Lists

In the Java standard library, the List is an interface rather than an implementation. Furthermore, the List is an indexed structure, allowing elements to be accessed by their positions. Here is a description of the List interface:

```
public interface List extends Collection {
  Object get (int index);
  Object set (int index, Object value); // optional
  void add (int index, Object value); // optional
  Object remove (int index); // optional
  boolean addAll (int index, Collection c); // optional

  int indexOf (Object value);
  int lastIndexOf (Object value);

  Iterator listIterator ();

  List subList (int from, int to);
}
```

Objects that support the List interface include the Vector and the class LinkedList. The latter is somewhat similar to the abstraction described in this book but has a much larger interface.

C.5 STACK, QUEUE, AND DEQUE

Rather than treating the *stack* as an interface, the standard library contains a Stack data type that is formed using inheritance from class Vector. Although this provides efficient implementation of the stack operations, it is not good software engineering, as nothing prevents a user from, perhaps inadvertantly, using the Vector operations on a stack data value. In fact, the data type almost encourages such use, as it provides a method to search for a value and to return its index!

The fact that it is an implementation also precludes discussion of alternative implementation techniques that result in the same interface. Users might get the mistaken impression that this is the only way to implement this data type.

The standard library Stack data type can be described as follows:

```
public class Stack extends Vector {
  public boolean empty (); // true if empty
  public Object peek (); // returns top object
  public Object pop (): // returns and removes top object
  public Object push (Object); // pushed new value onto stack
  public int search (Object); // finds index of value
}
```

The standard library does not have any explicit support for the *queue* abstraction. However, the class LinkedList does provide the ability to add and to remove elements to or from either end of a collection.

C.6 PRIORITY QUEUE

The standard library does not have any data type that matches the idea of a priority queue. However, as we saw in Chapter 15, a binary search tree can be used in the fashion of a priority queue. The standard library does provide examples of search trees.

C.7 BINARY SEARCH TREE

The class TreeSet implements the Collection interface using a red-black tree, which is similar to the AVL trees examined in Chapter 14.

The *Swing* graphical interface library introduces its own tree structures, formed using the interface `TreeNode`, which can be described as follows:

```
interface TreeNode {
  Enumeration children ();
  TreeNode getChildAt (int index);
  int getChildCount();
  TreeNode getParent();
  boolean isLeaf();
}
```

Although this would appear to be useful in developing a general-purpose data structure, there does not appear to be one.

C.8 HASH TABLES

The earliest versions of Java included a data type named `Hashtable`, but rather than supporting a set like `interface`, this was actually a form of map. Java 1.2 added the `HashSet` abstraction, which was closer to the hash table concept as discussed in Chapter 16, and also provided a `HashMap`, which has functionality very similar to the `Hashtable`. No explanation is given for the inconsistent use of capitalization.

C.9 SET

Java 1.2 introduced the `Set` interface. This is similar in intent to, but much larger than, the interface described in this book:

```
interface Set extends Collection {
  boolean add (Object val);
  boolean addAll (Collection c);
  void clear ();
  boolean contains (Object val);
  boolean containsAll (Collection c);
  boolean isEmpty ();
  Iterator iterator ();
  boolean remove (Object val);
  boolean removeAll (Collection c);
  boolean retainAll (Collection c);
  int size ();
  Object [ ] toArray ();
}
```

This interface is supported by the HashSet (hash table) and TreeSet (red-black tree) abstractions. Neither collection insists that all elements must be unique.

C.10 MAP

The class Dictionary provides a map abstraction implemented using a hash table:

```
public class Dictionary {
  Enumeration elements ();
  Object get (Object key)
  boolean isEmpty ();
  Enumeration keys ();
  Object put (Object key, Object value);
  Object remove (Object key);
}
```

In addition, there is a Map interface:

```
public interface Map {
  void clear ();
  boolean containsKey (Object key);
  boolean containsValue (Object value);
  Object get (Object key);
  boolean isEmpty ();
  Set keySet ();
  Object put (Object key, Object value);
  void putAll (Map t);
  Object remove (Object key);
  int size();
  Collection values ();
}
```

The Map interface is supported by TreeMap, which is an abstraction based on red-black trees.

BIBLIOGRAPHY

[Aho 83] Alfred V. Aho, John E. Hopcroft, and Jeffrey D. Ullman, *Data Structures and Algorithms*, Addison-Wesley, Reading, MA, 1983.

[Aho 86] Alfred V. Aho, Ravi Sethi, and Jeffrey D. Ullman, *Compilers: Principles, Techniques, and Tools*, Addison-Wesley, Reading, MA, 1986.

[Alexander 77] Christopher Alexander, Sara Ishikawa, and Murray Silverstein, *A Pattern Language*, Oxford University Press, New York, 1977.

[Ashenhurst 87] Robert L. Ashenhurst (Ed.), *ACM Turing Award Lectures, the First Twenty Years*, Addison-Wesley, Reading, MA, 1987.

[Beck 89] Kent Beck and Ward Cunningham, "A Laboratory for Teaching Object-Oriented Thinking," *Proceedings of the 1989 OOPSLA—Conference on Object-Oriented Programming Systems, Languages and Applications*; reprinted in *Sigplan Notices*, 24(10): 1–6, 1989.

[Beizer 90] Boris Beizer, *Software Testing Techniques*, Van Nostrand Reinhold, New York, 1990.

[Bellin 97] David Bellin and Susan Suchman Simone, *The CRC Book*, Addison-Wesley, Reading, MA, 1997.

[Bentley 86] Jon Bentley, *Programming Pearls*, Addison-Wesley, Reading, MA, 1986.

[Berman 97] A. Michael Berman, *Data Structures via C++*, Oxford University Press, New York, 1997.

[Budd 87] Timothy A. Budd, *A Little Smalltalk*, Addison-Wesley, Reading, MA, 1987.

[Budd 94] Timothy A. Budd, *Classic Data Structures in C++*, Addison-Wesley, Reading, MA, 1994.

[Budd 98] Timothy A. Budd, *Data Structures in C++ Using the Standard Template Library*, Addison-Wesley, Reading, MA, 1998.

[Campione 98] Mary Campione and Kathy Walrath, *The Java™ Tutorial*, 2nd ed., Addison-Wesley, Reading, MA, 1998.

[Campione 99] Mary Campione, Kathy Walrathm, and Alison Huml, *The Java™ Tutorial Continued*, Addison-Wesley, Reading, MA, 1999.

[Chan 96] Patrick Chan and Rosanna Lee, *The Java Class Libraries: An Annotated Reference*, Addison-Wesley, Reading, MA, 1996.

[Chan 99] Patrick Chan, *The Java Developer's Almanac 1999*, Addison-Wesley, Reading, MA, 1999.

[Cormen 90] Thomas H. Cormen, Charles E. Leiserson, and Ronald L. Rivest, *Introduction to Algorithms*, The MIT Press, Cambridge, MA, 1990.

[Cornell 96] Gary Cornell and Cay S. Horstmann, *Core Java*, Prentice-Hall, Englewood Cliffs, NJ, 1996.

[DeMillo 79] Richard DeMillo, Richard Lipton, and Alan Perlis, "Social Processes and Proofs of Theorems and Programs," *Communications of the ACM*, 22(5): 271–280, 1979.

[Dijkstra 59] Edsger W. Dijkstra, "A Note on Two Problems in Connection with Graphs," *Numerische Mathematik*, 1: 269–271, 1959.

[Dijkstra 76] Edsger W. Dijkstra, *A Discipline of Programming*, Prentice-Hall, Englewood Cliffs, NJ, 1976.

[Drozdek 96] Adam Drozdek, *Data Structures and Algorithms in C++*, PWS Publishing Company, Boston, 1996.

[Floyd 62] Robert W. Floyd, "Algorithm 97: Shortest Path," *Communications of the ACM*, 5(6): 345, 1962.

[Floyd 64] Robert W. Floyd, "Algorithm 245: Treesort," *Communications of the ACM*, 7: 701, 1964.

[Gabriel 96] Richard P. Gabriel, *Patterns of Software*, Oxford University Press, New York, 1996.

[Gamma 95] Erich Gamma, Richard Helm, Ralph Johnson, and John Vlissides, *Design Patterns: Elements of Reusable Object-Oriented Software*, Addison-Wesley, Reading, MA, 1995.

[Geurts 85] Leo Geurts, Lambert Meertens, and Steven Pemberton, *The B Programmer's Handbook*, Stichting Mathematisch Centrum, Amsterdam, 1985.

[Goldberg 83] Adele Goldberg and David Robson, *Smalltalk-80: The Language and Its Implementation*, Addison-Wesley, Reading, MA, 1983.

[Gonnet 91] Gaston H. Gonnet and Ricardo Baeza-Yates, *Handbook of Algorithms and Data Structures, in Pascal and C*, Addison-Wesley, Reading, MA, 1991.

[Goodrich 98] Michael T. Goodrich and Roberto Tamassia, *Data Structures and Algorithms in Java*, Wiley, New York, 1998.

[Gosling 96] James Gosling, Bill Joy, and Guy Steele, *The Java Language Specification*, Addison-Wesley, Reading, MA, 1996.

[Grand 98] Mark Grand, *Patterns in Java, Volume 1: A Catalog of Reusable Design Patterns Illustrated with UML*, Wiley, New York, 1998.

[Grand 99] Mark Grand, *Patterns in Java, Volume 2*, Wiley, New York, 1999.

[Gries 81] David Gries, *The Science of Programming*, Springer-Verlag, New York, 1981.

[Griswold 71] Ralph E. Griswold, James F. Poage, and Ivan P. Polonsky, *The Snobol4 Programming Language*, 2nd ed., Prentice-Hall, Englewood Cliffs, NJ, 1971.

[Griswold 90] Ralph E. Griswold and Madge T. Griswold, *The Icon Programming Language*, 2nd ed., Prentice-Hall, Englewood Cliffs, NJ, 1990.

[Harel 92] David Harel, *Algorithmics: The Spirit of Computing*, 2nd ed., Addison-Wesley, Reading, MA, 1992.

[Hartmanis 65] Juris Hartmanis and Richard E. Stearns, "On the Computational Complexity of Algorithms," *Transactions of the American Mathematical Society*, 117: 285–306, 1965.

[Hartsfield 90] Nora Hartsfield and Gerhard Ringel, *Pearls in Graph Theory*, Academic Press, Boston, 1990.

[Hoare 61] Charles Antony Richard Hoare, "Algorithm 63: Partition; Algorithm 64: Quicksort; Algorithm 65: Find," *Communications of the ACM*, 4(7): 1059–1062, 1961.

[Hoare 62] Charles Antony Richard Hoare, "Quicksort," *The Computer Journal*, 5: 10–15, 1962.

[Hopcroft 69] John E. Hopcroft and Jeffrey D. Ullman, *Formal Languages and Their Relation to Automata*, Addison-Wesley, Reading, MA, 1969.

[Knuth 97] Donald E. Knuth, *The Art of Computer Programming, Vol. 1: Fundamental Algorithms*, 3rd ed., Addison-Wesley, Reading, MA, 1997.

[Knuth 98a] Donald E. Knuth, *The Art of Computer Programming, Vol. 2: Seminumerical Algorithms*, 3rd ed., Addison-Wesley, Reading, MA, 1998.

[Knuth 98b] Donald E. Knuth, *The Art of Computer Programming, Vol. 3: Sorting and Algorithms*, 2nd ed., Addison-Wesley, Reading, MA, 1998.

[Kruse 99] Robert L. Kruse and Alexander J. Ryba, *Data Structures and Program Design in C++*, Prentice-Hall, Upper Saddle River, NJ, 1999.

[Lakoff 87] George Lakoff, *Women, Fire, and Dangerous Things*, University of Chicago Press, 1987.

[Langsam 96] Yedidyah Langsam, Moshe J. Augenstein, and Aaron M. Tenenbaum, *Data Structures using C and C++*, Prentice-Hall, Upper Saddle River, NJ, 1996.

[Lukasiewicz 29] Jan Łukasiewicz, *Elementy Logiki Matematyczny*, Warsaw, 1929; English translation: *Elements of Mathematical Logic*, Pergamon Press, London, 1963.

[McCulloch 43] William S. McCulloch and William Pitts, "A Logical Calculus of the Ideas Immanent in Nervous Activity," *Bulletin Mathematical Biophysics*, 5: 115–133, 1943.

[Meyers 98] Scott Meyers, *Effective C++*, 2nd ed., Addison-Wesley, Reading, MA, 1998.

[Nyhoff 99] Larry R. Nyhoff, *C++: An Introduction to Data Structures*, Prentice-Hall, Upper Saddle River, NJ, 1999.

[Pattis 88] Richard E. Pattis, "Textbook Errors in Binary Searching," *SigCSE Bulletin*, 20: 190–194, 1988.

[Perlis 60] Alan J. Perlis and Charles Thornton, "Symbol Manipulation by Threaded Lists," *Communications of the ACM*, 3(4): 195–204, 1960.

[Pohl 00] Ira Pohl and Charlie McDowell, *Java by Dissection*, Addison-Wesley, Reading, MA, 2000.

[Pugh 90] William Pugh, "Skip Lists: A Probabilistic Alternative to Balanced Trees," *Communication of the ACM*, 33: 668–678, 1990.

[Schaffer 91] Russel Schaffer and Robert Sedgewick, "The Analysis of Heapsort," Technical Report Number CS-TR-330-91, Department of Computer Science, Princeton University, January 1991.

[Sedgewick 78] Robert Sedgewick, *Quicksort*, Garland Publishing, New York, 1978.

[Sedgewick 92] Robert Sedgewick, *Algorithms in C++*, Addison-Wesley, Reading, MA, 1992.

[Shaffer 97] Clifford A. Shaffer, *A Practical Introduction to Data Structures and Algorithm Analysis*, Prentice-Hall, Upper Saddle River, NJ, 1997.

[Sleator 85] Donald D. Sleator and Robert E. Tarjan, "Amortized Efficiency of List Update and Paging Rules," *Communications of the ACM*, 28: 202–208, 1985.

[Sleator 86] Donald D. Sleator and Robert E. Tarjan, "Self-Adjusting Heaps," *SIAM Journal on Computing*, 15: 52–69, 1986.

[Velskii 62] Georgii M. Adel'son-Vel'skiĭ and Evgeniĭ Mikhaĭlovich Landis, "An Algorithm for the Organization of Information," *Soviet Mathematics Doklady*, 3: 1259–1263, 1962.

[Warshall 62] Stephen Warshall, "A Theorem on Boolean Matrices," *Journal of the ACM*, 9(1): 11–12, 1962.

[Wegner 86] Peter Wegner, "Classification in Object-Oriented Systems," *Sigplan Notices*, 21(10): 173–182, October 1986.

[Weiss 96] Mark Allen Weiss, *Algorithms, Data Structures, and Problem Solving with C++*, Addison-Wesley, Reading, MA, 1996.

[Williams 64] John W. J. Williams, "Algorithm 232: Heapsort," *Communications of the ACM*, 7: 347–348, 1964.

[Wirfs-Brock 90] Rebecca Wirfs-Brock, Brian Wilkerson, and Lauren Wiener, *Designing Object-Oriented Software*, Prentice-Hall, Englewood Cliffs, NJ, 1990.

[Wood 93] Derick Wood, *Data Structures, Algorithms, and Performance*, Addison-Wesley, Reading, MA, 1993.

[Wulf 81] William A. Wulf, Mary Shaw, Paul N. Hilfinger, and Lawrence Flon, *Fundamental Structures of Computer Science*, Addison-Wesley, Reading, MA, 1981.

INDEX